# Exploring Language and Linguistics

*Exploring Language and Linguistics* introduces the key concepts of linguistics and the application of these concepts to real-world settings. The first eight chapters cover the standard topics of introduction to linguistics courses, while subsequent chapters introduce students to applied topics such as media discourse, literary linguistics and psycholinguistics. Each chapter has been written by a subject expert and experienced teacher, ensuring that the text is both up-to-date and clearly presented. Numerous learning features provide extensive student support: exercises allow students to review their understanding of key topics; summaries encourage students to reflect on the main points of each chapter; figures, photos, tables and charts clarify complex topics; and annotated suggestions for further reading point students to resources for self-study. A companion website, with 170 self-test questions, suggested group exercises, audio files and links to additional web resources, completes the learning package.

NATALIE BRABER is a Senior Lecturer in Linguistics at Nottingham Trent University.

LOUISE CUMMINGS is Professor of Linguistics at Nottingham Trent University.

LIZ MORRISH is Subject Leader for Linguistics at Nottingham Trent University.

# Exploring Language and Linguistics

Edited by

**NATALIE BRABER**

**LOUISE CUMMINGS**

and

**LIZ MORRISH**

**CAMBRIDGE**
**UNIVERSITY PRESS**

University Printing House, Cambridge CB2 8BS, United Kingdom

Cambridge University Press is part of the University of Cambridge.

It furthers the University's mission by disseminating knowledge in the pursuit of education, learning and research at the highest international levels of excellence.

www.cambridge.org
Information on this title: www.cambridge.org/Exploring language



First published 2015

Printed in the United Kingdom by TJ International Ltd. Padstow Cornwall

*A catalogue record for this publication is available from the British Library*

*Library of Congress Cataloguing in Publication data*
Exploring language and linguistics / edited by Natalie Braber, Louise Cummings, Liz Morrish.
pages cm
ISBN 978-1-107-03546-1 (Hardback) – ISBN 978-1-107-66250-6 (Paperback)
1. Language awareness. 2. Linguistics–Study and teaching (Higher) 3. Language and languages–Study and teaching (Higher) 4. Applied linguistics. 5. Language acquisition.
I. Braber, Natalie, editor. II. Cummings, Louise, editor. III. Morrish, Liz, 1959– editor.
P53.454.I68 2015
400–dc23 2015002319

ISBN 978-1-107-03546-1 Hardback
ISBN 978-1-107-66250-6 Paperback

# CONTENTS

# FIGURES

# TABLES

# CONTRIBUTORS

KLAUS ABELS received his PhD in linguistics in 2003 from the University of Connecticut. He has held temporary appointments in Leipzig (Germany) and Tromsø (Norway) and has been at University College London since 2008, where he works as a reader in syntax. He is co-editor of the journal *Syntax*.

PATRICIA ASHBY, Emeritus Fellow of the University of Westminster and National Teaching Fellow of the UK Higher Education Academy, holds an MA and PhD in phonetics from University College London and a BA in English from the University of Lancaster. She has taught phonetics and phonology for over thirty years in countries all over the world, including Belgium, Poland, India, Germany and Japan. Her publications include *Speech Sounds* (1995, 2005) and *Understanding Phonetics* (2011). She has an international reputation in the field of phonetics pedagogy. Other research interests include English intonation. She is Examinations Secretary and a Member of Council of the International Phonetic Association, Director of the IPA Examination Strand on the UCL Summer Course in English Phonetics and a co-founder and organizer of the biennial Phonetics Teaching and Learning Conference.

ALLAN BELL is Professor of Language & Communication, and Director of the Institute of Culture, Discourse & Communication, at Auckland University of Technology, New Zealand. A dual career combining academic research with journalism and communications consultancy has led him to pioneering contributions on media language and discourse, as well as the theory of style (Audience Design) and New Zealand English. He is director of the World Internet Project New Zealand. He has published many papers and six books, including *The Language of News Media* (1991) and *Approaches to Media Discourse* (edited with Peter Garrett, 1998). His 2013 *Guidebook to Sociolinguistics* is a comprehensive, research-based map of the field. He is co-founder and editor of the *Journal of Sociolinguistics*.

ROGER BERRY is former Professor and Head of the Department of English at Lingnan University in Hong Kong where he taught courses in Applied Linguistics and English Grammar. His recent works include *Terminology in English Language Teaching* (2010) and *English Grammar: A Resource Book for Students* (2012). He was also editorial consultant for the *Collins Cobuild English Grammar* (3rd edition, 2011). His interests lie in language play, descriptive and pedagogic grammar, terminology and metalanguage. In his spare time he writes light verse about language, many pieces of which have been published.

NATALIE BRABER received her degree and PhD from the University of St Andrews. She first worked as a post-doctoral researcher and lecturer in Linguistics at the University of Manchester. Since 2005 she has worked at Nottingham Trent University as a Senior Lecturer in Linguistics. Her main research interest is language variation in the UK, specifically Glasgow and the East Midlands. She is also interested in identity and how this can influence a speaker's language usage as well as how emotion can affect language.

MICHAEL BURKE is Professor of Rhetoric at University College Roosevelt, a liberal arts and science honours college of Utrecht University. He has published articles on rhetoric, literary linguistics and cognitive poetics in numerous journals. His recent books include *Literary Reading, Cognition and Emotion: An Exploration of the Oceanic Mind* (2011), *Pedagogical Stylistics: Current Trends in Language, Literature and ELT* (edited with Csábi, Week and Zerkowitz, 2012) and *A Handbook of Stylistics* (edited, 2014). He is a former chair of the International Poetics and Linguistics Association (PALA).

CARMEN ROSA CALDAS-COULTHARD is Professor of English Language and Applied Linguistics at the Federal University of Santa Catarina, Brazil and was Senior Research Fellow in the English Department at the University of Birmingham, UK (1996 to 2012). She has published widely in the areas of critical discourse, media and gender studies. Her research interests are in social semiotics and gender representation, and visual communication. Her main publications are *Language and Sex* (1991), *News as Social Practice* (1997) and *Texts and Practices: Readings in CDA* (co-edited with Malcolm Coulthard, 1996). She is also co-editor of *The Writer's Craft, the Culture's Technology* (with Michael J. Toolan, 2005) and *Identity Trouble: Critical Discourse and Contested Identities* (with Rick Iedema, 2008). She is the co-editor (with Tommaso Milani) of *Gender and Language* (IGALA journal).

JONATHAN CULPEPER is Professor of English Language and Linguistics in the Department of Linguistics and English Language at Lancaster University, UK. His work spans pragmatics, stylistics and the history of English, and his major publications include *Language and Characterisation: People in Plays and Other Texts* (2001), *Early Modern English Dialogues: Spoken Interaction as Writing* (with Merja Kytö, Cambridge University Press, 2010) and *Impoliteness: Using Language to Cause Offence* (Cambridge University Press, 2011). He pursues research interests in historical pragmatics, especially historical politeness, and has written the textbook *History of English* (2nd edition, 2005). He is co-editor-in-chief of the *Journal of Pragmatics*.

LOUISE CUMMINGS is Professor of Linguistics at Nottingham Trent University. She teaches and conducts research in pragmatics and clinical linguistics. She is the author of several books: *Pragmatics: A Multidisciplinary Perspective* (2005), *Clinical Linguistics* (2008), *Clinical Pragmatics* (Cambridge University Press, 2009), *Communication Disorders* (2014), *Pragmatic Disorders* (2014), *The Communication Disorders Workbook* (Cambridge University Press, 2014) and *Pragmatic and Discourse Disorders: A Workbook* (Cambridge University Press, 2015). She has also edited *The Routledge Pragmatics Encyclopedia* (2010) and *The Cambridge Handbook of Communication Disorders* (Cambridge University Press, 2014).

JOHN FIELD is Senior Lecturer at the CRELLA research unit, University of Bedfordshire, where he advises on the cognitive processes elicited by tests of second language skills. He previously taught Psycholinguistics and Child Language at the University of Reading. He has long worked to make psycholinguistics accessible to readers with a non-specialist background; and has written several books on the subject, as well as numerous encyclopaedia and handbook entries. His main area of specialization is listening, particularly second language listening, on which he wrote his PhD at Cambridge. His *Listening in the Language Classroom* (Cambridge University Press, 2008) has become a standard text in that field.

HELEN GOODLUCK is Professor of Linguistics at the University of York. Her work has focused on language acquisition and on language processing, and the relationship between the two. Her research is primarily in syntax and has included studies of a range of languages, including Akan, Greek, Modern Irish and Serbian. She is the author of *Language Acquisition: A Linguistic Introduction* (1991) and has edited several volumes on language acquisition and adult psycholinguistics, as well as contributing articles to linguistics and psychology journals, including *Language, Cognition, Language Acquisition, Journal of Linguistics, Journal of Child Language* and *Journal of Psycholinguistic Research.*

S. J. HANNAHS is a Reader in Linguistics. He has worked over the past twenty years in theoretical phonology and morphology in the northeast of England, teaching at the University of Durham and currently at Newcastle University. His focus in recent years has been on the phonology of modern Welsh, leading to the publication of *The Phonology of Welsh* (2013). He is also the author of *Prosodic Structure and French Morphophonology* (1995) and co-author of *Introducing Phonetics and Phonology* (2010), and has published papers on Celtic and Romance phonology and morphology in various journals.

LESLEY JEFFRIES is Professor of English Language and Director of the Stylistics Research Centre at the University of Huddersfield. Her research has long straddled the twin topics of the stylistics of contemporary poetry and contemporary politics, though politics is currently the more time-consuming of the two. She has been working on a framework for critical stylistics for a number of years and is now working on integrating this into a general theory of language. Her work on the language of conflict includes the training of community mediators in language awareness and research into the language of war crimes tribunals.

DAN MCINTYRE is Professor of English Language and Linguistics at the University of Huddersfield, where he teaches stylistics, corpus linguistics and the history of the English Language. His major publications include *Stylistics* (with Lesley Jeffries, Cambridge University Press, 2010), *Language and Style* (co-edited with Beatrix Busse, 2010), *History of English: A Resource Book for Students* (2009) and *Point of View in Plays* (2006). He is reviews editor for the journal *Language and Literature*, series editor for *Advances in Stylistics and Perspectives on the English Language* and co-editor of *Babel: The Language Magazine* (www.babelzine.com).

LIZ MORRISH is Subject Leader for Linguistics at Nottingham Trent University. She teaches introductory courses in language and linguistics, and in phonetics. She also teaches a course in language, gender and sexuality, which is her primary research interest. At graduate level, she teaches and supervises work on language, gender, sexuality and Queer Theory. She is the author of *New Perspectives in Language and Sexual Identity* (with Helen Sauntson, 2007). She has also edited *Queering Paradigms: Queer Impact and Practices* (with Kathleen O'Mara, 2013).

JOHN SAEED is a Fellow of Trinity College Dublin, where he is a professor of linguistics. His doctorate was in African linguistics at London University's School of Oriental and African Studies and his first academic job was as a research fellow at the International African Institute. He is currently head of Trinity College's School of Linguistic, Speech and Communication Sciences. He has written on semantics and pragmatics in a number of languages, including Somali and Irish Sign Language, and is the author of *Semantics* (3rd edition, 2009) and *Irish Sign Language* (with Lorraine Leeson, 2012).

HANS-JÖRG SCHMID is Full Professor of Modern English Linguistics at Munich University, Germany. He is a graduate of the same university, where he also took his PhD (in 1992) and his *Habilitation* (in 1999). His research has been devoted to the fields of lexical semantics, cognitive linguistics, word-formation and pragmatics. His publications include: *English Abstract Nouns as Conceptual Shells: From Corpus to Cognition* (2000), *An Introduction to Cognitive Linguistics* (2nd edition, 2006), *English Morphology and Word-formation* (with Friedrich Ungerer, 2011) and *Cognitive Pragmatics* (edited, 2012).

PHILIPPA SMITH holds a number of positions at Auckland University of Technology, New Zealand. She is a senior lecturer in the School of Language and Culture, the research manager of the Institute of Culture, Discourse and Communication, and the executive director of the World Internet Project in New Zealand. Her research interests focus on media, national identity and discourse. She has published in a number of academic books and journals primarily examining discourse in reality television, animated sitcom, news stories and documentary programmes. In a recent project she used critical discourse analysis to compare constructions about New Zealand national identity in political documents, media texts and New Zealanders' online discussions during a period of increased multiculturalism.

# PREFACE

*Exploring Language and Linguistics* is designed to meet the needs of undergraduate students approaching linguistics for the first time. As teachers of first-year linguistics courses ourselves, we have always welcomed students from a range of academic backgrounds. The key challenge for instructors on introductory-level linguistics/English language modules is to introduce a wide range of topics, approaches and concepts in an accessible manner to students with little or no prior experience of studying language. Meanwhile, the key challenge for students lies in their ability to understand and then apply their learning to real-world settings. Our volume seeks to address these challenges with writing which is concise, accessible and richly illustrated with examples. We make no assumptions about prior experience with grammar or with learning foreign languages. In this book, we aim to provide readers with a thorough grounding in the terminology and techniques of linguistic description, as well as taking them forward into more specialist fields in the subject.

Linguistics is a developing subject, and new areas of enquiry are opening up. This book features chapters on language and ideology, media discourse, including a discussion of the language of computer-mediated discourse in social media, and clinical linguistics. Such wide but detailed coverage of developing areas makes this book stand out from other textbooks in linguistics.

The textbook is aimed at readers who are likely to be first-year undergraduates taking their first course in linguistics. Our students have told us that what excites them about the subject are the many applications to real-world problems. Each of these chapters is written by an expert in the field and will contain introductory as well as more challenging material. The first eight chapters introduce readers to the different *levels* of linguistic analysis: sound (phonetics and phonology), grammar (morphology, grammar, syntax), meaning (semantics and pragmatics) and structure beyond the sentence (discourse analysis). These chapters will all be preparatory reading for approaching the subsequent chapters, as students will be required to bring this body of knowledge to the study of applications of linguistics. The order in which the chapters are presented suggests the order of reading, but they may be read in any order.

Some unique features of the book will aid students in developing their understanding of each topic. Each chapter has: frequent boxes summarizing key points, exercises (with answers provided at the end of the chapter) so that students can check understanding and online exercises, including some designed to facilitate group work. Students will find themselves well prepared for second- and third-year undergraduate work in linguistics if they have worked through this book.

Most introductory textbooks in linguistics contain omissions in content which detract from their suitability, particularly as regards typical curricula in the UK. They also tend to discuss fewer applications of the theoretical concepts outlined. Also, in the UK strategies of teaching and learning in linguistics have evolved to the point where we wish to offer an approach which supports students' learning with both accessible content and interactive exercises. Most importantly, introductory textbooks tend to be written by generalists, that is, single authors or small groups of co-authors, who write about all the subdisciplines of linguistics in a general way. This textbook differs from the vast majority of competitor publications in that it features chapter contributions written by eminent experts in each of the subdisciplines of linguistics.

We have thought carefully about the features of a textbook which help students to learn, and we hope students will enjoy the following:

- An introduction to the fundamentals of the subject
- An introduction to a wide range of applications of the subject
- Key terms for each chapter
- A glossary which defines the key terms as well as specialist terminology
- A comprehensive index
- Chapters written by experts in the field
- Exercises to practise new skills and knowledge
- Online exercises which give feedback
- Tasks which stimulate group learning

As communication technologies continue to develop, there is likely to be a greater focus upon online learning, while at the same time encouraging interactivity and group work in the classroom. We include the in-text exercises in the expectation that instructors may choose to use these in classroom activities. Students may then follow up by doing the online questions independently.

# ACKNOWLEDGEMENTS

We wish to acknowledge the kindness and support of individuals at Cambridge University Press who have worked with us on this volume. We extend our gratitude to Dr Andrew Winnard (Executive Publisher, English Language and Linguistics) for his positive response to the proposal of a textbook in Linguistics. We also gratefully acknowledge the assistance of Valerie Appleby (Development Editor, Social Sciences), Bethany Gaunt (Assistant Editor, Language and Linguistics), and David Mackenzie (Production Editor) who have guided us during the preparation of this volume. We have benefited enormously from their advice and support. The contribution of the reviewers of each of the chapters has been invaluable, and we have included their insights wherever possible. We would also like to offer our thanks to Dr Dean Hardman who worked with us in the early stages of this project. Dean made a valuable contribution to the development of the proposal for this textbook. We have also received the encouragement of family members and friends during this project. Although they are too numerous to mention individually, we are grateful to them for their kind words during our many months of work on this volume. Finally, this volume would not have been possible without the professionalism and commitment of its contributing authors. We have enjoyed the experience of working with all of them, and hope these productive collaborations can be maintained.

# 1 Introduction: what is language? What is linguistics?

LIZ MORRISH

**KEY TERMS**

- arbitrary/arbitrariness
- descriptive
- design features for language, diachronic
- discreteness
- displacement
- duality
- paradigmatic
- prescriptive
- productivity
- semanticity
- signified
- signifier
- synchronic
- syntagmatic
- Universal Grammar

**PREVIEW**

Linguistics is the study of the structure, functions and acquisition of human language. This introductory chapter will introduce you to the enormous complexity of language and to the fact that our understanding of grammar depends on our world knowledge and on the context. This is followed by a discussion of the characteristics of human language and some ways of defining it. In comparing attempts to teach an ape human language with the language acquisition of small children, we ask whether human language has evolved from some shared, pre-existing communication system, or whether it is unlike anything that already exists in the animal world. The chapter discusses the views of Noam Chomsky on this question; we introduce evidence of native-speaker intuitions and children's errors in language acquisition which might support his argument that language is innate to humans. We then go on to discuss the approach and concerns of linguistics: that it is descriptive, and that it can be studied in its social context. The chapter ends by considering the rigorous and evidence-based methods, as well as the analytical tools, which linguists use to investigate language. Lastly, the chapter will introduce you to some of the uses and applications of linguistics. As you go through this chapter, and through the book, you will find exercises that allow you to practise these techniques of analysis.

## 1.1 INTRODUCTION

Any introductory textbook in linguistics will reveal to students that **language** is much more complex than speakers think it is, as they unself-consciously use it in their daily communication. As you work through this book, you will become aware that the different *levels of language* (discussed in Section 1.9 below) interact. You will learn that human language shows marked differences from animal communication systems. As speakers of English, or whatever our first language is, we all use it with a huge degree of proficiency. Some of us are able to use language in several different *modes*: speech, writing, email, or sign. Despite that, few of us could define what human language is. At the outset, it is important to make one clear distinction between the universal human faculty of language, which we all have, and the fact that different languages exist, and are used by different ethnic or national groups. Many readers will use more than one language on a regular basis, but even those readers who know only English will possess the same faculty of human language. We discuss this at length in Section 1.3. Definitions of that faculty of language are never really satisfactory. Instead the aim of this chapter is to raise some ideas that might not have occurred to you, which illustrate how complex human language is, and how it interacts with other forms of knowledge we have.

I wonder if that last sentence of the preceding paragraph exhausted you, or was difficult to understand? I hope that it was relatively straightforward, but if you have understood it, you will have been processing some very sophisticated syntax. For instance, that sentence contained a complex verb phrase, three relative clauses and a co-ordinated clause (these terms will all be explained in Chapter 5). But it probably did not seem out of the ordinary to you at all. Language users apparently do not expend much effort on language processing, despite dealing with an incredible volume of it all day long. As well as the ability to understand the grammar of utterances, we all carry around a huge mental lexicon of about 65,000 words (Amano and Kondo 1998). We retrieve words very fast when we plan our own utterances – up to five per second – and we make very few mistakes. We also recognize words very, very fast. In processing language, we store, retrieve, recognize and even create words all the time. And all users of language are brilliant at it. There are no linguistic dunces.

The sentence below illustrates one facet of the complexity of language:

(1) Can Spurs beat Manchester United without Wayne Rooney?

When I heard this utterance on a BBC Radio sports report, I was confused by the ambiguity of it. Perhaps as you re-read it, you are wondering how it could possibly be misunderstood, so let me try and explain the source of my confusion with some simple bracketing of the elements of the sentence. Example (2) demonstrates one of the ways I processed the sentence:

(2) Can Spurs beat (Manchester United) (without Wayne Rooney)?

In this *parsing* (meaning an analysis of the structure of the sentence), Wayne Rooney is assumed to play for Spurs. This, of course, reveals my ignorance about football, although I can be relied upon to identify Wayne Rooney in a line-up. Anyone who pays even casual attention to the UK national game will have understood the sentence without any attendant ambiguity, thus:

(3) Can Spurs beat (Manchester United without Wayne Rooney)?

In this parsing, the hearer understands that Wayne Rooney plays for Manchester United. As I write in 2014, this fact is part of most people's general knowledge, and so renders the meaning of the sentence clear and unambiguous. However, students who use this textbook ten years from now might find it difficult to understand if Mr Rooney is no longer a high-profile figure in football.

What the linguist understands from examples like this is that the hearer's grammatical analysis of a sentence takes place in conjunction with their knowledge about people, places, objects and events in the world. Language appears a very complex system when we take into account the numerous levels of language which interact when sentence processing takes place: phonology (sound patterns of the language), **lexis** (words in the language), syntax (grammatical relations between sentence elements), semantics and pragmatics (two types of meaning) and the individual's knowledge of the world. In other words, the complexity of linguistic knowledge involves a system characterized by the interaction of words + grammar + world knowledge

These interacting levels of language can explain our understanding of humour, particularly those jokes which exploit ambiguity predicated on world knowledge – what we know as 'double entendre'. The following example may require readers born later than 1990 to inform themselves of some of the relevant context. We suggest you do a Google search for 'Monica Lewinsky and President Clinton' before you proceed to the next example.

Example (4) was a joke circulating in 1998, at the height of the scandal involving former US President Bill Clinton and the 22-year-old White House intern Monica Lewinsky.

(4) What does President Clinton think about Monica Lewinsky? Answer – he thinks she sucks.

This joke works because adult native speakers of English will recognize that the answer displays ambiguity. The ambiguity lies in the grammatical possibilities of the verb *sucks*. There are two possible constructions – the first one we call *transitive,* meaning the verb requires a grammatical object to come after it, with the implication 'She sucks something.'

The second possibility for the verb is that no grammatical object follows it: 'She sucks', and this is a more colloquial usage taken to mean that the person so defined is not well thought of by the speaker. Notice that the meanings we are intended to access are only available to us if we have a rather detailed knowledge of the historical context, and this is the reason why younger readers are advised to inform themselves of the backstory first. The context is critical for supplying the elided object in the first construction! In other words, world knowledge and context will often work in conjunction with the grammar of an utterance to resolve ambiguity.

In a similar way, the current Minister for the Environment in the UK was heard on the radio saying, 'It is important to consider weather events connected to climate change', or did he in fact say this, 'It is important to consider whether events connected to climate change'? This sentence, or part of a sentence, could be analysed as *weather* behaving as a noun, or *whether* behaving as a subordinating conjunction, leaving us waiting for the next clause. In this case, our world knowledge was no help in enabling disambiguation – either analysis could have been equally likely in this instance.

Another example also takes the form of a joke. This joke was once rated the world's funniest, but again, its comprehension requires some complex linguistic processing and contextual knowledge:

(5) A couple of New Jersey hunters are out in the woods when one of them falls to the ground. He doesn't seem to be breathing, his eyes are rolled back in his head. The other guy whips out his cell phone and calls the emergency services. He gasps to the operator: 'My friend is dead! What can I do?' The operator, in a calm soothing voice says: 'Just take it easy. I can help. First, let's make sure he's dead.' There is a silence, then a shot is heard. The guy's voice comes back on the line. He says: 'OK, now what?' (Wikipedia)

The joke relies on listeners knowing that New Yorkers (more numerous and culturally powerful) consider their neighbours in the US state of New Jersey to be less intelligent than themselves. However, also at work is language understanding, and failure to interpret meaning in context. There are two meanings to the phrasal verb *make sure*: to *ensure that* X is dead, or, to *check if* X is dead. The joke rests on our (and the emergency operator's) assumption that the obvious interpretation is the latter, but the idiotic hunter acts on the former meaning.

As we see from the examples above, we cannot always rely on the same world knowledge, and the same perspective, being shared by all speakers, and so a speaker's intended meaning may not always be understood. This is a philosophical question discussed by, among others, Jacques Derrida.

## EXERCISE 1.1

(a) In the next conversation you have with a friend, note down two utterances which require contextual information or world knowledge in order to be understood. You will probably only have to think of what has been said in the past five minutes of conversation to find examples of something which might puzzle an overhearer.
(NB Linguists generally talk about utterances, unless they are referring to grammatically well-formed sentences of a language. Speakers, unless in a formal situation, do not usually speak in full sentences.)

(b) How many meanings can you identify for the following sentence?
Time flies like an arrow.
Can you explain why the meanings are different? Hint – some words can play more than one role in a sentence, e.g. they can be a verb or a noun. This sentence can be parsed in several ways, and because of this, is known as a **garden path sentence** (see Chapter 5 for further explanation).

WEBSITE: **Group exercise**

Visit the website and, in a small group discuss together and try and explain how grammar and world knowledge interact to lead us to the 'correct' interpretation of a joke.

**KEY POINTS: Complexity of language**

- Language is analysed on different levels of sound, words, grammar and meaning.
- These levels of language interact with each other, and also with context and an individual's knowledge of the world.
- These interactions allow language users to understand the utterances they hear.

## 1.2 Saussure and some important concepts in linguistics

Modern linguistics is thought to have begun with an extraordinary set of lectures from Ferdinand de Saussure, a Swiss **semiologist**, whose grateful students published the lectures after his death. He was the first to point out a seemingly obvious fact that a linguistic sign (for our purposes here, think 'word') is a combination of a ***signifier*** (a spoken or written form) and a ***signified*** (a thing or referent), but it is a crucial division which underpins the other insights developed in Saussure's famous lectures. For example, there is no inevitable or 'motivated' relationship between the signifier and the signified. This means that the relationship is an arbitrary, conventional one, for example, in English we have a word *book*, but in French it is *livre*, in German *Buch* and in Chinese *shū*. A motivated relationship between signifier and signified would mean that there is some necessary connection between the referent and the sound or symbol used to signify it. Examples would be onomatopoeic words like *choo choo* or *ding dong* – which, if the theory holds, we would expect to find are words which sound very similar across languages.

**EXERCISE 1.2**

Find onomatopoeic words in another language known to you. Do they sound similar to ones in English?

Another insight of Saussure's was that the value (meaning) of a sign is determined by the relationships it has with all the other signs in the system. As will be explained in Chapter 7 on semantics, words in a language fall into patterns of sense relations. Antonymy, or oppositeness, is one of these relations. The meaning of a word is not just determined by its referent, it is also determined by what it is not. So, a child learning the meaning of *hot* will learn to recognize all the items in their environment which attract this designation, but they will also learn that *hot* contrasts with *cold*, and that *clean* contrasts with *dirty*. There was a BBC television series in the 1970s called *Are You Being Served?* It was set in a department store, and featured the elderly store owner who only appeared to say to staff, 'You've all done very well!' He was so fragile he needed the support of his chauffeur to stand as he waved his cane. This, we learned, was 'young Mr Grace'. It was a brilliant visual gag, but the humour derived, not from the meaning that in absolute terms he was not young, but from the linguistic implication that there must be a contrasting 'old Mr Grace!'

Words, then, derive their meanings from the relationships they form with other words in a language. As words drop out of usage, others may need to widen their meanings to accommodate the lexical gap. We may need new coinages as language shifts to reflect changes in society, so, for example, since we now have 'gay marriage', we will need to specify a contrasting 'heterosexual marriage'. All of this means that the linguist can only make statements about the relations between words in a language at any one historical moment. Usually, in modern linguistics, we are concerned with the contemporary state of the language, and Saussure termed this a **synchronic** approach. As we will see in Chapter 10, language can also be studied historically, and Saussure called this a **diachronic** approach.

As well as relations of opposition, words enter into systems which Saussure termed **syntagmatic** and **paradigmatic**. The word 'syntagmatic' is related to *syntax*, which is covered in Chapter 6, and refers to the sequential relationships that words may have with each other. Here is an example from a notice outside a restaurant: 'shoes must be worn'. Anyone who knows English could expand this sentence based on their knowledge of words which can follow each other in combination, so we could expand to 'shirt and shoes must be worn'; 'a white shirt and black shoes must be worn'; 'a white shirt and black shoes must be worn by men at graduation'.

If syntagmatic relations are about the possibilities of combination of words, paradigmatic relations are about the choices we make when we choose a word to fit into a particular position in a sentence. So in the example above, it might read as follows if it was directed at women: 'a black dress and black shoes must be worn by women at graduation'. Meaning accrues to words according to their possibilities of combination with others, or their possibilities of substitution. We note the gendered messages encoded in the two examples above. We also note that a word substituted in this position, 'a ____ dress/shirt' would be an adjective – a word which qualifies or describes the following object. A number of different adjectives could fit into this slot, e.g. *black, white, grey, purple, smart, button-up*. These choices are said to contrast paradigmatically, in that they cannot be chained together, but they can contrast in the same grammatical slot. If items can fulfil this test of substitution, then we have diagnosed an adjective. Similarly, using a syntagmatic test, of what an adjective can combine with in the sentence, we find that *dress* or *shirt* can follow the adjective, and are nouns – usually names for persons, places or things. Linguists prefer this structural method of recognizing grammatical structures, and you will encounter this throughout the book.

### EXERCISE 1.3 PARADIGMATIC SUBSTITUTION

(a) When speakers of English construct *complex noun phrases* (see Chapter 5), they have intuitions (see Section 1.6) about the order in which the words must occur.

| A | long | sleek | red | convertible | sports | car |
|---|---|---|---|---|---|---|
| | | | | | | |
| | | | | | | |
| | | | | | | |

Using the following words, construct noun phrases similar to the one above by placing the words in the appropriate slot in the grid above (paradigmatic substitution):

*Some, many, the, tiny, heavy, table, wine, cloth, white, water, bed, firm, sensuous, large, swaying, overhanging, suspicious, bicycle, bald, ignorant, thief, convicted, menacing, physics, fragrant, teacher, deep, tall, handsome, cold, warm, green, grey*

(b) Can you make any generalizations about the order of occurrence of different types of premodifiers, e.g. do adjectives of shape come before adjectives of colour?

(c) The British comedian Barry Cryer told a story about a listener who tuned in to the radio and heard '*tits like coconuts*', and was immediately so offended she switched off. If she had listened further, she would have heard the full utterance, '*tits like coconuts and sparrows like nuts*' on a gardening programme. Explain, using the concepts of syntagmatic and paradigmatic relations, why the sentence fragment she heard caused her to opt for the wrong parsing of the sentence.

**KEY POINTS: Saussure's concepts in linguistics**

- There is an arbitrary relationship between a sign and its referent.
- The meaning of words in a language depends on the relationships between them.
- Words enter into systems of combination (syntagmatic relations) or choice (paradigmatic relations).

## 1.3 What are the characteristics of human language and animal communication?

The previous sections have laid out some of the complexities of human language, and some ways in which it can be studied. One way of illuminating the nature of human language, and its relationship to the human mind, is to compare it to naturally occurring animal communication systems. If we intend to make useful comparisons between human and animal communication systems, it is necessary to be very clear about criteria for differentiating the two.

Assuming that we all have experience of communication with a pet dog or cat, we know that this is limited in a way that communication with even a 3-year-old child is not. Our pet may be able to signal to us when it needs to eat, exercise, relieve itself, fight an aggressor or appeal to a potential mate. It will do this by means of bodily signals (tail wagging, standing on hind legs, arching its back), or by vocal signals (barking, mewing). Our toddler, while not yet able to offer an opinion on whether quantitative easing will have a corrective impact on the economic downturn, can argue, lie, joke, invent new words, tell imaginary stories, as well as being able to communicate all the needs that the dog can. Clearly, there are at least some qualitative differences between animal and human communication systems.

We dignify the human communication system with the term 'language', which we have used up to this point without explanation or justification. In order to make a comparison, and determine who or what possesses language, we must be able to define it by strict criteria. The most well-known attempt to do this was by anthropological linguist Charles Hockett (1960). Hockett was working at a time when others in the fields of linguistics and anthropology were interested in classifying and analysing natural phenomena by characteristics – an approach called 'taxonomics'. The thirteen (or fifteen, depending on who is writing) **design features** for human language that Hockett suggested, do not all have equal acceptance among linguists, but an agreed subset provides a way of differentiating human language from animal communication systems. Linguists continue to feel that human language is unique in displaying all of the following design features: **arbitrariness**, displacement, productivity, semanticity, discreteness and duality of patterning.

These features require further explanation and exemplification. Arbitrariness has already been discussed in Section 1.2 above. **Displacement** is the ability that humans have to refer to events, people, objects and places which are not currently present. These referents may be located elsewhere geographically – displacement in space – or they may be events which have taken place in the past, or may take place in the future – this is displacement in time. So, as I write this chapter in Nottingham, UK, in 2013, I can still discuss the ongoing conflict in Afghanistan (displacement in space) or the likely ways in which King Richard III met his end (displacement in time). Unlike other animals, human beings are not obliged to live within the confines of the here and now, although this may be an attribute of the language used by very small children.

**Productivity** is the ability to create novel utterances which may never have been spoken before. This feature relies on the fact that meaning in human language depends on structure, as we have also seen in the discussion of syntagmatic relations in Section 1.2 above. For example in an English sentence like *Shakespeare wrote ten tragedies*, we understand that Shakespeare is the agent – the person who did the writing. Similarly, we understand that *ten tragedies* is the outcome of the process of writing. In other words, we access the meaning because we understand the grammatical (syntagmatic) relations between the elements of the sentence. We also understand that this patterning is regular and rule based, and so we are able to make new and meaningful combinations of the elements of the language.

**Semanticity** is the capacity for the signs in the language system to mean something, in that they have reference to objects, concepts, places and people. Human languages have words and phrases which are linked in the minds of speakers to specific meanings. The feature of productivity also means that we can create new words whenever the need arises to name a new concept, e.g.*website, emoticon*.

**Discreteness** means that we recognize that the signs of the language are made up of discrete elements – ones which we recognize as different. For example, because /p/ and /b/ are different sounds in English (Chapter 3 will identify these as phonemes of English), we are able to recognize that *pat* and *bat* are different words. This allows us to recognize another feature of human language – **duality of patterning**. The smallest elements of a language – phonemes – combine to make morphemes (see Chapter 4). Morphemes combine to make words, and in turn, words combine to make sentences.

The next obvious question to ask is whether any other species has anything like language? This has been a question which has fascinated linguists, zoologists, cognitive and comparative psychologists, and much research has been done since the 1940s, largely in the USA. Zoologists have investigated the nature of animal communication systems and characterized the features of the various systems in much the same way as Hockett did with human language. Another approach, favoured by psychologists, is to try to replicate the process of child language acquisition with an animal, so that investigators might attempt to communicate with an animal using human language. Both these approaches are discussed below. As we will see, some animal systems display one or two of these features, but only all of the features in the subset can be identified in human language.

Human language is flexible and productive enough to communicate about any area of human experience. By contrast, animals can largely only send signals about food, predators and mating.

Various media or signalling channels are used by animals, e.g. sound (acoustic), smell (olfaction), electrical impulses (electroreception), movement (kinesics). Some animal communication systems which have attracted the interest of scientists are honey bees, vervet monkeys and whales and dolphins.

Honeybees were studied by Karl Von Frisch (1953), who found evidence of both arbitrariness and a degree of productivity. Bees are able to communicate about a source of nectar using an elaborate waggle dance. The intensity of the dance indicates to the members of the hive how sumptuous the nectar is, and the orientation of the body tells the other bees which direction to fly to find it. This might appear to be a case of signal arbitrariness, however, the intensity of the dance is analogically related to the richness of the nectar, which is not a strategy seen with any regularity in human language. We may occasionally say for effect, *it's a loooooong way away*, but this is exceptional. Another limitation of the bees' dance was that it seemed only to refer to the most recent source of nectar. Imagine how restricting it would be if you could only refer to your last beer, or party or game of football!

Semanticity has been claimed for the alarm calls of vervet monkeys in studies by Seyfarth et al. (1980). The researchers noticed that the monkeys responded in particular ways to different alarm calls emitted by the troop. For example, if a leopard was sighted, the other vervets would run up into the trees for safety. If a snake was seen on the ground, this would cause the monkeys to stand up and scrutinize the ground around them. Finally, if an eagle was circling overhead, the vervets would avoid trees, and instead conceal themselves on the ground in bushes. Seyfarth began to view these calls as being almost like individual words, and he decided to test these responses by playing recordings of the calls, in the absence of actual predators. Amazingly, the monkeys responded to the recordings in the same ways as they did to real calls. We may be able to regard this as semanticity, but it must be a very limited instance of it. We might predict that if another predator were to colonize the territory of vervets, they might fail to add another distinctive alarm call. This, of course, is very unlike the creativity which human beings exhibit in their use of language.

Animal communication is a broad topic which has been extensively studied, but it is beyond the scope of this chapter to pursue it in more detail. Interested readers may wish to read more widely on the nature of other animal communication systems (McGregor 2005), but we will now turn to the issue of whether an animal, in this case, an ape, can learn human language.

It is, perhaps, an enduring fantasy to have conversations with our nearest relatives, the great apes. Since the 1940s, comparative psychologists and primatologists have engineered experiments which aim to provide answers. Vicki, a chimp tutored by Keith and Catherine Hayes in the 1940s, was taught to try to vocalize a few words: *Mama, Papa, cup*. Vicki's difficulties with this soon became apparent; she was only able to produce the /k/ for *cup* by placing her hand over her nose. Research done by Philip Lieberman (2006) demonstrated that the problem lay with the chimpanzee vocal tract, which was not configured to facilitate the production of speech sounds.

However, the psychologists continued to probe the linguistic capabilities of the chimpanzee, and Alan and Beatrice Gardner procured a female baby chimp, named Washoe, with whom they used American Sign Language (ASL) to communicate, in order to bypass any vocal difficulties. A summary of their published work during the 1960s and 1970s details the training regimen that Washoe was exposed to (Gardner et al. 1989). A number of graduate student trainers were recruited to work with Washoe, and the rule was that they must only use ASL with her. Her hands were shaped into the correct signs, and her vocabulary grew rapidly over the course of the experiment. Interestingly, Washoe appeared to learn by observation, not just training, and also astonished her caregivers by appearing to invent new signs spontaneously. One such instance occurred when Washoe was walking by a river and saw a swan, whereupon she signed 'water bird'. In order to satisfy themselves that Washoe was able to use signs in a truly human way, the research team set up a double-blind test. This used an experimental rig involving mirrors so that Washoe could make an ASL sign when shown a picture, and a Deaf recipient was asked to interpret her response, but they were not able to see the stimulus picture. The results were put forward as convincing evidence that chimpanzees had propositional language, and certainly could exhibit semanticity. Washoe was seen to make signs in the absence of their first referents, so was able to generalize in a way similar to human children. She also signed 'dog' in the absence of a dog, and so displacement was added to the checklist of linguistic behaviours she demonstrated.

Project Washoe, however, left the scientific community unconvinced about one central question: could an ape demonstrate grammatical ability and create a sentence? Scepticism had increased with the publication of a set of results by Herbert Terrace (1987) who raised a chimpanzee called Nim Chimpsky (you will understand the punning intent when you read the next section of this chapter). Superficially, Nim seemed to have replicated the results of project Washoe, but on close analysis, Terrace viewed his signing behaviour as mere copying of his human trainers. Nim's signing showed very little structure and was characterized by frequent repetition of sequences, e.g. 'me banana you banana, me give me banana'. Terrace compared this signing to the dressage training undergone by show horses, and to a kind of operant conditioning which trained the chimp to respond to rewards and reinforcement. It was true that Washoe had been rewarded with favourite foods and tickling when she had correctly used signs, but the Gardners fiercely resisted suggestions that she had imitated her teachers.

The field of ape and human language research was left in a crisis after this debate broke out publicly. Another team of Sue Savage-Rumbaugh and Dwayne Rumbaugh presented their results of using language with a bonobo chimpanzee called Kanzi. Kanzi was a young male who was socialized by his trainers rather like a human child, and also trained to use an abstract symbolic system which worked by punching symbols on a large electronic keyboard. The Rumbaughs laid emphasis on word order and structure, in an effort to probe the question of whether an ape could understand and create a grammatical sentence. In a departure from the methods of previous ape language experimentation, Kanzi was spoken to in English by his trainers, but responded using his keyboard. The Rumbaughs produced video evidence that Kanzi could accurately respond to instructions like, 'Get the ball which is outside' (requiring Kanzi to ignore a ball inside the room), 'Give the doggie a shot' (with a hypodermic needle), or 'put the keys in the refrigerator'. In Savage-Rumbaugh et al. (1998), the authors firmly assert that this demonstrates a capacity for language on the part of Kanzi, and the other apes that they have raised over the years.

You will find different opinions offered by other linguists who argue that no animal has been able to demonstrate grammar in the same way that a human user of language does. It rather depends on how one chooses to define language, and in particular, the centrality or otherwise of the role attributed to grammar. Whatever view you arrive at, you will probably agree that Kanzi has a greater facility with language than your pet dog.

## EXERCISE 1.4

(a) A gorilla called Koko was taught to use American Sign Language by her trainer. She was filmed signing cigarette while looking at a cigarette advertisement in a magazine. What characteristic of language might that demonstrate?

(b) Washoe was offered a radish, and found that she disliked the hot, peppery vegetable. She signed *cry hurt food*. What characteristic of language might that demonstrate?

### KEY POINTS: Comparing human language and animal communication

- There are several key design features of human language.
- The most significant are: arbitrariness, displacement, productivity, semanticity and discreteness.
- Some animal communication systems demonstrate one or two of these features, but not the whole set. Only human language contains the whole set of design features.
- Researchers have achieved some limited success in teaching human language to apes.
- It remains uncertain whether an ape can be said to have demonstrated grammatical ability.

## 1.4 Where did human language come from?

As we have seen, some linguists and psychologists wish to contend that even our closest animal relatives do not have communication systems which resemble human language in structure and complexity. We have looked at the evidence for this assertion in the preceding section, and the argument does have substance. It does, however, raise an interesting paradox. By standard evolutionary theory, if we are assuming that human and animal communication systems are homologous (i.e. they share similarities of function *and* are derived from a common antecedent), then human language must have evolved from some pre-existing system in the animal world. Indeed, from the evidence of Washoe, Nim and Kanzi, it seems likely that the common ancestor of apes and humans would have had some capacity for propositional language. Lieberman's (2006) research has extended beyond investigating the anatomy of modern apes, to examining fossils of Neanderthals and Cro-Magnon hominids, and his results support this hypothesis. Nevertheless, if the contrary argument is defended – that human language is quite unlike any other communication system in the animal world – then the paradox is inaugurated. Put simply, what could human language have evolved from, if it is unlike the communication system which is the provenance of chimpanzees and other apes? This is, in effect, the point of view advanced by Professor Noam Chomsky, one of the foremost linguists of the last fifty years.

Chomsky (1968) (and now you understand the Nim Chimpsky pun) has argued that human language is so unlike anything else in the natural world that it must be considered an entirely separate ability. Indeed, he reasons that it is 'senseless' to seek to explain the evolution of human language by comparing it with more primitive animal communication systems. There are two separate ideas here: firstly, that language is innate to humans (discussed in Chapter 12); and secondly, that it is unique to humans. Chomsky also believes that language is an entirely separate faculty from any other human ability. For instance, some of us are better or worse at maths, or at making 3D jigsaws, or visualizing a 45 degree rotation of a rhomboid. However, as Chapter 13 details, we are all equally good at processing and understanding language, and processing is done with no perceptible effort on behalf of the speaker–hearer.

Chomsky believes that what enables human beings to do this is the possession of a 'language organ' which is present from birth. He believes we are born already equipped with a blueprint for language which he calls **Universal Grammar** (UG henceforth). It is stocked with a set of building blocks of language which set conditions on the form and organization of any human language; for example, we might expect to meet nouns, verbs, adjectives in our native language. Current research on hundreds of known languages across the world suggests that we are likely to find similar grammatical patterns and certain sentence permutations occurring across languages, e.g. questions, negatives and active/passive transformations of sentences. In other words, human beings are born with an innate faculty of UG which supplies them with the knowledge of what their first language is going to look like. At the time of publication (1968),

Chomsky's ideas had the effect of overturning some established ideas about language. American anthropologists, using their taxonomic methods, had made great claims about the diversity of languages on the evidence of much linguistic description of so-called exotic languages: Native American languages, Asian and African languages, and Pacific Island languages.

Chomsky's reasoning is based on the fact that human beings, from whatever social or linguistic background, all acquire language successfully, go through the same stages of language acquisition at more or less the same chronological age, and nobody misses out. None of us, really, is any better a user of language than anyone else. It is true that some of us may have larger vocabularies, or may sound more sophisticated or articulate than others, however, these are things that Chomsky calls 'performance' factors, and they cannot be held to indicate 'competence', which is a reflection of our mental model of language. Performance may be affected by situational factors like distractions, or the need to speak using a more formal register. He notes that the competence which children are able to demonstrate far exceeds the sum of actual linguistic experience they may have. This conclusion endorses the finding that imitation plays a very minor role in children's language acquisition, and adults are often surprised at the complexity of children's utterances. For example, at the age of 18 months, my niece was asked where her sister was. She replied, 'she's upstairs irritating mummy'. Let's unpack the grammatical complexity of this sentence. There is a pronoun *she*, a copula verb *is*, an adverb *upstairs*, then a non-finite clause initiated by the present participle *irritating*, and finally the object of that clause, *mummy*. It could be that this was an imitation, but the child was unlikely to have heard this construction from another adult in the house. It had all the hallmarks of a novel utterance, and it seemed remarkable to me at the time – I was still an undergraduate student of linguistics and fond of observing the early linguistic constructions of my nieces.

Competence is always in advance of performance, then. But as a consequence of his belief in a UG blueprint, Chomsky also advances his argument that all languages across the world, at a deep level, are structured in very similar ways. It seems that all that is needed for a child to acquire language is what Chomsky calls a 'rich environment' in terms of the language addressed to the child. Chomsky, however, prefers to view this in systems analysis terms as 'input' to the child's UG. The 'output', then, is a grammar of the child's first language.

**KEY POINTS: Where did human language come from?**

- There is a paradox if we argue that human language is unlike any other communication system in the natural world, and yet it must have evolved from some prior system.
- Chomsky prefers to argue that human language is unique and unlike any other animal – or human – cognitive system.
- Chomsky claims humans are born with a blueprint for language – Universal Grammar.

## 1.5 What happens when we acquire language?

Some of the evidence that a child is acquiring the grammatical rules of their first language comes from the errors that they make. Below are some errors which frequently appear in the speech of children acquiring English as their first language:

(6) *I swimmed

(7) *I goed

(8) *I sleeped

These past tense forms would be considered grammatically unacceptable for adult speakers of English, and hence these forms are prefixed by a '*'. This is generally a convention in linguistics to indicate a form which is not grammatically acceptable to a native speaker, and you may see it used again in this book. What the children's constructions reveal, however, is the fact that they have worked out the regular form for indicating past tense in English – by adding *-ed* to the end of the infinitive form of the verb. This demonstrates that children are doing more than imitating the adult forms they hear around them. It seems that they are able to process the linguistic evidence they hear around them (the 'rich environment'), and come up with hypotheses, some of which may be overgeneralized. When children acquire language, they do not make us think about the operant conditioning that Washoe and Kanzi seemed to demonstrate. Parents do not sit down and teach grammatical constructions and then give rewards for accurate reproduction. It is apparent that children acquire language despite a relative 'poverty of the stimulus' (another of Chomsky's assertions) in the language they hear around them. This is taken as evidence for the claim that the child's UG must be richly stocked with general principles and parameters of what languages must be like, and hence, children do not need to learn these. This is also offered as an explanation of why children acquire language so quickly.

As further evidence for UG, Chomsky was interested in the kinds of errors which children never make, for example, children do not make errors of this type: **I see doggie the*. The explanation, according to UG theory, is that there are limits set on the kinds of grammatical rules which languages use. English puts the article *the* before the noun *house*; by contrast, Norwegian puts the article after the noun, *huset*. Languages must conform to one of these two permutations for the order of article and noun, and the parameter is set when the child encounters positive evidence. If children arrive on earth already knowing from their UG that they can only meet these two parameters operating on the noun phrase, then this may explain the rapidity of language acquisition.

**KEY POINTS: What happens when we acquire language?**

- Children do much more than imitate adult models of language.
- Language acquisition is facilitated by Universal Grammar, according to Chomsky.
- All that is required is a 'rich environment' of language in order for language acquisition to progress.
- Children's errors are evidence of acquisition of a rule.
- Children make predictable errors, and this is evidence for **parameter setting** in their first language.

## 1.6 Language is studied in its social context

In any overview of linguistics, it is important to emphasize the study of language structure, and acquisition, but this book will also introduce you to the functions of language. Chapter 11 will focus on sociolinguistics – the study of language in its social context.

One of the things students find fascinating when they arrive at university is the linguistic variation they hear around them. For example, some students they meet are bilingual. In the UK there are many communities where more than one language is spoken within a family. Young people who grow up as second- or third-generation immigrants will use one language at school and outside the home (English, in the UK), and another language at home. Sometimes the choice is age stratified, so that children speak English with their siblings, but a community language (e.g. Urdu, Cantonese, Punjabi, Hindi) with grandparents who may not have learned English, or who no longer use it in retirement. In fact, most societies in the world are multilingual; the difference in the UK is that many of our institutions maintain an attitude and policy of monolingualism. As a result, a child's education may be impaired, or an elderly person's recovery from a stroke may not take full account of their linguistic background.

Another aspect of language variation is regional. Students always enjoy collecting new words they hear for the first time from friends who grew up in different parts of the country. You will find that a sandwich bread roll has different names according to region: *barm cake* (Manchester), *cob* (Midlands) or *bap* (Leeds). Language varies on all the levels of linguistic description (discussed in Section 1.1 above), and so we recognize different sound systems (regional accents) as well as word usage and grammatical choices. Together, variation on the levels of sound, grammar and lexis constitutes a dialect. Sometimes regional dialects are stigmatized, and are viewed as signifying low social status. By contrast, those who use Standard English, particularly accompanied by a BBC-type accent (Received Pronunciation) attract high social status.

In fact, the way we use language signals a great deal of social information about each of us as speakers. Gender is usually obvious in speech since men's and women's voices differ in pitch. Moreover, linguists have found other differences which take on the function of gender signification within particular cultures. For example, many gay and lesbian people report being able to tell when they meet another non-heterosexual person within the same culture. The linguistic indicators may not reside in the linguistic levels of sound system or grammar, but may emerge in lexical choice or in the level of pragmatics. Liang (1999) writes that gays and lesbians may avoid outing themselves by using the genderless pronoun *they* when referring to a partner. This may go unnoticed by the heterosexual listener, but the absence of gender reference raises an implicature (see Chapter 8) for the gay hearer.

The fact that social information is embedded in discourse (Chapter 9) and interaction is as important a part of the description of a language as the analysis of its grammatical structure. These are two key areas of emphasis in contemporary linguistics, and this book aims to cover both.

## 1.7 Linguistics is *descriptive* not *prescriptive*

One methodological difficulty for our linguist who is trying to write an account of the language is what they should use as evidence or data for the analysis. The problem is that the linguist wants to reproduce the native speaker's interior knowledge of their grammar (competence); however, the only available evidence is the data of utterances, or performance data as we discussed in Section 1.4. Chomsky finds this unreliable, since we often produce grammatically unacceptable utterances; we forget what we want to say, are distracted by our mobile phone ringing, or have our utterance interrupted by another speaker. Nevertheless, observed spoken data are as good a source of data as any linguist can get. Importantly, as sociolinguists would be keen to stress, the task of linguistics is to describe what contemporary speakers say; the linguist would never attempt to pass judgement on a speaker's use of language. The former is known as the **descriptive approach**, whereas the latter is known as the **prescriptive approach**. You will have met prescription either at home or at school. You may have been told that 'sentences do not end with prepositions' and yet heard the same speaker ask: *who did you sit next to?* Many of us have learned a kind of grammatical gymnastics trying to avoid split infinitives (*the tent is designed to comfortably accommodate four*), multiple negatives (*he doesn't know nothing*), or constructions like *didn't used to.* A descriptive approach would take a more enlightened view and ask, 'does this sound acceptable to a native speaker?' (see Chapter 5).

## 1.8 Linguistics is scientific in its approach

Linguistics is an empirical, evidence-based discipline, which means that researchers start their investigations by asking research questions and framing hypotheses. A hypothesis is a prediction which is usually expressed as a statement. Imagine I have formed the impression that my students are using a linguistic form more frequently than I and my older colleagues do. For instance, I hear them say *like* in a context such as 'I like, really enjoyed that lecture.' I might formulate a hypothesis based on this informal observation (a hunch, really), that would be expressed thus: 'Middle-class English speakers aged under 25 years will use *like* more frequently than middle-class speakers aged over 40 years.' My team of researchers would then go out into the field and record a random selection of speakers from the identified demographic groups. We would then analyse the results and compare them to the original hypothesis to see if this had been supported or not supported. It is important to recognize that you will probably never be able to collect sufficient data to be able to prove anything conclusively. It is for that reason that we are more cautious about making statements of supporting or not supporting a hypothesis, and we would probably also wish to justify our results by using statistical tests. In this way, researchers in linguistics are able to establish linguistic regularities on a scientific basis.

**KEY POINTS: Language indicates social information and linguistics is descriptive**

- Speakers give away information about their social characteristics: region, gender, sexual identity.
- Linguists *describe* what native speakers actually say; they do not *prescribe* what grammarians think they ought to say.
- Linguists pursue their research into language in a rigorous, scientific way.
- Linguistic research aims to identify regularities in language.

### EXERCISE 1.5

The exercise below presents you with some data of the way some younger speakers use *like*. It relies on using some of the concepts outlined in the last two sections – a descriptive approach and a scientific approach to linguistic data.

Look at the two sets of utterances in the data below.

Set (A)

- He was like, 'I'll be there in five minutes.'
- She was like, 'You need to leave the room right now!'
- I was like, 'Who do they think they are?'
- The car was like, 'vroom!'

Set (B)

- I, like, don't know what to do.
- There were four, like, really big guys outside.
- I can get, like, better qualifications.
- Kelly and I were, like, freaked.

(a) Does it seem to you that like is being used in the same way, or in a different way in sets (A) and (B)?

(b) Let's assume that the use of like is rule-governed. Can you explain e.g. to an older person, or to a non-native speaker of English what the rule might be?

(c) If, for example, an old-fashioned English teacher tried to criticize the speakers who use *like* in these two ways, would this be a prescriptive or a descriptive approach?

## 1.9 SUMMARY

This chapter has demonstrated some of the complexity of human language; how the levels of sound, lexis, grammar and meaning interact. We have discussed whether human language can be characterized by a set of design features, and whether these can also be used when comparing animal communication systems to human language. There is something of a demarcation debate over whether an ape can acquire human language and create a sentence. After reading the rest of the chapters in this book, you may feel informed and confident enough to enter into these debates yourself. We have seen that Chomsky has a firm view about the nature of the relationship between human language and the human mind. His theory that humans are born with a Universal Grammar is supported with evidence of child language acquisition. In the last three sections we have discussed the social nature of language, and the scientific and descriptive approaches to the study of language which linguistics employs.

## 1.10 Introduction to chapters of the book

These chapters are written by specialists in the field and they feature both introductory and more advanced material.

### Levels of linguistic description

Exercise 1.5 above looks at the organization of language, and this would be discussed in the subdiscipline of **discourse analysis**, which is the subject of Chapter 9. The approach you took to the analysis was to look for patterns and recurrences which can be distilled into a general rule about usage. Discourse analysis is the study of language used in a particular situation, and deals with both written and spoken language. Other topics in the study of discourse may involve the *genre* or *register* of a text – the formal features that are associated with the function of the text and its associated level of formality. For example, a pilot's manual for a Boeing 747 would have different linguistic features than a book review on a website. The former text is likely to include a large number of imperative forms of the verb, e.g. *raise the nose of the plane using the joystick at 10 meters from the ground*. The latter text may be characterized by a high number of evaluative adjectives, such as *interesting* or *thrilling*, and will give the author's opinion, rather than directions.

Linguistics offers the tools of analysis for making these kinds of studies at other *levels of language*. The structure of the rest of the book reflects these levels of language and Chapters 2–8 outline each of them in detail.

The most elemental (rather than lowest) level of linguistic description is that of sounds. The description of speech sounds, in articulatory, acoustic and perceptual terms, is the provenance of phonetics (Chapter 2). Sounds within a language form patterns of significance that are particular to that language. For example, in English we recognize two different sounds, /l/ and /r/ by the fact that in substituting one sound for the other, in the same phonetic context, we form a different word. By making this substitution in word-initial position, we get, for example *lake* and *rake*. We can be confident that these are two significant sounds of English – phonemes of the language. However, if the same two sounds were substituted in Japanese, the hearer would probably not hear the difference between them, and the substitution does not result in a new word. In other words, the two sounds are not phonemes of Japanese. This study of the patterns of sounds in a language is phonology, the subject of Chapter 3.

The next level of linguistic description is the level of grammar, which is usually discussed in terms of the structure and composition of words (morphology) and the structure and composition of sentences (syntax). These are discussed in Chapters 4–6.

Linguists also look for patterns of meaning (semantics) and the way words tend to be structured by meaning relations, e.g. of sameness of meaning (synonymy), oppositeness (antonymy) and inclusion (hyponymy). Another kind of meaning is pragmatic meaning which takes into account the role of personal, social and epistemic context (world knowledge) in accounting for meaning. The very earliest examples in this chapter demonstrated our understanding in context. Semantics and pragmatics are discussed in Chapters 7 and 8, respectively.

## Applied approaches to linguistics

Historical linguistics (Chapter 10) is the study of language change. In Saussure's terms, it is a diachronic approach to language, whereas most fields of linguistics study the present-day use of language, or synchronic study. You will find that language change can be seen at all levels of language: phonology, morphology, lexis (etymology), grammar. This chapter focuses mainly on change in English, although examples from other languages are brought in for comparative purposes.

Sociolinguistics (Chapter 11) is the study of synchronic language variation. The chapter will introduce the idea of internal variation within languages and how this relates to a number of social variables. Each section will consider the ways in which grammar and lexis can vary depending upon factors such as social class, geographical region, age, ethnicity and sexuality.

Child language acquisition (Chapter 12) will examine how children learn to use language. This chapter will examine 'normal' language acquisition and separate this into different phases. It will then examine theories of language learning and compare some of the most important schools of thought: behaviourism, empiricism, nativism and social interactionism. This will then allow for a study of 'wild children' to see what happens when children are brought up in unusual, isolated circumstances and how this can affect their language usage.

Psycholinguistics (Chapter 13). The chapter specifies the various areas covered by the term 'psycholinguistics'. The nature of language, including fundamental questions and issues such as whether other species possess language, the relationship between language and thought, and how language evolved, is explored. The notion of language storage is discussed, considering the ways in which phonological, lexical and syntactic knowledge are stored in the mind. The chapter goes on to consider how the mind enables language users to perform in two different modalities (speech and writing) and to comprehend as well as to produce utterances. The chapter then examines second language acquisition and the cognitive processes that are required when an individual with an established first language wishes to master a second language. The final section considers what neurolinguistics can tell us about the brain processes behind language and what happens in cases of brain damage or impairment.

Clinical linguistics (Chapter 14) begins with a discussion of the communication cycle and how breakdown can occur at various points in this cycle. This will lead the reader into an examination of the types of communication disorders that are studied by clinical linguists. A number of significant clinical distinctions will be examined. These include the distinctions between speech and language and a developmental communication disorder and an acquired communication disorder. In demonstration of how individuals are affected by communication disorders, two developmental disorders (communication in cleft palate children and children with specific language impairment) and two acquired disorders (communication after laryngectomy and aphasia) will be examined.

Language and ideology (Chapter 15) examines the assumption that ideologies manifest themselves in discourse on all levels of language and mark the stance and positioning of speakers/writers. The chapter will trace such manifestations in different genres (speeches, policy papers, conversations, ads, and posters as well as slogans) by exploring the persuasive means which are applied in context-dependent ways. Particular emphasis will be laid on rhetorical and argumentative devices, such as metaphors and other rhetorical tropes, presuppositions and implicatures, and the choice of argumentative schemes.

Media discourse (Chapter 16) will discuss the nature and influence of the mass media and consider reasons why it is important to study its linguistic features. The chapter then moves on to consider a variety of spoken, then written, media genres, such as news reports, magazine features and broadcasting, and considers some of the ways in which linguistic analysis can help to account for both their form and structure (in terms of genre). The chapter concludes by briefly considering how the language of media texts serves to construct and reflect social identities.

Literary linguistics (Chapter 17) first defines the concept of literary linguistics, also known as stylistics. It then sets out the historical development of the discipline starting with its classical rhetorical roots. The main focus in this historical overview though will be on its development during the twentieth century with regard to formal and functional aspects within both linguistic and literary theoretical paradigms. The chapter will then show how one goes about conducting a basic literary linguistic analysis. It ends with a discussion of a number of developments in contemporary literary linguistics including cognitive, corpus and pedagogical approaches.

WEBSITE: **Introduction**

Now go to the website and assess your knowledge of the material covered in the Introduction by completing the self-test questions!

## SUGGESTIONS FOR FURTHER READING

Aitchison, J. (2011). *The Articulate Mammal* (Routledge Classics). London: Routledge.
This book looks at some of the fascinating issues about the uniqueness of human language, and also discusses attempts to teach language to other species.

Crystal, D. (2007). *How Language Works: How Babies Babble, Words Change Meaning and Languages Live or Die*. Harmondsworth: Penguin.
This is a general and accessible introduction to a number of issues in language. It includes language acquisition, sign language, multilingualism and also some social aspects of language such as conversation and politeness.

Pinker, S. (1994). *The Language Instinct*. New York: William Morrow.
This would be a good place to start if you want to read more about language as an innate system, language acquisition and mental grammar.

# ANSWERS TO EXERCISES

## Exercise 1.1

(a) There will be a variety of answers appropriate for this question. Here is one example from an interaction I had today at the gym:

LIZ: Is the outside pool open today?

RECEPTIONIST: The engineers will be on site to rectify the fault today.

From this answer, I understood that, no, the pool was closed due to a fault, and that engineers had been called to fix it. In Chapter 8 on pragmatics, you will learn more about retrieving *implicatures*.

(b) At least three meanings:

There are things (noun) called *time flies* which like (verb) arrows.

It is an instruction to take a stopwatch and time (verb) some flies like an arrow.

It is a proverb that time (noun) itself flies (verb) like an arrow.

## Exercise 1.2

Many of these words are similar cross-linguistically.

### Doorbell ringing

- In English, *ding-dong, bing-bong*
- In Japanese, *pinpōn*
- In Russian, *din-don*
- In Swedish, *ding dong, pling plong*

### Water dripping

- In Dutch, *drup drup, drip, drop*
- In English, *drip drop, plink plonk*
- In French, *plic plic/ploc*
- In German, *plitsch, platsch, tropf*

Some are less similar:

### Pig grunting

- In Bulgarian, *gruh gruh*
- In Catalan, *oinc oinc*
- In Czech, *kvík kvík*
- In Danish, *øf øf*
- In Dutch, *knor knor*
- In English, *oink oink*

(Source: http://en.wikipedia.org/wiki/Cross-linguistic_onomatopoeias)

### Exercise 1.3 Paradigmatic substitution

(a) A range of combinations will be appropriate. Examples are shown in the grid.

| | | | | | | |
|---|---|---|---|---|---|---|
| A | long | sleek | red | convertible | sports | Car |
| the | tall | heavy | white | menacing | physics | teacher |
| some | cold | fragrant | white | sensuous | table | wine |

(b) The order appears to be determiner, length, attribute, colour, attribute, noun, head noun.

(c) On hearing this fragment, the hearer may have mistakenly assumed that *like* was filling the paradigmatic slot of a preposition introducing a comparison. In this case, the meaning would be rather lewd, as it would lead the hearer to assume that *tits* referred to a woman's breasts. In fact, it is a garden path sentence. As the rest of the sentence unfolds, we realize that the syntagmatic relation between *tits* and *like* is in fact one of Subject and Verb. As a result, it becomes clear that *tits* are in fact birds, and *like* is a main verb.

### Exercise 1.4

(a) Semanticity and perhaps also displacement as the actual object was not present.

(b) Productivity – she has coined a new phrase.

### Exercise 1.5

(a) It is being used in a different way.

(b) In set A, it is being used to introduce direct speech, and we would call this a *quotative* use. In set B, it is being used to draw the hearer's attention to an important part of the syntax – the noun phrase or the verb phrase. In this usage, we would call it a *focuser*.

(c) It would be a prescriptive approach. Note, though, that the answer to 1.5.b requires a descriptive approach.

## REFERENCES

Amano, S. and Kondo, T. (1998). Estimation of mental lexicon size with word familiarity database. *Proceedings of International Conference on Spoken Language Processing*, 5, 2119–22.

Chomsky, N. (1968). *Language and Mind*. San Diego, CA: Harcourt Brace Jovanovich.

Gardner, R. A., Gardner, B. and Van Cantfort, T. (1989). *Teaching Sign Language to Chimpanzees*. Albany, NY: State University of New York Press.

Hockett, C. (1960). The origin of speech. *Scientific American*, 203, 89–97.

Liang, A. C. (1999). Conversationally implicating lesbian and gay identity. In M. Bucholtz, A. C. Liang and L. Sutton (eds.), *Reinventing Identities*, pp. 293–310. Oxford University Press.

Lieberman, P. (2006). *Towards an Evolutionary Biology of Language*. Cambridge, MA: Harvard University Press.

McGregor, P. K. (ed.). (2005). *Animal Communication Networks*. Cambridge University Press.

Saussure, F. de (1959). *A Course in General Linguistics*, trans. Wade Baskin. New York: Columbia University Press.

Savage-Rumbaugh, S., Shanker, S. and Taylor, T. (1998). *Apes, Language, and the Human Mind.* Oxford University Press.

Seyfarth, R. M., Cheney, D. L. and Marler, P. (1980). Monkey responses to three different alarm calls: evidence of predator classification and semantic communication. *Science*, 210, 801–3.

Terrace, H. (1987). *Nim, a Chimpanzee Who Learned Sign Language.* New York: Columbia University Press.

Von Frisch, K. (1953). *The Dancing Bees: An Account of the Life and Senses of the Honey Bee*, 5th edn. New York: Harvest Books.

# 2 Phonetics

PATRICIA ASHBY

**KEY TERMS**

- acoustic phonetics
- airstream
- articulatory phonetics
- consonant
- intonation
- intonational phrase
- manner of articulation
- place of articulation
- stress
- tone
- transcription
- voice
- vowel

**PREVIEW**

Phonetics describes the sounds and melodies of the spoken word – how they are made (articulatory phonetics), their physical reality (acoustic phonetics) and how they are perceived (speech perception). Articulatory phonetics is a long-established discipline and the rudiments of general phonetic theory are relatively uncontentious. Phonetics impacts on many areas of linguistics including morphology (e.g. English plural and past tense endings), syntax (e.g. distinguishing between certain word classes, statements and questions), semantics (e.g. homographs, homophones) and pragmatics (e.g. context-sensitive intonational focus), also sociolinguistics (e.g. regional accents, styles of speech), psycholinguistics (e.g. speech errors, speech perception) and so forth. It makes sense, therefore, for students of language and linguistics to know something about the nature of the spoken word. Accordingly, against a background of examples drawn mainly (but not exclusively) from English, this chapter summarizes speech sound production, demonstrates key features in the speech waveform and in spectrograms, looks briefly at types of transcription, and introduces the contributions made by tone and intonation.

## 2.1 INTRODUCTION

The interconnected combination of mouth, throat and lungs is the **vocal tract**. The 'power' for speech is supplied by a stream of air from the lungs. To speak, we make deliberate movements of our throats and mouths (particularly the tongue and/or the lips) which act on the moving **airstream** to alter the way it flows. All speech sounds involve some kind of narrowing or approximation between active and passive organs in the vocal tract – the active/moveable tongue tip, for example, rising to touch the passive/immovable upper front teeth. This chapter aims to explain the nature of such gestures.

Phonetics is also inextricably linked with phonology (sometimes called linguistic phonetics). Phonology tells us which particular sounds are used with significance in the speech of different languages, contributing to the meanings of words – for example, 's' and 'z' are different sounds in English (represented in phonetic **transcription** as [s] and [z]) and distinguish word pairs like *bus~buzz, Sue~zoo, racer~razor*. Phonetics, however, tells us exactly how each sound is produced and about their physical characteristics. Phonology tells us that English also contrasts [ʃ] (e.g. in *sheep* or *mission*) and [ʒ] (in *vision*). Again, notice how the phonetic transcription of sounds isn't always like the spelling letters. The symbols and letters are similar for [s] and [z], but those for [ʃ] and [ʒ] are quite different. Instead of variable spellings, phonetics transcribes (writes) sounds using symbols drawn largely from the Extended Latin Alphabet on a strictly one-symbol:one-sound basis – the sound [ʒ] is always transcribed [ʒ].

This chapter will familiarize you with the basic articulatory phonetics of **vowels** and **consonants**, identifying some of their acoustic features in speech waveforms and spectrograms. It will also help you to 'read' the **International Phonetic Alphabet (IPA) Chart**[1] (page 26), understand about transcription of speech, and equip you to begin a more in-depth study of the subject. To hear all the sounds, you can use an interactive version of the IPA Chart such as http://web.uvic.ca/ling/resources/ipa/charts/IPAlab/IPAlab.htm.

## 2.2 Voice

**Voice** is fundamental to speech, thus providing a perfect place to begin the study of phonetics.

Speech is produced using a moving stream of air. If you hold your breath and try to talk, apart from a few unavoidable percussive noises, no one will hear you and no one will understand you. But as soon as you start to expel air from your lungs – just whispering, for example, producing what we would call a voiceless airflow – the message can be understood by the listener. So, this pulmonic egressive airstream is sometimes voiceless, as in *shh!* But at the top of the trachea or windpipe, it passes through the **larynx**, where it can be caused to vibrate by a particular alignment of the vocal folds, becoming voiced, as in *Ah!* Alternation between voiceless and voiced is fundamental in most languages – the difference between prolonged *sss* (a voiceless [s]-sound) imitating the hissing sound of a snake, and *zzz* (a voiced [z]-sound) imitating the buzzing sound of a bee, for example.

[1] This alphabet is maintained by the professional organization of phoneticians, the International Phonetic Association, http://www.internationalphoneticassociation.org, in order to provide 'the academic community world-wide with a notational standard for the phonetic representation of all languages'. The Association publishes a *Handbook* (IPA 1999).

# THE INTERNATIONAL PHONETIC ALPHABET (revised to 2005)

CONSONANTS (PULMONIC)



| | Bilabial | Labiodental | Dental | Alveolar | Postalveolar | Retroflex | Palatal | Velar | Uvular | Pharyngeal | Glottal |
|---|---|---|---|---|---|---|---|---|---|---|---|
| Plosive | p b | | | t d | | ʈ ɖ | c ɟ | k ɡ | q ɢ | | ʔ |
| Nasal | m | ɱ | | n | | ɳ | ɲ | ŋ | ɴ | | |
| Trill | ʙ | | | r | | | | | ʀ | | |
| Tap or Flap | | ⱱ | | ɾ | | ɽ | | | | | |
| Fricative | ɸ β | f v | θ ð | s z | ʃ ʒ | ʂ ʐ | ç ʝ | x ɣ | χ ʁ | ħ ʕ | h ɦ |
| Lateral fricative | | | | ɬ ɮ | | | | | | | |
| Approximant | | ʋ | | ɹ | | ɻ | j | ɰ | | | |
| Lateral approximant | | | | l | | ɭ | ʎ | ʟ | | | |

Where symbols appear in pairs, the one to the right represents a voiced consonant. Shaded areas denote articulations judged impossible.

CONSONANTS (NON-PULMONIC)

| Clicks | | Voiced implosives | | Ejectives | |
|---|---|---|---|---|---|
| ʘ | Bilabial | ɓ | Bilabial | ʼ | Examples: |
| ǀ | Dental | ɗ | Dental/alveolar | pʼ | Bilabial |
| ǃ | (Post)alveolar | ʄ | Palatal | tʼ | Dental/alveolar |
| ǂ | Palatoalveolar | ɠ | Velar | kʼ | Velar |
| ǁ | Alveolar lateral | ʛ | Uvular | sʼ | Alveolar fricative |

VOWELS

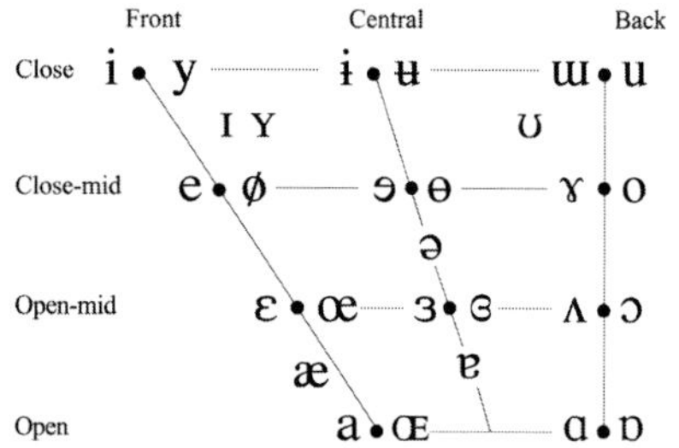

| | Front | Central | Back |
|---|---|---|---|
| Close | i • y | ɨ • ʉ | ɯ • u |
| | ɪ ʏ | | ʊ |
| Close-mid | e • ø | ɘ • ɵ | ɤ • o |
| | | ə | |
| Open-mid | ɛ • œ | ɜ • ɞ | ʌ • ɔ |
| | æ | ɐ | |
| Open | a • ɶ | | ɑ • ɒ |

Where symbols appear in pairs, the one to the right represents a rounded vowel.

OTHER SYMBOLS

ʍ Voiceless labial-velar fricative

w Voiced labial-velar approximant

ɥ Voiced labial-palatal approximant

ʜ Voiceless epiglottal fricative

ʢ Voiced epiglottal fricative

ʡ Epiglottal plosive

ɕ ʑ Alveolo-palatal fricatives

ɺ Voiced alveolar lateral flap

ɧ Simultaneous ʃ and x

Affricates and double articulations can be represented by two symbols joined by a tie bar if necessary. k͡p t͜s

DIACRITICS Diacritics may be placed above a symbol with a descender, e.g. ŋ̊

| | | | | | | | | |
|---|---|---|---|---|---|---|---|---|
| ̥ | Voiceless | n̥ d̥ | ̤ | Breathy voiced | b̤ a̤ | ̪ | Dental | t̪ d̪ |
| ̬ | Voiced | s̬ t̬ | ̰ | Creaky voiced | b̰ a̰ | ̺ | Apical | t̺ d̺ |
| ʰ | Aspirated | tʰ dʰ | ̼ | Linguolabial | t̼ d̼ | ̻ | Laminal | t̻ d̻ |
| ̹ | More rounded | ɔ̹ | ʷ | Labialized | tʷ dʷ | ̃ | Nasalized | ẽ |
| ̜ | Less rounded | ɔ̜ | ʲ | Palatalized | tʲ dʲ | ⁿ | Nasal release | dⁿ |
| ̟ | Advanced | u̟ | ˠ | Velarized | tˠ dˠ | ˡ | Lateral release | dˡ |
| ̠ | Retracted | e̠ | ˤ | Pharyngealized | tˤ dˤ | ̚ | No audible release | d̚ |
| ̈ | Centralized | ë | ̴ | Velarized or pharyngealized ɫ | | | | |
| ̽ | Mid-centralized | e̽ | ̝ | Raised | e̝ | | (ɹ̝ = voiced alveolar fricative) | |
| ̩ | Syllabic | n̩ | ̞ | Lowered | e̞ | | (β̞ = voiced bilabial approximant) | |
| ̯ | Non-syllabic | e̯ | ̘ | Advanced Tongue Root | e̘ | | | |
| ˞ | Rhoticity | ɚ a˞ | ̙ | Retracted Tongue Root | e̙ | | | |

SUPRASEGMENTALS

ˈ Primary stress

ˌ Secondary stress ˌfoʊnəˈtɪʃən

ː Long eː

ˑ Half-long eˑ

̆ Extra-short ĕ

| Minor (foot) group

‖ Major (intonation) group

. Syllable break ɹi.ækt

‿ Linking (absence of a break)

TONES AND WORD ACCENTS

| LEVEL | | | CONTOUR | | |
|---|---|---|---|---|---|
| e̋ or | ˥ | Extra high | ě or | ˩˥ | Rising |
| é | ˦ | High | ê | ˥˩ | Falling |
| ē | ˧ | Mid | e᷄ | ˦˥ | High rising |
| è | ˨ | Low | e᷅ | ˩˨ | Low rising |
| ȅ | ˩ | Extra low | e᷈ | ˧˦˧ | Rising-falling |
| ↓ | | Downstep | ↗ | | Global rise |
| ↑ | | Upstep | ↘ | | Global fall |

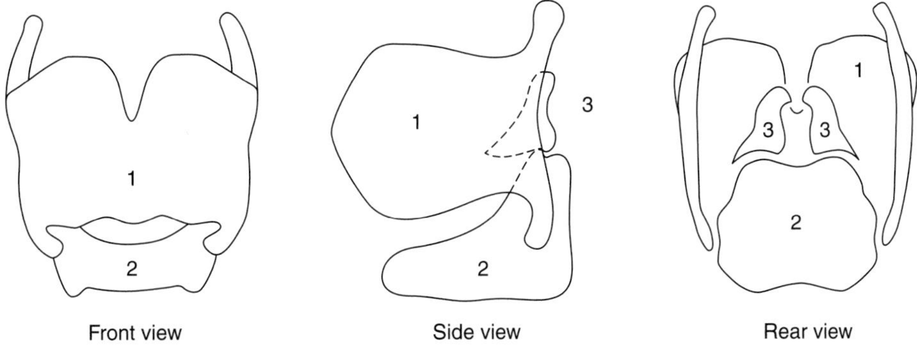


**Figure 2.1** Cartilages of the larynx: 1 thyroid cartilage; 2 cricoid cartilage; 3 arytenoid cartilages (adapted from G. J. Romanes, *Cunningham's Manual of Practical Anatomy*, vol 3: *Head and Neck and Brain*, Oxford University Press, 1986; reproduced by permission)

The structure of the larynx is, crudely, a 'box' made of cartilages, identified in Figure 2.1. The front and sides are formed by the thyroid cartilage (which forms the bump you can feel at the front of your neck, your Adam's apple), which is open at the back and sits on top of a complete circle of cartilage called the 'cricoid cartilage' (the topmost cartilage of the trachea). The cricoid cartilage is the base of the box and, like a ring, is open through its centre. Suspended inside the box, adjoining the cricoid cartilage from top to bottom at the front and the two arytenoid cartilages (which also sit on top of the cricoid cartilage) at the back, are the vocal folds, which can be drawn together or apart by movements of the arytenoids. When they are held open, voiceless sounds occur, and when they are drawn together, under gentle tension, a number of other qualities can be heard, one of which is the modal or normal voice.

Briefly, to produce modal voice you breathe in, filling your lungs with air, then draw the vocal folds together into a closed position (as in the first photo in Figure 2.2). The tension of the folds is such that when you start to expel air from the lungs, pressure from the airstream forces the folds apart, starting at the bottom and continuing to push upwards until it has forced them to open fully. When it reaches the top, although the same pressure is still being exerted from the lungs, there is no more work for the airstream to do and it flows rapidly into your pharynx (throat). This sudden acceleration in turn brings about a momentary drop in pressure at the bottom edges of the vocal folds which spring back together, like elastic – remember they are being held under tension by the arytenoid cartilages. They are then sucked back to the fully closed position and the opening process begins again. This vibratory sequence or cycle repeats 200–240 times per second for the average female voice and about 100–120 times for the average male. (The faster they vibrate, the higher the pitch of the voice.) The average female voice is therefore said to have a measurable **fundamental frequency** (f0) of 200–240 Hertz (Hz, meaning 'cycles per second') and the average male voice an f0 of 100–120 Hz. Seen using a laryngograph, modal voice produces a triangular looking waveform, the larynx waveform (Lx). One cycle of this is illustrated in Figure 2.2. The near vertical parts of the line show the rapid closing movement, and the less steep, bent line (starting from the top with complete closure) shows the gradual opening of the folds. Once open, the space between the folds is the

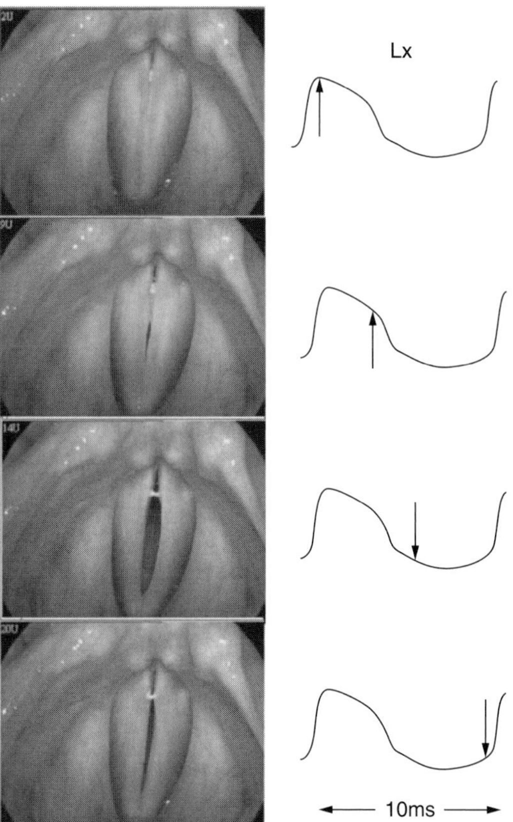


**Figure 2.2** The vocal folds and larynx waveform (Lx) (from Laryngograph Ltd)

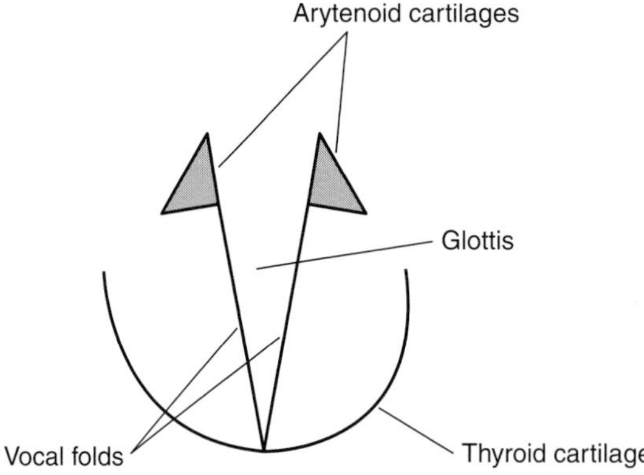


**Figure 2.3** Schematic view of the larynx from above with an open glottis

glottis, as in the third photo in Figure 2.2 and illustrated schematically in Figure 2.3. The regular repetition of cycles produces a waveform described as periodic. Voicing is visible as striations in the voice bar at the very bottom of a spectrogram (as in Figure 2.7).

Voice is mentioned explicitly in the name of each individual consonant sound ([s], [z], etc.) – each has a voice place manner (VPM) label. Vowels are normally voiced.

**KEY POINTS: Voicing and the role of the larynx in speech**

- Voice is fundamental to speech, contributing to meaning.
- All speech sounds are either voiceless or voiced.
- The larynx waveform (Lx) for normal/modal voice is a periodic (regular) waveform.
- The perceived pitch of a voice is related to the rate of vibration of the vocal folds (fundamental frequency, f0).

**EXERCISE 2.1**

Here is a voicing diagram for *fishing* [ˈfɪʃɪŋ]:

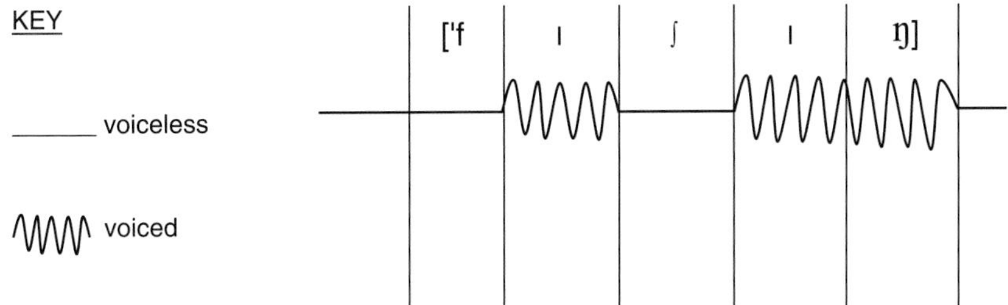


The flat line represents voiceless and the zig-zag (a bit like Lx) voiced. Try to draw voicing diagrams for the following words: (a) *slimy* [ˈslaɪmi], (b) *thoughtful* [ˈθɔːtfʊl], (c) *convince* [kənˈvɪns], (d) *monster* [ˈmɒnstə], (e) *sparrow* [ˈspæɹəʊ].

You will need to work out which sounds are voiceless and which are voiced. (If you are not confident that you can hear the difference, try making the sound while resting your fingertips on the front of your neck – can you feel a vibration?)

## 2.3 Consonants

Consonants are sounds produced with a constriction somewhere in the vocal tract usually sufficient to create an aperiodic waveform and resulting in audible noise – hissing, hushing, small 'explosions', etc. Repeated patterns (like those just seen in the Lx (see page 28 above)) are not found in pure aperiodic waveforms (see points marked '1' in Figure 2.7 showing the speech waveform and spectrogram of [ʃ] and [kʰ][2]).

There are three basic types of constriction (see **manner of articulation** below) – two almost exclusively consonantal in type and one shared with vowels by a small number of

[2] [ʰ] here represents the exhalation of breath heard after initial [p t k] sounds in English. This short interval of voicelessness is called **Voice Onset Time (VOT)**. The auditory characteristic when the next sound is a vowel, as here in *Ken* [kʰen], is an h-like sound called **aspiration**.

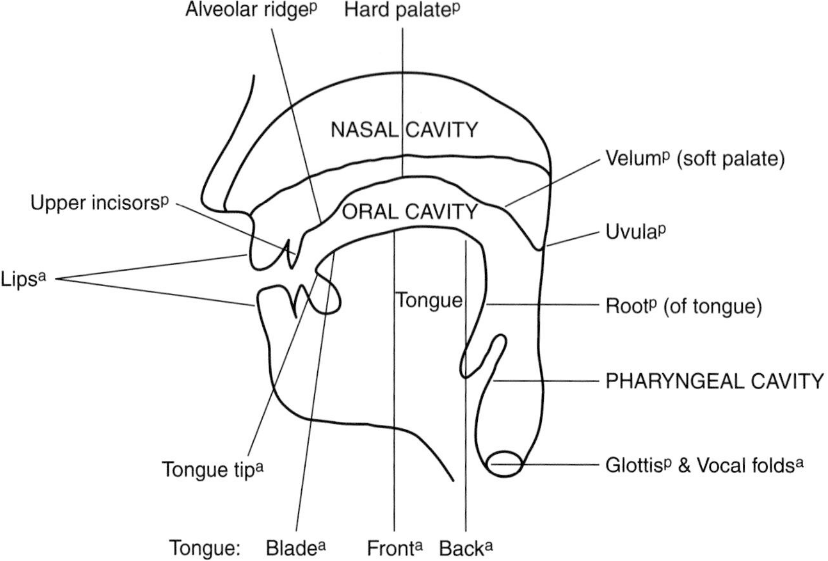


**Figure 2.4** Active[a] and passive[p] articulators in the supra-glottal cavities

vowel-like consonants. The constrictions are made at any point in the vocal tract from the glottis to the lips by movement of an active articulator towards a passive one (active/passive articulators are identified in Figure 2.4) – the lower lip towards the upper front teeth, for example, or the back of the tongue towards the velum or uvula.

We can summarize the eleven main places of articulation, following the horizontal axis of the pulmonic consonants' table on the IPA Chart:

- constrictions created between the upper and lower lips are called **bilabial** (literally 'two lips') – English has [p] in *pie,* [b] in *by*, and [m] in *my*; another bilabial sound is made when you blow out a candle, [ɸ].
- the lower lip rising to articulate with the upper front teeth is **labiodental** (literally 'lip-teeth') – English has [f] in *fly* and [v] in *vie*.
- the tongue tip rising to articulate against the upper front teeth is **dental** (interdental if the tip protrudes between the upper and lower incisors) – English has dental [θ] in *thigh* and [ð] in *thy*; many other languages make 't' and 'd' sounds here, e.g. French [t̪] in *thé* 'tea', [d̪] in *de* 'of'.
- the tongue tip (or sometimes the blade of the tongue) rising towards the alveolar ridge is called **alveolar** – English has [t] in *tie*, [d] in *dye/die,* [n] in *nigh,* [s] in *sigh,* [z] in *zip* and [l] in *lie*; and when the tip makes a constriction against the back of the alveolar ridge it's called postalveolar – English has [ɹ] in *rye*... notice that the articulators don't actually have to touch to make a constriction.
- Exceptionally, the highly flexible tongue tip may rise and curl over backwards to create a constriction against the hard palate. This gesture – the only one where a passive articulator moves out of the inherent alignment between the active and passive points that

you can feel in the rest position (sitting with your mouth closed and the jaws lightly clenched) – is an apico-palatal gesture (apex of the tongue towards the hard palate). This is given the name retroflex on the IPA Chart, distinguishing this from the regular palatal constrictions made using the front of the tongue. American and Irish English 'r' sounds are retroflex, [ɻ], and retroflexes are used in many Indo-Aryan and Dravidian languages (Hindi, Tamil, etc.).

- the front of the tongue rising towards the hard palate to create a constriction is called palatal – English has [j] in *yes*, and German [ç] in *ich* 'I'.
- the back of the tongue rising towards the velum is called **velar** – English has [k] in *kick*, [g] in *give*, and [ŋ] at the end of *sing*; and when it rises towards the uvula at the very end of the velum, the place of the constriction is called uvular – English has no uvulars, but the German 'r' sound is uvular [ʀ] as in *Rhein*.
- a constriction in the pharynx, tensing and retracting the root of the tongue (which reduces the space between the tongue root and the rear wall of the pharynx) is called pharyngeal (pharyngal by some) – pharyngeal sounds are rare but can be heard in Arabic which uses [ʕ] as in 'ayn' (the name of the letter which spells the sound).
- constriction between the two vocal folds (other than the approximation which results in voice production) is described as glottal – English has [h] in *hi!* and, in many accents (e.g. Popular London) the so-called glottal stop [ʔ], which replaces a final 't' sound as in *wha' a lo'* "what a lot".

Occasionally, two places are used simultaneously, for example lips acting simultaneously with a palatal gesture (labialpalatal – French [ɥ] as in *lui* 'him') or with a velar gesture (labialvelar – English [w] as in *we* and *away*). Such combinations are called double articulations – two simultaneous strictures of identical type. In this case, there is wide approximation (explained below) at both places.

The constriction itself can involve complete closure between the active and passive articulator, or a narrow gap being left, or a somewhat wider gap. These differences create a scale of strictures (constrictions) reflecting manner of articulation, which takes us from pure consonants, through more vowel-like sounds, to vowels themselves.

Before looking in detail at the different manners, it will be useful to take a closer look at the velum. So far, we have described its role as a **place of articulation**, but as Figure 2.5 shows, this soft part of the palate is also moveable. During normal breathing, it is in a lowered or open position as in the second and third diagrams, allowing air to flow freely in and out of the lungs via the nose. However, to stop airflow through the nose (or nasal cavities), we raise the velum into a closed position called velic closure (as in the first diagram). All air is then directed via the mouth (the oral cavity). Most consonants are oral speech sounds, produced with velic closure. But one group of consonants requires the velum to be in the open position. These are nasal sounds, such as [m] and [n] as in *many* [ˈmeni]. To produce nasal consonants, as well as an open velum, there is a complete obstruction one of the places of articulation described above. This stops the air from escaping via the mouth. In saying [m], for

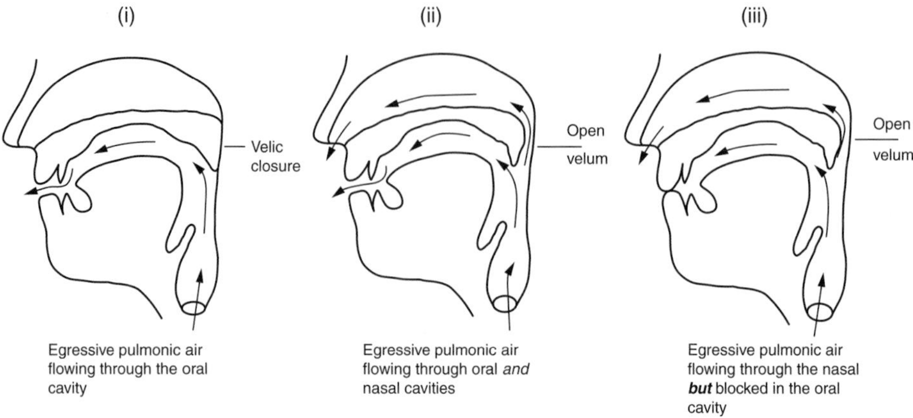


**Figure 2.5** Positions of the velum showing: (i) oral, (ii) nasalized and (iii) nasal airflow

example, the closure is bilabial (lips pressed firmly together, as in the third diagram) and a bilabial nasal is heard as all the air escapes via the nose (see (iii) in Figure 2.5). For [n], the closure is alveolar (see above), so [n] is an alveolar nasal. In the production of both of these sounds, the vocal folds are vibrating throughout for normal voice – remember you can check this by making a prolonged [m] sound, as when saying *Mm*... while resting your fingers lightly on your Adam's apple. You should feel a slight vibration against your fingertips. We can now give these two sounds their full and unique VPM labels: [m] is a voiced bilabial nasal, and [n] a voiced alveolar nasal. Look at the IPA Chart (page 26) – you will find nasals in the second row, [m] in the column headed bilabial, [n] in the alveolar column. Their position at the right side of their respective cells tells us they are voiced sounds, the space at the left being reserved for voiceless sounds. In fact, nasal consonants are typically voiced and for this reason have a periodic waveform, but because the airstream is working to resonate in two cavities at once (oral and nasal), the end-product is weaker-looking – the extent of vertical displacement seen in the waveform when the air comes only through the mouth, as for *Ah!*, is considerably reduced when it is flowing through both cavities. You can see this at points marked '2' in Figure 2.7 – the waveforms of [ŋ] and [n] are much less robust than those of the vowels preceding them. (Note the use of [ ̃] above the vowel symbol in *rang* [ɹæ̃ŋ] and *Ken* [kʰẽn] denotes the open(ing) velum, with air flowing simultaneously through both the oral cavity and the nasal cavity; sounds produced this way are called **nasalized** (see (ii) in Figure 2.5).)

All other consonants are made with velic closure which occurs along with another constriction in the oral or pharyngeal cavities. At the most extreme end of the scale, this constriction is a complete closure, just like that described for nasals. The velum closes, preventing nasal airflow, then the active articulator rises (the movement this time being called the approach phase) and seals firmly against the passive articulator, completely obstructing the oral airflow. This position is maintained for a brief interval of time (called

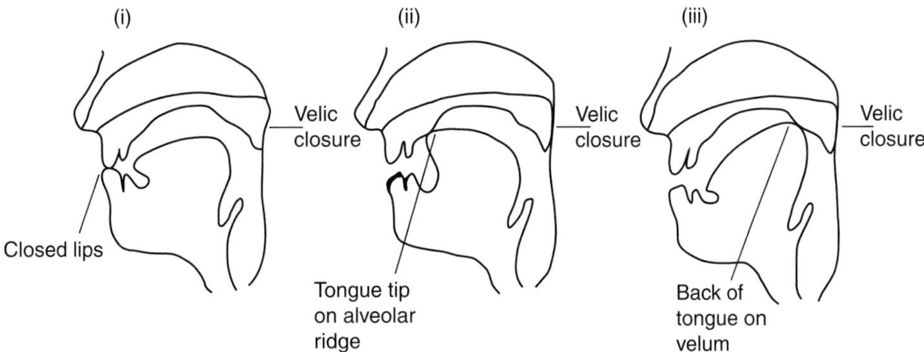


**Figure 2.6** Vocal tract diagrams showing positions of the articulators during production of plosives: (i) bilabial plosives [p b], (ii) alveolar plosives [t d] and (iii) velar plosives [k g]

the hold phase – visible as a flat line in the speech waveform and a blank in the spectrogram, at points '3' in Figure 2.7) before the active articular moves away (called the release phase). During the hold phase, air continues to flow from the lungs into a sealed space (there is an oral closure *and* velic closure, so the air is trapped). Air pressure in this sealed space therefore increases. When the articulators separate a transient, aperiodic noise is heard, called plosion. The compressed air is then released, intra-oral air pressure drops, and normal airflow resumes. Sounds made this way are called plosive and appear along the first row of the IPA Chart. Such sounds include [p] as in *pop-up* (remember, the location of the symbol in the left of the bilabial plosive cell tells us [p] is voiceless) and [b] as in *baby* (voiced bilabial plosives), [t] in *tighter* (voiceless alveolar plosive) and [d] in *deadly* (voiced alveolar plosives), [k] sounds in *cooker* (voiceless velar plosives) and [g] in *giggle* (voiced velar plosives). As well as symbols and labels, these sounds can also be represented by vocal tract diagrams showing the exact positions of the articulators, as in Figure 2.6.

If, instead of complete closure, the articulators are separated by a narrow gap, airflow is no longer blocked but becomes turbulent, giving rise to audible friction. Hissing and scraping sounds called 'fricatives' are heard (visible as aperiodicity in the resultant waveforms and spectrograms, as at points marked '1' in Figure 2.7). The nature of the gap may be slit-like, creating less noisy sounding friction, with the upper surface of the tongue smooth or slit as in English [θ] and [ð] (voiceless and voiced dental fricatives), or it can be more focused as when the upper surface of the tongue assumes a central groove, channelling the airflow along this groove. All the consonants we met in the preview are of the grooved, noisy kind, called sibilant. For [s] (voiceless alveolar fricative) and [z] (voiced alveolar fricative) the tongue tip or blade (speakers vary) with a narrow, shallow groove along the surface, articulates against the alveolar ridge. [ʃ] and [ʒ], for which the tongue surface assumes a rather deeper, wider groove, are described on the IPA Chart as voiceless and voiced postalveolar fricatives.

Other fricatives familiar from English include [f] and [v] (voiceless and voiced labiodental fricatives, see above) and [h] (called a 'voiceless glottal fricative') as in *high* and *who*.

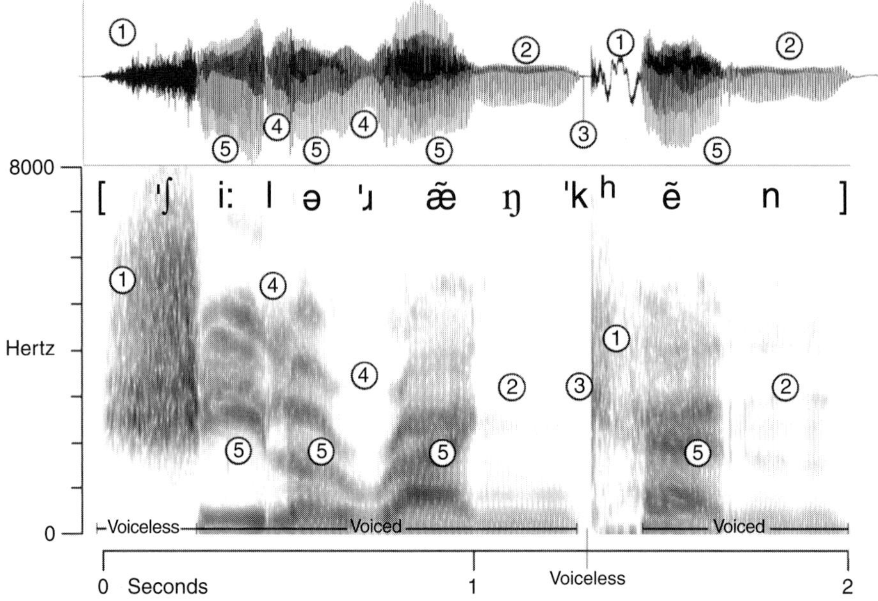


**Figure 2.7** Speech waveform (above) and spectrogram (below) of *Sheila rang Ken* (Speaker PA) 1 aperiodicity, 2 weak signal of nasal consonants, 3 hold-phase of plosive [k], 4 weaker signal of approximant consonants, 5 strong, robust image of vowels

In English, this becomes a voiced glottal fricative between other voiced sounds: [ɦ] as in *ahead, behind,* etc.

The third possible degree of stricture is wide approximation in which a substantial gap is left between the articulators enabling unimpeded airflow. In this case, the usually voiced airstream continues to flow smoothly, although like nasals (points '2' in Figure 2.7), the waveforms and spectrographic images of approximants tend to be feinter than those of vowels as you can see at points '4' in Figure 2.7. Consonants produced with wide approximation have much in common with vowels, and are called 'approximants'. English has four of these: voiced postalveolar approximant [ɹ] in *ray, arrow,* voiced palatal approximant [j] as in *yes, beyond,* voiced labialvelar approximant [w] as in *way, award,* and voiced alveolar lateral approximant [l] as in *lay, below.*

The approximant category subdivides into central (or median/mid-sagittal) approximants, where airflow is channelled straight along the centre line of the tongue ([ɹ], [j], [w] and all vowels) and lateral approximants where the tongue makes a complete central obstruction but lowers its side rims so that air flows unimpeded over the side. The two types are often referred to as simply approximants and laterals.

Wide central approximation is the position adopted by the articulators on release of a plosive sound when the following sound is often a vowel (think of English *pea, tea, key*) or sometimes an approximant consonant (think of English [kɹ-] in *cry,* [kj-] *cure,* [kw-] in *queen*). Sometimes, though, the active articulator moves only a fractional distance away from the passive one, creating a very narrow stricture in the release phase of the sort used to produce a fricative. This creates a further manner-type called 'affricate'. The technical definition of an affricate is a close-knit homorganic sequence (two consecutive gestures occurring at the same place of articulation) of stop plus friction agreeing in voice. This happens in English [t͡ʃ] as in *church* and [d͡ʒ] as in *judge* or *George*. In phonetic transcription, the use of the tie-bar shows that the sounds are close-knit – [t͡ʃ] in *Watch + Ed!* [ˈwɒt͡ʃ ˈed] rather than [-t ʃ-] in *What + shed?* [ˈwɒt ˈʃed]. In affricates, both the plosive component and the fricative component are shorter in duration than when they occur as separate sounds. Affricates are not entered separately on the IPA Chart because their symbols can be coined from related plosives and fricatives – [k͡x], for example, is a voiceless velar affricate.

Further manners include trill, tap and flap. The trill is quite widespread across languages and is more frequently used than English [ɹ], for example. For this reason, it is given the most straightforward of all the 'r' symbols on the IPA Chart, [r] – voiced alveolar trill. [r] consists of rapid, successive strikes by the tongue tip against the alveolar ridge. This contrasts with a single strike made for the sound called a 'tap', [ɾ] – voiced alveolar tap. The tap is a deliberate gesture, liking tapping once with your knuckles against a closed door. The trill, however, is inertial. The tongue tip rises towards the alveolar ridge and is held at just the right degree of stricture and under just the right amount of muscular tension for the passing airstream to cause it to bob up and down, striking repeatedly against the hard surface of the alveolar ridge. Neither sound is used routinely in English (although both are heard occasionally), but both are used in Spanish where they distinguish meanings such as [karo] *carro* 'cart' ~ [kaɾo] *caro* 'expensive'.

Flaps, such as [ɽ ], are also deliberate gestures. [ɽ ], for example, is a voiced retroflex flap, which is produced by curling the tongue tip up and back (much as for the retroflex American 'r' sound). This is then allowed to 'flap' back down into the rest position, striking once against the back of the alveolar ridge as it passes. Like other retroflexes, this is found in many Indo-Aryan and Dravidian languages.

In addition to each consonant sound being transcribed using a unique symbol, or having a unique VPM label, phoneticians also represent sounds by means of vocal tract diagrams showing the exact position of the principal articulators, the action of the vocal folds and arrows demonstrating air flow. Examples can be seen in Figures 2.4 and 2.5.

**KEY POINTS: Describing consonant sounds**

- Consonants are made by movement of an active articulator towards a passive articulator creating a stricture which affects the flow of the pulmonic egressive airstream.
- The point of stricture is the place of articulation.
- The type of stricture (wide, narrow, or complete closure) creates the manner of articulation.
- Airflow can be purely oral (with velic closure) or the velum can be open, enabling air to flow through the nasal cavities.
- The IPA Chart summarizes these characteristics and provides the phonetic symbol for each sound.

**EXERCISE 2.2**

Use the table of pulmonic consonants on the IPA Chart to complete the following transcriptions and VPM labels.

(a) English consonants

| | | | | |
|---|---|---|---|---|
| 1 | [m] | voiced | ________ | nasal |
| 2 | [ ] | voiced | velar | nasal |
| 3 | [k] | ________ | ________ | plosive |
| 4 | [ð] | voiced | ________ | fricative |
| 5 | [s] | ________ | alveolar | ________ |
| 6 | [l] | ________ | ________ | ________ |
| 7 | [ ] | voiceless | postalveolar | ________ |
| 8 | [ ] | ________ | postalveolar | approximant |
| 9 | [h] | ________ | ________ | ________ |
| 10 | [ ] | ________ | palatal | ________ |

(b) Non-English consonants

| | | | | | |
|---|---|---|---|---|---|
| 1 | [ɱ] | voiced | ________ | nasal | |
| 2 | [ ] | voiceless | palatal | plosive | |
| 3 | [χ] | ______ | ________ | fricative | |
| 4 | [ɣ] | voiced | velar | ________ | |
| 5 | [β] | ______ | bilabial | ________ | |
| 6 | [ɲ] | ______ | ________ | ________ | |
| 7 | [ ] | voiceless | ________ | lateral fricative | |
| 8 | [ʎ] | ______ | ________ | ________ | ________ |
| 9 | [ɖ] | ________ | ________ | ________ | |
| 10 | [ ] | ________ | labiodental | flap | |

## 2.4 Vowels

Speech is made up of sounds which in turn combine into syllables. Syllables are often multi-sound units, but almost always with a vowel at the centre. *Cap* [kæp], for example, is a single syllable with the structure [k]/consonant + [æ]/vowel + [p]/consonant. Phonologists (Chapter 3) present this as a CVC (consonant–vowel–consonant) syllable.

Because they have wide approximation, many vowels offer very little by way of tactile or kinaesthetic feedback – you can't feel anything touching, and there is often little impression of movement. This is quite different from the sensation of saying [mɑ mɑ mɑ] or [lɑ lɑ lɑ] where you can feel (and see) the lips touch for [m] and the tongue coming and going from the alveolar ridge for [l]. Accordingly, phoneticians describe vowels in rather different terms from those used for consonants. The first difference is that because vowels are usually voiced, there is no reason to mention voicing in the label at all. Instead, we rely more on what we hear, and we attribute particular auditory values to combinations of lip positions (spread, neutral or rounded) with the vertical displacements of the front, centre (mid-way between back and front) or back of the tongue, which we describe as adopting a close (that is, 'near' or 'close to'), close-mid, open-mid or open position (height) in relation to the hard and soft palates (see Figure 2.4). You should note here that you will encounter slightly different terminology in different books; phonologists, for example (as in Chapter 3 below) tend to refer to 'high' rather than close and 'low' rather than open vowels.

We judge the different auditory qualities in relation to fixed reference points called **Cardinal Vowels** which were established for this exact purpose over a century ago. You can hear the values for yourself by playing the eight peripheral vowel pairs around the vowel diagram (or quadrilateral) on the interactive version of the IPA Chart (see references). In auditory terms, the eight points around the edge of the vowel articulatory space are equidistant. In articulatory terms, the positions are often not so precise. Based on the original Cardinal Vowel system, the IPA Chart illustrates eight tongue gestures, each produced with unrounded (spread or neutral) or rounded lips, giving sixteen values in all.[3] On the IPA Chart, the unrounded symbol is presented systematically on the left of a pair, and the rounded one on the right. Each vowel quality can thus be given a backness openness roundness (BOR) label (the vowel equivalent of VPM labels for consonants).

Close vowels are produced with the high point of the tongue as close to the palate as possible without forming a stricture narrow enough to cause audible friction. As the high point of the tongue steps down, the jaw aperture also opens, moving from the narrow aperture associated with close vowels, through a medium aperture typical of the mid-height range (close-mid, mid, and open-mid), to a wide aperture for the production of the open vowels. Following the vowel diagram (Figure 2.8) round, starting at the top left corner, we find:

- [i] and [y] – front, close, unrounded and rounded vowels respectively, very like the vowels heard in French *vie* [vi] 'life' and *vue* [vy] 'view'
- [e] and [ø] – front, close-mid, unrounded and rounded, very like the vowels heard in French *thé* [t̪e] 'tea' and *deux* [d̪ø] 'two'
- [ɛ] and [œ] – front, open-mid, unrounded and rounded, very like the vowels heard in French *très* [tʁɛ] 'very' and *oeuf* [œf] 'egg'
- [a] and [ɶ] – front, open, unrounded and rounded; [a] is similar to the vowel heard in conservative Parisian French *patte* [pat̪] 'paw'; [ɶ] is rarely attested
- [ɑ] and [ɒ] – back, open, unrounded and rounded, very like the vowels heard in French *bas* [bɑ] 'low' and Non-regional British English (NBE) *hot* [hɒt]

[3] The IPA Chart rationalizes the original Cardinal Vowel diagrams, avoiding an arbitrary switch in lip position that occurred between positions 5 and 6.

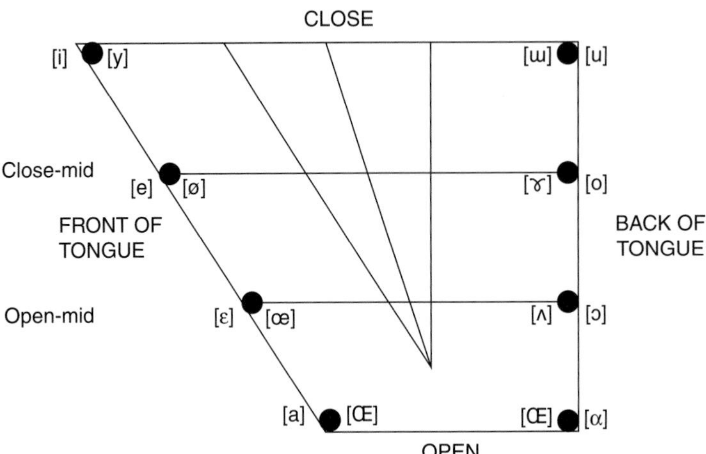


**Figure 2.8** A vowel quadrilateral showing the sixteen Cardinal Vowels, following the IPA Chart presentation

- [ɤ] and [o] – back, close-mid, unrounded and rounded; [ɤ] is very like the vowel heard in Vietnamese [tɤ]'silk' and [o] like French *beau* [bo] 'beautiful'
- [ɯ] and [u] – back, close, unrounded and rounded; [ɯ] is very like the vowel heard in Korean [ˈɯːmzig] 'food' and [u] near to French *doux* 'soft'

Note that these are absolute, Cardinal values. The fact that they are very similar to values attested in real languages does *not* mean that we can say some languages have Cardinal Vowels. Not at all! This simply allows us to keep certain more familiar values in mind as reminders of actual Cardinal values. In this way, we learn to judge values by ear. The vast majority of real language vowels fall in between these Cardinal and IPA reference values. The 'e' sound in English *bed*, for example, is approximately midway between Cardinal/IPA [e] and Cardinal/IPA [ɛ]. We represent this phonetically by saying it is mid-height, and we apply a diacritic to the main symbol to show this: [e̞] (the tiny-T below the symbol means 'more open than' the quality of the symbol itself). Likewise, the [i]-sound in English *bead* is more open, but also more centralized than Cardinal/IPA [i] (a point along the surface of the tongue, just behind the fully front point – so somewhat nearer to the centre – is the active articulator).

Vowels can be produced with or without velic closure. Vowels are usually oral sounds, produced with the velum closed, but some languages also use vowel sounds in which the velum is deliberately open. Air passes simultaneously through the oral and nasal cavities (see (ii), Figure 2.5). French, for example, has a small subgroup of nasalized vowels, [ɛ̃], [ɑ̃], [õ] and [œ̃] (heard in the utterance *un bon vin blanc* 'a good white wine' pronounced [œ̃ bõ vɛ̃ blɑ̃]). The nasalized values contrast with corresponding oral values: [bɑ] *bas* 'low' ~ [bɑ̃] *banc* 'bench', etc. In many languages, however, it makes no difference at all to the meaning whether the velum is open or closed – in English, for example, the velum will often remain fully open in words like *man* and *none* where the vowels are surrounded by nasal

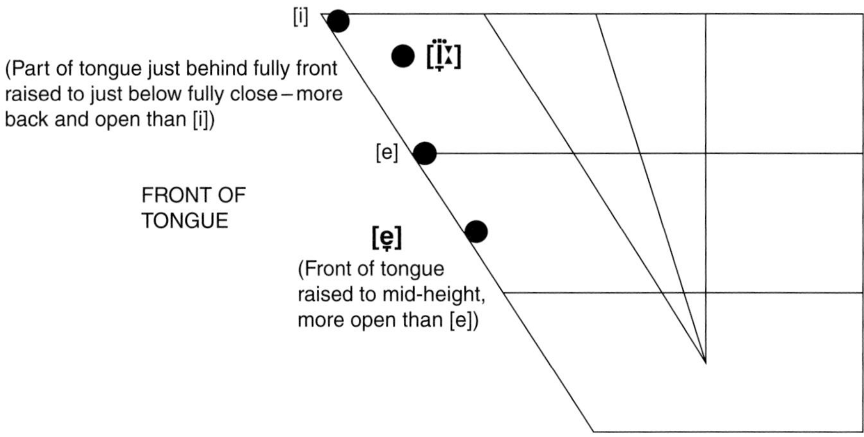


**Figure 2.9** Vowel diagram showing resonances of [ï̞ː] and [e̞]

consonants. Even in quite long utterances such as *one young man, on a runway,* etc., the velum can be left open throughout and the meaning is still clear. (The approximant consonants will also be nasalized, e.g. [ɒ̃n ə̃ ɹ̃ʌ̃nw̃ẽɪ̃].)

**KEY POINTS: Describing vowel sounds**

- Vowels are described in terms of auditory characteristics, and are judged/measured against the auditory values of Cardinal Vowels.
- Vowels are voiced, labelled in terms of backness, openness, and rounding:
  Backness – the active part of the tongue (front – centre – back).
  Openness – the nearness of the active part to the palate (close – close-mid – open-mid – open).
  Roundness – lip position (spread – neutral – round).

## EXERCISE 2.3

Complete the following transcriptions and BOR labels for the following vowels and try to position them on a vowel diagram:

| | | | | |
|---|---|---|---|---|
| (a) | [ä] | centralized front | ______________ | unrounded |
| (b) | [ ] | back | close | unrounded |
| (c) | [e] | ____________ | ______________ | unrounded |
| (d) | [ɒ] | back | open | ____________ |
| (e) | [ɔ̆] | ____________ | open-mid | ____________ |

### EXERCISE 2.4

This is a complete list of the symbols used here to transcribe English – the simplified phonemic versions used in pronunciation dictionaries, etc.

| Consonants | Keyword | Vowels | Keyword |
|---|---|---|---|
| p | *pie* | iː | *pea* |
| b | *buy, by(e)* | i | *happy* |
| t | *tie* | ɪ | *hit* |
| d | *die, dye* | e | *head* |
| k | *key, quay* | æ | *pat* |
| g | *guy* | ɜː | *purr* |
| f | *fee* | ə | *banana* |
| v | *V* (letter name) | ʌ | *hut* |
| θ | *thigh* | ɑː | *hard* |
| ð | *there* | uː | *who* |
| s | *sigh* | u | *usual* |
| z | *zoo* | ʊ | *put* |
| ʃ | *shy* | ɔː | *port* |
| ʒ | *usual* | ɒ | *pot* |
| h | *hi!* | eɪ | A (letter name) |
| ʧ | *cheer* | aɪ | *eye* |
| ʤ | *jeep* | ɔɪ | *boy* |
| l | *lie* | ɪə | *here* |
| r | *rye* | eə or ɛː | *hair* |
| w | *Wye, Y* (letter name) | ʊə or ɔː | *poor* |
| j | *you* | əʊ | *go* |

| | | | |
|---|---|---|---|
| m | *me* | aʊ | *how* |
| n | *no, know* | | |
| ŋ | *sing* | | |
| ʔ | *hotly, not now* (for some speakers) | | |

(a) Write VPM labels for each consonant not already labelled in Exercise 2.2.

(b) Try to give the orthographic version(s) of the following utterances:

1. /hɒt/ 2. /ˈevri/ 3. /siː/ 4. /weɪ/ 5. /red/
6. /kjuː/ 7. /ˈθæŋk ju/ 8. /ˈweðə(r)/ 9. /ˈzɪərɒks/ 10. /ˈsaɪkəʊ/

(c) A pair of words that differ in only one phoneme, such as *bed* vs *head*, are called a *minimal pair*. Find minimal pairs for the following contrasts – you can write the orthographic version of the words – the first one is done for you:

| | Initial position | Final position |
|---|---|---|
| 1. /p/ ~ /b/ | e.g. *pie* /paɪ/ ~ *buy/bye/by* /baɪ/ | *hop* /hɒp/ ~ *hob* /hɒb/ |
| 2. /s/ ~ /z/ | | |
| 3. /m/ ~ /n/ | | |
| 4. /n/ ~ /ŋ/ | (Not contrasted initially) | |
| 5. /m/ ~ /l/ | | |
| 6. /r/ ~ /w/ | | (Not contrasted finally) |
| 7. /ʃ/ ~ /tʃ/ | | |
| 8. /p/ ~ /f/ | | |
| 9. /d/ ~ /z/ | | |
| 10. /d/ ~ /t/ | | |

## 2.5 Tone and intonation

Language also exploits pitch variation. It does this in two ways: **tone** and **intonation**.

The deliberate use of pitch to change the meaning of a word is what happens in tone languages. Tone languages include all the Chinese languages (Modern Standard Chinese,

Cantonese, Hokkien, etc.), Thai, Vietnamese, many languages in Africa (Hausa, Yoruba, Zulu, the Khoisan languages, etc.) and a small number of indigenous languages of the Americas (Navajo, Mazatec, etc.). Tingsabadh and Abramson (1993) exemplify the five lexical tones of Thai (three static or register tones: high ´, mid ¯, low `, and two dynamic or contour tones: rising ˇ, falling ^):

kʰáː *to engage in trade*
kʰāː *to get stuck*
kʰàː *galangal* (a root from the ginger family)
kʰǎː *leg*
kʰâː *I*

But while only some languages use tone to distinguish word meaning, all languages have intonation. Intonation is the use of identifiable pitch patterns over (potentially longer) stretches of speech to convey attitude and feelings and, in some cases, also grammatical categories (statements vs questions, for example) or semantic content (completeness or finality vs incompleteness or non-finality, for example). Intonation is interpreted by listeners to determine the exact nature of the message intended by the speaker.

The first thing intonation does is to chunk speech into stretches short enough for listeners to process easily. In producing the utterance *the photo shows grey mice and brown mice*, the speaker might choose to break this down into two or three shorter units called **intonational phrases** (IPs): *the photo* |[1] *shows grey mice* |[2] *and brown mice* ||[3].This uses two non-final or minor boundaries (numbered 1 and 2) and one final or major boundary (3). The first two let the listener know the speaker hasn't finished (in Southern British English, the IPs will often be spoken using a rising melody line, a rising tone), while the third one traditionally signals 'this is the end of what I have to say' by use of a falling tone.[4] The speaker doesn't necessarily leave a gap at either of the first two boundaries, but there is a recognisable change in the melody line – a new tune starts after each boundary. Listeners, phonetically trained or not, are extremely sensitive to these cues. It is our intonation (deliberate or inadvertent) that gives offence, for example, provoking friends or loved ones to exclaim 'It's not what you said, it's the way that you said it!'

Each IP in English also has its own rhythm, determined by the number and distribution of stresses – this is known as **sentence stress**. The beats fall on the inherently stressed syllable of the word(s) in question, usually content words (nouns, verbs, adjectives, etc.). In English, the position of the **stress** in a word is free. For example, in the polysyllabic word *parliament*, stress falls on the first syllable [ˈpɑːləmənt], but in *parliamentary* it falls on the third syllable, [pɑːləˈmentri], and in *parliamentarian*, it is on the fourth [pɑːləmenˈteəriən]. This is quite different from a fixed stress language like Polish where the stress almost invariably falls on the penultimate syllable – *dobro*

[4] I say traditionally because of the increasing use of high rising terminals, or 'up-speak', in which the speaker completes a statement with a rising tone rather than a falling one. This is especially prevalent amongst younger speakers of English and may well be something you yourself do, and so you need to be aware of it. (Even I do it quite a bit, and I'm old!)

[ˈdɔbɾɔ] ‘good’, for example, but *dobroduszny* [dɔbɾɔˈduʃnɨ] ‘good-natured’, or *Latynos* [laˈtɨnɔs] ‘Latin-American (*n.*)’ but *latynoamerikański* [latɨnɔameɾiˈkaɲski] ‘Latin-American (*adj.*)’.

To get a feeling for stress and its role in English speech, the rhythm of the poetic limerick form is often helpful:

*There ónce was a yóungster called Óli*
*Who róde up to tówn on a trólley.*
*He spént his last díme,*
*And hád a great tíme,*
*But it ráined and he néeded his brólley!*

All limericks follow this pattern of five lines with three stresses (rhythmic beats) in the first, second and fifth, and two in each of the third and fourth – try clapping on the beats as you say it. Free stress also contributes to word class distinctions in English such as *permit* with first syllable stress in the noun variant [ˈpɜːmɪt] and second in the verb [pəˈmɪt], likewise *object* [ˈɒbdʒɪkt] (noun) and [əbˈdʒekt] (verb), etc.

The IPs in our data are very short and will probably have just one stress each. If we transcribe the data phonemically, this gives /ðəˈfəʊtəʊ |[1]ʃəʊz ˈgreɪ maɪs |[2] ən ˈbraʊnmaɪs ||[3]/.

Next, English intonation identifies the single most important item in each IP, again helping the listener to make sense of the message – in our limerick, there could be five IPs (one per line), with the most important stressed syllable the last in each, *Ol-, troll-, dime, time* and *broll-*. The most important item in an IP is usually the last content word with new information; it is the stressed syllable in this word that will be the **nucleus**. Intonation identifies this by giving pitch prominence to that particular stressed syllable, meaning it will have a noticeably different pitch (higher or lower than the pitch of the preceding syllable(s)) and/or a gliding tone. This syllable is called the nucleus. Every IP has just one nucleus, and the pitch movement or melody that begins there is called a nuclear tone.

In terms of chunking, IPs are usually short, around five words. In English, it’s very common for grammatical subjects to have their own IP, as is the case with IP1 in our data, ðəˈfəʊtəʊ|[1]. The IP has only one stressed syllable and so this, by default, will be the nucleus. It’s good practice to underline the nucleus, as here: ðəˈfəʊtəʊ |[1]. And because IP1 is incomplete – the speaker is only setting the scene and wants the listener to keep listening – it’s very likely that one of two so-called rising tones will be selected, either a low rise, or a fall-rise. Let’s use a fall-rise here: ðə$^{v}$fəʊtəʊ |. The stress mark is now a tonetic stress mark, in this case a small, raised v-shape showing that the syllable is stressed and that the speaker’s voice will begin a falling and then rising tonal movement here, the pitch high on *pho-* and going down to low on *–to* where it will glide up to a sort of mid-level within the speaker’s pitch range (illustrated in Figure 2.10). IP2 is also incomplete, so again a rising tone is most likely. This time it is the first item of a list, and will almost certainly be a low rise tone. The speaker will also avoid focusing attention on repeated items (English always avoids this) and so the nucleus will draw the listener’s attention to the different or new information being

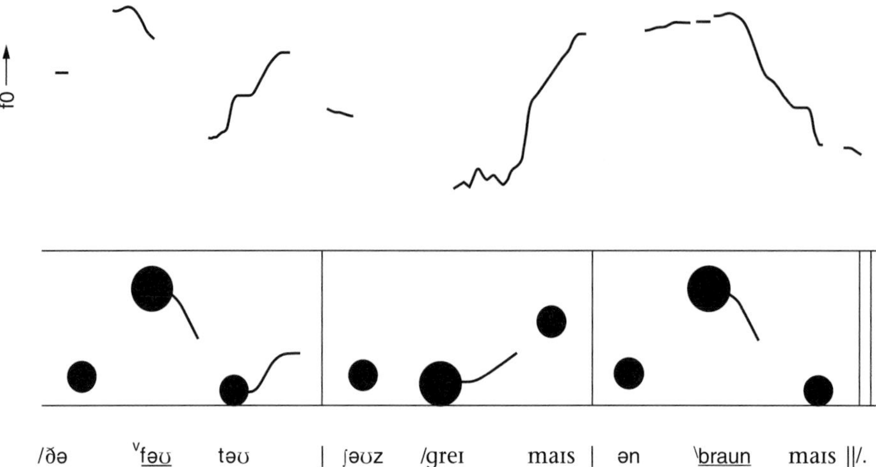


**Figure 2.10** An interlinear diagram showing the relation of the schematic representation to the actual f0 of the utterance (speaker PA)

given, the colour of the mice: ʃəʊz ˏgreɪ maɪs |[2]. Because English likes to alternate stressed syllables with unstressed ones, both the verb *shows* and the repeated word *mice* may be unstressed; the new tonetic stress mark now shows us 'low rise' – placed at the bottom of the line (implying 'low' in this system (Wells 2006)), the angle of the little line is pointing upwards, indicating 'rising' pitch. The speaker will pronounce the colour term at the bottom of his or her pitch range and then move up in pitch onto the final syllable *mice*. Again, you can follow these movements in the diagram in Figure 2.10. Then, the final IP which traditionally in English would have a falling tone: ən ˋbraʊn maɪs ||[3]. The nucleus picks out the only new (different) information here, *brown,* and the tonetic stress mark shows a high fall – the speaker's voice starts high and then falls down to fully low on the last syllable *mice* (as shown in Figure 2.10). Fully transcribed, we have /ðəᵛfəʊtəʊ | ʃəʊz ˏgreɪ maɪs | ən ˋbraʊn maɪs ||/. The actual f0 of this melody is shown in Figure 2.10, compared with the impressionistic representation using an interlinear diagram where the top line represents the speaker's highest pitch and the bottom line his or her lowest and each syllable is given a dot – large for stressed and smaller for unstressed.

The intonation of every language is unique. What is described here is specifically English. The descriptive system selected identifies some seven nuclear tones (high fall, low fall, rise-fall, mid-level, high rise, low rise, fall-rise). IPs subdivide into a maximum of four components of which only the nucleus is obligatory. Any remaining syllables following the nucleus constitute a tail (maintaining fully low, level pitch following all falling tones, and having a rising shape following all rising tones). Syllables before the nucleus can be stressed. The first stress, if that is not itself the nucleus, is called the onset and marks the beginning of one of four types of head: high (syllables on a level pitch, higher than mid pitch but below the starting pitch of a high fall nuclear tone), low (all syllables fully low), falling (starting from a high pitch, each syllable is a little lower in pitch than the one before) and rising (starting from fully low, each syllable is a little higher in pitch than the one before). Any syllables before the onset constitute a prehead and are usually lowish in pitch (although not fully low), forming a low or unmarked prehead, but can exceptionally be very high, forming a high or marked prehead. All four components occur in:

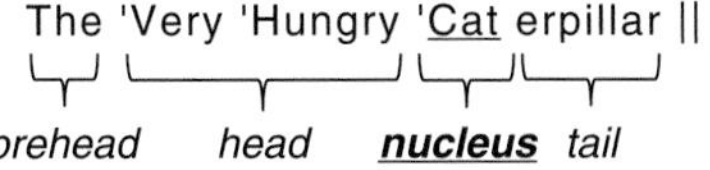


**KEY POINTS: Tone and intonation**

- Variation of pitch is used by some languages to distinguish word meaning – these languages are called tone languages.
- All languages use pitch variation over longer stretches of speech for accentual, grammatical or attitudinal purposes – this variation is called 'intonation'.

## EXERCISE 2.5

(a) Chunk the following limerick and identify the stressed syllables:

*There once was a baby called Tia*
*Who's mummy thought she was so dear*
*She had a pet cat*
*Who was sleepy and fat*
*And they found he had drunk her dad's beer*

(b) Try to think of more noun/verb pairs distinguished mainly by stress in English. You can give the orthographic versions of the words.

(c) Stress also distinguishes certain compound nouns from noun phrases. One such contrast is the sequence [bluːbɒtl̩] denoting either the compound noun identifying a type of fly, *bluebottle* [\bluːbɒtl̩] with the first component carrying the main stress (the nucleus), or a noun phrase identifying the colour of a bottle, *blue bottle* [bluː\bɒtl̩] with the nucleus in the second component. Can you think of a few more pairs of this kind? You can give the orthographic versions of the words.

(d) Identify the main stress in each of the following polysyllabic words:

1. photography 2. rhinoceros 3. beautiful
4. fellowship 5. remarkable 6. departmental
7. antisocial 8. conveniently 9. comprehensively
10. phonetics

WEBSITE: **Group exercise**

Professional phoneticians have usually undergone an extended period of ear-training – learning to identify, by ear, all the sounds encountered in human speech. To do this successfully, it helps to be what we could call 'speech aware' and sensitive to how you and the people around you pronounce things. This exercise will help you begin to cultivate and develop this important habit.

## 2.6 SUMMARY

This chapter has introduced you to the way in which phoneticians describe speech sounds and the techniques employed to identify and represent them. We looked first at the vocal tract and began and ended with consideration of the role played by the larynx in speech production. The contribution made by the vocal folds was fundamental here, acting on the stream of air being expelled by the lungs to enable speech and (as we saw later, in Section 2.5) to vary the pitch of the voice so as to enable the speaker to include tone and/or intonation.

Against the background of the IPA Chart, the chapter considered the various different ways the supraglottal speech organs act on the airstream to produce different qualities of sound (called manners of articulation) at different points in the vocal tract (called places of articulation). Looking first at the content of the pulmonic consonants table and the vowel diagram, we saw that consonants are described in a different way from vowels, using VPM descriptions to label consonants, and BOR labels (based in the first instance on the auditory perception of the sounds) for vowels.

The chapter also looked briefly at some of the effects of combining sounds in the speech continuum, at some of the changes that take place when sounds occur next to each other in rapid speech such as vowel nasalization in English. You were also able to begin to read transcription. Phonemic transcription also enabled us to see something of the relation between phonetics and phonology.

WEBSITE: **Phonetics**

Now go to the website and assess your knowledge of phonetics by completing the self-test questions!

## SUGGESTIONS FOR FURTHER READING

Ashby, P. (2005). *Speech Sounds*, 2nd edn. London: Routledge. This is a short, easy-to-read introduction to the basics of articulatory phonetics with plenty of in-text exercises (with answers) for further practice. *Speech Sounds* also briefly considers applications of phonetics in the workplace.

Ashby, M. and Maidment, J. (2005). *Introducing Phonetic Science*. Cambridge University Press. This book approaches phonetics from the acoustic viewpoint, introducing instrumental techniques for analysing speech. The book also covers the hearing mechanism and speech perception, linguistic universals relevant to phonetics and basic phonological (linguistic phonetic) concepts. The text is supported by plenty of practical exercises and has a companion website.

Cruttenden, A. (2014). *Gimson's Pronunciation of English*, 8th edn. London: Hodder Education. This book offers a detailed, in-depth study of the phonetics of English. As well as giving a general phonetic background and a sound-by-sound account, the book looks at the history of English sounds and aspects of connected speech including the stress, intonation and syllable structure. It offers a substantial final chapter on the teaching and learning of English as an additional language and the role of pronunciation.

# ANSWERS TO EXERCISES

## Exercise 2.1

**Key for all diagrams:**

______ voiceless

ΛΛΛΛΛ voiced

*slimy*

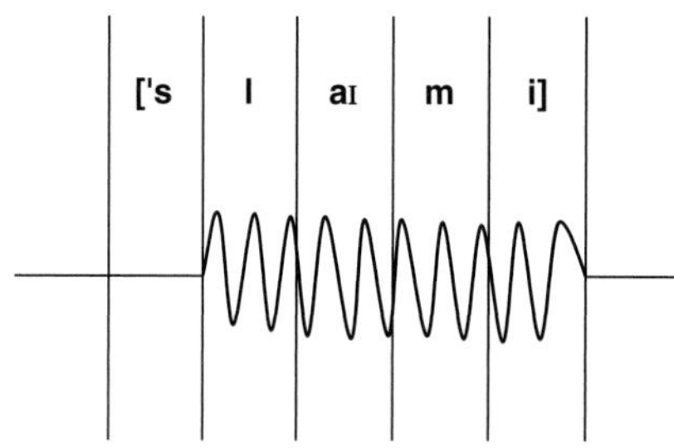


*thoughtful*

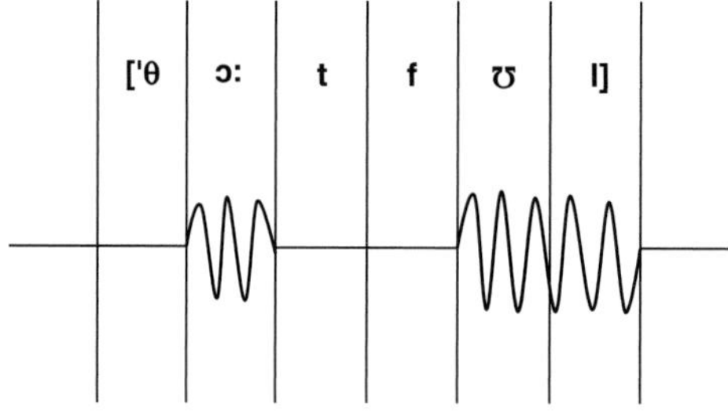


*convince*

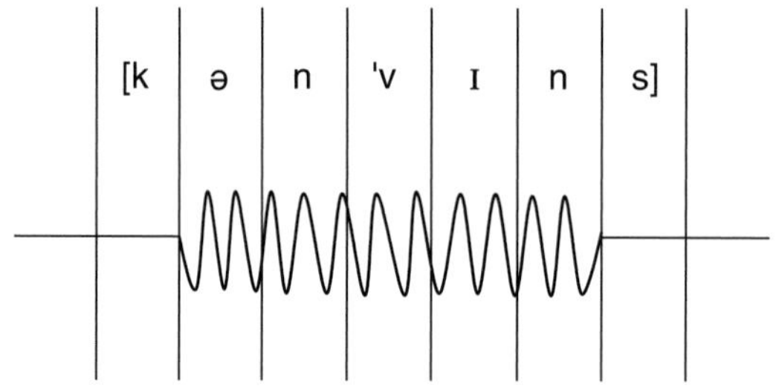

*monster*

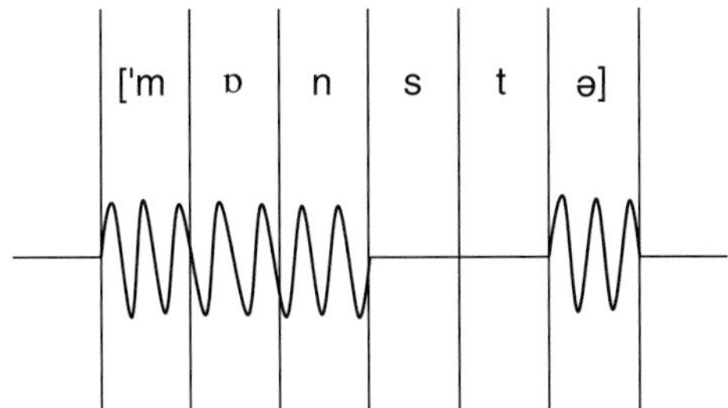


*sparrow*

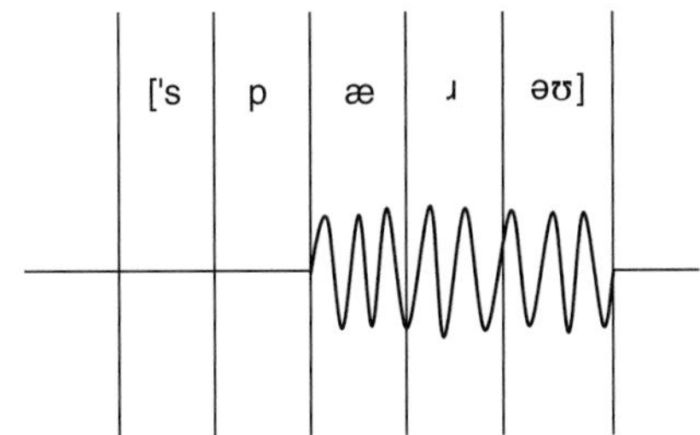


## Exercise 2.2

(a) English consonants

| | | |
|---|---|---|
| 1 | [m] | voiced **bilabial** nasal |
| 2 | [ŋ] | voiced velar nasal |
| 3 | [k] | **voiceless velar** plosive |
| 4 | [ð] | voiced **dental** fricative |
| 5 | [s] | **voiceless** alveolar **fricative** |
| 6 | [l] | **voiced alveolar lateral** (You can also call this **lateral approximant**) |
| 7 | [ʃ] | voiceless postalveolar **fricative** |
| 8 | [ɹ] | **voiced** postalveolar approximant |
| 9 | [h] | **voiceless glottal fricative** |
| 10 | [j] | **voiced** palatal **approximant** |

(b) Non-English consonants

| | | |
|---|---|---|
| 1 | [ɱ] | voiced **labiodental** nasal |
| 2 | [C] | voiceless palatal plosive |
| 3 | [χ] | **voiceless uvular** fricative |
| 4 | [ɣ] | voiced velar **fricative** |
| 5 | [β] | **voiced** bilabial **fricative** |
| 6 | [ɲ] | **voiced palatal nasal** |
| 7 | [ɬ] | voiceless **alveolar** lateral fricative |
| 8 | [ʎ] | **voiced palatal lateral (approximant)** |
| 9 | [ɖ] | **voiced retroflexplosive** |
| 10 | [ⱱ] | **voiced** labiodental flap |

## Exercise 2.3

(a) [ä] centralized front **open** unrounded

(b) [ɯ] back close unrounded

(c) [e] **front close-mid** unrounded
(d) [ɒ] back open **rounded**
(e) [ɔ̈] **centralized back** open-mid **rounded**

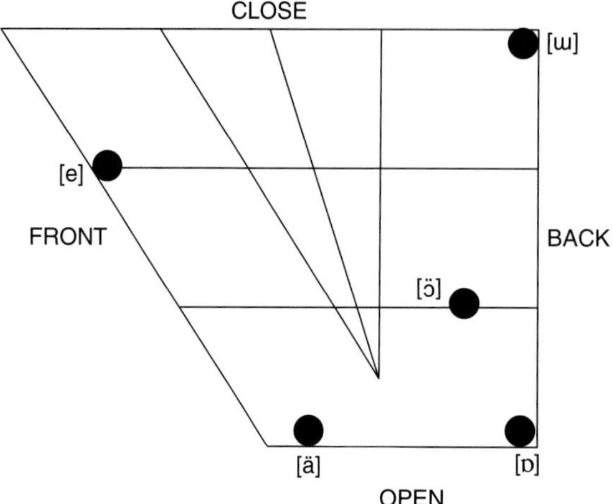


## Exercise 2.4

(a) [p] voiceless bilabial plosive — [b] voiced bilabial plosive
[t] voiceless alveolar plosive — [d] voiced alveolar plosive
[k] (see Exercise 2.2) — [g] voiced velar plosive
[ʔ] voiceless glottal plosive
[f] voiceless labiodental fricative — [v] voiced labiodental fricative
[θ] voiceless dental fricative — [ð] (see Exercise 2.2)
[s] voiceless alveolar fricative — [z] voiced alveolar fricative
[ʃ] (see Exercise 2.2) — [ʒ] voiced postalveolar fricative
[h] (see Exercise 2.2)
[tʃ] voiceless postalveolar affricate — [dʒ] voiced postalveolar affricate
[m] (see Exercise 2.2) — [n] voiced alveolar nasal — [ŋ] (see Exercise 2.2)
[ɹ] (/r/) (see Exercise 2.2) — [l] (see Exercise 2.2)
[j] (see Exercise 2.2) — [w] voiced labialvelar approximant

(b) 1. hot 2. every 3. see, sea, C 4. way, weigh, whey 5. red, read
6. cue, queue, Q 7. thank you 8. weather, whether 9. Xerox
10. psycho

(c) You will probably have chosen different words in answer to this question, but to help you decide whether your answers are right, here are some further examples of these contrasts – the transcription of each word is given so that you can compare the sound sequences and see how just one symbol/one sound is different in each pair.

## Exercise 2.5

(a) There ˈonce was a ˈbaby called ˈTia |
Who's ˈmummy thought ˈshe was so ˈdear |
She ˈhad a pet ˈcat |
Who was ˈsleepy and ˈfat |

| | *Initial position* | *Final position* |
|---|---|---|
| 2. /s/ ~ /z/ | sue /suː/ ~ zoo /zuː/<br>seal /siːl/ ~ zeal /ziːl/ | base /beɪs/ ~ bays, baize /beɪz/<br>niece /niːs/ ~ knees /niːz/ |
| 3. /m/ ~ /n/ | moon /muːn/ ~ noon /nuːn<br>meat /miːt/ ~ neat /niːt/ | rum /rʌm/ ~ run /rʌn/<br>lame /leɪm/ ~ lane /leɪn/ |
| 4. /n/ ~ /ŋ/ | (Not contrasted initially) | sin /sɪn/ ~ sing /sɪŋ/<br>ban/bæn/ ~ bang /bæŋ/ |
| 5. /m/ ~ /l/ | mean /miːn/ ~ lean /liːn/<br>make /meɪk/ ~ lake /leɪk/ | aim /eɪm/ ~ ale /eɪl/<br>hum /hʌm/ ~ hull /hʌl/ |
| 6. /r/ ~ /w/ | ray /reɪ/ ~ way /weɪ/<br>rink /rɪŋk/ ~ wink /wɪŋk/ | (Not contrasted finally) |
| 7. /ʃ/ ~ /tʃ/ | shoe /ʃuː/ ~ chew /tʃuː/<br>ship /ʃɪp/ ~ chip /tʃɪp/ | dish /dɪʃ/ ~ ditch /dɪtʃ/<br>wash /wɒʃ/ ~ watch /wɒtʃ/ |
| 8. /p/ ~ /f/ | pin /pɪn/ ~ fin /fɪn/<br>pat /pæt/ ~ fat /fæt/ | cop /kɒp/ ~ cough /kɒf/<br>leap /liːp/ ~ /leaf /liːf/ |
| 9. /d/ ~ /z/ | deal /diːl/ ~ zeal /ziːl/<br>do /duː/ ~ zoo /zuː/ | raid /reɪd/ ~ raise, rays /reɪz/<br>said /sed/ ~ says /sez/ |
| 10. /t/ ~ /d/ | ten /ten/ ~ den /den/<br>town /taʊn/ ~ down /daʊn/ | feet /fiːt/ ~ feed /fiːd/<br>rot /rɒt/ ~ rod /rɒd/ |

And they ˈfound he had ˈdrunk her dad's ˈbeer ||

(b) Other pairs include: ˈsubject/subˈject, ˈcontract/conˈtract, ˈimport/imˈport, ˈcontest/conˈtest, ˈremake/reˈmake, ˈsurvey/surˈvey, . . .
Also, pairs such as ˈfly-past/fly ˈpast, ˈsit-in/sit ˈin, ˈrunaway/run aˈway, ˈclimbdown/climb ˈdown, . . .

(c) Colours frequently feature in these pairs, such as: ˈgreenhouse/green ˈhouse, ˈBlackpool/black ˈpool, ˈblackbird/black ˈbird, ˈblue-stocking/blue ˈstocking, ˈyellow-hammer/yellow ˈhammer, ˈwhiteboard/white ˈboard . . .
But there are also pairs such as: ˈbighead/big ˈhead, ˈwholemeal/whole ˈmeal, ˈfairway/fair ˈway, ˈlighthouse/light ˈhouse, ˈflatpack/flat ˈpack . . .

(d) 1. phoˈtography 2. rhiˈnoceros 3. ˈbeautiful
4. ˈfellowship 5. reˈmarkable 6. departˈmental
6. antiˈsocial 8. conˈveniently 9. compreˈhensively
10. phoˈnetics

# Web resources

## Exercises and tutorials

University College London's Educational Resources in Speech, Hearing and Phonetic Sciences can be found at: www.phon.ucl.ac.uk/resource/educational.php. This site offers a range of pages on phonetics, including web tutorials on voicing and different aspects of plosives, plus a large range of interactive exercises relating to sound recognition, intonation and transcription.

## The International Phonetic Association

The IPA's homepage can be found at http://www.internationalphoneticassociation.org. There is a great deal of useful, interesting and informative information here regarding the wider discipline and world of phonetics. The page will give you access to the association's *Handbook* and recordings of the specific language illustrations this contains, as well as informing you about the history of the association, its *Certificate* examination, and much more.

## The IPA Chart

### Interactive charts

There are several different sites offering interactive versions of the IPA's alphabet chart where you can hear the different sounds represented by the symbols.

- http://web.uvic.ca/ling/resources/ipa/charts/IPAlab/IPAlab.htm

This is one of the best interactive charts, freely available to the general public. It is produced and maintained by John Esling and hosted at the University of Victoria in Canada. The recordings accompanying this chart are accurate, clear and dependable.

- www.phonetics.ucla.edu/course/chapter1/consonants1.html

This is another chart offering good, clear and extremely accurate recordings made by the late Peter Ladefoged. It is a little bit more fiddly to use than the Esling chart, above, but excellent for hearing another voice/speaker producing the different cardinal sound qualities.

- www.paulmeier.com/ipacharts/

Meier's recordings of the IPA sound values are often much less accurate than those of Esling and Ladefoged, but they are nonetheless valuable for comparative purposes. Additionally, by hovering your mouse over the symbol, this chart provides you with the full label for each sound (vowels and consonants) as well as the agreed name of each symbol – it's well known, for example, that [ə] is called *schwa*, and [æ] *ash*, but less well known are the names of other symbols such as [ŋ] *eng* and [ɲ] *left hook N* or [ʊ] *upsilon* or *turned omega*, etc. (Sometimes these names can be useful, but other times they are less convenient – the dental diacritic [̪], for example, is memorable because it looks like a tiny tooth, but it has the rather formal name *underscore bridge*. . .)

This page is also accessible, along with other phonetics pages, via the homepage of Eric Armstrong, the Canadian phonetician who made the recordings, at the York University (Canada): www.yorku.ca/earmstro/

- www.ipachart.com

One more interactive chart, the work of Peter Isotalo at the UCLA Phonetics Lab Archive, can be found on this web page. Not all pronunciations are equally reliable here.

### Hard copies

Hard copies of the IPA Chart (on page 26 of this book) and of what is often called the ExtIPA ('Extensions' to the IPA Chart – a further range of symbols used to supplement the basic alphabet by speech and language therapists) can be downloaded and printed from: http://web.uvic.ca/ling/resources/ipa/handbook.htm or from the Association's homepage at: http://www.internationalphoneticassociation.org

## Typing phonetic/phonemic transcriptions

To make the most of Unicode fonts and make typing phonetic transcriptions easier, you are recommended to download and use the phonetic keyboard, free from the UCL phonetics resources website: www.phon.ucl.ac.uk/resource/phonetics/

You can also download the free Charis SIL fonts by following this link. These fonts were designed specifically for phonetics and they overcome problems with alignment and stacking of diacritics commonly found in regular Unicode fonts.

## Speech analysis

If you are interested in trying to make your own speech waveforms and spectrograms, like the one you have seen in this chapter in Figure 2.7, or intonation curves like the one in Figure 2.10, there is free software that you can download and use.

- *Speech Filing System* (SFS), authored by Mark Huckvale, runs on PCs using Windows and Unix systems. SFS is available from UCL at: www.phon.ucl.ac.uk/resource/sfs/
- A simpler version of SFS, called WASP (*Waveforms Annotations Spectrograms and Pitch*), again authored by Mark Huckvale, and which also runs on PCs, is also available from UCL at: www.phon.ucl.ac.uk/resource/sfs/wasp.htm
- A rather more complex program, but one favoured by many phoneticians is *Praat: Doing Phonetics by Computer*. Authored by Paul Boersma and David Weenink, *Praat* is available from the University of Amsterdam at: www.fon.hum.uva.nl/praat/. *Praat* is available for both PCs and Macs.

## Visible speech...

There is a lot of good quality visual imaging of speech accessible on the internet today:

- ***Voicing and the vocal folds*** – some excellent photographs and video clips of the vocal folds in action can be found at: www.voicemedicine.com/normal_voice_functioning.htm#2
- ***Articulation*** – the University of Oxford's Phonetics Laboratory website contains excellent MRI scans of speakers producing short words and phrases in which the movements of the velum and the articulators in the oral cavity can be seen at: www.phon.ox.ac.uk/mri

  You can also follow the many links from this website which offer a wealth of imagery, both static and dynamic. (Bear in mind that not all links play equally well/easily on both PCs and Macs, so you might need to experiment.)

  Other URLs for the Oxford MRI materials include: www.phon.ox.ac.uk/dynamic_mri (which also has a link to a list of other sites).

  A further copy of the short Oxford MRI video – a speaker saying *Answered a door* – can also be found at: http://linguistics.berkeley.edu/acip/appendix/vocal_tracts/oxford/

  On the University of Maryland's School of Dentistry website, you can find an excellent clip of an electropalatography recording of a speaker saying *My pal Al saw the SS Pinafore*: http://speech.umaryland.edu/epg.html

  Electropalatography (EPG) requires speakers to wear a personalised acrylic palate – like a removable dental prosthesis – fitted with contact electrodes. The film shows the tongue making contact with the roof of the mouth as the speaker talks. You can see a picture of a sample palate on the same web page.

## Phonetics of other languages

Helpful for students of these modern foreign languages who are keen to understand more about their phonetics and pronunciation, a site maintained by the Centre for Languages, Linguistics and Area Studies and hosted by the University of Southampton offers a course in the phonetics of French, German and Spanish, authored by Rodney Ball: www.llas.ac.uk/resources/mb/296

The course manual, which includes lots of excellent exercises to supplement the exercises in Chapter 2, can be found at: http://humbox.ac.uk/62/1/PhoneticsFull.pdf

More generally, you can download the audio files of the languages used to illustrate use of the IPA's alphabet in its *Handbook* from: http://web.uvic.ca/ling/resources/ipa/handbook.htm

## Resources – general

An excellent and regularly updated website listing online phonetics resources of every imaginable kind is maintained by Jennifer Smith at the University of North Carolina:

www.unc.edu/~jlsmith/pht-url.html

## REFERENCES

http://web.uvic.ca/ling/resources/ipa/charts/IPAlab/IPAlab.htm

IPA (1999). *Handbook of the International Phonetic Association*. Cambridge University Press.

Laver, J. (1994). *The Phonetic Description of Voice Quality*. Cambridge University Press.

Tingsabadh, M. R. K. and Abramson, A. S. (1993). Thai. *Journal of the International Phonetic Association*, 23(1), 24–8.

Wells, J. C. (2006). *English Intonation: An Introduction*. Cambridge University Press.

(2008). *Pronunciation Dictionary*, 3rd edn. London: Longman.

# 3 Phonology

S. J. HANNAHS

**KEY TERMS**

- coda
- complementary distribution
- conditioning factors
- contrastive distribution
- flapping
- minimal pair
- neutralization
- obstruent
- onset
- phoneme and allophone
- phonotactics
- rhyme
- sonorant
- stress
- syllable
- underlying vs surface forms

**PREVIEW**

The focus of the last chapter was on phonetics, examining the characteristics of speech sounds, how they are produced and their physical properties, along with important related issues such as tone and intonation, and the crucial distinction between (phonetic) transcription and (orthographic) spelling systems like English writing. In this chapter we turn to phonology, which focuses on the systematic organization of speech sounds. As we will see, there are systematic behaviours in the speech sounds of language that cannot be attributed to the phonetics alone. We will also see that some aspects of the sound system of language – for instance, native speakers' intuitions about the relationships among the sounds of their language which may be at odds with phonetic reality – can be best understood at an abstract level of representation.

## 3.1 INTRODUCTION

In the previous chapter it was pointed out that phonetics deals with the characteristics of speech sounds themselves, while phonology deals with the organization of speech sounds into systems. There are aspects of the sound systems of human languages that cannot be explained by phonetics alone. Consider first the Greek word *πτέρυγα* [ˈptɛrɪɣɑ] > 'wing', the French word *psychologie* [psikɔlɔʒi] > 'psychology' and the German word *Knie* [kniː] 'knee' (and remember that the symbols in square brackets [ ] show how the words are pronounced). And now consider English: there are no words beginning with the sounds [pt], [ps] or [kn]. Since Greek, French and German are human languages, it cannot be the case that [pt], [ps] and [kn] are impossible (for human beings) to pronounce. Rather, it is a fact about the organization of the sound system of English that initial [pt], [ps] and [kn] are disallowed. Looking more closely, it is not really a fact about words, but a fact about **syllables**: English syllables do not begin with [pt], [ps] or [kn]. Recall from Chapter 2 that English spelling does not accurately represent how words are pronounced. There *are* words of English spelt with <pt>, <ps> and <kn>, as in *pterodactyl, psychology* and *knee*, but there are no words of English in which these sequences are routinely pronounced at the beginnings of words or even at the beginnings of syllables. In these cases only one of the initial consonants is pronounced: [tɛɹəˈdæktəɫ], [saɪ ˈkɔlɔʤiː], [niː].

To return to the point that phonetics alone does not explain all aspects of sound systems of language, what is going on here is that the phonology of English – the system organizing the sound patterns of the language – does not allow these particular combinations in specific positions. Take the sequence [pt] for instance. It is fine at the end of a word, like *kept, stepped, flipped*, etc. It can also occur in words like *apt* or *captain*, or in phrases like *hop to it!* or *up town*. What is the difference? In the cases where the sequence is allowed, the [p] and the [t] are either at the end of a syllable (where the dot indicates a syllable boundary) – [.kɛpt.], [.æpt.] – or in different syllables – [.ˈkæp.tən.], [.ʌp.ˈtaʊn.]. In none of these cases do the [p] and [t] occur together at the beginning of a syllable.

Interestingly, it is not just specific combinations that are disallowed in specific places, particular segments may also be disallowed in specific positions within a syllable. Take English again: words may begin with the sound [h] – *hat, head, hot, heavy, heartfelt, happy* – but words do not end with [h] in English. Again, spelling does not count! Words like *verandah* and *savannah* which may be spelt with <h> at the end are not pronounced with a word-final [h]. Note, though, that we can find non-initial [h] pronounced in English, in words like *ahead, behind, perhaps*. So, it is not the case that [h] in English can occur only at the beginnings of words. In all of these cases, the [h] occurs at the beginning of a syllable: *a. head, be.hind, per.haps, head, ha.ppy*.

Looking once again at the beginnings of words, consider the velar nasal, [ŋ], the final sound in *thing* [θɪŋ], *hang* [hæŋ], and so on. English words happily end with [ŋ], but they do not begin with that sound. Again, though, we can find [ŋ] in the middles of words, e.g. *finger, ringtone*, but once more, the syllable is crucial: the [ŋ] appears only at the ends of syllables, i.e. [ˈfɪŋ.gə], [ˈɹɪŋ.toʊn].

The facts about [h] and [ŋ] could, of course, be facts about phonetic possibilities in human language. And if we never found initial [ŋ] or final [h] in any language we would be supported in that conclusion. Unfortunately for that hypothesis, there are languages which routinely pronounce final [h], e.g. Navajo, with words like *gah* [kɑh] 'rabbit' and *tooh* [$t^h$oːh] 'lake'. Likewise, there are languages which regularly pronounce initial [ŋ], e.g. Samoan, in words like [ŋaŋana] 'language' and [ŋaːlue] 'to work'.

Throughout this chapter we will explore various ways in which speech sounds are organized into systems, and ways in which that organization goes beyond the phonetic facts.

## 3.2 Phonotactics and syllables

The illustrations above are to do with **phonotactics**, in other words, the allowable combinations of speech sounds in a particular language. Again, it is important to recognize that phonotactics are language specific. That means that the allowable combinations of speech sounds can vary from language to language, just as we have seen that Greek, French and German allow syllable-initial [pt], [ps] and [kn], respectively, but English does not.

Consider another illustration of this. In English there are no native words beginning with *[pw], *[bw], *[fw], *[vw], *[mw] (here the asterisk means 'does not occur'). That is, words like *[pwiːm], *[bwaɪf], *[fwɪɫ], *[vwɔt] and *[mwæp] are not possible words of English – despite the fact that English speakers can easily (learn to) pronounce them. How can we tell that this is a fact about English? Because other languages allow words beginning with [pw], [bw], etc. For instance, Spanish is perfectly happy with words like *puedo* [pweðo] 'I can' and *bueno* [bweno] 'good, masc.' Note, too, that forms like *[pwiːm] and so forth are not just non-occurring words of English, they are impossible words of English. Compare, for instance, something like [stɹɪɫp], which is a perfectly acceptable English word but which happens not to exist. So, we can say that [stɹɪɫp] is a possible but non-occurring word of English.

There are at least two questions you can ask about the restriction in English on words like *[pwiːm], *[bwaɪf], *[fwɪɫ], *[vwɔt] and *[mwæp]. Is it a restriction on any sequence of p+w, b+w, f+w, etc.? In other words, is it some general prohibition on [w] following [p], [b], [f], [v] and [m]? Or can the sequence occur in some contexts? The second question is this: can we observe anything about these particular combinations of sounds? That is, is there some generalization we can make about these words, and specifically these combinations of sounds, to help us understand the restriction?

Let us look first at the question of the sequence of p+w, b+w, and the others. In fact, we can find sequences of these sounds in English, both in phrases like *sleep well, live with, slim wife*, and in words like *leafworm, labworker, livewire*. What is it that makes these sequences different from those in *[fwɪɫ], *[pwiːm], etc.? The difference is that in *sleep well* and *live with*, and the other occurring sequences, there is a syllable boundary between the [p] and the [w] and between the [v] and the [w], [.sliːp.wɛɫ.], [.lɪv.wɪð.]. The [fw] and [pw] in *[.fwɪɫ.], *[.pwiːm.], on the other hand, are not separated by a syllable boundary. So the generalization seems to be this: the sequences [pw], [bw], [fw], [vw], [mw] can occur in English provided that they are in different syllables.

Can we say anything more about this? Yes. As a logical puzzle, it might be the case that English disallows syllables to begin with a combination of consonant + [w]. But consider this: there are consonants of English that can occur at the beginnings of words, and therefore syllables, followed by [w], such as *twine* [twaɪn], *dwell* [dwɛɫ], *sweep* [swiːp], *queen* [kwiːn], *Gwen* [gwɛn]. How do these words differ from the impossible words above, *[pwiːm], *[bwaɪf], *[fwɪɫ], *[vwɔt] and *[mwæp]?

Recall in the previous chapter, Section 2.3, different places of articulation were discussed. Now consider the sounds we are interested in here. As we have just seen, the consonants [t], [d], [k], [g] and [s] can all occur before [w] at the beginning of a word. These consonants,

[t], [d], [k], [g] and [s], are all '**obstruents**', in other words oral stops or fricatives. Do these consonants have some shared property, apart from simply that of being obstruents? Not really one that would help us here: [t], [k] and [s] are voiceless while [d] and [g] are voiced; [t], [k], [d] and [g] are stops while [s] is a fricative. Place of articulation, is also not shared, as [t], [d] and [s] are alveolars while [k] and [g] are velars.

But now consider the consonants that cannot precede [w]: [p], [b], [f], [v], [m]. They are also a mixture of voiced and voiceless, they also include stops and fricatives – and a **sonorant**. But what about place of articulation? The consonants [p], [b] and [m] are bilabial, while [f] and [v] are labiodental. What about [w] itself? It was described in the last chapter as labialvelar. So, [p], [b], [m], [f], [v], *and* [w] all involve a 'labial articulation', i.e. the lips. It would seem, then, that the prohibition on the cooccurrence of [p], [b], [m], [f], [v] followed by [w] is a restriction on two labial segments occurring together at the beginning of a syllable. In other words, we can state a phonotactic generalization about the facts we have been considering here: a labial consonant followed by a labial approximant in the same syllable is disallowed in English.

Without going into the details of syllables and syllable structure, we have seen that phonotactic restrictions can be stated in terms of syllables, for instance that in English [h] can occur only at the beginning of a syllable and [ŋ] only at the end. We have also seen that allowable combinations of speech sounds can be stated in terms of syllables, that for instance in English a labial consonant can be followed by [w] only when the two are in different syllables.

**KEY POINTS: Co-occurrence restrictions and the syllable**

- Languages have 'phonotactic restrictions', allowable combinations of speech sounds that may occur in specific positions in syllables.
- Languages also have restrictions on the occurrence of specific segments or segment types in specific syllable positions, for instance restricted to occurring in an onset or a coda.
- Phonotactic restrictions are language-specific and may differ from language to language.
- The syllable is the key to understanding these restrictions.

### EXERCISE 3.1 COUNTING SYLLABLES

For each of the words below state how many syllables it has and indicate where you think that the syllable boundaries fall. For instance, *elephant* has three syllables, [.ˈɛ.lə.fənt.]. (It is probably easiest to represent the syllable boundaries using a transcription, since English writing does not always clearly reflect the sounds involved.) And please do not use a dictionary – rely on your own knowledge of English!

| | | | |
|---|---|---|---|
| (a) table | (b) town | (c) mobile | (d) transept |
| (e) rhinoceros | (f) idea | (g) psychic | (h) conundrum |
| (i) lemon | (j) telephone | (k) honesty | (l) punitive |

## 3.3 Phonemes and allophones

In the last section we looked at syllables and phonotactics. Interestingly, syllables and syllable boundaries are not always clearly identifiable phonetically, yet syllables can help us make phonological generalizations, for instance about the phonotactics of a language. Another place where phonetics and phonology differ has to do with native speaker intuitions, where native speakers of a language may consider phonetically different sounds 'the same' in some real sense. Let us turn now to this and to the distinction between **phonemes** and **allophones**, which will be explained below.

Consider two set of words of English, *tack, stack* and *cat*, and *leaf* and *fill*. As an experiment, ask some speakers of English (who are not studying language and linguistics!) whether the 't'-sounds in *tack, stack* and *cat* are the same. Then ask them if the 'l'-sounds of *leaf* and *fill* are the same. It is very likely that in both cases the native speakers you ask will answer that, yes, the 't'-sounds in *tack, stack* and *cat* are the same, and the 'l'-sounds of *leaf* and *fill* are the same.

Now consider the phonetic transcription of the words in question: [t$^{h}$æk], [stæk] and [kæʔ],[1] and [liːf] and [fɪɫ]. As you learned in the previous chapter, phonetic transcription is done on a strictly one-symbol:one-sound basis. If two different symbols are used, that means that there are two different sounds. So here the 't'-sounds are phonetically [t$^{h}$], [t] and [ʔ]. The 'l'-sounds are phonetically [l] and [ɫ]. In other words, there are three phonetically different 't'-sounds and two phonetically different 'l'-sounds. Why, then, should native speakers of English think that these different 't'-sounds are the same, or that these different 'l'-sounds are the same? And more importantly for our purposes, how can we resolve this apparent contradiction that phonetically different sounds are perceived by native speakers as 'the same'?

The answer lies in the phonology, the abstract system underlying the speech sounds of, in this case, English. Let us assume that in some respect native speakers are correct that there is one 't'-sound and one 'l'-sound. Let us also assume that the native speaker's 't'-sound somehow corresponds to the phonetically different 't'-sounds, and the native speaker's 'l'-sound likewise maps onto the phonetically different 'l'-sounds. In doing so, we could say that the 't'-sound = [t$^{h}$], [t] and [ʔ], and the 'l'-sound = [l] and [ɫ]. Using a diagram, we might represent these relationships as in (1):

(1)
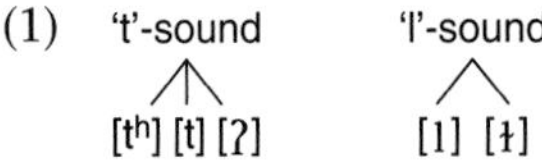


In a sense this allows us to represent the relationship between the native speakers' intuition about there being a 't'-sound and an 'l'-sound, because the diagram in (1) shows that the native speakers' 't'-sound corresponds to three different sounds, and that their 'l'-sound corresponds to two different sounds. But we also need to ask if we are

[1] For some speakers the last sound in words like this tends to be an 'unreleased' [t̚], rather than a glottal stop,[ʔ].

justified in doing this. In other words, is a representation like this merely a convenience for us to try to understand the organization of the speech sounds of English, or can we find further justification for it?

If the behaviour of native speakers were random, a diagram like that in (1) might be just a convenience. But, crucially, the occurrence of the 't'-sounds and the 'l'-sounds in native speakers' speech is not random, it is entirely predictable on the basis of where the sound occurs (also taking into consideration some variation across dialects of English). In other words, the aspirated [tʰ] occurs only in specific places, for instance at the beginning of a word like *tap* [tʰæp]. It also occurs at the beginning of a stressed syllable as in *attack* [əˈtʰæk]. (Stress here refers to syllable prominence, that the second syllable of *attack* is more prominent. For English, stress corresponds to higher pitch and greater volume.) Importantly, aspirated [tʰ] does not show up at the ends of words in English, e.g. *[kætʰ] or following [s] at the beginnings of words (or more precisely, syllables), as in *[stʰæk]. Similarly, the 'l'-sounds of *leaf* and *fill* cannot change places: *[ɫiːf], *[fɪl][2]. This tells us that not only is the occurrence of 't'-sounds and 'l'-sounds not random, since we can predict on the basis of phonetic environment which phonetic 't'-sound we will find in which position.

To formalize this a bit, what we have been calling the native speaker's 't'-sound we can refer to as 'phoneme /t/'. The 'l'-sound recognized by the native speaker is 'phoneme /l/'. Note the formalism of the slashes, / /: a symbol appearing between slashes is considered to be a 'phoneme', an abstract phonological unit distinct from actual phonetic production. In the two cases we have been looking at we can say that phoneme /t/ is related to three speech sounds, [tʰ] [t] and [ʔ]. These are known as 'allophones', the concrete phonetic speech sounds related to a particular phoneme. Likewise, phoneme /l/ has two allophones, 'clear-l' [l] and 'dark-l' [ɫ].

We are now in a position to express the relationships in (1) more formally as in (2). Here the native speakers' intuition is represented as a phoneme, which corresponds to one or more allophones.

(2) *phonemes* /t/ /l/

*allophones* [tʰ] [t] [ʔ] [l] [ɫ]

We noted above that speakers' use of specific allophones is not random. So, the one thing that is still missing at this point is a statement about the distribution of the allophones, in other words, information about the context in which each of the allophones is found. There are various ways of encoding this information. For our purposes, let us rely on 'distribution statements', descriptive statements about the context in which each allophone of a particular phoneme is found. For phoneme /t/ we need to say that the [tʰ] allophone occurs at the beginning of a syllable, the [t] allophone occurs following [s], and the glottal stop allophone [ʔ] occurs at the end of a syllable. This information is given in

[2] Some varieties of English tend to have either clear-l, [l], or dark-l, [ɫ] . For such varieties there is only one 'l'-sound, even phonetically.

(3), where the forward slash means that what follows is the relevant context, the underscore indicates the position of the allophone relative to its surroundings. The '${}_{\sigma}[$' means 'at the beginning of a syllable'; '$]_{\sigma}$' means 'at the end of a syllable'; lower-case sigma, σ, stands for 'syllable'.

(3) phoneme /t/: [t$^{h}$] / ${}_{\sigma}[$__ e.g. *tack*
[t] / ${}_{\sigma}[$s__ e.g. *stack*
[ʔ] / _ $]_{\sigma}$ e.g. *kat*

There are some important properties associated with phonemes and allophones. Phonemes are said to be in '**contrastive distribution**', while the allophones of a given phoneme are said to be in '**complementary distribution**'. Let us see what this means. In English, /t/ and /p/ are both phonemes. We can be sure of this because they occur in '**minimal pairs**', i.e. in words where there is a difference in meaning but a phonetic difference in only one sound. For example, *tack* and *pack* differ only in the first sound, [t$^{h}$æk] vs [p$^{h}$æk], while *stat* and *spat* differ only in the second sound, [stæt] vs [spæt]. So, we can say that /t/ and /p/ contrast in English; this sort of contrast, or contrastive distribution, is a property of phonemes.

Now consider the allophones of /t/. Do they contrast in the way we just saw for /t/ and /p/? No. We are able to say that /t/ and /p/ contrast because they can occur in exactly the same environment – e.g. at the beginning of a word, or following [s] – and when they do so they change the meaning of the word. On the contrary, the allophones of /t/, that is [t$^{h}$] [t] and [ʔ], cannot do this. Where one allophone of /t/ occurs, a different allophone of /t/ does not occur. So, [t$^{h}$] occurs in *tack* [t$^{h}$æk] but not in *stack* [stæk], where unaspirated [t] occurs. Interestingly, even if you did pronounce [stæk] as [st$^{h}$æk] it would not become a different word with a different meaning, it would just be a weird pronunciation of *stack*. That is because, as allophones, [t$^{h}$] [t] and [ʔ] are in complementary distribution. If, on the other hand, you pronounced *tack* as [p$^{h}$æk] it *would* be a different word and therefore misunderstood, because phoneme /t/ and phoneme /p/ are in contrastive distribution.

As we saw earlier in the chapter, phonotactic restrictions differ between languages. Similarly, the distribution of speech sounds and the relationship between phonemes and allophones are also language-specific. In other words, two sounds that are allophones in one language may be separate phonemes in a different language. For example, both English and Thai have the sounds [t$^{h}$] and [t]. However, although [t$^{h}$] and [t] in English are allophones of phoneme /t/, we find a different relationship in Thai. In that language [t$^{h}$] and [t] are separate phonemes. We can tell this because [t$^{h}$] and [t] contrast to form minimal pairs in Thai, e.g. [tûː][3] 'cabinet' vs [t$^{h}$ûː] 'blunt', [tam] 'to pound' vs [t$^{h}$am] 'to do', [tɔ̀j] 'punch' vs [t$^{h}$ɔ̀j] 'despicable'. So, for Thai we have to say that these two sounds are separate phonemes, /t/ and /t$^{h}$/, unlike English where [t] and [t$^{h}$] are allophones of the same phoneme /t/.

[3] The accent marks here indicate tones. They can be safely ignored for our purposes.

**KEY POINTS: Phonemes & allophones**

- The speech sounds of a language can be divided into 'phonemes' and 'allophones'.
- Phonemes contrast with each other – as seen in minimal pairs.
- Allophones do not contrast with each other and although they are phonetically different, native speakers often hear allophones of a single phoneme as 'the same'.
- The identification of phonemes and allophones is language specific; allophones in one language may be phonemes in another.

## EXERCISE 3.2 PHONEMES VS ALLOPHONES

### (i) Spanish (Indo-European; Spain and Latin America)

We know that [d] and [ð] are separate phonemes in English because they contrast in minimal pairs like *doze* and *those*, *ladder* and *lather.* Consider the same two sounds of Spanish in the following data and decide whether [d] and [ð] are separate phonemes or allophones of the same phoneme. Explain your decision. The data are given in transcription, not Spanish orthography, and you have enough data to decide.

| | | | | | |
|---|---|---|---|---|---|
| 1. naða | 'nothing' | 4. dezde | 'since' | 7. roðar | 'to roll' |
| 2. deðo | 'finger' | 5. donde | 'where' | 8. de | 'from' |
| 3. dɑr | 'to give' | 6. deðonde | 'whence' | 9. kwɑndo | 'when' |

### (ii) Tojolabal (Mayan; Mexico)

Consider the sounds [k] and [kˀ] (glottalized-k) in the following data and determine whether they are allophones of a single phoneme or separate phonemes. What kind of argument(s) can you develop for your position?

| | | | |
|---|---|---|---|
| 1. kisim | 'my beard' | 7. ʧakˀa | 'chop it down' |
| 2. kˀak | 'flea' | 8. koktik | 'our feet' |
| 3. pˀakan | 'hanging' | 9. kˀaʔem | 'sugar cane' |
| 4. sak | 'white' | 10. kˀiʃin | 'warm' |
| 5. kˀuutes | 'to dress' | 11. skuʧu | 'he is carrying it' |
| 6. snika | 'he stirred it' | 12. ʔakˀ | 'reed' |

There is one final point to mention with respect to phonemes and allophones, and that is '**neutralization**'. Neutralization is not terribly important, but it can be a confounding factor when trying to decide on the status of some segment as either a phoneme or an allophone. A contrast between two phonemes is said to be neutralized when, in a particular context, the two phonemes share a single allophone. Consider **flapping** in American or Irish English (there are other varieties that have flapping, too, but these two dialects are often cited). As you can easily establish, [t] and [d] are phonemes – /t/ and /d/ – in English, as supported by words like *tear* and *dear, bat* and *bad*. All varieties of English have this sort of contrast between /t/ and /d/. But what about *ladder* and *latter, Adam* and *atom*? In varieties of English with flapping, both /t/ and /d/ occur as flap, [ɾ], between two vowels when the first vowel is stressed. So, in American English both *ladder* and *latter* are pronounced as [ˈlæɾəɹ], *Adam* and *atom* are both [ˈæɾəm]. Even though /t/ and /d/ contrast elsewhere, in this position the contrast is neutralized. Consequently, we can say that /t/ and /d/ are phonemes of English, but that the contrast is neutralized between two vowels when the first vowel is stressed. Note, too, that there is further evidence that the [ɾ] in *atom* really is an allophone of phoneme /t/: compare the related word *atomic* [əˈtʰɑmɪk]. In *atomic*, the /t/ shows up as [tʰ] before a stressed vowel. Here, [ɾ] and [tʰ] occur in complementary distribution with each other: [ɾ] occurs following the stressed syllable, while [tʰ] occurs before the stressed syllalble. Given this complementary distribution, that means that [ɾ] is a further allophone of /t/ in these varieties. Just as [ɾ] is also an allophone of /d/ occurring in *ladder* and *Adam*. The neutralization refers to the fact that both phoneme /d/ and phoneme /t/ share the allophone [ɾ] in this particular position.

WEBSITE: **Group exercise**

Visit the website and, in a small group, examine the data from Welsh. Like Spanish in Exercise 3.2 (i), Welsh also has [d] and [ð]. This exercise encourages you to think about the phonological relationship between these two sounds in Welsh, and how this compares to the relationship between these sounds in Spanish and English.

## 3.4 Alternations and conditioning factors

Allophones are contextual variants of specific phonemes. For instance, as we have seen, [tʰ] is an allophone of /t/ which occurs in the context of the beginning of a syllable; [t] is an allophone of /t/ which occurs in a consonant cluster following [s]. In other words, a specific allophone of a particular phoneme occurs in a precise environment or set of environments. These environments may be purely phonetic, meaning that the only relevant information is the phonetic context. Or they may be a combination of phonetic conditioning together with morphological information, for instance the presence of a particular kind of prefix or suffix or grammatical marker (Chapter 4 focuses on morphology). Or the alternations can be associated with phonetic, morphological and lexical factors, where only specific words exhibit a certain alternation. We will look at these different **conditioning factors** in the next few sections.

### 3.4.1 Phonetic conditioning

The environment in which a particular allophone occurs may be defined purely phonetically. In this case, the conditioning context can be said to be phonetic. Take for instance the allophones of /n/ in English. Phoneme /n/ has several distinct allophones, including [n], [m], [ŋ], depending on the place of articulation of a following obstruent. So, phoneme /n/ occurs as [n] in words like *indeed* [ɪnˈdiːd] and *onto* [ˈɔntuː], but shows up as [m] in words like *input* [ˈɪmpʊt] and *unbroken* [ʌmˈbɹoʊkən]. Phoneme /n/ also occurs as [ŋ] in words like *ink* [ɪŋk] and *uncle* [ˈʌŋkl̩].

It becomes particularly clear that this is phonetic conditioning when we consider what happens in a different sort of syntactic context, but where the shape of /n/ can still be attributed to a following obstruent. Consider the preposition *in* of English. In isolation, or when followed by a vowel, this preposition is pronounced [ɪn]. It is also pronounced [ɪn] when followed by an alveolar consonant, e.g. [t] or [d] or [n]:

(4) [ɪn] Africa [ɪn] Texas [ɪn] Durham [ɪn] Norwich

However, in normal speech, that same preposition is pronounced [ɪm] before a bilabial consonant, [p], [b], [m], and it is pronounced [ɪŋ] before the velars [k] or [g] (presumably it would also be pronounced [ɪŋ] before [ŋ], but as we noted earlier, there are no [ŋ]-initial nouns in English).

(5) [ɪm] Paris [ɪm] Boston [ɪm] Manchester
[ɪŋ] Crete [ɪŋ] Greece . . .

We can see from the examples in (4) and (5) that the allophones of phoneme /n/: [n], [m] and [ŋ], are phonetically conditioned. The shape of /n/, that is, whether it occurs as alveolar [n], bilabial [m] or velar [ŋ], is determined entirely by the phonetic characteristics of the segment that follows /n/. In this case, the important phonetic characteristic is the place of articulation of the following consonant.

Another example of phonetic conditioning in English involves the alternation between oral and nasal vowels. In English, unlike some other languages like French, Polish, Navajo, the difference between nasal vowels and oral vowels is not phonemic – there are no minimal pairs in English based solely on whether a vowel is oral or nasal. Nonetheless, phonetically English does have both oral vowels and nasal vowels, as shown in (6), where the nasal vowels are shown with a tilde, ˜, over the vowel.

(6) *cat* [kʰæt] *can* [kʰæ̃n]
*sit* [sɪt] *sin* [sɪ̃n]
*suit* [sut] *soon* [sũn]

If you need convincing that the vowels in *can, sin,* and *soon* really are nasalized, try pronouncing those words while pinching your nose. The airflow, in particular the effect of stopping the airflow through the nose, indicates that the vowels are nasalized. And the words in (6) show the phonetic conditioning of vowel nasalization in English: the words ending with a nasal consonant, here [n], have a nasal vowel, while those ending in an obstruent have an oral vowel. The same is true of words ending with the nasals [m] or [ŋ], like *ham* and *hang*. Compare both of these words with *hat,* which has an oral vowel.

(7) *ham* [hæ̃m] *hang* [hæ̃ŋ] *hat* [hæt]

The phonetic environment is not the only type of conditioning factor that can influence the distribution of allophones of a specific phoneme. That distribution can also be affected by a combination of phonetic factors together with morphological considerations.

### 3.4.2 Phonetic and morphological conditioning

Linguistic morphology – the study of word-formation – is the topic of Chapter 4. Nonetheless, for the moment we only need to recognize a single suffix, the plural marker of English, written *-s* or *-es*. The first thing to notice is that there are three ways of pronouncing this suffix, as shown in (8):

(8) *tree*[z] *hedg*[ɪz] *bat*[s]
*field*[z] *ditch*[ɪz] *wasp*[s]
*maple*[z] *ash*[ɪz] *oak*[s]

The shape of the suffix, i.e. its pronunciation, depends on two things. First, it depends on the final segment of the noun that it is attached to. So, following a voiced segment such as a vowel, as in *tree*, or a voiced stop, as in *field*, or a sonorant, as in *maple*, the suffix appears as [z]. Following a voiceless stop, as in *bat*, *wasp* and *oak*, the suffix appears as [s]. What about *hedge*, *ditch* and *ash*? In each of these cases the final segment is a 'sibilant', an affricate in the case of *hedge* and *ditch*, a fricative in the case of *ash*. In each case when it follows a sibilant, the suffix appears as [ɪz]. Try this with other nouns of English, ending with other segments that we have not considered in (8). You will find the same pattern: [z] following a voiced non-sibilant, [s] following a voiceless non-sibilant, and [ɪz] following a sibilant.

There are two interesting things to note at this point. First of all, we can tell that this is not a purely phonetically conditioned alternation, since normal English phonology does allow a voiced segment followed by [s], as in *hence* [hɛns] and *since* [sɪns]. It is only when the [n] is noun-final and the following sibilant is the plural marker that we need to have [z], as with the noun *hen*, the plural of which is *hen*[z], not **hen*[s]. The second interesting point is that as a morphologically governed alternation, selection of the correct shape for the plural marker is productive. If you invent a new word of English, it will behave according to the patterns seen above. So, the word *bleem* will be pluralized as [bliːmz], not *[bliːms], *trat* will be [tɹæts], not *[tɹætz], and *plotch* will be [plɒtʃɪz]. So although the alternation is slightly complex, involving both phonetics and morphology, it is entirely systematic for regular noun pluralization in English.

### 3.4.3 Morphological and lexical conditioning

Before leaving the topic of phonological alternations, there is one more type of conditioning to briefly consider: morphological and lexical conditioning. We have already seen that morphological conditioning refers to some phonological alternation involving some morphological object, in the example above this was the regular plural marker of English.

Sometimes an alternation can be restricted to a specific set of lexical items, i.e. words, in a language. Consider the words in (9).

(9) *leaf* [li:f] ~ *leaves* [li:vz]
*thief* [θi:f] ~ *thieves* [θi:vz]
*house* [haʊs] ~ *houses* [haʊzɪz]
*hoof* [huf] ~ *hooves* [huvz]

With the words in (9) there is an alternation in the stem-final consonant, [f] alternating with [v], and [s] alternating with [z]. This is considered to be lexically conditioned, because only a small, closed set of words in the language participate in the alternation. Consider, for instance, the words *kiss* and *cliff*. They are not members of the set of words which participate in this alternation, so they have regular plurals, [kisɪz] and [klɪfs], not *[kizɪz] and *[klɪvz].

**KEY POINTS: Conditioning factors**

The alternations between allophones of a phoneme may be associated with different sorts of 'conditioning factors'. These include:

- Phonetic conditioning, where the relevant factor is phonetic context
- Morphological conditioning, where specific morphological factors are relevant
- Lexical conditioning, where the alternation is specific to a particular word or type of word

## EXERCISE 3.3 PHONEMES AND ALTERNATIONS

**Kurdish (Indo-Aryan; Iraq, Iran, Turkey and Syria)**

Consider the alternations between the final consonant in the words in the left-hand column and the corresponding consonant in the right-hand column (underscored):

[kɨtep] 'book' [kɨtebaka] 'the book'
[bart] 'stone' [barda] ' it is stone'
[sak] 'dog' [sagakat] 'your dog'

What are the two possible analyses, assuming that for each alternation, [t] ~ [d], [p] ~ [b], [k] ~ [b], there is a single **underlying phoneme**?

Now consider these further data. They support one of the possible analyses. Which analysis do they support, and what evidence do they provide?

[kup] 'cup' [kupaka] 'the cup'
[dɨrk] 'thorn' [dɨrka:wi] 'thorny'

## 3.5 The syllable

In earlier sections of this chapter we referred to the syllable as playing a role in determining phonotactic restrictions, in particular, that certain combinations of segments such as [p]+[w] in English could occur across syllables, but not within a single syllable. In this section we will look a little more closely at the syllable and see that there are other important aspects to the syllable beyond phonotactics and syllable boundaries alone, and that the syllable itself has internal structure.

Consider the following words of English: *bit, bid, hat, had, bet, bed, seat, seed, see, suit, sued, sue.* If we look at transcriptions of these words, we see an interesting pattern emerging.

(10) bit [bɪt] bid [bɪ:d]
hat [hæt] had [hæ:d]
bet [bɛt] bed [bɛ:d]
seat [sit] seed [si:d] see [si:]
suit [sut] sued [su:d] sue [su:]

What is interesting here is that the phonological contrast – as supported by minimal pairs – is between [t], [d] or zero at the end of the word. Nonetheless, there is something else going on as well, a difference in vowel length. *Bit, hat, bet, seat* and *suit* all have short vowels, while *bid, had, bed, seed, sued, see* and *sue* all have long vowels. Where the syllable, or more precisely syllable structure, comes in is that in those cases with short vowels, there is a voiceless obstruent at the end of the syllable. When the vowel is long, the syllable is either closed with a voiced obstruent, or the syllable is open. This is shown in (11).

(11)
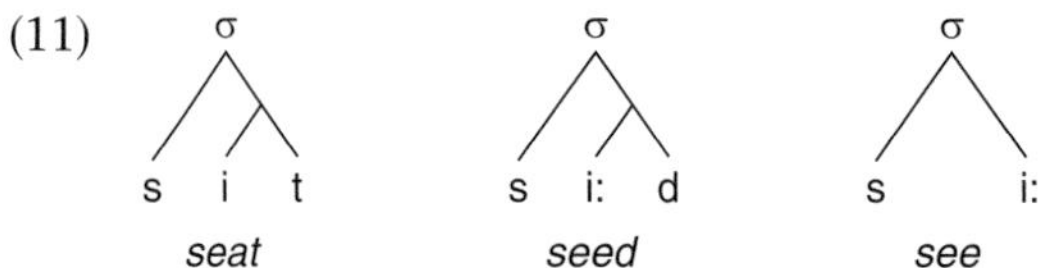


The lower-case sigma, σ, represents the 'syllable node', i.e. the whole constituent of the syllable. As noted in the previous chapter, the nucleus of the syllable, the most important part, is usually a vowel; here it is the [i] or [i:]. The beginning of the syllable, if there is material before the nucleus, is known as the '**onset**', while any material following the nucleus is called the '**coda**'. The node dominating both the nucleus and the coda is called the '**rhyme**'.

(12)
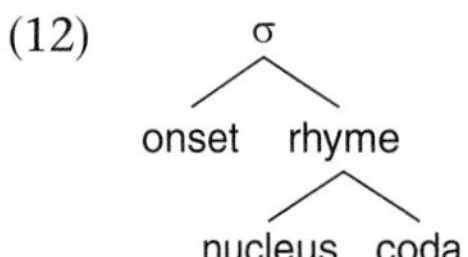


So, what appears to be happening in the data in (10) is that when a syllable is closed with a voiceless obstruent in the coda in English, the preceding vowel is short. Otherwise, when the syllable is open (lacking a coda) or when the syllable is closed with a voiced obstruent in the coda, the vowel is long. This is a systematic occurrence in the phonology of English.

Recall the earlier discussion of the allophones of phoneme /l/, and that the difference was between 'clear-l', [l], in *leaf* as phonetically distinct from the 'dark-l', [ɫ], in *fill*. We're now in a position to be a bit more precise about the distribution of these two allophones. Clear-l, [l], is found in onset position, dark-l, [ɫ], in coda position.

(13)

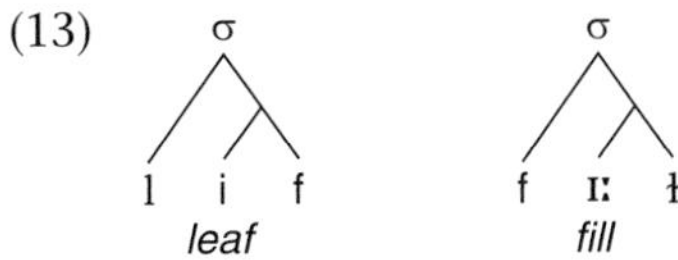


There are certain aspects to the syllable that are assumed to be universal: for instance that all spoken languages contain syllables consisting of an onset and nucleus, i.e. CV, where 'C' stands for 'consonant' and 'V' for 'vowel'; that all languages allow vowels in the nucleus. At the same time, there are also many language-specific aspects to the syllables of particular languages, such as the number of consonants allowed in onsets or codas; whether onsetless syllables are allowed. As to number of consonants in onsets and codas, English, for example, allows a maximum of three consonants in the onset, of which the first must be [s], the second a voiceless stop, [p], [t] or [k], and the third a sonorant, either [l] or [ɹ], as in *split* [splɪt], *strike* [stɹaɪk], or *scream* [skɹiːm]. Some languages allow a maximum of two consonants in the onset. Others, e.g. Polish, allow up to four consonants in the onset, e.g. [vzglɑ̃d] 'consideration' and [drgnɑ̃ts] 'shudder'. Some languages, like English and French, allow vowel-initial syllables, e.g. *eye* [aɪ] and *eau* [o] 'water', while others, e.g. German and Arabic, require an onset, so words spelt with a vowel at the beginning are nonetheless pronounced with an initial glottal stop, e.g. German *Adler* [ˈʔɑdlʌ] 'eagle', *ohne* [ˈʔoːnə] 'without' and Arabic *akhbar* [ʔɑxbɑr] 'news' and *eid* [ʔiːd] 'festival'.

The number of consonants permitted in the coda, too, is language-specific. Some languages, e.g. Fijian and Hawai'ian, allow no coda consonants, meaning that all words must end in a vowel. Other languages permit varying numbers of consonants in the coda. English, for instance, allows up to four, e.g. in a word like *sixths* [sɪksθs] (although words like this in English are relatively rare).

Along with language-specific aspects of syllable structure, like required vs permitted numbers of segments in onsets and codas, remember too that certain other aspects of phonology, like the distribution of allophones, are also language-specific. It is a fact about English that clear-l occurs in onsets and dark-l in codas; it is a fact about English that vowels are lengthened in open syllables and in syllables closed with a voiced segment. We can also find language-specific phenomena related to both fairly general aspects of syllable structure, e.g. French 'closed syllable adjustment', which distinguishes simply between open and closed syllables, and phenomena associated with specific segments occurring in specific positions, e.g. vowel length in Welsh monosyllabic words. In the Welsh case, native monosyllabic words with [p, t, k, m, ŋ] in the coda, or with more than one consonant in the coda, have a short vowel; monosyllabic words with no coda or with any of the other consonants of Welsh in the coda, have a long vowel.[4]

[4] In fact, things are slightly more complicated than this, in that [n] and [r] in the coda of a monosyllabic word may follow either a long or a short vowel.

As a final illustration of the importance of syllable structure, let us look at French closed syllable adjustment. Among the vowels of French we find the mid central vowel [ə], as in the first syllable of *petit* [pəti] 'small, masc.', [e] as in *été* [ete] 'summer'and [ɛ] as in *lait* [lɛ] 'milk'. While all three of these vowels can occur in open syllables, as in the examples given, in a closed syllable we find only one of them, [ɛ]. Thus we can find an alternation between [ə] and [ɛ] and between [e] and [ɛ]. Such an alternation is most clearly shown in related words in which the vowel in question is [ə] or [e] in an open syllable, but appears as [ɛ] in a closed syllable. This is illustrated in (14), where the relevant syllable boundaries are shown and the alternating vowel underlined.

| | | | |
|---|---|---|---|
| (14) | *sécher* [.se.ʃe.] 'to dry' | but | *sèche* [.sɛʃ.] 'dry, fem.' |
| | *premier* [.prə.mje.] 'first, masc.' | but | *première* [.prə.mjɛʁ.] 'first, fem.' |
| | *peser* [.pə.ze.] 'to weigh' | but | *pèse* [.pɛz.] 'I weigh' |
| | *mener* [.məne.] 'to lead' | but | *mène* [.mɛn.] 'I lead' |

In this French case, the relevant factor is simply the occurrence of the vowel in question in either an open or a closed syllable. The specifics of that syllable, e.g. type of consonant in the coda, are irrelevant.

**KEY POINTS: Syllable structure**

- Recognizing the syllable and syllable structure help in accounting for phonological alternations.
- Syllable position, for instance occurrence in an onset as opposed to occurrence in a coda, may be relevant in characterizing an alternation.
- Open vs closed syllable may be relevant in accounting for an alternation.
- The characteristics of a segment in a particular position may be important, such as between a voiced segment in a coda as compared with a voiceless segment in a coda.

## EXERCISE 3.4 STRESS AND SYLLABLE STRUCTURE

**Mohawk (Algonquian; North America)**

Note the interaction between stress and syllable structure. A stressed vowel is indicated with an acute accent, ´, over the vowel. In particular, how do stress and syllable structure predict the occurrence of long vowels?

| | | | |
|---|---|---|---|
| .wísk. | 'five' | .ké:.saks. | 'I look for it' |
| .í:.raks. | 'he eats it' | .jék.reks. | 'I push it' |
| .rá:.kʌs. | 'he sees her' | .ra.jʌ́t.hos. | 'he plants' |

Now consider the following words of Mohawk. For each case, say whether the underlined vowel should be long or short, and explain why.

| | | | |
|---|---|---|---|
| .ra.ké.tas. | 'he scrapes' | .ro.jóʔ.teʔ. | 'he works' |

## 3.6 Syllable weight

Apart from syllable structure itself, whether a syllable is open or closed, whether or not it has an onset, and so on, there is also a distinction made between 'light' and 'heavy' syllables. We can see this distinction in stress assignment in English. In English a syllable counts as 'light' if it is an open syllable with a short vowel. So, the first syllable of *between* [.bə.ˈtwiːn.], *about* [.ə.ˈbaʊt.] and *elegy* [.ˈɛ.lɪ.ʤiː.] is light. A heavy syllable, on the other hand, has either a long vowel or diphthong in the nucleus, or is closed with a consonant. So, the first syllable of *open* [.ˈoʊ.pən.], *island* [.ˈaɪ.lənd.], *easel* [.ˈiː.zəɫ.] and *athlete* [.ˈæθ.liːt.] is heavy.

While the stress system of English as a whole is rather complex, and there are various exceptions to the generalizations, there are nonetheless some interesting observations that can be made about stress assignment to specific classes of English words relative to syllable weight. Let us look briefly at the patterns of stress assignment to nouns and verbs. Typically, nouns of two syllables have stress on the first syllable, regardless of the weight of that syllable, e.g. *island* and *athlete*, with a heavy initial syllable, but also *carrot* and *forest* with light initial syllables. For nouns of English of more than two syllables, stress typically falls on the penultimate syllable, if that syllable is heavy, e.g. *computer* [.kəm.ˈpjuː.tə.],[5] *enclosure* [.ɛn.ˈkloʊ.ʒə.], *navigation* [.næ.vɪ.ˈgeɪ.ʃn̩.]. If, on the other hand, the penultimate syllable is light, stress falls on the antepenultimate syllable, even if that syllable itself is light, e.g. *elephant* [.ˈɛ.lə.fənt.], *testament* [.ˈtɛ.stɪ.mənt.], *precedent* [.ˈpɹɛ.sɪ.dənt.].

Turning to verbs, here too we can find some interesting patterns associated with heavy and light syllables – and some further complexities. Where the weight of the penultimate syllable is important in nouns, for verbs the weight of the final syllable is important. With verbs like *reveal* [.ɹɪ.ˈviːɫ.], *defend* [.dɪ.ˈfɛnd.] and *respect* [.ɹɪ.ˈspɛkt.], the final syllable is heavy and stress falls on that syllable. With verbs like *envy* [.ˈɛn.vi.], and *pity* [.pɪ.ti.], where the final syllable is light, stress falls on the penultimate syllable.

The verbs of English also illustrate an interesting situation in which phonetic material is phonologically invisible, referred to as **extrametricality**, meaning literally outside the assignment of stress. Take the verbs *enlighten, nourish* and *imagine*. According to what was said in the last paragraph, we might expect these words to be stressed on the final syllable which appears to be heavy: **enlighTEN, *nouRISH, *imaGINE*. What appears to be happening here though is that the final consonant is ignored by the stress assignment process. It is as if the words were *enlighte, nouri* and *imagi*. But note that these words fall into line with the pattern observed above if the final consonant is ignored. Without the final [n], [ʃ] and [n], *enlighten, nourish* and *imagine* have a final light syllable consisting of a single short vowel. Note, too, that this is not a trick of analysis either. Consider the words listed earlier as illustrating verbs with heavy final stress-attracting syllables, *reveal, defend* and *respect*. Even if the final consonant is removed from these words, they still have a heavy final syllable, i.e. [.ɹɪ.ˈviː.], [.dɪ.ˈfɛn.] and [.ɹɪ.ˈspɛk.]. So, it appears to be the case that, for whatever reason, the final consonant of verbs is ignored by the phonological process

[5] Pronouncing the final <r> here makes no difference to the stress: [.kəm.ˈpjuː.təɹ.]

assigning stress to English words. If, with the final consonant ignored, the final syllable is still heavy, it attracts the stress. If, with the final consonant ignored, the final syllable is light, stress retracts to the penultimate syllable.

Although as we have seen there are some interesting generalizations to be made concerning syllable weight and English stress assignment, not all stress systems are sensitive to syllable weight. Some, like Welsh and Czech, are purely positional systems, insensitive to the weight of the syllables involved. In Welsh, the penultimate syllable typically bears the main stress of the word, regardless of whether that syllable is heavy or light. Czech, on the other hand, stresses the initial syllable in a word. Again, the weight of that syllable, whether heavy or light, is irrelevant.

Even in English we can find apparent instances of stress by position. Consider the nominalizing suffix *-ity*, that is, the suffix attached to adjectives to create nouns, for example *electric* > *electricity*, *curious* > *curiosity*, *human* > *humanity*. In each of these cases stress falls on the syllable immediately to the left of the suffix, *elecTRIcity*, *curiOsity*, *huMAnity*, which sounds like it could be positional stress assignment. Interestingly, too, the stress on the noun in each of these cases is different from the stress on the adjective – *eLECtric*, *CURious*, *HUman*. But is this really stress by position? The suffix *-ity* consists of two syllables, a light penultimate syllable [ɪ] followed by a further final light syllable [ti]. So, nouns formed with the suffix *-ity* simply conform to the basic stress placement algorithm for nouns: if the penultimate syllable is light, stress normally falls on the antepenultimate. In these cases, the antepenultimate syllable happens to systematically correspond to the final syllable of the stem.

**KEY POINTS: Syllable weight**

In addition to syllable structure, syllable weight can also play a role in phonology.

- Syllables can be light or heavy.
- The distinction between light and heavy is different from the distinction between open and closed syllables.
- Some stress assignment systems are sensitive to syllable weight; in such systems stress is often attracted to a heavy syllable.

## 3.7 SUMMARY

In this chapter we have considered a number of aspects of the organization of the sound system of spoken language typically referred to as 'phonology'. We have seen that there is more to understand with respect to the speech sounds of language than simply the physical properties of those sounds, their articulation, their mutual influence on each other, their perception and so on, as important as those aspects are. Understanding that the sounds we produce when speaking our language are related to abstract phonemes allows us to reconcile the fact that native speakers of any language will regard certain sounds as 'the same' despite demonstrable phonetic difference between those sounds. As we have seen, it helps us understand that despite the phonetic fact that the sounds [tʰ], [t] and [ʔ] are distinct, English speakers nonetheless consider them in some sense 'the same'. We can account for this by assuming that in English the phoneme /t/ occurs as [tʰ], [t] or [ʔ] in specific environments.

We have also seen that phonology allows us to understand something about phonotactics, the permissible combinations of speech sounds in a language. Including, for instance, the fact that in a particular language a specific sequence of sounds may be perfectly permissible provided that that sequence does not occur within a syllable. Recognition of the syllable as a unit of analysis then led us on to consider other aspects of the systematic organization of speech sounds, including the role of syllable structure in phonological processes themselves, such as French closed syllable adjustment, the relationship between syllable structure and vowel length in English, as well as the phenomenon of vowel nasalization in English. We saw further that syllable structure, specifically syllable weight, allowed us to describe typical stress assignment for nouns and verbs in English.

As a final illustration of the distinction between phonetics and phonology, and the role of phonology beyond the surface phonetic structure, consider the following sentence of English in two different dialects:

(15) (a) [ðə ɹɛd kɑːˈkw̥ɪkliː stɒpt ðɛn ˈstɑːtəd əˈgɛn]
(b) [ðə ɹɛd kɑɹˈkw̥ɪkliː stɑpt ðɛn ˈstɑɹɾəd əˈgɛn]

The transcription in (15a) is standard British English. The transcription in (15b) is General American. Note first of all the differences between the two. Even in this very short sentence, there are some differences both in the vowels and in the consonants. In the transcription of *car* and *started* (15a) has a long vowel where (15b) has a short vowel followed by [ɹ]. The two transcriptions have a different vowel in the word *stopped*, and (15b) has a flap, [ɾ], in one case where (15a) has a [t], in the word *started*, but the other [t]s match in both transcriptions. Although this is a brief comparison, and although the differences are few here, consider the implications of it: how is it that British and American speakers of English can understand each other? How can the British listener come to understand that the American flap corresponds to the British [t]? Or that the British [ɒ] vowel may correspond to the American [ɑ]? Indeed, take two more divergent varieties of English than standard British and General American and, apart from differences in the words used, speakers of those two varieties will (with some practice) come to understand each other's variety with few difficulties. How is that possible? We certainly cannot do it with a foreign language. The answer lies in the phonology, in the correspondence between the abstract phonological representations and the **surface phonetics**.

Assuming that each speaker of English has unconscious knowledge of their phonological system, in particular the correspondence between their surface phonetics and the phonological representations, e.g. phonemes, the task of understanding another variety of English boils down to this: becoming familiar enough with the other variety to map the phonetic surface structure of that variety to the phonological representations of one's own dialect. It is very hard to see how this could happen relying on the surface phonetics alone. But by means of the phonology, it becomes a more straightforward exercise, mapping from a different dialect to your own phonological system.

(16) (a) ⟶ [ðəɹɛd kɑːˈkw̥ɪkliː stɒpt ðɛn ˈstɑːtəd əˈgɛn]
→ / ðəɹɛd kɑɹ kwɪkli stɒpt ðɛn stɑɹtəd əgɛn / ⟶
(b) [ðəɹɛd kɑɹˈkw̥ɪkliː stɑpt ðɛn ˈstɑɹɾəd əˈgɛn] ←

The illustration in (16) is simply meant to indicate that a speaker of one dialect could come to understand a speaker of a different dialect through the abstract underlying structures common to both. This suggests that at least with respect to the sound system, even a language with very divergent dialects may have a relatively unitary phonology.

In this chapter we have briefly examined aspects of the systematic organization of speech sounds. As we have seen, there are systematic behaviours in the speech sounds of language that cannot be attributed to the phonetics alone. We have also seen that some aspects of the sound system of language can be best understood at an abstract level of representation.

WEBSITE: **Phonology**

Now go to the website and assess your knowledge of phonology by completing the self-test questions!

## SUGGESTIONS FOR FURTHER READING

Carr, P. and Montreuil, J.-P. (2013). *Phonology*, 2nd edn. Basingstoke: Palgrave Macmillan. This is an introduction to phonology and phonological theory, assuming some knowledge of phonetics

Davenport, M. and Hannahs, S. J. (2010). *Introducing Phonetics and Phonology*, 3rd edn. Oxford: Routledge. This is an introductory text to both phonetics and phonology, covering the material of Chapters 2 and 3 in greater depth and introducing the reader to phonological theory.

McMahon, A. (2002). *An Introduction to English Phonology*. Edinburgh University Press. This is a textbook of phonology focusing on the sound patterns of English.

# ANSWERS TO EXERCISES

## Exercise 3.1

(a) two: .ˈteɪ.bɫ̩.
(b) one: .taʊn.
(c) two: .ˈmoʊ.baɪɫ.
(d) two: .ˈtɹæn.sɛpt.
(e) four: .ɹaɪ.ˈnɔ.sə.ɹəs.
(f) three: .aɪ.ˈdi.ə.
(g) two: .ˈsaɪ.kɪk.
(h) three: .kə.ˈnʌn.dɹəm.
(i) two: .ˈlɛ.mən.
(j) three: .ˈtɛ.lə.foʊn.
(k) three: .ˈɔ.nɛ.stiː.
(l) three: .ˈpju.nɪ.tɪv.

## Exercise 3.2

### (i) Spanish

The sounds [d] and [ð] in Spanish appear to be allophones of a single phoneme, since [ð] appears only between two vowels, whereas [d] never appears in that position; [d] appears word initially and next to a consonant, environments in which [ð] doesn't appear. Moreover, you can see an alternation by comparing (5) [donde] 'where' with (6) [deðonde] 'whence': the second consonant in [deðonde] alternates with the first consonant in [donde]. Recognizing this as an alternation is supported by the meanings 'where' and 'whence' = 'from where'.

### (ii) Tojolabal

Plain [k] and glottalized [kʾ] can be said to be separate phonemes. In the first place, both appear word-initially, compare items (1) and (10) – indeed these two words are almost a minimal pair. Secondly, both appear between two vowels: items (3) and (7) contrast these two sounds between the vowel [a]. Thirdly, plain [k] and glottalized [kʾ] both appear word-finally, compare items (2) and (4) with item (12). Finally, there is no indication of an alternation involving these two sounds.

## Exercise 3.3 Kurdish

Since in each case the voiced and voiceless stops appear in related words, there appears to be an alternation between [p] and [b], between [t] and [d], and between [k] and [g]. Assuming that one of each pair is the phoneme, the two possible analyses are either (i) that the voiceless member of each pair is the phoneme (for instance /p/), with a voiced allophone occurring between two voiced sounds (either a vowel or a sonorant) (e.g. [b]), as in the words in the right-hand column, or (ii) that the voiced member of each pair is the phoneme (e.g. /b/), with a voiceless allophone occurring at the end of the word (e.g. [p]), as in the words in the left-hand column.

The further data show no alternation: the words for 'cup' and 'the cup' both have [p], while the words for 'thorn' and 'thorny' both have [k], even when the [p] and [k] are between two voiced sounds. That supports the position that in the alternating cases the phoneme is the voiced member of the pair; the voiceless one occurs word finally. Note, too, that this is a type of neutralization: there is reason to believe that both voiced and voiceless stops occur as phonemes, but in word-final position only the voiceless stop occurs.

### Exercise 3.4 Mohawk

A stressed vowel is long in an open syllable. The stressed vowels in [.wísk.], [.jék.reks.], and [.ra.jʌ́t.hos.] appear in closed syllables, so they are short. The stressed vowels in the remaining words appear in open syllables, so they are long. The underlined vowel in [.ra.ké:.tas.] is stressed and in an open syllable, so it is long; the underlined vowel in [.ro.jóʔ.teʔ.] is stressed and in a closed syllable, so it is short.

## REFERENCES AND DATA SOURCES

Tojolabal data from: Supple, J. and Douglass, C. M. (1949). Tojolabal (Mayan): phonemes and verb morphology. *International Journal of American Linguistics*, 15, 168–74.

Mohawk data from: Postal, P. (1968). *Aspects of Phonological Theory*. New York: Harper and Row.

Spanish data from: Quilis, A. and Fernández, J. A. (1972). *Curso de fonética y fonología españolas*. Madrid: Consejo superior de investigaciones científicas.

Kurdish data on final devoicing from Twana Hamid, personal communication

Thai data on phonemic status of stops from Pak Tong Sen, personal communication

# 4 Morphology

HANS-JÖRG SCHMID

**KEY TERMS**

- acronym
- allomorph
- analytic languages
- back-formation
- blending
- clipping
- compounding
- conversion
- derivation
- inflection
- morpheme
- prefixation
- synthetic languages
- word-formation
- suffixation

**PREVIEW**

In this chapter you will first learn to segment words into their smallest meaningful parts, their morphemes. Different types of morphemes will then be distinguished on a number of dimensions. The classes arising from such distinctions are useful because they allow us to formulate generalizations about the properties shared by the members of these classes and the restrictions they are subject to. A second type of generalization covered in this chapter concerns the patterns and rules which underlie the formation of complex lexemes, i.e. words that are made up of more than two lexical morphemes. This is the realm of word-formation. You will be introduced to the range of word-formation patterns that can be used to form new words with the help of existing words and morphemes, including compounding, i.e. the joining of two or more words to form a new complex lexeme (e.g. *interest rate, washing-machine* or *watertight*), prefixation, yielding words such as ***dis**agree,* ***un**just* or **ex**-*minister*, and suffixation (e.g. *agree**ment**, just**ify**, minister**ial***). Further word-formation patterns, which are less regular and transparent, include conversion (*hammer* $_{N}$ → *to hammer* $_{V}$ or *empty* $_{Adj}$ → *to empty* $_{V}$), back-formation (e.g. *to sightsee* ← *sightseeing*; *to burgle* ← *burglar*), blending (e.g. *infotainment* ← *information + entertainment*), clipping (e.g. *ad* ← *advertisement, phone* ← *telephone*), and the formation of acronyms or initialisms from fixed sequences of words (*URL* ← *unique resource locator; NATO* ← *North Atlantic Treaty Organization*).

## 4.1 INTRODUCTION

Generally speaking, the linguistic discipline of morphology – the term is derived from the Greek word *morphos* meaning 'form' – examines the internal makeup and structure of words as well as the patterns and principles underlying their composition. In doing so, morphology straddles the traditional boundary between grammar (i.e. the rule-based, productive component of a language) and the lexicon (i.e. the idiosyncratic, rote-learned component). Morphology looks at both sides of linguistic signs, i.e. at the form and the meaning, combining the two perspectives in order to analyse and describe both the component parts of words and the principles underlying the composition of words.

Unlike phonology, morphology does not analyse words in terms of syllables but in terms of **morphemes**, i.e. components of words that are carriers of meanings. For example, while the words *father* and *teacher* both consist of two syllables, *father* represents only one morpheme (meaning 'male parent'), whereas *teacher* consists of two: the verb *teach* ('instruct') and the nominalizing suffix *-er* ('someone who does something'). The most frequently found definition of the notion of morpheme states that it is the 'smallest meaning-bearing unit' in a given language. As the example of *father* has shown, morphemes can coincide with simple words, or more precisely, **simple lexemes**, i.e. abstract representations of words uniting forms and (bundles of related) meanings, but they can also constitute parts of **complex lexemes**, which are in turn defined as lexemes consisting of more than one morpheme. Unlike *father*, then, *teacher* is an example of a complex lexeme.

The study of morphology is traditionally divided into two major areas. The first is known as **inflectional morphology** and deals with the markers of grammatical categories such as CASE, NUMBER, TENSE and ASPECT. These inflectional morphemes are attached to lexical stems and create word-forms (rather than new words). For example, the verb *employ* can occur in the base-form *employ* when no inflectional morpheme is added, in the form *employs* when the morpheme marking agreement with a third person singular subject is attached, in the form *employed* when marked by the past tense or the past participle morpheme, and in the *ing*-form *employing*, used, among other things, for encoding the progressive aspect. The second major branch of morphology is **word-formation**, whose scope includes the direct terminological counterpart to inflectional morphology, **derivational morphology**, but goes beyond that. The field of word-formation deals with the patterns and rules guiding the formation of new words (rather than just word-forms of existing words). From this perspective, the word *unemployment*, for instance, would first be segmented into the base *employ* and the derivational morphemes *un-* and *-ment*, and it would be stated that the affixes *un-* and *- ment* are added to the base *employ*, thus manifesting the word-formation types of **prefixation** and **suffixation** respectively. In addition to derivational morphology, word-formation encompasses the study of **compounding** (e.g. *employment agency*) and also those word-formation types that do not use morphemes as their basic building blocks, i.e. non-morphemic types such as **blending** (e.g. *infotainment* ← *information* and *entertainment*) and **clipping** (e.g. *flu* ← *influenza*). The scope of the fields of morphology and word-formation is summarized in Figure 4.1. In appreciating this figure you should keep in mind, however, that the situation is not quite as simple and clear as suggested by the neat division: firstly, the word-formation type of compounding does not really fall within the scope of derivational morphology, but is placed in the same branch as prefixation and

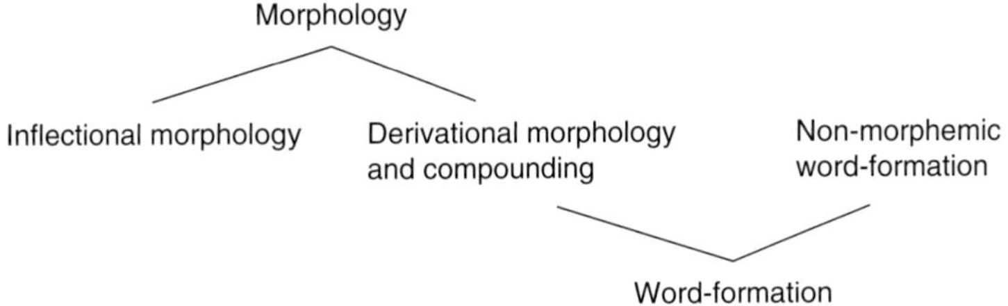


**Figure 4.1** The scope of morphology and word-formation (adapted from Schmid 2011: 15)

suffixation because it shares with these the property that it uses morphemes as basic building blocks. Secondly, **conversion**, i.e. the transfer of a word from one word class to another without the addition of a morpheme, and **back-formation**, as in the verb *to sightsee* derived from the longer noun *sightseeing*, could be seen as relying on morphemes, too, but this is much less straightforward than is the case in the other types of morphemic word-formation patterns.

## 4.2 Morphemes and other morphological building-blocks

As has been pointed out above, morphemes are defined as smallest meaning-bearing units. Morphemes can be classified in various ways. One common classification you have already learnt about above separates those morphemes that mark the grammatical forms of words (*-s, -ed, -ing* and others) from those that form new lexemes conveying new meanings, e.g. *un-* and *-ment*. The former morphemes are **inflectional morphemes** and form a key part of grammar, the latter are **derivational morphemes** and play a role in word-formation, as we have seen. The following criteria help you to distinguish the two types:

- Effect: inflectional morphemes encode grammatical categories and relations, thus marking word-forms, while derivational morphemes create new lexemes.
- Position: derivational morphemes are closer to the stem than inflectional morphemes, cf. *amendments* ($amend_{\text{stem}}$ – $ment_{\text{derivational}}$ – $s_{\text{inflectional}}$) and *legalized* ($legal_{\text{stem}}$ – $ize_{\text{derivational}}$ – $ed_{\text{inflectional}}$).
- Productivity: inflectional morphemes are highly productive, which means that they can be attached to the vast majority of the members of a given class (say, verbs, nouns or adjectives), whereas derivational morphemes tend to be more restricted with regard to their scope of application. For example, the past morpheme can in principle be attached to all verbs; suffixation by means of the adjective-forming derivational morpheme *- able*, however, is largely restricted to dynamic transitive verbs, which excludes formations such as **bleedable* or **lieable*.
- Class properties: inflectional morphemes make up a closed and fairly stable class of items which can be listed exhaustively, while derivational morphemes tend to be much more numerable and more open to changes in their inventory.

Both inflectional and derivational morphemes must be attached to other morphemes; they cannot occur by themselves, in isolation, and are therefore known as **bound morphemes**. **Free morphemes**, on the other hand, are autonomous, can occur on their own and are thus also words at the same time. Technically, bound morphemes and free morphemes are said to differ in terms of their 'distribution' or 'freedom of occurrence'. As a rule, lexemes consist of at least one free morpheme.

A third way of classifying morphemes relies on the kinds of meanings they encode. **Grammatical morphemes** serve the purpose of signalling grammatical categories and encoding relational meanings, while **lexical morphemes** carry richer conceptual, more autonomous meanings. Note that this distinction overlaps partly, but not fully, with the one between inflectional and derivational morphemes. In fact, as shown in Table 4.1, inflectional morphemes form the subclass of bound grammatical morphemes, whereas derivational morphemes are bound lexical morphemes.

Table 4.1 gives a survey of a widespread way of classifying morphemes in terms of a cross-tabulation of the dimension of distribution/freedom of occurrence (free vs bound) and meaning (lexical vs grammatical).

The table also indicates that the class of free grammatical morphemes contains so-called function words such as *the*, *of* or *to*, which mark grammatical relations, cannot be inflected and are semantically and distributionally much more restricted than free lexical morphemes (i.e. so-called content words). Content words belong to the word classes of nouns, adjectives and adverbs and form the large majority of verbs, while function words comprise articles, conjunctions, prepositions and particles as well as the so-called primary verbs *be*, *have* and *do*, which contribute to the encoding of grammatical categories such as TENSE and ASPECT (*I* ***have been*** *running*), NEGATION (*She* ***does*** *not eat shrimp*), VOICE (*He* ***was*** *scratched by the dog*) or sentence MOOD (***Does*** *she eat garlic?*).

**TABLE 4.1** A cross-classification of types of morphemes

| | Lexical morphemes | Grammatical morphemes |
|---|---|---|
| Free morphemes | = content words (e.g. *paper, slim, run*)<br>• semantically and distributionally more autonomous<br>• can be inflected<br>• rich conceptual content | = function words (e.g. *to, the, of*)<br>• semantically and distributionally less autonomous<br>• cannot be inflected<br>• mark grammatical relations |
| Bound morphemes | = derivational morphemes (e.g. *re-, -ize, -able*)<br>• create new lexemes<br>• closer to the stem<br>• more restricted productivity<br>• more open class | = inflectional morphemes (e.g. *-s, -ed, -est*)<br>• mark word-forms<br>• more distant from the stem<br>• highly productive<br>• closed class |

While the distinctions introduced so far seem straightforward enough, it turns out that implementing the definition of morphemes as *smallest meaning-bearing components of words* is not an easy task. One complication arises from the fact that short and seemingly simple word forms can express sets of meanings which are encoded by several morphemes in other words. Consider, for example, the form *sang* carrying the meanings of the lexical morpheme {sing} and the grammatical morpheme {past}, which are expressed by two morphemes in *shouted, kissed* and many other verbs.

Secondly, as will be discussed in greater detail in Section 4.3, morphemes are not always realized by the same form but by a number of variants, so-called **allomorphs**, depending on the environment in which they occur. This is particularly relevant for inflectional morphemes. The form *sang* mentioned above can in fact be treated as a rather unpredictable allomorph of the {past} morpheme. More regular allomorphs can be identified in the forms *smiled, laughed* and *greeted*, where the past morpheme is realized by the allomorphs /d/, /t/ and /ɪd/ respectively.

Thirdly, you can face difficulties when trying to segment words into morphemes because a seemingly reasonable formal analysis is not matched by a semantic one, or because your segmentation does not leave you with a free morpheme, as is usually required. The word *refer* is a case in point. You may well be inclined to divide this word into the morphemes *fer*, which you also find in *transfer, infer, confer* and *prefer*, and the derivational prefix *re-* occurring in large numbers of other verbs. What you soon realize, however, is that neither of these two potential morphemes is free, and that you will not find it easy to work out a meaning for the form *fer* which is shared by all the verbs in which it occurs (unless you happen to know that it is derived from Latin *ferre* 'to carry', but even then things do not quite make sense). Many of these cases have to do with the fact that English borrowed large numbers of words from Latin which were already prefixed and suffixed in that language, but did not bother to borrow the bases – cf., e.g., *describe, inscribe, subscribe, prescribe* but **scribe* (as a verb) or *insist, desist, consist, persist, resist* but **sist*. To solve this analytical dilemma, in some accounts of morphology (e.g. Stockwell and Minkowa 2001: 61–2) the bases of these lists of forms are given the special status of bound roots, which can be considered as somewhat untypical kinds of lexical morphemes.

Fourthly and finally, analytical problems arise because some forms can be put to use as both lexical and grammatical morphemes. The form - *ing*, for example, functions as a grammatical, inflectional morpheme participating in the formation of progressives (*she was knocking on his door*) and as a lexical, derivational morpheme forming adjectives from verbs (*interesting, exciting*) or nouns from verbs (*meeting, building*). In this case you could argue that the two functions are closely related and that the morpheme has several similar meanings. You could say that the morpheme is polysemous. In contrast, the use of *-er* as a nominalizing derivational suffix (as in *teacher*) is clearly unrelated to its use in the formation of the comparatives of adjectives (*wider, rougher*, etc.). Two different morphemes happen to have the same form, which is a case of homonymy rather than polysemy.

**KEY POINTS: Morphemes**

- Morphemes are the smallest meaning-carrying units of a language.
- Simple lexemes consist of one morpheme only, while complex lexemes have at least two lexical morphemes.
- Inflectional morphemes can be distinguished from derivational morphemes on the basis of their effects on the base (marking of word forms vs creation of new lexemes), their position vis-à-vis the stem (more distant vs closer), their productivity (highly productive vs restricted) and their class properties (closed class vs open class).
- Free morphemes are autonomous, while bound morphemes cannot occur in isolation.
- Grammatical morphemes mark grammatical categories and relations, lexical morphemes carry conceptual meanings.

**EXERCISE 4.1**

Using the information provided in this section and keeping in mind the four complications, you can now tackle the task of segmenting the following passage into morphemes and classifying them along the lines summarized in Table 4.1. Follow the format suggested below the text. (List of abbreviations: gr = grammatical; lex = lexical; fr = free; bd = bound.)

*While his granddaughters were still playing with their laptops and desktop computers in the living-room, Granddad found the necessary picnic supplies in the fridge and began to take them to his beloved flashy BMW convertible.*

| gr | gr | lex | lex | gr | ... |
|---|---|---|---|---|---|
| *while* | *his* | *grand* | *daughter* | *s* | ... |
| fr | fr | fr | fr | bd | ... |

## 4.3 Inflectional morphology

Languages differ considerably with regard to the extent to which they employ inflectional morphemes to mark grammatical categories and the way in which these morphemes are combined. On one end of a continuum are **analytic languages**, which do not signal grammatical categories and relations by means of inflectional morphemes but instead by other strategies such as fixed word order, auxiliaries and particles. As present-day English can muster only a relatively small number of inflectional morphemes, it comes quite close to acting as a representative of such a language. The full inventory of bound grammatical morphemes, which is listed in Table 4.2, amounts to less than ten items.

Controversial further candidates are the form {-th}, which forms ordinal numbers (*fourth*, *fifth*) and the adverb-forming suffix {-ly}, which is sometimes treated as a derivational

**TABLE 4.2** Inflectional morphemes in present-day English

| Word class | Morpheme | Functions/meanings | Grammatical category |
|---|---|---|---|
| noun | {plural} | marking of plural | NUMBER |
| | {genitive} | marking of genitive, possession, part-of, etc. | CASE |
| verb | {3rd person} | 3rd person singular present, marking agreement with subject | PERSON, AGREEMENT |
| | {ing} | present participle, marking of progressive aspect | ASPECT |
| | {$ed_1$} | simple past | TENSE |
| | {$ed_2$} | past participle, used for present perfect and passive voice | TENSE |
| adjective | {er} | comparative | GRADATION |
| | {est} | superlative | |

morpheme because it causes a change of word class, and sometimes as an inflectional suffix because its productivity is almost unrestricted and the changes in meaning and grammatical function are very limited.

**Synthetic languages**, on the other hand, encode large numbers of grammatical categories by attaching inflectional morphemes. German, for example, differs substantially from English in this respect, as it can mark four CASES (nominative, accusative, genitive and dative), NUMBER (singular and plural) as well as the GENDER of nouns (masculine, feminine and neuter). Adjectives can be marked for CASE and NUMBER, and the type of marking differs depending on whether the weak or strong declension is required (cf. *ein gutes Buch* 'a good book' vs *das gute Buch* 'the good book'). Verbs are marked not only for TENSE by inflectional morphemes, but also for PERSON, NUMBER and MOOD (indicative vs conjunctive). In addition, articles and pronouns are important markers of CASE, PERSON, GENDER and NUMBER. While many of these distinctions have collapsed into the same forms (a phenomenon known as syncretism), there can be no doubt that the grammar of German relies on inflectional marking to a much greater extent than English does. Languages which are even richer in inflectional markers, especially markers of much larger numbers of CASES, are by no means uncommon, both within the branch of Indo-European languages and elsewhere. Russian, for example, has inflectional markers for as many as six cases, Hungarian for more than a dozen.

Within the group of synthetic languages, we can distinguish between so-called **fusional languages** like German or Latin, which often express a whole set of grammatical meanings in one form – as is the case in the Latin *bonus* ('good') where the form *-us*

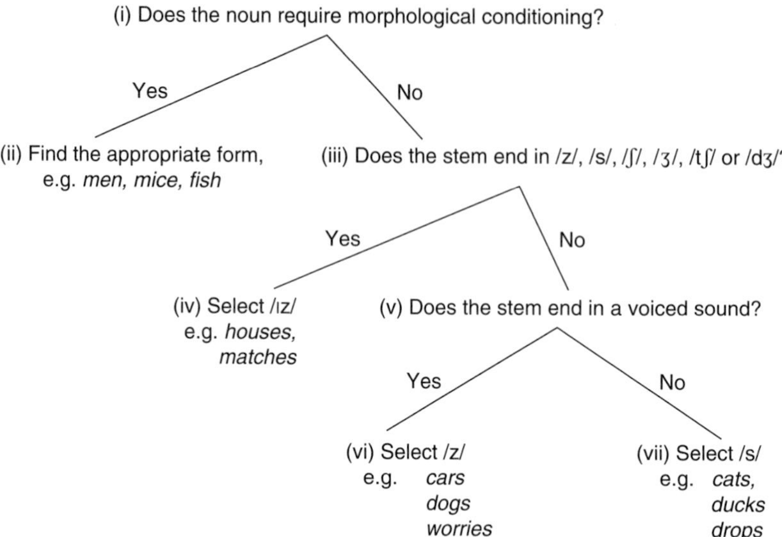


**Figure 4.2** Rules of allomorphy illustrated for the English plural morpheme

encodes the morphemes 'masculine', 'singular' and 'nominative' – and **agglutinating languages**. In these languages, examples of which include Turkish, Finnish, Mongolian and Japanese, word forms and even phrases and clauses are produced by joining sequences of morphemes that neither overlap nor collapse into forms expressing several meanings (e.g. the Turkish form *evlerinizin* 'of your houses', joining the morphemes *ev* 'house', *ler* 'plural', *in* '2nd person poss. pron.', *iz* 'plural' and *in* 'of').

In the course of its historical transition from Old English to Modern English, the English language has undergone a shift from more synthetic to more analytic. This entails that it has not only lost most of its inflectional morphemes, but has also become more 'regular' by leaving behind a massive number of allomorphs. Almost the entire system of differently conjugated classes of strong verbs and differently declined classes of nouns which were once typical of Germanic languages has disappeared. Irregular forms such as the past tense forms *sang, stood* or *told* and the plural forms *mice* and *oxen* are indeed only small remnants of the complex system of former allomorphs. Today, the choice of the remaining variants can be determined either by the stem as such (**morphological conditioning**) or by the final sound of the stem to which an inflectional morpheme is added (**phonological conditioning**). All the 'irregular' forms cited above are morphologically conditioned, since the stems *sing, stand, tell, mouse* and *ox* are responsible for how they are modified in order to mark the past or plural. Phonological conditioning is less idiosyncratic and can be captured in terms of a small set of rules, which are illustrated for the plural morpheme in Figure 4.2.

The allomorph systems of other languages are again much more complex. Once more taking German as an example, Table 4.3 lists the more systematic allomorphs of the plural morpheme.

**TABLE 4.3** Extract of the system of German plural allomorphy

| Declination and allomorph | Gender | Examples without umlaut | Examples with umlaut |
|---|---|---|---|
| *N*-declension: | masc. | *der Bär/die Bären* 'the bear/bears' | - |
| *-n* or *–en* | fem. | *die Pfeife/die Pfeifen* 'the pipe/pipes' | |
| | neutr. | *das Auge/die Augen* 'the eye/eyes' | |
| *E*-declension: | masc. | *der Stein/die Steine* 'the rock/rocks' | *der Hut/die Hüte* 'the hat/hats' |
| *-e* | fem. | *die Erkenntnis/die Erkenntnisse* 'the insight/insights' | *die Maus/die Mäuse* 'the mouse/mice' |
| | neutr. | *das Rohr/die Rohre* 'the tube/tubes' | - |
| *R*-declension: | masc. | *der Leib/die Leiber* 'the body/bodies' | *der Mann/die Männer* 'the man/men' |
| *-er* | neutr. | *das Bild/die Bilder* 'the picture/pictures' | *das Glas/die Gläser* 'the glass/glasses' |
| zero-declension:-Ø | masc. | *der Rahmen/die Rahmen* 'the frame/frames' | *der Boden/die Böden* 'the floor/floors' |
| | neutr. | *das Fenster/die Fenster* 'the window/windows' | - |
| *S*-declension: | masc. | *der Park/die Parks* 'the park/parks' | - |
| *-s* | fem. | *die Bar/die Bars* 'the bar/bars' | |
| | neutr. | *das Auto/die Autos* 'the car/cars' | |

A wide variety of further forms and rules have to be used for other nouns depending on an intricate combination of factors including meaning, derivational suffixes, origin (native or foreign) and others. Arguably, it is this comparative morphological complexity and unruliness of German that has caused judgements of the type 'Life is too short to learn German', found on T-shirts and attributed variously to Richard Porson, Mark Twain and Oscar Wilde.

### KEY POINTS: Inflectional morphology

- Synthetic languages have a large number of inflectional morphemes, while analytic languages can only muster few of them.
- German is located further towards the synthetic end of the continuum than present-day English, which has gradually become more analytic over the past fifteen centuries.
- Among the synthetic languages, fusional languages like Latin often encode several grammatical meanings in one form, while agglutinating languages such as Turkish join sequences of morphemes.
- Inflectional morphemes have allomorphs whose forms can depend on the stem (i.e. be morphologically conditioned) or on the final sound of the stem (i.e. be phonologically conditioned).

EXERCISE 4.2

Figure 4.2 has provided a maximally systematic and economical way of describing the allomorphy of the English plural morpheme. Try to transfer the logic behind this figure to the English past tense morpheme and produce a similar figure. You can use the following dataset as a basis for your classification: *kissed, loved, watched, smiled, sat, put, sang, laughed, was, cost, ruined, rated, rode, pleaded.* Make sure you pay attention to how the sounds represented by *-ed* are pronounced. For example, in *kissed* the ending *-ed* is realized by the sound /t/, in *loved* by the sound /d/, and in *rated* by the sounds /ɪd/. Try to determine how these choices are conditioned. Irregular forms (e.g. *sang, was*) can also be treated in analogy to Figure 4.2.

## 4.4 An analytical and descriptive system for the study of word-formation

Before we can look at the different types of word-formation patterns in more detail, it will be helpful to introduce a diagnostic system (see Schmid 2011: 95ff.). This essentially serves two main functions, one related to the analysis of existing words and one related to the way in which new words are created. Obviously, these two functions are intertwined. Firstly, the system helps to reveal similarities and differences in the body of existing complex words; here it has an analytical and descriptive function. Secondly, we can use the information gained from such analyses to formulate general ideas concerning how new words can be formed. The rationale behind this is that the way in which existing words have been formed will not be too different from the way in which new words can and will be formed. Irrespective of the format in which generalizations are stated, e.g. as patterns, rules or schemas, they essentially have the function of capturing speakers' tacit knowledge about how to decompose and form words. This means that the system to some extent reflects some sort of 'grammar' of word-formation. Note that since the system ultimately aims at the description of regularities, it is more applicable to the more regular and predictable field of morphemic word-formation than to that of the more haphazard and unpredictable non-morphemic patterns.

*Morphological form.* The first level in the proposed system concerns the analysis and description of word-formation products in terms of their morphological form or shape. This is done by segmenting complex lexemes into their morphemes and other potentially meaning-bearing constituents, and classifying them. The description of the morphological form can either be presented in terms of the morpheme classification introduced in Section 4.2, or can make use of the terms *base, affix, prefix, suffix,* etc. It is helpful for further analytical steps to mark the word classes of free lexical morphemes and the word-class changes caused by bound lexical morphemes, especially suffixes. Table 4.4 provides illustrations of the terminology and the kinds of elements that can be used for this part of the analysis. The examples will be taken up for further discussion below.

**TABLE 4.4** Illustrating the analysis in terms of morphological form

| | | | | |
|---|---|---|---|---|
| *disappointment* | *dis-*<br>lexical bound<br>prefix | *appoint*<br>lexical free<br>base$_V$ | *-ment*<br>lexical bound<br>suffix$_N$ | |
| *unemployment* | *un-*<br>lexical bound<br>prefix | *employ*<br>lexical free<br>base$_V$ | *-ment*<br>lexical bound<br>suffix$_N$ | |
| *armchair* | *arm*<br>N | *chair*<br>N | | |
| *paperback* | *paper*<br>N | *back*<br>N | | |
| *trade union leader* | *trade*<br>lexical free<br>N | *union*<br>lexical free<br>N | *lead*<br>lexical free<br>base$_V$ | *-er*<br>lexical bound<br>suffix$_N$ |

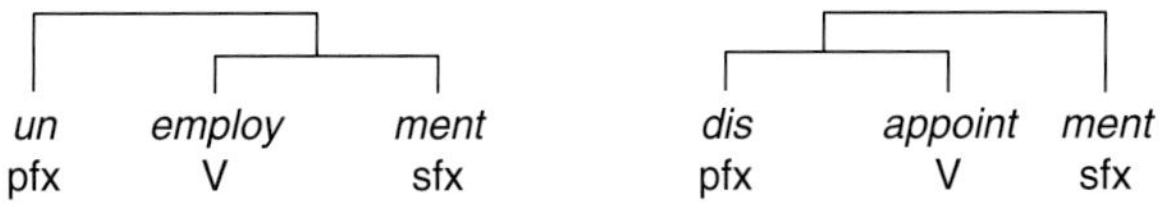

*un* *employ* *ment*
pfx V sfx

*dis* *appoint* *ment*
pfx V sfx

**Figure 4.3** Comparing the morphological structures of *unemployment* and *disappointment*

*Morphological structure.* The descriptions in Table 4.4 fall short of accomplishing the mission of teasing apart things that look similar but are in fact different. Consider the two examples *disappointment* and *unemployment*. Table 4.4 renders identical analyses in terms of morphological forms for these two nouns. However, these analyses conceal the fact that the two nouns differ with regard to their internal constituent structure, i.e. with regard to the question as to which elements belong together more closely than others. Looking at *unemployment* first, you will realize that here the suffix belongs more closely to the base than the prefix does, because the verb **to unemploy*, which would have to serve as a base for the suffixation does not exist. The formation history, so to speak, must therefore be *employ* → *employment* → *unemployment*. This means, as is shown in Figure 4.3, that *employ* and *-ment* are so-called immediate constituents. For *disappointment*, the situation is different. Here it is much more likely that the prefix was added to the base first, yielding the verb *to disappoint*, with the suffix being added in a second step, since the noun *appointment* does not seem to be semantically related to *disappointment*. The morphological structures of the two nouns thus differ, as is shown in Figure 4.3.

Adequate descriptions of the morphological structures of complex lexemes require even more information, however. The two compounds *armchair* and *paperback*, which are identical in terms of morphological form and immediate constituents, lend themselves to an illustration of this aspect. In the case of *armchair*, the first constituent *arm* modifies the second constituent *chair*. Both grammatically and semantically, *chair* can be considered

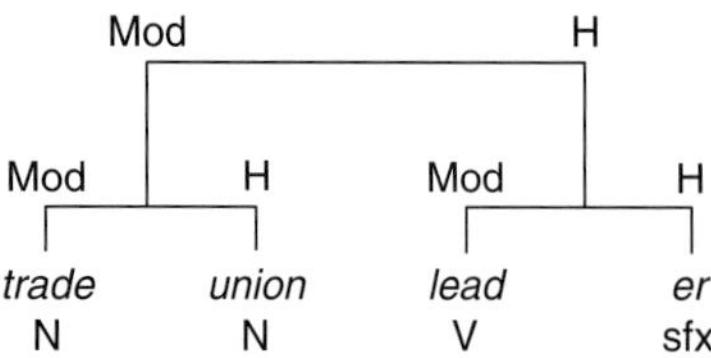


**Figure 4.4** Illustration of description in terms of morphological form and structure: *trade union leader*

the **head** of the compound, while *arm* functions as a **modifier**. A suitable paraphrase of the meaning of this compound could begin with the head and add the extra information provided in the modifier: 'a chair that has arms'. An analogous paraphrase is clearly impossible for *paperback*, since the meaning of this word is certainly not 'a back that is made from paper' but rather 'a book that has a back made from paper'. This indicates that the head of the compound *paperback* is not *back*, but could be *book* despite the fact that this is not part of the morphological form of *paperback*. The exemplary comparison of the two modifier–head structures reveals that *armchair* and *paperback* are not two of a kind and should therefore not be lumped together.

The distinction between modifier and head is an important general descriptive principle in word-formation, which, just like the idea of immediate constituents, has been taken over from syntax. As in syntactic structures, in English it is generally the case that in complex lexemes modifiers also precede heads. Heads are therefore the right-most constituents of complex lexemes and determine their word-classes. In the fairly complex formation *trade union leader* it is the last constituent *-er* which marks the whole unit as a noun. Furthermore, again as in the syntactic analysis of sentences, in the morphological analysis of complex lexemes we generally strive for a binary, i.e. two-way branching of constructions into immediate constituents. Lexemes consisting of more than three morphemes can usually be accounted for by several hierarchical layers of binary modifier–head combinations. This is shown in the exemplary analysis given in Figure 4.4, which demonstrates the whole scope of the analysis in terms of morphological form and structure.

While the analytical steps described so far already go a long way towards an adequate account of complex lexemes, they do not yet tell the whole story. What is needed to obtain the full picture is a description of the internal semantic structure of complex lexemes, including the semantic relations between the constituents. Consider as a first illustration the compounds given in (1), all of which have the noun *chair* as head. Using the system set up so far, you would be able to come up with a number of interesting observations: that all of these compounds consist of two free lexical morphemes; that they all represent a modifier–head structure; and that *high chair* and *swivel chair* differ from the rest of the group in that they have an adjective and a verb respectively as modifiers, rather than a noun. This account would miss out on important further differences, however, which concern the semantic relations linking the constituents of these compounds. As we have seen, the meaning of *armchair* can be paraphrased as 'a chair that has arms', indicating that the relation between *arm* and *chair* can be described as a possessive or part–whole one. As is pointed out in (1), however, the other compounds in the list encode distinctly different semantic relations, including comparison, identity and others:

| (1) | *armchair* | 'a chair that has arms' | → | POSSESSION/PART–WHOLE |
|---|---|---|---|---|
| | *barrel chair* | 'a chair that is shaped like a barrel' | → | COMPARISON |
| | *bedchair* | 'a chair that can be turned into/is also a bed' | → | IDENTITY |
| | *cane chair* | 'a chair made from cane' | → | SUBSTANCE, MATERIAL |
| | *deck chair* | 'a chair that is found on the deck of a ship' | → | LOCATION |
| | *high chair* | 'a chair that is unusually high' | → | SIZE |
| | *swivel chair* | 'a chair that allows you to swivel' | → | FUNCTION |

A similar problem arises in the analysis of suffixations and prefixations, where form–meaning ambiguities are also very common. The noun *declaration* is a good example of the widespread phenomenon that nominalizations can highlight different aspects of activities, processes and states:

(2) *declaration* 'action of declaring something', e.g. *his declaration took two hours*
'result of declaring something', e.g. *I did not believe his declaration*
'product of declaring something', e.g. *they signed a declaration*

The relations between prefixes and their bases can also vary considerably, even when the same prefix is used. What this shows is that an analysis and description of the internal semantic structures and relations must complement that of the morphological forms and structures.

**KEY POINTS: Analysis and description of word-formation types**

An adequate account of the structure of complex lexemes should consist of information on

- their morphological forms
- their morphological structures in terms of immediate constituents and modifier–head relations
- their internal semantic structures and relations

This now puts us in a position to have a systematic look at the system of word-formation in English, beginning with a general survey of the basic patterns.

## 4.5 Survey of English word-formation patterns

Figure 4.5 renders the most common way of classifying word-formation patterns in English and is to serve as a frame for the following sections (see Plag 2003, Lieber 2005, Schmid 2011).

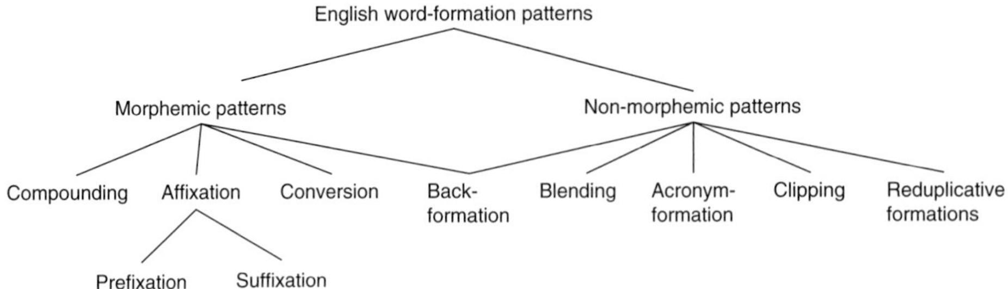


**Figure 4.5** Survey of basic word-formation patterns in English

## 4.5.1 Compounding

Compounding is the process of joining at least two free lexical morphemes or simple lexemes to form a complex lexeme. Compounds can be distinguished from syntactic phrases with the help of a number of criteria: in compounds, the main stress is typically, but not always, on the first constituent (e.g. *ˈblackbird* vs. *blackˈbird*); the first constituent cannot be inflected (e.g. *wallspaper*); the head cannot be replaced by *one* in coordination (e.g. *let's buy a newspaper and a wall one*); and compounds are typically lexicalized, which means that the meaning of the compound tends to differ and go beyond the meanings of its parts. For example, a *holiday* is not just, or no longer, a *holy day*, as its components suggest, but typically extends over several days and is mainly marked by the fact that people do not work.

In terms of morphological form, if compounds consist of nothing else than two lexemes (e.g. *wallpaper, mousemat, daydream*), they are commonly called **root compounds** and described in terms of the word-classes of their constituents (see Table 4.5). Compounds containing bound morphemes in addition to free ones, e.g. *meeting point, theatre-goer* or *good-looking*, are known as **synthetic compounds**.

The most frequent and productive types of compounds are listed in Table 4.5 (Schmid 2011: 122).

True verbal compounds, i.e. complex lexemes with verbs as heads which are actually the result of a compounding process, do not seem to exist in English or are in any case very rare. Potential candidates such as *to sightsee, to babysit* or *to handmake* are not verbal compounds, but result from the back-formation or conversion of nominal or adjectival compounds, here *sightseeing, babysitting* and *handmade.*

With regard to morphological structure, **determinative compounds**, in which the first constituent actually modifies the second, stand out as the most common type of compounds. All examples in Table 4.5 are of this type, which are also known as **endocentric compounds**, which means that the head is actually part of the compound. Counterparts to endocentric compounds are **exocentric compounds**, whose head does not appear in the morphological form of the compound. Although it presumably results from a clipping from *paperback book*, the word *paperback* can be used as an illustration of this type. As we have seen in Section 4.4, the head of *paperback* is

**TABLE 4.5** Most frequent and productive types of compounds in terms of morphological form

| **Nominal compounds:** |
|---|
| N + N: *backbone, barman, nutshell, pony tail, seat-belt, timetable, wallpaper* |
| Adj + N: *greenhouse, high-chair, smalltalk, stronghold* |
| [V + ing] + N: *dancing girl, building-block, dressing gown, racing car* |
| V + N: *cease-fire, copyright, showroom, stopgap* |
| N + [V + ing]: *credit rating* |
| **Adjectival compounds:** |
| N + Adj: *accident-prone, carefree* |
| N + [V + ing]: *awe-inspiring, eye-catching, time-consuming* |
| Adj + [V + ing]: *good-looking, hard-drinking* |

located outside the compound, and this is what the term 'exocentric' means. Many exocentric compounds rely on a possessive or 'has a'-relation: consider *redhead* 'person with red hair', *paleface* 'person who has a pale face', *redbreast* 'bird that has a red breast'. Compounds of this type are therefore also known as **possessive compounds** or **bahuvrihi compounds**, a term which comes from the ancient Indian language Sanskrit and exemplifies the phenomenon itself, as it literally expresses the notion of 'having a lot of rice' but means 'rich man'. The third type of compound is also often referred to by a Sanskrit term, **dvandva**, meaning 'pair'. Dvandva compounds are compounds in which there is no modifier–head relation, but both constituents are considered as heads on a par, e.g. *study-bedroom, singer-songwriter, bitter-sweet* or *deaf-mute*. They are also known as **copulative compounds** when they denote the sum of the two meanings (e.g. *bitter-sweet*), or as **appositional compounds** when they combine two different descriptions of the referent (e.g. *singer-songwriter*). Unlike determinative compounds, dvandva compounds are typically stressed on both elements of the pair. As is shown in Table 4.6, the three major types of compounds can also be differentiated in terms of the logical relations between the constituents and the compound.

A special challenge for the analysis of morphological structure arises in synthetic compounds of the nominal types *theatre-goer* and *shareholding* and the adjectival types *eye-catching* and *dark-haired*, all of which involve verbal elements and bound lexical morphemes. The problem concerns the branching in binary immediate constituents and the allocation of modifier and head roles. In all four cases, an analysis in terms of a compound consisting of a simple modifier (*theatre, share, eye* and *dark*) and a suffixed head is ruled out, as the potentials heads *goer, holding, catching* and *haired* are at least doubtful with regard to their status as existing lexemes. Analyses in terms of suffixations with complex modifiers (*to theatre-go + -er, to sharehold + -ing, to eye-catch + -ing* and *dark-hair + -ed*) are equally unsatisfactory on the same grounds that the potential bases do not exist. In these cases, and also in those innumerable ones where a

**TABLE 4.6** Survey of types of compounds differentiated by internal morphological and semantic structure

| Type | Internal structure | Logical relation (A = first constituent; B = second constituent; AB = compound) | Example and paraphrase |
|---|---|---|---|
| **determinative** compounds | modifier–head structure, endocentric (head is part of compound) | AB is a type of B | *mousemat* 'a mousemat is a type of mat' |
| **bahuvrihi** compounds | exocentric (head is found outside compound) | AB is neither A nor B but a type of C | *egghead* 'an egghead is neither a type of egg nor a type of head but a type of person' |
| **dvandva** compounds, either copulative or appositive | two-headed structure, endocentric | AB is both A and B | *singer-songwriter* 'a person who is both a singer and a songwriter' |

compound analysis seems at least possible, for instance for *bus driver*, it may seem advisable to argue that compounding and suffixation take place at the same time, so to speak, and to regard these lexemes as synthetic compounds formed by compressing major components of sentences into one word (e.g. *theatre-goer* → 'someone who goes to the theatre').

Further, somewhat less typical classes of compounds include so-called phrase compounds (e.g. *father-in-law, rough-and-ready, man-in-the-street, good-for-nothing*) and particle compounds derived from phrasal verbs (*take-away, breakthrough, handout, take-off*), which present a serious problem for modifier–head analysis. Neoclassical compounds are formations that also combine two concepts in a manner very similar to compounds, but these are not encoded by free lexical morphemes, but rather by bound forms derived from Greek and, less frequently, Latin. Examples of these somewhat learned and often technical words include *democrat, photograph, biography, technology* and *microscope*.

The types of semantic structures and internal relations that can be realized by compounds are virtually unlimited. Nevertheless, some tendencies concerning particularly frequent types can be identified. The examples of root compounds featuring *chair* as head have already given you a glimpse of some of the most dominant relations. More examples are provided in Table 4.7.

Note that the semantic interpretation of compounds, especially root compounds, often offers several equally plausible options.

**TABLE 4.7** Frequent semantic relations in root compounds

| Relation | Examples |
|---|---|
| FUNCTION | *gunpowder, breadbasket, toothbrush* |
| PART–WHOLE | *coat-collar, door-knob, picture-frame* |
| COMPARISON | *bell skirt, frogman, pot-belly* |
| TIME | *nightclub, morning coffee, midnight feast* |
| LOCATION | *water-rat, garden-party, tombstone* |
| MATERIAL | *ironware, gold ring, stone wall* |
| CONTAINMENT | *apple cake, sandpaper, picture book* |
| SOURCE | *spring water, seafood* |

**KEY POINTS: Compounding**

- Compounds are complex lexemes consisting of at least two free lexical morphemes, i.e. lexemes.
- Root compounds consist of free morphemes only, while synthetic compounds include bound lexical morphemes.
- Endocentric compounds include a constituent encoding the head; in contrast, the head is not expressed on the morphological surface of exocentric compounds.
- The major types of compounds are determinative, bahuvrihi and dvandva compounds.
- Compounds can exhibit a variety of internal relations including FUNCTION, PART–WHOLE, COMPARISON and others

## EXERCISE 4.3

Describe the following compounds in terms of their morphological forms and structures and classify them as determinative, possessive or copulative compounds. Provide the information in a table following the two models given:

| Compound | Morphological form and structure | Classification |
|---|---|---|
| a. *credit card* | *credit* *card*<br>N N<br>Mod H | determinative noun compound |

*(cont.)*

| Compound | Morphological form and structure | | | Classification |
|---|---|---|---|---|
| b. *answering machine* | | | | |
| c. *lemon-yellow* | | | | |
| d. *roller blade* | | | | |
| e. *actor-director* | | | | |
| f. *hard-working* | *hard*<br>Adj<br>[Mod | *work*<br>V<br>[Mod | *ing*<br>sfx (Adj)<br>H]H] | determinative adjective compound, synthetic |
| g. *birdbrain* | | | | |
| h. *shareholder value* | | | | |

## 4.5.2 Prefixation

Prefixation is the word-formation pattern which attaches a bound lexical morpheme at the front of a base, which typically includes at least one free lexical morpheme, i.e. lexeme. Only very few prefixes go hand in hand with a change of word-class: *a-* (*asleep*), *be-* (*beloved*), *en-* (*encourage*) as well as *de-* (*deform*), *dis-* (*displace*) and *un-* (*unsaddle*) in certain uses, while the large majority of prefixes are word-class-maintaining. Prefixation thus has first and foremost semantic, rather than grammatical, effects on a base.

With regard to morphological form and structure, we can distinguish nominal, adjectival and verbal prefixation patterns. Table 4.8 (from Quirk, Greenbaum, Leech and Svartvik 1985: 1540–6) provides a survey of frequent prefixes, which is organized in terms of semantic groups. It provides information on the word classes of the bases with which they occur and contains information on their major meanings or semantic relations.

Looking at the table, you will perhaps realize that the vast majority of those prefixes that still exist in present-day English and are also still productive and thus used to form new lexemes are of Latin, French and Greek rather than of native Germanic origin. Exceptions are the forms *fore-* as well as *under-*, *over-* and *out-*. You may also have noticed that the prefix *in-* has a number of variants depending on the first sounds of the base to which it is attached (e.g. *indirect*, *illegal*, *impossible*, *irresponsible*). These assimilations often took place in Latin or French before the words were borrowed into English. From a synchronic descriptive point of view, the variants can be considered allomorphs of bound lexical morphemes.

**TABLE 4.8** Frequent types of prefixes (from Quirk et al. 1985: 1540–6)

| Semantic type | Prefix | Meaning | Nominal examples | Adjectival examples | Verbal examples |
|---|---|---|---|---|---|
| negative | *a-* | 'lacking in' | - | *amoral, asexual* | - |
| | *dis-* | 'the converse of' | *disorder, discontent* | *disloyal* | *disobey* |
| | *in-* | 'not', 'the converse of' | – | *incomplete, illogical, irresponsible, impossible* | – |
| | *non-* | 'not' | *non-smoker* | *non-degradable* | – |
| | *un-* | 'the converse of' | – | *unfair, unexpected* | – |
| reversative and privative | *de-* | 'reversing the action' | attached to deverbal nouns, e.g. *de-nationalization* | - | *defrost, de-escalate* |
| | | 'remove from' | – | – | *delouse, degasify* |
| | *dis-* | 'reversing the action' | – | – | *disconnect, disinfect* |
| | *un-* | 'reversing the action' | – | – | *unzip, unpack, unwrap* |
| | | 'depriving of' | – | – | *unseat, unmask, unman* |
| pejorative | *mal-* | 'badly', 'bad' | *malnutrition* | *malodorous* | *maltreat* |
| | *mis-* | 'wrongly', 'astray' | *misconduct* | *misleading* | *mishear* |
| | *pseudo-* | 'false', 'imitation' | *pseudo-intellectual* | *pseudo-scientific* | – |
| degree or size | *co-* | 'joint' | *co-pilot* | – | *co-exist* |
| | *hyper-* | 'extreme' | – | *hypersensitive* | – |
| | *mini-* | 'little' | *mini-skirt* | – | - |
| | *out-* | 'surpassing' | *outnumber*$_V$ | – | *outgrow* |

**TABLE 4.8** *(cont.)*

| Semantic type | Prefix | Meaning | Nominal examples | Adjectival examples | Verbal examples |
|---|---|---|---|---|---|
| | *over-* | 'excessive' | – | *over-confident* | *overreact* |
| | *sub-* | 'below' | - | *subnormal* | – |
| | *super* | 'more than' 'very special' | *superman* | *supernatural* | – |
| | *under-* | 'too little' | – | *underprivileged* | *underplay* |
| orientation and attitude | *anti-* | 'against' | *anti-war* | *anti-social* | – |
| | *contra-* | 'opposite' | *contradistinction* | *contrafactual* | *contraindicate* |
| | *counter-* | 'against' | *counter-espionage* | *counter-clockwise* | *counteract* |
| | *pro-* | 'for', 'on the side of' | - | *pro-American* | - |
| locative | *inter-* | 'between', 'among' | *inter-war* | *international* | *intermarry* |
| | *sub-* | 'under' | *subsection* | *subnormal* | *subdivide* |
| | *super-* | 'above' | *superstructure* | – | *superimpose* |
| | *trans-* | 'across' | – | *transatlantic* | *transplant* |
| time and order | *ex-* | 'former' | *ex-husband* | – | – |
| | *fore-* | 'before' | *foreknowledge* | – | *foretell* |
| | *post-* | 'after' | *post-war* | *post-Freudian* | *postpone* |
| | *pre-* | 'before' | *pre-war* | *pre-marital* | *pre-heat* |
| | *re-* | 'again', 'back' | *re-analysis* | – | *rebuild* |
| number | *bi-, di-* | 'two' | *biplane, dioxide* | *bilateral, divalent* | – |
| | *poly-, multi-* | 'many' | *polytechnic, multiform* | *multi-racial* | – |
| | *semi-, demi-* | 'half' | *semivowel, demigod* | *semi-conscious* | – |
| | *tri-* | 'three' | *tricycle* | *tripartite* | – |
| | *uni-, mono-* | 'one' | *unisex, monoplane* | *unilateral, monosyllabic* | – |

**KEY POINTS: Prefixation**

- Prefixation is a word-formation process in which a bound lexical morpheme is attached to the front of an existing lexeme.
- In the vast majority of cases, prefixation does not change the word class of the base but has an effect on its meaning.
- Most prefixes in present-day English are not of Germanic origin but come from Greek, Latin and French.

## 4.5.3 Suffixation

With regard to morphological form, suffixation appears to be a perfect mirror image of prefixation: a bound lexical morpheme is attached at the end of a base which consists of at least one free lexical morpheme. However, the effects of suffixation on the base are so fundamentally different from the effects of prefixation that to stress this similarity would indeed be rather misleading. Although there are a number of suffixes that keep the word class of the base intact, including the nominal suffixes-*ship* (*lordship*), *-let* (*droplet*) and *-ing* (*tubing*) and the adjectival suffix *-ish* (*greyish*), these make up a comparatively small portion of the full set of derivational suffixes, whose main function arguably is to bring about a change in word class. A survey of English suffixes is therefore also more reasonably arranged in terms of their target word-classes, i.e. the word-classes of the products of the derivation process, and the word class of the base (see Table 4.9). The most precise and economical way of describing specific suffixation patterns follows the format '*de*-base target word-class formation'. For example, *signify* would be described as the product of a de-nominal verb-formation, *amendment* as a de-verbal nominalization, *manageable* as a de-verbal adjective formation.

If you study the examples in this list very closely, you will not fail to notice a number of peculiarities about suffixation which deserve special attention: firstly, some suffixes bring about changes in the pronunciation of the base concerning the quality and length of vowels and/or the allocation of the main stress. Cases in point include *explore – exploration, atom – atomic* and *sane – sanity*. Secondly, a small number of suffixes, mainly *-ee, -ation* and *-esque,* attract the main stress, while others shift it (e.g. *-ic, -ian, -ity*) or leave it unchanged. Thirdly, compared to the large number of noun-forming and adjective-forming suffixes, the list of verb-forming suffixes is quite short. As you will see, this is compensated for by the process of conversion (see Section 4.5.4), which has produced massive numbers of verbs derived from nouns and adjectives. Fourthly, unlike prefixes, suffixes frequently occur in sequences of several types, each bringing about a change of word class. The adjective-forming suffix *-able* is frequently followed by the noun-forming suffix *-ity* (e.g. *washability*, *debatability*); the verb-forming suffix *-ize* is added to the adjective-forming suffix *-ar* and frequently followed by the noun-forming suffix *-ation* (e.g. *pol(e)-ar-iz(e)-ation*). Finally, from a semantic point of

**TABLE 4.9** Frequent types of suffixes (extracted from Quirk et al. 1985: 1546–58)

| | | | |
|---|---|---|---|
| Noun-forming suffixes | de-nominal | abstract | *-age: mileage, footage*<br>*-ery: drudgery, slavery*<br>*-ful: spoonful, glassful*<br>*-hood: brotherhood, widowhood*<br>*-ing: carpeting, farming*<br>*-ism: idealism, impressionism*<br>*-ship: friendship, membership* |
| | | concrete | *-er: Londoner, villager*<br>*-ess: actress, lioness*<br>*-ette: kitchenette*<br>*-let: booklet, piglet*<br>*-ster: trickster, gangster* |
| | de-verbal | abstract | *-age: drainage, leverage*<br>*-al: refusal, dismissal*<br>*-ation: exploitation, exploration*<br>*-ment: amazement, embodiment* |
| | | concrete | *-ant: contestant, informant*<br>*-ing: building, opening*<br>*-ee: employee, payee*<br>*-er, -or: driver, writer, computer, actor* |
| | de-adjectival | abstract | *-ity: sanity, mobility*<br>*-ness: happiness, kindness* |
| Noun/adjective-forming suffixes | de-nominal or – de-adjectival | reference to persons and membership qualities | *-ese: Japanese, Chinese*<br>*-(i)an: Darwinian, Elizabethan, Russian*<br>*-ist: violinist, stylist*<br>*-ite: socialite, Raffaelite* |
| Adjective-forming suffixes | de-nominal | native | *-ed: wooded, simple-minded*<br>*-ful: useful, delightful*<br>*-ish: foolish, snobbish*<br>*-less: careless, restless*<br>*-like: childlike, monkeylike*<br>*-ly: brotherly, friendly*<br>*-y: sandy, wealthy* |
| | | foreign | *-(i)al: dialectal, professorial*<br>*-esque: romanesque, Kafkaesque*<br>*-ic: atomic, heroic*<br>*-ous: desirous, ambitious* |
| | de-verbal | | *-able: washable, debatable*<br>*-ive: attractive, explosive* |
| Adverb-forming suffixes | de-adjectival | | *-ly: extremely, calmly* |

| | | |
|---|---|---|
| | de-nominal | *-wards: northwards*<br>*-wise: clockwise, crosswise* |
| Verb-forming suffixes | de-nominal | *-ate: orchestrate, hyphenate*<br>*-ify: codify, beautify*<br>*-ize: hospitalize, symbolize* |
| | de-adjectival | *-en: broaden, harden*<br>*-ify: simplify, amplify*<br>*-ize: legalize, publicize* |

view frequent noun-forming suffixes fall into two basic categories, those producing concrete nouns referring to people and objects (e.g. *-er, -or, -ant, -ee* and *-ing*) and those forming abstract nouns (e.g. *-ation, -ment, -age, -ism, -ity* and also *-ing*). Adjectival formations typically refer to qualities and characteristics attributed to people, objects and ideas, and to notions such as ability and potentiality ( *-able, -ive*). Verb-forming suffixes show a strong tendency to form transitive verbs incorporating a causative element that can be paraphrased by 'make', e.g. *simplify* 'make simple' or *harden* 'make hard'.

As the list in Table 4.9 also suggests, suffixes are of course restricted with regard to the types of bases with which they can combine. In more technical parlance, suffixes – like prefixes in fact – are subject to productivity restrictions (e.g. Bauer 2001). These concern first and foremost the word-class properties of bases. For instance, while the suffix *-er* can be added to nouns to form concrete nouns denoting a typical quality of persons or, less frequently, objects (e.g. *Londoner, villager*) and to verbs in order to refer to the agents of actions (*driver, teacher*) or instruments (*computer, dish-washer*), de-adjectival formations (**consistenter, *patienter*) are unacceptable. Knowledge about such restrictions can be very useful in the analysis of word-formation products, because it allows you to predict, for example, that the nominalization *cleaner* must be derived from the verb *to clean* rather than the adjective *clean*. Most suffixes have further productivity restrictions concerning more specific grammatical or semantic properties. The noun-forming suffix *-ee*, for instance, typically combines with bases expressing the patient rather than agent role in a paraphrase: *employee* denotes 'someone who is employed, *interviewee* 'someone who is interviewed'. The adjective-forming suffix *-able* tends to require transitive rather than intransitive verbs as bases. However, as formations like *sleepable* and *livable* indicate, these productivity restrictions are often not hard and fast rules.

**KEY POINTS: Suffixation**

- Suffixation is a word-formation process which attaches a bound lexical morpheme at the end of an existing lexeme.
- In the vast majority of cases suffixation changes the word class of the base.
- Suffixation typically creates nouns and adjectives rather than verbs.
- Suffixes are subject to productivity restrictions.

**EXERCISE 4.4**

Give descriptions of the following complex lexemes using the format provided in the models:

(a) *countless* de-verbal adjective formation
(b) *unfair* negative adjective prefixation
(c) *darkness*
(d) *subcategory*
(e) *foreigner*
(f) *mispronounce*
(g) *Australian*
(h) *simplify*
(i) *carbonize*
(j) *re-open*
(k) *dishonest*
(l) *painting*

### 4.5.4 Conversion and zero-derivation

Not only can words be transferred from one word-class to another by the addition of a suffix, but this also takes place without any visible changes to their form. The nouns *hammer, bottle* and *father,* for instance, have been turned into verbs with no formal change, and so have the adjectives *clean, tidy* and *dirty*. The process of conversion is made responsible for these changes. It is defined as a word-formation process which transposes a lexeme to a new word-class without the addition of an overtly marked suffix. That this change has actually taken place can mainly be gleaned from the new grammatical functions that the converted lexeme can fulfil. In many cases, the semantic paraphrase also gives a hint: *to bottle* can be glossed as 'to put into a bottle', *to father* as 'to act as father to'. These paraphrases can often be used as a guide in determining the direction of derivation of a given conversion, as the base lexeme is usually part of a felicitous paraphrase of the derived lexeme. To paraphrase the noun *father* by something like 'someone involved in an act of fathering' would be decidedly odd; the same applies to a potential paraphrase 'result of an act of cleaning' for the adjective *clean*. Not all products of conversion lend themselves to this test, however. Particularly tricky to work out with regard to the direction of derivation are a huge number of abstract noun-verb pairs including *love, aim, plan, attempt, doubt, hope* and *fear,* which more or less defy all attempts to allocate the roles of base and derivative. The grouping of words of this type in Table 4.10, which gives a survey of the dominant types of conversion (Quirk et al. 1985: 1560–3), is therefore potentially controversial.

There has been some controversy in linguistics as to how the phenomenon of conversion should be explained theoretically. The approach presented so far regards it as some kind of invisible transfer process very similar to overt suffixations. Another possibility is to argue that many lexemes in the English lexicon have either multiple word-class

**TABLE 4.10** Frequent patterns of conversion

| | |
|---|---|
| **De-verbal nouns** | |
| 'state', 'state of mind' | *desire, dismay, doubt, love, smell, taste, want* |
| 'event/activity' | *attempt, fall, hit, laugh, release, search, swim* |
| 'object of V' | *answer* ('that which answers'), *bet, catch, find* |
| 'subject of V' | *bore* ('s.o./s.th. who/that bores'), *cheat, coach* |
| 'instrument of V' | *cover* ('s.th. with which to cover things'), *paper* |
| 'manner of V-ing' | *walk* ('manner of walking'), *throw* |
| 'place of V' | *divide, retreat, rise, turn* |
| **De-nominal verbs** | |
| 'to put in/on N' | *bottle, corner, catalogue, floor, garage* |
| 'to give/provide with N' | *butter (bread), coat, commission, grease, oil* |
| 'to deprive of N' | *core, peel, skin* |
| 'to . . . with N' | *brake, elbow, fiddle, hand, finger, glue* |
| 'to be/act as N with respect to' | *chaperone, father, nurse, parrot, pilot* |
| 'to make/change . . . into N' | *cash, cripple, group* |
| 'to send/go by N' | *mail, ship, telegraph; bicycle, boat, canoe* |
| **De-adjectival verbs** | |
| 'to make (more) Adj' (trans. V) | *calm, dirty, dry, humble, lower* |
| 'to become Adj' (intrans. V) | *dry, empty, narrow, weary (of), yellow* |

membership or are not determined with regard to word classes anyway, but only acquire word-class properties when used in syntactic contexts (Farell 2001). Extreme cases supporting the latter view include the form *round*, which can be used as a noun, verb, adjective, adverb and preposition or particle. Yet another approach, which emphasizes the similarity to overt suffixation, works with the notion of **zero-morpheme** and claims that the word-class change is brought about by a suffix that does not have a formal substance (Marchand 1969: 360ff.). The verb *to empty*, for example, would be explained as a result of the addition of the zero-morpheme to the adjective *empty* (*empty* – *empty* + {Ø}) in analogy to cases like *legal* – *legalize* or *public* – *publicize*. An argument in favour of this approach is that the semantic change effected by the zero-morpheme ('cause to be empty') is also identical to the one taking place in overt formations.

**KEY POINTS: Conversion and zero-derivation**

- Conversion is a word-formation process which transfers a lexeme to a new word class without the addition of an overtly marked suffix.
- While conversion frequently produces verbs from nominal or adjectival bases, for many cases it can be difficult to determine the direction of derivation.
- An alternative account is the idea of zero-derivation which claims that a zero-morpheme is responsible for the observable change of word class.

**EXERCISE 4.5**

Paraphrase the meanings of the following conversions as illustrated in (a) and (b):

(a) *pocket* V ← *pocket* N: 'put in N'

(b) *kick* N ← *kick* V: 'an act/instance of V-ing'

(c) *nail* V ← *nail* N

(d) *progressive* N ← *progressive* Adj

(e) *grant* N ← *grant* V

(f) *model* V ← *model* N

(g) *warm* V ← *warm* Adj

## 4.5.5 Back-formation

Like suffixation and conversion, back-formation is a word-class-changing process. In contrast, however, this process is not marked by the addition of morphological material or by keeping the surface form unchanged, but by the elision of material. It can be defined as the process whereby the deletion of a morpheme or morpheme-like element results in a transposition of a lexeme to a new word class. The verb *babysit,* which is derived from the noun *babysitter* by means of back-formation, and the verb *to sightsee* derived from *sightseeing* have already been mentioned above. Other frequently quoted examples include *to burgle* → *burglar, to edit* → *editor, to laze* → *lazy* and *to televise* → *television.* As these examples indicate, back-formation joins conversion as a predominantly verb-forming process.

Of course, back-formation is much more difficult to spot and identify than additive word-formation processes. Deficient inflectional paradigms can be an indicator, as is indicated by the rather unusual forms *I babysat last week* or *we sightsaw in London.* Paraphrases can also contribute as an argument: while 'to sit by the baby' is a rather poor gloss of *to babysit,* a paraphrase that includes the noun *babysitter,* e.g.

'to act as a babysitter' is quite plausible. If you keep in mind that genuine verbal compounds do not exist in English, this will also help you to realize that verbs like *bottle-feed, house-hunt* or *chain-smoke* might be the results of a back-formation process.

### 4.5.6 Non-morphemic word-formation types

The hallmark of non-morphemic word-formation processes, in addition to the fact that they do not obey morpheme boundaries, is that they are less regular and therefore less predictable. This means that given a recent verb like *to desktop-edit*, you can easily envisage that someone may eventually find it convenient to coin the adjective *desktop-editable*. However, knowledge of the words *floor* and *wardrobe* will not have put you in a position to foretell that someone has actually found it funny to coin the blend *floordrobe* to refer to an untidy room where lots of clothes are scattered all over the floor.

Four main types of non-morphemic word-formation processes are commonly distinguished: blending, clipping, acronym-formation and reduplication.

The term blending subsumes a number of ways in which two or more words can be merged or telescoped into each other. In the most typical cases, overlapping segments of words are exploited, as for example in the classic *smog* → *smoke* and *fog* or the more recent *wintertainment* → *winter* and *entertainment*, and the meanings of the blended lexemes are also blends of the meanings of the source lexemes. In *sexploitation*, both source words are retained in their full forms. The example *floordrobe* mentioned above illustrates the type of blend in which there is no or only a very superficial kind of overlap. A further example is the well-known noun *brunch* → *breakfast* and *lunch*, which differs from *floordrobe*, however, in that *floor* finds its way into the blend without being subject to a change. From a formal perspective, the latter example could in principle also be seen as a combination of *floor* and *drobe*, a clipped form of *wardrobe*, but the merged meaning of 'floor that serves as a wardrobe' speaks against that.

The process of clipping is responsible for a number of entirely common everyday words, whose sources are hardly known today. For example, *car* is a front clipping of *motor car* and *bus* a front clipping of *omnibus*; *pub* is a back clipping of *public house* and *zoo* a back clipping of *zoological garden*. *Flu* has emerged from *influenza* by way of a combination of front and back clipping.

**Acronym-formation** is an extremely productive process, especially in technical and institutional registers, but also increasingly in youth language and computer-mediated communication (e.g. *FAQs* ← *frequently asked questions, lol* ← *laughing out loud, brb* ← *be right back* and many other examples). Regarding the pronunciation of these formations we can distinguish those that are pronounced as words, e.g. *NATO* (← *North Atlantic Treaty Organization*), *AIDS* (← *Acquired Immunodeficiency Syndrome*), *PEN* (← *poets, essayists, novelists*), from cases where the letters are pronounced separately (e.g. *TV* ← *television*, *UK* ←*United Kingdom*, *BBC* ←*British Broadcasting Corporation*). The former are sometimes labelled as acronyms in a narrow sense, the latter as **initialisms**

(Bauer 1983: 223). Usually, the capital letters are used as a sign that a compound or phrase has been reduced to the initial letters, but there are also highly lexicalized forms like *radar* (from ***ra**dio **d**etection **a**nd **r**anging*) or *laser* (from ***l**ight **a**mplification by **s**timulated **e**mission of **r**adiation*).

Finally, **reduplication** is a quite minor type of word-formation pattern illustrated by lexemes such as *hush-hush, hip-hop* and *walkie-talkie*. As the examples indicate, the pattern subsumes cases where an element is repeated in identical form (*hush-hush*), cases where we have a vowel change (*hip-hop*) and those where the two components rhyme (*walkie-talkie*).

**KEY POINTS: Back-formation and non-morphemic word-formation types**

- Back-formation is a word-class-changing word-formation process which deletes a morpheme or morpheme-like element.
- In blending, the forms and meanings of words are merged.
- In clippings, parts of words are deleted without a change in meaning.
- Acronyms and initialisms are shortened forms retaining the initial letters of compounds and other fixed sequences of words; the former are pronounced as words, the latters as sequences of letters.
- Reduplication is a fairly rare word-formation process repeating a word or word-like element either identically or in a slightly varied form.

## EXERCISE 4.6

Classify the following lexemes in terms of their formation pattern:

(a) *tick-tick*

(b) *ad*

(c) *Oxbridge*

(d) *USA*

(e) *lab*

(f) *higgledy-piggledy*

(g) *grannie*

(h) *IRC*

(i) *prefab*

(j) *fanzine*

(k) *fridge*

(l) *IMO*

(m) *hi-fi*

## 4.6 A note on theoretical issues

Although it may not have struck you while reading the chapter, the approach presented here is largely a practical, down-to-earth one, which focuses on the methods and background knowledge required to carry out morphological analyses and appreciate the system behind the structures of words. Only very little has been said about the manifold theoretical disputes concerning the precise characteristics of this system. Back in the 1970s and 1980s, the discussion was dominated by the question of whether morphology and word-formation work essentially on the basis of principles similar to those postulated for syntax, thus producing members of phrasal categories, or whether morphology and word-formation have their basis in the lexicon, the storehouse of lexical categories. A more recent controversy concerns the format of the system described in this chapter and, specifically, the nature of the morphological knowledge which individual speakers and speech communities as a whole apparently have at their disposal – otherwise they would constantly coin ill-formed words. For a long time, this knowledge was modelled in the form of strict and abstract rules operating over entities defined in terms of equally abstract categories; work on morphology was very much preoccupied with defining these rules and the prerequisites for their input, and with determining the nature of their output. Individual words and how they are coined, used and propagated had hardly any role to play in this model. More recently, this approach has been rivalled by one which proceeds from the assumption that morphological knowledge is available in the form of more flexible schemas (Bybee 2007, Kemmer 2003) or constructions (Booij 2010) which are extracted or distilled by speakers from their constant exposure to inflected word-forms and complex lexemes (Schmid 2011: 85, 93–5). While these schemas provide them with the knowledge to distinguish well-formed from ill-formed novel creations, speakers are still free to coin creative new words but will then be more likely to have to face the possibility that their creations are not taken up by other speakers and therefore do not catch on.

WEBSITE: **Group exercise**

Visit the website and, in a small group, attempt the exercises on word-formation patterns, and the meaning and morphological status of word endings.

## 4.7 SUMMARY

This chapter has introduced you to inflectional morphology and word-formation, including derivational morphology. You should now be familiar with different types of morphemes and their characteristics, as well as different types of word-formation patterns.

The section on inflectional morphology has shown that languages differ considerably with regard to the extent to which they rely on inflectional morphemes to mark grammatical categories and relations. Different examples that will help you remember the major types were

English (increasingly analytic), German (more synthetic than English), Latin (fusional) and Turkish (agglutinating). Complexity in the field of inflectional morphology is not only caused by the number of inflectional morphemes but also by their variants, the allomorphs.

The section on word-formation has demonstrated the need to analyse complex lexemes systematically at the levels of morphological form, morphological structure and semantic structure. You have seen that the more regular, morphemic word-formation types of compounding, prefixation, suffixation and conversion differ in their effects on the grammatical, formal and semantic structures of the elements involved. Essentially, the function of compounding is to join words and concepts in order to create more specific words and concepts; the main function of prefixation is to modify the meanings of existing words in a number of basic ways; the main effect of suffixation and conversion is to change the word class of the base. The non-morphemic word-formation patterns (blending, clipping, acronym-formation and reduplication) are less regular and more creative, sometimes also more playful, than the morphemic ones. The idea, hinted at in the final section, that knowledge about word-formation patterns is available in the form of rough schemas and blueprints rather than strict rules seems particularly plausible for these flexible formation types but is also applicable to the more regular ones.

WEBSITE: **Morphology**

Now go to the website and assess your knowledge of morphology by completing the self-test questions!

## SUGGESTIONS FOR FURTHER READING

Bauer, L. (2003). *Introducing Linguistic Morphology*, 2nd edn. Edinburgh: Edinburgh University Press. An accessible, richly illustrated introduction to linguistic morphology containing examples from a wide range of European and other languages. The book covers inflectional and derivational morphology as well as compounding and discusses the relation of morphology to phonology.

Bauer, L., Lieber, R. and Plag, I. (2013). *The Oxford Reference Guide to English Morphology*. Oxford: Oxford University Press. This handbook, written by three of the leading authorities in the field of English morphology, is a very useful resource for finding out more about all aspects relating to the field of morphology.

Schmid, H.-J. (2011). *English Morphology and Word-Formation: An Introduction*. Berlin: Erich Schmidt. This introduction covers inflectional morphology from a synchronic and diachronic point of view, as well as word-formation. The discussion is based on authentic examples taken from a corpus, which is also used for quantitative analyses of data. With regard to theory, special emphasis lies on cognitive-linguistic approaches and socio-pragmatic aspects, while the generative tradition is clearly kept in the background. One chapter offers a systematic description of the processes involved in the establishment of new words.

# ANSWERS TO EXERCISES

## Exercise 4.1

Comments are given below:

| gr | gr | lex | lex | gr | [gr + gr][1] | lex | lex | gr[2] | gr |
|---|---|---|---|---|---|---|---|---|---|
| *while* | *his* | *grand* | *daughter* | *s* | *were* | *still* | *play* | *ing* | *with* |
| fr | fr | fr | fr | bd | [fr + bd] | fr | fr | bd | fr |

| gr | lex | lex | gr | gr | lex | lex | lex | lex | gr |
|---|---|---|---|---|---|---|---|---|---|
| *their* | *lap* | *top* | *s* | *and* | *desk* | *top* | *compute* | *er* | *s* |
| fr | fr | fr | bd | fr | fr | fr | fr | bd | bd |

| gr | gr | lex | lex[2] | lex | lex | lex | [lex + gr][3] | gr |
|---|---|---|---|---|---|---|---|---|
| *in* | *the* | *live* | *ing* | *room* | *Grand* | *dad* | *found* | *the* |
| fr | fr | fr | bd | fr | fr | fr | [fr + bd] | fr |

| lex | lex | lex | gr | gr | gr | lex | gr | [lex + gr][3] | gr |
|---|---|---|---|---|---|---|---|---|---|
| *necessary* | *picnic* | *supply* | *s* | *in* | *the* | *fridge* | *and* | *began* | *to* |
| fr | fr | fr | bd | fr | fr | fr | fr | [fr + bd] | fr |

| lex | gr | gr | gr | lex | lex | lex | lex | lex | lex |
|---|---|---|---|---|---|---|---|---|---|
| *take* | *them* | *to* | *his* | *be* | *love* | *ed* | *BMW* | *convert* | *ible* |
| fr | fr | fr | fr | bd | fr | bd | fr | fr | bd |

1. *were* functions as an auxiliary verb here. The root *be* is therefore classified as a (free) grammatical morpheme. In addition, the form incorporates the morpheme marking past tense, which is a bound grammatical morpheme.
2. The form *-ing* functions as a grammatical marker of the progressive in *playing* but as a derivational suffix in *living room*. It is thus classified as bound grammatical in the former case, and as bound lexical in the latter.
3. The forms *began* and *found* are analogous to *were* in their capacity of encoding a free morpheme and the past tense marker.

## Exercise 4.2

The forms *sat, put, sang, was, cost* and *rode* are 'irregular' and thus morphologically conditioned. While *sit–sat* and *sing–sang* exhibit some commonalities, it is very difficult to come up with generalizations here.

The other forms are phonologically conditioned according to the following system:

Rules of allomorphy for the English past tense morpheme

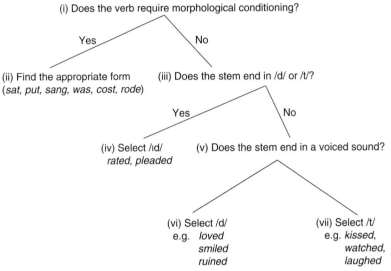

(i) Does the verb require morphological conditioning?

Yes → (ii) Find the appropriate form (*sat, put, sang, was, cost, rode*)

No → (iii) Does the stem end in /d/ or /t/?

Yes → (iv) Select /ɪd/ *rated, pleaded*

No → (v) Does the stem end in a voiced sound?

→ (vi) Select /d/ e.g. *loved smiled ruined*

→ (vii) Select /t/ e.g. *kissed, watched, laughed*

## Exercise 4.3

Key to abbreviations: Mod = modifier; H = head; sfx = suffix; N = noun; V = verb; Adj = adjective

| Compound | Morphological form and structure | Classification |
|---|---|---|
| (i) *credit card* | *credit card*<br>N N<br>Mod H | determinative noun compound |
| (j) *answering machine* | *answer ing machine*<br>N/V sfx (V) N<br>[[Mod H]Mod H] | determinative noun compound, synthetic |
| (k) *lemon-yellow* | *lemon yellow*<br>N Adj<br>Mod H | determinative adjective compound |
| (l) *roller blade* | *roll er blade*<br>V sfx (N) N<br>[[Mod H]Mod H] | determinative noun compound, synthetic |
| (m) *actor-director* | *act or direct or*<br>Vsfx (N)Vsfx (N)<br>[[ModH]Mod[ModH]H] | copulative noun compound |
| (n) *hard-working* | *hardworking*<br>Adj V sfx (Adj)<br>[Mod [Mod H]H] | determinative adjective compound, synthetic |
| (o) *birdbrain* | *bird brain*<br>N N<br>[[Mod H]mod H] | possessive noun compound ('person that has a brain like a bird'), metaphorical |
| (p) *shareholder value* | *share hold er value*<br>N V sfx (N) N<br>[Mod [Mod H]H] H] | determinative noun compound, synthetic |

Notes:

1. The copulative compound *birdbrain* is described in terms of an internal modifier-head structure and an external head.
2. It is doubtful whether the constituent structure of the synthetic compound *shareholder* can be described in terms of binary branching, as neither *sharehold* nor *holder* can serve as a base.

### Exercise 4.4

| | |
|---|---|
| (a) *countless* | de-verbal adjective formation |
| (b) *unfair* | negative adjective prefixation |
| (c) *darkness* | de-adjectival nominalization |
| (d) *subcategory* | locative noun prefixation |
| (e) *foreigner* | de-adjectival nominalization |
| (f) *mispronounce* | negative verb prefixation |
| (g) *Australian* | de-nominal adjective formation |
| (h) *simplify* | de-adjectival verb formation |
| (i) *carbonize* | de-nominal verb formation |
| (j) *re-open* | temporal verb prefixation ('iterative') |
| (k) *dishonest* | negative adjective prefixation |
| (l) *painting* | de-verbal nominalization |

### Exercise 4.5

| | |
|---|---|
| (a) *pocket* V ← *pocket* N | 'put in N' |
| (b) *kick* N ← *kick* V | 'an act/instance of V-ing' |
| (c) *nail* V ← *nail* N | 'fasten with a N' |
| (d) *progressive* N ← *progressive* Adj | 'person who is Adj' |
| (e) *grant* N ← *grant* V | 'sth that has been V-ed' |
| (f) *model* V ← *model* N | 'act as a N' |
| (g) *warm* V ← *warm* Adj | 'become/make Adj-er' |

### Exercise 4.6

| | |
|---|---|
| (a) *tick-tick* | identical reduplication |
| (b) *ad* | back-clipping ← *advertisement* |
| (c) *Oxbridge* | blend ← *Oxford* and *Cambridge* |
| (d) *USA* | initialism ← *United States of America* |
| (e) *lab* | back-clipping ← *laboratory* |
| (f) *higgledy-piggledy* | rhyming reduplication |
| (g) *grannie* | back-clipping ← *grandmother* + suffix-formation |
| (h) *IRC* | initialism ← *internet relay chat* |
| (i) *prefab* | back-clipping ← *prefabricated house* |
| (j) *fanzine* | blend ← *fan magazine* |
| (k) *fridge* | back- and front-clipping ← *refrigerator* |
| (l) *IMO* | acronym ← *in my opinion* |
| (m) *hi-fi* | acronym ← *high fidelity* |

## REFERENCES

Bauer, L. (1983). *English Word-Formation*. Cambridge University Press.

(2001). *Morphological Productivity*. Cambridge University Press.

(2003). *Introducing Linguistic Morphology*, 2nd edn. Edinburgh University Press.

Booij, G. (2010). *Construction Morphology*. Oxford University Press.

Bybee, J. (2007). *Frequency of Use and the Organization of Language*. Oxford University Press.

Farell, P. (2001). Functional shift as category underspecification. *English Language and Linguistics*, 5, 109–30.

Kemmer, S. (2003). Schemas and lexical blends. In H. Cuyckens, Th. Berg, R. Dirven and K.-U. Panther (eds.), *Motivation in Language: Studies in Honor of Günter Radden*, pp. 69–97. Amsterdam: Benjamins.

Lieber, R. (2005). English word-formation processes. In P. Štekauer and R. Lieber (eds.), *Handbook of Word-Formation*, pp. 375–427. Dordrecht: Springer.

Marchand, H. (1969). *The Categories and Types of Present-Day English Word-Formation: A Synchronic-Diachronic Approach*, 2nd edn. Munich: Beck.

Plag, I. (2003). *Word-formation in English*. Cambridge University Press.

Quirk, R., Greenbaum, S., Leech, G. and Svartvik, J. (1985). *A Comprehensive Grammar of the English Language*. London and New York: Longman.

Schmid, H.-J. (2011). *English Morphology and Word-Formation: An Introduction*. Berlin: Erich Schmidt.

Stockwell, R. and D. Minkova (2001). *English Words: History and Structure*. Cambridge University Press.

# 5 Grammar

ROGER BERRY

**KEY TERMS**

- adjective
- adverb
- clause
- descriptive grammar
- meaning
- noun
- object
- phrase
- preposition
- prescriptive
- sentence
- subject
- verb
- word class

**PREVIEW**

'Grammar' is a word that is known to almost everyone, but it is clear that people have different attitudes towards and preconceptions about it. This chapter tries first of all to tease these out before attempting to identify what grammar really 'is'. A definition is offered which emphasizes the role of grammar as a resource for creating meaning. A number of approaches to grammar, which help to conceptualize it, are then discussed. This is followed by a description of some of the most important aspects of English grammar: word classes, clause elements and clause combination. Grammar is not treated as a monolith, however, and several dimensions of variation are examined. There is then a section showing how all this can be applied to solving problems. Finally, a revised set of attitudes is put forward for consideration.

## 5.1 INTRODUCTION

'Grammar' is a troublesome and emotive word, with many meanings and implications for different groups of people. It is more in the public domain than any of the other chapter titles in this book. Few people can come to the study of grammar without preconceived notions. Here are just some of the potential attitudes to the discipline.

For some linguists,'grammar' is a cover term for syntax and morphology (see Chapters 4 and 6, this volume). But grammar is more than just a combination of these two areas. Its function and purpose are what counts, as the rest of this chapter will demonstrate. Indeed, it is clear that most people's conception of grammar is at odds with that of linguists.

For some teachers of English as a foreign language (EFL), grammar is a crutch to rely on in difficult circumstances. For others, it is a distraction from the real task of learning languages. For still others, grammar is a tool to be used occasionally to make generalizations. And for yet others – though they are a dying breed – grammar is an inseparable part of learning a foreign language.

For learners of foreign languages, grammar is a collection of separate rules ('rules of thumb'), given by their teachers and textbooks (and usually simplified, though they do not know it), which may occasionally be helpful (though there is the danger, long recognized, that learners may take the learning of such rules as a substitute for learning the language – see the distinction between primary and secondary grammar below). There is also the issue of whether such conscious learning can be applied anyway.

For students of English as an academic subject at university (i.e. in the secondary sense to be described below), grammar is a surprisingly complex subject which is full of terms and concepts (and, if they are foreign language learners, totally unlike the grammar they studied at school), but which is indispensable for further study of the language. (It is hard to imagine studying discourse analysis, for example, without a foundation in grammar.)

For EFL textbook writers and planners, grammar used to be (and still is for some) the organizing principle around which they structure their syllabus. Their textbooks have units proactively introducing or reactively explaining various traditional structures such as the tenses, reported speech, the comparison of adjectives, the use of conjunctions, and so on.

For many native speakers of English, grammar was once an essential part of the school curriculum, which went out of fashion fifty years ago, but which has now resurfaced in some parts of the world in a milder, more enlightened form under the heading of Language Awareness or Knowledge about Language. Outside school, grammar is a guide to 'correctness' for some. But for others, it is something to beware of, because they do not know it as well as they think they ought to, and it may trip them up. For some politicians, grammar (or rather its absence in education) is a pretext for all that is wrong with education.

The following sections try to work out a realistic and coherent appreciation of what grammar is, which will encompass all of these concerns while also going far beyond them.

**EXERCISE 5.1**

What is your own personal experience of 'grammar'? In what capacity or capacities have you experienced grammar? What do you feel about the following statements?

(a) I make grammatical mistakes in my first language.

(b) You should use *were* after *if*, not *was*.

## 5.2 What is grammar?

### 5.2.1 Towards a definition

In linguistics, 'grammar' has been regarded as one of the three traditional areas of language study, alongside phonetics and semantics. But while phonetics is the study of pronunciation, or the sounds of speech (see Chapter 2), and semantics is the study of meaning (see Chapter 7, but also Chapter 8 on pragmatics), it is not so obvious what grammar is the study of. The best answer is that grammar is the study of grammar, i.e. 'grammar' refers not only to the discipline but also to the subject matter of the discipline. (This is another of the confusions that bedevils the word, alongside all the different interpretations of it described above.) But what is grammar? What actually is it that we study under the heading of grammar?

Let's take an example in which English and Chinese are compared. The name of one university in Hong Kong is *Lingnan* in Mandarin, which roughly translates as *south of (the) mountain(s)* (referring to its original location). A literal translation, however, would be *mountain south*, reflecting the order of the two elements *ling* and *nan*. It is possible to reverse the order of these two elements to get *nanling*, which equates to *(the) south mountain(s)*. Thus, in Mandarin (and other Chinese languages) the two elements can be combined in two ways to achieve two different meanings, illustrating one of the major grammatical resources languages possess: changing the order of elements. English uses word order a lot too, but in this case it keeps the same basic word order but uses another technique to achieve the different meanings: the insertion of function words, in this case *of* (we can ignore *the* here). The point is that while English and Mandarin do things differently, they both do it grammatically. They achieve different meanings by altering the form of language in a productive, systematic way, i.e. they use a rule. We can see this in (1) to (6) if we take other similar elements:

(1) hebei = *north of the river*
(2) hunan = *south of the lake*
(3) shandong = *east of the mountain*
(4) beihe = *the north river*
(5) nanhu = *the south lake*
(6) dongshan = *the east mountain*

In Mandarin the order of the two elements is simply reversed, with the first element acting as a **premodifier** to the second element, which is the head (the most important word). In English the expressions on the right above follow the same pattern, but in those on the left there is a **postmodifier** (e.g. *of the river*) following the head.

Based on this we can attempt a tentative definition: grammar is the system of rules that relates forms to meanings. There are two important words here. The first is 'system'. The rules are not just a random phenomenon. Rather, they are connected and interact with each other. The other important word is 'meaning'. Though some aspects of grammar must simply be accepted (e.g. the way verb tenses are formed, or the formation of irregular forms), grammatical choices are largely related to the creation or interpretation of meaning. Very often we see cases where a difference in grammar parallels a difference in meaning. Some approaches to grammar play down the meaning element altogether, but this is not an approach taken here.

## EXERCISE 5.2

(a) What do the following Mandarin phrases mean in English? *nanshan, hubei*

(b) How would *south of the river* be translated into Mandarin?

## 5.2.2 How do languages 'do' grammar?

The above examples show two mechanisms or strategies whereby, according to Swan (2005), words can be turned into language. The first mechanism is that the word order can be changed, as in the classic example: *the dog bit the man* vs *the man bit the dog*. English and Chinese both make extensive use of this device to show relationships between words and phrases. Both languages generally have the same basic word order, such as subject–verb–object (as in the 'dog' example), or modifier–head (as in the *lingnan* example). However, other languages differ. For example, French usually places adjective modifiers after noun heads (e.g. *le mot juste*), while Japanese and other languages place the object before the verb rather than after it.

The second mechanism that can be used to change words into language is that words such as *of* can be inserted, e.g. *the success of their plan* (see the distinction between **content words** and **function words** below). There is a third strategy where the form of words can be altered, such as the addition of *-(e)s* to form the third-person singular of verbs in English (e.g. *dies*). These three strategies are used to a different extent by different languages. English uses the first extensively in a number of ways, as the above examples show, and also makes much use of the second strategy. However, English also makes limited use of the second strategy (less than it used to) in the morphology of **nouns**, verbs and **adjectives**. The Chinese languages also make little use of the third strategy, while Latin and the Slavonic languages use it extensively in the shape of their extensive verb and noun endings. A fourth technique that is used in English – intonation – is discussed below Section 5.5.4.

**KEY POINTS: Grammar in different languages**

- All languages use the same three basic strategies to 'do' grammar, i.e.
  changing the word order
  inserting function words
  changing the form of words

but to different extents.

- In all languages grammar is a resource for the creation of meaning, thereby helping to turn words into language.

**EXERCISE 5.3**

What is the function/meaning of *of* and *to* in these sentences?

(a) The death <u>of</u> the Prime Minister surprised everyone.

(b) I want <u>to</u> go.

## 5.3 Approaches to grammar

Many words can premodify 'grammar'. Some refer to a particular approach to, or theory of, grammar. Out of this confusion of epithets we can discern three distinctions that are relevant to a proper understanding of grammar.

### 5.3.1 Primary versus secondary grammar

This distinction is taken from McArthur (1983: 73–5), or rather the terms for it are, as this is a long-established dichotomy. It is also characterized as 'operational grammar' versus 'analytical grammar'. **Primary grammar** is the knowledge we all possess unconsciously and intuitively about our first languages. Some people say they do not know the grammar of their own language. This is nonsense. If they did not, they could not use it to communicate fluently and correctly, as per the definition above. What they perhaps mean is that they do not know anything *consciously* about the language. This conscious knowledge is secondary grammar. **Secondary grammar** derives from the deliberate study of a language and results in a body of knowledge found in grammar books or more simply in foreign language teachers' rules of thumb.

'Secondary' is an appropriate term because secondary grammar is derived from primary grammar. All languages have a primary grammar which is contained in the 'heads' of their speakers. But many do not have a codified secondary grammar. For those that do, even the most comprehensive grammar books (e.g. Quirk et al. 1985 for English), which nowadays approach 2,000 pages, do not account for all the subtle nuances that a native speaker knows intuitively. All forms of secondary grammar should therefore be an attempt to capture primary grammar. When this does not happen, problems occur (see Section 5.3.2 below).

The difference between primary and secondary grammar is not quite as straightforward as it may seem. It is not just about the perfect intuitive knowledge of the native speaker versus the imperfect conscious knowledge of the grammarian or learner of the language. Some native speakers do have a partial conscious knowledge of their first language (though they are fewer now than they used to be when 'grammar' was seen as an indispensable part of the school curriculum). And language learners do acquire a certain intuitive knowledge about the language they are learning, one that, for example, allows them to judge correctly the acceptability of sentences they are presented with (without knowing consciously any rule).

### 5.3.2 Prescriptive versus descriptive grammar

As described in Section 5.1, some native speakers (and learners too) see the role of grammar as being a source to turn to for advice on matters of correctness. In this approach certain personages are accorded, or claim, the authority to decide on linguistic matters. For English there is a long list of authoritative figures who from the eighteenth century onwards have written influential books on what should be considered grammatical and what should not.

Over the years a number of usages in English have been stigmatized by this 'prescriptive' tradition and have given rise to complaints to media outlets whenever so-called solecisms have been spotted. Their injunctions include:

- not to end sentences with a preposition (e.g. *They are people we can do business with*)
- not to split infinitives, as in the famous phrase from *Star Trek*: *to boldly go*
- not to use *hopefully* to mean *I hope that* or *it is to be hoped that*
- not to use double negatives (e.g. *I don't know nothing*)
- not to use *less* with count nouns (e.g. *There were less people there that night*)

However, many of these injunctions were derived from a comparison with Latin grammar and had no historical basis in English, i.e. there was no reference to primary grammar.

Against this **prescriptive grammar** we must set a more recent tradition, but one which is more in accordance with modern linguistics. The aim of so-called descriptive grammar is to describe the language as it is and to base descriptions on evidence of usage rather than on opinions. It is embodied in the great **descriptive grammars** of the late twentieth and early twenty-first centuries such as Quirk et al. (1985), Biber et al. (1999) and Huddlestone and Pullum (2002). The debate has continued in this century with the publication of books by John Humphrys (2004, 2006) for the prescriptivists (albeit in a more moderate form) and David Crystal (2006) for the descriptivists. Humphrys rightly gives up on some of the less tenable prescriptive injunctions such as 'no prepositions at the end of sentences' and 'no splitting of infinitives'. However, he still decries the 'misuse' of *hopefully*. A brief look at this word will be instructive.

The prescriptive claim is that *hopefully*, as with similar words, is an adverb of manner and should only be used to mean 'in a hopeful way'. Thus, the sentence *He looked at the toy hopefully* is grammatically correct, while the sentence *Hopefully his parents will buy him the toy* is not.

The descriptive evidence, however, is that *hopefully* is used regularly in the manner illustrated by the second of these sentences and has been for a long time. It is one of a number of words that may be called 'disjunct' or 'comment' adverbs that allow speakers to express their attitude towards a proposition. In debunking the prescriptivist's claim, Crystal (1984) lists a number of other such words and phrases that are used in this way: *thankfully, happily, regrettably, wisely, funnily enough, incredibly, luckily*. We can also add *fortunately, stupidly* and *frankly*.

It is clear that this is an extensive and important use of adverbs in English. Indeed, it is one that Humphrys also employs, perhaps inadvertently, as the examples in (7) to (9) from his book, *Lost for Words* (2004), demonstrate:

(7) Oddly enough, politicians don't much like the word 'money'. (p. 194)

(8) He is, sadly, extinct... (p. 217)

(9) What they'll get (thankfully) is... (p. 239)

Presumably (another example of this use) in this last example he did not mean that 'they' would get something 'in a thankful manner'. This illustrates a tendency among prescriptivists: to unwittingly commit the very 'crime' they are decrying.

Such controversies may seem a storm in a teacup (especially to those who deal with the problems of non-native speakers). However, they can cause a loss of confidence in speakers, especially those of non-standard varieties. And other languages do not seem to occasion the same obsession in their speakers. Imagine the reaction of speakers of French, Russian and other Slavonic languages if they were told that the multiple negatives that are standard in their language were illogical and incorrect.

**EXERCISE 5.4**

Examine these sentences and state what prescriptive injunction they break. (Some are taken from the text of this chapter; did you notice them?) What alternatives are there?

(a) 'Grammar' is a difficult word to be objective about.

(b) This was not a subject I was prepared to spend much time on.

(c) This illustrates a tendency in prescriptivists: to unwittingly commit the very 'crime' they are decrying.

(d) I have tried to distribute the roles evenly, but if anyone feels that they should be given more work, they should let me know.

(e) They failed to completely understand the problem. (from Crystal 2006: 127)

(f) This is not to be sneezed at.

## 5.3.3 Pedagogic versus scientific grammar

This third distinction relates to the purpose of grammatical description and the intended audience. Is it meant for fellow linguists and grammarians, in which case there is no limit to the level of sophistication in the account, or is the aim to teach learners of the language, in which case some level of simplification is required? The former can be called **scientific grammar** and the latter **pedagogic grammar**. It should be emphasized that there are as many variants of pedagogic grammar as there are different target groups, and the difference between the two is not absolute but rather more of a cline.

By way of example, we can take a rule of thumb that is sometimes presented to learners (in slightly varying guises) about the difference between two common words in English, *some* and *any*: use *some* in positive sentences and *any* in negatives and questions. This would seem to account for sentences such as (10) to (12):

(10) I know some answers.

(11) Do you know any answers?

(12) I don't know any answers.

where *some* seems to be replaced by *any* because of the context. First of all, though, we need to recognize that we have not exhausted all the contexts in which *any* and its compounds are used. Conditionals and words with a negative implication also seem to allow *any*:

(13) If anyone does turn up, we'll be delighted.

(14) I've seldom seen anything so ridiculous.

This is a pointer to the real difference between the two words; that it is to do with their meaning. *Some* 'asserts' the existence of something, while *any* does not. This explains the apparent exception in offers where it would be normal to ask (15) rather than (16):

(15) Would you like some tea? (i.e. I have some)

(16) Would you like any tea?

And there are further contradictions to the rule where, given the right circumstances and with the appropriate intonation, it is possible to say (17) and (18):

(17) Do you know some answers?

(18) I don't know some answers. (I know all of them.)

In fact, the rule seems to have so many 'exceptions' that its value can be called into question. This is the case with many rules of thumb. This also illustrates how pedagogic rules tend to be presented in isolation, whereas scientific ones apply more generally and can be combined with others. Thus, the concept of 'assertion' applies not just to *some* and *any* but also to compounds of the words (*somebody, anybody*) and, more interestingly, to other apparently unrelated words: *already* (assertive) and *yet, ever, at all* (non-assertive).

However, there is a link between prescriptive and pedagogic grammar. Since learners of a language cannot be presented with the full truth (and some educators would argue that they should not be presented with any grammatical formulations, simplified or otherwise), some simplification is necessary. This may involve advice which is economical with the truth, i.e. prescriptive (see the rule about the comparison of adjectives in Section 5.5.5).

Fortunately, most of the prescriptive 'rules' cited above have not passed into pedagogic grammar for non-native speakers. However, one that has, at least in some regions, is the injunction to use *were* instead of *was* after *if*; this forms the topic of the next exercise.

**KEY POINTS: Grammatical distinctions**

- All native speakers of a language know its grammar (in the primary sense); otherwise they could not use it to communicate. However, they are unlikely to know much about its grammar in the secondary sense (an explicit account of the rules).
- In modern linguistics (secondary) grammatical accounts are based on description, not prescription.
- Many prescriptive injunctions are not based on evidence.
- Pedagogic grammar is tailor-made for particular target audiences and so may legitimately contain some simplification.

**EXERCISE 5.5**

How do you feel about the following two sentences? Use your intuitions, or feelings, about what is acceptable. Is there any situation where one might be preferable to the other?

(a) If I was correctly informed, this is the place.

(b) If I were correctly informed, this is the place.

If you are familiar with using a corpus (a collection of texts that can be searched electronically), check the usage there by searching for the strings *if I was, if I were, if she was, if she were.* There are several corpora available free of charge online, for example, the Corpus of Contemporary American English (COCA, available at corpus.byu.edu/coca).

## 5.4 Describing English grammar

What follows is an attempt to capture the secondary grammar of English descriptively and scientifically (though on a necessarily selective and introductory level), while at the same time reviewing pedagogic and prescriptive accounts. But before we do so, we must note that there are different approaches to description, some complementary and overlapping, and some with different explanations for the same phenomena (and sometimes, confusingly, different terminology). Which approach is chosen depends on a number of factors: its efficiency, its ability to explain other factors, its simplicity, and its purpose or aims (description and explanation versus universal applicability).

### 5.4.1 The structure of grammar

It is traditional to arrange units of grammar into a hierarchy of five levels:

*morphemes* (see Chapter 4), which make up...
*words*, which make up...
*phrases*, which make up...
*clauses*, which make up...
*sentences* (there is some disagreement about whether this constitutes a valid level)

At each level the unit may consist of one or more units of the lower level. An example of a sentence with one clause, one phrase, one word and one morpheme would be *Stop!* The fact that language can be analysed according to a number of hierarchical levels indicates that grammatical structure is not a simple matter of linearity, whereby one word is followed by another, then by another, and so on (even though that is how it is actually represented in speech and writing). Grammatical structure is (at least) two-dimensional, as in the tree diagram example of a **noun phrase** shown in Figure 5.1.

Various names are given to this idea of how words 'go together': phrase structure, immediate constituents, constituent structure. This chapter goes beyond a simple aligning of constituents, however, by explaining how they relate to one another.

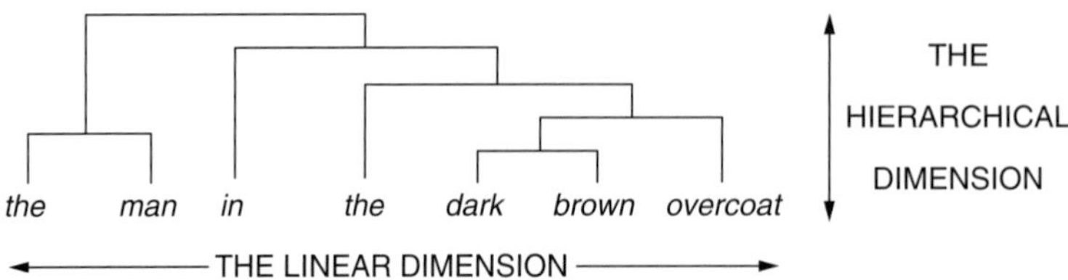


**Figure 5.1** Tree diagram of a noun phrase

The remainder of this section concentrates on three areas that are central to any description of English grammar: word classes (i.e. dealing with words, and how they make up phrases), clause elements (i.e. how phrases make up clauses) and clause combination (i.e. how to make up sentences). For other important areas, such as verb forms, noun and verb phrase construction, you will need to refer to some of the more extensive grammars described in the annotated suggestions for further reading.

## 5.4.2 Classifying words: word classes

When the ancient Greeks and Romans first started to think about language objectively, they took the basic elements, the words, and classified them into a number of 'parts of speech'. This classifying tradition is still with us today, though we prefer to use the term 'word classes' for the different groupings. It is not a perfect or complete approach to the description of languages, and there are numerous disagreements about what constitutes a **word class**, but it is a good place to start.

One broad distinction that can be made first of all is between content and function words. **Content words** are those which contain the major part of the message in a text, such as nouns, verbs, adjectives and adverbs. **Function words**, such as prepositions, convey less meaning and may have a grammatical function (though it is not true to say they have no meaning at all). Function words tend to be shorter, less numerous but more frequent than content words. This corresponds to a distinction between open and closed word classes. Content word classes are more open to accepting new members than closed ones. For example, it is relatively easy to add new nouns and verbs (*selfie* and *twerk* are recent examples, respectively).

The major word classes that may be established for English are:

noun, verb, adjective, adverb, preposition, conjunction, auxiliary, determiner, pronoun

The first four are open word classes; the last five are closed. Some grammarians would disagree in part with this list. Some would like to conflate determiners with pronouns, arguing that their membership overlaps greatly. The separation of auxiliary (verbs) from (main) verbs will raise some eyebrows. The justification for it is that auxiliaries are a closed class, while verbs are an open class. And a case can be made for extending the list by adding '**numerals**' and other classes.

Before looking at the word classes individually, we need to consider two approaches to defining them: notional and formal. Let us take 'noun' as an example. Traditionally nouns are said to represent the names of people, places or things. Setting aside the issue of what names are, there are clear problems with this notional definition. There are many words which are clearly nouns but which this definition would not apply to, such as words referring to feelings (*boredom*), actions (*reading*), and so on. What we actually use to identify word classes (and other linguistic phenomena) are formal criteria, i.e. how the words behave linguistically. These formal criteria can be of two kinds: morphological criteria (i.e. to do with the shape of the words, in particular what inflectional endings they may have), and structural criteria (i.e. the other words it 'goes' with).

Nouns can be identified morphologically by the ending for the plural and, in writing, for the **genitive**, or apostrophe-*s*, as it is better known, e.g. *dog/dogs/dog's/dogs'*. Structurally nouns are commonly found as the head in a noun phrase, where they can be preceded by determiners and adjectives, e.g. *a good woman*. One major subclassification of nouns distinguishes between **count nouns** and **noncount nouns** (or countable and uncountable nouns, respectively). A word such as *table* is count because it can be plural (*tables*) or preceded by the determiner *a* (*a table*), while *furniture* is noncount because it cannot. In many cases a noun can be both, and sometimes this indicates a different meaning. Thus, while *dog* is normally count, it can be reclassified as noncount to mean the meat rather than the animal. (Thus there is a great difference between saying *I like dogs* and *I like dog*.) This is a good example of how grammar changes with meaning. See also the example with *room* in Section 5.6.

Verbs such as *go* and *want* can be identified morphologically by the way they change for the past tense (*went, wanted*), by the third person singular (*goes/wants*), and by the *-ing* and *-ed* participles (*going/wanting; gone/wanted*); these are sometimes misleadingly referred to as the present and past participles. Verbs can also be identified structurally by the fact that they can be preceded by auxiliaries to form **verb phrases**, e.g. *has gone*.

Adjectives can be identified morphologically by their ability to take the endings *-er* and *-est* for the so-called comparative and superlative forms, e.g. *big/bigger/biggest*. They can also be identified structurally by their occurrence in two positions: in front of nouns as 'attributive' adjectives, e.g. *the big apple*, and after the verb *be* and similar verbs, e.g. *It is big*. They are also common after a certain group of adverbs called intensifiers: *very/so/fairly big*.

Adverbs are harder to identify. Traditionally they have been identified as having the ending *-ly* added to adjectives (e.g. *happy, happily*), but this does not apply to all adverbs (e.g. *soon, there, yet*), and many words ending in *-ly* are adjectives (e.g. *friendly, costly*). The endings *-wise*, *-ways* and *-wards* are clearer indicators of some adverbs, but they are rarer. In fact, adverbs are a rather amorphous class of words, consisting of a number of subclasses (see the above discussion of *hopefully*) with only tenuous interconnections. Words such as *please* and *yes* are included simply because there is nowhere else to put them.

The closed word classes are harder to identify since they generally do not have different forms.

Prepositions are found at the start of prepositional phrases, that is, a group of words consisting of a preposition and a noun phrase (e.g. *in the room*). They help to relate their noun phrase to a preceding verb, adjective or other noun and to indicate the meaning relationship. Sometimes they are separated from their noun phrase and left at the end of their clause.

Auxiliaries can be identified by their position in front of (main) verbs. They are often described as 'helping' to form verb phrases. They include modal auxiliaries (e.g. *can, will*), which do not change their form, and primary auxiliaries (*be, have* and *do*) which assist in the formation of tenses, negatives and questions.

Determiners include words such as *the, a, some, many, this, these,* and so on, which indicate the start of a noun phrase (e.g. *some good ideas*). In some cases they agree with the following noun (e.g. *this idea, these ideas, many ideas*). Their function is to specify in the most general terms (i.e. more generally than adjectives) the nature of the noun phrase they introduce: via its quantity, whether it is known or not, or close or far, and so on.

Pronouns are sometimes said to take the place of nouns. This is not accurate, however. What they may replace is noun phrases (e.g. *I like the girl / I like her*), though in many cases it is hard to identify anything that has been replaced (e.g. *It is windy*). Conjunctions are best dealt with when talking about clause combinations (see Section 5.4.4).

One problem with word class analysis is that all of the apparent members do not exhibit all of the formal features described above. Thus some adjectives do not fulfil all the conditions. For example, *snap* can only be used attributively (*a snap election* but not *the election was snap*) whereas the reverse is true of *asleep* (*he's asleep* but not *he's an asleep person*). For this reason it is usual to make a distinction between central (or prototypical) and marginal members of a word class.

A far more important issue with word class analysis is the fact that many words (especially the more frequent ones) can belong to more than one word class. For example, *access* is a word that has relatively recently acquired membership of the verb class in addition to being a noun (see the concept of conversion in Chapter 4):

(19) I need access to the database. (noun)

(20) I need to access the database. (verb)

However, this is not necessarily a problem. In fact, the different word class labels can be used effectively to show how a word behaves differently.

## EXERCISE 5.6

Identify the word classes in this sentence (taken from the text in Exercise 5.9): *He released his smelly load outside the palace.*

## EXERCISE 5.7

Distinguish the word class of *down* in these sentences. You may not be familiar with all the meanings, but you can use your knowledge of word classes to distinguish the different uses. Which features described above did you use?

(a) They sounded really down.

(b) Put down your weapons.

(c) In winter we use a down duvet on our bed.

(d) Down the street there was quite a commotion going on.

(e) I saw him down five whiskies in ten minutes.

### 5.4.3 Analysing clauses: clause elements

What is a clause? The notional definition suggests that it is something that contains 'a complete idea'. However, this is very hard to substantiate, and units at other levels, i.e. phrases or sentences, might also fit this description. The formal definition is that clauses contain at least a subject (except for **imperatives**) and a verb, as well as other elements according to the requirements of the verb. The theory of clause elements, as expounded in Quirk et al. (1985), though not described as such, is that all clauses in English can be analysed in terms of five elements: subject, verb, object, predicative (or complement) and adverbial. These are explained below (with their abbreviations in brackets).

In trying to define **subject** (S), we encounter the same problem of inaccurate notional definitions as was the case with word classes. A subject is often thought to be the person or animal that carries out an action, i.e. is the 'doer' or 'agent', as in (18):

(21) They solved the problem.

But this is a very restricted view of subjects, since in addition they can fill a wide range of roles, such as experiencer (e.g. *We saw the accident* where 'we' actually did nothing), instrument (e.g. *The key opened the door*) and location (e.g. *This chapter contains a discussion of...*). Another possible confusion is to think of a 'subject' of a sentence in its normal, non-technical meaning, where it refers to what the sentence is about. Here, however, subject is a grammatical concept, with the following formal characteristics in English: they are usually placed at the start of clauses in front of the verb; they 'agree' with the verb such as the so-called third-person *-s* (e.g. *she knows*); and they change places ('invert') with auxiliaries to form questions (e.g. *Can you come?*)

The verb (V) corresponds to the **verb phrase** described in Section 5.4.2, although here we are talking about its role in clauses. It is the most important part of a clause since it determines which of the remaining three other elements occur in a sentence. So, for example, a **transitive verb** will have one or more objects such as in (22) and (23):

(22) They like us.

(23) I bought my daughter a bike.

while an **intransitive verb** will have no object as in (24):

(24) We laughed.

Many verbs, especially the more frequent ones, can occur as both transitive and intransitive, e.g. *She explained the problem. / Please explain.* Two more types of verb are described below under predicative.

**Objects** (O) usually occur after verbs. They generally denote something directly affected by an action or event, e.g. *A husband and wife team run the company*. They can usually become the subject of a **passive voice** construction, e.g. *The company is run by a husband and wife team.*

The function of **predicatives** (P), sometimes called 'complements', is to describe something already mentioned as subject or object, rather than to introduce a distinct entity (as with objects). Adjectives as well as noun phrases are common:

(25) He's rich/a banker. (a subject predicative following a link verb)

(26) They drove her crazy. (an object predicative following a link transitive verb)

They are the least frequent of the five elements. Object predicatives, in particular, occur only with a rather limited range of verbs.

**Adverbials** (A), which are not to be confused with adverbs, generally refer to less central circumstances of actions, states and events, such as location, timing, manner, cause, effect or reason. While subjects, objects and predicatives generally respond to questions beginning *Who* or *What*, adverbials respond to other *wh*-word questions such as *Why*, *Where*, *When*, *How*, etc. They can be represented by adverb phrases as in (27):

(27) I saw him (very) briefly. (How long. . .?)

but prepositional phrases as in (28) are also common:

(28) I saw him in the garden. (Where. . .?)

Adverbials are generally optional in clauses – they are rarely specified as obligatory by verbs – and there can be more than one. While they usually come after the verb, they are fairly free in terms of word order, as can be seen in (29):

(29) In winter these animals are never seen in the daytime outside their burrows.

To illustrate, let's take an example of how the application of clause elements can explain an ambiguous sentence as in (30):

(30) I will ask her to pay the bills on Monday.

The ambiguity resides in whether the asking will take place on Monday or the payment of the bills. In the first interpretation *on Monday* is an adverbial and the whole sentence would be analysed as:

I (S) will ask (V) her (O) to pay the bills (O) on Monday (A).

In the second, *on Monday* would be analysed as part of the object.

I (S) will ask (V) her (O) to pay the bills on Monday (O).

This can be shown by asking two different questions focusing on the object using *what*:

What will you ask her on Monday? (To pay the bills.)
What will you ask her? (To pay the bills on Monday.)

Another way to distinguish these is to move the elements around, e.g. *On Monday I...*

**EXERCISE 5.8**

Analyse these sentences according to their clause elements. State what type the verb is.

(a) He became a brilliant teacher.

(b) I have found your wallet.

(c) The court found him guilty.

(d) They bought me a smartphone for Christmas.

(e) You've been swimming all day.

(f) The man in the dark brown overcoat is very secretive.

## 5.4.4 Building sentences: clause combination

What is a sentence? To say that it is a string of words between a capital letter and a full stop (or question mark, etc.) is inadequate, since it only applies to writing; it cannot apply to speech. What is needed is a grammatical definition, one that applies to both modes equally, namely: sentences are strings of words that obey the rules of clause construction (see Section 5.4.3) and clause combination. So what are the rules of clause combination? To understand this, we need to consider a final word class: conjunctions. **Conjunctions** are said to join two clauses together. This is certainly true of co-ordinating conjunctions (*and, but* and *or*). However, it would not apply to the subordinating conjunctions (*when, if, because*, etc.), since they introduce subordinate clauses, that is, clauses which are part of another, larger clause, as in (31):

(31) Wash your hands before you eat.

Here *before you eat* functions as an adverbial in the main clause. It is called an adverbial clause since it indicates a circumstance (in this case time), just like other adverbials. There are also a number of words that are called subordinators, such as *that* and *whether*, and relative pronouns *who, which,* etc. which can also have the same function as subordinating conjunctions of placing one clause inside another, e.g. *Reports said that she would keep the baby*. Here the subordinate clause introduced by *that* functions as the object of *said*. In fact, clauses are very common as objects. Subjects and predicatives can also be clauses but they are less common.

**KEY POINTS: Describing English grammar; word classes to sentences**

- The structure of grammar is not merely a question of one word following another. Words may be grouped together in various ways to form a hierarchical structure.
- The concept of word classes helps to explain how words behave differently and how they group together in phrases.
- The concept of clause elements helps to show how different phrases perform different functions in making up clauses. Verbs are central to the way clauses are constructed.
- The concept of clause combination explains how clauses are combined, using conjunctions and subordinators, into sentences.

**EXERCISE 5.9**

Look at the following text and identify the clauses in it – whether they are subordinate or not – and the conjunctions or subordinators that introduce them. (Hint: check the verb phrases. As per the definition above, every (full) clause must have one in addition to a subject.)

> The driver was apprehended by police after he released his smelly load outside the palace that houses the National Assembly. It was unclear what was behind the protest, but it comes as the President faces a scandal over revelations that he is having an affair with an actress…

(Abridged and adapted from the *South China Morning Post*, 19 January 2014)

## 5.5 Variation in grammar

The above discussion might be seen as implying that grammar is a monolith, that it is an unvarying, one-size-fits-all phenomenon that affects all speakers of a language identically. This is emphatically not the case. Grammar varies along a number of different, interrelated dimensions: in time; among the speakers of different dialects; across levels of formality; and between different modes, most obviously between speech and writing.

### 5.5.1 Historical change

Perhaps the most obvious dimension is the historical one. Grammar changes over time, as does language generally. Prescriptivists who complain that language is in decay because of certain changes that they object to do not realize that they themselves are using forms that earlier prescriptivists objected to. Languages change inexorably, and there is little that 'authorities' can do to stop them. Most changes pass without notice. Three recent innovations in English are:

- so-called 'quotative' *like* (e.g. *He looked at me and I'm like: what's your game?*)
- *you guys* as a second-person-plural pronoun (with *you* being restricted to singular use)
- *I'm so out of here* (where *so* is used as a different type of adverb)

Only the first of these has drawn much fire. It remains to be seen if any of them will gain general acceptance. However, since they are used widely by the young, it seems likely that resistance to them will die out.

### 5.5.2 Standard versus non-standard varieties

The grammar that has been described in this chapter is largely that of standard British English. This is just one particular variety (a dialect) of English that has acquired a certain prestige worldwide because of its association with powerful sections of society, with education and so on. Along with standard American English it is the variety that is generally taught in EFL classes. However, there is nothing superior linguistically about standard English. It is chosen for description simply because it is more widely encountered and studied. Non-standard varieties of English have equally valid grammars. Here are some features that are common in other English dialects:

- The use of double or multiple negatives. Many dialects of English employ this device. It is merely a different way of expressing negation which creates a negative 'prosody' throughout a clause.
- The use of *ain't* as a multi-purpose negative contraction (to replace forms of *be* and *have*), e.g. *I ain't going / I ain't seen him.*
- Different verb forms such as past tenses, e.g. *I done it, We seen it* or *We was cheated.*
- Different personal pronouns such as *y'all, 'em, hisself* (more consistent with other forms than *himself*)

We need to accord the same status to the grammar of varieties of non-native English such as the use of *isn't it* as a universal tag question in Singaporean and other varieties of English, e.g. *He was guilty, isn't it? She knew him, isn't it?* (instead of the far more complex range of forms in standard English: *...wasn't he*/*...didn't she*).

### 5.5.3 Appropriateness

Another dimension along which grammar varies is according to the situation. Certain grammatical forms may be appropriate in one situation but not in another. The level of formality is one aspect of this form of variation. The use of contractions is an obvious example: to write *do not* rather than *don't*, or to say *Can you not* ... rather than *Can't you...* implies a more formal situation. The use of *were* rather than *was* after *if* is similar: *If he were here...*

Particular genres of English have conventions that should be observed by users. In some academic writing, for example, the use of the passive to achieve objectivity is recommended over more personal styles which use personal pronouns such as *I*. Thus, the use of *Fifty learners were given a questionnaire...* is preferred over *I gave a questionnaire...* (though *We gave...* is acceptable). Similarly, in film and book reviews it is normal to use the present tense to describe events in the plot, e.g. *Although they have little in common, they end up living together.*

### 5.5.4 Spoken versus written grammar

In Section 5.2.2 above, it was suggested that there are three ways in which languages 'do' grammar. But for English there is a fourth way: intonation. A difference in intonation can make a difference in grammar. Thus, *do it* with a falling intonation would be interpreted as an imperative (an instruction in this case), whereas with a rising intonation it would be a question (checking what was said before). The addition of a question mark to the latter in writing indicates that punctuation can have a similar function to intonation in speech. However, punctuation is a poor cousin by comparison, as it is unable to match all the subtleties that intonation supplies. And sometimes it serves other purposes. Commas, for instance, while they sometimes indicate phrase or clause boundaries, also indicate pauses (a phonetic feature).

Stress is another feature of speech that can have a grammatical function which is unmatched in writing. Crystal (2006: 119) gives the example of the sentence in (32) that would be unclear in writing because we do not know whether *only* refers to *advised* or to *Mary*:

(32) I only advised Mary.

but which would be clear in speech depending on whether *advised* or *Mary* was stressed.

The difference between intonation/stress and punctuation is just one example of grammatical variation between speech and writing. There are many other features which can be represented in both but which are more typical of spoken than written English. An example is dislocation where an element is taken out of a sentence for emphasis and replaced by a pronoun, e.g. *That game you're playing – what is it?* By contrast, lengthy noun phrases and sentences with multiple subordinate clauses are more common in writing. There is a link to formality here: contractions, for example, are much more common in spoken English.

### 5.5.5 Tendencies

A final strand of variation is one where there seems to be no obvious motivation, where absolute rules seem to be replaced by relative tendencies. An excellent example is the rules for the formation of the comparative and superlative of adjectives. Most textbooks (for learners) will state a rule something like: Add *-er* and *-est* to adjectives of one syllable, and to those of two syllables ending in *-y*, *-ow*, *-er*, etc. (e.g. *kinder, happier, shallower, cleverer*); with other adjectives of two syllables and more use *more* and *most* (e.g. *more extreme, more beautiful*). Depending on the level of sophistication, the rules given do allow for some variation (e.g. *commoner/more common*). However, a study of actual usage by Hilpert (2008) showed a great amount of variation, with many adjectives having both possibilities. In addition, there were several unexpected (but intuitively correct) forms that directly contradicted the rules. Here are just a few examples: *more real* (not *realer*); *more likely* (much more common than *likelier*, while other such adjectives seem to obey the rule, *happier* being more likely than *more happy*); and *unhappier* (almost as frequent as *more unhappy*).

**KEY POINTS: Variation in grammar**

- Grammar is not a monolith; it varies in many ways.
- Grammatical change occurs over time; new forms are introduced while others die out.
- Different dialects have different grammars. There is nothing inherently better about the grammar of standard English or worse about that of non-standard varieties, for example the use of double negatives.
- Grammar varies according to the situation language is used in. Thus something may be appropriate in one situation but not another, especially in terms of the level of formality.
- While speech and writing generally have the same grammar there may be differences; intonation is a factor that generally cannot be replicated in writing.
- Some grammatical behaviour is the result, not of hard and fast rules, but of subtle tendencies.

**EXERCISE 5.10**

Why are the forms at the end of Section 5.5.5 in breach of the so-called rules? Do they correspond to your intuitions? Can you think of any reason why they might be preferred to the prescribed form? Also, did you notice two other comparatives that were used in explaining the text above? Which form was used: *-er* or *most*?

## 5.6 Why does grammar matter?

We have already seen a number of areas where a principled approach to grammar can be applied in various situations to relieve people of hang-ups they may have about the way they speak, or to understand language change and variety. There are other applications.

### 5.6.1 Debunking myths about language

Grammar can also be applied to debunk myths. One very tenacious myth about English grammar is that it has a future tense, namely *will*. This belief began at a time when people thought Latin was the perfect language and went searching for reflections of it in English, especially for its tenses. Thus English 'acquired' a future, conditional, pluperfect, future perfect, and so on. The other terms have largely disappeared, but the future tense seems to be with us still. Yet if we examine the evidence we see that the case is very weak. Firstly, tense in English elsewhere (as in Latin) is a question of morphology, of adding a suffix to the basic form of verbs to form the past tense (*want/wanted*), not of placing an auxiliary in front of the verb (*will want*). Secondly, *will* behaves exactly like all the other modal verbs, and is best treated along with them. Thirdly, it does not always refer to future time (e.g. *That'll be the postman* – a deduction about the present), and when it does there is always another element of meaning, e.g. promise (*I'll do it for you*). Fourthly, there are other candidates, such as *going to* (*It's going to rain*) which, though rarer, seems to have a purer idea of futurity. Nowadays textbooks for learners tend to have units on 'future with *will*' and 'future with *going to*' rather than promoting *will* as a tense, and no scientific grammars use the term.

### 5.6.2 Explaining language play

We can also apply the concepts of grammatical description in explaining jokes and other forms of language play. For example, take this classic joke from Groucho Marx: *Yesterday I shot an elephant in my pyjamas. How he got into my pyjamas I don't know.* The ambiguity depends on whether *in my pyjamas* is interpreted as an adverbial in the first sentence (i.e. 'he' was in his pyjamas) or as part of the object (*an elephant in my pyjamas*). The second sentence makes it clear that the elephant was wearing them. As with all language-based jokes, the first part 'leads us up the garden path', making us expect something which the second part then undermines, making us realize that we should have interpreted the first part differently.

Advertisers are also very playful with language. Some years ago at the Hong Kong Rugby Sevens tournament there was a very effective advert for a beer. It showed a bunch of thirsty rugby supporters converging on an empty bar where one very nervous waiter is holding what is obviously the last bottle of beer in the place. Then a voice proclaims: *One game, one tournament, one beer.*

While this slogan may not appear at first sight to have much of interest to grammarians, there is an ambiguity in the word *beer* that is highly grammatical. *Beer* is normally a noncount noun (*I can't drink beer*), but it can be converted to count status to mean a unit (glass, bottle or can) or a type of beer. The language and the visual used cleverly create the possibility of both interpretations: one (bottle of) beer or – the intended outcome – one (unique type of) beer.

### 5.6.3 Understanding ambiguity

We can also use grammar in understanding and solving other ambiguities and paradoxes. Here are a few ambiguous and paradoxical sentences in (33) to (36). You might like to pause before reading the solution and try to work them out yourselves, though in some cases you will need additional concepts.

(33) There's no room in that room.

This apparent paradox (if there is 'a room' how can there be 'no room') can be explained by reference to the distinction between count and noncount nouns, as described in Section 5.4.2 above, but with the added factor that the distinction can sometimes involve quite different meanings. Thus the first 'room' is a noncount noun meaning 'space', whereas the second is a count noun, referring to a unit in a building. This is a good example of how grammar parallels meaning.

(34) She has a duty to perform.

The ambiguity here depends on whether (a) 'she' is going to perform a duty, or (b) performing is her duty. Grammatically, *perform* is a transitive verb in (a) but is intransitive in (b).

(35) What do we want to improve most of all?

This sentence is ambiguous. In one interpretation, 'we' want to improve something (i.e. 'we' is the hidden subject of 'improve'). In the other interpretation, 'we' want something to improve (i.e. 'what' is the hidden subject). This ambiguity is possible because *improve* is a so-called ergative verb: it can be both transitive (*we improved the situation*) and intransitive but where the object replaces the subject (*the situation improved*).

(36) I'll pass on your offer.

Does this mean (a) 'I won't accept your offer', or (b) 'I'll convey it to someone else'? This ambiguity rests on the nature of the word *on* and its relationship to the verb *pass*. In (a) *on* is a preposition linked to the following noun phrase. In (b) it is actually an adverb more closely linked to the verb. We can see the difference if we move *on* to the end, i.e. *I'll pass your offer on*. Then only interpretation (b) is possible. This combination of verb and adverb is sometimes called a phrasal verb. Interestingly, if we turn the noun phrase into a pronoun, then the two meanings are represented differently. *I'll pass on it* could only be (a) while *I'll pass it on* could only be (b).

WEBSITE: **Group exercise**

Visit the website and, in a small group, examine the data from a corpus of English texts. Use this evidence to evaluate an account, commonly given to learners of English, of the way conditional sentences are constructed.

## 5.7 SUMMARY

This chapter has taken two broad approaches to grammar. The first was to look outwards to how it relates to people in general, how it affects them; this is a theme that was taken up again in the final sections. In between, the chapter turned inwards, by attempting to work out what the essence of grammar is. In this respect, it concluded that grammar is a resource found in all languages (though they use different techniques) for the expression of meaning. The three distinctions that were then made, between primary and secondary grammar, between prescriptive and descriptive grammar, and between scientific and pedagogic grammar, helped to pin down why grammar appears in different guises to different people, for example how learners of English only see a small, unsystematic, simplified and sometimes incorrectly explained part of grammar (the 'tip of the iceberg'); how native speakers should be considered to possess a complete knowledge of the grammar of their language; how this knowledge is as good as the next person's; and how unhelpful, prescriptive notions have come about.

The central portion of the chapter concentrated on three of the most important areas in the description of English grammar: word classes, clause elements and clause combination; a number of important concepts and terms were introduced here. This section was an inevitably brief introduction to these areas, and several other important areas had to be omitted. Nevertheless, these concepts are extremely useful in gaining an insight into how grammar works in English and, most importantly, into how it may be applied. Thus grammar is a useful tool in debunking myths and prescriptive notions, in accounting for variation and in solving various 'problems'. It may be claimed that an understanding of grammar is essential in acquiring an understanding of language and that it is at the heart of explaining how language works. Above all, grammar is not a dry academic discipline; it is about people – the choices they make to express their meaning, and the attitudes they have towards the languages around them.

WEBSITE: **Grammar**

Now go to the website and assess your knowledge of grammar by completing the self-test questions!

## SUGGESTIONS FOR FURTHER READING

Crystal, D. (2006). *The Fight for English*. Oxford University Press. This text, which is aimed at the general reader, is full of wise words on the debate between prescriptive and descriptive grammar. It also covers more than just grammar, being partly a response to Lynne Truss's book on punctuation entitled *Eats, Shoots and Leaves*. See chapters 15–19 in particular, and chapter 23 for his 'disagreement' with John Humphrys (discussed in Section 5.3.2).

Swan, M. (2005). *Grammar*. Oxford University Press. This is an excellent text for the uninitiated reader about grammar in general. It covers much of the same ground as this chapter, but also includes sections on the learning of grammar and historical language change.

# ANSWERS TO EXERCISES

## Exercise 5.1

People sometimes 'slip up' in their first language when, for example, they start off a sentence one way and change course in mid-stream. But when people make statement (a) – and a lot do – they are usually referring to some prescriptive rule of style, such as that in (b), which has been imposed on the language from outside. As should be clear from Section 5.3.1, native speakers by definition 'know' the grammar of their language.

## Exercise 5.2

(a) *the south mountain, north of the lake*

(b) *henan* (Like other examples, this is the name of a Chinese province.)

## Exercise 5.3

*Of* is usually thought of as a preposition that indicates possession (e.g. *the pen of my aunt*). But in fact it indicates a whole range of relationships between two noun phrases such as an attribute (e.g. *the height of the building*), or a personal relationship (e.g. *the leader of the gang*). Here the relationship is one of an underlying subject (*the Prime Minister*) and verb (*died*).

*To* is likewise thought of as a preposition, but here it is nothing of the sort. Its function is to mark (note this further example) the following word as an infinitive after certain constructions (such as the verb *want*). It is hard to see what meaning it could add here. Without it the sentence is perfectly understandable (as many learners of English would claim).

## Exercise 5.4

(a), (b) and (f) all end with a preposition (because the noun phrases they accompany have been placed earlier in the sentence). These are perfectly normal constructions. With (a) and (b) it would be possible to have a more formal alternative with the preposition placed earlier: ... *a difficult word about which to be* ... and ... *a subject on which I was prepared* ... These are relative clauses. But for (f) no alternative is possible (because this is a passive).

(c) and (e) have a 'split' infinitive. In (c) it would be possible to say ... *unwittingly to commit* ..., but in (e) to say *They failed completely to understand* ... would change the meaning, while ... *to understand completely the problem* sounds awkward.

(d) has an example of *they* referring back to a singular word with an indefinite meaning (*anyone*). This is of some antiquity in English and sounds completely normal. The alternatives are all problematic:

...*if anyone feels he should*... (sexist? but the prescribed form in American English)

*...if anyone feels he or she should...* (clumsy? especially if the pronoun is repeated, as in the example)

*...if anyone feels s/he should...* (unpronounceable and, I am told, falling into disuse)

### Exercise 5.5

*Were* in this situation is a remnant of an old grammatical form called the 'subjunctive' which was used extensively in Old English to express hypothetical situations. But *was* is also of some antiquity. In fact, in modern usage *was* appears to be more common and the use of *were* (where there is a choice, so not *you were*) sounds distinctly formal. One situation where *were* is possibly preferable, however, is in *If I were you* ... This is a fixed expression. *If I was you* ... while possible, may sound non-standard.

### Exercise 5.6

*he*: pronoun
*released*: verb
*his, the*: determiners
*smelly*: adjective
*load, palace*: nouns
*outside*: preposition

### Exercise 5.7

(a) is an adjective meaning 'depressed'. It occurs after a link verb.
(b) is an adverb, accompanying a verb.
(c) is actually a noun, although it looks like an adjective because of its attributive position. But it is referring to the feathers of young birds. We could say *a duvet made of down.* Nouns are actually quite common premodifying other nouns.
(d) is a preposition, preceding a noun phrase.
(e) is a verb in its infinitive form (meaning 'drink').

### Exercise 5.8

| | |
|---|---|
| (a) He (S) became (V) a brilliant teacher (P). | link |
| (b) I (S) have found (V) your wallet (O). | transitive |
| (c) The court (S) found (V) him (O) guilty (P). | link transitive |
| (d) They (S) bought (V) me (O) a smartphone (O) for Christmas (A). | transitive (with two objects) |
| (e) You (S) have been swimming (V) all day (A). | intransitive |
| (f) The man in the dark brown overcoat (S) is (V) very secretive (P). | link |

### Exercise 5.9

The verb phrases are underlined below.

> The driver (1) <u>was apprehended</u> by police after he (2) <u>released</u> his smelly load outside the palace that (3) <u>houses</u> the National Assembly. It (4) <u>was</u> unclear what (5) <u>was</u> behind the protest, but it (6) <u>comes</u> as the President (7) <u>faces</u> a scandal over revelations that he (8) <u>is</u> <u>having</u> an affair with an actress...

There are therefore eight clauses, as indicated by the numbered verb phrases above. The corresponding clauses are as follows:

(1) is a main clause (containing incidentally a passive verb)
(2) is an (adverbial) subordinate clause introduced by *after*

(3) is a relative subordinate clause introduced by the relative pronoun *that*
(4) is a main clause
(5) is a subordinate extraposed clause introduced by *what*. This clause could replace *it* as the subject of clause (4): *What was behind the protest was unclear...*
(6) is a main (co-ordinated) clause introduced by *but*
(7) is an (adverbial) subordinate clause introduced by *as*
(8) is a complement subordinate clause introduced by *that*. It is part of the noun phrase headed by *revelations* (in the same way that clause (3) is part of the noun phrase headed by *palace*). Note that this clause, though similar to (3), is not the same. A clue is that *that* could not be replaced by *which* in (8) but could be in (3). However, they are similar in that neither functions as a distinct clause element. They are both postmodifiers in noun phrases.

All the subordinate clauses are part of larger clauses. Thus clause (8) is part of clause (7), which is part of clause (6); clause (5) is part of clause (4); and clause (3) is part of clause (2), which is part of clause (1).

### Exercise 5.10

(a) is 'wrong' because the base adjective, *real*, has only one syllable. In fact, there are several such adjectives which prefer *more* and *most* (*You couldn't be righter!?*). This may be something to do with their rarity, with *more* and *most* being the default rule.
(b) contradicts the rule that adjectives ending in *-y* should have *-er*. In fact, most adjectives of this type have some such variation, but *likely* is an extreme case. Hilpert surmises that this is because it is often followed by a *that* clause (*It is more likely that...*), unlike other *-y* adjectives.
(c) contradicts the rule about three-syllable adjectives taking *more* and *most*. This is almost certainly due to the influence of *happier*.

The two other comparatives were *more common* and *more likely*.

The choice between the two types of comparison is therefore based on a complex of factors, too many to be condensed into one simple rule in scientific description. However, for pedagogic purposes some simplification may be justifiable. But rather than stating that simplification in the form given above, it may be better to simply state that, unless users are familiar with the *-er* and *–est* forms, they should use *more* and *most*.

## REFERENCES

Biber, D., Johansson, S., Leech, G., Conrad, S. and Finnegan, E. (1999). *The Longman Grammar of Spoken and Written English*. Harlow: Longman.
Carter, R. and McCarthy, M. (2006). *Cambridge Grammar of English*. Cambridge University Press.
Celce-Murcia, M. and Larsen-Freeman, D. (1999). *The Grammar Book*. 2nd edn. Boston: Heinle and Heinle.
*Collins Cobuild English Grammar* (2011). 3rd edn. Glasgow: Collins.
Crystal, D. (1984). *Who Cares about English Usage?* London: Penguin.
(2006). *The Fight for English*. Oxford University Press.
Hilpert, M. (2008). The English comparative – language structure and language use. *English Language and Linguistics*, 12, 395–417.
Huddlestone, R. and Pullum, G. K. (2002). *The Cambridge Grammar of the English Language*. Cambridge University Press.

Humphrys, J. (2004). *Lost for Words*. London: Hodder & Stoughton.
(2006). *Beyond Words*. London: Hodder & Stoughton.
McArthur, T. (1983). *A Foundation Course for Language Teachers*. Cambridge University Press.
Quirk, R., Greenbaum, S., Leech, G. and Svartvik, J. (1985). *A Comprehensive Grammar of the English Language*. Harlow: Longman.
Swan, M. (2005a). *Grammar*. Oxford University Press.
(2005). *Practical English Usage*, 3rd edn. Oxford University Press.
Yule, G. (1998b). *Explaining English Grammar*. Oxford University Press.

# 6 Syntax

KLAUS ABELS

**KEY TERMS**

- c-command
- constituent
- gloss
- grammar
- movement
- parameter
- principle
- tree diagram
- Universal Grammar

**PREVIEW**

This chapter examines the question of what limits there are in the ways in which languages can differ from each other structurally. Whenever we utter a sentence in any language, the words come in a particular order and are grouped into phrases in a particular way. While it is obvious that words in a sentence are ordered, the organization into phrases is less obvious, often imperceptible. This chapter argues that the variation between languages is largely confined to perceptible properties of word order, while the imperceptible organization into phrases is the same – or very nearly so – in all languages. Whether this view is true and, if so, why, is at the heart of some of the most fundamental debates in linguistics with implications for all of cognitive science. The chapter starts by motivating the existence of abstract phrase structure and by outlining what kinds of facts the syntactic description of a language must account for. A sufficiently explicit discussion requires some technical tools and notions, which will be introduced. The chapter then explains the goals of a general syntactic theory: to delimit and explain the range of variation found in human languages. This is followed by a case study of the word order found in noun phrases across languages. The case study focuses on the idea that languages differ in word order but resemble each other in phrasal organization.

## 6.1 INTRODUCTION

This chapter introduces you to a problem that has driven research in theoretical linguistics since the middle of the twentieth century. This problem and its potential solutions have shaped the field of theoretical syntax, giving rise to some of the most important debates within linguistics and with neighbouring disciplines.

The problem arises from tension between two basic observations: Firstly, human languages differ immensely in how words are arranged into sentences and ordered.

Secondly, children pick up the language spoken in their environment quickly, at a young age; they end up with remarkably complex and largely similar **grammars** in the absence of explicit instruction.

The first observation suggests that grammars are very different from each other. The second observation suggests the exact opposite; if children acquiring a language had to sift through a vast space of radically different grammars in order to acquire their language, the process should be slow and error prone and it should require explicit instruction. Since it does not, grammars must be very similar to each other, despite appearances. The problem then is to find the underlying unity among the superficial diversity of grammatical systems.

The chapter proceeds by first illustrating the kinds of facts that the grammatical description of a language must account for. Along the way it illustrates the remarkable complexity and abstractness of speakers' grammatical knowledge. To describe such facts adequately, tree graphs and some terminology about such graphs are introduced. The fact that languages vary across a broad range is illustrated on the basis of the variety of neutral word orders found in noun phrases across languages. It is then shown how the diversity of word orders can be factored into a set of very abstract rules that are true across all languages and a set of superficial and easily learnable rules, which vary across languages.

## 6.2 Syntax: the study of sentence structure

Syntax is the study of how phrases and sentences are constructed. The syntax of any given language is a precise and rigorous description of the rules that characterize the phrases and sentences of that language. More broadly, a general theory of syntax specifies the types of rules and rule systems found across all languages.

To see why linguists think about the syntax of languages in terms of rules, that is, in terms of ways of constructing sentences, rather than in terms of the sentences themselves, we need to consider an everyday fact about what it means to know a language: when you know a language, this knowledge enables you to understand and produce sentences you have never heard before. For example, you have never before heard or read the sentences in this chapter. Yet you have no trouble determining that they are English and interpreting them. This usually happens so automatically and easily that we rarely stop to notice. Not only do we produce and understand sentences that we have never heard before, we can also judge whether a particular sentence is a sentence of our language or not:

(1) a. Hyperintelligent jellyfish from Mars fly quickly.
 b. *Hyperintelligent from quickly fly Mars jellyfish.

The first example is recognizably a sentence of English; it has a clear enough, even if fairly odd meaning. The second example is not a sentence of English at all but merely a list of words. Knowing English, you know the difference. Example (1a) conforms to the rules by which English sentences are constructed but (1b) does not. Following standard practice in syntax, example (1b) has an asterisk (*) in front of it to indicate that it is felt to be deviant by native speakers of English.

Importantly, this judgement of deviance is not a judgement about meaning. Example (2a) is a grammatical, nonsensical sentence of English. Example (2b) on the other hand is ungrammatical in standard English though perfectly interpretable.

(2) a. Complicated triangles are confusing for small dreams.
    b. *Complicated games is confusing for small children.

Everybody who speaks English can easily make these judgements and many more like them. This indicates that to know English means to know, subconsciously, the rules of English sentence construction.

The grammatical rules that enable you to distinguish between the examples in (1) and (2) depend in part on word classes, since the rules governing the placement of nouns in a clause are different from those governing the placement of verbs, adjectives or prepositions. Furthermore, the rules of the grammar must also ensure that the meaning of a sentence depends on its structure. Otherwise, all sentences that use the same words should mean the same thing, but this is clearly not true: *The cat caught a mouse.* does not mean the same thing as *The mouse caught a cat.*

Based on this, it is clear enough what it means to say that a sequence of words is a sentence of a particular language: we mean that native speakers of the language recognize that sequence of words as belonging to their language. Since the set of sentences that belong to any given language is infinite, linguists don't construe languages as sets of sentences but as rule systems, that is, grammars. For syntacticians this means that they study the rules and rule systems that allow the construction and interpretation of sentences.

Everybody who speaks a language tacitly knows the rules of the language, since it is the rules that allow them to produce and understand novel sentences. The grammar is therefore an abstract characterization of the computations going on in the speaker's and hearer's minds when producing and understanding sentences. The grammar makes claims about which sentences are part of the language and which ones aren't, what the structure is of the ones that are part of the language and what meaning they have. It does not make claims about how the grammar is implemented, what algorithms are used in the mind to compute these results, or how the computation unfolds in real time. Part of this task falls to the psycholinguistic modelling of real-time language production and perception. The grammar also does not model how the brain realizes these algorithms in its synaptic structure, of course.

This brief bird's-eye characterization should be sufficient to place the following discussion of the rules governing noun phrase structure in various languages. We start by looking at some English examples. The examples have the recurrent sequence of words *those three green jellybeans* in them. Together these four words behave as a unit in the sentences; they form a phrase, also called a **constituent**. We can see that they behave as a unit because they can be replaced by a single word without changing the meaning. Thus in (3b) and (3c), *them* stands for *those three green jellybeans*.

(3) a. Those three green jellybeans are tasty.
    b. Rosa is looking at them.
    c. She will give them to her mother.

The constituent *those three green jellybeans* is called a noun phrase. Even if you have never thought about this before, you can easily see that there are rules about how to construct noun phrases. For example, in any combination of the noun *jellybeans* with one of the other three words, *jellybeans* has to come last.

(4) a. (i) Those jellybeans are tasty.
(ii) *Jellybeans those are tasty.
b. (i) Three jellybeans are tasty.
(ii) *Jellybeans three are tasty.
c. (i) Green jellybeans are tasty.
(ii) *Jellybeans green are tasty.

Similarly, the order between the demonstrative *those*, the numeral *three*, and the adjective *green* is fixed:

(5) a. (i) Rosa is looking at those three jellybeans.
(ii) *Rosa is looking at three those jellybeans.
b. (i). Rosa is looking at those green jellybeans.
(ii) *Rosa is looking at green those jellybeans.
c. (i). Rosa is looking at three green jellybeans.
(ii) *Rosa is looking at green three jellybeans.

When all four elements are present, their relative order is, again, completely fixed. Of course, the grammar of English doesn't have special rules about the relative ordering of the words *those, three, green* and *jellybeans*. These words are members of classes all of whose members behave the same way. All nouns behave like the word *jellybeans* in the examples above, all descriptive adjectives behave like *green*, all numerals – like *three*, and all demonstratives – like *those*. This explains why (6a) is acceptable while (6b) is not; in (6a), the object noun phrase shows the order demonstrative before numeral before adjective before noun, in (6b), it does not.

(6) a. Jason scratched those five red cars.
DEM NUM A N
b. * Jason scratched five those cars red.
NUM DEM N A

Notice, as an aside, that example (6) introduces a very useful notation. You will notice that below the English example there is a line that indicates the category of each of the relevant words: DEM – demonstrative, NUM – numeral, A – adjective, and N – noun. This line is called the **gloss**. As you will see below, examples from foreign languages that you do not speak make little or no sense unless they come with a gloss. The gloss informs you of the function and category of each word or morpheme.

We can now return to our discussion of the rules of English. In addition to the facts about word order mentioned above, the grammar of English has to capture the way words are grouped into constituents. We saw above that the words *those three green jellybeans* behave as a unit and, therefore, form a constituent. There is evidence for further organization within that constituent.

Consider the following example. The verb *eat* appears twice. The first time it takes the complete noun phrase *two green jellybeans* as its object. The second time the noun phrase is incomplete and consists only of the numeral *three*.

Underlining in the examples indicates which parts of the sentence to compare with each other and small caps indicate stress.

(7) I'll eat TWO green jellybeans and you can eat THREE.

Think about the interpretation of the incomplete object in (7). It is natural to interpret it to mean *three green jellybeans*. Here, the missing part of the noun phrase means *green jellybeans*. *Green jellybeans* thus behaves as a unit and the words that form this unit can either be present or missing together.

The same can be seen in the next example, where the incomplete object is naturally interpreted to mean *those green jellybeans* with the unit *green jellybeans* missing.

(8) I'll eat THESE green jellybeans and you can eat THOSE.

We have now established two facts: example (3) shows that *those three green jellybeans* is a constituent and examples (7) and (8) demonstrate that *green jellybeans* is a constituent.

We can also show that *three green jellybeans* is a constituent. Example (9) makes this point. The incomplete noun phrase can mean *those three green jellybeans*, with the constituent *three green jellybeans* missing as a unit.

(9) I'll eat THESE three green jellybeans and you can eat THOSE.

What we see is that *green jellybeans*, *three green jellybeans* and *those three green jellybeans* are all constituents. One can imagine the combining of words in terms of packing them together into boxes: two things that are packed into one box form a unit. We thus have the following:

(10)

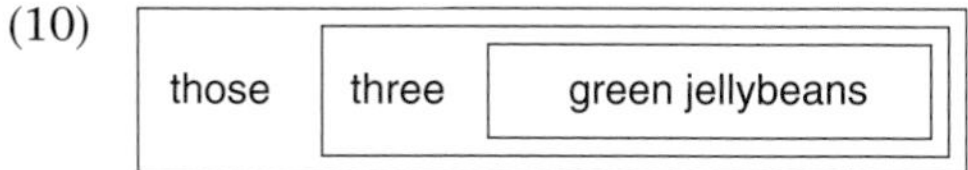


Instead of drawing boxes around groups of words, syntacticians usually express these facts using **tree diagrams**. The tree diagram below expresses the same information as (10).

(11)

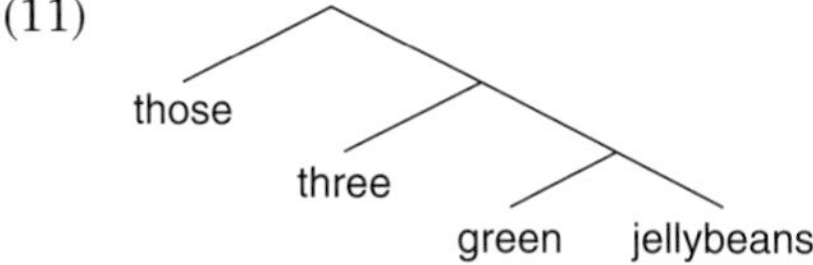


We will use such diagrams in the rest of this chapter, so it is worth introducing them in some detail. Every point in such tree diagrams where a line (called an edge) ends or where several edges meet is called a node.

(12)

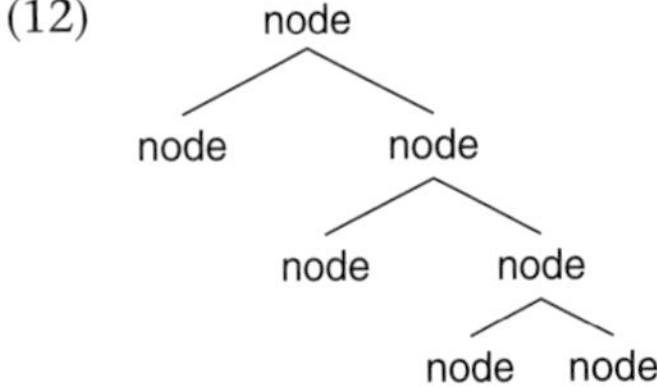


The nodes at the bottom and at the top of the tree are special. The ones at the bottom are called the leaves of the tree, (13), and this is where all the words that make up a sentence are drawn, as you can see in (11). The node at the very top of the tree is called the root.

(13)

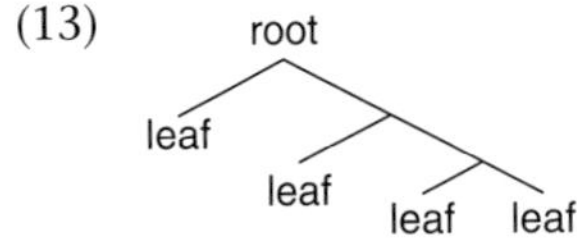


If the leaves represent words, what do the remaining nodes represent? Each one of the remaining nodes in (11) corresponds to one of the boxes in (10). You can see this correspondence quite clearly in (14). Each node is the root of its own tree; each such tree corresponds to a structural unit, a constituent.

(14)

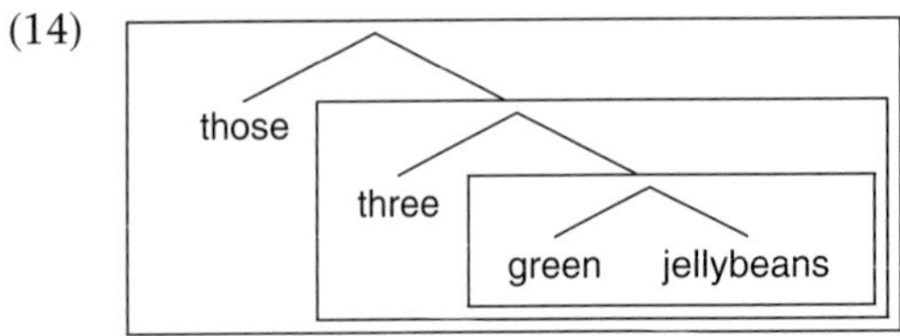


In the next tree, the nodes are numbered for ease of reference. We say that a node is the **mother** of all the nodes that it is connected to and which are immediately below it. Therefore, the root node 1 is the mother of nodes 2 and 7; node 2 is the mother of nodes 3 and 6; node 7 is the mother of node 8;... The leaves (nodes 4, 5, 6 and 8) are not the mother of any other node. A node is the **daughter** of any node that it is connected to and that is directly above it. Thus, nodes 4 and 5 are the daughters of node 3; node 8 is the daughter of node 7; nodes 2 and 7 are the daughters of the root node 1. The root node is not the daughter of any other node. Finally, two nodes that have the same mother are called **sisters**. In the tree below nodes 4 and 5, nodes 3 and 6, and nodes 2 and 7 are sisters.

(15)

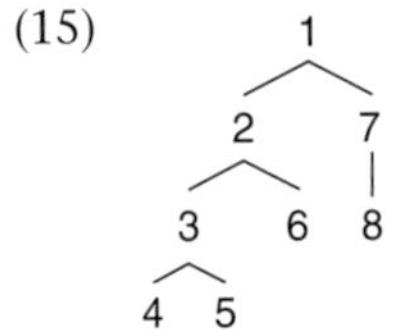


The edges of syntactic trees never cross. Diagram (16) is therefore not a permissible syntactic tree.

(16)

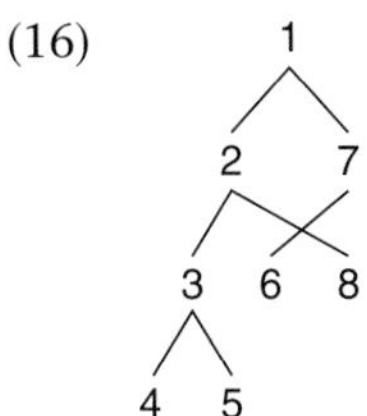


What matters for syntactic trees is which nodes are the mothers, daughters and sisters of which other nodes and the order in which sisters come. The lengths or angles of edges play no role so long as branches don't cross. So all of the following trees mean the same as (11): the left-to-right order of the leaves represents the word order of the phrase.

(17)

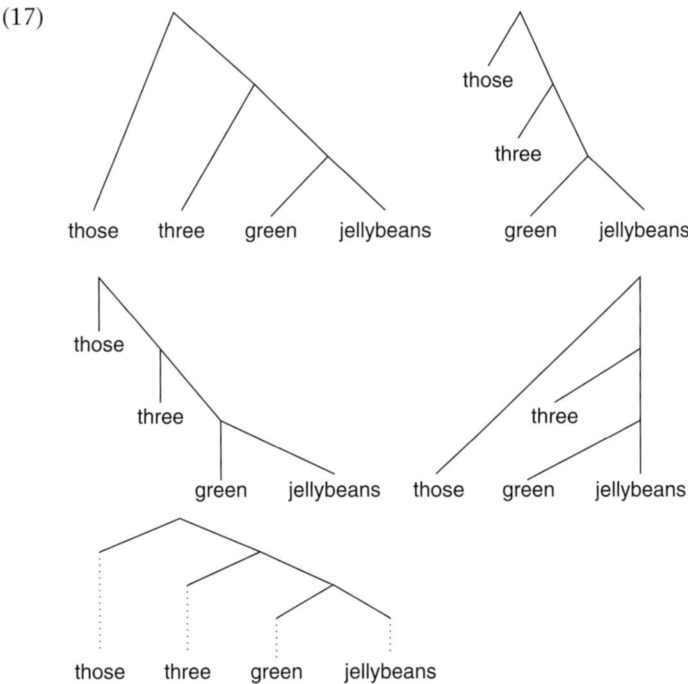


The final tree is particularly perspicuous, as it makes it easy to read off both the word order and the constituent structure of an expression. The dotted lines in the diagram have no significance, they are just a visual device connecting each leaf in the hierarchical structure of the tree to the word representing that leaf on the horizontal axis. Like edges in the tree, dotted lines may not cross. I will use trees like the final one from now on.

While the trees in (17) all look different but express exactly the same information, the following trees represent different information, because they either group or order the nodes differently. The structures in (11) and (17) all depict a constituent containing all and only the words *three green jellybeans*. We concluded that this is correct on the basis of example (9). None of the structures in (18a)–(18c) shows such a constituent. Instead, all three group the leaves *those* and *three* together. But there is no evidence that they form a constituent. The structures in (18b) and (18c) additionally group *those three green* together – a grouping that is not supported by the behaviour of the noun phrase. (18b)–(18d) fail to group *green* with *jellybeans* – a constituent whose existence is supported by examples like (7). And (18d) claims that *three green* is a constituent – a claim for which there is no factual basis. Finally, (18e) is particularly interesting, since it gets the constituent structure exactly right – there is a constituent made up of *green* and *jellybeans*, one made up of *three*, *green* and *jellybeans*, and one made up of *those*, *three*, *green* and *jellybeans* – but the word order is wrong.

(18) a.

b.

c.

d.

e.

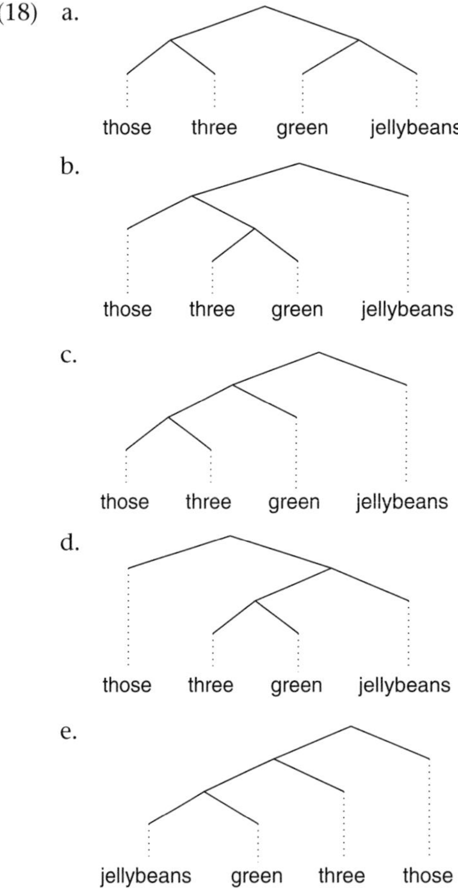


As we saw, the grammar of English dictates that the only way to combine a demonstrative, numeral, descriptive adjective and a noun into a single noun phrase is with the order and hierarchical structure in (11) and (17). (This is actually a simplification. Certain adjectives, like the words *visible* or *present*, can appear after the noun, others may appear after the noun only under special circumstances, yet others, like *other*, appear before the numeral. We will not deal with these complications here.) In the correct tree diagram for the English noun phrase, the demonstrative *those* is 'higher' than the other elements. What is meant by higher is that all the remaining words are contained in the sister of the demonstrative. Furthermore, the numeral is higher than the adjective and the noun. And the noun is (or, in more complex cases, is contained in) the adjective's sister. Moreover, the demonstrative, numeral and adjective all precede their respective sisters.

Since being 'higher' than another element is a very important concept in syntactic theory, syntacticians have coined a technical term for it. We say that one node in a tree **c-commands** another node if the second node is or is contained in the first node's sister. Technically, we say that a node **dominates** all the nodes that it contains, or, in other words, all those nodes that are below it and can be reached by following a continuous path of edges that always go down and never up. Thus, in (19) B c-commands nodes C, F, G, H and I, and no other nodes. This is so, because C is B's sister, and F, G, H and I are contained in – that is dominated by – C. B only has one sister, so the remaining nodes (A, B, D and E) are not B's sisters. They are also not contained in B's sister because, in order to reach them from B's sister one would have to go up the tree at least once. Therefore, B does not c-command either A, B, D or E.

Similarly, node C c-commands B, D and E. D and E c-command each other and nothing but each other. Node A c-commands none of the nodes in the tree. etc.

(19)

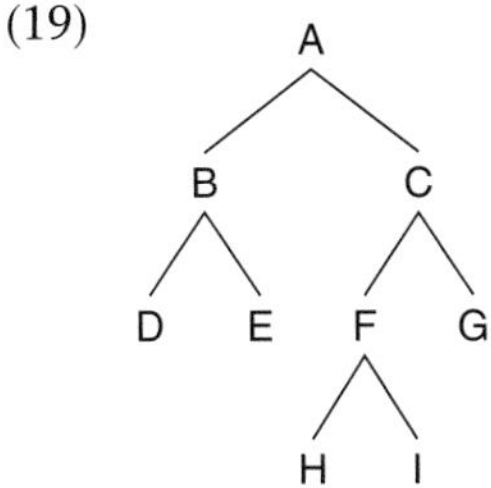


We can therefore rephrase our description of a correct English noun phrase by saying that the demonstrative must c-command any numerals, adjectives and the noun within its noun phrase. The numeral must c-command any adjectives and the noun within its noun phrase. Adjectives must c-command the noun. Demonstratives, numerals and adjectives precede their sister.

**KEY POINTS: Syntax**

- Linguists characterize grammars in terms of rules.
- Rules are necessary to explain why speakers can produce and understand novel sentences.
- The rules rely on abstract categories (nouns, verbs, adjectives,. . .).
- The rules characterize the word order and the abstract grouping of words into units.
- The structures of sentences formed according to such rules are usually represented by tree diagrams.

**EXERCISE 6.1**

Each of the examples below contains a clue that the underlined material is a constituent. Identify this clue and describe in what way the underlined material acts as a unit. Provide a gloss for the underlined material and classify the examples according to the types of constituent that they identify.

(20) He praised the student's fanciful suggestion but ignored the professor's.

(21) These new products passed the test, but those failed.

(22) You should read these two complicated papers because I cannot understand them.

(23) I suggest we divide the work evenly so that I solve these two problems and you– those.

(24) The customer preferred these red tiles, so we ordered them.

## 6.3 Syntactic theory and its goals

The approach taken in the previous section might seem foreign. The grammatical categories and tree diagrams introduced above have no direct analogue in your introspective everyday experience of language.

To explain this disconnect between your experience and those theoretical tools, we need to remind ourselves that linguistics is the scientific study of language. This means that we approach language with the same attitude of curiosity and detachment that is common to all of science: we should study language in the same way we investigate pendulums, chemical reactions or the anatomy of beetles. Our introspective judgements and everyday experience of language can provide data but they should never be confused with the theory.

Precise descriptions of the rules that characterize the phrases and sentences of a given language provide answers to the question of what the grammar of that language is. They also lead to a number of further questions, all of which guide research in syntactic theory to a greater or lesser extent: what is the range of rule systems that we find in different languages? Are the rule systems similar or different? And why? How are these rule systems learned by children acquiring the language? How are the rules deployed by speakers in the real-time production and comprehension of utterances? To what extent are the rule systems shaped by the fact that they must be implemented in human brains and deployed in real time? To what extent are such rule systems shaped by the functions language has?

Different linguistic schools of thought emphasize some of these questions more strongly than others, but in some form, these questions define the broader goals of all current syntactic theorizing.

The answers to these questions are quite strongly interconnected. If it turned out that the rule systems of different languages varied in arbitrary and unpredictable ways, then children trying to learn a particular language would face a large and difficult task. If on the other hand it turned out that the rule systems of different languages vary only in relatively minor ways or that the variation is constrained systematically, then children acquiring language face a much more narrowly circumscribed, and hence easier, task.

Noam Chomsky, the father of modern linguistic theory, has argued that the variation between languages must be fairly narrowly circumscribed. He reaches this conclusion on the basis of the assessment that language acquisition is relatively easy for children. This can be seen from a number of facts. Firstly, language is acquired early by children: by the time they enter school, they have essentially acquired their native language. Secondly, language is acquired in much the same way by children with a rich and by those with a poor linguistic environment and the ultimate level of attainment is comparable. Finally, children are able to acquire language on the basis of degenerate data; some of the sentences they hear are actually ungrammatical, because speakers make errors; some of the constructions that linguists have found to be highly revealing about the structure of sentences are very rare in everyday speech; children have no direct access to the intended meaning of sentences.

We have good reasons to believe that children get an important leg up in the process of acquiring language. Linguists generally believe that children are greatly assisted in their task by the fact that variation between languages is constrained and that there are grammatical properties shared across all languages. Grammatical properties that are shared across all languages are usually referred to as **principles** while points where we find restricted variation are called **parameters**. The system of principles and parameters together with a method for learning how the variable parameters are set for a given language is called **Universal Grammar**. In the next two sections we will discuss some of the principles and parameters that enter into the syntax of noun phrases.

The terminology of principles, parameters, and Universal Grammar introduced above is associated with the work of Noam Chomsky. Chomsky has sometimes suggested that Universal Grammar is innate and that it is task specific. The claim that Universal Grammar is innate is uncontroversial. Among other things, it explains why language disorders are heritable and therefore run in families (McMahon and McMahon 2006) and why humans but no other species can acquire language with a syntactic organization. The question of whether Universal Grammar is a language specific capacity or whether the same mental mechanisms have more general application remains open at present (see, for example, Elsabbagh and Karmiloff-Smith 2006). To answer the question, one needs to find out whether the principles and parameters discovered in language and the learning strategies used in language acquisition also characterize how we do other things like recognizing faces, planning movements, navigating in space, understanding social interaction, solving geometrical problems, solving ethical dilemmas, etc. Progress on this will come from constructing separate theories of the principles, parameters and learning strategies involved in all of these different tasks and then analysing carefully to what extent they can be unified. In what follows, we will consider only the task of constructing an explicit account of the principles and parameters of linguistic structure.

There are a number of strategies researchers pursue to construct such an account. Conceptually the simplest approach is to construct grammars of different languages and to compare them carefully. We illustrate this method later on in this chapter using the noun phrase as an example.

A different, less obvious, strategy is to construct the grammar of only a single language and to assess to what extent its properties could be learned by a child hearing a representative sample of sentences of the language. If we discover properties that could not reasonably be learned that way and yet all native speakers end up acquiring these properties, we conjecture that those properties are in fact not learned but are given. Such properties have to form part of (or follow from) Universal Grammar.

The goals of syntactic theory are therefore to describe the grammars of different languages, to analyse which parts of the grammar are universal (the principles) and which parts are subject to variation across languages (the parameters), to create an account of how children acquire the grammar(s) of their native language(s), and to explain these findings in terms of language-specific or more generally available cognitive constraints and processes.

The next two sections illustrate the search for linguistic universals.

**KEY POINTS: Syntactic theory**

- The central goal of syntactic theory is to explain the way in which grammars are similar to each other and to circumscribe the ways in which they can differ from each other.
- Properties that characterize all grammars are called principles.
- Points of variation between grammars are called parameters.

## EXERCISE 6.2

Consider the following thought experiment:

> Suppose that biologists discovered a species of apes on an unexplored island who can communicate with each other but not with humans. The biologists study the apes' communication system and attempt to figure out its rules. Eventually, they come up with a grammar of the apes' language. The grammar is successful in capturing which utterances the apes accept as part of their language and which utterances they reject, as well as in correctly capturing the meaning the apes attribute to their utterances. Suppose furthermore that, to achieve this, the grammar has to posit complex rule systems and abstract entities (like the tree structures and syntactic categories of the previous section) of which the apes profess to have no introspective awareness.

Discuss to what extent the apes' lack of awareness of a complex rule system of categories and abstract structures invalidates the biologists' findings and calls their truth into question.

## 6.4 Universal and language-specific properties of phrase structure

Section 6.2 has shown that the grammar of English must represent the phrase *those three green jellybeans* as in (25).

(25)

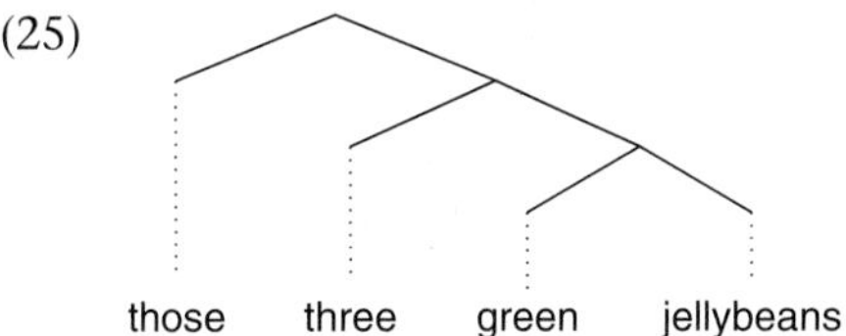


We turn to noun phrases in Spanish now. In Spanish, the order of elements differs somewhat from English.

(26) esos dos libros interesantes
those two books interesting
'these two interesting books'

The gloss indicates that the demonstrative and the numeral precede the noun, as they do in English, but the adjective follows it.

What structure should we assign to the Spanish noun phrase?

We know from (18a)–(18d) that a given sequence of words could logically be associated with a variety of structures. To decide which of them is correct, we used examples that reveal the grouping of words. Specifically, we considered the interpretation of incomplete noun phrases. Examples (7)–(9) showed that the adjective forms an exclusive unit with the noun and that the numeral forms an exclusive unit with the adjective–noun unit. We can use the same method to investigate Spanish.

The following example illustrates that the noun can be missing from a noun phrase in Spanish.

(27) Yo voy a leer ESTE libro y tu – ESE.
I go to read this book and you – that
'I am going to read this book, and you are going to read that book.'

With only a single word missing the example cannot tell us how words are grouped. We need to look at examples with several words missing. Relevant examples show that the noun and the adjective form a unit, because they can be left out together: (28a). Likewise, numeral, noun, and adjective form a unit, because they can be left out together: (28b).

(28) a. Yo voy a comer estos TRES chupa chuses rojos y tu – estos DOS.
I go to eat these three lollipops red and you – those two
'I am going to eat these three red lollipops and you are going to eat those two red lollipops.'

b. Yo voy a comer ESTOS tres chupa chuses rojos y tu – ESTOS.
I go to eat these three lollipops red and you – those
'I am going to eat these three red lollipops and you are going to eat those.'

We depict the Spanish noun phrase by the following tree:

(29)

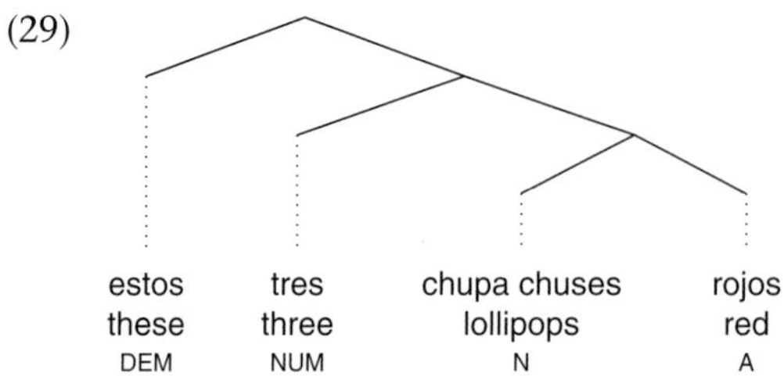


The diagram for the English noun phrase, (25), and that for the Spanish noun phrase, (29), differ in linear order but the hierarchical structure is identical.

Both in English and in Spanish the demonstrative c-commands any numerals, adjectives and the noun; the numeral c-commands any adjectives and the noun; adjectives c-command the noun; demonstratives and numerals precede their sister. The only difference is the relative order of the adjective and its sister. In English, the adjective precedes, in Spanish, it follows its sister.

A useful analogy might be that of a mobile. Depending on the way the arms of the mobile are turned, the words suspended at the bottom will appear in different orders, but its hierarchical organization in terms of what is attached to what remains constant. Phrased in the terminology of principles and parameters, we can say that the way an element is ordered with respect to its sister is a parameter while the hierarchical organization of the noun phrase, which is the same in Spanish and in English, is a candidate for a linguistic universal, a principle.

Of course, drawing any conclusions just on the basis of two languages would be rash. Nevertheless, we can consider the plausibility of the idea that the hierarchical organization of phrases is a principle. This idea makes good sense from the perspective of language acquisition: word order is directly given to the child in the data she hears and is hence learnable, but it is impossible to infer the hierarchical structure of a phrase solely on the basis of readily observable properties of sequences of words alone. Such considerations of learnability can provide an indirect argument for considering the hierarchical structure of noun phrases a linguistic principle .

In the remainder of this and the following sections, we will further explore the idea that the hierarchical structure but not the word order of the noun phrase represents a principle of Universal Grammar by looking at noun phrases from languages across the globe. The characterization of the facts builds on a large amount of work comparing different languages, inspired by Greenberg (1963). The more specific claims come from Cinque (2005) as reinterpreted in Abels and Neeleman (2006). It is important to note that the only orders we consider are unmarked orders, that is, orders that can be used without putting special emphasis on any of the elements within the noun phrase. Special emphasis allows additional word order possibilities not discussed below.

We have already seen that, in Spanish, noun phrases have the same hierarchical organization as in English but the adjective follows its sister instead of preceding it. In other words, there is a parameter regulating the relative order of the adjective and its sister. We expect to find similar parameters regulating the order of demonstratives and numerals relative to their sisters. The following examples from the languages Dulong, a Tibeto-Burman language spoken in parts of China and Tibet, and Sranan, a creole language from Suriname, show that this expectation is borne out. In these languages word order in the noun phrase is like in English except that Dulong numerals and Sranan demonstratives follow the noun.

(30) Dulong (simplified, based on LaPolla 2003: 676)

| kɔ̄ | tə́i | zə̆ɟɛ́ | ə̆sɯ̄mpə̄ŋ |
|---|---|---|---|
| that | big | book | three |
| DEM | A | N | NUM |

'those three big books'

(31) Sranan (simplified, based on Voorhoeve 1962: 33–6)

| den | dri | moi | fooru | dati |
|---|---|---|---|---|
| the | three | beautiful | chickens | these |
| | NUM | A | N | DEM |

'these three beautiful chickens'

The noun phrases for these languages would be represented as follows:

(32) a. Dulong

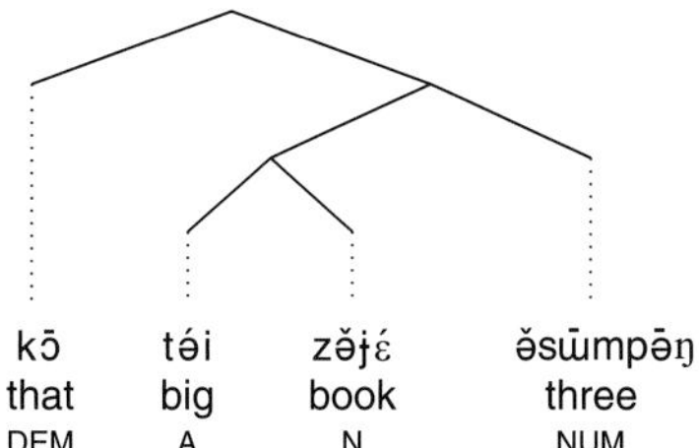


b. Sranan – leaving out the article *den* 'the', since it does not concern us here

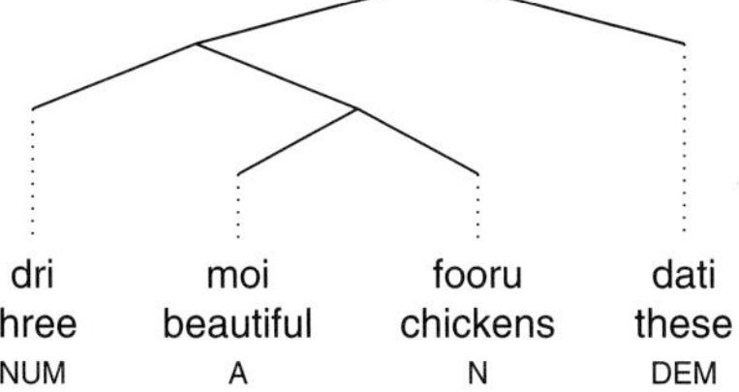


Hierarchically these structures are identical to their English and Spanish counterparts. What sets Dulong and Sranan apart from English is only the position of the numeral and the demonstrative, respectively.

Of course, there is no reason to think that languages can set only a single ordering parameter differently from English. In many languages, all elements follow their sisters instead of preceding them. Gungbe, a Kwa language from Benin, is an example of this type. In this language, the order of demonstrative, numeral, adjective and noun is the mirror image of that found in English. This order type is very common among the languages of the world.

(33). Gungbe (Aboh 2004: 78)
távò ɖàxó xóxó àtɔn éhè lɔ́ lɛ́
table big old three DEM SPF.DF PL
'these specific three big old tables'

The tree structure for Gungbe is given in (34). This structure is simplified in that it ignores the morphemes *lɔ́* and *lɛ́* which have no direct correspondences in English. The glosses stand for specific definite and plural, respectively.

(34) Gungbe

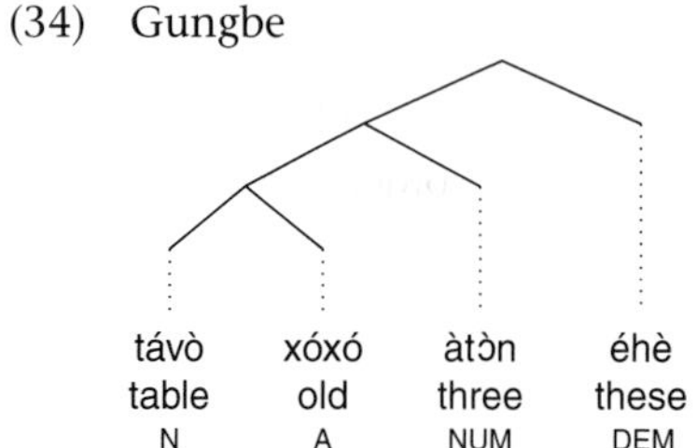


As before, this tree is identical to the structures we have seen above for English, Spanish, Dulong and Sranan in hierarchical terms; only the order of elements is different.

There are three more logically possible orders that the single hierarchical structure we have been assuming produces without crossing any branches. The orders in question reverse those found in Spanish, Dulong and Sranan: adjective–noun–numeral–demonstrative, numeral–noun–adjective–demonstrative and demonstrative–noun–adjective–numeral, respectively. Indeed, languages with the word orders in question exist. The order adjective–noun–numeral–demonstrative is found in Sango, one of the official languages of the Central African Republic, numeral–noun–adjective–demonstrative is found in Basque, a language isolate spoken in regions of Spain and France, and demonstrative–noun–adjective–numeral in Burmese, a Sino-Tibetan language spoken in Myanmar.

(35) Sango: *these two good families* (simplified from Thornell 1997: 71 using Samarin, 1967, pp. 57–83)

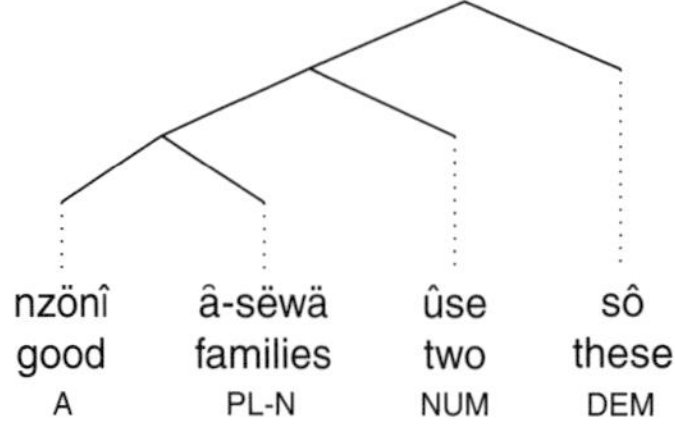


(36) Basque: *these four red apples* (Oyharçabal 2012: 269)

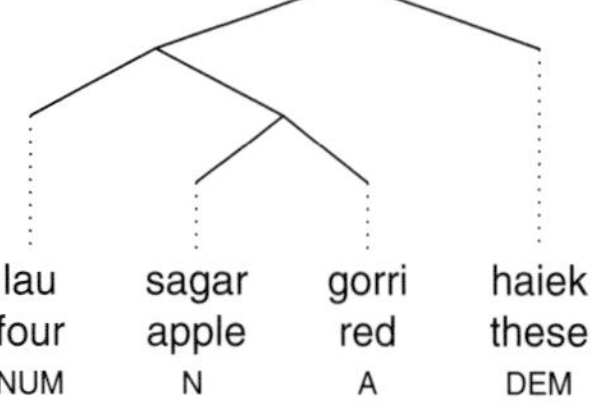

(37) Burmese: *these three big persons* (simplified from Jones 1970: 5)

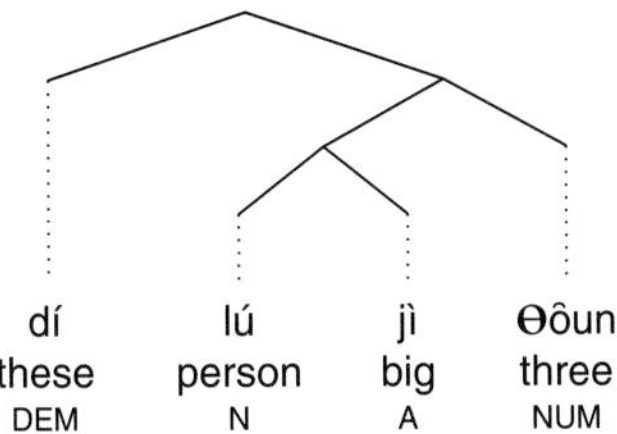


Again, the hierarchical structure in terms of c-command of the noun phrases above is identical to the now familiar structure, only the word order is different.

The idea that the hierarchical syntactic structure is a linguistic universal with the linear order being subject to parametric variation has produced the expectation that all of the above eight word orders should occur in some languages. As we saw, this expectation is borne out.

The proposed principle of Universal Grammar creates a second and far more important expectation. If the hierarchical structure of the noun phrase is universally fixed and the word order varies only in the way we have observed so far, then the eight orders given above should be the only orders we find since no further orders are possible without crossing any branches. To appreciate this point fully, we need to consider the fact that given four elements belonging to different classes, there are twenty-four logically possible orders (4!=4x3x2x1=24). We have now discussed eight of these orders and seen that, in line with our expectations, they occur as the unmarked word order in some languages. We have so far left the remaining sixteen orders aside. The proposed linguistic principle clearly predicts that none of them should occur.

According to Cinque (2005), this expectation is partially correct; ten of the sixteen remaining word orders conform with our expectations and never occur as the unmarked order. For example, no language employs the orders adjective–demonstrative–noun–numeral, adjective–numeral–noun–demonstrative, demonstrative–adjective–numeral–noun and numeral–adjective–demonstrative–noun as the unmarked word order. If we try to construct trees corresponding to the unattested orders, such trees invariably either have crossing branches, (38a), or violate the linguistic principle according to which the demonstrative c-commands everything in the noun phrase, the numeral c-commands everything but the demonstrative, and the adjective c-commands the noun, (38b).

(38) a.

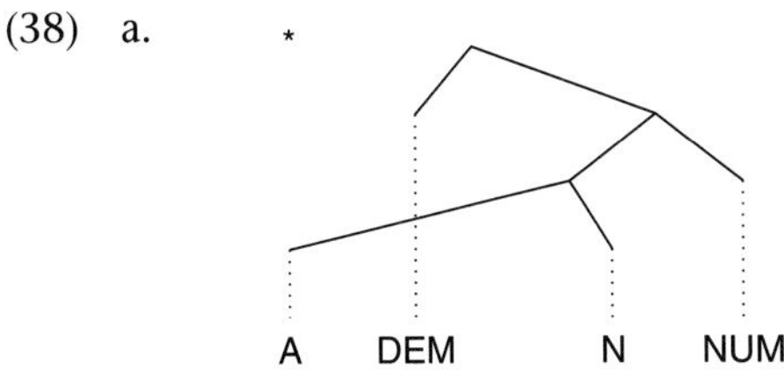

b.

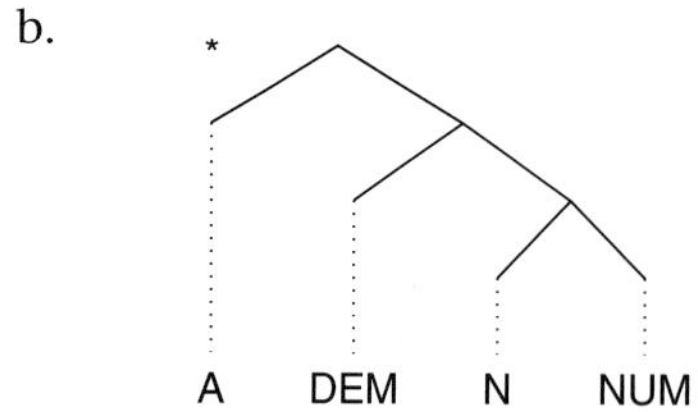


This section has illustrated what linguistic universals, the principles of Universal Grammar, might look like and what the locus of language variation might be. We argued that, from the perspective of language learnability, the proposed structural principle of Universal Grammar makes sense as it simplifies the acquisition task greatly. At the same time, the variations resulting from the linear parameters are readily learnable. The system explored so far has the right key ingredients. It offers explicit and correct analyses for the languages discussed so far. It answers the question of which aspects of the grammar are universal and which aspects vary between languages. Finally, it provides a straightforward answer to the problem of language acquisition.

We have seen partial support for the proposed system of principles and parameters in so far as all expected word orders are attested as the unmarked order in some languages. Furthermore, some of the word orders that are expected to be impossible have indeed been claimed never to occur as the unmarked word order in any language (see Cinque 2005 and references cited there). In the next section, we will discuss the six word orders that form counterexamples to the principles and parameters discussed so far and extend the system carefully so that it covers those orders but retains its pleasing properties of restrictiveness and easy learnability.

**KEY POINTS: Phrase structure**

- The neutral word order within the noun phrase in the vast majority of languages can be described by a set of abstract principles and superficial parameters as follows:
- Principles
  - Within a given noun phrase, the demonstrative c-commands all other elements.
  - Within a given noun phrase, the numeral c-commands all other elements except for the demonstrative.
  - Within a given noun phrase, the adjective c-commands the noun.
- Parameters
  - The order of demonstrative, numeral, and adjective with respect to their respective sisters is subject to cross-linguistic variation.

WEBSITE: **Group exercise 1**

Visit the website and, in a small group, investigate what motivation there is for the claim that demonstrative–numeral–noun is the neutral word order in English despite the fact that it is not, strictly speaking, the only possible word order.

**EXERCISE 6.3**

The word order and structures for the eight languages mentioned so far are repeated next to each other below.

(39)

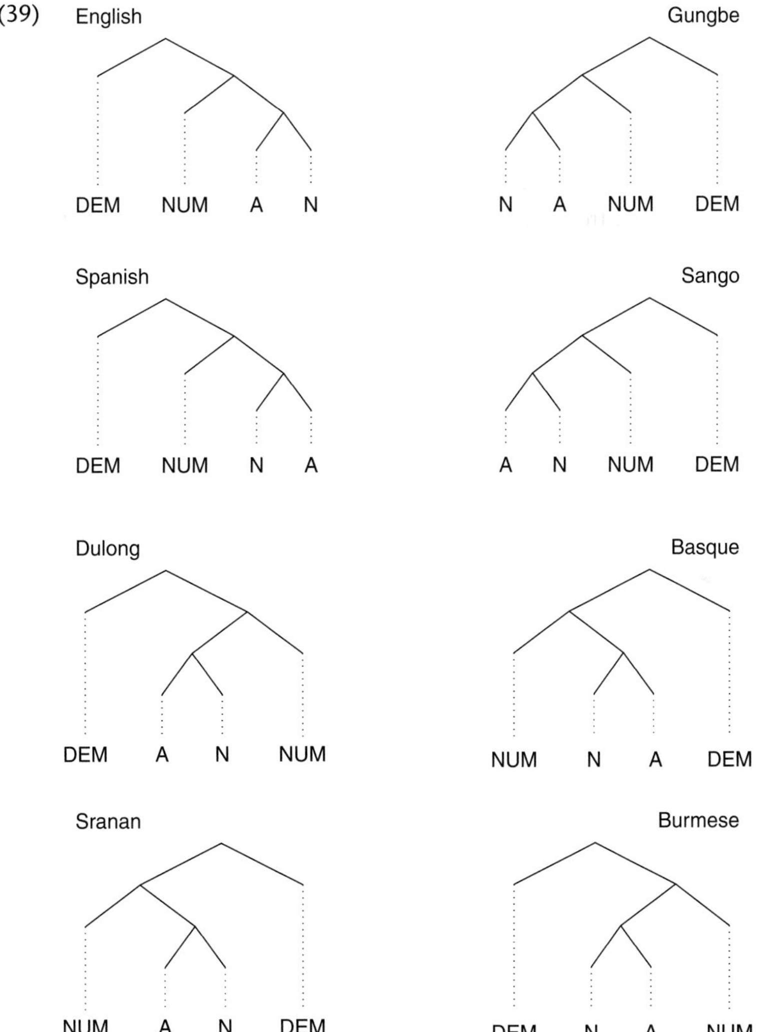


Verify for yourself that no further orders are possible without changing the structure and without illicitly crossing branches.

## 6.5 Universal and language-specific properties of movement

Section 6.4 ended with a mixed conclusion. On the one hand, the idea that noun phrase structure but not the order is universally fixed finds support in the fact that all eight predicted orders are actually attested and that it solves the problem of learnability in the face of variation. Furthermore, some of the word orders that are not expected to occur are indeed unattested cross-linguistically. However, Cinque (2005) documents six word-order patterns that our current model does not predict. We turn to these orders now.

The first four new patterns are fairly simple variations on those already discussed.

The languages Maasai, a Nilo-Saharan language spoken in Kenya and Tanzania, Kĩĩtharaka, a Bantu language from Kenya, Kele, a nearly extinct Austronesian language of Papua New Guinea, and Pitjantjatjara, an Australian language, illustrate four of the attested word orders not previously discussed.

(40) Maasai (Koopman 2003)

| kù-n-dâ | mɛ́sa-i | àré | sìdân |
|---|---|---|---|
| PL-F-that | table-F.PL.ACC | F.PL.two.ACC | nice.PL.ACC |
| DEM | N | NUM | A |

'those two nice tables'

(41) Kĩĩtharaka (Peter Muriungi p. c.)

| i-kombe | bi-bi | bi-tano | bi-tune |
|---|---|---|---|
| 8-cup | 8-this | 8-five | 8-red |
| N | DEM | NUM | A |

'these five red cups'

(42) Kele (Ross 2002: 132)

| pihin | ha-mow | il | tóti |
|---|---|---|---|
| woman | one-CLF | old | this |
| N | NUM | A | DEM |

'this one old woman'

(43) Pitjantjatjara (based on Eckert and Hudson 1988: 89)

| Tjitji | pala | tjukutjuku | kutjara |
|---|---|---|---|
| child | that | small | two |
| N | DEM | A | NUM |

'those two small children'

These orders are beyond the reach of the theory developed so far. The following table compares the four new orders with attested orders from the previous section. Languages and orders already discussed are in unmarked rows, new orders are in rows marked with a double right arrow (⇒). The table is organized in such a way that all the ordering types that share relative ordering of demonstrative, numeral, and adjective are grouped together.

(44)

| | Language | Order | | | | | | |
|---|---|---|---|---|---|---|---|---|
| | English | | Dem | | Num | | A | N |
| | Spanish | | Dem | | Num | N | A | |
| ⇒ | Maasai | | Dem | N | Num | | A | |
| ⇒ | Kĩĩtharaka | N | Dem | | Num | | A | |

| | | | | | | | |
|---|---|---|---|---|---|---|---|
| | Sranan | | Num | | A | N | Dem |
| | Basque | | Num | N | A | | Dem |
| ⇒ | Kele | N | Num | | A | | Dem |
| | Dulong | | Dem | | A | N | Num |
| | Burmese | | Dem | N | A | | Num |
| ⇒ | Pitjantjatjara | N | Dem | | A | | Num |

A simple generalization governs the table: In the four new patterns, the noun appears earlier in the string of words than our current theory allows. It seems as though the noun moves 'to the left'. Comparable movement of the noun 'to the right' never occurs: languages with the order shared in common by Sranan, Basque and Kele or Dulong, Burmese and Pitjantjatjara but with the noun all the way at the end do not exist. This suggests that there is a principle banning postposing the noun.

The two remaining orders documented by Cinque (2005) are illustrated here using Aghem, a Niger-Congo language from Cameroon, and Banda-Linda, another Niger-Congo language from the Central African Republic.

(45) Aghem (based on Hyman 1979: 28)

| nwɨ́n | fìdú'ú | fɨ́n | fɨ́mɔ̣̀ |
|---|---|---|---|
| bird | big | this | one |
| N | A | DEM | NUM |

'this one big bird'

(46) Banda-Linda (constructed based on Cloarec-Heiss 1986: 185–200)

| ōgbōrō | yāʃē | sə́yē | bīʃì |
|---|---|---|---|
| tall | women | these | two |
| A | N | DEM | NUM |

'these two tall women'

Again it is useful to compare these orders to the ones we discussed in the previous section. The table groups languages together where the relative order of demonstrative and numeral on the one hand and of adjective and noun on the other hand is the same as in the languages with the new orders.

(47)

| | Language | | Order | | | |
|---|---|---|---|---|---|---|
| | Spanish | | Dem | | Num | N A |
| | Burmese | | Dem | N A | Num | |
| ⇒ | Aghem | N A | Dem | | Num | |
| | English | | Dem | | Num | A N |
| | Dulong | | Dem | A N | Num | |
| ⇒ | Banda-Linda | A N | Dem | | Num | |

Again there is a simple generalization. It appears that the constituent made up of noun and adjective in its language-specific order appears earlier than our theory allows in both Aghem and Banda-Linda. (I should point out that Cloarec-Heiss (1986), where the information on Banda-Linda word order comes from, does not analyse *ōgbōrō* 'tall' as an adjective but instead as a relational noun, which leads to an overall meaning more like *these two giants of women*. Though cross-linguistically rare, the order A N DEM NUM has also been reported for the languages Bai (Wiersma 2003) and Koiari (Dutton 1996).)

There are no further attested, unmarked word order patterns.

How can we account for this state of affairs? How do we allow the six new orders without threatening our conclusions about the universal structure of the noun phrase, which provided a solution to the learnability problem?

As a first step towards a solution, we observe that the new data from this section in some sense reinforce rather than challenge the significance of the universal hierarchical structure; this is so, because the additional orders can be given a very simple characterization in terms of this universal structure, but not otherwise: In the noun phrase, the noun or a constituent containing the noun may appear earlier than expected under the theory of noun phrase structure from Section 6.4.

Since, for example, the numeral by itself is not a constituent containing the noun it never occurs earlier in the string of words than the theory from Section 6.4 would predict: the order NUM DEM N A is unattested as an unmarked word order. Similarly, there is no constituent made up of noun and numeral to the exclusion of the adjective, even in those languages in which noun and numeral always occur right next to each other. Consequently, we do not find languages where just the numeral and the noun occur too early and hence, N NUM DEM A never occurs as the unmarked order.

When an element appears earlier in the sequence of words than phrase structure theory would lead us to expect, syntacticians speak of movement. In English, the object of a verb usually appears immediately after the verb, but in questions it can be moved to the beginning of the clause. This accounts for the different placement of the object in *John read the book.* and *What did John read?*. If movement only impacted the word order without changing the structure, we would account for movement by allowing, in restricted circumstances, crossing branches in syntactic trees after all. However, there is strong evidence that movement changes order and structure.

In keeping with the conventional notation for movement structures in tree diagrams, the six new orders are drawn as shown in (48). The position indicated by *t* (mnemonic for 'trace') is an unpronounced, silent position. Its function is to indicate what the hierarchical position of the displaced element according to the basic phrase structure theory would be. There are also arrows connecting the trace and the movement element. These arrows differ from branches of the tree, since arrows are allowed to cross branches.

(48). a. Maasai

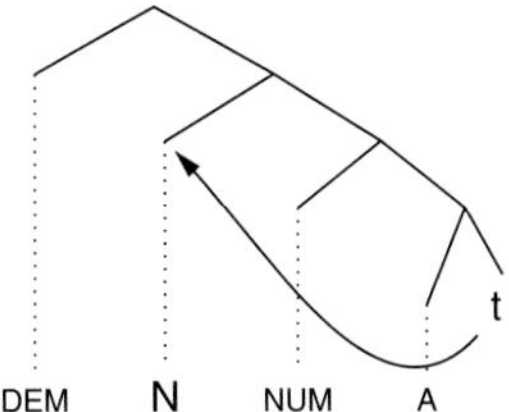


b. Kîîtharaka

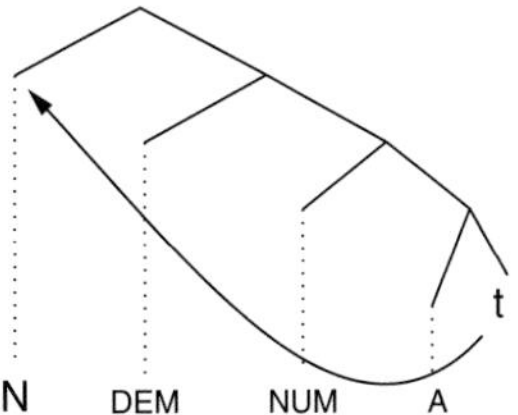


c. Kele

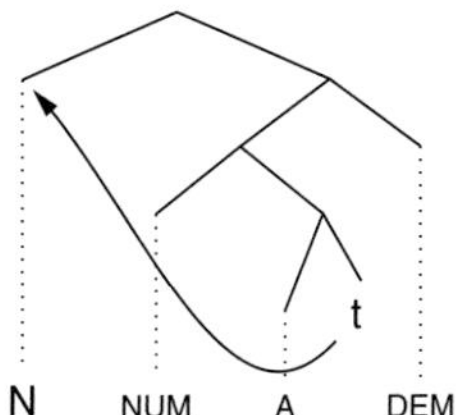


d. Pitjantjatjara

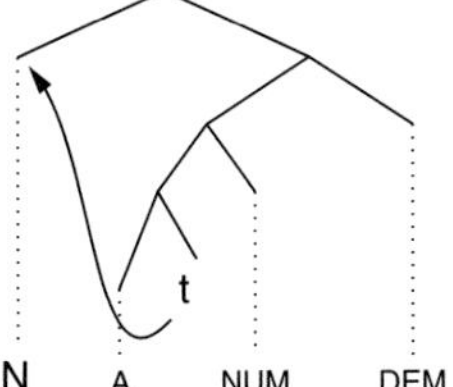


e. Banda-Linda

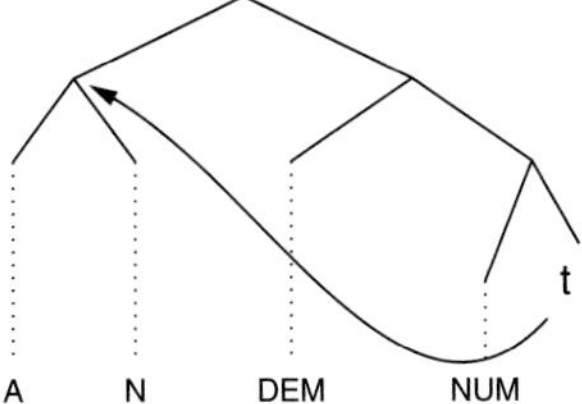


f. Aghem

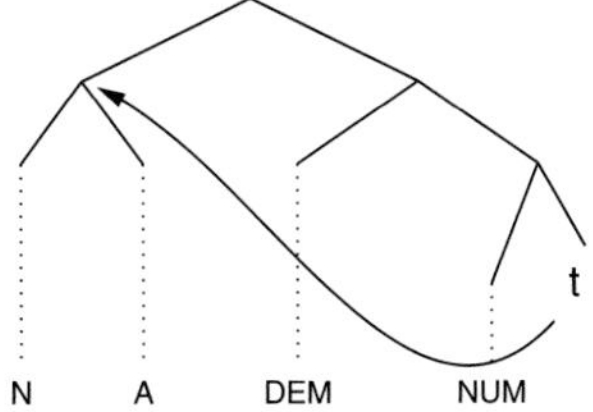

We can summarize our exploration of the syntax of noun phrases as follows.

(49) a. Universal principles of noun phrase construction:
(i) Ignoring the result of movement operations, noun phrases are hierarchically structured with any demonstrative c-commanding all other elements, any numeral c-commanding everything but the demonstrative, and any adjectives c-commanding the noun.
(ii) If **movement** occurs, the moved constituent occurs earlier in the sequence than it would have without movement, never later.
(iii) If movement occurs, the displaced constituent is or contains the noun.

b. Language-particular parameters of noun phrase construction:
(i) The linear order of demonstrative, numeral, and adjective with respect to their sisters is subject to language-specific variation.
(ii) Whether movement happens or not is subject to language-specific variation.
(iii) If movement happens, the exact target position and the size of the moving constituent are subject to language-specific variation.

The system has a number of very pleasing properties. Firstly, it derives the correct range of word order patterns. All and only the attested word order patterns can be derived within this system; we have seen how it derives the fourteen attested word orders. The remaining ten logical possibilities cannot be derived without violating one of the universal principles .

## EXERCISE 6.4

Reconsider the order A DEM N NUM. The last section, in particular the discussion of the structures in (38), showed why the simple model of the noun phrase as a mobile could not produce this order. The order is unattested as an unmarked order and it remains outside the reach of the system even with the addition of movement.

The structures in (50) illustrate this. Which order would have resulted from (50a) if movement had not happened? Which of the languages discussed in Section 6.4 exemplified this order? Which of the elements moves in (50a)? Which of the conditions on movement in (49) is violated by this operation?

Now consider the structure in (50b), where movement has applied twice. Which order would have resulted if the second step of movement, that is, noun movement, hadn't occurred? Which language discussed in this section exemplifies this order? Which order would have resulted if neither of the movements had taken place? Which language from Section 6.4 exemplifies this order? Which condition on movement stated in (49) is violated by (50b)?

(50) a.

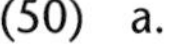

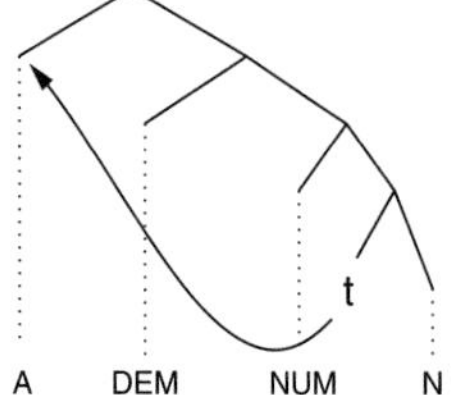

b.

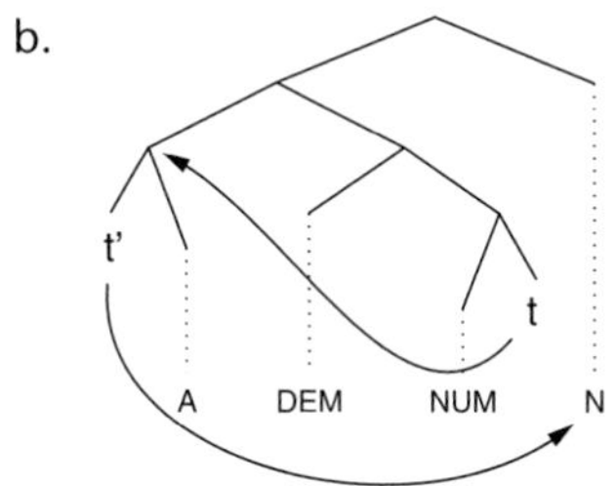


## EXERCISE 6.5

Show that the even when the effects of movement are taken into account, the order A–NUM–DEM–N cannot be derived. (Hint: you will probably want to use the property that in (39) the English type of order is the only n-final one.)

In Section 6.4, the idea was introduced that those properties of the noun phrase that vary across languages should be easily detectable in the input for the language learner. This idea underpinned our account of the noun phrase as a uniform hierarchical structure with varying linearization. The same idea emerges again from (49): exactly which constituents move in a given language and where are easily detectable properties; they can be allowed to be parameterized. The effectively unlearnable hierarchical structure must be kept as a universal principle. The system now delivers precise analyses of all existing language types, rules out the inexisting ones, and solves the learnability problem. We have reached the end of our exploration of the noun phrase.

You may wonder at this point whether the principles and parameters discussed are valid outside the narrow confines of the syntax of noun phrases. Indeed, many of them are. Consider the following example:

(51) Who are you talking to?

The example shows two things. Firstly, the question word *who* moves to the beginning of the sentence to form a question. Secondly, the preposition does not move together with the question word – and, in fact, in normal colloquial English it cannot. We saw above that in the noun phrase there is a parametric choice of whether movement happens to begin with, (49b(ii)), and if so, whether the noun moves by itself or together with additional material, (49b(iii)). The same type of parametric choice is also found in question formation. Some languages, like German, are very similar to English in that they, too, move their question words to the beginning of the sentence to form a question. However, unlike in English, prepositions have to front together with the question word.

(52) German

a. Mit wem redest du?
with who talk you
'Who are you talking with?'

b. *Wem redest du mit?
who talk you with

Other languages, like Chinese, are less similar to English and German in that they do not front their question words at all. This is shown in (53). Like English, Chinese generally shows the order subject–verb–object. This order is maintained in questions, (53). Leaving the question word at the end of the sentence in the English counterpart to this sentence would be impossible in a regular question.

(53) Chinese (Huang 1982: 253 ex. 159)
ni kanjian-le shei?
you see-ASP who
SUBJ VERB OBJ
'Who did you see?'

These brief remarks illustrate that the system of parameters developed above has broader validity within syntax than just the narrow domain that we initially used to motivate them.

**KEY POINTS: Movement**

- Together with the structural principles and parameters developed in Section 6.4, the following provides a comprehensive characterization of the neutral word order within the noun phrase across languages.
- Movement, which is invoked here, is regulated by a set of abstract, structural principles together with superficial, easy-to-learn parameters.
- Principles of movement:
  - To derive neutral word orders, only movement of the noun or a constituent containing the noun is licit.
  - To derive neutral word orders, only preposing movement is allowed.
- Parameters of movement:
  - The exact landing site of movement is subject to cross-linguistic variation.
  - The exact size of the moving constituent is subject to cross-linguistic variation.

WEBSITE: **Group exercise 2**

Visit the website and, in a small group, investigate the question to what extent the layered, hierarchical structure for the noun phrase contributes to the explanation of cross-linguistic word order patterns discussed in this chapter.

## 6.6 SUMMARY

This chapter characterized syntax as the study of how phrases and sentences are constructed. We analysed English noun phrases and discovered the need for abstract structures and categories, which we represented with the help of tree diagrams. Section 6.3 introduced some of the broader, more ambitious goals of syntactic theory. These goals are tied to the questions of language learnability, of the role played by nature and nurture in language acquisition and in variation between languages, and of the relative importance of language-specific and domain-general cognitive operations in shaping language.

The remaining two sections proceeded to develop an account of the neutral word order within noun phrases across the languages of the world. The account provides explicit analyses of noun phrases across languages, rules out unattested word order patterns, and provides a solution to the learnability problem. The presentation relied heavily on the tree notation from section 6.2, underscoring its usefulness.

Section 6.4 motivated and developed a model of the commonalities and differences between noun phrases in different languages. The model assumed that the hierarchical structure of noun phrases constitutes a principle of Universal Grammar and that the only variation between languages lies in the choice of the order in which two sister constituents appear. This model is partly successful but turns out to be slightly too restrictive.

Section 6.5 extended the model to achieve better cross-linguistic coverage without giving up the ability to solve the learnability problem. To this end further universal principles and a number of parameters of cross-linguistic variation in the realm of movement were posited. As a description, the system is very successful, since it allows all and only the actually attested word order patterns. The system remains sufficiently constrained to allow a neat solution to the learnability problem: those properties of noun phrase syntax that are very abstract are universally fixed whereas those that vary correspond to easily detectable properties of the input, namely, word order.

The theory of noun phrase syntax presented in this chapter illustrates the logic of the Principles and Parameters approach to language. The approach was first articulated by Noam Chomsky in the 1980s and developed into the Minimalist Program. All modern formal theories of syntax adopt the core idea of universal principles combined with a constrained set of parameters allowing cross-linguistic variation.

The success of this core idea comes from its descriptive strength and from its ability to explain the otherwise mysterious fact that children manage to acquire highly complex grammars of their native languages on the basis of poor and degenerate input.

The success of a theory is not only measured by the questions that it answers but also by the novel questions that it gives rise to.

After reading this chapter, you may wonder about the following questions, which would hardly have occurred to you before reading it and many of which couldn't be asked without the explicit account of noun phrase syntax provided here. Where do the principles that govern the hierarchy within the noun phrase come from? Is the syntactic mobile describing hierarchical aspects of the noun phrase learned or innately given? Does it characterize only language or other aspects of cognition, such as perception, as well? How would we find out? Does movement in the noun correlate with other properties found in the languages that have it? Why do we find movement of the noun or a constituent containing it in some languages but not in others? Where does the restriction come from that the moved element has to move forwards in the sequence of words rather than backwards? Can the theory of word order in the noun phrase be generalized to other syntactic categories such as verb phrases or adjective phrases?

Some of these questions are syntactic by nature others can be addressed only through interdisciplinary work across the cognitive sciences. Linguists have long thought that the study of language can provide insights into the workings of the human mind. Such insights cannot be won without describing the rules characterizing different languages carefully or without delineating the boundary between possible and impossible linguistic systems. Likewise, the broad question of whether the principles invoked in syntactic theory are specifically linguistic or characterize cognition more broadly can only be answered on the basis of the kind of articulated syntactic theory with a broad coverage of data hinted at in this chapter, but not without such a theory.

WEBSITE: **Syntax**

Now go to the website and assess your knowledge of syntactic theory by completing the self-test questions!

## SUGGESTIONS FOR FURTHER READING

Hurford, J. R. (1994). *Grammar: A Student's Guide*. Cambridge: Cambridge University Press. This book contains short articles on descriptive grammatical terminology. Among many other things, it treats adjectives, demonstratives, numerals, and nouns. The book contains exercises and is a useful guide to terminology.

Pinker, S. (1994). *The Language Instinct*. New York: Morrow. This book introduces the central problems and goals of syntactic theory. It is also a very readable polemic in defence of the position that many of the principles and parameters characterizing language are specifically linguistic and do not reduce to general cognitive mechanisms.

Larson, R. K. (2010). *Grammar as Science*. Cambridge, MA: MIT Press. This book gives you an in-depth introduction to the syntactic concepts used in this chapter including phrase structure rules, tree relations, grammatical categories and movement rules.

# ANSWERS TO EXERCISES

## Exercise 6.1

In (20) 'the professor's' is naturally interpreted as 'the professor's fanciful suggestion.' 'Fanciful suggestion' behaves as a group, as the words are missing together. In (21) 'those' is naturally interpreted as 'those new products.' 'New products' behaves as a group, as the words are missing together. In (22) 'them' is naturally interpreted as 'these two complicated papers,' which behaves as a group, since it can be replaced by a single pro-form. In (23) 'those' is naturally interpreted as 'those two problems'. 'Two problems' acts as a group, since the words are missing together. Finally, in (24) 'them' is naturally interpreted as 'these red tiles'. 'These red tiles' acts as a group, as it can be replaced by a single pro-form: 'them.'

Glossed examples, grouped according to the type of constituent that is picked out:

(54) [A N]
  (20) fanciful suggestion
    A N
  (21) new products
    A N

(55) [NUM N]
  (23) two problems
    NUM N

(56) [DEM NUM A N]
  (22) these two complicated papers
    DEM NUM A N

(57) [DEM A N]
  (24) these red tiles
    DEM A N

## Exercise 6.2

All of the elements, DEM, NUM and A, can either precede or follow their sister. We start at the top left of (39) with the English order, where all of the above precede their sister. Moving counter-clockwise, we invert only A for Spanish, only NUM for Dulong and only DEM for Sranan. The languages in the right column represent the mirror image of those in the left column. Burmese inverts A and NUM, Basque inverts A and DEM, Sango inverts NUM and DEM, and Gungbe inverts all three. This exhausts all the options of what can be switched with what. Therefore, no further orders can be produced from this structure.

### Exercise 6.3

The biologists in our thought experiments are constructing an abstract, computational, symbolic theory of what is going on inside the apes' heads. They treat the apes as (complicated) information processing devices and come up with what Marr (1982) would have called a 'computational theory' of their language. Marr points out that a proper understanding of any information processing device necessarily includes a computational theory. He gives the example of a cash register. The computational theory of a cash register is simply provided by the mathematical function of addition. This is true, despite the fact that cash registers do not know that they are computing addition or how they are doing it. Likewise, the biologists computational theory of the apes' communication system can be true or false completely independently of the apes' beliefs about it.

### Exercise 6.4

In (50a), [A] moves. Without [A]-movement, the English order DEM–NUM–A–N results. Movement of [A] alone violates the condition that only constituents containing the noun may move.
Without [A]-movement, the Aghem order N–A–DEM–NUM results. Without both movements, the Spanish order DEM–NUM–N–A results. The second step in (50b) violates the condition that movement must result in an order where N appears earlier in the string than it would have, had movement not taken place (49a(ii)).

### Exercise 6.5

Derivations with movement necessarily start with one of the structures in (39). The target order of the exercise is A–NUM–DEM–N. This is a structure with N in final position. Since movement always has the effect that N is pronounced earlier than it would otherwise be, only N-final structures in (39) are possible source structures. The only such structure corresponds to the English type of order: DEM–NUM–A–N. Moving any of the constituents containing N leftward ([N], [A N], [NUM A N], [DEM NUM A N]) results in an order where N is no longer final. Deriving an N-final order from there would require illicit rightward movement . Therefore, A–NUM–DEM–N cannot be derived.

## REFERENCES

Abels, K. and Neeleman, A. (2012). Linear asymmetries and the LCA. *Syntax*, 15(1), 25–74.
Aboh, E. O. (2004). *The Morphosyntax of Complement–Head Sequences: Clause Structure and Word Order Pattern in Kwa* (Oxford Studies in Comparative Syntax). Oxford University Press.
Brown, K. (ed.) (2006). *The Encyclopedia of Language and Linguistics*. Amsterdam: Elsevier North-Holland.
Cinque, G. (2005). Deriving Greenberg's universal 20 and its exceptions. *Linguistic Inquiry*, 36(3), 315–32.
Cloarec-Heiss, F. (1986). *Dynamique et équilibre d'une syntaxe: le banda-linda de Centrafrique* (Descriptions de Langues et Monographies Ethnolinguistiques). Cambridge and Paris: Cambridge University Press and Éditions de la maison des sciences de l'homme.
Dutton, T. E. (1996). *Koiari* (Languages of the World – Materials, vol. 10). Munich and Newcastle: LINCOM Europa.
Eckert, P. and Hudson, J. (1988). *Wangka Wiru: A Handbook for the Pitjantjatjara Language Learner*. Underdale: South Australian College of Advanced Education.
Elsabbagh, M. and Karmiloff-Smith, A. (2006). Modularity of mind and language. In K. Brown (ed.), *The Encyclopedia of Language and Linguistics*, pp. 218–24. Amsterdam: Elsevier North-Holland.

Greenberg, J. (1963). Some universals of grammar with particular reference to the order of meaningful elements. In J. Greenberg (ed.), *Universals of Language*, pp. 73–113. Cambridge, MA: MIT Press.

Huang, C.-T. J. (1982). Logical relations in Chinese and the theory of grammar. Doctoral dissertation, MIT.

Hurford, J. R. (1994). *Grammar: A Student's Guide*. Cambridge University Press.

Hyman, L. (1979). Aghem grammatical structure. *Southern California Occasional Papers in Linguistics*, 7.

Jones, R. B. (1970). Classifier constructions in Southeast Asia. *Journal of the American Oriental Society*, 90(1), 1–12.

Koopman, H. (2003). *On the parallelism of DPs and clauses: Evidence from Kisongo Maasai*. MS, UCLA.

LaPolla, R. J. (2003). Dulong. In G. Thurgood and R. J. LaPolla (eds.), *The Sinto-Tibetan Languages* (Routledge Language Family Series), pp. 674–82. London: Routledge.

Larson, R. K. (2010). *Grammar as Science*. Cambridge, MA: MIT Press.

Marr, D. C. (1982). *Vision: A Computational Investigation into the Human Representation and Processing of Visual Information*. New York: Freeman.

McMahon, A. and McMahon, R. (2006). Genetics and language. In K. Brown (ed.), *The Encyclopedia of Language and Linguistics*, pp. 21–4. Amsterdam: Elsevier North-Holland.

Oyharçabal, B. (2012). Word order in Basque determiner phrases. In U. Etxeberria, R. Etxepare and M. Uribe-Etxebarria (eds.), *Noun Phrases and Nominalization in Basque* (Linguistik Aktuell vol. 187), pp. 267–82. Amsterdam: Benjamins.

Pinker, S. (1994). *The Language Instinct*. New York: Morrow.

Ross, M. (2002). Kele. In J. Lynch, M. Ross and T. Crowley (eds.), *The Oceanic Languages*, pp. 123–47. Richmond, Surrey: Curzon Press.

Samarin, W. J. (1967). *A Grammar of Sango* (Janua Linguarum). The Hague and Paris: Mouton & Co.

Thornell, C. (1997). *The Sango Language and Is Lexicon* (Travaux de l'Institut de Linguistique de Lund 32). Lund University Press.

Thurgood, G. and LaPolla, R. J. (eds.) (2003). *The Sinto-Tibetan Languages* (Routledge Language Family Series). London: Routledge.

Voorhoeve, J. (1962). *Sranan Syntax*. Amsterdam: North-Holland.

Wiersma, G. (2003). Yunnan Bai. In G. Thurgood and R. J. LaPolla (eds.), *The Sinto-Tibetan Languages* (Routledge Language Family Series), pp. 651–73. London: Routledge.

# 7 Semantics

JOHN SAEED

## KEY TERMS

- aspect
- denotation
- lexeme
- lexical relations
- lexical semantics
- linguistic truth
- literal meaning
- metaphor
- metonymy
- non-literal meaning
- reference
- semantic roles
- sense
- situation type
- tense
- truth conditions

## PREVIEW

This chapter provides an introduction to semantics, which we define as the study of meaning in language. The chapter begins by drawing a fluid boundary between semantics and pragmatics, characterizing the former as knowledge of the linguistic system and the latter as its use in real-life situations. An important distinction is made between reference, the act of using language to identify items in the world, and sense or meaning, which allows the link to be made between sounds and reality. The chapter discusses meaning at the levels of word and sentence. At the word or lexical level, a number of semantic relations are identified, such as synonymy, antonymy and hyponymy. These relations structure a language's vocabulary. We will see how some relations, such as hyponymy, have effects at both word and sentence level. At the sentence level, the chapter introduces some of the rich repetoire of semantic systems which allow speakers a choice in characterizing situations, including situation type, aspect, tense and semantic roles. A central theme will be construal, the choice of semantic options made by a speaker when talking about a situation or event. The discussion moves on to examine the proposal that the philosophical notion of truth should be used to characterize sentence meaning. The chapter closes with the distinction between literal and non-literal language, looking briefly at the cognitive semantics position that questions this traditional and longstanding distinction. By the end of the chapter you will have been introduced to a range of semantic systems that are embodied in speakers' knowledge of their native language.

## 7.1 INTRODUCTION

Semantics is the study of linguistic meaning. It shares this interest with pragmatics, which is the subject of the next chapter. The dividing line between the two areas is fluid and depends in part on the type of linguistic theory we employ. However, in advance of both chapters we can say that in studying semantics we try to model what speakers implicitly know about the meanings of words, phrases and sentences in their native languages. A primary concern of pragmatics, on the other hand, is how speakers integrate contextual and non-linguistic knowledge in the communication of meaning. Another way of making the distinction is to say that semantics is concerned with language as a system, while pragmatics is concerned with how speakers use language. Both of these distinctions are rather rough and ready but they give us an outline which our subsequent discussions will help to flesh out.

Since classical times writers have discussed the sophisticated links that human beings are able to make between words, strings of sounds, and what they perceive in the world around them. We begin this chapter by discussing aspects of this link between language and the world. We then move on to what traditionally has been the main focus of linguistic semantics: word meaning, or lexical semantics. Speakers are aware that there are connections between words in their languages: that for example English *tall* and *short* are different in meaning but in some way related too. Words are also borrowed from language to language, so that we find different words for similar meanings, such as *cemetery* and *graveyard*. Dictionary writers try to capture the knowledge speakers have about similarities and differences in word meaning. When speakers combine words into sentences they are able to employ a range of sentence-level semantic systems. We will look at some of these, for example tense, which allows us to position events in time, and aspect, which allows us to describe how the events unfold. When we discuss the meaning of sentences it is difficult to avoid the importance of context, such as the assumptions hearers make about the speaker's intentions and knowledge. This is especially clear when we go on to look at figurative uses of language, such as metaphor, where hearers routinely seem to make sense out of nonsense.

## 7.2 Reference and sense

There are two aspects of describing what someone means by an expression. Take, for example, what a speaker might mean by saying the noun phrase (NP) *the President of France* in the sentence below:

(1) I saw *the President of France* on television last night.

If the speaker had said this sentence in January 2012, she would be using the italicized NP to refer to Nicolas Sarkozy. However, if she had said it in January 2013, she would refer to François Hollande. This use of a noun phrase or name to pick out someone or something is called **reference**. Though the person identified, called the **referent**, would be different, clearly there is something in common between the 2012 and 2013 versions of the noun phrase used. We can call this its meaning or, to use a term due originally to Frege (1980), its **sense**. We can characterize the difference in simple terms as follows:

REFERENCE: the act of using language to identify or pick out individuals
SENSE: the linguistic knowledge which allows the act of reference

So, when we investigate what a speaker means by a word or phrase, we will have to take account of both its reference and its sense. So our imaginary speaker's two uses of the italicized NP could be described as below:

2012: sense: political leader of France
referent: Nicolas Sarkozy
2013: sense: political leader of France
referent: François Hollande

In this example, the NP is being used to refer to an individual. We could also take the uttering of the whole sentence in (1) to be referring to an event or a situation. However, not all parts of linguistic expressions can be used to refer independently. In the NP *the President of France*, parts of the NP like *the* and *of* do not refer to anything themselves, though they are necessary to the referring potential of the whole NP. We can reflect this by saying that while all expressions have sense, not all can be used to refer.

There is another way in which linguistic expressions can be applied to 'real-world' phenomena. Instead of picking out a specific phenomenon in a particular context, an expression may be used to identify a whole class of phenomena. Compare, for example, the sentences in (2a) and (2b):

(2) a. I ate a banana for breakfast this morning.
b. A banana is a type of fruit.

In uttering (2a), a speaker is using *a banana* to refer to or pick out a particular banana, but in (2b) we have a non-referring use of the same NP. Here, *a banana* relates the observation to any one of a class of things. We could paraphrase (2b) as *Any banana is a kind of fruit* or *All bananas are a kind of fruit*. Many linguists call this latter kind of relationship **denotation**, and term the class of entities to which an expression may be applied its **extension**. However, it should be noted that the terms 'refer', 'reference' and 'referent' are sometimes used in a loose sense to cover both reference as defined earlier and denotation. In our current use we can characterize different types of linguistic expression as having different types of extension. Proper nouns, or names, would have entities as their extensions and common nouns would have sets of things. So the name *Beijing* would have the city as its extension, while the noun *tiger* would have as its extension the set of all tigers. It is possible to extend this to other types of words, so that the verb *live* would have as its extension the set of things that live and the adjective *purple* would have the set of all purple things. Sometimes an expression can be understood either as referential or denotational, as in:

(3) I am looking for a cat.

Somebody saying this sentence could either have a particular cat in mind or be looking to select from a set of cats. Listeners would have to infer which was meant in a particular context.

In this chapter, we will concentrate on sense rather than reference. For convenience, we will often say that such-and-such an expression has a particular meaning. It is important though to remember that only a speaker's use of an expression will convey meaning, and that the actual meaning will depend greatly on the context in which it is being uttered. It is useful here to make a distinction between utterances and sentences. Utterances are produced when a person says something. They represent behaviour and produce physical data that can be recorded in various ways. Sentences, on the other hand, are abstractions from utterances. A simple example is the English sentence *I love you*. This has been spoken countless times and each time produces a unique utterance, which needs contextual information to be meaningful, including clearly who is referred to by *I* and *you*. The single sentence is what is common to all those utterances. It can be written down, as here, and it provides us with a guide to some aspects of those real utterances, but it also omits much, for example the phonetic features of speakers that indicate gender, accent, age, etc. When we use examples of language in this chapter, they also appear as sentences on the page, or individual words that can appear in sentences. However, you should remember that when we talk about the meaning of those examples, we are talking about their meaning potential when uttered. We begin by looking at word meaning and then go on in later sections to look at aspects of sentence meaning.

**KEY POINTS: Reference and sense**

- Two important aspects of meaning are reference and sense.
- Denotation is the relationship between words and the world that makes reference possible.
- The person or thing identified by uttering a noun phrase or name is called the 'referent'.
- The class of entities to which an expression may be applied is called its 'extension'.
- Sentences are abstractions from utterances.
- While sentences have meaning, their full interpretation only emerges when they are uttered in context.

## EXERCISE 7.1

For each of the following sentences imagine a situation in which it is uttered by a speaker. Which of the expressions in bold would the speaker be using to refer to a particular entity?

(a) **A seagull** just stole **my sandwich**.

(b) **I** don't like living in **a city**.

(c) **No politician** is completely honest.

(d) **The dugong** doesn't look anything like **a mermaid**.

(e) **A police spokesman** said they are looking for **a one-armed man**.

## 7.3 Word meaning

The study of word meaning is called **lexical semantics**. The basic aims of semantics at this level are (i) to represent the meaning of each word in the language, and (ii) to show how the meanings of words in a language are interrelated. For convenience, we will talk of word meaning. This is despite the fact that lexical semantics goes beyond individual words to include unitary semantic units below and above the word: the meaning of morphemes and **multiword units**. Morphemes are the minimal meaningful units which make up words and larger units. Thus, we can identify the word *manlike* as being composed of the two morphemes *man* and *like*, each of which has meaning. Some morphemes are words, traditionally called free morphemes, like *man* and *bird*. While these may combine in compounds, such as *businessman* and *blackbird*, they have the potential to occur alone. Other morphemes are bound morphemes, parts of word like *un-* and *pre-* in *unlikely* and *precook*, which cannot occur alone. A semantic unit may also be larger than a word. In this case, two or more words have a unitary meaning which does not correspond to the meaning of their parts, like the English phrasal verbs in (4a) or the idioms in (4b):

(4) a. give up, show off, do in
b. red herring, old flame, bury the hatchet

When the meaning of a complex expression is predictable from its parts, its meaning is said to be **compositional**. Multiword expressions are therefore non-compositional.

### 7.3.1 Types of words

It is clear that grammatical categories, though defined at the level of syntax and morphology, do reflect semantic differences. For this reason, different categories of words must be given different semantic descriptions. Examples include names, common nouns, pronouns and logical words, all of which show different characteristics of reference and sense. Some examples of these words are shown below:

(5) a. Names, e.g. *Joan of Arc, Nelson Mandela, Poland*
b. Common nouns, e.g. *dog, banana, tarantula*
c. Pronouns, e.g. *you, they, her*
d. Logical words, e.g. *not, all, if, and, or*

Looking at these types of words we can say that they operate in different ways: some kinds may be used to refer, others may not (names versus logical words); some can only be interpreted in particular contexts, while others are very consistent in meaning across a whole range of contexts (pronouns versus logical words), and so on. It seems too that semantic links will tend to hold between members of the same group rather than across groups. So the semantic relations between common nouns like *man, woman, animal*, etc. are clearer than between any noun and words like *and, or, not*. Note too that these are only a selection of categories: we will have to account for others like verbs, adjectives, adverbs, prepositions, etc. Having said this, we will deal in this section mainly with nouns, verbs and adjectives. You should bear in mind that this is not the whole story.

## 7.3.2 The lexicon

The word '**lexicon**' is from the Classical Greek word λεξικόν (lexicon), which basically means 'dictionary', and is used by linguists as a convenient label for the knowledge speakers have about the meanings of the words of their language. Words can be identified at the level of writing, where in many languages, including of course English, they are identified by being separated by space on the page. They may be identified at other linguistic levels, for example phonology, where they are strings of sounds which show unifying features such as stress patterns. At the level of grammar, words in a language like English act like a unit because they show internal stability, with morpheme order tending to be fixed, and external mobility, since they may take up various positions in sentences. We can say that in (6) below, there are three grammatical words, represented as three written words, which could be pronounced as three phonological words:

(6) talks, talked, talking

However, for semantics we will want to say that these are three instances of the same semantic unit, which we can represent in capitals to show that it is an unpronounceable abstraction, i.e. TALK, and for which we use the term '**lexeme**'. Dictionaries are composed of lists of lexemes, with information about them forming **lexical entries**. So our lexicon will be a collection of lexemes with, among other things, (i) a representation of the lexeme's meaning, and (ii) a representation of its meaning relations with other lexemes. Many writers also include the lexical rules for the creation of new vocabulary, for example, the very general rule in English that allows adjectives ending in *-al* to form related verbs ending in *-ize*, e.g. *radical→radicalize*. For each lexeme we include any information that cannot be predicted by general rules of the language's grammar. This would include pronunciation, exceptional morphological behaviour, and what grammatical categories it belongs to. For now we are just interested in semantic information: what is the meaning of the word and what semantic relations does it enter into with other words in the same language? We can begin by looking at the second question: the semantic relations that can hold between lexemes.

## 7.3.3 Lexical relations

Speakers of a language implicity know various kinds of relations between words and their associated lexemes. We outline some of these in this section. We begin with relations between lexemes and the forms of words by looking at homonymy.

*Homonymy*. Homonyms are words which are identical in form but which have different meanings and thus belong to separate lexemes. So, for example, the word *bark* is pronounced the same whether it means the sound made by a dog or the covering of a tree. This sharing of one form by distinct lexemes is called homonymy. From the point of view of semantics, there are two items here: *bark*$^1$ 'cry of a dog' and *bark*$^2$ 'covering of a tree'. Some authors distinguish further between **homophones**, words sharing the same pronunciation but not the same spelling and **homographs**, words sharing just the same written form. In fact, if we add the level of grammatical category, there are several types of homonymy, as shown below:

## Types of homonymy:

(7) a. Same grammatical category, same pronunciation, same spelling, e.g. the distinct meanings of the noun *bark*
b. Different category, same pronunciation, same spelling, e.g. the noun *bear* and the verb *bear*
c. Same category, same pronunciation, different spelling, e.g. the nouns *pair* and *pear*
d. Different category, same pronunciation, different spelling, e.g. *to* and *two*
e. Same category, different pronunciation, same spelling, e.g. the nouns *row* 'line' and *row* 'quarrel'
f. Different category, different pronunciation, same spelling, e.g. the verb *lead* and the noun *lead* (denoting the metal)

We can identify types (7a) and (7b) as homonyms, types (7c) and (7d) as homophones, and types (7e) and (7f), where only the spelling unites the two lexemes, as homographs.

There is a traditional distinction made between **homonymy** and **polysemy** that is important to lexicographers in the creation of dictionaries. Both terms identify multiple meanings for the same phonological word, but polysemy is used when the meanings are judged to be related by one or more critera. These criteria include speakers' intuitions and what is known about the historical development of the items. Lexicographers usually assign independent entries in their dictionaries to homonyms, while examples of polysemy are listed under the same entry. Entries from an imaginary dictionary are shown in (8) below:

(8) seal$^1$ *noun* 1. Tight or complete closure. 2. Special closure that reveals tampering. 3. Certifying stamp. 4. Piece of wax showing the mark of a stamp. 5. Symbol of office.
seal$^2$ *noun* Fish-eating sea mammal.

These entries treat one set of meanings, or senses, of *seal* (closure, stamp, etc.) as polysemy and list them under one lexical entry. A separate sense (sea mammal) is treated as unrelated, therefore a case of homonymy, and is assigned a separate entry. So we have two distinct lexemes. Such decisions are not always as clear-cut as this and lexicographers also take into account the history or etymology of the words. Semantic change over time can multiply and diversify the senses of words so that their relatedness becomes obscured. Speakers of English, for example, may feel that *right* 'opposite of *left*' and *right* 'correct' are not related, even though they are etymologically derived from the same ancestor. Alternatively, shifts in pronunciation can make words from different origins resemble each other, so for example Modern English *ear* (the organ of hearing) from Old English *ēare* 'ear' and Modern English *ear* (of corn) from Old English *ēar*' ear of corn' have converged, leaving some speakers unsure whether they are related and therefore polysemous. Speakers' intuitions and the known history of words may be in conflict and published dictionaries differ in weighing between them.

*Synonymy*. Synonyms are different words that have the same or very similar meanings. Some examples might be the pairs in (9) below:

(9) answer–reply gratuity–tip abdomen–belly disaster–catastrophe

In fact, there are rather few exact synonyms, as we might expect from considerations of economy of effort in language learning and communication. Many differ by being associated with particular regions where a language is spoken, such as differences between English *vineyard* and *winery* or *rubbish* and *garbage*. The candidates for **synonymy** may differ in register, that is formality, or by specialized contexts of use. So a speaker may say *I was dismissed* or *I was sacked* according to context, or use *cranium* rather than *skull*. Other differences reveal a speaker's attitude like using *squander* versus *waste* or *insurgent* rather than *rebel*. A particular feature of the history of English is the presence of loanwords from French following the Norman Conquest, which in some cases form synonyms with words with an older Germanic origin, such as in (10). This is an example of language contact producing synonyms.

(10) lawful–legal freedom–liberty understand–comprehend baby–infant

*Antonymy*. In general, and in traditional terms, antonyms are lexemes which are opposite in meaning. It is useful, however, to identify several different types of opposition under the label '**antonymy**'. Binary antonyms, as the name suggests, are in a complementary relationship where the assertion of one lexeme implies the denial of the other and vice versa. Two lexemes in this relationship can be seen as forming a two-term classification, like the examples in (11). Such pairs are also called simple antonyms or complementary antonyms.

(11) dead–alive pass–fail moving–still true–false

Gradable antonyms are in an opposition, which implies the possibility of gradations or intermediary stages between them. This relation is found most typically in adjectives with pairs like *small* and *large*. We know from buying clothes that in this context there can be intermediate terms like *medium*. Similar pairs are shown in (12):

(12) cold–hot tall–short fast–slow cheap–expensive

Gradable antonyms are usually relative, so a *cold* cup of coffee might not be much colder than a *hot* day. Their gradability means that they can be used with intensifying words, like *very*, *so*, etc. as in *so expensive*, *really tall*. Gradable adjectives may also be used in comparative forms, such as *taller* or *slowest*. Gradable antonyms are sometimes called polar antonyms.

Relational opposites allow different perspectives on the same relationship, such as *lend* and *borrow* in English. So the sentences *Fred lent the money to Michael* and *Michael borrowed the money from Fred* can offer different perspectives on the same situation. Some other examples are shown in (13):

(13) buy–sell  above–below  before–after  give–receive  doctor–patient

Reverse antonyms are lexemes which describe both phases of reversible processes, such as the movement verbs *come* and *go*, or *ascend* and *descend*. Other examples are the verbs in (14) below:

(14) heat–cool  inflate–deflate  build–demolish  close–open

*Hyponymy*. **Hyponymy** is a relation of inclusion between more specific and less specfic terms, for example, the hyponym *poodle* and the superordinate term (or hyperonym), *dog*. We can also capture this relationship by saying that a poodle is a (kind of) dog. Co-hyponyms of *poodle* would be *boxer, bulldog, schnauzer*, etc. These relations can have several levels, so that dog is a hyponym of mammal, which is itself a hyponym of animal. The resulting network is upwardly transitive so we know automatically that a poodle is also a mammal and an animal. We can see that these are conceptual and cultural rather than natural networks since words can be in several networks. *Dog*, for example, is also a hyponym of *pet*, where its co-hyponyms might be *cat, turtle, hamster*, etc. These hierarchical networks in the lexicon of a language have been of great interest in anthropology and psychology since they can be seen to reflect the conceptual classifications of the world embedded in particular languages.

### 7.3.4 Word meaning and concepts

Earlier we said that part of a word's meaning comes from its contribution to a speaker's ability to refer to things in the real world. This contribution varies according to the type of word, so that names denote individual entities fairly directly, nouns denote categories of entities, while other words, such as logical words, enable speakers to create and use sentences to refer to the world. The other aspect of meaning is a lexeme's sense and the last section shows us that at least some of this derives from relationships in the lexicon. A lexeme's sense is partially defined through relations like synonymy, antonymy and hyponymy. It is also clear to many semanticists that there is a conceptual element to sense and a number of different approaches have tried to characterize this. One traditional way, which comes down to us from the Classical world, is to identify basic features or attributes that define a word's sense. We commonly find correspondences such as (15) in the lexicon:

(15) man–woman–child  ram–ewe–lamb  dog–bitch–pup

This suggests that semantic distinctions like MALE/FEMALE and ADULT/YOUNG might be part of lexemes' meanings. Similarly, when we look at verbs, we can identify patterns such as in (16) below:

(16) kill–die lift–rise feed–eat fell–fall

In these pairs, the first verb seems to describe the causing of a process described in the second, suggesting a semantic feature CAUSE. This feature might explain correspondences between adjectives and verbs like those in (17) below. In these pairs, the derived verb seems to mean 'cause the state described by the corresponding adjective'.

(17) a. sharp–sharpen tight–tighten light–lighten damp–dampen
b. real–realize actual–actualize ideal–idealize brutal–brutalize

The problem has been that while it seems useful to identify abstract features like MALE, FEMALE, CAUSE that impact upon the grammar of a language and which seem to be shared by lexemes, it has proved impossible to come up with a list of such features that exhaustively describe the senses of lexemes.

A distinct approach, characteristic of cognitive semantics as described by Ungerer and Schmid (2006), is to identify the sense of a lexeme as a concept and to apply to lexemes the models of concepts developed in the cognitive psychology literature. One influential approach is Rosch's (1978) **prototype theory**, which views concepts as having an internal structure with a central core about which people have clear intuitions, but also peripheral elements about which people demonstrate less clarity in their judgments. Well-discussed examples include the concept BIRD, where the core element might be a small flying bird like a sparrow or robin. More peripheral members might include the ostrich, which shows non-typical features such as being large relative to humans, conspicuously unfeathered in parts and unable to fly. In some cases, speakers might be uncertain about judging the borderline between concepts, for example, between the extensions of the words *tree* and *bush*. In this approach, a concept might be seen as organized around actual examples, or exemplars, but other versions might be organized around images and other sensory experiences, or information structured as **propositions**. The central idea in this approach is that the word is a label for the concept, however it is structured.

### KEY POINTS: Word meaning

- Lexical semantics is the study of word meaning and meaning relations between words in the vocabulary.
- The store of knowledge about a language's words is called the 'lexicon'.
- The semantic unit at word level is called the 'lexeme'.
- Meaning relations in the lexicon include homonymy, polysemy, antonymy and hyponymy.
- The meaning of a word is usually equated with a concept, with no common agreement about how this is structured.

**EXERCISE 7.2**

Part A: For each of the following words, identify a synonym. Then try to find a context where one of each pair could be used but not the other.

marry (verb)

tall (adjective)

decay (noun)

food (noun)

limp (adjective)

dead (adjective)

Part B: Classify the following pairs of antonyms as binary, gradable, relational or reverse:

| | |
|---|---|
| high–low | debtor–creditor |
| sink–float | advance–retreat |
| rich–poor | succeed–fail |
| husband–wife | teacher–student |
| same–different | enter–exit |
| dress–undress | young–old |
| complete–incomplete | lead–follow |
| easy–difficult | freeze–thaw |

WEBSITE: **Group exercise**

Visit the website and, in a small group, attempt the group exercise. This involves dividing into pairs and conducting some semantics fieldwork on word meaning.

## 7.4 Sentence meaning

Speakers combine words into phrases and sentences, and sentences allow us to describe the world in different ways. One important notion is **construal**, that is the particular viewpoint that a speaker chooses when describing something. Every language offers its speakers a range of ways to classify situations and events, and to describe the roles of the people and objects involved. In this section, we look at some important ways in which semantic systems allow these choices, beginning with situation type.

### 7.4.1 Classifying the situation

One basic distinction available to the speaker is between identifying static situations (or states) and dynamic situations. Talking about states involves viewing a situation as existing at a time. It allows the speaker to relate individuals to locations, or to attribute to them qualities as in (18) below:

(18) a. The book is in the library.
b. Joan feels sea-sick.
c. She's a doctor.
d. Rudolf has a red nose.

There are many different types of states. Some are temporary, others are permanent; some relate to location, still others to possession or description.

Dynamic situations involve the identification of change. They can be viewed as processes, where the change is spread over time, as in sentence (19a), or as events, where something happens at a particular point or points in time, as in (19b), or as actions, where someone or something is identified as causing the process or action, as in (19c):

(19) a. Snow was falling all night.
b. The rat ran up the drainpipe.
c. Ayesha is feeding the goldfish.

How are these semantic distinctions marked? One way is by the use of different grammatical categories. For example, there is a tendency in English for states to be described by adjectives and dynamic situations by verbs. Compare the two sentences in (20) below:

(20) a. Frank died.
b. Frank is dead.

Sentence (20a) identifies an event and uses a verb, while (20b) identifies a state and uses an adjective. Sometimes, this relationship between a verb and an adjective is marked by a morphological relation, as shown below:

***Situations and categories***

| Verb (dynamic) | Adjective (static) |
|---|---|
| *rot* | *rotten* |
| *shrink* | *shrunken* |
| *break* | *broken* |
| *freeze* | *frozen* |

Often, such derived adjectives describe a state resulting from the process or event described by the verb. However, there is no one-to-one match between semantic distinctions and grammatical categories, and there are a number of stative verbs which describe static situations, for example, the verbs in the sentences in (21):

(21) a. He knows his way home.
b. Water consists of hydrogen and oxygen.
c. My brother owns a car.

As can be seen from our definitions of dynamic situations, distinctions of situation type crucially involve different ways of viewing time. The linguistic markers of such views are traditionally called **aspect** and **tense**. We can distinguish them by saying that aspect allows different views of how a situation is distributed over time, while tense allows the positioning of situations in time relative to some reference point. In a language like English aspect and tense are marked together on verbs and, as we shall see, tend to co-occur in combined forms, so separating them is not always easy. We begin with the aspect.

It is useful to distinguish two levels of aspectual distinction: lexical aspect and grammatical aspect. Lexical aspect refers to a classification of situations encoded in the words of a language, and is called by some writers **situation type**, or described by the German term **Aktionsart**. An important distinction is between durative, which describes situations spread over time, and punctual, which describes something taking place instantaneously. The adjectives and stative verbs we discussed earlier are inherently durative and static. Verbs which describe processes, like *walk* and *talk* in (22) below, are durative and dynamic:

(22) a. I walked to work.
b. Joan is talking to her mother.

Other verbs are punctual in that they denote processes that are conceptualized as being instantaneous or so compressed in time as to display no internal structure, as in (23):

(23) a. The car crashed.
b. The sprinter crossed the finish line.

Durative verbs can combine with other expressions, such as nouns, to form either bounded and unbounded types. The term 'bounded' describes events or processes that have an inherent endpoint at which a new state comes into being. These are sometimes called 'telic', after the Classical Greek word τέλος (telos) meaning 'end, purpose, goal'. By contrast, unbounded situations are called 'atelic'. Some examples of bounded situation types are in (24):

(24) a. James painted a portrait of his mother.
b. Sean filled the glass.
c. Marcela cleared the counter.

These sentences imply an end to the action where the portrait was painted, the glass was full and the counter cleared. In a classification derived from Vendler (1957, 1967), this situation type is given the label 'accomplishment'. Unbounded types describe dynamic situations that have no inherent endpoint, such as in (25). These situation types are called 'activities' in the same classification system.

(25) a. James painted.
b. Sean poured beer.
c. Marcela wiped the counter.

Punctual verbs can be divided into two types. The first identifies instantaneous events that involve a new state, as in (26). These events are termed 'achievements'.

(26) a. Jeff smashed the window.
b. The building collapsed.

Other punctual events are instantaneous but involve no change of state, as in (27). These are termed 'semelfactives', from a term used in Slavic linguistics.

(27) a. The teacher coughed.
b. Joan's mobile phone rang.

When sentences are constructed, lexical aspect combines with grammatical aspect. The latter is typically marked by morphology and the use of specific auxiliary verbs. Grammatical aspect distinguishes the speaker's viewpoint on an event and its profile over time. Perhaps the commonest distinction in languages is between perfective aspect, which allows the speaker an external focus on the situation as a complete unit, and imperfective, which allows a focus on the internal phases of a situation. We can compare the sentences (28a) and (28b) below:

(28) a. Robinson built a raft.
b. Robinson was building a raft.

Both sentences describe a situation in the past. But they differ in that (28a) views the raft building as a completed event, while (28b) views it as an ongoing process and gives no information about whether the raft ever got finished. The verb forms are each at a different intersection of the aspect and tense systems of English: *built* is in a simple past tense/aspect form and *was building* is in a past progressive tense/aspect form. The former is a type of perfective aspect and the latter a type of imperfective. Another example of an imperfective aspect is the habitual, through which a speaker views an event or state as repeated over a period of time. In English, this can be marked by the auxiliary verbs *will* in the present and *would* in the past, as in (29):

(29) a. He will wear that old suit to every wedding.
b. She would bring her dog along to parties.

The examples so far have shown that the marking of aspect is inextricably linked to tense, which allows a speaker to locate a situation in time. The location is always relative to the act of speaking (or writing). This makes tense one of the deictic systems of language, which anchor an utterance to a specific time and place. Some deictic expressions are simply adverbs of time and space, such as English *now*, *then*, *here* and *there*. Tense is a form of temporal **deixis** that is incorporated into the grammar of the language. In English, tense distinctions, such as the basic distinction between past, present and future, are marked by a combination of verb endings and auxiliary verbs in the same way as grammatical aspect. As a result, individual verb forms in English carry information about both aspect and tense and are given composite labels like 'past progressive'. The simple present/past/future distinction, as in *She eats/ate/will eat*, is anchored relative to the current act of speaking or writing. Complex tense forms like *She had eaten* and *She will have eaten* allow a speaker to locate a situation prior to a reference point in the past or the future. As described by reference grammars like Huddleston and Pullum (2002), tense systems are rich and flexible, and interact with lexical and grammatical aspect to allow speakers choices in their portrayal of situations and events.

### 7.4.2 Classifying participants

Another range of semantic options allows the speaker to characterize the roles of various entities in a situation. There are certain **semantic roles** available to a speaker, which can be associated with verbs. Some common labels used for these are given below:

AGENT: initiator of some action, typically capable of acting with volition
PATIENT: entity undergoing the effect of some action, typically undergoing a change of state
THEME: the entity which is moved by an action, or whose location is described
EXPERIENCER: an entity aware of the action or state described by the predicate but not in control of it
BENEFICIARY: the entity benefiting from some action
INSTRUMENT: the means by which an AGENT causes something to come about
LOCATION: the place in which something is situated or takes place
GOAL: the entity towards which something moves
SOURCE: the entity from which something moves
STIMULUS: the entity causing an effect in the EXPERIENCER

In (30), some examples with the semantic roles identified are given:

(30) a. A rock star$_{\text{AGENT}}$ threw the television$_{\text{THEME}}$ from the window$_{\text{SOURCE}}$.
b. The takeoff$_{\text{STIMULUS}}$ frightened the passengers$_{\text{EXPERIENCER}}$.
c. The conspirators$_{\text{AGENT}}$ assassinated Julius Caesar$_{\text{PATIENT}}$ with daggers$_{\text{INSTRUMENT}}$.

There are some other types of role identified by semanticists, for example, NATURAL FORCE for a physical force that is neither an agent nor an instrument, as in *The tide*$_{\text{NF}}$ *swept away the raft*. However, those above are characteristic of the variety of roles in which participants in a situation can be viewed. Some writers use other terms for these roles, including **participant roles** and **thematic roles**.

One important reason for identifying these roles is the insight they provide into the lexical semantics of verbs. Representing semantic roles can help capture facts about verb classes and argument structure possibilities. So, for example, we can distinguish in English between *kill*, which allows an INSTRUMENT subject, and *assassinate*, which does not, by giving them as part of their lexical entries appropriate semantic role templates. This is shown in (31a) and (31b) below where the underlined element corresponds to the semantic role that is represented by the grammatical subject:

Lexical specification: *kill* versus *assassinate*

(31) a. *kill* V: <AGENT, PATIENT, INSTRUMENT>,
<INSTRUMENT, PATIENT>
Doctors killed the virus with a mystery drug.
A mystery drug killed the virus.

b. assassinate V: <AGENT, PATIENT, INSTRUMENT>
The anarchist assassinated the emperor with a bomb.
? The bomb assassinated the emperor.

In (31a) we see that *kill* shows two different argument structures: one with the AGENT as subject, the other with the INSTRUMENT. However, in (31b) *assassinate* only allows the first. This can be viewed both as a semantic difference between the verbs and as a difference in the viewpoints on a situation that they allow to the speaker.

Such differences in semantic role templates can be more systematic and identify whole subclasses of verbs. For example, the English verb *shatter* allows the three mappings between semantic roles and grammatical roles in (32a–c) below:

(32) a. The child shattered the window with a stone.
Subject = AGENT, Object = PATIENT, Prepositional Phrase (Oblique) = INSTRUMENT

b. The stone shattered the window.
Subject = INSTRUMENT, Object = PATIENT

c. The window shattered.
Subject = PATIENT

The verb *shatter* in (32a) above is a **causative** verb describing a caused change of state and it allows two other argument possibilities. The first in (32b) allows the INSTRUMENT role to occur as subject. The second in (32c) involves *shatter* as a change of state verb, where no agency is identified. This type is termed an **inchoative** verb and has the PATIENT as subject.

This particular pattern of correspondences is called the causative–inchoative alternation. It involves transitive causative verbs and their corresponding intransitive inchoatives, including verbs like *break, snap, open, melt, freeze, burn* and *grow*. However, not all inchoative intransitives have transitive causative alternants, as can be seen in (33):

(33) a. The Roman Empire decayed.
b. ?The Germanic tribes decayed the Roman Empire.

Furthermore, not all transitive causative verbs allow an inchoative version, as can be seen in (34):

(34) a. The developer demolished the building.
b. ?The building demolished.

Semantic roles help characterize these alternations, which are an important aspect of verbal semantics.

Linguists have also been able to make cross-linguistic generalizations about the mapping of semantic roles to grammatical relations. For example, the implicational hierarchy below makes predictions about the possibility and likelihood of semantic roles being able to occur as subjects in different languages:

*Subject hierarchy*
AGENT > EXPERIENCER >THEME/PATIENT > INSTRUMENT > LOCATION

This is a cross-linguistic observation, which among other things predicts that moving left to right is a movement from more typical to less typical subjects. The hierarchy also predicts that if a language allows one position on the chain it will allow all others to the left. So if a language allows LOCATION as subject, as in the English example in (35) below, it will allow also INSTRUMENT, PATIENT and AGENT, which our earlier examples have shown:

(35) This house sleeps eight.

Many languages do not allow semantic roles like LOCATION and INSTRUMENT to occur in subject position and translators and language learners have to adopt strategies to cope with the mismatches produced by such differences.

### 7.4.3 Meaning relations between sentences

In addition to the **lexical relations** described earlier, speakers also have tacit knowledge of semantic relations between sentences. So, for example, synonymy can be recognized at both lexical and sentence levels. Some sentential synonymy derives from lexical synonymy, as in (36) below, where the sentences are synonymous because of the antonymy between the adjectives *dead* and *alive* and the use of negation:

(36) a. The parrot is dead.
b. The parrot is no longer alive.

Other sentential synonymy is caused by the relationship between grammatical constructions, as between the active and passive sentences in (37):

(37) a. The tiger attacked the visitor.
b. The visitor was attacked by the tiger.

Lexical antonymy is mirrored at sentence level by **contradiction**. The example in (38) is a case of contradiction within a sentence:

(38) ? The door is open and is shut.

Sentences like this can be used of course, but their semantic anomaly forces hearers to search for a non-literal meaning, which we discuss a little later on. Negation will by its nature cause a **contradictory** relation between sentences, as in (39a) and (39b):

(39) a. Nairobi is the capital of Kenya.
b. Nairobi is not the capital of Kenya.

An important sentential relation is **entailment**. This describes a relation between two sentences where the second follows automatically from the first, without any need for reasoning. This can be seen in (40), where we assume that the names in the two sentences are used to refer to the same individuals:

(40) a. Jane is Patrick's wife.
b. Patrick is Jane's husband.

The entailment in (40) follows from the fact that the nouns *wife* and *husband* are relational opposites. Other lexical relations can also cause entailment, such as the hyponymy in (41) below, where (41a) entails (41b) because *poodle* is a hyponym of *dog*:

(41) a. Harold has bought a poodle.
b. Harold has bought a dog.

Finally, we can mention **presupposition**, which was traditionally viewed as a semantic relation, though there are reasons for viewing it as a pragmatic notion, as we will see. This term has been used for when a speaker's sentence seems to signal an assumption, as in (42a) and (42b):

(42) a. The President of Ruritania is a woman.
Presupposition: There is a President of Ruritania.
b. Michael has stopped smoking.
Presupposition: Michael used to smoke.

These presuppositions seem to be outside the scope of the speaker's assertion, so that they survive when the main clause is negated. The negative sentences in (43a) and (43b) still carry the same presupposition:

(43) a. The President of Ruritania isn't a woman.
Presupposition: There is a President of Ruritania.
b. Michael hasn't stopped smoking.
Presupposition: Michael used to smoke.

Hearers can challenge or reject a speaker's presupposition, for example, by replying as in (44):

(44) Michael hasn't stopped smoking, because he never smoked.

This form of rejection or contradiction of a presupposition has been called **meta-linguistic negation** to distinguish it from the simple negation of the speaker's main assertion, which here would be *Michael has stopped smoking.*

It has been convincingly proposed that presuppositions should be described within pragmatics rather than semantics because they show sensitivity to contextual, non-linguistic knowledge. For example, in the sentence in (45), *before* presupposes the content of the following clause:

(45) Isabel peeled the apple before she ate it.

However, real-world knowledge means that this not true in (46):

(46) The architect was fired before he completed the design.

This sensitivity to real-world knowledge, it is argued, is more characteristic of speakers' pragmatic abilities than their purely linguistic, i.e. semantic, knowledge.

### 7.4.4 Linguistic truth and meaning

One approach to characterizing the sentential relations described in the last section is to use the philosophical notion of truth. Philosophers have identified two basic types of truth. The first relates to correspondence with the facts of situations in the world. If a statement corresponds to the facts it is true, otherwise it is false. Being true or false is called the **truth value** of the statement. This can be called **contingent truth** because it is dependent on the conditions holding in the situation. Alternatively, it can be called **empirical truth** because we have to check the fit between the statement and the situation. So the truth value of an uttered sentence *It is snowing* depends on the context it is uttered in, including crucially of course whether it is snowing there. In contrast, we can identify another kind of truth, **linguistic truth**, where truth or falsity follows from the meaning relations within and between words and sentences. This second type of truth can be used to characterize the sentence relations in the last section. So, for example, entailment can be characterized as a truth relation between sentences, as shown below:

#### ENTAILMENT AS A TRUTH RELATION

A sentence P entails a sentence Q when the truth of the first (P) guarantees the truth of the second (Q), and the falsity of the second (Q) guarantees the falsity of the first (P).

Applying this to our earlier example in (41), we can see how it works. If *Harold has bought a poodle* is true, it is automatically true that *Harold has bought a dog*. If it is false that *Harold has bought a dog* then it is automatically false that *Harold has bought a poodle*. If we understand what the sentences mean the relationship is guaranteed. Note that this relationship has a specific quality: if it false that *Harold has bought a poodle* we do not know anything about the truth or otherwise of *Harold has bought a dog*. It depends on the situation: he may have bought a different kind of dog or no dog at all.

Entailment, defined in terms of truth, can be used to characterize other semantic relations. Sentence synonymy, for example, can be defined as mutual entailment. So the two sentences in (47), which do entail one another, are synonymous:

(47) a. Frédéric Bartholdi designed the Statue of Liberty.
b. The Statue of Liberty was designed by Frédéric Bartholdi.

You can check that these two sentences entail one another by working through the entailment definition for each. In short, these sentences when uttered will be true or false together. In contrast, two sentences are contradictory if the truth of one necessarily entails that the other is false. So we know that *It is snowing* and *It is not snowing* contradict each other, without checking the weather. These truth relations are thus independent of empirical truth. In another terminology, empirical truth is called **synthetic truth** and linguistic truth is analytic truth called **analytic truth**.

**KEY POINTS: Sentence meaning**

- Aspect is a semantic system that allows speakers to characterize how situations are profiled over time.
- Some aspectual distinctions are part of a verb's basic meaning (lexical aspect), while others are marked by verb inflection and auxiliary verbs (grammatical aspect).
- One influential system, based on Vendler (1967), divides situation types into states, accomplishments, achievements and semelfactives.
- Tense is a semantic system expressed in grammar that allows speakers to locate situations in time, relative to the act of utterance.
- Semantic roles like AGENT, PATIENT, INSTRUMENT, etc. reflect a semantic classification of how entities in a situation relate to the verb.
- It has been proposed that the philosophical notion of truth can characterize semantic relations between sentences, including synonymy, contradiction and entailment.

## EXERCISE 7.3

Part A: Typically, the semantic role of AGENT is carried by an entity that is animate, acts deliberately and employs force or movement. For each of the sentences below, decide whether the subject of the sentence corresponds to this characterization and is, hence, a typical AGENT:

(a) The angler pulled the salmon from the river.

(b) The tsunami destroyed the hotel.

(c) Anastasia is mowing her lawn again.

(d) George accidentally knocked over my pint of Guinness.

(e) She smelled smoke in the hall.

Part B: For each of the following pairs of sentences, say whether the first entails the second. When the same noun phrases, names and pronouns occur in both, assume they are being used to refer to the same individuals and entities.

(1) a. Dublin Zoo borrowed a male panda.

b. Dublin Zoo borrowed an animal.

(2) a. Peter and Mary got married.

b. Peter and Mary got married to each other.

(3) a. Peter fed his pet python a rat.

b. Peter's pet python ate a rat.

(4) a. Harry met Sally.

b. Sally met Harry.

(5) a. She donated most of her books to the library.

b. She donated many books to the library.

## 7.5 Non-literal meaning

We have used the symbol ? to mark sentences as semantically anomalous. This makes the apparently uncontroversial assumption that speakers know which sentences will make sense when uttered and which will not. However, this is not always straightforward in practice. Some of the difficulty arises from pragmatic principles of conversational cooperation, as described by Grice (1989), Wilson and Sperber (2012) and other writers. These principles lead hearers to try to make sense of a speaker's words, under the assumption that the utterance is spoken with a goal in mind. So hearers will ignore slips of the tongue, fill in gaps and follow hints in order to reconstruct the speaker's intended meaning. It is hard to say out of context how far hearers' interpretive efforts will take them. In addition, speakers may say things that are contextually implausible if not impossible, such as in (48):

(48) a. We've seen this movie millions of times.
  b. They are in talks with Seoul again.
  c. Your landlady is a dragon.

Such examples are, of course, very common and since hearers do not usually reject them, there is a tradition of distinguishing between **literal meaning** or utterances and **non-literal meaning** or utterances. The former are held to be semantically transparent while the latter are not, yet still are meaningful. There is a long tradition of viewing non-literal language as a form of verbal special effect, done to excite unusual reactions or as an ornament to style. In this tradition, a taxonomy of strategies or tropes is identified, wherein (48a) would be an example of exaggeration, often termed **hyperbole**, (48b) is an example of **metonymy**, where an associated noun is used to refer indirectly, in this case perhaps to the South Korean government, and (48c) is an example of **metaphor**.

In recent work in semantics and pragmatics this view of non-literal language as an extra layer of rhetorical ornament has been challenged. Scholars working in cognitive semantics, for example, have claimed that such processes as metonymy and metaphor are integral both to thought and language and see them as integral to ordinary language. Metaphor is then characterized as a strategy of coping with new or difficult areas of knowledge by relating them to existing and more accessible knowledge. In this view, metaphor is the linguistic reflection of analogical reasoning. In a famous example used by Lakoff and Johnson (1980), talk about a lovers' relationship may be organized by a metaphorical transfer to a physical journey, with the correspondences shown below, as discussed by Evans and Green (2006: 294–6):

LOVE IS A JOURNEY metaphor

| | | |
|---|---|---|
| love | → | journey |
| co-travellers | → | lovers |
| the vehicle | → | the relationship |
| the journey | → | phases in relationship |
| physical obstacles | → | difficulties experienced |
| distance covered | → | progress in relationship |
| decisions on routes | → | choices about what to do |
| destination | → | goal of relationship |

In this view, metaphor is a structured mapping between domains of knowledge, rather than a single comparison. The mapping, called a conceptual metaphor and shown in small capitals (LOVE IS JOURNEY), licenses a whole range of individual uses, as in (49):

(49) a. This relationship isn't going anywhere.
b. We will have to go our separate ways.
c. Their marriage is on the rocks.

In this example, love is called the target domain and the journey is the source domain. Linguists have identified a tendency for the source domains to be more concrete and familiar, allowing a kind of cognitive control over the target domain. To take another example, in an earlier phase of personal computing, designers employed the metaphor A COMPUTER INTERFACE IS AN OFFICE DESK, thus enabling the use of terms like *desktop, clipboards, file folders, trashcans,* etc. Other conceptual metaphors discussed in the literature include TIME IS MONEY, IDEAS ARE COMMODITIES and ARGUMENTS ARE BUILDINGS. The claim is that such conceptual metaphors are learned and internalized so that they will be used unconsciously by speakers talking about these domains. In this view, speakers are not conscious of speaking metaphorically when they say *So this is how you spend your time!* This is quite a different picture of metaphor than the traditional one of a speaker consciously coining a figure of speech to make a rhetorical effect. Metaphorical mappings are an important source for the creation of new words. The human being is a common source domain so that when talking of tools and machines we speak of the *hands* of a clock, *face* of a watch, and *memory* of a computer.

A similar approach may be taken to metonymy so that rather than viewing it as a rhetorical trope, it is characterized as a systematic referential strategy that relies on bodies of knowledge. Speakers select contextually salient associations to guide hearers to the intended referent. Metonymic reference can be divided into several types, including those below, where the metonymic element is underlined:

## Types of metonymy

(50) a. PART FOR WHOLE
They rely on air power not <u>boots</u> on the ground.
b. WHOLE FOR PART
<u>The police</u> are at the door.
c. PRODUCER FOR PRODUCT
He drives a <u>Hyundai</u>.
d. PLACE FOR INSTITUTION
The Government has urged <u>Beijing</u> to acknowledge the hacking of US firms.
e. CAUSE FOR EFFECT
Give me <u>a hand</u> with this cleaning up.
f. EFFECT FOR CAUSE
I can't listen to this terrible <u>bore</u> any longer.

The expression used, for example *boots* in (50a) above, is termed the vehicle and the intended referent, soldiers, the target. The first two referential strategies, PART FOR WHOLE and vice versa, are traditionally called **synecdoche**. Although the examples in (50) represent systematic strategies, any kind of contextually salient association may be used, as in the often cited example of a waiter referring to a customer as *the ham sandwich at table four*. It has been argued that the estimation of contextual salience is influenced by some general principles, including a preference for identifying human agents in descriptions of actions, as in (51):

(51) Why did George Bush invade Iraq?

In this example, an individual, President George Bush, is used to direct reference to the US armed forces, of which he is commander-in-chief. Another proposed principle is preference for the concrete over the abstract, as in (52):

(52) The Minister volunteered to lend her voice to the campaign.

In (52), the concrete noun *voice* is used to refer to the more general notion of support.

Some of the examples above represent lexicalized metonymy, such as *give a hand* and *bore*. Like metaphor, metonymy is a means of adding new lexemes to the lexicon. The lexicon contains many instances of this, for example, things named for their materials such as an *iron* (for clothing), a *glass* (for drinking), and for names of associated people or places, such as *diesel*, *guillotine*, *sandwich* and *bikini*.

**KEY POINTS: Non-literal meaning**

- A traditional view of language distinguishes between literal language, where speakers try to make their meaning clear, and non-literal or figurative language, where special techniques are used to appeal to the senses or emotions.
- Lists of non-literal uses of language, sometimes called tropes, have been established, including metaphor and metonymy amongst many other.
- Cognitive semanticists reject the traditional literal/non-literal distinction and instead view metaphor and metonymy as linguistic reflections of very general cognitive processes.

## EXERCISE 7.4

Find or make up an example for each of the following types of metonymy:

PLACE FOR INSTITUTION

PART FOR WHOLE

PRODUCER FOR PRODUCT

WHOLE FOR PART

EFFECT FOR CAUSE

## 7.6 SUMMARY

This chapter has presented a range of important topics in semantics, which it is hoped gives a flavour of the nature of enquiry in this field. An important section of the chapter was devoted to lexical semantics, exploring the knowledge speakers have about the meaning of individual words in their language and the relationships between them. The relations introduced here include homonymy, polysemy, synonymy, antonymy and hyponymy, each of which describes a semantic relationship tacitly known by speakers and which underpins their use of language.

Moving on to semantics at sentence level, the chapter outlined some of the options a speaker has in deciding how to characterize a situation or event. Lexical aspect allows portrayals of situations as static or dynamic, having a natural end point or not, while grammatical aspect allows the speaker to profile a situation relative to time, to see it as ongoing or completed, and repeated or not. Intimately linked to these, tense systems permit the situating of situations in time relative to the act of utterance and to other points in time. Within the depiction of a situation various semantic roles can be assigned to entities, reflecting choices of verbs to describe the actions and processes.

The discussion outlined some semantic relations between sentences, notably entailment, and reviewed the proposal to use truth to characterize both these relations. Finally we noted the rejection by cognitive semantics of the traditional distinction between literal and non-literal meaning, using metaphor and metonymy as examples. This approach sees these not as stylistic figures or tropes but as examples of more general cognitive processes, exemplified both within and outside language.

WEBSITE: **Semantics**

Now go to the website and assess your knowledge of semantics by completing the self-test questions!

### SUGGESTIONS FOR FURTHER READING

Portner, P. H. (2005). *What Is Meaning? Fundamentals of Formal Semantics*. Oxford: Blackwell. This is an accessible and lively introduction to formal, logic-based semantics.

Saeed, J. I. (2009). *Semantics*, 3rd edn. Oxford: Wiley-Blackwell. This book provides a broad introduction to semantics, including the topics covered in this chapter. It is written for readers new to the field.

Ungerer, F. and Schmid, H-J. (2006). *An Introduction to Cognitive Linguistics*, 2nd edn. London: Longman. This book presents a general survey of cognitive linguistics, including its treatment of semantics, and introduces this approach's account of metaphor and metonymy.

# ANSWERS TO EXERCISES

## Exercise 7.1

In (a), both *a seagull* and *my sandwich* would be used to refer, or in other words be referring expressions.
In (b), *I* refers to the speaker but *a city* is not used to refer, since it denotes any city.
In (c), *no politician* is not used to refer: it helps relate the assertion to the whole class of politicians.
In (d), *a mermaid* is not used to refer and identifies a whole class of entities. In this sentence, the expression *the dugong* is ambiguous. In one reading, it is used to refer to a specific animal and is therefore a referring expression. In the other reading, *the dugong* identifies the whole class and is therefore not being used to refer. In this second reading, the speaker is taken to be making a general statement about all dugongs.
In (e), *a police spokesman* is used to refer; a *one-armed man* is ambiguous. In one reading, the police are looking for a specific individual: in this case, it is a referring expression. In the other reading, the police do not know the fugitive's identity just that he belongs to the class of one-armed men. In this case, it is not being used to refer.

## Exercise 7.2

Part A:

| | |
|---|---|
| *marry* (verb) | synonym: *get hitched* |
| Odd use: | #The minister will say: 'Since it is your intention to get hitched, join your right hands and declare consent.' |
| *tall* (adjective) | synonym: *lanky* |
| Odd use: | #the world's lankiest buildings |
| *decay* (noun) | synonym: *rot* |
| Odd use: | #Our new formula toothpaste helps prevent tooth rot. |
| *food* (noun) | synonym: *nutrients* |
| Odd use: | #Shall we go home and make some nutrients? |
| *limp* (adjective) | synonym: *floppy* |
| Odd use: | #floppy wristed |
| *dead* (adjective) | synonym: *deceased* |
| Odd use: | #There was a deceased badger by the roadside. |

Part B:

The following pairs are binary antonyms since the use of one necessarily involves the negation of the other: *sink–float, same–different, complete–incomplete, succeed–fail.*
The following pairs are gradable antonyms since the use of one necessarily involves the negation of the other, and there are intermediate terms: *high–low, rich–poor, easy–difficult, young–old.*
The following pairs are relational antonyms: *husband–wife, debtor–creditor, teacher–student, lead–follow.*
The following pairs are reverse antonyms: *dress–undress, advance–retreat, enter–exit, freeze–thaw.*

### Exercise 7.3

Part A:

In sentence (a), the subject *the angler* is a typical AGENT, since he is animate, acts deliberately and uses force or energy. Informally, we can say that he controls the action of the sentence. In sentence (b), *the tsunami* is not a typical agent since it is inanimate and does not act deliberately. Some writers use a label NATURAL FORCE for this kind of semantic role. In (c), Anastasia is a typical AGENT. In (d), George is not a typical agent because he does not act deliberately, or in another terminology, with volition. We could call this role a non-volitional AGENT. In (e) she is not a typical agent since the subject does not deliberately cause the activity described by the verb smell but is affected by it. Writers often use the label EXPERIENCER for this kind of semantic role.

Part B:

Remember from our truth-based definition of entailment that when a sentence *A* entails a sentence *B*, then negating the entailment *B* will make the entailing sentence *A* false. Using this as a test, we can see that (1a) does entail (1b), because if the zoo didn't borrow an animal then it couldn't have borrowed a panda. However, (2a) does not entail (2b), because even if Peter and Mary did not marry each other they could still have got married. On this basis, sentences (3a) and (4a) entail (3b) and (4b), respectively, while sentence (5a) does not entail (5b).

### Exercise 7.4

Some sample answers are:

PLACE FOR INSTITUTION:

The White House denies nuclear talks with Iran.

PART FOR WHOLE:

We need some new faces on this committee.

PRODUCER FOR PRODUCT:

Joyce is difficult to read.

WHOLE FOR PART:

America loves a winner.

EFFECT FOR CAUSE:

That looks like death in a cup.

## REFERENCES

Evans, V. and Green, M. (2006). *Cognitive Linguistics: An Introduction*. Edinburgh University Press.

Frege, G. (1980). *Translations from the Philosophical Writings of Gottlob Frege*, ed. P. Geach and M. Black. Oxford: Blackwell.

Grice, P. (1989). *Studies in the Way of Words*. Cambridge, MA: Harvard University Press.

Huddleston, R. D. and Pullum, G. K. (2002). *The Cambridge Grammar of the English Language*. Cambridge University Press.

Lakoff, G. and Johnson, M. (1980). *Metaphors We Live By*. University of Chicago Press.

Rosch, E. (1978). Principles of Categorization. In E. Rosch and B. B. Lloyd (eds.), *Cognition and Categorization*, pp. 27–48. Hillsdale, NJ: Lawrence Erlbaum.

Ungerer, F. and Schmid, H-J. (2006) *An Introduction to Cognitive Linguistics*, 2nd edn. London: Longman.

Vendler, Z. (1957). Verbs and times. *The Philosophical Review*, 66, 143–60.

(1967). *Linguistics in Philosophy*. Ithaca, NY: Cornell University Press.

Wilson, D. and Sperber, D. (2012). *Meaning and Relevance*. Cambridge University Press.

# 8 Pragmatics

LOUISE CUMMINGS

**KEY TERMS**

- constative utterance
- context
- cooperative principle
- deixis
- felicity condition
- implicature
- maxim
- performative utterance
- presupposition
- speech act

**PREVIEW**

This chapter examines how language users employ aspects of context in the production and interpretation of utterances. Context pervades every aspect of language use, from the lexical choices that we make to the way in which we disambiguate linguistic expressions. Its pervasive character is such that it has been shown in recent years to permeate those aspects of meaning that were once thought to be strictly semantic in nature. In fact, the debates which take place at the semantics–pragmatics interface are some of the most contentious in modern linguistics. This chapter begins by delineating the contributions of semantics and pragmatics to this interface. A simple cleavage between these disciplines is neither possible nor desirable, it will be argued. The chapter will then turn to the notion of context. More often than not, context is alluded to, rather than directly examined, in discussions of pragmatics. Context will be characterized along social, physical, linguistic and epistemic aspects in this chapter. Several pragmatic concepts exemplify the influence of context on language meaning. These concepts include deixis, presupposition, speech acts and implicatures. Speech acts and implicatures reflect the influence on the development of pragmatics of the language philosophies of John L. Austin, John Searle and H. Paul Grice. The views of these philosophers of language will be briefly examined. By the end of the chapter, you will have an understanding of the significant contribution of pragmatics to the study of language meaning as well as the key concepts and ideas that have shaped this linguistic discipline.

## 8.1 INTRODUCTION

This chapter will introduce you to a key set of ideas and concepts that has come to define the discipline of pragmatics. Many of these ideas emerged from a dissatisfaction about how far semantics could take us in the study of language meaning. One of the earliest insights to shape the emerging discipline of pragmatics was the idea that linguistic utterances can do more than merely describe states of affairs in the world. Rather, utterances can be used to perform a range of actions such as issuing requests and warnings, undertaking promises and apologies and extending congratulations and threats to others. None of these **speech acts** are possible without permitting a role for language users in an account of meaning. These users must attend to aspects of **context** as they produce utterances and interpret the utterances of others. For example, they must be aware of their social relationship to other conversational participants, the particular setting in which an utterance is produced, the beliefs and knowledge that are presumed to hold between speakers and hearers and of how an utterance relates to other parts of a conversation.

These various dimensions of context permeate the interpretation and expression of linguistic utterances and are the means by which speakers are able to implicate something more than an utterance explicitly states. These so-called **implicatures** are the basis of some of our most creative uses of language, including irony and metaphor. Alongside speech acts and implicatures, you will be introduced to how speakers 'point' to aspects of context through the use of deixis in language. Speakers and hearers must also make inferences about the knowledge they share, and represent this shared knowledge in the form of **presuppositions** of an utterance. By the end of this chapter, you will have an understanding of each of these pragmatic concepts as well as an appreciation of how these concepts contribute to the meaning of utterances. But as a first step, we must consider the relationship of pragmatics to that other linguistic discipline which studies meaning, namely, semantics.

## 8.2 Semantics and pragmatics: a viable distinction?

Before proceeding to examine pragmatic concepts, it is important to emphasize that the interface between semantics and pragmatics is one of the most theoretically contested areas in modern linguistics. The relationship between semantics and pragmatics is typically characterized in terms of a number of distinctions between literal and non-literal meaning, sentence meaning and utterance meaning, and truth-conditional meaning (meaning based on truth conditions) and non-truth-conditional meaning. In the standard characterization, semantics is described as the study of the first component in each of these distinctions, while pragmatics is taken to be the study of the second component:

| ***Semantics*** studies: | ***Pragmatics*** studies: |
|---|---|
| Literal meaning | Non-literal meaning |
| Sentence (propositional) meaning | Utterance (speaker) meaning |
| Truth-conditional meaning | Non-truth-conditional meaning |

These distinctions have the effect of characterizing semantics as the study of a basic level of meaning in the sentence (the **proposition**) to which pragmatics contributes a further component of non-literal or speaker meaning. Most importantly, pragmatics is not portrayed as playing any role in arriving at the proposition of the sentence. Rather, pragmatics merely adds something extra to the level of meaning that is independently specified by semantics. The model of language meaning that is motivating these descriptions can be characterized as follows:

Propositional meaning + speaker meaning = complete utterance meaning

It is now widely accepted by theorists in both semantics and pragmatics that this is a somewhat simplistic characterization of how language meaning works. Two simple examples serve to demonstrate how pragmatic factors play an important role in specifying the proposition that is expressed by a sentence. Consider (1) and (2) below:

(1) I will be there tomorrow.

(2) She parked next to the bank.

To assign referents to the personal pronoun *I*, the adverb *there* and the calendrical term *tomorrow* in (1) above, the listener must know who the speaker is, the location to which the speaker refers and the day on which the utterance has been produced, respectively. These factors are all part of the wider context of utterance, a context that even the semanticist must acknowledge if he or she is to specify the proposition that (1) is expressing. The identification of the referents of these so-called deictic expressions is not the only aspect of propositional meaning that requires the semanticist to step beyond the strict confines of his or her discipline. In order to achieve the disambiguation of the word *bank* in (2) above, the hearer must again look to the wider context to decide if the speaker means a financial institution or the side of a river (of course, the hearer must consider context if he or she is to establish the referent of the pronoun *she* in (2) as well).

What these cases of reference assignment and disambiguation demonstrate is that pragmatic factors intrude into the propositional meaning of a sentence in a very powerful way. These factors are not merely 'added onto' the proposition, as standard characterizations of pragmatics would tend to suggest. Rather, they are integral to determining what proposition is being expressed by any sentence. Pragmatic factors, it thus emerges, go well beyond determining the speech act that is being performed by an utterance (for example, that the speaker of (1) is undertaking a promise) to include an altogether more fundamental role in specifying the propositions expressed by sentences.

To the extent that a hearer must look to context to determine the propositions expressed by (1) and (2) above, we need to say something about this key pragmatic notion. Context will be discussed in the next section.

## EXERCISE 8.1

It is increasingly being recognized by theorists who work at the semantics–pragmatics interface that pragmatic factors play an important role in propositional meaning. For example, pragmatic factors must be acknowledged in order to assign referents to deictic expressions and to achieve the disambiguation of terms within sentences. For each of the following sentences, state if pragmatic factors are used to achieve either reference assignment or disambiguation:

(a) We leave for Paris in the morning.

(b) John missed the ball for the third time.

(c) Stan leapt with great force over the bar.

(d) I present the argument in the next chapter.

(e) Bill worked here for ten years.

(f) After much deliberation, Mary decided she needed another bulb.

(g) Yesterday was a bitterly cold day.

(h) Fran found two bats in the shed.

(i) Jack wondered how he would manage without his old vice.

(j) That claim is unsubstantiated. You need to justify it in the revision.

## 8.3 Context and meaning

Context may be defined as any aspect of the knowledge, physical environment, and social relationships of speakers and hearers that is relevant to the interpretation of an utterance. It was seen in Section 8.2, for example, how a hearer needed to know the date on which an utterance was produced in order to establish the referent of *tomorrow* in *I will be there tomorrow*. This temporal dimension forms part of the physical context of this utterance. Other elements that are part of physical context include the people who are present in a particular situation, the setting in which a conversation takes place, and the artefacts and natural phenomena (e.g. weather) that attend different conversational exchanges. It is an aspect of physical context, for example, that allows a hearer to infer that a speaker who utters *What lovely weather we're having!* in the middle of a snow storm is doing so with considerable ironic intent.

Speakers and hearers must also be aware of features of social context as they construct utterances and interpret the utterances of others. In this way, the decision to use an indirect speech act to make a request (e.g. *Can you open the window?*) rather than a direct speech act (e.g. *Open the window!, I want you to open the window*) bears testament to the fact that in the normal course of events, speakers are both aware of, and concerned to maintain, good social relationships with hearers during conversation. The requirement to observe politeness constraints during conversation and to reflect the social standing of hearers in our choice of linguistic utterance is so pervasive that any speaker who fails to comply with this requirement is judged to have deviant communication skills. This can be seen in the following extract of language which has been produced by an adult with schizophrenia. The extract is taken from Thomas (1997: 41) and has been produced as part of a doctor–patient interview:

(3) Then I left San Francisco and moved to ... where did you get that tie? It looks like it's left over from the 1950s. I like the warm weather in San Diego. Is that a conch shell on your desk? Have you ever gone scuba diving?

This speaker neglects social context when he makes comments about the doctor's tie which are likely to be viewed as impolite. In fact, the somewhat formal nature of a medical interview normally prohibits personal remarks about a participant's attire. Of course, the extract is problematic in a further respect in that it contains a number of irrelevant comments. We will discuss relevance again in Section 8.7 when we come to examine Grice's cooperative principle and maxims. In the meantime, this example illustrates an important application of pragmatics to the study of language and communication disorders (Cummings 2005, 2007, 2009, 2012).

Beyond physical and social dimensions of context, speakers and hearers must also be aware of the beliefs and knowledge of conversational participants. As might be expected, this knowledge includes general facts (e.g. dogs are mammals) and specific facts (e.g. Obama is the US president), but much else besides (knowledge of how human beings behave, knowledge of events in the world, etc.). It is aspects of epistemic context that permit *A* in the exchange below to recover a certain implicature from *B*'s utterance, an implicature to the effect that *B* will not be joining *A* in Rome:

(4) A: Do you want to stay with us in Rome next summer?
B: Sally's mother is having hip replacement surgery.

It is *A*'s background knowledge which is the basis of this particular implicature, specifically his knowledge that hip replacement is major surgery, that people who undergo major surgery require extensive recuperation, that recuperation is made possible through the assistance of others (particularly family members), and that caring for a sick relative precludes foreign travel. This implicature is even more strongly reinforced as the implicature intended by *B* if, in an earlier part of the conversational exchange between *A* and *B*, *B* mentions that his partner Sally is very concerned about her mother's health and that she is visiting her on a daily basis at home. This prior linguistic context sets in place certain conditions (namely, that Sally has family responsibilities which have precedence over holidays) which make it possible for *B* to implicate that he will not be staying with *A* in Rome. Finally, it is an aspect of social context, particularly a concern to maintain amicable social relationships with *A*, which leads *B* to decline *A*'s invitation to Rome indirectly by way of implicature rather than through the use of the more direct, but less polite, form of *No!*.

*A*'s utterance in the above exchange uses several linguistic expressions which may be said to 'point' to aspects of context, namely, the personal pronouns *you* and *us* and the noun phrase *next summer*. These so-called deictic expressions are commonplace in language. They will be examined further in the next section.

**EXERCISE 8.2**

Context pervades every aspect of the production and interpretation of utterances. Although it is not possible to describe context in its entirety, it is possible to identify physical, social, epistemic and linguistic dimensions of this notion. Read the paragraph below. Indicate what Mary may be taken to implicate by way of her response to Sue's question. Then characterize the aspects of physical, social, epistemic and linguistic context that helped you establish the likely implicature of Mary's utterance:

> John had never previously attended one of his chief executive's dinner parties. So it was with some trepidation that he and his wife Mary arrived at the executive's home. At the party, John met an old school friend whom he hadn't seen in twenty years. Mary discussed future holiday plans with Jill, another guest at the party. It was 11 o'clock by the time Sue, the executive's wife, began to serve tea and coffee. With the exception of John everyone had coffee to drink. It was nearly midnight when Sue asked Mary 'Would you like another coffee?'. Mary replied 'Coffee would keep me awake.'

## 8.4 Deixis

The notion of **deixis** in pragmatics captures a range of expressions that 'describe entities within the wider social, linguistic or spatiotemporal context of an utterance' (Cummings 2005: 22). It was seen in Section 8.2 that it was only by examining these different dimensions of context that the referents of deictic terms could be established. In this way, *I* in the utterance *I always leave a tip* has a context-invariant meaning of {speaker of the utterance}. Yet the identification of the actual speaker of this utterance can only be achieved by looking to the context in which this utterance is produced. Deictic expressions belong to several grammatical categories including pronouns (e.g. *I*, *you*), adverbs (e.g. *here*, *there*), **demonstratives** (e.g. *this*, *that*), adjectives (e.g. *next*, *last*) and verbs (e.g. *come*, *bring*). These linguistic forms are variously used in personal, spatial, temporal, social and discourse deixis. Consider the following utterances:

(5) You must stop talking now.

(6) Frank moved here last year.

(7) Sally must behave for Mummy.

(8) I will argue for a related view in the next chapter.

(9) I'm going to church this Sunday.

(10) I'm going to church this way.

(11) I present the case in this chapter.

The pronoun *you* in (5) above exemplifies personal deixis. Although *you* has a context-invariant meaning of {addressee of the utterance}, the identification of that addressee requires us to have knowledge of who the participants are in a conversational exchange. Spatial deixis is evident in utterances (6) and (10) above. In (6), the adverb *here* refers to a location that is proximal to the speaker (a town, city or housing estate, for example), while in (10) the demonstrative noun phrase *this way* refers to a route to the church that is closest to the speaker. In temporal deixis, a speaker refers to a time that is prior to, concurrent with or subsequent to the point of utterance. In (5), for example, the speaker intends that an action should take place at a time concurrent with the speaking of the utterance. In (6), the noun phrase *last year* refers to the year prior to the one in which the utterance is produced. In (9), the demonstrative noun phrase *this Sunday* relates to a 24-hour period of time that is subsequent to the point of utterance.

Social deixis is typically demonstrated using languages which encode social attributes of speakers and hearers in certain lexical items. The *tu/vous* distinction in French and the *du/Sie* distinction in German reflect a personal pronoun system in these languages which varies the use of pronouns in accordance with the formality of the speaking situation and the social standing of the addressee of an utterance. The forms *tu* and *du* indicate an addressee with whom the speaker is familiar, while *vous* and *Sie* reflect an addressee with whom the speaker lacks acquaintance or an addressee whose social standing exceeds that of the speaker (*Wie heißen Sie?*, for example, is the standard, polite way of asking for someone's name in German). Notwithstanding the fact that English does not encode social relationships in its pronoun system (all addressees are referred to by *you*), English can nonetheless indicate social deixis in other ways. In (7) above, the use of third-person noun phrases *Sally* and *Mummy* instead of *you* and *me* indicates the less powerful status of the child in relation to her mother. Utterances of the type used in (7) are often found in child-directed speech. They illustrate an important application of the discipline of pragmatics to child language acquisition (see Chapter 12, this volume).

In discourse deixis, speakers or writers use linguistic expressions to refer to some part of wider (spoken or written) discourse. In (8), the writer in this case is using the noun phrase *next chapter* to refer to the chapter that follows the current one. Sentence connectors can also perform a discourse deixis function. For example, the word *moreover* in *Moreover, the plans were not economical* refers to another attribute of the plans which is mentioned previously and which is also negative in nature. It is important to recognize that one and the same linguistic expression can perform two or more deictic functions. In (9), (10) and (11) above, the demonstrative determiner *this* is serving a temporal deixis function in *this Sunday*, a spatial deixis function in *this way* and a discourse deixis function in *this chapter*.

As well as pointing to context through the use of deixis, speakers can also assume aspects of context in the utterances they produce. These assumptions form part of the presuppositions of an utterance and will be examined in the next section.

**KEY POINTS: Deixis**

- Deictic expressions refer to entities in social, linguistic or spatiotemporal context; listeners must have knowledge of context to identify the intended referent.
- There are five types of deixis: personal, spatial, social, temporal, discourse.
- Languages encode deixis in different ways, e.g. English has no equivalent of the *tu/vous* distinction in French.
- Deictic expressions include pronouns (e.g. *I*), adverbs (e.g. *there*), demonstratives (e.g. *this*), adjectives (e.g. *next*), verbs (e.g. *come*).
- Some expressions perform more than one deictic function, e.g. *this week* and *this way*, where *this* is performing temporal and spatial deixis, respectively.

## EXERCISE 8.3

A range of linguistic expressions can be used to point to entities within the wider context of an utterance. Amongst these expressions are words and phrases that point to people (personal deixis), to social relationships between speakers and hearers (social deixis) or to units of time (temporal deixis). Other expressions make reference to aspects of spoken and written discourse (discourse deixis) or to locations that are either proximal to, or distal from, the speaker (spatial deixis). For each of the utterances below, identify the linguistic expressions that are performing a deictic function. Also, indicate which type of deixis is exemplified by the expressions that you have identified:

(a) I plan to travel to Spain next year.

(b) The last section revealed a lack of understanding of the issues.

(c) Marjorie lives here because the rent is cheap.

(d) Little boys must be well behaved to get ice cream from granny (uttered by granny).

(e) Bring the book to me if you want help with the exercises.

(f) We hope the performance will go ahead this Friday.

(g) If you walk this way, you will get home quicker.

(h) Pupils must attend class to get help from Mr Rolston (uttered by Mr Rolston).

(i) We want to live there for another year.

(j) Take the book back to the library!

## 8.5 Presupposition

Verbal communication between speakers and hearers would be inefficient if certain information could not be assumed in advance of formulating messages and had to be explicitly stated. In general, speakers and hearers are adept at identifying this information and handling it through the use of a pragmatic device called 'presupposition'. Semantic and pragmatic definitions of presupposition abound. Some definitions emphasize that a presupposition is a proposition that is backgrounded or taken for granted. Other definitions state that a presupposition is only appropriate in a particular context if the proposition that is presupposed is part of the mutual knowledge of the speaker and the hearer. Still other definitions require the assumed truth of a presupposition to be a precondition for the felicitous utterance of a sentence. Notwithstanding the different emphases of these definitions, in general a presupposition can be taken to be information that is assumed to be the case, or exists prior to, the making of statements and other utterances.

The following examples capture features from all three definitions of presupposition. If a speaker and hearer are both standing in front of a vandalized bus shelter, the speaker may safely assume that the hearer accepts the truth of the proposition {someone vandalized the bus shelter}. If the speaker then goes on to utter *It was the gang from Eastwood that vandalized the shelter*, he or she may be said to do so appropriately or felicitously in that particular context (the truth of the proposition {someone vandalized the bus shelter} can be 'taken for granted'). However, if the truth of the proposition presupposed by an utterance is in any way contentious, or is not likely to be accepted by the hearer, then the speaker who produces an utterance that presupposes that proposition may be said to do so inappropriately. A classic example from the literature in pragmatics is *Have you stopped beating your wife?*. This question presupposes that the hearer has been beating his wife. If this presupposition is not accepted by the hearer, it cannot be said to be part of the mutual knowledge of the speaker and hearer.

A range of lexical items and linguistic constructions can trigger presuppositions. These so-called 'presupposition triggers' are demonstrated by the following utterances:

(12) The castle on the hill is in need of restoration.

(13) It was the caretaker who lost the keys.

(14) When did you begin exercising?

(15) She regretted failing her exams.

(16) The scientist managed to isolate the chemical compound.

(17) Bill was as drunk as Joe.

(18) Sally failed her driving test again.

(19) After he escaped from prison, the convict went into hiding.

(20) Dettori is a better jockey than Fallon.

(21) If I were a millionaire, I would own several mansions.

In (12) above, the definite noun phrase *the castle on the hill* triggers a presupposition of existence, namely, that there exists a castle on the hill. The cleft construction *It was...* in (13) triggers a presupposition that someone lost the keys. The change-of-state verb *begin* in (14) presupposes that there was a time when the hearer did not exercise. In (15), the factive verb *regret* triggers a fact as its presupposition, the fact that she failed her exams. The implicative verb *manage* in (16) presupposes that the scientist tried to isolate the chemical compound. In (17), the use of a comparison of equality (*as* + adjective + *as*) triggers the presupposition that Joe was drunk. The iterative expression *again* in (18) triggers the presupposition that Sally failed her driving test before. In (19), the temporal clause *After he escaped* ... gives rise to the presupposition that the convict escaped from prison. The comparative *is a better jockey than* in (20) triggers the presupposition that Dettori is a jockey and Fallon is a jockey. Finally, the counterfactual conditional *If I were a millionaire* ... in (21) presupposes that the speaker is not a millionaire.

Two features of presupposition are noteworthy: constancy (survival) under negation and defeasibility or cancellability. The first of these features can be used to distinguish the presuppositions of an utterance from the other inferences that are generated by an utterance. For example, the utterance *The workers managed to repair the wall* presupposes that the workers *tried* to repair the wall, but entails that the workers *repaired* the wall. This is because the presupposition alone survives the negation of the original utterance – *The workers didn't manage to repair the wall* still presupposes that the workers *tried* to repair the wall. Unlike the presupposition, the entailment follows the truth-value of the original utterance – {the workers repaired the wall} is true when the utterance *The workers managed to repair the wall* is true, and is false when this utterance is false.

Presuppositions can be defeated or cancelled if (a) they are inconsistent with background knowledge, (b) they are inconsistent with the implicatures of an utterance or (c) they occur in certain linguistic contexts (Marmaridou 2010). As an example of (a), the temporal clause in *John died before he completed the project* would normally trigger the presupposition that John *completed* the project. However, our world knowledge – namely, that one cannot complete something if one is dead – blocks the generation of this particular presupposition. In demonstration of (b), the implicature associated with the utterance *If Fred has stolen the money, his mother will be angry that he has done so* (namely, that Fred may not have stolen the money) blocks the presupposition that Fred *has stolen* the money which is normally triggered by the factive adjective *angry*. As an example of (c), the factive verb *know* in *The teacher knows/did not know that the pupils returned late* presupposes that the pupils *returned* late. However, in a different linguistic context, one in which the verb is used in the first-person subject (*I do not know that the pupils returned late*), the presupposition no longer holds.

As well as presupposing aspects of meaning, linguistic utterances can also perform a range of meanings. The idea that speakers can perform different meanings through the utterances they use is the basis of speech act theory, which will be examined in the next section.

**KEY POINTS: Presupposition**

- Proposition that is in the background of an utterance, or that is taken for granted or assumed in the saying of an utterance; part of speaker and hearer mutual knowledge.
- Certain lexical items and linguistic constructions can 'trigger' presuppositions.
- Presupposition triggers include definite noun phrases; cleft constructions; change-of-state/factive/implicative verbs; comparisons of equality; iterative expressions; temporal clauses; comparatives; counterfactual conditionals.
- Two features of presupposition: constancy (survival) under negation; defeasibility or cancellability.

## EXERCISE 8.4

A number of words and grammatical constructions in language act as presupposition triggers. For each utterance below, (i) state the presupposition of the utterance, (ii) identify the word or construction that triggers the presupposition in question and (iii) provide a linguistic characterization of the trigger (e.g. regret is a factive verb):

(a) She forgot to submit her essay.

(b) The lake beside the garden always attracted visitors.

(c) Jack is as sexist as Tom.

(d) Are you continuing to smoke?

(e) Bill Clinton was a better president than George Bush.

(f) After he left the office, Tom headed to the pub with his friends.

(g) It was the teenager who smashed the window.

(h) He realized that his situation was hopeless.

(i) If I were prime minister, I would abolish child poverty.

(j) The teacher explained the maths exercises again.

## 8.6 Speech act theory

Until the middle of the twentieth century, the dominant semantic view of language meaning was judged to be the only type of meaning that was philosophically interesting and worthy of consideration. This view held that the meaning of the sentences in a language consists in the conditions under which these sentences are true. In fact, to know what any sentence means is just to know its truth conditions. This view of language meaning assumed that all sentences are declarative in nature and describe states of affairs in the world. In the 1940s and 1950s, a group of ordinary language philosophers at Oxford University, which included John L. Austin, began to challenge the assumptions which had motivated the dominant semantic conception of meaning. These philosophers believed that the idea that sentences are only used to describe states of affairs in the world and that the meaning of a sentence consists in its truth conditions – Austin called this idea the 'descriptive fallacy' – served to overshadow the large range of other actions that speakers intend to undertake by way of producing utterances.

To capture the fundamental distinction between sentences which report or describe states of affairs and sentences which perform actions, Austin introduced the terms '**constative utterance**' and '**performative utterance**'. Only constative utterances described states of affairs in the world and were true or false. Performative utterances did not report or describe states of affairs and, as such, were not true or false. Rather, these utterances performed actions. This is how Austin ([1962] 1975: 5) captures performative utterances in his now classic book *How to Do Things with Words*. These utterances:

A. do not 'describe' or 'report' or constate anything at all, are not 'true' or 'false'; and
B. the uttering of the sentence is, or is a part of, the doing of an action, which again would not normally be described as, or as 'just', saying something.

Austin's distinction between constative and performative utterances can be demonstrated by the following example. The utterance *I name this ship the Queen Elizabeth II* is a performative utterance, the uttering of which constitutes the act of naming. The act of naming is itself not true or false. Rather, it can be performed felicitously or infelicitously in accordance with whether or not certain conditions are observed (these so-called **felicity conditions** specify, for example, who must say and do what and in what circumstances and the thoughts, feelings and intentions that must be present in all parties). However, the result of the act of naming having been performed – that there is a ship called the Queen Elizabeth II – is something which can be true or false (and in this case, it is true).

Later in *How to Do Things with Words*, Austin takes a step which leads to the abandonment of the distinction between constative and performative utterances which he initially proposed. Having first used the notion of a performative utterance to challenge ideal language philosophy (a formal approach to the study of natural language that employs logical and mathematical languages), Austin then goes on to argue that there is no way in which to distinguish constative and performative utterances, and that all utterances are performative in the sense that he intends (Wharton 2010a). To the extent that all utterances are performative, Austin argues that in speaking we simultaneously perform locutionary, illocutionary and, on occasion, perlocutionary acts. The first of these acts is closest to the traditional, semantic notion of meaning. Austin ([1962 ] 1975: 109) states that a **locutionary act** 'is roughly equivalent to uttering a certain sentence with a certain sense and reference, which again is roughly equivalent to "meaning" in the traditional sense'. For example, in the utterance in (22) below:

(22) The river has burst its banks.

the locutionary act consists in a description of a state of affairs in which there exists a river which has burst its banks. At the level of the locutionary act, the speaker is using the words in this utterance to refer to the river and its banks and to describe how the latter have been compromised. However, in performing a locutionary act, Austin ([1962] 1975: 109) argues that we 'also perform illocutionary acts such as informing, ordering, warning, undertaking, etc., i.e. utterances which have a certain (conventional) force'. One can easily imagine a situation, for example, in which an emergency worker might produce the above utterance with a view to warning local residents of the impending danger posed by the river. Certainly, the **illocutionary act** of a warning cannot be achieved if the words in the above utterance lack 'a certain sense and reference'. Yet the sense and reference of these words do not capture the particular type of interactional move that the speaker intends to contribute by way of producing this utterance.

Finally, we may also on occasion, according to Austin ([1962] 1975: 109), 'perform perlocutionary acts: what we bring about or achieve *by* saying something, such as convincing, persuading, deterring' (italics in original). If the emergency worker manages to persuade local residents to evacuate their homes by way of producing the above utterance, then his utterance has additionally performed a **perlocutionary act**. Of course, one can readily imagine how the emergency worker may manage to warn residents through the use of the above utterance without thereby persuading them to leave their homes, i.e. perform an illocutionary act in the absence of a perlocutionary act.

John Searle developed and revised many of Austin's ideas following Austin's death in 1960. Indeed, it was through Austin's tutelage of Searle at Oxford that the seeds of Searle's (1969) book *Speech Acts* were first sown. Searle went further than Austin not only in developing a general framework for a theory of speech acts, but also in achieving a more detailed specification of the structures of speech acts (Smith 2003: 9). Felicity conditions were further distinguished according to conditions on the performance of a speech act and conditions on the satisfaction of a speech act. Searle (1969: 63) discussed conditions on the performance of speech acts in terms of preparatory, propositional content, sincerity and essential rules. To the extent that a speaker promises to deliver the groceries, the hearer must want the groceries to be delivered, the speaker must believe this to be the case, and both speaker and hearer must believe that the speaker would not otherwise deliver the groceries (so-called 'preparatory rules' on the performance of a promise).

Additionally, the speaker's utterance *I promise to deliver the groceries* must predicate the right sort of act on the part of the speaker (a 'propositional content rule' of the speech act of promising). The speaker must also entertain a sincere intention to deliver the groceries (a felicity condition called the 'sincerity rule'). Finally, the speaker's utterance must count as an undertaking to perform the action being promised (an 'essential rule' on the performance of a promise). Searle (1979: 45–8) also describes how by exploiting shared knowledge of these rules, speakers can produce **indirect speech acts**. For example, a preparatory condition on the performance of directives (that the hearer is able to undertake the action being requested, for example) can be used to request that the hearer pass the salt by way of asking *Can you pass the salt?*. The hearer knows that the speaker knows that he can pass the salt. Accordingly, the hearer concludes that this is not a question about his ability to pass the salt, but is instead a request to do so.

Searle (1979) also devised a revised taxonomy of illocutionary acts which included assertives, directives, commissives, expressives and declarations. These acts differed according to their illocutionary point, their direction of fit with the world and their expressed psychological state. The direction of fit of an utterance describes if an utterance aims to match the world (word-to-world) or to have the world match it (world-to-word). The class of assertives (word-to-world) represents something as being the case and includes statements. Directives (world-to-word) get the audience to do something and include commands and requests. Commissives (world-to-word), such as promising, commit the speaker to doing something. Expressives (no direction of fit) express a psychological state and include congratulations, apologies and condolences. Declarations such as appointing, baptizing and marrying aim to make something the case. Declarations have a dual direction of fit, because they not only bring something about (world-to-word) but they are also used to represent what they have brought about (word-to-world).

The notable contribution of Austin and Searle to the study of language meaning was matched only by the work of another philosopher of language, H. Paul Grice. Grice's contribution to a theory of meaning will be examined in the next section.

**KEY POINTS: Speech act theory**

- Austin challenged the dominant semantic view of meaning in which sentences in a language are only used to report or describe states of affairs in the world.
- Austin introduced a distinction between constative and performative utterances; only the former utterances report or describe states of affairs.
- Later in *How to Do Things with Words*, Austin abandoned this distinction: all utterances are performative in the sense he intended.
- To the extent all utterances are performative, Austin argued that we perform locutionary, illocutionary and perlocutionary acts when speaking.
- Searle developed and revised Austin's ideas in his book *Speech Acts.*
- Searle stated conditions on the performance of speech acts in terms of preparatory, propositional content, sincerity and essential rules; speakers can perform indirect speech acts by exploiting shared knowledge of rules.
- Searle devised a revised taxonomy of illocutionary acts: assertives, directives, commissives, expressives and declarations.

## EXERCISE 8.5

The work of Austin and Searle has been fundamental to the study of pragmatics. These philosophers of language have contributed ideas such as performative utterances, felicity conditions and indirect speech acts to this field of linguistics. Using your knowledge of the work of these philosophers, indicate if the utterances in (A) qualify as examples of Austin's constative or performative utterances. Give one felicity condition for each of the utterances in (B). State if the utterances in (C) are direct or indirect speech acts.

Part A. Constative and performative utterances

(a) I will be on time tomorrow.

(b) I bet you £20 that Quantitative Easing won't even finish the race!

(c) The girl threw a coin into the well.

(d) The field yielded a bumper crop.

(e) I apologise for that remark.

Part B. Felicity conditions

(a) I pronounce you man and wife.

(b) I promise to complete the painting next week.

(c) You are under arrest.

(d) I baptise this child John Smith.

(e) I name this ship the Queen Elizabeth II.

Part C. Direct and indirect speech acts

(a) Can you tell me the time?

(b) It's very warm in here.

(c) Open the door!

(d) I want you to leave now.

(e) That cake looks very appetising.

## 8.7 Grice on meaning

The views of another philosopher of language, Herbert Paul (H.P.) Grice, have had a profound influence on the development of modern pragmatics. Grice's views were first set out in his 1957 paper entitled 'Meaning', and were further developed in Grice (1968, 1969, 1975). (These latter publications contain revised forms of the William James Lectures, which Grice delivered at Harvard University in 1967.) It was in his paper 'Meaning' that Grice attempted to characterize the notion of non-natural meaning (meaning$_{NN}$) that was to be integral to his theories of meaning and conversation. For Grice (1957: 385), 'A meant$_{NN}$ something by X' is equivalent to saying:

> A intended the utterance of X to produce some effect in an audience by means of the recognition of this intention.

The expression and recognition of communicative intentions were for the first time to play a key role in defining meaning. To the extent that the meaning of words was to be construed in terms of the intentions of those who utter them, human verbal communication could no longer be viewed as simply the coding and decoding of utterances. Rather, it was an inferential activity that had the mutual exchange and recognition of intentions at its heart. Grice believed that human beings were essentially rational in their interactions with each other and that the processes by means of which communicative intentions were established should embody certain rational expectations. It was in the second of his William James Lectures that Grice set out what these expectations should be in the form of his **cooperative principle** and **maxims**. This is how Grice captures the cooperative principle in that lecture (reprinted in Grice 1989: 26):

> Our talk exchanges do not normally consist of a succession of disconnected remarks, and would not be rational if they did. They are characteristically, to some degree at least, cooperative efforts; and each participant recognizes in them, to some extent, a common purpose or set of purposes, or at least a mutually accepted direction ... We might then formulate a rough general principle which participants will be expected (ceteris paribus) to observe, namely: Make your conversational contribution such as is required, at the stage at which it occurs, by the accepted purpose or direction of the talk exchange in which you are engaged. One might label this the Cooperative Principle.

By itself, the cooperative principle does not stipulate exactly what constitutes a 'cooperative' conversational contribution. This principle was fleshed out in the same lecture in terms of four maxims of quality, quantity, relation and manner, which Grice captured as follows (reprinted in Grice (1989: 26–7)):

> The category of Quantity relates to the quantity of information to be provided, and under it fall the following maxims:
>
> 1. Make your contribution as informative as is required (for the current purposes of the exchange).
> 2. Do not make your contribution more informative than is required...
>
> Under the category of Quality falls a supermaxim – 'Try to make your contribution one that is true' – and two more specific maxims:
>
> 1. Do not say what you believe to be false.
> 2. Do not say that for which you lack adequate evidence.
>
> Under the category of Relation I place a single maxim, namely, 'Be relevant.' ...
>
> Finally, under the category of Manner... I include the supermaxim – 'Be perspicuous' – and various maxims such as:
>
> 1. Avoid obscurity of expression.
> 2. Avoid ambiguity.
> 3. Be brief (avoid unnecessary prolixity).
> 4. Be orderly.

The combined operation of the cooperative principle and maxims is the means by which speakers may be taken to implicate meanings beyond that expressed by the words used in an utterance. This can be demonstrated by returning to example (4) discussed in Section 8.3, which is repeated below:

(4) A: Do you want to stay with us in Rome next summer?
B: Sally's mother is having hip replacement surgery.

B's response to A's question appears to violate two of Grice's maxims. It appears not to satisfy the maxim of quantity in that it is insufficiently informative to address A's question. Furthermore, it fails to satisfy the maxim of relation in that information about hip replacement surgery appears not to relate to a question about staying in Rome. Notwithstanding these apparent violations of the maxims, *A* still assumes that *B* is observing the cooperative principle. *A* uses this assumption of cooperation as the starting point in an inferential process that ends in the recovery of *B*'s likely implicature, namely, that *B* will not be taking up *A*'s invitation to stay with him in Rome next summer. Specifically, by reasoning that *B* has family commitments which have precedence over foreign travel, commitments which prevent *B* from accepting *A*'s invitation, *A* is able to interpret *B*'s utterance as a rational, cooperative contribution to the conversational exchange. In doing so, *A* interprets *B*'s apparent violations of the maxims, not as an aberration of rational behaviour, but as a means of directing *A* to a level of implied meaning beyond that which *B* has directly stated.

In the example above, *B*'s implicature is generated by the *apparent* violation of maxims (*A* presumes that *B* is observing the cooperative principle and maxims). However, Grice identified four ways in which speakers may fail to fulfil the maxims (Wharton 2010b). Speakers may violate a maxim covertly, such as the maxim of quality when they are lying. They may opt out of the cooperative principle and maxims as when a politician responds *No comment* to waiting journalists. Speakers may experience a clash of maxims, and have to suspend one maxim in an effort to fulfil another maxim. Consider the following exchange:

(23) A: Has the postman called yet?
B: I heard the dog barking a few minutes ago.

*B*'s response may be taken to violate the maxim of quantity, as it falls short of providing *A* with the information that he or she requires. However, for *B* to furnish *A* with that information would require that *B* say something for which he or she lacks adequate evidence (a violation of the quality maxim). In this particular clash, the quality maxim wins out over the quantity maxim with the speaker choosing to produce an under-informative utterance rather than an utterance which may be false.

The fourth way in which a speaker may fail to fulfil the maxims involves an overt (as opposed to apparent) violation of one of the maxims. Overt violations of maxims are a particularly important source of implicatures, as they are the basis of irony, metaphor, hyperbole and understatement in language. For example, if Sue and Fran both know that Jack is a pessimistic, depressed individual and Sue utters *Jack is such a positive human being!*, Sue may be taken to implicate a meaning which is the exact opposite of that expressed by her utterance (i.e. Jack is anything but a positive human being). The irony of Sue's utterance is made possible by her overt violation of the quality maxim. Humorous effects are often achieved by the overt violation of maxims. Attardo (2010) describes how relevant information can be withheld in order to produce a surprising punch line, as in the joke in which Holmes wakes Watson and asks what he can observe. Watson notes the position of the stars, the clouds in the night sky, and similar details. Holmes replies 'No, Watson, someone stole our tent.'

Grice distinguished several types of implicature. He called implicatures that depend upon a particular context **particularized conversational implicatures**. Returning to the 'hip replacement' exchange between *A* and *B*, it is easy to imagine how a slightly different context – one in which *A* knows that *B* dislikes his mother-in-law and also knows that she will be staying with *B* for a period of recuperation following surgery – can generate a quite different implicature. In that case, *B* may be taken to implicate that he *will* stay with *A* in Rome next summer. **Generalized conversational implicatures** require no special context for their generation. In the utterance *The woman helped a child across the road*, there is an implicature that the child, which the woman helped, was not her own. This implicature is not the result of a particular context, but stems from the use of the indefinite article *a*. According to Gazdar (1979), the referent of a noun that is modified by the indefinite article *a* is not closely associated with any person who is contextually identifiable.

**Scalar implicature** is a particular type of generalized conversational implicature that is generated by a set of terms which differ in informational strength. One such set of terms is <*all, most, many, some*> in which *all* is the semantically strongest term and *some* the semantically weakest term. A speaker may be taken to negate any term that is semantically stronger than the term used. So the utterance *Mike bought some of the books for the module* generates the scalar implicature that Mike did not buy all/most/many of the books for the module. Finally, the category of **conventional implicatures** captures those meanings that are attached by convention to particular lexical items. For example, *but* in the utterance *Mary got pregnant but John was pleased* generates the implicature that it was not expected that John would be pleased. In the utterance *Even Sam passed the pragmatics exam*, the word *even* carries a conventional implicature to the effect that it was not expected that Sam would pass the exam.

Implicatures exhibit several properties including cancellability (defeasibility), non-detachability, calculability and non-conventionality. In the exchange below, the first clause in *B*'s response generates the implicature that *B* won't be going to Lottie's birthday party. However, this implicature is immediately cancelled by the second clause without the appearance of anomaly:

(24) A: Are you going to Lottie's birthday party?
B: I have to submit an essay tomorrow, but I'll drop by later on.

Non-detachability describes the fact that linguistic expressions with the same semantic content will generate the same implicatures. Implicatures cannot be detached from an utterance simply by replacing expressions within the utterance by their synonyms. The utterance *Freddie almost won the race* carries the implicature that Freddie did not quite win the race. But so, too, does the utterance *Freddie nearly won the race*. The property of calculability describes the fact that it must be possible to derive the implicature of an utterance using the cooperative principle and maxims. The implicature of the first part of *B*'s response to *A*'s question in (24) – that *B* will not be going to Lottie's birthday party – is derivable from *A*'s assumption that *B* is observing the cooperative principle along with the apparent violation of the maxim of relation. The non-conventionality of implicatures captures the fact that implicatures are not coded in 'what is said' by an utterance; rather, they are generated by the saying of an utterance. For example, the implicature that *B* will not be going to Lottie's birthday party is not part of what is said in *B*'s utterance, even though it is generated by the saying of that utterance.

**KEY POINTS: Grice on meaning**

- Grice advanced the notion of non-natural meaning, in which communicative intentions were to play a key role for the first time in defining meaning.
- Grice captured rational expectations between speakers and hearers within his cooperative principle and maxims.
- Cooperative principle and maxims are the means by which speakers may be taken to implicate something beyond what is said.

- Speakers can (a) violate a maxim covertly, (b) opt out of the cooperative principle and maxims, (c) experience a clash of maxims, (d) violate a maxim overtly.
- Grice recognized different types of implicatures: particularised conversational implicatures; generalised conversational implicatures (GCI); scalar implicatures (a type of GCI); conventional implicatures.
- Implicatures exhibit several properties: cancellability (defeasibility); non-detachability; calculability; non-conventionality.

## EXERCISE 8.6

Grice's views on meaning and conversation have been particularly significant in the development of modern pragmatics. His ideas about the expectations that guide rational cooperative behaviour are given shape in his cooperative principle and maxims. Grice also characterized different types of implicatures (e.g. particularized and generalized conversational implicatures). Using your knowledge of Grice's views, state which maxims are being flouted, exploited or violated by the speakers and writers of the utterances in (A). Identify the types of implicatures generated by the utterances in (B).

Part A. Maxims of conversation

(a) A: Did you bring wine and beer? B: I brought beer.

(b) (Written instructions for the assembly of a table) Screw panels A and B together. Before doing so, attach three hinges to panel A.

(c) (Verbal instructions to gardener) I want you to prune the roses and trim the back hedge. That rose bush was given to me last year by my uncle. He is a keen horticulturalist and he judges entries in the Flowers in Bloom competition in town. He hopes to go to Spain this year to see some new varieties of hydrangea. Please also add fertilizer to this bed of pansies.

(d) (Uttered in presence of speaker's child) We will say this toy is from S-A-N-T-A.

(e) (Uttered in the middle of a thunder storm) This really is a glorious day!

Part B. Types of implicature

(a) The teacher marked some of the exam scripts. Implicature: the teacher did not mark all the exam scripts.

(b) Even Joseph passed the driving test. Implicature: it was not expected that Joseph would pass the driving test.

(c) A: Would you like more cake? B: I'm watching my calories this week. Implicature: I would not like more cake.

(d) The woman was overweight but healthy. Implicature: it was not expected that the woman would be healthy.

(e) Bill met a woman in the restaurant. Implicature: the woman was not Bill's wife, mother, etc.

WEBSITE: **Group exercise**

Visit the website and, in a small group, examine the data from a child with pragmatic disorder. Discuss the pragmatic errors committed by this child. Then answer the questions based on the data.

## 8.8 SUMMARY

This chapter has presented an overview of the main ideas and concepts that have shaped the field of pragmatics. Among linguistic disciplines, pragmatics is a relative newcomer. Its emergence has been the result of dissatisfaction with a formerly dominant, semantic account of language meaning. According to this account, the meaning of the sentences (largely declaratives) in a language is based on the conditions in the world that make those sentences true (truth conditions). This semantic view of meaning overlooked the many ways in which utterances can be used to do things beyond merely report or describe states of affairs in the world. By the middle of the twentieth century, this approach to meaning was beginning to be challenged by a group of ordinary language philosophers. The new approach to meaning proposed by these philosophers took the form of the speech act theories of John Austin and John Searle, and the radical views on meaning and conversation of H. Paul Grice. This pragmatic revolution in the philosophy of language is the basis of many of the concepts that are now included as standard in pragmatics.

As well as examining the substantial contributions of Austin, Searle and Grice to pragmatics through a discussion of speech acts and implicatures, this chapter has addressed a number of other issues and concepts in pragmatics. The relationship of pragmatics to semantics continues to challenge theorists who are working on the semantics–pragmatics interface. It was described how pragmatic factors have increasingly been found to intrude into the propositional content of sentences, a situation that has forced semanticists to revise their views of meaning. The notion of context pervades every aspect of the production and interpretation of utterances, and yet it continues to evade satisfactory explanation. Several aspects of context were examined in this chapter. Finally, the chapter also described the roles of deixis and presupposition in language, two pragmatic concepts which are intimately connected to the wider contexts in which utterances are used.

WEBSITE: **Pragmatics**

Now go to the website and assess your knowledge of pragmatics by completing the self-test questions!

## SUGGESTIONS FOR FURTHER READING:

Cummings, L. (ed.) (2010). *The Routledge Pragmatics Encyclopedia*. London and New York: Routledge. This volume contains short, accessible entries on the pragmatic concepts examined in this chapter: context, deixis, implicature, presupposition, semantics-pragmatics interface and speech act theory.

Huang, Y. (2007). *Pragmatics*. Oxford University Press. This book will give you a more detailed introduction to implicature (chapter 2), presupposition (chapter 3), speech acts (4) and deixis (chapter 5). It also examines the relationship of pragmatics to semantics.

Grundy, P. (2008). *Doing Pragmatics*, 3rd edn. London: Hodder Education. This book examines deixis (chapter 2), presupposition (chapter 3), speech acts (chapter 4) and implicit meaning (chapter 5). The discussion is supported by examples based on real data and there are exercises that you can undertake.

# ANSWERS TO EXERCISES

### Exercise 8.1

(a) Reference assignment – listener must establish referent of pronoun 'we'
(b) Disambiguation – listener must resolve ambiguity of 'ball' (dance event vs. spherical object) and 'missed' (failed to attend vs. failed to catch or kick)
(c) Disambiguation – listener must resolve ambiguity of 'bar' (metal bar vs. bar in public house)
(d) Reference assignment – listener must establish referents of pronoun 'I' and adjective 'next'
(e) Reference assignment – listener must establish referent of adverb 'here'
(f) Disambiguation – listener must resolve ambiguity of 'bulb' (light bulb vs. bulb for planting)
(g) Reference assignment – listener must establish referent of the calendrical term 'yesterday'
(h) Disambiguation – listener must resolve ambiguity of 'bats' (flying mammal vs. racquet used in sport)
(i) Reference assignment and disambiguation – listener must establish referent of pronoun 'he' and resolve ambiguity of 'vice' (moral flaw vs. tool)
(j) Reference assignment – listener must establish referents of demonstrative 'that', pronoun 'you' and pronoun 'it'

### Exercise 8.2

It is most likely that Mary is attempting to implicate that she does not wish to have more coffee. This implicature is supported by the fact that it is nearly midnight (*physical* context) when Sue offers Mary more coffee. While many people can drink coffee late in the evening without being kept awake, Sue will know that coffee contains caffeine, that caffeine is a stimulant and that the ingestion of a stimulant can prevent some people from sleeping (*epistemic* context). Mary and Sue do not have a pre-existing friendship, so the relationship between them is characterized by social distance (*social* context). Also, the setting of a dinner party at the chief executive's home (*physical* context) is likely to be quite formal in nature (*social* context). The combination of these contextual factors is the reason why when Sue asks Mary if she would like more coffee (*linguistic* context), Mary decides to decline Sue's offer indirectly by way of implicature rather than through the use of the more direct, but less polite, response of saying 'No!'.

### Exercise 8.3

(a) I (person deixis); *next* year (temporal deixis)
(b) *last* section (discourse deixis)
(c) here (spatial deixis)
(d) 'little boys' and 'granny' used instead of 'you' and 'me' (social deixis)
(e) bring (spatial deixis); me (person deixis); you (person deixis)
(f) we (person deixis); *this* Friday (temporal deixis)
(g) you (person deixis); *this* way (spatial deixis)
(h) 'pupils' and 'Mr Rolston' used instead of 'you' and 'me' (social deixis)

(i) we (person deixis); there (spatial deixis)
(j) take (spatial deixis)

### Exercise 8.4

(a) She should have submitted her essay. 'forgot' (implicative verb)
(b) There is a lake beside the garden. 'The lake beside the garden' (definite description)
(c) Tom is sexist. 'as sexist as' (comparison of equality)
(d) The addressee has smoked in the past. 'continuing' (change-of-state verb)
(e) Bill Clinton was a president and George Bush was a president. 'was a better president than' (comparative)
(f) Tom left the office. 'After he left the office' (temporal clause)
(g) Someone smashed the window. 'It was' (cleft construction)
(h) His situation was hopeless. 'realized' (factive verb)
(i) The speaker is not prime minister. 'If I were...' (counterfactual conditional)
(j) The teacher explained the maths exercises before. 'again' (iterative)

### Exercise 8.5

Part A. Constative and performative utterances
(a) performative
(b) performative
(c) constative
(d) constative
(e) performative

Part B. Felicity conditions
(a) speaker must be someone who has the legal or religious authority to conduct the ceremony of marriage (e.g. vicar)
(b) speaker must intend to complete the painting next week
(c) speaker must be an officer of the law
(d) speaker must have the religious authority to conduct the ceremony of baptism
(e) speaker must smash bottle of champagne against the side of a ship

Part C. Direct and indirect speech acts
(a) indirect
(b) indirect
(c) direct
(d) direct
(e) indirect

### Exercise 8.6

Part A. Maxims of conversation
(a) quantity
(b) manner
(c) relation, quantity
(d) manner
(e) quality

Part B. Types of implicature
(a) scalar implicature
(b) conventional implicature

(c) particularized conversational implicature
(d) conventional implicature
(e) generalized conversational implicature

## REFERENCES

Attardo, S. (2010). Humour. In L. Cummings (ed.), *The Routledge Pragmatics Encyclopedia*, pp. 199–201. London and New York: Routledge.

Austin, J. L. ([1962] 1975). *How to Do Things with Words*. Oxford University Press.

Cummings, L. (2005). *Pragmatics: A Multidisciplinary Perspective*. Edinburgh University Press.

(2007). Pragmatics and adult language disorders: Past achievements and future directions. *Seminars in Speech and Language*, 28, 98–112.

(2009). *Clinical Pragmatics*. Cambridge University Press.

(ed.) (2010). *The Routledge Pragmatics Encyclopedia*. London and New York: Routledge.

(2012). Pragmatic disorders. In H.-J. Schmid (ed.), *Cognitive Pragmatics* (Handbooks of Pragmatics, vol. 4), pp. 291–315. Berlin and Boston: Walter de Gruyter.

Gazdar, G. (1979). *Pragmatics: Implicature, Presupposition, and Logical Form*. London: Academic Press.

Grice, H. P. (1957). Meaning. *Philosophical Review*, 66, 377–88.

(1968). Utterer's meaning, sentence meaning and word meaning. *Foundations of Language*, 4, 225–42.

(1969). Utterer's meaning and intentions. *Philosophical Review*, 78, 147–77.

(1975). Logic and conversation. In P. Cole and J. Morgan (eds.), *Syntax and Semantics 3: Speech Acts*, pp. 41–58. New York: Academic Press.

(1989). *Studies in the Way of Words*. Cambridge, MA: Harvard University Press.

Marmaridou, S. (2010). Presupposition. In L. Cummings (ed.), *The Routledge Pragmatics Encyclopedia*, pp. 349–53. London and New York: Routledge.

Searle, J. R (1969). *Speech Acts: An Essay in the Philosophy of Language*. Cambridge University Press.

(1979). *Expression and Meaning: Studies in the Theory of Speech Acts*. New York: Cambridge University Press.

Smith, B. (2003). John Searle: From speech acts to social reality. In B. Smith (ed.), *John Searle*, pp. 1–33. New York: Cambridge University Press.

Thomas, P. (1997). What can linguistics tell us about thought disorder. In J. France and N. Muir (eds.), *Communication and the Mentally Ill Patient: Developmental and Linguistic Approaches to Schizophrenia*, pp. 30–42. London: Jessica Kingsley Publishers.

Wharton, T. (2010a). Speech act theory. In L. Cummings (ed.), *The Routledge Pragmatics Encyclopedia*, pp. 452–6. London and New York: Routledge.

(2010b). Maxims of conversation. In L. Cummings (ed.), *The Routledge Pragmatics Encyclopedia*, pp. 256–9. London and New York: Routledge.

# 9 Discourse analysis

CARMEN ROSA CALDAS-COULTHARD

**KEY TERMS**

- communication
- discourse/s
- discourse analysis
- exchange
- exchange structure
- genre
- speech role
- social practices
- social semiotics
- text/s

**PREVIEW**

In the last four decades, the focus of linguistic studies has changed from the description of formal properties of language as a code to the description of how people communicate through semiotic systems. This chapter will introduce some of the most important developments in language studies that contributed to a new approach to the analysis of interaction called discourse analysis. Key notions about communication will be presented so that the concepts of text, genre and discourse can be discussed. Since all discourse is multimodal, in other words, we communicate our meanings through different semiotic modes, some of the differences between these modes will be addressed, especially between the oral and written modes. Another important topic in the area of discourse analysis is the question of how interactants exchange meanings. We will be discussing therefore how participants and roles are realized linguistically.

## 9.1 INTRODUCTION

This chapter introduces you to important aspects of recent research in the areas of **discourse analysis** and suggests practical applications to the interpretation and production of **texts**. The main purpose of this chapter is to consider the relationship between language, other **semiotic** signs, and society. You will be introduced to theories of discourse analysis and spend time doing textual analysis. This chapter will enable you to develop a critical understanding of some key concepts involved in discourse analysis and to understand how language reflects, mediates and creates our everyday reality. The first objective of the chapter is, then, to make you aware of communicative processes. The second objective is to review some different approaches to **communication**, written and oral. We will also be mentioning the important issue of how we communicate through other means that do not involve the linguistic expression.

The final aim is that by being exposed to current approaches to the analysis of interaction, you should improve your own production, both oral and written, and become more aware of what is involved when we use our linguistic resources to communicate our meanings.

## 9.2 How do we communicate?

Language is only one of the ways we communicate meanings in our daily lives. We use the resources of our bodies and the environment we are placed in at the moment of communication to send a message to somebody else. It is very interesting to look at babies and see how they use their physical resources to start and to maintain interactions with others (see Chapter 12 on child language acquisition). By using an index finger and pointing, for example, an 11-month-old baby 'says' to her mum – 'this is my toy' or 'I want that toy'. Or by choosing to dress their baby in blue, parents signify that it is a boy (see Chapter 15 on language and ideology).

We therefore communicate meanings through the choices we make in the ways we dress, accessorize, the ways we walk (think of the different meanings between the ways soldiers march and the ways common people walk or the difference between ordinary women and models on the catwalk), the ways we cut our hair, etc. . .

When we talk about **discourse**, we refer to the ways people use different semiotic resources, or different signs, to communicate. The linguistic system is, of course, one of the most salient modes of communication.

One important fact about communication is that it always takes place in a context. Native speakers of all languages 'know' how to communicate in certain social situations, being appropriate most of the time. This is because communication and society are a unified concept – one does not exist without the other. So we can state that all texts have contexts, and even when we are examining surface linguistic features, we need to be aware of what there is outside the text informing the text, and affecting the way it is written or spoken. For example, we need to consider:

- who wrote the text?
- who did the author write it for?
- who is saying what to whom on what occasion?
- who are the participants and what kind of outcome is expected from their discourse?
- when, where, and why did they write it?
- where has the text appeared and in what format?

Michael Halliday (1975, 1978, 1985), the main proponent of the systemic functional view of communication and language, refers to two types of contexts where communication occurs, the *context of culture* and the *context of situation*. Figure 9.1 exemplifies his theory.

The **context of culture** is the outside location where ways of doing things according to specific cultural rules happen (see also Chapter 8 above for further discussion on the notion of context).

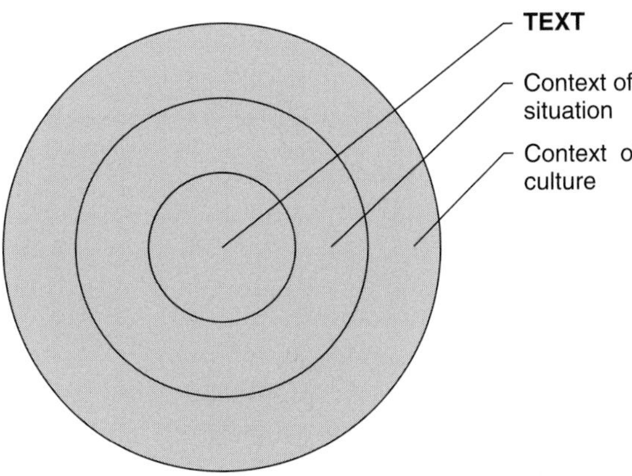


**Figure 9.1** Halliday's context of situation and culture

The **context of situation** is the inner circle where the immediate location will determine ways of interacting (things going on in the world outside the text which make the interaction what it is). Language is itself inseparable from its sociolinguistic context. In other words, we will have different ways of interacting if we are at a party or in a classroom. The combination of the two contexts will produce differences in communication. Halliday proposes in all his books that when we notice that language is different in different situations, we are taking a **functional view of language**. A functional view focuses on what makes a piece of language different from another in social contexts. For Halliday, language is a systematic semiotic resource for expressing and exchanging meaning through varying contexts and linguistic usage. *Language*, according to the functional theory of language (Halliday 1985: xvii), is a 'system for making meaning'. Meaning derives from the relationships and the interactions people have with each other. Whenever we communicate, we take a particular point of view or perspective on whatever we want to transmit. This 'perspective taking' signals our views of the world and consequently our ideologies. To be competent in one language is not simply to know the grammar and words of a linguistic code. 'Variability' and 'multiplicity', concepts fundamental to language, account for different ways of saying things according to different situations. These different language 'styles' are tied to signals of status and solidarity. When we communicate, we manipulate the sociolinguistic variables in order to display various identities. Therefore, when we speak, we express and reproduce social structure.

Another important aspect of communication or '**forms of discourse**' is the fact that our communications will depend not only on cultural and situational contexts but also on the ways in which we were raised as people (socialization patterns), on our beliefs and values (ideologies) and on the ways we use our social skills to maintain good relationships with other people – face and politeness systems (Goffman 1955) in other words, how polite or rude you can be to the people you are talking to. Figure 9.2 summarizes these relationships.

Finally, our forms of discourse will also depend on the ways we identify ourselves in given situations. Our **discourse identities** depend on the ways we interact with others and these are linked to our ways of being: our gender, age, profession and social relations,

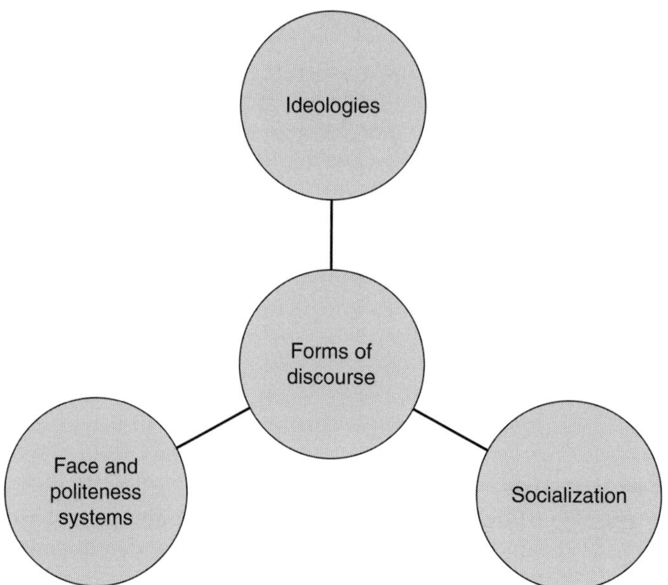


**Figure 9.2** Identity relationships in discourse

our nationality, our religion, among others. In fact, we can say that 'because' of our forms of discourse we have multiple identities. So, when we refer to 'modes of discourse', we are talking about the kind of text that is being made, the channel of communication adopted, the people involved in the interaction and finally the place and time where this interaction takes place.

## EXERCISE 9.1

Read the following five short text fragments, and say what *general kind* of writing you think each comes from. How easy is it to decide? How sure are you on a scale from 1–5?

In what contexts would you expect to find these fragments? What clues are there in the fragments to their contexts?

(a) **Espionage** (n uncount) is the activity of finding out the political, military or industrial secrets of your enemies or rivals by using spies, e.g. *The Swiss threatened to throw them in jail for espionage*

(b) Halliday's (1978, 1985) theory of social semiotics explained that words mean not only on their own but as part of a network of meanings.

(c) **New detective put on Pistorius case**
South Africa's top detective is to take over the Oscar Pistorius investigation amid attempted murder accusations against the current lead officer.

(d) **Rosemary crusted lamb chops –** Rub with some chopped herbs, garlic, salt and pepper, and olive oil, let sit for a bit, sear all over on high heat, let rest a few minutes, and serve. A lamb chop is such a lovely tender cut of meat, you just don't have to do much to it. In fact, the only thing you really have to take care with is to not overcook it.

(e) Poor Mr Worry. Whatever happened, he worried about it. If it rained, he worried that his roof was going to leak. If it didn't rain, he worried that all the plants in his garden were going to die. If he set off he worried that the shops would be shut when he got there. One day, he went for a walk. . .

I hope that you find this relatively straightforward and that you recognized these fragments as coming from one of the following (number them according to the presentation above):

academic writing (a linguistics textbook)
cookery book
dictionary
newspaper report
children's story

It is also very important to keep in mind the fact that all texts have *purposes*. These will, of course, range widely and sometimes they can have more than one purpose. Fairy tale narratives have the main purpose of entertaining, but they also have a moral purpose – to change behaviour. A humorous column in a magazine may be intended purely to entertain, whereas a document such as an Act of parliament is intended to establish a binding principle of law.

**KEY POINTS: Communication**

- All forms of communication are multimodal, in other words, we communicate our meanings through different semiotic modes (language being the main one, colour, fonts, gestures among others).
- Meanings are communicated through the different choices we make (different ways of talking, walking, dressing).
- Communication and society are a unified conception – one does not exist without the other. So all texts only exist in contexts. In other words, language is inseparable from its sociolinguistic context.
- We take a FUNCTIONAL view of language when we consider that language is different in different situations.
- Language is a 'system for making meaning' (Halliday 1985: xvii)
- When we communicate, we manipulate sociolinguistic variables in order to display our various identities.
- All discourses have purposes.

## 9.3 Text, genre (text types) and discourse: introducing the main concepts

Before we go any further, we need to establish what we mean by discourse and what we mean by text.

When we talk about text, we are mainly referring to language, although as we will see later, other semiotic systems can also produce 'texts' (a painting, for example can tell a story). When we study text, we study its formal characteristics: in particular, its structure and its grammatical and lexical choices. A course book, a poem, a lecture, an advertisement, an instruction leaflet, a courtroom trial are all texts: that is, we can consider them as individual semiotic units (although normally, of course, we react to them in the context of other texts, or in the light of our awareness of other texts, and not in isolation). This chapter can be considered as a text, as can all the other chapters in this book. We can summarize the definition of text by saying that a text is a collection of meanings appropriate to a context. The *purpose* of any communication will determine its structure and will contain certain obligatory elements to create meaning.

**Genres** are a socially acceptable way of using language in connection with a particular kind of social activity. Through different 'genres', people use language to achieve culturally recognized goals. When texts share the same obligatory and optional structural elements, they belong to the same genre. Stories, comments, anecdotes, for example, share the same generic structure and share the same social purposes.

Martin provides an interesting definition, which focuses on culture:

> A genre is a staged, goal oriented, purposeful activity in which speakers engage as members of our culture . . . Virtually everything you do involves you participating in one or other genre. Culture seen in these terms can be defined as a set of generically interpretable activities. (Martin 1985: 25)

Longacre (1976, 1983) was one of the first scholars to suggest that there are four broad types of prose texts (or genres): narrative, expository, persuasive or behavioural, and procedural. He says that

> Narrative is story telling and the most vivid kind of discourse. Expository includes essays, scientific articles and descriptive material. Persuasive includes sermons, pep talks, etc. . . Procedural is how-to-do-it or how-it-is-done text. (Longacre 1976: 358)

The primary aims of these genres are different:

- narrative (and drama) aim at entertaining or informing
- expository, at explaining or describing
- persuasive, at influencing conduct and
- procedural, at telling 'how to do'

All text types are classified by Longacre according to two major parameters, contingent temporal succession (to do with the sequence of time – is there a sequence?), and agent orientation (to do with people involved in the text – are there people in the text?).

Table 9.1 summarizes his model.

When we talk about discourse (in the singular) we are referring to texts and genres in their social context. That is, we are not just considering the *language* and *structure* of the text, but also how it relates to the society and culture that it belongs to. When we study discourse, we

**TABLE 9.1** Summary of Longacre's model **(adapted from Longacre 1983)**

| | +Agent orientation | -Agent orientation |
|---|---|---|
| **+ Succession** (chronological) | **Narrative** (many types)<br>1. Third persons<br>2. Actor oriented<br>3. Accomplished time encoded as past or present<br>4. Chronological linkage | **Procedural** (many types), includes instructional<br>1. Non-specific person<br>2. Goal oriented<br>3. Projected time encodes as past, present or future<br>4. Chronological linkage |
| | **Drama**<br>1. Multiple second persons<br>2. Accomplished time as concurrent<br>3. Dialogue without quotation | |
| **-Succession** (non-chronological) | **Persuasive**<br>1. Second person<br>2. Addressee oriented<br>3. Commands, suggestions encodes as imperatives<br>4. Logical linkage | **Expository**<br>1. Any person<br>2. Subjectmatter<br>3. time not focal<br>4. Logical linkage |

study the way a text creates meanings and reflects the views and ideology of its writer and his/her society. If we were to consider this book as a discourse, we would investigate how the authors project their view of their topic, of linguistics, and of the world, at the same time as explaining the issues they are presenting. From reading the whole of my text, you can conclude that I am a critical social semiotician since I am interested in discourse studies that investigate how identities are constructed through semiotic choices.

In this sense discourse is always part of *social action*: every text is an instrument of communication placed in a social context, being influenced by it and, at the same time, influencing it. In fact, one of the major proponents of a critical stance to discourse, Norman Fairclough, suggests: 'Discourse is for me more than *just* language use; it is language use seen as a type of social practice' (1992:28).

But we also talk about **discourses.** For Van Leeuwen (2005: 95) discourses are:

> resources for representation, knowledges about some aspect of reality, which can be drawn upon when that aspect of reality has to be represented.

He also suggests that 'discourses are plural. There can be different discourses, different ways of making sense of the same aspect of reality, which include and exclude different things and serve different interests' (ibid.).

This is the distinction between text, genre and discourse that we will be making in this chapter. Two other terms that you will come across during your studies in discourse analysis and your readings are:

- **Discourse domain**, which is the socially recognized context within which the discourse takes place – (scientific discourse– domain of science);
- **Social practice**, which can be defined as things that people (*social actors*) *do* with/to other people, in specific *places* following *conventions/rules* in *time* and *space.*

Linguistic aspects (vocabulary, grammar, semantics and text structure) and paralinguistic aspects (intonation and voice quality) together with other *semiotic* systems (like typefaces, colour, diagrams, etc.) help create structure and meaning in all discourses. All of these aspects of communication reflect **social practices** or ways of doing things, power relations and ideologies. A simple example of how semiotic choices help to reflect social practices is the cover of the children's book *Little Miss Naughty* from the famous series *Little Miss* books. Differently from the *Mr Men* books, where the majority of covers are white, the cover of *Little Miss Naughty* is bright pink, a serif font is used for the subtitle and the illustration is a fairy with glittering wings. These choices indicate 'girlhood', especially the colour pink, and reflect the common assumption that girls are associated with romance.

**KEY POINTS: Discourse – concepts**

- A text is a collection of meanings appropriate to a context. The *purpose* of any communication will determine its structure, which will contain certain obligatory elements to create meaning.
- Genres are a socially acceptable way of using language in connection with a particular kind of social activity. When texts share the same obligatory and optional structural elements, they belong to the same genre.
- Discourse (in the singular) is the production of texts and genres in their social context. Discourse is always part of social action.
- Discourses (in the plural) are resources for representation that also contain practice-specific knowledge (for example, legal discourses, media discourses) or are ideologically motivated (sexist discourses, racist discourses).

## EXERCISE 9.2

List the genres and purposes of the texts from which the fragments in exercise 9.1 were taken.

## EXERCISE 9.3

Choose a text from a newspaper, an advert, a piece of literature, an instruction manual, or any other text you that interests you.

1. Decide what is the macro structure of the text in the terms of Longacre's typology.
2. Explain your decision – use Table 9.1 to help you.

## 9.4 An overview of the development of discourse analysis research

Since the first studies done in Birmingham, UK, during the 1970s, with the pioneering work of John Sinclair and Malcolm Coulthard on classroom discourse, discourse analysis expanded to include within the field of language studies, the areas of applied linguistics, **social semiotics**, conversation analysis and narratology. Discourse analysis is now considered to be a multidisciplinary approach to communication and interaction. Many other academic areas claim to 'do' discourse analysis, although in most of the cases, the semiotic/linguistic meanings are not the focus of their studies:

- Anthropology
- Business studies
- Cultural geography
- Cultural studies
- Psychology
- Sociology of interaction

After almost four decades of research on discourse, studies have indisputably demonstrated that all types of interactions are systematically structured and socially organized. Before these studies, however, crucial assumptions that underpinned mainstream theories of text production and interpretation were that texts were unproblematically established and fixed. Language was viewed as an autonomous, self-contained system, separated from other semiotic and social systems. Discourse analysis as a new area of research changed all these assumptions.

There are many theoretical **approaches to discourse analysis** and the variety of descriptive methods is extensive (see for a detailed discussion, Wodak and Meyer 2005). Conversational analysis and text analysis are the most prominent ones. The methods are, however, bound to the specificity of the different disciplines.

The first studies (in the 1970s and 80s) concentrated mainly on how sociocultural knowledge was related in the performance of what are called speech acts (see Chapter 8).

American conversation analysts (for example, Sacks, Schegloff and Jefferson 1974) and sociolinguists (Gumperz 1982) investigated the production and interpretation of everyday action through conversation while European linguists (Hoey 1983; Coulthard 1985, 1994 among others) looked at texts in terms of their internal organization and were interested in what happens above the sentence level. In both cases, these studies were concerned with the description of the forms and structures of oral and written interaction.

This research demonstrated that both oral and written texts are systematically structured and socially organized (classroom and casual talk, doctor–patient interaction, lectures, meetings, etc.). Texts were seen as products and there was not a lot of interest on the social contexts the texts were embedded in.

From the 1990s on however, scholars turned to the application of discourse analysis to social practices and to the implications of linguistic analysis for social understanding and change. The current concern with the social nature of language demonstrates that 'language is not only a product, but it shapes and is shaped by society' (Fairclough 1993: 134). Discourse is now thus seen as socially constructive since social subjects and social relations are constituted in and by it.

The body of research on discourse can, therefore, be divided into two groups according to the nature of their social orientation to language studies. We can distinguish between non-critical and critical approaches. The non-critical approaches simply describe discursive phenomena, while critical approaches not only describe but also show how discourse is shaped by relations of power and ideologies.

Examples of non-critical discourse analysis are the American work on conversational analysis, on therapeutic discourse, on the classroom discourse analysis and on text description.

The critical approaches include:

- critical linguistics (Fowler et al. 1979, 1996; Kress and Hodge 1979)
- the work on discourse, power and ideology (Van Dijk 1985; Fairclough 2003; Caldas-Coulthard and Coulthard 1996; Caldas-Coulthard and Iedema 2008; Wodak 1989; Machin and Mayer 2012)
- the social semiotics work and multimodality of Kress and Van Leeuwen (1990, 2001),
- the works on language and gender (Cameron 1990, 1992; Mills 1995)
- the work on language and discrimination in legal contexts, also known as forensic linguistics (Coulthard and Johnson 2007).

According to Fairclough (1992: 1929), critical language studies demonstrate 'the constructive effects discourse has upon social identities, social relations and systems of knowledge and belief, neither of which is normally apparent to discourse participants'.

To begin with, let's consider some of the previous linguistic studies which led to the current focus on how social actors construct themselves and are constructed through discourse.

### 9.4.1 The sociolinguistics turn

Sociolinguistics (see Chapter 11), which first presented the basic principles later developed by discourse analysts, claimed to consider language in a social context. Sociolinguistics, mainly developed in America, was a reaction against the practice of 'linguistics proper'. William Labov and his team felt that a more socially relevant discipline, concerned with the problems of disadvantaged groups, was necessary. Interactional sociolinguistics (derived from the work of Goffman 1955, Gumperz 1982 and Hymes 1971) suggested the notions of communicative competence, where interaction was the main focus of analysis. These studies demonstrated that factors like the social context and social roles determine linguistic production. It is thanks to 'interactional sociolinguistics' therefore that the socially constituted nature of language practice became a focus of empirical study and discourse analysis was born.

### 9.4.2 The functional turn: language is a way of behaving and making others behave

From the 1980s onwards, especially in British studies, there was an increasing concern with language and society, which began with the work of Michael Halliday in particular. Halliday first proposed that language is a social semiotic, taking his inspiration from the work of Firth (1957), the academic who turned linguistics into a recognized distinct discipline in Britain. Firth and his colleague Malinowski (1923) were interested in investigating how languages function as social acts. For Malinowski, a language, in its primitive use, 'functions as a link in concerted human activity… It is a mode of action and not an instrument of reflection' (1923: 312). One of Firth's assertions was that language is 'a way of doing things and getting things done', of 'behaving and making others behave in relation to surroundings and situations' (1957: 35). Halliday, continuing in the same tradition, postulates that linguistic form is affected systematically by social circumstances. He says that the nature of language is closely related to the demands that we make on it, the functions it has to serve.

The model developed by the Birmingham school of discourse analysis is an example of the application of Hallidayan functional–systemic linguistics to real data (classroom interaction) since it proposed the first linguistic descriptive and systematic theory of the structure of spoken discourse in a specific social context. Known as 'exchange structure theory', the model was further developed and extensively applied to other kinds of social contexts.

### 9.4.3 The exchange structure

Halliday claims (1985: 68) that in the act of speaking, the speaker adopts for himself/herself a particular speech role, and in so doing assigns to the listener a complementary role which s/he wishes him to adopt in his/her turn. There are, for him, two fundamental types of speech role: giving (when a speaker is giving something to a listener – a piece of information, for example) and demanding (when the speaker requires something from the listener). An act of speaking, therefore, can be called 'an interact': 'it is an exchange, in which giving implies receiving and demanding implies giving in response' (ibid.).

Another fundamental distinction for Halliday is the one that relates to 'the nature of the commodity being exchanged' (ibid.), which may be either 'goods-and-services' or 'information'. These two types define the four primary speech functions, OFFER, COMMAND, STATEMENT and QUESTION, which in turn are matched by a set of responses. According to Halliday, of the responses, only 'answer' is essentially verbal, though even 'answers' can be realized nonverbally, for example a 'yes, no' head movement to polarity questions, or responses to 'Where is X?' by gesture. The other options are often realized non-verbally, though all possibilities can be verbalized.

Based on Halliday's theory of speech roles, Sinclair and Coulthard (1975) studied the 'exchange' in detail and their work became internationally known as the Birmingham model of discourse analysis, now widely publicized and developed (in Coulthard 1994, Coulthard and Montgomery 1981, and in Sinclair, Hoey and Fox 1993).

The original Birmingham model analyses the interactive structures which characterize formal teaching in authentic classroom environments, in terms of their organization and relationship. The researchers were also interested in describing how discourse is controlled (by whom, when and why speaker/listener roles change) and in the linguistic evidence for the discovery of discourse units longer than the sentence.

Discourse for Sinclair et al. (1972) and Sinclair and Coulthard (1975) meant the 'systematic way in which a number of speakers order their contributions so as to produce a coherent text' (Sinclair et al. 1972: 150). Their choice of data (the discourse of teachers and pupils) is based on the fact that the interactive mechanisms of classroom communication are apparent: 'one participant has acknowledged responsibility for the direction of the discourse, for deciding who shall speak when, and for introducing and ending topics' (1972: 6). Speakers, according to the researchers, interpret utterances according to structural expectations, observing if they succeed or fail to fulfil these expectations.

The typical **exchange structure** for classroom discourse was described as having three parts, where the third part functions to evaluate or comment upon the fit between the first and the second and it is sometimes optional.

1. Initiation
2. Response
3. Follow up

The exchange (I/R/F), for Sinclair and Coulthard, is the minimal unit of interaction. In the teaching situation, most of the time information transfer is the main purpose of the discourse. Typical classroom exchanges are realized like the following:

TEACHER: Can you tell me why do you eat all that food? (Initiation)
PUPIL: Too keep you strong. (Response)
TEACHER: To keep you strong. Yes. To keep you strong. (Follow up)

(Sinclair and Coulthard 1975: 21)

TEACHER: Can you point to a piece of metal in this room, anybody, a piece of metal in this room? (Initiation)
PUPILS: non-verbal – pointing (Response)
TEACHER: Yes. (Follow up)

(Sinclair and Coulthard 1975: 91)

In naturally occurring interactions, although there are some differences according to the speech event (see Stubbs 1983; Burton 1980) the exchange can also be realized in terms of the three-part I/R/F structure, as in:

DOCTOR: And how long have you had these? (Initiation)
PATIENT: Well I had 'em er a week a week last (Response)
Wednesday.
DOCTOR: A week last Wednesday. (Follow-up)

(Coulthard and Montgomery 1981: 20)

The researchers were interested in describing how discourse is handled by the participants (by whom, when and why speaker/listener roles change) and in the linguistic evidence for the discovery of discourse units longer than the sentence. In this sense, therefore, the Birmingham school, although not explicitly using these terms, initiated the first studies on power relations, demonstrating for instance how teachers control the talking in the classroom.

## EXERCISE 9.4

Writers, when representing dialogue, rely heavily on the reader's ability to interpret utterances according to structural expectations, in other words according to the I/R/F structure. Written interaction (or reported speech) at exchange level is characterized by chains of initiations and responses. It is interesting to note that as in real conversational interaction, F (follow-up) is an optional part of simulated exchanges. In classroom talk, however, F is quite frequent, while in reported interaction, it is not, although sometimes F is also present.

The following examples show the chains:

(i) 'What animals were they'? (*Initiation*)
'There were three animals altogether', he (*Response*) explained. 'There were two goats and a cat and then there were four pairs of pigeons.'
'And you had to leave them?' (*Initiation*)
'Yes, because of the artillery. The captain (*Response*) told me to go because of the artillery.'
'And you have no family?' (*Initiation*)
'No', he said, 'only the animals.'(*Response*) (Ernest Hemingway, 'The Old Man at the Bridge', p. 79)

(ii) 'Aren't you going back to work, dear?'(*Initiation*) asked the doctor's wife, from the room where she was lying with the blinds drawn.
'No.' (*Response*)
'Oh! Was anything the matter?'(*Follow up*) (Ernest Hemingway, 'The Doctor And The Doctor's Wife', p. 51)

Read the written dialogues below and classify them according to the I/R/F structure:

(a) 'But why are you such a lonely bird?' ...............
Connie asked him and again he looked at
her, with his full searching hazel look.
'Some birds are that way', he replied ................
Then with a touch of familiar irony,
'Aren't you by way of being ...............
a lonely bird yourself?'
Connie a little startled, thought about it
for a few moments and then said:
'Only in a way, not altogether like you. ............... (D. H. Lawrence, *Lady Chatterley's Lover*, p. 26)

(b) The kitchen phone was on the counter in a
corner behind the roasting pan. He moved the
roasting pan and picked up the receiver.
'Is Charlie there?', the voice said ………………
'No', Burt said ………………
'Okay', the voice said ……………… (Raymond Carver, 'What We Talk When We Talk About Love', p. 110)

### 9.4.4 Voloshinov and social semiotics

At the beginning of the twentieth century Saussure, considered by many the founding father of linguistics, postulated that a language was a sign system, a kind of entity which sociologists call *social facts*. Social facts, according to Durkheim ([1895] 1966), are ideas (representations) in the collective mind of a society.

Saussure placed the investigation of symbolic systems such as languages at the centre of a new science, the science of signs – semiology (also known as semiotics). Although Saussure was referring to the sign as a social fact, the linguists of the first part of this century, up to the 1950s and even into the 1960s as we have seen before, developed theories of language based exclusively on the Saussurean notion of *langue* (the abstract system, which is a social contract, and not the property of an individual) and not of *parole* (the actualization of this system, an individual's behaviour regulated by language, or particular instances of speech).

At around the same time Saussure was postulating the theory of the sign, another very important scholar was suggesting that the utterance is a social phenomenon. Voloshinov, writing in 1929, pointed out that the problem with the Saussurean tradition, which he labelled 'abstract objectivism', was that there was a rejection of the *parole* in the dichotomy '*langue* and *parole*'. He proposed that 'the form of signs must be conditioned by the social organization of the people involved and also by the conditions of their interaction' (1973: 21).

Voloshinov made a close connection between the study of language as semiotics (the study of signs) and the study of ideology. For him, the social dimension is essential in any semiotic analysis. He says that:

1. Ideology may not be divorced from the material reality of the sign.
2. Signs may not be divorced from the concrete forms of social intercourse (seeing that the sign is part of organized social intercourse, and cannot exist as such, outside it).
3. Communications and the forms of communication may not be divorced form the material basis (Voloshinov 1973).

For Voloshinov, therefore, language and ideologies are not monolithic phenomena. Society is characterized by conflicts and people are constantly renegotiating their roles and relations within a community. A certain way of dressing or a certain way of speaking reflect social meanings and, at the same time, create other meanings by their interactions with other signs.

Voloshinov's basic ideas can be considered as a basis for any investigation into the semiotic act. He leaves unexplored, however, as Hodge and Kress (1988) pointed out, the relationships between speech roles and social interactions in class societies. Social semioticians and critical discourse analysts, like Hodge and Kress (1988), Kress and Van Leeuwen (2001) and Van Leeuwen (2005, 2008), who are interested in social meanings, proposed an alternative social semiotics which will incorporate the following components:

1. Culture (society and politics) as intrinsic to semiotics
2. other semiotic systems alongside verbal language
3. parole (the act of speaking) and concrete signifying practices in other codes
4. diachrony, (time, history) process and change
5. the material nature of signs. (Hodge and Kress 1988: 18)

## 9.4.5 Critical discourse analysis

**Critical discourse analysis** (CDA) is, according to Fairclough (1992), an orientation towards language which associates linguistic text analysis with a social theory of the functioning of language in political and ideological processes. It criticizes linguistics proper 'for taking conventions and practices at face value, as objects to be described in a way which obscures their political and ideological investment' (Fairclough 1992: 7).

The first studies, known nowadays as 'critical linguistics', were developed by a group based at the University of East Anglia in the 1970s (Fowler et al. 1979; Kress and Hodge 1979). This work, which was linguistically centred, drew heavily upon the functionalist theory of Halliday.

Critical discourse analysts see discursive practices or discourses (in the plural) as

> modes of behaviour which place us in determined social groups. They operate to integrate people in societies . . . Interacting, valuing, thinking, believing, speaking and often reading and writing that are accepted as instantiations of particular roles by specific groups of people, whether families of a certain sort, lawyers of a certain sort, bikers of a certain sort, etc. Language, as well as literacy, is always and everywhere integrated with and relative to *social practices* constituting particular Discourses. (Gee 1990: xix)

The social group determines the discursive practices we are socialized into. Gee (1990) suggests that every cultural group has its own home-based discourse which is connected to that particular group's ways of behaving in and acting upon the world. This discourse marks its identity. However, each one of us is also a member of many discourses – school, work, church, etc., are sites where discourses operate to integrate people. Since we act in many different sites, discursive practices represent our many identities. However, discourses in general often do not have compatible values and in many instances, they can be conflictive. This has a crucial significance for education in general. The white middle-class home-based discourses in many ways share features of the white middle-class school discourse – children of white middle-class parents value books, for instance. A black, working-class child, who comes from a different home-based discourse (where, for example, oral communication is more appreciated than written communication), when entering the white middle-class school discourse, will be at a disadvantage in relation to the white child. The whole process of literacy for this black child can be hindered, therefore.

All institutions and social groupings thus have specific meanings and values which are articulated in 'language' and other semiotic codes in systematic ways. If we want to practise any kind of linguistic analysis, therefore, we must not dissociate linguistic production from ideological values.

Power relations and the effect they have upon social practices is a main concern of CDA. The main objective of a critical reading is, therefore, to expose misrepresentation and discrimination in different types of discourse and by doing so, produce social change. Everything we say, think, feel and do, is always dependent on the social context we live in.

**KEY POINTS: An overview of the development of discourse analysis**

- Discourse analysis is a multidisciplinary approach to communication and interaction.
- American conversation analysts in the 1970s and1980s studied everyday action through conversation. European text analysts described interaction by analysing structural properties above the sentence level. Both schools contributed to what is known as discourse analysis.
- Functional scholars became interested in how languages function as social acts and in the semiotic resources speakers use to communicate.
- Critical discourse analysis, social semiotics, multimodality and forensic linguistics are the latest developments in discursive studies and are concerned with meaning being realized in multiple modes and in how discourse identities are construed and construe new meanings.
- All past discourse studies have indisputably demonstrated that all types of interaction are systematically structured and socially organized.

**EXERCISE 9.5**

Think about the ways that your language changes when you talk to:
Your doctor/teacher

Your family members

Friends and colleagues

Make a note of these differences.

# 9.5 Doing discourse analysis: some interesting areas

## 9.5.1 Interaction in discourse: participants and roles

According to Jakobson (1960: 353), an act of communication involves:

> The *addresser* who sends a message to the *addressee*. To be operative the message requires a *context* referred to ('referent'), accessible to the addressee, and either verbal or capable of being verbalized, a *code* fully, or at least partially, common to the addresser and addressee (or in other words, to the encoder and decoder of the message); and finally, a *contact*, a physical channel and psychological connection between the addresser and the addressee, enabling both of them to stay in communication.

In discourse, the addresser constructs an imagined addressee (listener or reader)

> to whom s/he attributes knowledge of certain facts, memory of certain experiences, accurate recall of certain parts of certain other texts, plus certain opinions, preferences and prejudices and a certain level of linguistic competence. From this point on all decisions about content, expression, sequencing and rhetorical devices are made with reference to this imagined reader. Thus, once completed, every text defines its own imagined reader. (Coulthard 1994: 9)

However, this imagined reader is not a real person in the world, you or me reading a text, but a construction of the addresser. Coulthard (1994: 10) goes on to make an analogy with what happens in spoken interaction, where there are three major relationships: those between the *addressee* (the person to whom the message is encoded), *the listener* (an acknowledged participant in a conversation who is not the addressee for a particular utterance) and the *overhearer* (an unacknowledged participant who 'listens in' to the conversation). So the relationships could be represented as:

In written communication, the relationships can be represented as:

writer → text → (imagined reader) → real reader

## 9.5.2 Imagined readers and real readers

Discussions of written communication are often presented in terms of a writer communicating directly with his/her readers by means of a written text. In this model the text carries the writer's ideas and intentions and any problems that readers have with the text tend to be seen as deficiencies in the reader, deficiencies which are obviously compounded if the reader is not a native reader of the language in which the text is written.

However, it is in fact an unhelpful formulation to see a writer as creating a text for *those who actually read it*. As I create this text I have no way of knowing anything about you, nor of when or where you will read my text. My only guess is that you are interested in learning about language. The only strategy open to me, therefore, is to *imagine* a reader, and to create my text for that imagined reader. Only in this way can I decide what I need to make explicit and what I can assume, what parts of our argument must be spelled out in detail and what can be passed over quickly or even omitted completely – a writer can't begin at the beginning of everything every time.

Because texts are written for a specific audience, once a text exists it defines its audience; indeed, no writer can create even a single sentence without a target imagined reader, so almost every sentence provides some clue(s) about the imagined reader which allows any real reader to build up gradually a picture of his/her imagined counterpart.

**EXERCISE 9.6**

Select a 100–150-word article from an international newspaper written about a recent major event. Now imagine you are going to rewrite this article for young readers in South America. Make notes about your target imagined reader in terms of age, gender, education, knowledge of the topic area of the article, etc. and then decide what you will need to add to the text, and also what you will need to omit, in order to produce a version of the article which reads as if it had been written originally for your imagined reader. What are the major types of addition? *After completing this activity, write it down.*

### 9.5.3 The difference between text and talk

Although the differences between speech and writing may seem obvious, it is worth thinking, very briefly, about what the differences are, before we begin considering some features specific to written text. First, read the following texts:

**Text 1**

BUSH: Yo, Blair. How are you doing?
BLAIR: I'm just...
BUSH: You're leaving?
BLAIR: No, no, no not yet. On this trade thingy...[indistinct]
BUSH: Yeah, I told that to the man.
BLAIR: Are you planning to say that here or not?
BUSH: If you want me to.
BLAIR: Well, it's just that if the discussion arises...
BUSH: I just want some movement.
BLAIR: Yeah.
BUSH: Yesterday we didn't see much movement.
BLAIR: No, no, it may be that it's not, it may be that it's impossible.
BUSH: I am prepared to say it.
BLAIR: But it's just I think that we need to be an opposition...

BUSH: Who is introducing the trade?

BLAIR: Angela [Merkel, the German Chancellor]

BUSH: Tell her to call 'em.

BLAIR: Yes.

BUSH: Tell her to put him on, them on the spot. Thanks for the sweater – it's awfully thoughtful of you.

BLAIR: It's a pleasure.

BUSH: I know you picked it out yourself.

BLAIR: Oh absolutely – in fact I knitted it!!!

(laughter)

...............................................

BLAIR: [indistinct]

BUSH: We are not blaming the Lebanese government.

BLAIR: Is this. . .? [Blair taps the microphone in front of him and the sound is cut.]

## Text 2

In the light of the moon a little egg lay on a leaf.

One Sunday morning the warm sun came up and pop, out of the egg came a tiny and very hungry caterpillar.

He started to look for some food.

On Monday he ate through one apple, but he was still very hungry.

On Tuesday he ate through two pears, but he was still very hungry.

On Wednesday he ate through three plums, but he was still very hungry.

On Thursday he ate four strawberries, but he was still very hungry.

On Friday he ate through one piece of chocolate cake, one ice cream cone, one pickle, one slice of Swiss cheese, one piece of salami, one lollipop, one piece of cherry pie, one sausage, one cupcake, one slice of watermelon.

That night, he had a stomach ache.

Then he ate through one nice green leaf and after that he felt much better.

Now he wasn't hungry anymore. He was a big, fat caterpillar.

He built a small house, called a cocoon, around himself. He stayed inside for more than two weeks. Then he nibbled a hole in the cocoon, pushed his way out and

HE WAS A BEAUTIFUL BUTTERFLY.

## Text 3

Apparently he didn't hav2be there2day. I'll ask paul if its ok4us2meethere. I'm workin l8r so it'l be a good excuse2get away. Maybe paul willbe able2giv u greg's perspective if u don't know it. Xxx saythanks2sally4me. Xx are u doing ok? Xx

## Text 4

Mother is victim of sex attack.

A young mother of two stood screaming in a city street after being attacked by a sex-fiend as passers-by turned a deaf-ear to her pleas for help, police revealed last night.

. . . Now police have appealed for witness . . .

### EXERCISE 9.7

First, classify texts 1–4 above. Are they written or spoken oral texts?
Now, think:

1. What features do written texts have, which are not shared by spoken interactions?
2. What features do spoken interactions have, which are not shared by written texts?

List some of them before you continue reading.

These are very broad questions. You may in fact have objected to them: you may argue that it all depends on what kind of written text and what kind of spoken language. Or that in some cases, written texts have characteristics of spoken texts. Examine with care text 3. What is special about it?

Let's narrow down the question a little and consider some situations where there are fairly close parallels in form or content.

Think of the most striking differences between:

- a conversation and the script of a play
- a conversation in which someone is talking about their reactions to a new novel that they have just read, and a review of that same novel in a newspaper or magazine
- a monologue in which someone recounts their experiences when on holiday, and an article in the travel section of a newspaper
- a cookery demonstration in a store about how to make pancakes, and a recipe for pancakes in a cookery book
- an academic lecture on, say, discourse analysis in English, and this chapter

Each of these pairs has its own differences and distinctions. But amongst your comments, you have probably thought about the fact that in the spoken situations the intended audience is actually present and that the addresser can adjust his/her message in real time depending on the reaction of the audience, in the 'here and now', whereas in the written presentation, they are remote in both place and time and the text was completed long before they started reading it. You have probably also said something about the fact that many spoken situations allow for feedback in some form, such as questions and comments, or 'repairs' when misunderstandings or problems arise. Even in monologues and lectures, the speaker is able to monitor the audience's attention and adjust his/her presentation accordingly. Also, the fact that oral delivery, even when it is scripted or semi-scripted rather than spontaneous, allows some of the meaning to be conveyed by intonation, stress, pace and pauses, gestures, hesitations, repetitions and facial expressions, whereas in written text this has to be conveyed more explicitly in the words and structures themselves and there is linearity in the written mode. You may have commented on how spoken language is a one-off experience, unfolding for the listener in real time from beginning to end, whereas a reader has the opportunity to go back over passages and to reread, or to change the order in which the text is read.

One of the important questions that you have to consider when you 'do' any discourse analysis is the issue that all discourses, as we have seen in the sections above, written or spoken, are interactive and dialogic. In other words, every act of communication involves participants that will be interacting explicitly or implicitly (as in the case of monologues). And that there is no discourse that does not have values and points of view. You always select and organize according to your position in the world what you want to communicate.

**KEY POINTS: The interactive nature of discourse**

- All discourse is essentially interactive and dialogic. Any written or oral text creates and depends on a relationship between participants, and the meaning of the text arises out of that relationship: not just what the writer writes or the speaker speaks, but also the interpretation made by addressees. The meaning is a matter of negotiation, as it were, between addresser and addressee. This is a crucial point.
- Discourse operates within an interactional framework. We often think of discourse in terms of its purpose. It is designed to give information to the reader or listener, or to persuade of some point of view or to entertain them. But some discourses are primarily social in their functions. The main purpose is to create and maintain social relationships. This is the main purpose of a personal phone call. This entails that people may at different times draw on different discourses about the same practice or practices, choosing the one they see as most appropriate to their own interests in the given context.
- Texts, genres and discourses are means of talking, writing about and acting upon the world. Through language and consequently discourse, we construct social practices, which in turn, construct us as members of a society and as individuals.

WEBSITE: **Group exercise**

Visit the website and, in a small group, examine the three written texts on display. Discuss the features of these texts and answer the questions that relate to them.

## 9.6 SUMMARY

Michael Stubbs (1983: 1) defined discourse analysis as

1. concerned with language use beyond the boundaries of a sentence/utterance
2. concerned with the interrelationships between language and society and
3. concerned with the interactive or dialogic properties of everyday communication.

I would add that discourse analysis is also concerned, not only with describing linguistically or semiotically what goes in communication, but also with understanding what people 'do' socially through their ways of communication. For me, discourse is socially constructive, constituting social subjects, social relations and systems of knowledge and belief. Discursive practices (like the media and other institutional practices) have effects on social structures – they can produce and reproduce unequal relations through the way they represent people, things, events, since 'all texts code the ideological position[s] of their producers' (Caldas-Coulthard (1996: 228). One of the ways women are discriminated against in discourse, for example, is by the ways their nomination is associated with sexuality – *bitch, cougar, tart, dishy* and many others.

Discourse analysts, especially critical ones, are concerned therefore with deconstructing ideologies, power relations, discrimination and exclusion in interaction. Van Leeuwen (2008: 6) states:

> [Discourses] not only represent what is going on, they also evaluate it, ascribe purpose to it, justify it, and so on, and in many texts these aspects of representation become far more important than the representation of the social practice itself.

As discourse analysts, it is our duty to understand how this is done and to reveal the strategies used by participants in interaction. In this sense, discourse analysis is not only an academic subject but also a tool that we can use to bring about change in society.

I hope that this chapter has presented an overview of the main ideas and concepts of this fascinating area of study and that you will apply some of these notions to your everyday interactions and practice.

WEBSITE: **Discourse analysis**

Now go to the website and assess your knowledge of discourse analysis by completing the self-test questions!

## SUGGESTIONS FOR FURTHER READING

Coulthard, M. (1985). *An Introduction to Discourse Analysis*. London: Longman. This is the essential book for discourse students since it introduces the main concepts discussed in this chapter clearly and appropriately.

Caldas-Coulthard, C. R. and M. Coulthard (eds.) (1996). *Texts and Practices: Readings in Critical Discourse Analysis*. London: Routledge. This is one of the first collections that introduced critical discourse analysis. The chapters discuss theory and some very interesting applications.

Van Leeuwen, T. (2005). *Introducing Social Semiotics*. London: Routledge. This very interesting book introduces you to the area of social semiotics and multimodality. The main analyses concentrate on different types of semiotic resources: visual, graphic and musical.

# ANSWERS TO EXERCISES

## Exercises 9.1 and 9.2

(a) word taken from *The Essential English Dictionary*, Collins Cobuild (Glasgow: Collins, 1988). Since this is a dictionary text, its purpose is to inform and resolve doubts about meaning.

(b) extract from D. Machin and A. Mayer, *How to Do Critical Discourse Analysis* (London: Sage, 2012), p. 39. The purpose of an academic text is to describe theory and inform about new discoveries.

(c) written news taken from BBC On line, 25 February 2013. News have the main purpose to inform readers about current events. Some news can also entertain readers (news that inform about celebrity lives, for example).

(d) recipe taken from www.simplyrecipes.com. This is an instructional text and tells you how to do things. So, the main purpose is to instruct.

(e) extract from Roger Hargreaves, *Mr Worry* (London: Thurman Publishing, 1978). This is a children's narrative, therefore, its main purpose is to entertain its readers.

| | |
|---|---|
| academic writing (a linguistics textbook) | (b) |
| cookery book | (d) |
| dictionary | (a) |
| newspaper report | (c) |
| children's story | (d) |

## Exercise 9.4

| | |
|---|---|
| (a) 'But why are you such a lonely bird? ' | *Initiation* |
| Connie asked him and again he looked at | |
| her, with his full searching hazel look. | |
| 'Some birds are that way', he replied. | *Response* |
| Then with a touch of familiar irony, | |
| | |
| 'Aren't you by way of being | *Initiation* |
| a lonely bird yourself?' | |
| Connie a little startled, thought about it | |
| for a few moments and then said: | |
| 'Only in a way, not altogether like you.' | *Response* |
| (D. H., Lawrence, *Lady Chatterley's Lover*, p. 26) | |
| | |
| (b) The kitchen phone was on the counter in a | |
| corner behind the roasting pan. He moved the | |
| roasting pan and picked up the receiver. | |
| 'Is Charlie there?' the voice said. | *Initiation* |
| 'No', Burt said. | *Response* |

| | |
|---|---|
| 'Okay', the voice said. | *Follow up* |
| (Raymond Carver, 'What We Talk When We Talk About Love', p. 110) | |
| 'Aren't you going back to work, Dear?' asked the doctor's wife, from the room where she was lying with the blinds drawn. | *Initiation* |
| 'No'. | *Response* |
| 'Oh! Was anything the matter?' | *Follow up/Initiation* |
| 'I had a row with Dick Bouton.' | *Response* |
| 'Oh!' said the wife. | *Follow up* |
| 'I hope you didn't lose your temper.' | *Initiation* |
| 'No', said the doctor. | *Response* |
| (Ernest Hemingway, 'The Doctor and the Doctor's Wife', p. 51) | |

## Exercise 9.5 Commentary

When you talk to your doctor or anyone in authority, your choice of vocabulary, for example, is very different from when you talk to your family or friends. You will certainly address your doctor by the term of address *Doctor*, while you will address your friends by their first names. In certain cultures, in-laws are addressed by their first names, while in others, as in the Brazilian context, this would be inconceivable. In-laws have to be addressed as Mr or Mrs, indeed in some parts of Brazil adult children even address their parents in this way. These choices and many others reflect power relations and place speakers in given roles. Think of other semantic and even grammatical choices that point to these relations.

## Exercise 9.7

Text 1 is a transcript of a dialogue (conversation) between US President George W Bush and UK Prime Minister Tony Blair during a break at the G8 conference in Russia.

Text 2 is a fictional written narrative for children, *The Very Hungry Caterpillar*, by Eric Carle (Penguin, 1980)

Text 3 is a text message (SMS) – although is a written text, it has very marked characteristics of a spoken text (this text message comes from the data collected by Tagg's (2009) PhD Thesis). Mixed genre, therefore.

Text 4 is a piece of written narrative news, taken from the newspaper the *Birmingham Daily News*, 12 February 1987.

## REFERENCES

Burton, D. (1980). *Towards an Analysis of Casual Conversation*. London: Routledge & Kegan Paul.

Caldas-Coulthard, C. R. and Coulthard, R. M. (eds.). (1996). *Texts and Practices*. London: Routledge.

Caldas-Coulthard, C. R. and Iedema, R. (eds.). (2008). *Identity Trouble: Critical Discourse and Contested Identities*. London: Palgrave.

Cameron, D. ([1985] 1992). *Feminism and Linguistic Theory*. London: Macmillan.

(ed.). (1990). *The Feminist Critique of Language. A Reader*. London: Routledge. Coulthard, R. M. (1985). *An Introduction to Discourse Analysis*. London: Longman.

(1994). *Advances in Written Text Analysis*. London and New York: Routledge.

Coulthard, R. M. and Johnson, A. (2007). *An Introduction to Forensic Linguistics*. London: Routledge.

Coulthard, R. M. and Montgomery, M. (eds.). (1981). *Studies in Discourse Analysis*. London: Routledge & Kegan Paul.

Durkheim, É. ( [1895] 1966) *The Rules of Sociological Method*. London: Collier-Macmillan.
Fairclough, N. (2003). *Analysing Discourse: Textual Analysis for Social Research*. London: Routledge.
(1993). Critical discourse analysis and the marketisation of public discourse. *Discourse and Society*, 4, 133–68.
(1992). *Discourse and Social Change*. Cambridge: Polity Press.
Firth, J. R. (1957). *Papers in Linguistics 1934–1951*. London: Oxford University Press.
Fowler, R. (1996). On critical linguistics. In C. R. Caldas-Coulthard and M. Coulthard (eds.), *Texts and Practices: Readings in Critical Discourse Analysis*. London: Routledge.
Fowler, R., Hodge, B., Kress, G. and Trew, T. (eds.). (1979). *Language and Control*. London: Routledge and Kegan Paul.
Gee, J. (1990). *Social Linguistics and Literacies: Ideology in Discourses*. London: Falmer Press.
Goffman, E. (1955). On face-work: an analysis of ritual elements in social interaction. *Psychiatry: Journal of Interpersonal Relations*, 18(3), 213–31.
Gumperz, J. (1982). *Discourse Strategies*. Cambridge University Press.
Halliday, M. A. K. (1975). *Learning How to Mean*. London: Edward Arnold.
(1978). *Language as Social Semiotic*. London: Edward Arnold.
([1985] 1994). *An Introduction to Functional Grammar*. London: Edward Arnold.
Hodge, R. and Kress, G. (1988). *Social Semiotics*. Cambridge: Polity Press.
Hoey, M. (1983). *On the Surface of Discourse*. London: Allen and Unwin.
Hymes, D. (1971). Sociolinguistics and the ethnographies of speaking. In E. Ardener, (ed.), *Social Anthropology and Linguistics* (Association of Social Anthropologists, monograph no. 10), pp. 7–98. London: Tavistok.
Jakobson, R. (1960). Linguistics and poetics. In T. Sebeok, (ed.), *Style in Language*, pp. 350–77. Cambridge, MA: MIT Press.
Jaworski, A. and Coupland, N. (eds.). (1999). *The Discourse Reader*. London: Routledge.
Kress, G. (1985). *Linguistic Processes in Socio-Cultural Practice*. Victoria, Australia: Deakin University Press.
Kress, G. and Hodge, R. I. V. (1979). *Language as Ideology*. London: Routledge.
Kress, G. and Van Leeuwen, T. (1990). *Reading Images*. Victoria, Australia: Deakin University Press.
(2001). *Multimodal Discourse: The Modes and Media of Contemporary Communication*. London: Arnold.
Labov, W. (1972). *Language in the Inner City*. University Park, Philadelphia: University of Pennsylvania Press.
Longacre, R. E. (1976). *The Anatomy of Speech Notions*. Lisse: Peter de Ridder Press.
(1983). *The Grammar of Discourse*. New York: Plenum.
Machin, D. and Mayer, A. (2012). *How to Do Critical Discourse Analysis*. London: Sage.
Malinowski, B. (1923). The problem of meaning in primitive languages. In C. K. Ogden and I. A. Richards (eds.), *The Meaning of Meaning*. London: Routledge & Kegan Paul.
Martin, J. R. (1985). *Factual Writing: Exploring and Challenging Social Reality*. Sydney: Deakin University Press.
Mills, S. (1995). *Feminist Stylistics*. London: Routledge.
Sacks, J., Schegloff, E. A. and Jefferson, G. (1974). A simplest systematics for the organisation of turn-taking for conversation. *Language* 50, 696–735.
Sinclair, J. McH. and Coulthard, R. M. (1975). *Towards an Analysis of Discourse*. Oxford University Press.
Sinclair, J. McH., Forsyth, I. J., Coulthard, R. M. and Ashby, M. C. (1972). *The English Used by Teachers and Pupils*. Final Report to SSRC, mimeo, University of Birmingham.
Sinclair, J. McH., Hoey, M. and Fox, G. (eds.). (1993). *Techniques of Descriptions: Spoken and Written Discourse*. London: Routledge.

Stubbs, M. (1983). *Discourse Analysis: The Sociolinguistic Analysis of Natural Language*. Oxford: Blackwell.

Tag, C. (2009). *A corpus linguistics study of SMS text messaging*. Unpublished PhD thesis, University of Birmingham.

Van Dijk, T. A. (ed.) (1985). *Handbook of Discourse Analysis: Dimensions of Discourse,* vol. 2. London: Academic Press.

Van Leeuwen, T. (2008). *Discourse and Practice: New Tools for Critical Discourse Analysis*. Oxford University Press.

(2005). *Introduction to Social Semiotics*. London: Routledge.

Voloshinov, V. I. ( [1929] 1973). *Marxism and the Philosophy of Language*. New York: Seminar Press.

Wodak, R. (1989). *Language, Power and Ideology: Studies in Political Discourse*. Amsterdam: Benjamins.

Wodak R. and Meyer, M. (2005). *Methods of Critical Discourse Analysis*. London: Sage.

# 10 Historical linguistics

JONATHAN CULPEPER AND DAN MCINTYRE

**KEY TERMS**

- actuation
- chain shift
- corpora
- diachronic
- economy
- expressiveness
- grammaticalization
- lenition
- lexicalization
- linguistic reconstruction
- primary data
- propagation
- secondary data
- synchronic

**PREVIEW**

This chapter explains the insights and techniques of historical linguistics, the study of how language changes over time. We begin with a brief explanation of the value of historical linguistics before going on in Section 10.2 to describe the background to its development. In Section 10.3 we examine some key explanations for why languages change over time. In so doing we discuss how changes come about and how they then spread throughout speech communities. Following this, we describe some of the types of change that languages go through. Here we focus particularly on change at the levels of phonology, grammar, lexis and semantics. We give examples of changes that have occurred at these levels of language and describe some influential theories that have sought to explain such developments. We then move on in Section 10.5 to describe some of the main techniques that historical linguists use to study language change. By the end of this chapter you should have a good knowledge of the variety of ways in which languages change, as well as an insight into the methods that linguists use to study such changes.

## 10.1 INTRODUCTION

Primarily, historical linguistics involves describing how and explaining why language changes over time. Much work has focused on sound change, such as the fact that Germanic languages, past and current, have the sound [t] at the beginning of the number 'two' (e.g. Gothic *twai*, English *two*, Dutch *twee*, German *zwei* (pronounced [tsvaɪ])), whereas other Indo-European languages past and current typically have [d] (e.g. Latin *duos*, Italian *due*, French *deux*, Spanish *dos*, etc.). But other linguistic areas – grammar, semantics and lexis – have also received significant attention, and most recently areas such as pragmatics have come into focus.

Why bother with historical linguistics? Importantly, it helps explain language that is used today. For example, why is it that when we say the English word *knight* we do not pronounce the <k>? Historical linguistic detective work has been able to establish that the <k> used to be pronounced. But that sound has been subject to a regular process of sound change, mapped out by historical linguists, until it reached the final endpoint of complete loss. Today's spelling simply retains the <k> as an archaeological relic. Further, differences in accent and dialect can often be accounted for by the fact that change does not proceed at the same pace for all communities of speakers of a language. Additionally, we might note that historical linguistics helps us to read and understand old texts, including literary texts – in English, texts such as *Beowulf* (somewhere between the eighth and eleventh centuries), the work of Chaucer (fourteenth century), Shakespeare (*c.*1600) and Jane Austen (early nineteenth century).

Most examples in this chapter are English for the obvious reason that they are more accessible to most readers. We will occasionally deploy the conventional labels for particular periods of the development of English, namely, Old English (OE) (700–1100), Middle English (ME) (1100–1500) and Early Modern English (EModE) (1500–1750). Needless to say, the concepts, processes and factors we discuss in relation to language change are not specific to English.

This chapter is divided into three parts. The first is designed to give a sense of some of the theories and ideas that historical linguists have grappled with. The second looks more closely at change at specific linguistic levels. The third discusses data and method, enabling you to conduct your own studies.

### EXERCISE 10.1

Ask a friend who isn't a linguist to explain how they think language has changed within their lifetime. What sort of linguistic changes do they talk about and what does this suggest about the difficulty of studying historical linguistics?

## 10.2 The historical background to historical linguistics

In its broader definition, historical linguistics encompasses more than the issues outlined in the first sentence of our introductory section. It accounts for any historical aspect of language, including the state of language at a particular moment in past time, as well as change over time. For example, the 'state' of the infinitive form of the verb 'to have' was *habere* in Latin, a language that was thriving as a spoken language 2,000 years ago, whilst it is *avere* in modern Italian. The idea of studying the state of the language at a particular moment in time has its roots in an important precursor to historical linguistics, namely, **philology**, the study of historical texts, literary or otherwise. Famous figures who were philologists include J. R. R. Tolkien (of hobbit fame) and Henry Sweet (in part the model for the linguist in George Bernard Shaw's play *Pygmalion*). Historical linguistics uses insights from philology but draws primarily on the methods of modern linguistics, of which Ferdinand de Saussure was one of the founders (see his *Cours de Linguistique Générale*, published posthumously in 1916).

Saussure proposed a distinction between **synchronic** and **diachronic** linguistics. Essentially, synchronic linguistics studies language at one point in time, and diachronic linguistics studies language over time. Note that synchronic linguistics is not confined to present-day language; it can involve any point in time. Historical linguistics has made diachronic linguistics its central concern. However, the two approaches to language are in fact inextricably linked. For example, the fact that in the UK some people might use the term *radio* whilst others use the term *wireless* is a matter of synchronic variation. The fact that in the twentieth century *radio* made its way into British English from American English or that we can trace the word back at least as far as Latin *radius*, meaning 'ray', is a diachronic matter. Similarly, the formation of *wireless* through a combination of *wire* and the suffix *-less* is a diachronic matter. Note here that the synchronic account of *radio* and *wireless* makes no mention of the fact that it is on-going change that is driving the variation. There was no variation until *radio* arrived in British English, and now *wireless* is confined to the older generation, itself an indication of change in progress. Observe that the diachronic accounts in the previous two sentences make no connection between *radio* and *wireless*. *Radio* and *wireless* denote the same concept. Languages do not need several words with exactly the same meaning. Instead, one or both words shift their meanings, or one word disappears, as seems to be happening in this case.

The general point is that a full account of what is going on needs both a synchronic and a diachronic perspective. A synchronic snapshot of language at one point in time is often in fact a slice of diachronic change. Saussure was not interested in the issues we have been outlining in the above paragraph; he was interested in language as an abstract system and not in the variation you get in its realization, which is more the preserve of sociolinguistics. The relationships between synchronic variation and diachronic change were famously elaborated in Uriel Weinrich, William Labov and Marvin Herzog (1968), and have been developed in the work of William Labov (e.g. 1963, 1978, 1994, 2001).

Some grand theories of change have held sway for decades, even centuries. One such theory relates to **economy**. Here, there is an obvious connection with Darwinism, centred on the idea of the survival of the fittest. In his 1871 book *The Descent of Man*, Darwin draws a parallel between evolutionary biology and language. He approvingly quotes Max Müller's words:

> A struggle for life is constantly going on amongst the words and grammatical forms in each language. The better, the shorter, the easier forms are constantly gaining the upper hand, and they owe their success to their own inherent virtue. (Darwin 1871: 58)

In fact, it is indeed likely that economy plays some role in language change. **Lenition**, which describes the weakening of sounds such as the [k] of *knight*, is a case in point: less effort is required to produce the newer sound compared with the older. And there are many other examples of reduction (e.g. *God be with you* > *goodbye* > *bye*). However, economy cannot be the single explanation for all language change. It would not account for why [k] is alive and well in many words. Moreover, counterevidence is in the fact that new forms are often not the most economic. For example, compounding is a regular process by which two shorter elements evolve into a longer one (e.g. *green* + *house* > *greenhouse*). Also, with respect to English, consider that many new words were adopted from Latin, and were often less economic (longer and more effortful) than their English counterparts (compare, for example, *urine* and *faeces* with *piss* and *shit*).

For these reasons, modern historical linguistics has been less focused on grand all-encompassing theories as to why language change occurs. Instead, the focus has been on the influence of particular contexts of change, both linguistic and extralinguistic, and often on establishing that change is not random by identifying particular paths of change.

**EXERCISE 10.2**

In his *Cours de linguistique générale,* Saussure makes the point that diachronic analysis requires initial synchronic analysis but synchronic analysis doesn't require initial diachronic analysis. Why is this?

## 10.3 Explanations for change: actuation and propagation

The questions 'how' and 'why' languages change presuppose that they do. Indeed this is the case; only dead languages (e.g. Latin, Sanskrit) do not. Change occurs at all levels of language, though it is not equally observable. Relatively rapid changes in vocabulary are easily observed; relatively slower changes in grammar are less easily observed. It's likely that you saw this in your answer to exercise 10.1.

How does a change begin? Or, to look at it another way, why do some things change and others don't? And when exactly did the change begin and where? This issue is one of innovation or **actuation**, and it is the site of much controversy. A way of thinking about language is that it is in a continual state of change yet consists of stepping-stones or states along the way. The first step is that somebody produces a novel form – they innovate. However, it would not be reasonable to describe actuation as all there is to language change. If one person starts using a new word – let's say 'pokey-chops' for people who like trying different foods – would it count as a change? Or is that person simply being creative with language? Shakespeare, for example, is cited in the *Oxford English Dictionary* as being the only recorded user of over 300 words, including *askance* (as a verb) *unhaired* and *non-come*. For a word or other linguistic item to count as a new form in the language, it needs to be conventionalized to a degree, that is, the new form and its relationships with particular meanings need to be shared amongst members of a speech community. Language is a matter of shared conventions; it enables people to communicate meanings with, for example, words, even when those words have an arbitrary relation with their meanings.

Dark clouds in the sky may non-arbitrarily 'mean' rain, as there is a natural physical connection between the two, but there's an entirely arbitrary relationship between the word *rain* and the wet stuff it denotes (onomatopoeic words such as *buzz* perhaps have a semi-arbitrary relationship with their denotations). So, a full language change can hardly stop at actuation; it must spread across the entire community of users of a particular language, something which is called **propagation** or diffusion. Propagation involves speakers selecting to use somebody else's linguistic material (including any innovations) themselves. Note here that propagation, the sharing of linguistic conventions, is in itself a mechanism working against change – it is a matter of replication. Language change, then, involves both actuation and propagation. Distinguishing them is tricky, not least because the evidence trail is clearer for propagation than it is for actuation.

### 10.3.1 Actuation

Explanations for the actuation of change seem to fall roughly into three camps according to the degree of involvement of the speaker in communication.

One set of explanations treats language as an abstract system. A subset of these, in tune with structuralist approaches to language, appeals to **teleological mechanisms**, that is, mechanisms that preserve the internal balance of the linguistic system. One such mechanism is the preservation of uniformity. The process of analogy, or linguistic copying, can help enhance uniformity. For example, today in English the generally uniform means of making a noun plural is to add the <s> inflection. But in Old English that was one of the inflections for one particular set of nouns; other inflections existed for other sets (e.g. the plural of *eye* was *eyen*). Over time, speakers seem to have extended the <s> plural inflection to all other sets of nouns. Another mechanism is hole-filling (see Martinet 1952). Clear examples of this are **chain shifts** in sound systems (see Section 10.4.1). For example, the vowel of the word *I* used to rhyme with that of *tea*. When it, and many other words with the same vowel, shifted to its current pronunciation, it left a hole in the sound system, and so other adjacent sounds shifted to fill it. We will look further at this moment when we consider the **Great Vowel Shift** in Section 10.4.1. Yet another mechanism is the avoidance of homonymy – that is, words that share the same spelling and pronunciation but have different meanings (e.g. *left*, meaning either the opposite of right or the past of the verb *leave*) – so that there is a neat one-to-one mapping of meanings and forms. There are particular problems with teleological explanations, including, for example, the fact that cross-linguistic empirical work reveals languages with long-standing gaps, not to mention the fact that teleological mechanisms are not actually that abstract (we avoid homonymy in order not be misunderstood). It is also worth observing that the teleological explanation does not ultimately account for change: a perfectly balanced system is one that does not change. Yet languages do change.

Another subset of explanations treating language as a relatively abstract system appeals to child language acquisition. The basic assumption here, in tune with generative approaches to language, is that an adult's grammar is fixed; changes only occur during the phase of child language acquisition. Regarding change, the idea is that there is not necessarily a straightforward transmission of the grammatical system from one generation to another. Children sometimes get the wrong end of the grammatical stick, which can lead to them changing a grammatical parameter. When this happens, there is abrupt and radical change to the abstract grammatical system. This account, however, has a number of problems. For example, the idea that grammatical change is restricted to the phase when a child acquires language is controversial (sociolinguistic studies, such as Labov 1994, have shown actuations amongst adults). It is also not clear why children sometimes suddenly act in unison to create an abrupt change in the language system, whereas at other times they do not. The most famous application of the child-based approach to matters of language change is Lightfoot's (e.g. 1979) account of the modal verbs in English. Lightfoot's account runs thus: the core modal verbs (*will, shall, may, can, must*) were very different in Old English, failing to exhibit many of the characteristics they have today (e.g. they could not act as auxiliary verbs, they could express tense); but in the sixteenth century they underwent abrupt change, becoming like the auxiliary modal verbs we know today; more precisely, they underwent **reanalysis**, that is to say, the surface form remained the same, but their underlying grammatical category changed (e.g. full verb to auxiliary verb). There has been, however, considerable criticism of this account, including empirical work showing that already in Old English these verbs did not quite behave as full lexical verbs, and that there was no abrupt change (see, for example, Fischer 2003).

The remaining two actuation explanation camps have in common the fact that they assume the site of change to be the context of communication: i.e. the context in which a speaker produces an utterance which is understood by a hearer. Where they differ is in the degree of intentionality or consciousness involved in producing the actuation. An area at the more intentional end of the scale involves increased **expressiveness** or creativity. Using the words *bad* or *wicked* to mean 'good' are examples of expressiveness. Expressiveness, however, is partly constrained by the desire for clarity, the desire to avoid being misunderstood. Less intentional is economy. Economy can be seen in terms of physical effort, but also in terms of achieving one's goal in the least amount of time possible. It is often mentioned in relation to elliptical or eroded forms. To return to an example from Section 10.2, the fact that Latin *habere* ('to have') has evolved into modern Italian *avere* involves a process of lenition (see Honeybone 2008) in which the plosive [b] weakens to fricative [v]. The final step in this path of change is complete loss. This has happened to the initial [h] of *habere*; this is already a weak sound which simply weakened to nothing.

The final actuation explanation camp involves little intentionality. Ohala (1981), for example, suggested that people misperceive sounds and then reproduce those sounds in their speech. Note, however, that Ohala was thinking about pronunciation, and there is much variability in the production of sounds, especially vowels, and hence greater potential for error than in other areas of the language system.

### 10.3.2 Propagation

Change is never fully predictable (though one can state what is probable). An actuation need not propagate; it can fizzle out. For example, one of the last words recorded in the 1989 second edition of the *Oxford English Dictionary* is *hoolivan*. This is created by a blend of *hooligan* and *van*, and denotes the van with which the police force collected up hooligans. The dictionary makers clearly thought that this lexical item would become established – that it would propagate across the bulk of the English-speaking community, but it fizzled out almost immediately. Note the implications of this: if a particular change does not work its way across all relevant items, we are left with irregularities. For example, today the inflection <s> in English marks plurality, but not quite for all nouns. Nouns such as *oxen*, *deer* and *geese* deploy alternative ways of marking plurality, ways which once used to apply to many more nouns (recollect the earlier example of *eyen*, to which we could add many others like *shoen* or *treen*).

The causes of propagation – the factors that favour a particular form being adopted by members of a speech community – are social. People select particular variants in order to achieve particular social aims. One factor involves acts of identity: using language to identify with, or conversely distance oneself from, a particular social group (see LePage and Tabouret-Keller 1985). Those acts of identity often involve prestige, another important factor (see Labov [1966] 2006). Prestigious forms are often associated with people in dominant, high-ranking social groups, and conversely stigmatized forms are often associated with people in low-ranking social groups. Social aspirers emulate those groups, and thus those prestigious forms trickle down the social hierarchy. This is what Labov ([1966] 2006) refers to as change from above. Here, this means 'above the level of consciousness'; people knowingly select a prestigious variant (or avoid the stigmatized variant). In the development of standard British English, for example, the prestigious variants of dominant social groups played a key role (Nevalainen and Raumolin-Brunberg 2003). There were some exceptions, however. The eventual rise of the present tense singular verb inflection *s* (e.g. *he talks*) was fuelled by the mass of the population, especially in London, using it without any kind of conscious emulation of prestige (Nevalainen and Raumolin-Brunberg 2003). This is what Labov ([1966] 2006) refers to as change from below (i.e. 'below the level of consciousness'). It is not, however, always the case that the most prestigious forms are associated with the dominant social groups. Labov (1963) introduced the idea of covert prestige, referring to cases where speakers choose non-standard forms that have prestige in specific contexts. Sometimes speakers wish to identify with the regional or the local social group, even if it may not have broader social prestige. It is worth noting that the notion of prestige need not apply simply to prestige variants within a language. Speakers are likely to imitate prestige languages. Classical Latin and Greek have been hugely influential on many modern European languages for exactly this reason.

Propagation does not happen without contact. A hermit is not going to propagate! Let us first consider contact between people speaking the same language. What is important here is how people organize themselves in social networks. People who talk to one another tend to talk like one another: they accommodate to each other's speech habits. So, people who just talk to the same people again and again, as for example in isolated communities, are not going to come into contact with new forms but simply replicate the old ones. Conversely, those who talk to a variety of people are more likely to come into contact with new forms and adopt them. The difference is between social networks with fewer and stronger links and social networks with more and weaker links (see Milroy and Milroy 1985). The consequences of this can be seen in the development of accents and dialects in the

British Isles. Urbanization has created large cities, most notably London, which comprise social networks with numerous weak links. It is no surprise then that in the melting pot of London changes progress rapidly across the region, whereas in areas more remote from London with sparser populations much older features can still be found (in Scottish English the pronunciation of *house* is /hus/).

Social networks can operate on a larger scale. Invasion, migration and settlement can lead to contact with new language communities, as well as the loss of contact with old ones. Sometimes the speaker and hearer are not using the same language. For instance, as a result of the Hungarian conquest of the Carpathian Basin between the ninth and tenth centuries, the Hungarian language came into close contact with other speech communities. This facilitated the borrowing of words from the languages of these neighbouring communities, which included Slavic, Romanian and Turkic. Contact with communities speaking different languages is an important part of the history of English. Trudgill (1989) suggests that a high number of adults acquiring a second language in a contact situation is a cause of simplification. This factor is one of the classic explanations for the simplification of the inflectional complexity English used to have, notably with the arrival, starting in the late eighth century, of the Norse-speaking Viking invaders and later the Norman French following the conquest of 1066 (though it should be noted that simplification for one speech community may not be recognized as such by another, and the more neutral term regularization may be more appropriate). The borrowing of words is a typical feature of contact situations, especially when one of the languages has prestige. This is most obviously the case for French loanwords in English.

Issues of prestige and contact often overlap with issues of power. Prestige languages and dialects can be imposed by those in power. Power can bring about conquest: effectively, enforced contact, as happened in Britain with the Roman, Anglo-Saxon, Viking and Norman conquests. The language of the dominant invader can gain prestige, as happened notably with Latin and French. An interesting converse example concerns the Celtic languages (e.g. Welsh) of Ancient Britain. The Anglo-Saxons settled in Britain in various waves, mostly in the centuries around the sixth century, and brought with them the Germanic dialects that formed the foundation for English. However, Celtic languages made very little impact on English, especially with respect to vocabulary, possibly because they had little prestige (recently, scholars, such as Juhani Klemola or Peter Schrijver, have argued for greater impact in areas of phonology and grammar than hitherto acknowledged). Prescriptive rules, which are coined by authorities, self-appointed individuals (e.g. the eighteenth-century English grammarian Robert Lowth) or institutions (e.g. language academies, educational bodies) often gain prestige, and may well be followed by certain social groups. For example, from EModE onwards the English increasingly avoided multiple negation, a change which seems to have been led by the professional ranks, gentry and royal court (see Nevalainen and Raumolin-Brunberg 2003). (It is possible that some prescriptive rules partly reflect aspects of contemporary usage; it might be that descriptive norms of usage feed prescriptive stipulations, which in turn feed descriptive norms, and so on.)

Finally, we briefly note the development of communication technologies to facilitate contact. With respect to English, William Caxton's establishment of a printing press near

Westminster in 1476 marks the beginning of printing in England. Printing increased opportunities for communication, of bringing many people into contact with one form of a text, and thereby helping facilitate the standardization of English. The development of transport networks (e.g. tarmac roads, railways) can facilitate contact. More recently, the telegraph and the telephone have offered further opportunities for communication. The advent of radio broadcasting in the UK (the first BBC broadcast was in 1922) is credited with fuelling the establishment of Received Pronunciation, a prestigious social dialect that is not regionally marked. We should also mention the advent of television and also satellite communications. These later developments have been credited with fuelling the Americanization of British English.

**KEY POINTS: Explanations for change**

- Actuation refers to the initiation of linguistic change through the production of a novel form.
- Important mechanisms of actuation include analogy, hole-filling, reanalysis, misperception, economy and expressiveness.
- For a linguistic innovation to become part of the language of a community it needs to be selected by other speakers and thus propagated.
- Through propagation linguistic innovations come to be shared by a majority of the speech community and thus become conventionalized.
- Propagation requires contact between speakers.
- Propagation can result if speakers choose to emulate a form that they believe to be high-status in social terms. This is what William Labov calls 'change from above'.
- Alternatively, a form may be propagated simply by a significant mass of speakers choosing to use it. This is what Labov calls 'change from below'.
- Prestige is an important propellant of propagation, whilst communication technologies are important facilitators.

## EXERCISE 10.3

(a) Have a guess as to how the word *outrage* came about. Now go to a dictionary with historical information, such as the *Oxford English Dictionary*, and discover what type of language change this is.

(b) Write down some examples of new language features which seem to be driven by expressiveness.

(c) Investigate the effect of contact with speakers of other languages on regional dialects. In the case of Britain, investigate northern dialects in the light of the fact that the Norse-speaking Vikings only settled in the northern and eastern areas of Britain. Write down some northern dialectal words, and then investigate their heritage (note down similar cognate forms) (an obvious resource to use is the *Oxford English Dictionary*).

## 10.4 Types of linguistic change

In this section we examine change at specific linguistic levels, paying particular attention to phonology, grammar, lexis and semantics, as it is here where most work has focused. Change, needless to say, can occur in any area of language.

### 10.4.1 Phonological change

Phonological changes rarely happen in isolation. A change in one part of the sound system of a language is likely to affect other sounds too, and a change in the phonology of one language can affect the phonology of a neighbouring language.

In 1822, Jacob Grimm (one half of the Brothers Grimm, of fairy tale fame) published a systematic account of a phonological change in Germanic, an ancestor of modern languages such as English, German, Dutch, Danish, Swedish and Norwegian. This phonological change explains why Germanic became distinct from the other branches of the **Proto-Indo-European** (PIE) language, such as Italic and Celtic. According to Grimm, at some unknown point in the past, the consonants of Germanic shifted. That is, they began to be pronounced differently to the consonants in PIE. For example, PIE [bh] (an aspirated voiced stop) started to be pronounced in Germanic as [b] (an unaspirated voiced stop). PIE [b] shifted in Germanic to a [p] (a voiceless stop). And PIE [p] shifted in Germanic to [f] (a fricative). Grimm's description of this process has become known as Grimm's Law and explains why, for example, the word for 'foot' in Latin and Greek begins with a [p] (*pod-* and *ped-*, respectively), while in English and German it begins with a [f] (*foot* and *fuss*). (Grimm also accounts for the examples given in the first paragraph of Section 10.1.)

Grimm's Law is an example of what historical linguists call a chain shift, a teleological mechanism of language change. This model imagines the phonemes of a language to be like links in a chain. Because they are connected, moving one link of the chain inevitably means that the others move too. That is, if the pronunciation of one phoneme changes, then others will also change. Theoretically there are two types of chain shift (i.e. two variants of the model). These are drag chains (also known as pull chains) and push chains. The idea behind the drag chain model is that when the pronunciation of one phoneme changes (i.e. when it moves position in the chain), it 'drags' the other phonemes with it. In effect, one phoneme fills the hole left by the movement of another, and so on. The push chain model suggests the opposite, i.e. that one phoneme moves into the 'slot' already occupied by another, causing that phoneme to be pushed into another slot in order to avoid merging with the new phoneme. The idea of drag chains and push chains was originally proposed by Martinet (1952). Many historical linguists prefer the drag chain model because of a theoretical problem with the notion of a push chain. Remember that the idea behind a push chain is that phonemes are pushed out of their existing position into a new one in order to prevent them merging phonemically with the phoneme that has moved into their slot. While it may be possible for two vowel sounds to occupy the same position while one is in the process of moving, Aitchison (2001: 190) makes the point that it is harder to envisage this happening with consonant sounds. For these reasons, the drag chain model is often seen as a more plausible description of sound changes in language. Applying this to Grimm's description of the movement of consonants in Germanic, it is likely that one consonant dragged the others in its wake. In practice, however, phonemic mergers do happen in language (e.g. in many varieties of English the first sound of *which* is now indistinguishable from *witch*, but once they used to be distinct). Aitchison (2001) also discusses cases where a sound change might involve both a drag and a push chain.

Phonological changes in a language can offer insights into why other levels of language are as they are. For example, the sound change in English known as the Great Vowel Shift (GVS) helps to explain why the pronunciation of English words often seems at odds with their spelling. Why, for instance, is the Present-day English word *tide* pronounced [taɪd] and not [ti:də]? Why should *name* be pronounced [neɪm] and not [na:mə]? The answer is that at some point in the fifteenth century, the way in which people pronounced the long vowels began to change. This change took place over a long period of time (approximately 1400 to 1650) and the end result was that the pronunciation of the long vowels was raised. Raising refers to the height in the mouth at which your tongue is when you produce a particular vowel sound (this affects the size of the resonating cavity which then impacts on the sound that is produced). As an example, during the period of the GVS the pronunciation of [a:] was raised so that by the Early Modern English period it sounded more like [ɛ:]. (If you pronounce the two sounds, you should feel that your tongue is closer to the roof of your mouth for [ɛ:] than it is for [a:].) Over time, [ɛ:] was also raised, eventually becoming a diphthong [eɪ], hence the Present-day English pronunciation [neɪm].

During the GVS, each of the seven long vowels shifted to take the position of the one immediately above it in height. When it came to the highest vowels, [i:] and [u:], since these had no higher place to move to, they developed into diphthongs. The long vowels, and the changes that they underwent during the GVS, are outlined in Table 10.1:

**TABLE 10.1** Raising of the long vowels during the Great Vowel Shift

| Middle English → | Early Modern English → | Present-day English → | Examples |
|---|---|---|---|
| [a:] | [ɛ:] | [eɪ] | [na:mə] → [nɛ:m] → [neɪm] *name* |
| [ɛ:] | [e:] | [i:] | [mɛ:t] → [me:t] → [mi:t] *meat* |
| [e:] | [i:] | [i:] | [fe:t] → [fi:t] *feet* |
| [i:] | [əɪ] | [aɪ] | [ti:də] → [təɪd] → [taɪd] *tide* |
| [ɔ:] | [o:] | [əʊ] | [rɔ:b] → [ro:b] → [rəʊb] *robe* |
| [o:] | [u:] | [u:] | [go:s] → [gu:s] *goose* |
| [u:] | [aʊ] | [aʊ] | [hu:s] → [haʊs] *house* |

The GVS took place over a long period of time. During this period, English spelling became standardized as a result of a number of factors, including the impact of William Caxton's printing press (see Section 10.3.2). However, the phonological developments of the GVS continued until at least the midseventeenth century (and arguably continue today), long after standardized spelling had become widely accepted. This meant that the new standard spellings often preserved much earlier pronunciations, hence *name* reflecting the older pronunciation [na:mə]. Had spelling been standardized *after* the GVS, we might have expected a spelling that reflected the modern pronunciation – perhaps *neim*.

The motivation for phonological change in language is complex and encompasses both language-internal (e.g. teleological mechanisms in actuation) and language-external factors (e.g. propagation, contact, prestige, power). The chain shift model describes the former. For the latter we need to look to sociolinguistic explanations. Romaine (1982: 122–3) extends, perhaps controversially, the **Uniformitarian Principle** (the assumption that the general properties of language have been the same throughout history) to encompass sociolinguistic practices. In this respect, just as there are prestige varieties of language today, so too must there have been prestige varieties in the past. Assuming this to be the case, it is reasonable to suppose that the actuation of the GVS may have been the aspiration on the part of the merchant classes in London to emulate what they considered to be more prestigious sociolects (see Labov 1978).

### 10.4.2 Grammatical change

Old English was a synthetic language, in which word order was much less constrained than it is in Present-day English. Grammatical function was marked instead by a system of inflections (more like Latin or Modern German). This inflectional system gradually broke down as a result of numerous factors, including phonological change in OE that resulted in inflections becoming unstressed, and language contact with Scandinavian settlers. By the Middle English period OE had developed from being a largely synthetic (i.e. inflectional) language to an analytic one (i.e. one in which grammatical function was indicated through syntactic structure rather than inflections). This development is an example of grammatical change. For example, nouns in Old English not only varied according to **number** (e.g. singular, plural), but also **case**. Compare these two sentences: *The hunter saw the deer* and *The deer saw the hunter*. We know that in the first sentence the hunter is the subject doing the seeing, whereas in the second the hunter is the object being seen because of word order – where they are positioned in the sentence. The unmarked order of sentence elements today is subject–verb–object (**SVO**). In Old English, the nominative case was used for subject functions (thus *hunta*), and the accusative for object functions (thus *huntan*). Note that if words themselves are thus marked by inflections, one can move them to various positions in the sentence yet still know whether they are the subject or object.

Much recent work has focused on **grammaticalization**. Antoine Meillet (1912: 132) defined grammaticalization as 'the attribution of a grammatical character to a formerly independent word'. Grammaticalization is the gradual process whereby linguistic items, typically contentful lexical items, become more grammatical, and as they do so undergo other linguistic changes. Hopper and Traugott (2003: 7) proposed a particular grammaticalization cline or path of change (finer gradations are possible within these steps):

content word → grammatical word → clitic → inflectional affix

An important point about the cline is the unidirectional hypothesis – the hypothesis that change develops in the direction of being more grammatical not less. We have already encountered an example of the first stage, when we noted the core modals (e.g. *shall, will, may*) in English shifting from full lexical verbs to auxiliary verbs. The modals also illustrate some of the associated linguistic changes involved in grammaticalization:

- *Reduction in syntactic freedom*. Modals, as auxiliary verbs have less freedom than full lexical verbs. Consider that one can say *Go!* and still form a sentence, but *Shall!* does not. Auxiliary verbs, by definition, work with lexical verbs.
- *Semantic bleaching*. For example, the original sense of *shall* in Old English was obligation (a sense that lingers in relics such as 'thou shalt not commit adultery'). But that original sense has been bleached out of most current usages, such as 'we shall finish this chapter soon', which have much more to do with marking the future. In fact, it is not the case that semantic meaning is bleached out to leave nothing, but rather that there is a shift from more concrete meanings to more abstract.
- *Phonological reduction*. In speech, *shall* is almost always reduced to the clitic *'ll*, as in 'we'll finish this chapter soon'. (Note that *'ll* has even less syntactic freedom, as it cannot stand on its own).

Perhaps grammaticalization sounds like a fairly obscure process. In fact, it encompasses a large range of features. Here are some rapid examples: the intensifying adverb *very* evolves from an adjective with the sense of 'truly' or 'really'; the indefinite article *a/an* evolves from the numeral adjective *one* with the sense of a single thing; the negative form *not* evolves from the negative form *ne* plus the noun *aught* meaning 'anything', giving *naught*, i.e. 'not anything' (*nowt* and *aught* can still be heard in Northern English).

### 10.4.3 Lexical change

Lexical change encompasses the expansion of a language's vocabulary and the development of its constituent words. There are a number of ways in which vocabularies can be developed. New words can be borrowed from other languages, consequently having the status of **loans**. Examples include *weekend* and *computer*, borrowed from English into French, *Allee* ('avenue') and *Beton* ('cement') borrowed from French into German, and *kindergarten* and *sauerkraut* borrowed from German into English. And it is not simply words that can be borrowed. Loans into English include inflections (e.g. French plural *aux*, as in *gateaux*), prefixes (e.g. German *über*), suffixes (e.g. French *ette*, as in *cigarette*), phrases (e.g. Latin *summa cum laude*, particularly in American English), acronyms (e.g. French *RSVP*) and even whole sentences (e.g. French *C'est la vie!*). Some loans are borrowed without change, as in the above examples, and some are adapted (e.g. *music* from French *musique*). This process of adaptation can sometimes involve transliterating a word or expression into the target language. The resulting lexeme is known as a calque. For example, Spanish *tarjeta de crédito* is a calque of English *credit card,* while *long time no see* is an English calque from Cantonese. Motivations for borrowing were discussed at the end of Section 10.3.2.

In addition to simply borrowing words, the vocabulary of a language can be expanded through a number of internal word-formation processes. These include:

## Acronymization

The formation of a word from the initial letters of some or all of the words in a given phrase. E.g. *ET* (Extra Terrestrial), *KANUKOKA* (Kalaallisut *Kalaallit Nunaanni Kommunit Kattuffiannit* = Greenlandic Communities Association), *RSVP* (French *Répondez s'il vous plaît*), *SNCF* (French *Société nationale des chemins de fer français* = French National Railways Society). Some acronyms are so commonly used that many speakers fail to recognize them as such. Examples include *laser* (light amplification by stimulated emission of radiation) and *scuba* (self-contained underwater breathing apparatus).

## Back-formation

The formation of a word by the removal of an affix from an existing word, e.g. *choreograph<choreography, euthanize<euthanasia, edit<editor, enthuse<enthusiasm*. Note that back-formation usually involves changing the part-of-speech of the original word (in all of the particular examples given the change is from noun to verb).

## Blending

The process of taking elements from two existing words to form a new one, e.g. *genome* (gene + chromosome), *pixel* (picture + element), *wifi* (wireless + fidelity), Spanish *cantautor* (*cantante* [singer] + *autor* [author] = singer-songwriter), Swedish *Hemester* (*hem* [home] + *semester* [holiday] = staycation) and Danish *mokost* (*morgenmad* [breakfast] + *frokost* [lunch] = brunch).

## Clipping

The removal of syllables from a polysyllabic word to create a new one. While similar in essence to back-formation, clipped words (clips) do not differ in part-of-speech from their original form. E.g. *bus* (*omnibus*), *doc* (*doctor*), *exam* (*examination*), *flu* (*influenza*), *pub* (*public house*).

## Coinage

Coinages are invented words with no etymology, and are thus extremely rare. Examples are often product names, such as *Teflon* and *Xerox*.

### Conversion

The practice of using an existing word as a different part-of-speech, e.g. *ask* and *blog* (originally nouns) as verbs. Conversion is common in analytic languages and is sometimes referred to as zero-derivation. In synthetic languages, conversion is not possible, since indicating a change of word class involves the addition of inflections.

### Derivation

The formation of a new word through the addition of derivational morphemes, or affixes, to an existing word, e.g. *im* + *possible* = *impossible*, *hope* + *less* = *hopeless*, *impressive* + *ly* = *impressively*. Derivational morphemes differ from inflectional morphemes in that the former generate new words while the latter simply generate grammatical variants of the same word (for example, plural forms of a noun, past tense forms of a main verb).

### Compounding

Combining words (free morphemes) to form another word. Note that this is not the same as blending, which does not combine the entire words at the outlet. Examples are *head-hunter* (noun–noun compound), *greenhouse* (adjective–noun compound), *spoonfeed* (noun–verb compound). Over time compounds can lose material as they coalesce (e.g. *goodbye* began as a compound of 'god be with you (ye)').

Brinton and Traugott (2005) argue the process of **lexicalization** is a common feature of language change. We have already seen that grammaticalization is the process by which a lexical item takes on a grammatical function (for example, the negative clitic *n't* – as in *haven't* – is a grammaticalization of *not*). Lexicalization describes the process by which a meaning comes to be realised in a single word or morpheme rather than in a grammatical construction. For example, the word *cupboard* was originally a noun phrase (*cup board*), meaning 'a board on which to place cups'. However, by the sixteenth century, the [p] of *cup* had assimilated to the [b] of *board*, and *board* had lost its full stress (evidence for this can be seen in seventeenth-century spellings such as *cubbard* and *cubbert*). As a result of these changes, today's English speakers no longer understand the meaning of the word as being a compound of *cup* and *board* (compare, for example, *ironing board*); *cupboard* has become lexicalized. Other examples of lexicalization in English include *holiday*, *about*, *bridegroom*, *husband*, *goodbye* and many more. The process can also be observed in many other languages. In Hungarian, for instance, the greeting *csókolom* ('I kiss your hand') is arguably lexicalized. Coalescence of form and idiomatization of meaning are typical of lexicalization. For example, OE *god* ('god') has fused with *sib(b)* ('relation') to give *gossip*, which has a meaning that is not predictable – it is idiomatic. Lexical developments in language are inextricably linked to semantic change, which we turn to next.

## 10.4.4 Semantic change

Semantic change refers to the changes in meaning over time. Historical linguists are interested in two main questions here: what types of semantic change occur and why?

To begin with the first issue, a number of different types of semantic change have been identified. Two basic categories of semantic change are broadening and narrowing. Broadening describes the process by which the meaning of a word becomes more general than it originally was. For example, the word *dial* was originally a noun derived from Latin *diale* and described a flat disc engraved with units of measurement (as in a sundial). When the telephone was invented, *dial* broadened in usage to become a noun to describe the moveable disc on the face of a telephone and a verb to describe the action of using the dial to call up a number. With the advent of mobile technology, *dial* underwent a further broadening so that it could now be used to describe the action of typing a number into a mobile phone keypad.

Narrowing describes the opposite process, by which the meaning of a word becomes more specific than it originally was. The noun *to starve*, meaning 'to die or to suffer severely from a lack of food', had a much more general meaning in OE, where *steorfan* meant simply to die.

In addition to these two superordinate categories, we can identify a number of other types of semantic change. Amelioration is the process of meaning becoming more positive over time, as has happened with the words *nice* and *pretty*, which originally meant 'foolish' and 'sly', respectively. Pejoration, on the other hand, refers to meaning becoming less positive over time. *Bully*, for instance, was originally a term of endearment and familiarity, only acquiring its negative meaning in the seventeenth century. Hungarian *jobbágy* originally meant 'soldier' before acquiring the more pejorative meaning of 'peasant'. These processes are ongoing all the time. The meaning of *criticize*, for example, is arguably becoming more pejorative over time, moving from simply meaning 'to appraise something' to its more common sense now of negative appraisal.

Weakening is another common process of semantic change and involves meanings becoming weaker over time. For example, *blitz*, a clipping of *blitzkrieg*, was borrowed from German into English during the Second World War to describe a violent air attack. Over time its meaning has weakened so that it is now often used fairly trivially to describe intense campaigns generally, such as 'a blitz on benefits cheats'. In this particular case, the original meaning of *blitz* has not been lost completely from English. This can sometimes happen, as in the case of *slip* as an intransitive verb, which used to mean 'to escape' (note that this meaning is still preserved in the expression 'to give someone the slip'). Weakening may be seen as a type of semantic shift, in which some aspect of the original meaning of a word is lost whilst a related meaning develops.

Another common tendency in the process of semantic change is for words to become metaphorized over time. For example, the meaning of the verb *starve* (see above) has not only narrowed over time but has become metaphorized too (for example, to be starved of affection). It goes without saying that the same processes can be observed in all languages. For example, the meaning of Hungarian *fejvadász* ('headhunter') is, like its English, German and doubtless other counterparts, now primarily metaphorical to refer to someone who directly approaches a senior executive with a job offer.

It is relatively straightforward to identify trends in semantic change. It is much harder to determine the causes of semantic development. Blank (1999) suggests a variety of potential motivations. Perhaps the most obvious of these is when a new concept in the world calls for a new word, such as *blog* or *wifi*. Indeed, sociocultural changes generally can drive semantic development, as in the case of OE *haligdæg* ('holy' + 'day' → 'holiday') broadening to mean a period of leave from work, rather than a religious festival specifically, a change that parallels the secularization of society. Close conceptual relations can also facilitate semantic change, as when *infer* is used to mean *imply*, or *affect* to mean *effect*. These are the kinds of changes that prescriptivists often rail against. Blank (1999) also notes that emotionally marked concepts can be drivers of semantic change, as speakers seek euphemisms to avoid embarrassment; hence, *throne* to refer to *lavatory* and *take a leak* to refer to urinating. Blank (1999) describes the overarching motivation of his typology for semantic change as a search for increased efficiency and expressivity (cf. the discussion of economy and expressivity in Section 10.3.1).

Recent work on semantic change, especially by Traugott (e.g. 1989, 1995), has been focused on the idea that semantic change normally proceeds in the direction of increased subjectivity, that is, expressions of the speaker's attitudes and evaluations. Traugott (1989) identified three general tendencies or paths of semantic change. We give these below in a simplified form. The first is reminiscent of our discussion of grammaticalization above.

- *Towards more abstract meanings*, e.g. the word *bureau* changed from something physical, something tangible (a type of cloth), to something which is abstract and untouchable (an agency).
- *Towards more textual meanings*, e.g. the word *and* originally meant 'in the presence of' (a spatial preposition), but it is now used to join two bits of discourse (it is now primarily a conjunction).
- *Towards more attitudinal meanings*, e.g. the word *well* has changed from meaning a positive state (e.g. good fortune, health), which it can still do today, to also being able to mark the speaker's attitudes and beliefs about something, as when one says 'Well I never!'

Of these tendencies, Traugott views the third as the most important. It is the one that encapsulates **subjectification**: the 'development of a grammatically identifiable expression of speaker belief or speaker attitude to what is said' (Traugott 1995: 32). Most recently, scholars, including Traugott, have been turning to the notion of **intersubjectivity**, a further stage of development by which subjectified items take on meanings which encode attitudes towards the addressee. One can see something of this with the item *well*, which can display reluctance to the addressee to say something negative, as in 'It was a bit ... well ... tasteless.'

**KEY POINTS: Types of change**

- Change can occur at any level of language.
- Phonological change is often described using the chain shift model, which imagines linguistic elements (typically phonemes) to be like links in a chain. If one link changes position, the others do too.

- There are two variants of the chain shift model: drag chains and push chains. In the former, the movement of the target phoneme drags the others in its wake. In the latter, the target phoneme moves into an already occupied slot, pushing that phoneme to a different position.
- A key theory of grammatical change is grammaticalization, a gradual process whereby an item becomes more grammatical in character.
- A key theory of lexical change is lexicalization, a gradual process whereby an item becomes more lexical in character.
- A key theory of semantic change is subjectification, a gradual process whereby the meanings of an item become more attitudinal in character.

## EXERCISE 10.4

### (a) Grammatical change

Why might the expression *gonna*, as in for example 'I'm gonna switch the light off', have anything to do with grammaticalization?

### (b) Lexical change: borrowing

What motivates the borrowing of lexical items from other languages? And in what ways is the term *borrowing* an inaccurate description of the process? Can you think of a better term?

### (c) Lexical change: word-formation

Here are some words first recorded in the *Oxford English Dictionary* between 2000 and 2013. Choose the word-formation process (or processes) that best explains how it was created (it may help to look the words up in a dictionary first).

i. defriend (*verb*, 2005)
ii. goji (*noun*, 2002)
iii. goldendoodle (*noun*, 2001)
iv. iPod (*noun*, 2001)
v. metabolomic (*adjective*, 2001)
vi. SARS (*noun*, 2003)
vii. Sudoku (*noun*, 2000)
viii. waterboarding (*noun*, 2004)

### (d) Semantic change

King James II, upon seeing Sir Christopher Wren's St Paul's Cathedral, described it as 'amusing, awful and artificial', by which he meant it was wonderful. Describe the shifts in meaning these three words have undergone.

## 10.5 Data and method

How do you investigate linguistic change over time? Historical linguists use a combination of **primary data** (records of actual language use), **secondary data** (commentaries on language use) and **linguistic reconstruction**.

With regard to primary data, two important caveats need to be borne in mind. First, historical texts were usually repeatedly published over the years, often without the original publication date, thus giving the impression that they are not as old as they are in fact are. Moreover, editors, especially in the nineteenth century, often re-published historical texts with the original publication date, but also with editorial interference. Some editors were better than others, but there was often the urge to tidy up the original, to get rid of that nasty variation. However, it is often that very variation that is of interest to the historical linguist.

The second caveat relates to genre. Historically important genres include religious texts (e.g. the Bible), legal texts (e.g. laws, courtroom proceedings), literary texts, scholarly writings (notably histories), scientific writing and correspondence (both personal and official). These are important because they span centuries, are present in several languages and survive in reasonable quantities. Tracking linguistic change within genres is the basis for much more solid conclusions than change across genres and time. Comparing a legal text from 1600 with an email from 2000 confuses two variables, time and genre. One of the genres that has a remarkably good survival rate across time and languages is religious language, specifically, the Bible (see, for example, Görlach 1997). However, to analyse what is happening across multiple genres, we need to use corpora (singular corpus). Broadly speaking, a **corpus** is a large body of texts in electronic form, often designed to represent particular genres and periods (for an excellent list of historical corpora, see: www.helsinki.fi/varieng/CoRD/corpora/index.html). With a computer, one can investigate linguistic features in a corpus, including its frequencies in the categories of a corpus, and thus, assuming those categories pertain to different periods, over time. But there are caveats. Spelling variation can be a problem (e.g. searching for *sweet* would not retrieve instances of *sweete*, *svveet*, etc.). Searching for a grammatical feature or an aspect of word meaning is even harder, and arriving at frequencies of occurrence is not the endpoint, as we must examine the function in context of whatever linguistic feature we are searching for. Also, absence of occurrence is not a guarantee that an item is completely obsolete. The problem could be with the corpus not happening to contain that item. With respect to this point, we should remember that historical records, beyond relatively recent times, are written records – they do not record what was happening in everyday speech. Some linguists argue that spoken interaction is the powerhouse of linguistic change. Indeed, the bulk of communication takes place in speech, and speech is learnt before reading/writing – it is primary in various senses. For early periods of language use, historical linguists are forced to look for clues in speech-based genres such as trial proceedings and plays, or in secondary data.

Secondary data include works like dictionaries, grammars, and commentaries on pronunciation, elocution, spelling and correctness of use. Sometimes secondary data reveal as much about attitudes towards language as the language itself. For example, William Bullokar's *Pamphlet for Grammar* (1586) reveals how early grammarians were in the thrall of Latin, and so attempted to see other languages, even those with markedly different grammatical systems, through the prism of Latin. For instance, the early English grammarians typically distinguished grammatical gender in nouns and adjectives. This is nonsense from today's perspective, as we know from primary data that the situation was more or less the same then as it is now.

What happens when we have no suitable primary or secondary data? In such instances, linguistic reconstruction must fill the gaps. This is essentially calculated guesswork made on the basis of indirect evidence. In the case of sound change, for example, the indirect evidence sources are as follows:

## Spelling

Not all languages involve systematic correspondences between phonemes and graphemes but some do. Moreover, the fact that older stages of spelling were less standardized means that spelling systems were more likely to reflect people's pronunciation. Thus, regarding the word *nut*, the presence of initial <h> in some varieties of OE (thus *hnutu*) gives us a clue that the word originally had an initial sound approximating to [h], and regarding the word *was*, the presence of <æ> in some varieties of OE (thus *wæs*) gives us a clue that the vowel quality approximated to [æ].

## Rhymes and rhyming dictionaries

The following rhyming couplet offers evidence for the shift in English from [æ] to [ɒ] in words such as *was* and *Swan*.

> Then, as her Strength with Years increas'd, began
> To pierce aloft in Air the soaring Swan: (Dryden, *Aeneis* 1697)

The fact that *Swan* rhymes with *began* seems to be good evidence for the fact that in this period it was still [æ]. Of course, this evidence only works if one can be sure about the pronunciation of one half of the rhyme (in this case *began*), and we need to establish how accurate the poet's rhyming technique is (e.g. watch out for eye-rhymes).

## Puns

The following pun offers evidence for the shift in English from [i:] to [aɪ], a shift that falls under the umbrella of the Great Vowel Shift:

PRO. But what said she?
SP. I.
PRO. Nod-I, why that's noddy.
SP. You mistooke Sir: I say she did nod;

And you aske me if she did nod, and I say I.
PRO. And that set together is noddy.
(Shakespeare, *Two Gentlemen of Verona*, act 1, scene I, First Folio 1623)

The pun exploits the fact that the letter *I* could either represent the first-person pronoun or could represent an affirmative 'aye' (i.e. roughly today's 'yes'). Today, of course, *I* and 'aye' sound the same. Speed's answer to Protheus's question is that she gave the affirmative 'aye' (it is written I, but Speed clarifies 'she did nod', so the sense is most likely 'aye' not *I*). Protheus then wittily draws out the fact that Speed has presumably nodded as he said 'aye', and a nod plus 'aye' sounds the same as the word *noddy*, meaning foolish. The last vowel sound of *noddy* is [i:], so now we are in a position to infer that affirmative *aye* is pronounced [i:]. Speed seems to think that Protheus thinks he mistakenly meant *I* as a first-person pronoun. He clarifies by saying *I say I*, which we could clarify today by writing 'I say aye'. *Set together* this does sound a bit odd, or *noddy*, because both the first person pronoun *I* and the affirmative *I* (i.e. 'aye') are said the same way. This being so, we have evidence that in this period the first person pronoun *I* was pronounced [i:].

## Statements made by grammarians and spelling reformers

Consider the evidence from John Hart's *An Orthographie* (1569) that the spelling <ee> was pronounced [i:]:

> We call thee, in learning the A.B.C. in the sound of i, and do double thee, for that sound, as in see the Bee doth flee.

Here, he is saying that the letter <e> represented the sound 'i', that is to say, [i:] (we know from elsewhere in Hart's work that the letter was used for that sound). What he then reveals is that words such as *bee* and *flee* have that sound, as they do today. This is interesting because we know that <ee> originally had the value [e:] in ME. Hart, then, helps pinpoint when this change might have taken place. Of course, such evidence is dependent on the scholar's interpretation and attitudes, as well as the accuracy of the transcription used.

## Clues from other languages

If we know the pronunciations of words in particular languages and in particular periods, we may be in a position to infer across languages. For example, words imported from French have given clues about the timing of pronunciation changes in English. When the French word *age* was borrowed into the English language its first vowel was closer to [a:]. The pronunciation of this word in English has followed a whole group of words like *name* (OE *nama*), words that have been part of the Great Vowel Shift. So, given that *age* fell in line with this development, there seems to be some tangential evidence that when it arrived words such as *name* had not yet changed their vowel to the diphthong [eɪ].

## Following paths of development

Sometimes we might have some evidence to suggest that the changes in the pronunciation of a word or group of words has followed a particular path. We might not have evidence of pronunciations at each stage of the path, but often we can infer the missing links. A case in point would be the Great Vowel Shift, where we might not have evidence for all stages of the shift for any particular item, but we can infer what is missing on the basis of the well-established general path of change.

Of course, none of these individual sources of evidence is particularly robust. The ideal scenario for any specific case is where one can bring several sources of evidence to bear.

Linguistic reconstruction, relying especially on the indirect evidence mentioned in the last two points of the list in the previous paragraph, has been the mainstay of comparative philology or **comparative linguistics**. One idea is that different languages from very different geographical areas of the world are 'genetically' related, and by systematic comparison of forms we can reconstruct linguistic genealogies, such as the Proto-Indo-European (PIE) family tree. Table 10.2 gives a sense of some of the evidence used in deriving PIE. Use of the asterisk is a convention to indicate that we have no attested form – it is a reconstructed member of the proto-language.

Note that the focus is on some kind of core lexicon – numbers, close kinship terms and 'basic' words (e.g. *blood, egg, tail, ear, hand, sun, water*) – as core items are more likely to represent the language variety in hand, being more resistant to borrowing, something that would confuse the language variety categories (various lists of supposedly core items can be found here: http://cals.conlang.org/word/list/). Reconstructing the forms of the proto-language has partly been done on the basis of examining existing forms for commonalities.

**TABLE 10.2.** Language families

| Language group | Language | 'father' | 'mother' | 'two' | 'three' | 'tooth' |
|---|---|---|---|---|---|---|
| Germanic | Old English | *fœdar* | *meder* | *twá* | *þrí* | *tóþ* |
| | Old Saxon | *fadar* | *m⌧der* | *twâ* | *thrie* | *tand* |
| | Old Norse | *faðer* | *móðir* | *tveir* | *þrír* | *t⌧nn* |
| Italic | Latin | *pater* | *m⌧ter* | *duo* | *tr⌧s* | *dens / dents* |
| Hellenic | Greek | πατ⌧ρ (*pater*) | μaτέρ (*mater*) | δύο (*duo*) | τρε ς (*treis*) | ὀδούς (*odous*) |
| Celtic | Old Irish | *athir* | *m⌧thir* | *dá* | *tri* | *dét* |
| Indic | Sanskrit | *pitr* | *matr* | *dwau* | *trayas* | *dans / danta* |
| Proto-Indo-European | - | **p∂t⌧r* | **m⌧tér* | **dwou* | **trejes* | **dentis* |

Thus one might suppose that similarities amongst the items listed in the columns of Table 10.2 reflect an earlier word. In addition, reconstruction has proceeded on the basis of identifying paths of change. A famous case of this is Grimm's Law, described in Section 10.4.1. Note that in Table 10.2 Germanic forms seem to be the odd ones out in having word-initial <f> instead of <p>, which is also the PIE form.

Still, linguistic reconstruction remains calculated guesswork, and remains dependent on how good the initial evidence is in the first place. In particular, it rests on the assumption that particular words represent specific languages and only those languages. But work in dialectology has shown repeatedly that languages rarely if ever have sharp edges; instead, one blurs into another, giving rise to a dialect continuum.

**KEY POINTS: Data and methods**

- Primary data are records of actual language, such as archival records, letters, prose and poetry.
- Secondary data are commentaries on the language, such as dictionaries, grammars and style guides.
- Electronic corpora of primary data allow for the computational analysis of large quantities of language data.
- Linguistic reconstruction involves piecing together direct and indirect evidence to generate a sense of what a language was like at an earlier point in its history.

## EXERCISE 10.5

### (a) Comparing texts within a genre

Compare the two versions of an extract from the English Bible below. What is different? At what linguistic level is it different?

> But Peter sate vvithout in the court: and there came to him one vvenche, saying: Thou also vvast vvith IESVS the Galilean. But he denied before them all, saying, I vvot not vvhat thou sayest. (The Rheims Bible 1582)
>
> Meanwhile Peter was sitting outside in the courtyard when a serving-maid accosted him and said, 'You were there too with Jesus the Galilean.' Peter denied it in face of them all. 'I do not know what you mean', he said. (New English Bible 1961)

### (b) Reconstructing old pronunciations

Read the first stanza from Christopher Marlowe's poem 'The Passionate Sheepheard to his Love' (1600). What might the rhyme scheme suggest about the pronunciation of *prove* in Early Modern English? How certain can you be and what other evidence would help to confirm your hypothesis? (It might help to read the full poem online.)

> Come live with mee, and be my Love,
> And we will all the pleasures prove,
> That Vallies, groves, hills and fieldes,
> Woods, or steepie mountaine yeeldes. (quoted in Keegan 2001: 174)

**WEBSITE: Group exercise**

Visit the website and, in a small group, examine the text in Early Modern English. You will be asked to complete two tasks. They are designed to get you to think about how usage and meaning (pragmatics) can influence formal elements of language in historical texts.

## 10.6 SUMMARY

The techniques of historical linguistics have allowed linguists to (i) determine how languages change over time and (ii) suggest reasons for why such changes might occur. In this chapter we have introduced some of the main theories, models and findings from historical linguistics, as well as given you an insight into how historical linguists go about investigating language change.

What makes historical linguistics so challenging is that, as Aitchison (2001: 21) points out, explaining language change is fraught with the potential for misinterpreting evidence. Even Aitchison does not manage to avoid this danger completely. Discussing how rhymes can indicate older pronunciations, she notes that a 'tongue/wrong' rhyme in an EModE poem tells us that *tongue* used to be pronounced to rhyme with *wrong*, the implicit assumption being that this is not the case anymore. But this claim overlooks the fact that *tongue* is still pronounced to rhyme with *wrong* in many varieties of northern English. This particular case highlights the importance of not prioritizing the standard language at the expense of regional varieties, something which Crystal (2004) points out has been a particular problem in the study of the history of English (the same charge might be levelled at the diachronic study of many languages). Sometimes, of course, in cases where data are so scarce that we are relying on linguistic reconstruction, there may be a limit to what we can legitimately claim about regional varieties. But in cases where enough evidence exists for us to consider other possible variations, it is important not to focus on standard forms at the expense of regional variation. This issue underlines the importance of triangulation in historical linguistics; that is, using as many checks as is possible (e.g. primary data, secondary data, reconstruction, etc.) to increase the confidence we can have in our claims.

Finally, it should be noted that there is a significant degree of crossover between historical linguistics and some of the concerns of other subdisciplines of language study. Although historical linguists have traditionally focused more on formal change in language, functional change is increasingly being investigated (see, for example, the studies in Watts and Trudgill 2000), for which it is necessary to draw on disciplines such as pragmatics, stylistics, sociolinguistics and literary studies. It is also the case that language change is sometimes deliberately affected (or at least an effect is deliberately attempted), by governmental or non-governmental organizations imposing policies to influence language use. A recent well-known example is the German spelling reform imposed collectively in 1996 by the governments of Austria, Germany, Lichtenstein and Switzerland. Such macro-level language planning brings its own complications, not least of which is the issue of whether such interventions in linguistic development are either feasible or desirable. The same issues are faced by linguists engaged in trying to preserve endangered languages. And the common factor in all investigations of language development is that change is both inevitable and fascinating.

WEBSITE: **Historical linguistics**

Now go to the website and assess your knowledge of historical linguistics by completing the self-test questions!

## SUGGESTIONS FOR FURTHER READING

Aitchison, J. (2012). *Language Change: Progress or Decay?*, 4th edn. Cambridge University Press. This book is a highly readable introduction to the how and why of language change, covering all of the issues described in this chapter in a genuinely accessible way.

McColl Millar, Robert (2007). *Trask's Historical Linguistics*. London: Hodder. This is a revised version of R. L. Trask, *Historical Linguistics* (1996). It is a good, readable introduction with examples from many languages.

Campbell, L. (2013). *Historical Linguistics: An Introduction*, 3rd edn. Edinburgh University Press. This is an accessible introductory textbook, very much focused on explaining how to *do* historical linguistics.

# ANSWERS TO EXERCISES

## Exercise 10.1

Most people will respond by talking about new words that have entered the language – and these will often be words that are foregrounded by virtue of their relatively rapid arrival and possibly the creativity that has gone into their formation. So, for example, they might mention new blends such as *braggadocious* or conversions such as *to sex up*. It's unlikely that they will talk about sound changes or grammatical developments. The reason for this is that because such developments take place gradually, it is difficult to perceive them, not least because change here tends to be relatively slow. One of the consequences of this for historical linguists is that we often need an awful lot of data, gathered over a long period, before we can confirm, describe and explain a change.

## Exercise 10.2

Imagine you walk into a pub where two people are playing a game of pool (pocket billiards if you're reading this in North America!). You don't need to know how the game began in order to observe which player is winning. You simply look at the number of remaining red and yellow balls (or stripes and solids) on the table. By the same token, if you want to study language use at a particular point in time, you don't necessarily need to know how that language began (i.e. synchronic analysis doesn't require initial diachronic analysis). But if you want to study language change over time, not only do you need to track developments diachronically, you also need to know what that language was like at an earlier stage (i.e. diachronic analysis requires initial synchronic analysis).

## Exercise 10.3

(a) Most people assume that the word *outrage* is a compound of *out* plus *rage*, and this seems to be consistent with the current sense (i.e. out of the normal bounds of rage, a kind of super rage). The word is in fact the word *outr* (from Latin *ultra*, meaning 'beyond') plus the noun-forming suffix *-age*, the sense being to be in a state of being beyond any kind of norm. This is a case of reanalysis; people have reanalysed the word in a different way. (This particular example is discussed in a number of books, including McColl Millar 2007.)

(b) To continue the kind of examples mentioned in Section 10.3, the use of *sick* as a positive evaluation is a good case of expressiveness. But expressiveness need not only apply to the lexical items. Recent years have seen the advent of the 'high rising tone', a rising pitch in the final elements of a sentence with the result that statements sound more like questions. This phenomenon is present in Southern California, especially amongst teenagers, and also in Australia, and seems to be spreading to other Englishes too. One of its functions seems to be to create interest for listeners and encourage their participation, hence it is a matter of expressiveness.

(c) A striking case is the very frequent northern variant of the word *no*, i.e. *nay*. Consider that modern Danish and Swedish have *nei*, which sounds identical. Similarly, we might point to the northern word *laik*, meaning 'to play', and Swedish *leka*, the northern *kirk*, for a church, and Danish *kirke*, or the northern *beck*, for a brook or stream, and Swedish *bäck*. These, and others, are clues to the Viking settlement of northern areas, given that the Vikings come from the area of modern Denmark, Sweden and Norway.

## Exercise 10.4

### (a) Grammatical change

The expression *gonna* is an example of grammaticalization. It is originally formed from 'going to', with the original, more concrete sense of moving from one place to another. Today, it has no sense of changing place but forms the more grammatical function of marking reference to the future. Note it has also undergone phonetic reduction.

### (b) Lexical change: borrowing

Borrowing is facilitated by contact, and often motivated by prestige (we copy items that are perceived to be prestigious in order to sound more prestigious ourselves). Other factors can include a kind of hole filling, where the borrowed item fills a need created by changes in the environment (e.g. the arrival of a new concept or item). In some respects, *borrowing* is an odd term to use to describe the practice of taking words from other languages, since there is little sense in which the loans are ever given back. *Copying* may better describe the process.

### (c) Lexical change: word-formation

i. Derivation (*de* + *friend*)
ii. Borrowing (from Chinese *gǒuqǐzǐ* [goji berry])
iii. Blending (*golden* + *doodle*; note that the first part of the blend is from *Golden Retriever* while the second part is derived from the morphological reanalysis of another blend: *labradoodle* = *Labrador* + *Poodle*)
iv. Compounding (*i* + *Pod*; note that the first compound is an initialization of *internet* and is potentially undergoing a degree of semantic bleaching, such that *i* can simply be a prefix to indicate cutting-edge technology)
v. Derivation (*metabolome* + *ic*)
vi. Acronymization (*S*evere *A*cute *R*espiratory *S*yndrome)
vii. Borrowing (from Japanese *Sūdoku*)
viii. Compounding, followed by inflection (*water* + *board* + *ing*)

### (d) Semantic change

*Amusing* and *awful* originally refer to something that could cause a state of: musing or staring in astonishment; awe, dread or reverential fear, whilst *artificial* meant that something was full of artifice or skill. James's statement is mildly humorous today largely because of the second and third items which have undergone pejoration, but even today's sense of *amusing*, causing laughter, is hardly appropriate for a magnificent cathedral. More generally, it should be noted that all of them have shifted towards greater subjectivity, that is, away from merely describing an emotional state or property of the building towards a strong evaluation of it.

## Exercise 10.5

### (a) Comparing texts within a genre

A wealth of observations are possible. For example, in the 1582 version we see: *sate* vs *was sitting* (progressive forms had not been established); *vvenche* vs *serving-maid* (today, *wench* has a more pejorative meaning); *thou* vs *you* (*you* was not the only second-pronoun form); *IESVS* vs *Jesus* (now, the letter *has now given rise to the letter <j> and <v> is only used for the consonant); denied* vs *denied it* (the verb *denied* now must take an object, it is transitive); *vvot* vs *know* (*vvot* is now obsolete) and so on.

### (b) Reconstructing old pronunciations

The rhyme scheme of the poem is AABB, and in the second and third stanzas the end-rhymes are full rhymes. This structure suggests that *love* and *prove* also rhyme. (It is possible that they may be eye-rhymes, though this is unlikely at a time when spelling was still not standardized.) The question then concerns the value of the vowel sound in both words. The likelihood is that it was [ʊ] rather than [u:]. Crystal (2009) draws on secondary data to ascertain this, quoting from Ben Jonson's *English Grammar* in which Jonson notes that the letter <o> 'soundeth...akin to *u*; as *cosen, dozen, mother, brother, love, prove*'. Of course, we cannot discount the possibility of other regional pronunciations where *love* may have been pronounced [u:], but the evidence from Jonson at least confirms that /prʊv/ was an accepted pronunciation at the time.

## REFERENCES


Aitchison, J. (2001). *Language Change: Progress or Decay?* 3rd edn. Cambridge University Press.

Blank, A. (1999). Why do new meanings occur? A cognitive typology of the motivations for lexical semantic change. In A. Blank and P. Koch (eds.), *Historical Semantics and Cognition*, pp. 61–89. Berlin: Mouton de Gruyter.

Brinton, L. J. and Traugott, E. C. (2005). *Lexicalization and Language Change*. Cambridge University Press

Crystal, D. (2004). *The Stories of English*. London: Penguin.

(2009). Sounding the sonnets. *Around the Globe* 43, 26-7.

Darwin, C. (1871). *The Descent of Man*. New York: D. Appleton and Company.

Fischer, O. (2003). The development of the modals in English: radical versus gradual changes. In D. Hart (ed.), *English Modality in Context*, pp. 17–32. Bern: Peter Lang.

Görlach, M. (1997). *The Linguistic History of English*. Basingstoke: Macmillan.

Honeybone, P. (2008). Lenition, weakening and consonantal strength: tracing concepts through the history of phonology. In J. Brandão de Carvalho, T. Scheer and P. Ségéral (eds.), *Lenition and Fortition*. Berlin: Mouton de Gruyter.

Hopper, P. J. and Traugott, E. C. ([1993] 2003). *Grammaticalization*, 2nd edn. Cambridge University Press.

Keegan, P. (ed.) (2001). *The New Penguin Book of English Verse*. London: Penguin.

Labov, W. (1963). The social motivation of a sound change. *Word*, 19, 273–309.

(1978). On the use of the present to explain the past. In P. Baldi and R. N. Werth (eds.), *Readings in Historical Phonology*, pp. 275–312. Pennsylvania State University Press.

([1966] 2006). *The Social Stratification of English in New York City*. Cambridge University Press.

(1994). *Principles of Linguistic Change: Internal Factors*. Oxford: Blackwell.

(2001). *Principles of Linguistic Change: Social Factors*. Oxford: Blackwell.

Le Page, R. B. and Tabouret-Keller, A. (1985). *Acts of Identity: Creole-based Approaches to Language and Ethnicity*. Cambridge University Press.

Lightfoot, D. (1979). *Principles of Diachronic Syntax*. Cambridge University Press.

Martinet, A. (1952). Function, structure and sound change. *Word*, 8, 1–32.

Meillet, A. (1912). L'évolution des formes grammaticales. *Scientia*, 12(26) [Reprinted as *Linguistique historique et linguistique générale*, pp. 130–48, Paris: C. Klincksieck, 1951].

Milroy, J. and Milroy, L. (1985). Linguistic change, social network and speaker innovation. *Journal of Linguistics*, 21, 339–84.

Nevalainen, T. and Raumolin-Brunberg, H. (2003). *Historical Sociolinguistics: Language Change in Tudor and Stuart England*. London: Pearson Education.

Ohala, J. J. (1981). The listener as a source of sound change. In C. S. Masek, R. A. Hendrick and M. F. Miller (eds.), *Papers from the Parasession on Language and Behaviour, Chicago Linguistics Society*, pp. 178–203. Chicago Linguistic Society.

Romaine, S. (1982). *Socio-historical Linguistics: Its Status and Methodology*. Cambridge University Press.

Traugott, E. C. (1989). On the rise of epistemic meanings in English: An example of subjectification in semantic change. *Language*, 65(1), 31–55.

(1995). Subjectification in grammaticalisation. In D. Stein and S. Wright (eds.), *Subjectivity and Subjectivisation: Linguistic Perspectives*, pp. 31–54. Cambridge University Press.

Trudgill, P. J. (1989). Interlanguage, interdialect and typological change. In S. Gass, C. Madden, D. Preston and L. Selinker (eds.), *Variation in Second Language Acquisition: Psycholinguistic Issues*, pp. 244–53. Clevedon: Multilingual Matters.

Watts, R. and Trudgill, P. (2000). *Alternative Histories of English*. London: Routledge.

Weinreich, U., Labov, W. and Herzog, M. I. (1968). Empirical foundations for a theory of language change. In W. P. Lehmann (ed.), *Directions for Historical Linguistics: A Symposium*, pp. 95–195. Austin: University of Texas Press.

# 11 Sociolinguistics

NATALIE BRABER

**KEY TERMS**

- accent
- age grading
- apparent time
- covert prestige
- crossing
- dialect
- ethnolect
- free variation
- idiolect
- overt prestige
- real-time
- RP
- structured variation
- verbal repertoire
- vernacular

**PREVIEW**

This chapter looks at the relationship between language and society. This means that we will be examining language in its social contexts – how it is actually used by people (rather than how grammarians may prescribe language 'should' be spoken). Sociolinguistics investigates how the language practices of one individual differ from situation to situation or how they differ within one community. This involves looking at the social characteristics of language users or speakers – such as social class, gender and sexuality – as well as the social context in which language use changes. We will also discuss how we can adapt our language to fit a situation and the people we are speaking with. We all have a verbal repertoire of speech styles and ways to use language, which allow us to switch, depending on the person we are talking to and the situation we are in, and we frequently do so without being aware of it. Issues such as language policy, language planning and education can also be included within sociolinguistics, although we will not be looking at these in this chapter.

## 11.1 INTRODUCTION

We may think of languages as single entities – English, French and Yoruba for example – but things are not as simple as this. If we think specifically about English, we may think of the English used in education, law courts, on the media or the English that is taught to foreign speakers as 'being' English. But this is just one **variety** – in this case, **Standard English**. It is the English used in dictionaries and grammar books. Most people who speak English can understand other English speakers, but that is not to say that we all speak the same; consider the differences in the English spoken in the UK, USA, Canada, South Africa and India to name just a few examples. We pronounce words differently and use different words or grammatical constructions, but we are all speaking 'English'.

The unique characteristics of the spoken language of an individual person are called a speaker's **idiolect**. Although everybody has a range of styles, also known as their **verbal repertoire**, we see that individuals tend to share their linguistic practices with others. This means there are groups of speakers who use language in a similar way, but differently from the standard form. For example, people from a certain part of the country or a particular youth group may use language in a distinctive way. The interesting thing about this phenomenon is that these differences are not random, rather they show systematic variation. As sociolinguists we examine this variation. We look at different groups (or different situations) and examine how language changes – we think about the how and why and where of language variation. Sociolinguists are descriptivists, not prescriptivists. We do not prescribe how people *should* speak, but we describe how people *actually* use language. Rather than condemning a certain type of language usage as wrong, sociolinguists would instead view it as *non-standard*.

When analysing language from a sociolinguistic perspective we can do so on several levels:

- Sound system: the particular phonemes speakers use (and do not use);
- Grammar: this refers to morphology, grammar and syntax;
- Lexis: words used by speakers;
- Discourse: we can investigate issues such as turn-taking, topic introduction and narratives.

In this chapter we will examine patterns of variation by using case studies, which show the systematic changes we can find within a particular language. These case studies will focus on English, but sociolinguistic studies can, of course, be carried out on all languages, as all languages show systematic variation in ways which will be outlined in this chapter.

## 11.2 What is sociolinguistics?

It is difficult to say exactly what the first sociolinguistic study was, but many linguists believe the first systematic study of the relationship between language variation and social organization was made in 1958 by John Fischer, a sociologist, who noted that school children in New England (northeastern United States) said either *running* or *runnin'*. He found correlations between these linguistic forms and the students' gender and social class. This indicated that rather than **free variation** (where the choice between forms is arbitrary and unpredictable), he had come across **structured variation** (where the choice between forms is linked to other factors). Most often, though, William Labov is credited with inaugurating modern sociolinguistics with ground breaking studies in the USA (in Martha's Vineyard and also in New York; see Labov 1972 and 1966 respectively). Labov obtained recordings of natural speech and correlated aspects of linguistic variation with social characteristics of speakers, examining in detail the relationship between how people speak and how they fit into their speech community.

We all have a class, ethnic, gender, age and sexual identity; additionally we come from places and may now live in other places. These social characteristics may be manifest in ways that allow sociolinguists to investigate how speakers define themselves, and how they identify themselves through language use. We can also consider the function of language in a particular situation – is it being used to talk to a stranger, give a lecture, scold a child, seduce a lover or talk to a grandmother? Although many of these variables will interact, we will try to examine them individually to determine how they affect our language usage.

Sociolinguistics, like all academic disciplines, requires the learner to become familiar with new terminology which practitioners use with precisely defined meanings. Here we will talk about different *varieties* of a language, for example of English. The word '**dialect**' can evoke a stigma, especially for non-linguists, but we will use the term in a specific way, as will be discussed below. We also use terms to explain language variation. In this chapter we will introduce particular **social variables** (such as class or ethnicity) and the different ways of using aspects of language: pronunciation, word choice or grammatical choices, which are known as the **linguistic variables**. In short, sociolinguistics investigates the extent to which there is systematic variation involving social variables by examining which speakers use which linguistic variables and the contexts which condition the different usages.

**KEY POINTS: Sociolinguistics**

- All languages show variation.
- This variation is not random and will be determined by the speaker and/or the situation.
- All speakers have their own idiolect(s) which make up their verbal repertoire.

## 11.3 Regional variation

In the previous section we have seen that the varieties of English spoken, for example, in Canada and South Africa, are likely to show differences from each other. However, these differences also occur on a smaller scale. Within a country like the UK there are regional differences between speakers. We can often tell where a speaker comes from by hearing the language they use. In this section we will discuss what this diversity entails and how it has been examined.

All living languages are in a constant state of change and sociolinguists are interested in how they change and why. When language change occurs, it is not necessarily spread uniformly throughout the wider speech community. Regional diversity can develop when people are separated geographically and socially. Some changes will take place in certain locations but not in others. Some changes will spread and others will not. Some changes will be adopted by some speakers but not by others. Another force may run counter to that of diversification: in recent years many sociolinguistics have been interested in the concept of **dialect levelling**. This refers to a movement towards greater uniformity and less variation among language varieties. It has been suggested that it is the influence of the mass media that is causing increased dialect levelling, but this may not be the case. Other factors could play a role too. For example, more so than in the past, people are moving around the country and travelling more widely, and this could also affect how language changes. Furthermore, although it seems certain that in the UK some rural dialects are disappearing, urban dialects are still continuing to be reinforced. In any case, dialect levelling is just one of the ways in which language use can change. What is important for us is that we can look at where people live and who they mix with to examine how and why language change spreads.

### 11.3.1 Issues around terminology

Before we explore regional variation in greater detail, we should expand on the way sociolinguists use specific terminology. The question here is really what do we call different varieties of language? Many non-linguists use the word *language* to refer to the *standard* form of the language, for example Standard English, while referring to other varieties of the language as *dialects*. There are usually value-judgements attached to these references in the sense that the standard variety can be seen as 'proper' and governed by rules, whereas the other varieties are perceived as 'broken', 'improper' or 'wrong'. A standard variety of a language is usually the one that is codified, that is, dictionaries and grammar books describe this variety and it is frequently used in the fields of education, law and the media.

In this chapter we refer to all the different dialects of English as varieties, and we recognize Standard English as just one variety, not 'the' variety. We use the term '**accent**' to refer to pronunciation, and dialect to refer to a system of differences related to word choice, morphology and grammar. We also use the term '**vernacular**'; this refers to a usually low-status variety, which has features that are different from the standard variety. It is often used by younger, urban, working-class speakers. An important thing to remember is that all speakers have an accent. Many speakers consider **RP** (Received Pronunciation) the 'best' and most correct variety, however, it is an accent like any other, but one with a considerable amount of prestige attached to it. Only a very small proportion of the English-speaking population use RP (in England, for example, between 3 and 5 per cent of the total population) and it is hard to associate any regional area with this variety – it is considered a 'social accent' linked with people at the top end of the social scale. At this end of the scale we see the least amount of regional variation, whereas at the lower social levels, we see much more regional variation (see Figure 11.1). We tend to associate specific accents with specific dialects; for example, a Scouse accent with a Liverpudlian dialect. Nevertheless, an accent can be spoken with any dialect and anyone can speak Standard English with any kind of regional accent.

It can be difficult to distinguish a language from a dialect. Linguists invoke the criterion of **mutual intelligibility**, whereby, if speakers can understand one another, they are speaking the same or different dialects of a language. By contrast, if speakers cannot understand one another, they are speaking different languages. Unfortunately the situation is not always so straightforward. We have all been in situations where we have not

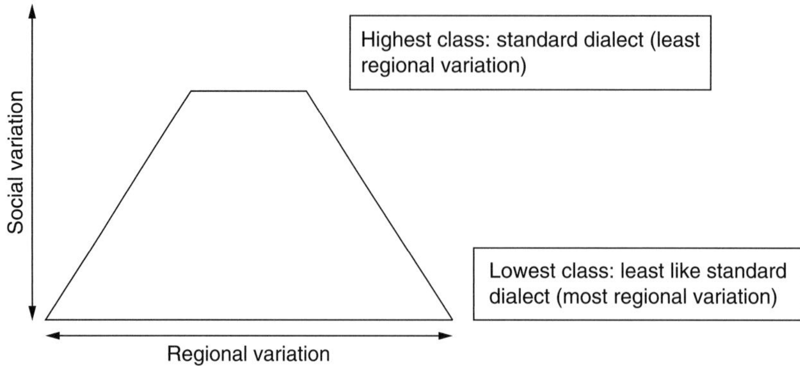


**Figure 11.1** Social and regional dialect variation (adapted from Trudgill 2000: 30)

understood someone (or they have not understood us), but we were both speaking the same language. Furthermore, many of the distinctions made between a language and a dialect are political in nature rather than based on linguistic criteria. For example, Danish, Norwegian and Swedish are treated as different languages even though speakers can understand one another, and many different dialects of Chinese are not mutually intelligible, especially if geographically widely separated, but Chinese is considered to be one language because of its political unity.

## 11.3.2 How can we examine regional variation?

Our awareness that people from other parts of the country speak differently can lead to jokes about the way people speak. People associate particular varieties with social characteristics and stereotypes. Many studies have illustrated the link people can make between a linguistic variety and the perceived characteristics of a speaker, for example, whether they are well-educated, trustworthy, funny or likeable (see, for example, Lambert et al. 1960). When examining regional variation, we look for consistent features, which are found in one region but may not be used in another region. This method allows us to establish where different words are used, or where words are pronounced differently, for example where in England people say *put* and *putt* the same way, which vowel they use for *grass* in the UK, how a New Zealander's pronunciation of the word *bad* can sound like *bed*, or how in certain parts of the US *god* will sound like an RP *guard*. Because language change is much more likely to be gradual, we cannot always draw lines on a map and say that everything on one side of the line is 'Variety A' and everything on the other side is 'Variety B'. However, this type of analysis does allow us to make generalizations about regional variation and present the findings in a graphical format. We can do this, for example, by drawing a line on a map to show where different pronunciations, words or grammatical structures can be found. Such a line is called an **isogloss** (see Figure 11.2 which shows which varieties in the UK and Ireland pronounce the [r] sound in words like *car* and *farm*).

**Figure 11.2** Postvocalic [r] in the UK and Ireland (adapted from Hughes, Trudgill and Watt 2012: 64)

Theoretically speaking, when you cross an isogloss, you cross a linguistic boundary. Sometimes several isoglosses coincide, and they may also coincide with political or natural boundaries (for example, borders, rivers or mountains). Such bundles of isoglosses can define a regional dialect. In the UK, the biggest bundle of isoglosses is found on the border between Scotland and England. Although we can look at language and dialect boundaries and see how language varies regionally and nationally, it is important to realize that definitive borders are often not apparent. Rather than having sharp boundaries, languages or dialects often seem to merge from one to the other. This is what is called a language or **dialect continuum**, where we see gradual change as we move through a country, or from country to country. The varieties at the opposite ends of the continuum may be very different, but the varieties next to each other are much more similar.

### 11.3.3 Case study: [r]

Regional variation is an important aspect of a speaker's identity and many sociolinguistic studies have been carried out to examine attitudes towards different varieties. In this section we will look at an example of regional variation that has been the subject of much research. This relates to the map in Figure 11.2. It illustrates which varieties of English pronounce the [r] sound after vowels in words like *car* and *farm*, also known as postvocalic [r]. Traditionally, the majority of the UK was rhotic, meaning speakers pronounced the r-sound in these words. This has gradually changed over the last few centuries, beginning in the southeast of England and spreading to other parts of the country. In the UK there are now only a few areas which remain rhotic, such as parts of southwest England, Ireland, Scotland and a small pocket in Lancashire. However, even in these areas, recent research has shown that this may be changing and these varieties may be lost. We are more likely to hear postvocalic [r] in the language of older, working-class rural speakers than in younger middle-class urban speakers, and so, in the UK, this pronunciation feature is associated with lower prestige. However, a study in New York revealed that the reverse is true in that city. The study, carried out by Labov and published in 1966, showed that if any two subgroups of New York City speakers are ranked on a scale of social stratification, they will use certain variables differently. By collecting data from staff in three different department stores (which were ranked from Saks Fifth Avenue, a high-status store in an exclusive part of town, to Klein's, a shop aimed at poor people), Labov discovered that employees of the high-end stores were more likely to use postvocalic [r] than those at the low-end stores. Although Labov's study examined this variable in relation to style and formality, it has shown clearly that one variable can be seen as having a higher prestige in one area than another. Therefore, there is linguistically nothing 'good' or 'bad' about certain ways of pronouncing words or sounds, but rather, that this type of variation can be associated with specific speakers and contexts.

Sociolinguists distinguish different kinds of prestige, namely **overt prestige** (where speakers aim towards the standard varieties of a language) and **covert prestige** (where speakers are more likely to move away from standard varieties – this has often been associated with working-class male speakers as will be discussed in Section 11.4). The fact that aspects of non-standard varieties could be emblematic and signal regional origin and covert prestige can also be illustrated by our example of postvocalic [r]. As mentioned above, certain varieties of Scottish English still use postvocalic [r]. This can closely reflect a sense of local identity. The pop band *The Proclaimers* is made up of identical twin brothers, Charlie and Craig Reid, who are known for singing their songs using their local dialect. They are also known for their strong sense of Scottish identity, their support for Scottish independence and that they have been at various stages of their lives activists for the Scottish National Party. One of their songs is entitled 'Throw the R away'. The lyrics state that they have been told that their accent is bad, but that 'I wouldn't know a single word to say if I flattened all the vowels and threw the "R"away'. For these speakers, their way of speaking and therefore their regional identity are important parts of who they are. However, other aspects of our identity can also influence our language use, and these will be discussed in the sections which follow.

**KEY POINTS: Regional variation**

- Although some linguists have identified dialect levelling, regional variation is still clear in varieties of English.
- The term *accent* is used to refer to pronunciation and *dialect* refers to grammar, morphology and syntax as well as pronunciation.
- Rather than clear-cut boundaries, most varieties will show gradual changes, which can be referred to as a language or dialect continuum.
- We can use isoglosses on maps to plot regional variation in a language.
- Standard English is just one variety of English.

WEBSITE: **Group exercise**

Visit the website and, in a small group, follow the link to the British Library website. Follow the instructions to examine a particular linguistic variety and discuss this with your group.

## EXERCISE 11.1

1. Can you think of a situation where you suddenly became aware that your linguistic variety was different from that of other people? For example, now you are at university – perhaps you have moved to a new town, or met people from other areas? Do they/you use words that are unfamiliar or do they have different ways of pronouncing things?
2. Have you been in a situation where you have not understood someone who spoke the same language? Which levels of language are most likely to cause difficulty in understanding: pronunciation, grammar or vocabulary?
3. British English and American English are usually considered to be the same language. Think of one reason why this might be the case, and one reason why US and UK Englishes might be considered to be different languages

## 11.4 Gender and sexuality

In the early 1970s, Robin Lakoff published one of the first works specifically concerned with women and the way they use language (Lakoff 1973). Since that publication many linguists have focused on language and gender in sociolinguistic research. In western societies, most of us will spend much of our time talking to both men and women, but this does not mean that males and females use language in the same way. The idea that men and women use language differently is present in popular beliefs about language. The sort of things that have been said about men and women in relation to language is that women talk more, are more likely to use certain types of words, are more polite, are less assertive, gossip more and swear less (Lakoff 1973).

When we consider the differences between men and women, one thing we can immediately note is the generally higher pitch used by women, and this is mainly due to them having shorter vocal folds. However, studies have shown that differences in pitch between male and female voices are on average greater than could be accounted for by physiology alone, suggesting that social factors may be involved too.

### 11.4.1 Issues around terminology

Some of the earlier work related to this topic referred to 'language and sex'. However, we will use 'sex' as a biological category and 'gender' as a socially constructed identity. There is also 'grammatical gender', which means that many languages require certain nouns to be linguistically marked as feminine, masculine or neuter – but this final category is something we will not examine in this chapter. We are going to consider whether language differences related to gender and sexuality (later in the chapter) are things that we just 'do'. There are many prescriptions inherent in British culture related to gender or sexuality, for example, that boys and girls 'should' speak or act in a particular way. These types of behaviour are acquired (they are not innate, that is to say, we are not born with these types of behaviours). We will see that 'becoming' a social gender involves understanding how to perform this linguistically. We should note that much historical sociolinguistics was carried out from a male perspective, where male speakers (particularly NORMS – non-mobile, older, rural males) were used for data collection. Other groups, such as different ethnic groups and women were regarded as using language differently from 'the norm'. An alternative approach, which we will explore, considers the ways in which speakers use language to identify themselves and communicate with others.

### 11.4.2 Gender-exclusive and gender-preferential forms

One theme language and gender research has looked at is how gender differences in language can reflect social status or power differences between speakers. If a particular community is very hierarchical (and men typically are more powerful than women in many cultures), then linguistic differences may be just one aspect of distinctiveness in the social hierarchy as a whole. There are two types of gendered variation: **gender-exclusive language** and **gender-preferential language**.

Gender-exclusive language refers to a situation where men and women only use one variety, for instance, particular words or pronunciations, which the other gender does not use. For example, in Japanese, women may choose to speak a distinct variety even though they are fully aware of the standard dialect which can be used by men and women. Also, when referring to themselves, Japanese men have traditionally used *boku* and women *watashi* or *atashi* (although this may now be changing). In Koasati, a Native American language spoken in Louisiana, some words end in an [s] when used by men but end in an [l] or [n] when spoken by women. For example, the word meaning 'lift it' is *lakawhol* for women and *lakowhos* for men. In Sidamo (spoken in Ethiopia), some words are only used by men or women, so the translation of the word *milk* would be *ado* when spoken by a man, but *gurda* when used by a woman (see, for example, Yule 2010).

Gender-exclusive usage is fascinating, but not typical of gendered linguistic variation generally. More common cross-linguistically are gender-preferential forms where one gender is more likely to use certain features of language in particular situations. This occurs more in typically western societies, where men's and women's social roles overlap. Rather than using forms that are linked specifically to one gender, speakers will manifest different frequencies of the same forms. We can find this in English, where men may be more likely to drop the [h] sound in word-initial positions, e.g. house → *'ouse*, or use *-in'* instead of *-ing* in words such as *running*. This was found, for example, by Peter Trudgill during his studies in Norwich (Trudgill 1972). He established that in every social class, men are more likely to use vernacular (non-standard) forms than women. This is not just the case for English; similar examples have been found in French Canadian in Montreal, where women are less likely to drop the [l] in phrases such as *il y a* and *il fait*. In these examples, research has shown that women have a tendency to use forms closer to the standard, which we will examine below. Trudgill reports that this finding is the single most consistent finding to emerge from sociolinguistic studies.

It seems that gender is something we do and we actively construct gender difference, using language as an important way to identify ourselves. There can also be implications for sexual identity. We will return to this later in the chapter.

### 11.4.3 Examining language variation and gender

As explained in the previous section, in English we do not often come across gender-exclusive forms, but many researchers have investigated how gender may influence language usage. As we discussed, research in this field was inaugurated by Lakoff's early work. Her main argument was that there is such a thing as *women's language* and that it differs from the way men use language. She proposed that women's language is characterized by a specific group of linguistic features, which included:

- Hedges (*sort of, kind of*)
- Intensifiers (*that is soooo funny!*)

- Fillers (*you know, well*)
- Tag questions (*that's good, don't you think?*)
- Rising intonation in non-question sentences
- 'Empty' adjectives (*lovely, divine, cute*)
- Precise colour terms (*magenta, cerise*)

Lakoff also stated that women were more prone to use standard language forms, use super-polite forms, avoid swear words and avoid interrupting their communicative partners. She stated that these features could be linked to women's generally subordinate role in society and signalled a lack of confidence on behalf of the speaker.

Further studies by other researchers have shown mixed results. Some support Lakoff's theories and others seem to disprove them. Many researchers have suggested that differences are due to a cooperative method of communicating, rather than uncertainty, and this is the basis of the apparent differences in women's language.

### 11.4.4 Case studies: gender and standard language

When we look at gender variation in pronunciation, in the context of a variable which has a higher and a lower prestige variant, we see that women seem to use the higher–prestige forms with higher frequency than men. That is not to say that women do not use non-standard varieties. However, as Trudgill's studies in Norwich suggested, regardless of social class, women use standard forms more than men, and also report using standard forms more than they may actually use them (this is called over-reporting). Men, on the other hand, seem to use vernacular, non-standard forms more, and under-report using standard varieties if questioned. This pattern already occurs among children and teenagers. Studies carried out by Jenny Cheshire in Reading (Cheshire 1982) with groups of teenagers revealed that adolescent males are more likely to use non-standard grammatical forms than adolescent females. These differences have been found in every social class in English (although the differences between men and women tend to be highest in the middle classes) and the results seem relatively consistent. We might ask why this is. Some have suggested it may be to do with women's socialization, their awareness of social status and of how others may judge them. Or it could be that men have better access to other ways of marking their social status (for example, their jobs), so that women have to use language to do this. Or perhaps the jobs that women have are more likely to encourage them to use a variety closer to the standard as they are more likely to be public-facing. Some researchers have suggested that it may be linked to the social expectation that men should be strong and tough. Certain forms associated with working-class speech may be preferred by men because of their association with manual work and strength.

However, we also see that where linguistic change is in progress, female speakers tend to lead in the use of innovative forms. For example, changes in high rise 'up-speak' intonation (where intonation rises at the end of a sentence even if it's not a question), and an increased use of the quotative *like* (*he was like 'don't go to the party'*) are being led by female speakers in New Zealand and Canada respectively, and these changes are also found among young female speakers in the UK (see, for example, Tagliamonte and Hudson 1999).

### 11.4.5 Mixed-gender interaction

Another research theme is the study of how men and women interact with one another. We can investigate this by looking at gender variation in discourse. When we look at interaction between children, we see that they already show a preference for talking to those of the same gender, and that the hierarchies between groups of boys and groups of girls are already quite different. Boys tend to play together in larger groups and have a 'leader', whereas girls are more likely to play in smaller groups of twos and threes. It is therefore not surprising that there are differences in the way the genders approach interaction with each other.

Many studies have examined what happens when men and women communicate with each other. In same-gender discussion (groups of just males or just females) there is very little difference in the number of times speakers interrupt each other. However, that is not always the case in cross-gender interaction. Studies discussed in Zimmerman and West (1975) show that, in mixed-gender conversations among American college students, 96 per cent of interruptions can be attributed to the male speakers. Women ask more questions but get fewer responses from men. Topic changes initiated by men were more likely to be accepted than women's topic changes. Reports by Zimmerman and West (1975) and Fishman (1983) have argued that women do not have the same conversational rights as men and women are 'expected' to be supportive in conversations, and that these issues all reflect the differential power that society affords them.

A study by Maltz and Borker (1982) showed that back-channels and minimal responses (such as *really, hmm, oh*) are used differently by men and women. Men produce fewer back-channels, but when they do they appear to use them as indicators of agreement. Women use them more and as signs of listening. This means in cross-gender interactions, the absence of back-channels from men tends to make women think that men are not listening to them, while the frequent production of back-channels by women lead men to think that the women are agreeing with what they are saying. Much of this suggests that men are silencing the women, or it can seem that men and women's conversations have different purposes. More of men's conversation seems to be direct, rather than cooperative. For example, a study which examined medical conversations between doctors and patients showed that male doctors were more likely to use imperatives such as *take this series of pills*, whereas female doctors were more likely to use suggestions like *why don't we try using this type of medication* (West 1998). It seems that many of the features identified as typical of women facilitate the exchange of turns and allow others to speak, whereas men's talk appears more hierarchical. However, if women use directness they are frequently labelled as aggressive.

Some research (for example, Lakoff 1973) suggested that women's language is more polite and that this is reflected by the increased usage of tag questions, fillers and hedges. However, such language must be reviewed in context. A statement like *Let's see what he says, shall we?* can have quite different connotations in different situations, and they may not always be more polite or friendly. It is crucial we examine such forms in context of the speakers and the situation.

More recently, researchers have been examining single-sex interaction, particularly informal talk between friends. In same-sex groups studied by Pilkington (1992) men's conversation appears to be competitive whereas women's appears to be supportive. It is believed that this is the case for conversation more generally; women's language may invite participation rather than state assertions (which is seen as more masculine). The purpose of these conversations is the same, which is to build solidarity, bearing in mind that much of our socialization is carried out in single-gender groups.

These studies show broad tendencies; they suggest that men and women use language differently but of course not all men and not all women use language in the same way (or for the same purposes) and the way people talk can change in context. Nevertheless these studies have suggested there are differences that are worth researching.

### 11.4.6 Dominance vs deficience vs different?

One more approach to language and gender research has claimed that gender differences in language reflect different cultures of conversation. Some of the earliest work carried out on women's language, for example by Lakoff, is typical of the *deficit* approach, which states that women's language is somehow deficient when compared to male language. The *dominance* approach sees women as an oppressed group; it interprets linguistic differences as being due to women's subordination in society. The approach examined by Tannen (1990) is known as the *difference* approach. Tannen has claimed that men and women belong to different cultures and their language reflects this socialization. Women are more likely to use language to build and maintain relationships, which is known as a 'rapport' style, while men are more likely to use language to communicate factual information, the 'report' style. The most recent approach is the *social constructionist* approach. It regards gender identity as a social construct (all these approaches can be applied to many other subfields of sociolinguistics, for example, ethnicity, sexuality and age). This means that people 'do' gender rather than 'be' a gender. There is a large body of research focusing on the role of women's language in performing 'femininity'. Men's language has long remained under-researched (as it was seen as being the 'norm'), but recently theories on men's language and performing 'masculinity' have been rising as there has been a growing awareness of the role played by language in the construction of gender.

### 11.4.7 Language and sexuality

The thought that gender is a social or cultural construct rather than a binary opposition has made linguists think about how speakers 'perform' and 'do' gender and use linguistic resources to do so. Rather than there being a binary opposition of gender identities of male or female, there seems to be a range of femininities and masculinities that can intersect with other social variables. This has also influenced theories of *queer linguistics*, which examines the language of gay, lesbian, bisexual and transsexual communities because gender and sexuality are closely interlinked.

The approaches to language considered in the previous section, the dominance/difference/deviance approaches, tend to examine subjects that are 'different'. For example, it is assumed that the language of homosexuals is different to that of heterosexuals, and in fact, most research on sexuality involves looking at the language use of gay men. However, when we look at language and sexuality, we also need to consider other fields, for example the language of heterosexuality and masculinity, which for many years was regarded as the norm and therefore not studied. In this way, queer linguistics puts at the forefront of linguistic analysis the regulation of sexuality by hegemonic heterosexuality and the ways in which non-normative sexualities are negotiated in relation to these regulatory structures. It also submits for examination the normative gender and sexuality categories.

### 11.4.8 Performing identity

Sexual identity is an important aspect of modern western thinking. Sexuality (being straight, gay or bisexual) is not just an observation about someone's sexual behaviour, but also an identity that structures other aspects of life, just as gender and ethnicity do. This also means that our sexuality can emerge through language, as well as in other ways, for example how we move or dress. Researchers such as Judith Butler (1990) argue that identities like 'man', 'woman', 'gay' or 'transsexual' are not just pre-existing attributes of individuals that their behaviour expresses, but are brought into being, and sustained, by the repeated actions an individual performs.

We can examine how language can be used to perform a particular identity for speakers who are gay or lesbian. Similarly, we can also examine masculinity and heterosexuality. Very little research has been carried out on straight, white, male speakers (as they are considered 'the norm'). However, research by linguists such as Kiesling (2004) has shown how men can 'perform' a heterosexual identity. This requires the assertion of a certain type of masculinity, the main characteristics of which are that speakers differentiate themselves from women and from gay men. There is also work by Eckert (1996) which examines how communities of practice (groups of people who engage with each other for a particular function) can use language to construct and perform identity. This work is extremely detailed and nuanced. For example, Eckert discusses a particular vowel used by Trudy, a core member of a group, in her journey from childhood to adolescence, and how pronunciation changes. This style used by the speaker is a linguistic resource that has a particular social meaning, and in early adolescence it demonstrates belonging to a heterosexual marketplace. This vowel comes to index that particular identity and other speakers also use it to display central membership of the group. What is interesting is that only other members of the group can accurately decode its meaning.

**KEY POINTS: Gender and sexuality**

- We consider gender and sexuality as socially constructed identities, that is to say, people 'do' their identity rather than it being something they are born with.
- Some cultures have gender-exclusive forms, where men and women may use different words, and others have gender preferential forms, where men and women will use the same linguistic varieties but in different amounts.
- Studies show different results when looking at whether men and women are more or less likely to use certain linguistic features, such as tag questions and hedges.
- Women are more likely to use standard forms and report using them, whereas men are more likely to use vernacular forms and report using these.
- Women's language is said to be more cooperative, whereas men's language is said to be more competitive.
- Language and sexuality is about more than looking at language use of gay men.
- In sociolinguistics, the deficit/difference/dominance/social constructionist approaches are important in many fields of study.

**EXERCISE 11.2**

1. A common response to early language and gender work as carried out by Lakoff is to say that society has changed and that these arguments are not relevant any more. To what extent do you think that this is correct or not? Have things changed since the 1970s or remained the same?
2. What are some of the problems with just using NORMS in a sociolinguistic study?

## 11.5 Age

Age has frequently been treated as a biological fact and not as something which needs to be regarded as an aspect of our identity. Perhaps because of this, age has often been omitted from sociolinguistic study. This is strange, because we are usually capable of guessing the age of a speaker when we hear their voice, so it is worth considering how language use influenced by age affects how people are perceived and treated. There are several features of language that vary with age. Biological differences, which influence the sound of a voice (i.e. voice quality), ways of pronouncing words and also the use of grammar (including the use of non-standard grammar) can differentiate age groups from one another. For example, language use which is acceptable for children or for teenagers may not be deemed suitable for adults, and these differences are known as age-graded patterns. **Age grading** occurs when a pattern is repeated every generation, rather than being an actual change in the language. For example, in every generation young people may use more vernacular forms, which they use less in adulthood, and this is reproduced in every generation.

Another approach is to examine speakers of different ages to see how a language might be changing (and we know that language is always in a process of change). If we compare speakers of different ages in a particular community, we can show how language change is progressing. This is known as **apparent-time change**. A comparison of differently aged speakers is quicker than examining **real-time change**, because that would mean recording a speaker at different points in their life to see if their language use changes. Also, if we have recordings from an area fifty years ago, we can use these data to make a comparison with current speakers, which would also allow us to examine the rate of change and the directions they have taken.

### 11.5.1 Life stages

To simplify the study of how age can affect language use, we can divide the lifespan into four stages: childhood, adolescence, adulthood and old age (there are of course problems with such stages – people are different and two 18-year-olds are not necessarily going to be the 'same'; these stages are also broad and may not contain people in similar stages of their lives, for more detail see Llamas et al. 2007). Researchers have examined the acquisition of sociolinguistic competence in the first stage. They have looked at how children learn to use the language(s) that surround them. From a very young age, children are sensitive to the variation they hear, and reflect it in different ways of pronouncing words. From around the age of 4, children can style-shift, that is to say, they can change their language depending on who they are talking to. They will change their speech depending on whether they are talking to someone younger than them, the same age, or to an adult. It seems that there is a critical age for acquiring sociolinguistic competence, in the same way as for acquiring language in general. For example, in the case of children who move, the older they are when they move, the harder they find it to adopt the new language system that surrounds them in their new place (see, for example, Kerswill 1996).

In sociolinguistic studies we can look at all ages – older and younger speakers – and this allows us to also look at the first issue mentioned above, how language might be changing. As children get older they tend to rely on people their own age (or slightly older) for speech models. Non-standard language seems to peak in adolescence, and among younger speakers there is often covert prestige attached to particular non-standard aspects of language, certain types of pronunciation or grammar (th-fronting, where words like *three* and *free* sound the same or double negatives for example, *I ain't seen nothing*). For many groups the frequency of non-standard forms is lowest in adulthood and middle age and gradually increases again in old age when social pressures reduce and people leave the workforce (for a visual representation see Holmes 2013: 178). For many younger speakers these types of non-standard language usage are not just to do with age, but they can also indicate membership of close-knit social groups. Typically, the adult group is the least examined group, as it is assumed to be 'the norm' against which other age groups are compared.

Most studies on language and ageing have focused on the clinical problems of ageing and associated language problems – hearing loss, memory loss and degenerative conditions such as dementia and Alzheimer's disease, features that have contributed to an attitude about the elderly in western societies that gives them a less important status in society than younger people. Many studies have collected data from older participants, but these data have generally been used to examine apparent-time change rather than the state of being an older speaker. Studies by Coupland and colleagues (1991) have examined how people, for example staff in nursing homes, change their language to fit in with these apparent stereotypes about older persons, which could damage communication and relations between different age groups such as the staff and residents of nursing homes. However, matters which may improve with age such as increased vocabulary or narrative skills are often overlooked and require more research.

## 11.5.2 Case study: slang

The term *jargon* tends to be used for specialized vocabulary used by people in established social groups, and it can be linked to professional areas, whereas *slang* is used for groups of younger speakers and other groups with special interests, particularly those outside higher-status groups. There may be particular types of slang used to strengthen bonds between groups – and make language less comprehensible to outsiders (i.e. adults!). The use of slang can signal membership of a particular age group and can sound odd when used by an older speaker. Just like clothes and music, language is subject to fashion and the use and meaning of terms change quickly. Slang can include taboo language considered to be obscene, or can contain words and phrases that people avoid for reasons related to religion, politeness and prohibited behaviour. In a study of adolescents, Eckert (2000) found regular use of taboo words among male and female speakers. In higher-status groups, some male speakers used them when talking with other males, but used them much less when females were present, and higher-status females were far less likely to use them. Eckert has suggested that these differences are already apparent in adolescence.

Using slang (and this applies to many groups, not just youth groups) has a particular function; it signals coolness, opposition to mainstream groups, excludes certain speakers and bonds those within the group. Some of the specialized terms in a group will enter mainstream culture, others will not. Some will remain, and other terms will change. Much interesting research has been carried out on different groups examining their particular language usage.

**KEY POINTS: Age**

- The lifespan is frequently separated into: childhood, adolescence, adulthood and old age.
- Language is in a constant process of change and we can compare the usage of different age groups to examine this.

- Apparent-time studies use speakers of different ages in a community to examine which features may be entering or leaving a community.
- Real-time studies examine speakers over time to examine language change.
- Adulthood tends to be seen as the period where speakers are more likely to use 'standard' forms, it is also the least examined age group.

**EXERCISE 11.3**

1. Ask three people who are over 65 and three people who are around 20 from similar social backgrounds to tell you which words they would use in the following situations:

(a) I've just got a new car. It's ____________________ (meaning they think it's great).

(b) I saw a film at the cinema yesterday – what a waste of money, it was __________ (meaning it was terrible).

(c) You won't believe David yesterday, he was ________________ (meaning he was drunk).

2. If you were interested in carrying out a study looking at language change in a particular location, explain how it would be different to use an apparent-time study as opposed to a real-time study.

## 11.6 Ethnicity

In Section 11.3 we discussed regional variation, for example in the UK, and saw that although there are different varieties of English, this does not tend to stop communication between different groups and networks. Diversity, notably in urban areas, is the result of significant in-migration during the last fifty years. Immigrants, refugees and asylum seekers now live side by side with the native population, who themselves do not necessarily live in places where their predecessors were born and all have different cultural and ethnic backgrounds. Some varieties of English can be linked to specific indigenous ethnicities, including Scottish English, Welsh English and Irish English. For many speakers, language is a crucial part of their identity. Many speakers are bilingual or bidialectal, and the survival of minority languages is closely bound to ethnicity and culture. For some speakers, a complete conversation in an ethnic language might not be possible, but they might use particular words or markers to signal ethnic affiliation (for example Maori people in New Zealand who are not able to speak the Maori language fluently or non-Gaelic speakers in certain parts of Scotland). It can be difficult, however, to separate ethnicity from other social variables as it is embedded within different relationships and cultures.

### 11.6.1 Case study: African American Vernacular English (AAVE)

Much research has been carried out in different countries examining how language influenced by ethnicity varies and how this can change down the generations. For some speakers, maintaining a separate ethnic identity means using a distinct language (for example, Urdu or Polish), but in other cases speakers have a linguistic repertoire which is a continuum between the majority variety and an ethnically marked variety. Much of this research has been carried out on Black English, both in the UK (Edwards 1986; Kerswill 2013) and the USA (Wolfram 2004; Thomas and Beckford Wassink 2010). AAVE (African American Vernacular English), as it is referred to in the USA, varies from Standard English on levels of pronunciation, grammar and discourse. Many such non-standard varieties and their particular features have been stigmatized and have been considered 'bad language' or 'corrupt grammar', but it is important to note that these varieties are rule-governed and are legitimate varieties in their own right.

Experiments have shown that people in general are quite accurate when it comes to identifying speakers from different ethnicities (see for example Llamas et al. 2007), but we must remember that not all members of a particular group or community will use the same language. A black child raised in an environment where Standard English is spoken will speak Standard English, and a white child raised in an environment where AAVE is spoken will speak that variety.

AAVE can be recognized on the basis of its linguistic characteristics. A typical phonological feature of AAVE and other such varieties is the tendency to reduce consonantal clusters, e.g. (*left hand* → *lef han*). Certain initial consonants such as initial *th-* as in *think* or *that* can be replaced with *t-* and *d-* (for example, *think* → *tink*, *fink* or *that* → *dat*). The copula verb BE can be omitted → *he angry*, or *he be angry*, but they mean different things (the first means he is angry at the moment and the second that he is generally an angry person). Double negatives are common and may actually be used to emphasize the negative → *he don't never do nothin'*.

Although we can examine these varieties from a linguistic point of view, we can also consider them from an identification perspective. These varieties can be used to perform a particular ethnicity (as well as other aspects of identity such as social class, gender, age and geographical origin). For some groups Black English has become associated with youth and coolness, and this may be represented in other aspects of culture (such as hip hop, rap and associated performances). We can also examine the use of **patois** and creole in speakers as many people use such varieties or code-switch between them to show affiliation to a particular group. At the moment Jamaican patois is frequently used as a form of slang for young people. This can lead into the examination of **crossing** (Rampton 1995), where speakers from specific ethnicities use varieties associated with another ethnic group (for example, white and Asian speakers using Black English for particular in-group activities).

Many features of AAVE also feature in other varieties of non-standard English. For example, some varieties in the UK contain double negation and different verb endings (*he love cars*) or cases where plural markers do not agree (*three pound, four mile*). The fact that we locate different ethnicities in specific urban or rural centres, such as

'Chinatown' around the world or 'Scotland' in Barbados, shows that society has a name for ethnic groups which are seen as different from 'the norm'. This marking suggests that everything else is 'unmarked' or 'normal' (as we have seen, something similar happens with gender and sexuality). Some recent research looks at whiteness (Hill 1998; Bucholtz 2011), which has often been seen as an absence of ethnic identity and associated with standard varieties.

A final example to illustrate the link between language, ethnicity and identity comes from the House of Commons. Following a comment during a debate about the referendum for Scottish independence made by Scottish MP Jim Sheridan in 2013, who stated that the SNP (the Scottish National Party) were 'big feartigs' (which means someone who is scared of someone), the scribe who had to transcribe this discussion for Hansard sent a note to the MP in question (see Figure 11.3), asking what he had said and whether he had meant 'a big fairy'. Here, a vocabulary item from a specific **ethnolect** had confused a speaker who expected Standard English. We might speculate that a Scottish Nationalist MP might deliberately use this word as an 'act of identity' (Le Page and Tabouret-Keller 1985).

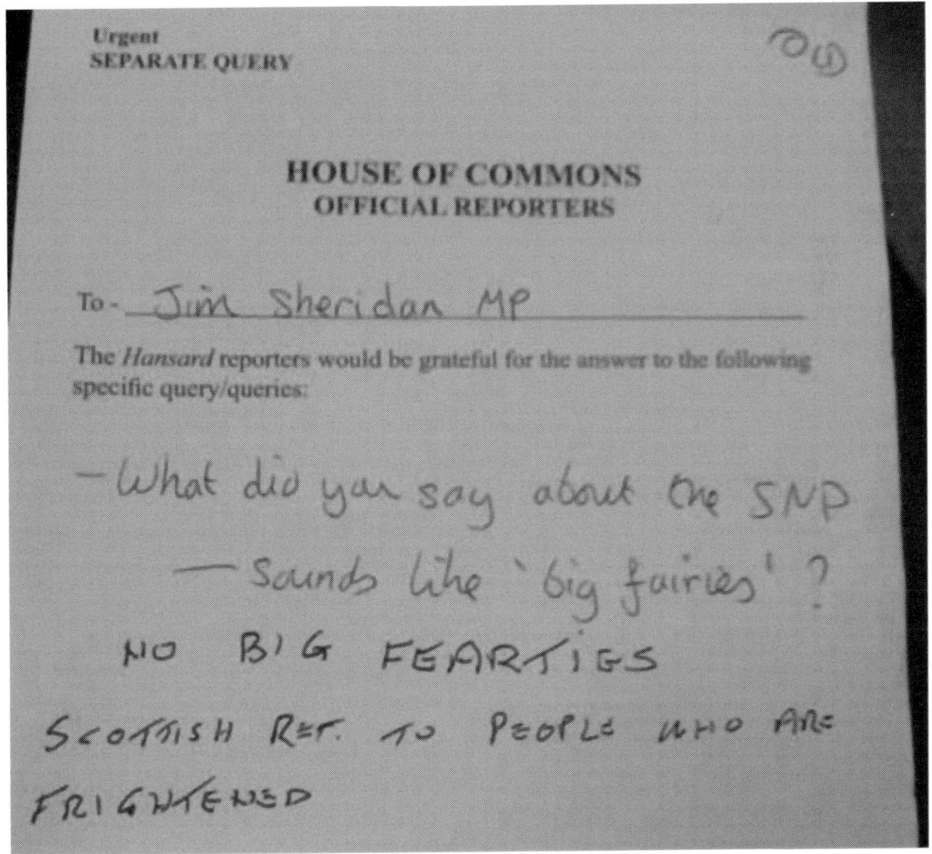

Urgent
SEPARATE QUERY

HOUSE OF COMMONS
OFFICIAL REPORTERS

To - Jim Sheridan MP

The *Hansard* reporters would be grateful for the answer to the following specific query/queries:

- What did you say about the SNP
— Sounds like 'big fairies'?

NO BIG FEARTIGS
SCOTTISH REF. TO PEOPLE WHO ARE
FRIGHTENED

**Figure 11.3** House of Commons document (reproduced with permission from Pamela Nash, MP)

**KEY POINTS: Ethnicity**

- Diversity in language may signal ethnicity of speakers and difference from the identified mainstream or standard.
- Many ethnic varieties were treated as illogical or incorrect for many years and as subordinate in relation to the standard.
- Using such features can create a strong sense of identity and can lead to 'crossing' where members of other ethnic groups may also start using aspects of these varieties.

**EXERCISE 11.4**

1. Think of different ethnic groups who use English (or another language you know) and list the linguistic differences from your own variety. Try and specify whether the differences are phonetic, lexical, grammatical or on the level of discourse.
2. Why do you think that many non-standard varieties have been labelled as 'slang', 'lazy' or 'ungrammatical'?

## 11.7 SUMMARY

Wardhaugh comments 'language is complex because it's a social thing, and society is complex' (2006). In this chapter we have discussed sociolinguistics, which investigates language variation and the ways people use language in context. We have seen that language variation is not free variation and sociolinguistics can investigate the reasons why language differs for specific groups. For example, different varieties of English are governed by rules that determine their sound system, grammar, lexis and discourse. No variety is more expressive, logical or complex than another variety. The same applies to accents and dialects of a language, for that matter. In the past varieties such as those spoken by white, middle-class and male speakers have been treated as unmarked, with all other varieties seen as being different and marked by their differences from the assumed 'norm'. However, a judgement about a variety – about its inherent superiority or inferiority – is a social value judgement, which has no place in the study of sociolinguistics (although we may look into the causes and extent of such value judgements).

To use language appropriately involves knowing the sociolinguistic rules for speaking in a community. As speakers we can use language to construct our identity or emphasize similarities with and differences from other speakers. This variation depends on our region, gender, sexuality, age, or ethnicity. However, we all have more than one identity in terms of the characteristics mentioned in the previous sentence and we can also belong to overlapping social groups, for example class and gender. We have seen in this chapter that some of issues related to language are complex and interwoven with other issues such as social divisions. Perhaps we cannot answer all questions, but by studying the relationship between language and society and by using different approaches we can inform ourselves about the way that language works.

WEBSITE: **Sociolinguistics**

Now go to the website and assess your knowledge of sociolinguistics by completing the self-test questions!

## SUGGESTIONS FOR FURTHER READING

Holmes, J. (2013). *An Introduction to Sociolinguistics*. Harlow: Pearson. This book will give you very accessible information about all aspects of sociolinguistics, with in-depth discussion of case studies and illustrations to support understanding.

Llamas, C., Mullany, L. and Stockwell, P. (2007). *The Routledge Companion to Sociolinguistics*. London: Routledge. This book contains chapters on all the topics covered in this chapter written by subject experts. It also contains chapters on analysing language and other topics which deal with issues related to sociolinguistics.

Van Herk, G. (2012). *What is Sociolinguistics?* Chichester: Wiley-Blackwell. This book is a very well written and comprehensive study of sociolinguistics. It contains many real-life examples which help relate this to the theory discussed.

# ANSWERS TO EXERCISES

## Exercise 11.1

1. Depending on which students you speak to, you will find that they may have quite different ways of pronouncing words or different words for particular items. Which word someone uses for a bread roll differs significantly around the country. You can also ask people from other English-speaking countries for their input. Non-native speakers who have just arrived in the UK may struggle with terms that we use normally every day as they have been taught Standard English.
2. The level of language which causes most confusion is that of vocabulary. If someone uses a word we have not heard of before we will need to ask them what it means. Differences in pronunciation and grammar tend to cause less of a problem as the overall meaning is still clear. This will of course depend on how different these features are from your own variety.
3. British and American English tend to be considered to be the same language because of the concept of mutual intelligibility. Although there are differences on all levels of language, we tend still to be able to understand one another. However, when speakers of very different dialects speak to one another, they may feel as if they are speaking different languages as they can have great problems communicating with one another.

## Exercise 11.2

1. There are many different viewpoints to such a question. Some people consider that the linguistic situation of men and women has changed and that they are more likely to use a similar form of language (particularly in western cultures). Many people agree that young women are much more likely to swear than would have been the case in the past. Other researchers think that what is expected of male and female speakers is still different. It is interesting to put this question to men and women, of older and younger ages, to see if there are any differences in their opinions. You can also try recording conversations between single-gender and mixed-gender groups to see what results you find.
2. If you only use NORMS, you miss out a large section of the population – females, younger speakers, people who move around a lot, people from other ethnic backgrounds – and these speakers make up a large proportion of a population. This means that data collected from a limited group can't be used to make generalizations about the population in general.

## Exercise 11.3

1. From your responses, see what your findings are. Which words are currently being used and which are no longer being used? Have meanings of words changed (for example, a word like *gay* has changed meanings many times over the years)? Have meanings become wider or narrower? What do speakers from different age groups say when you tell them words that others use?
2. If you carry out an apparent-time study, you could examine older and younger speakers in a population to see if any linguistic features are appearing or disappearing. This would allow you to

make some hypotheses about the direction of language change. In a real-time study you would collect data from a group of speakers and then revisit them a certain number of years later to see whether changes had occurred. For both of these you have to bear in mind age grading where certain changes may occur as part of every speaker's lifespan. If you have access to a collection of data from a number of years ago, you can compare this to contemporary data to see whether there are differences. For all of these studies you would have to ensure that other linguistic variables (such as geographical location and social class) are constant to isolate the particular social variable you are interested in: age.

### Exercise 11.4

1. You may want to think about the similarities and differences of these varieties to each other as well as to Standard English.
2. If the standard form of a variety is seen as being the most correct and right form of a language, it tends to have a lot of prestige attached to it. The fact that it is associated with the media, law, education and bureaucracy will also elevate its status. If other varieties do things differently, these have been seen as not being 'true' to the standard variety and therefore can be stigmatized. Their role is not generally as powerful in society (although don't forget about covert prestige). Many attitudes to language reveal a lot about people's attitudes to the people who use that variety.

## REFERENCES

Bucholtz, M. (2011). *White Kids: Language, Race and Styles of Youth Identity*. Cambridge: Cambridge University Press.

Butler, J. (1990). *Gender Trouble: Feminism and the Subversion of Identity*. New York: Routledge.

Cheshire, J. (1982). *Variation in an English Dialect: A Sociolinguistic Study*. Cambridge: Cambridge University Press.

Coupland, N., Coupland, J. and Giles, H. (1991). *Language, Society and the Elderly: Discourse, Identity, and Ageing*. Oxford: Blackwell.

Eckert, P. (1996). Vowels and nail polish: The emergence of linguistic style in the preadolescent heterosexual marketplace. In N. Warner, J. Ahlers, L. Bilmes, M. Oliver, S. Wertheim and M. Chen (eds.), *Gender and Belief Systems*, pp. 183–90. Berkeley Women and Language Group.

(2000). *Linguistic Variation as Social Practice: The Linguistic Construction of identity in Belten High*. Malden, MA: Blackwell.

Edwards, V. (1986). *Language in a Black Community*. Clevedon: Multilingual Matters.

Fischer, J. (1958). Social influences on the choice of a linguistic variant. *Word*, 14, 47–56.

Fishman, P. (1983). Interaction: the work women do. In B. Thorne, C. Kramarae and N. Henley (eds.), *Language, Gender and Society*, pp. 89–101. London: Newbury House.

Hill, M. (1998). 'Souls undressed': the rise and fall of the new Whiteness studies. *Review of Education/Pedagogy/Cultural Studies*, 20, 229–39.

Holmes, J. (2013). *An Introduction to Sociolinguistics*. Harlow: Pearson.

Hughes, A., Trudgill, P. and Watt, D. (2005). *English accents and dialects*. Oxford: Hodder Arnold.

Kerswill, P. (1996). Children, adolescents and language change. *Language Variation and Change*, 8, 177–202.

(2013). Identity, ethnicity and place: the construction of youth language in London. In P. Auer, M. Hilpert, A. Stinkenbrock and B. Szmrecsanyi (eds.), *Space in Language and Linguistics*, pp.128–64. Berlin: De Gruyter.

Kiesling, S. (2004). 'Dude'. *American Speech*, 79, 281–305.

Labov, W. (1966). *The Social Stratification of English in New York City*. Washington, DC: Center for Applied Linguistics.
(1972). *Sociolinguistic Patterns*. Philadelphia: University of Pennsylvania Press.
Lakoff, R. (1973). *Language and Woman's Place*. New York: Harper & Row.
Lambert, W. E., Hodgson, R,. Gardner, R. C. and Fillenbaum, S. (1960). Evaluational reactions to spoken languages. *Journal of Abnormal and Social Psychology*, 60, 44–51.
Le Page, R. B. and Tabouret Keller, A. (1985). *Acts of Identity*. Cambridge: Cambridge University Press.
Llamas, C., Mullany, L. and Stockwell, P. (2007). *The Routledge Companion to Sociolinguistics*. London: Routledge.
Maltz, D. and Borker, R. (1982). A cultural approach to male-female miscommunication. In J. Gumperz (ed.), *Language and Social Identity*, pp. 196–216. Cambridge: Cambridge University Press.
Meyerhoff, M. (2011). *Introducing Sociolinguistics*. London: Routledge.
Pilkington, J. (1992). 'Don't try and make out that I'm nice!' The different strategies women and men use when gossiping. *Wellington Working Papers in Linguistics*, 5, 37–60.
Rampton, B. (1995). *Crossing: Language and Ethnicity among Adolescents*. London: Longman.
Tagliamonte, S. and Hudson, R. (1999). *Be like* et al. beyond America: the quotative system in British and Canadian Youth. *Journal of Sociolinguistics*, 3, 147–72.
Tannen, D. (1990). *You Just Don't Understand: Women and Men in Conversation*. New York: William Morrow.
Thomas, E. and Beckford Wassink, A. (2010). Variation and identity in African-American English. In C. Llamas and D. Watt (eds.), *Language and Identities*, pp. 157–65. Edinburgh University Press.
Trudgill, P. (1972). Sex, covert prestige and linguistic change in the urban British English of Norwich. *Language in Society*, 1, 175–95.
(1974). *The social differentiation of English in Norwich*, Cambridge: Cambridge University Press.
(2000). *Sociolinguistics: An Introduction to Language and Society*. London: Penguin.
Van Herk, G. (2012). *What is Sociolinguistics?* Chichester: Wiley-Blackwell.
Wardhaugh, R. (2006). *An Introduction to Sociolinguistics*. Malden, MA: Blackwell.
West, C. (1998). When the doctor is a 'lady': Power, status and gender in physician-patient encounters. In J. Coates (ed.), *Language and Gender: A Reader*, pp. 396–412. Oxford: Blackwell.
Wolfram, W. (2004). The grammar of urban African American Vernacular English. In B. Kortmann and E. Schneider (eds.), *Handbook of Varieties of English*, pp. 111–32. Belin: Mouton de Gruyter.
Yule, G. (2010). *The Study of Language*, 4th edn. Cambridge: Cambridge University Press.
Zimmerman, D. and West, C. (1975). Sex roles, interruptions and silences in conversation. In B. Thorne and N. Henley (eds.), *Language and Sex: Difference and Dominance*, pp. 105–29. Rowley, MA: Newberry House.

# 12 Child language acquisition

HELEN GOODLUCK

**KEY TERMS**

- cross-linguistic variation
- innateness
- innovation
- input
- language processing and acquisition
- learning from input
- special populations
- theories of language acquisition
- trajectories of learning
- Universal Grammar

**PREVIEW**

This chapter will summarize arguments in favour of an innate mechanism for language learning. This is not a general mechanism for learning, but is dedicated to language – the name given to the innate mechanism is Universal Grammar. Universal Grammar must be able to deal with the fact that languages differ quite dramatically in their structural properties, and that learning paths can vary for different languages. Evidence for an innate, language-specific mechanism comes from children's innovations during development, lack of negative evidence from caregivers, creation of signed languages and creoles, and first language learners who have various deficits in their cognitive abilities. We consider the need for a better integration of language acquisition theory with the theory of language processing.

## 12.1 INTRODUCTION

Chimpanzees are our closest relatives. Yet chimpanzees cannot learn a human language. With training, they can develop a repertoire of signs, and they can combine these signs in meaningful ways. But chimpanzees have never been shown to use the abstract structural relations between signs (words) that are characteristic of human language.

In this chapter, we argue that humans are equipped with an innate ability to construct a grammar, and that this ability is generally independent of intelligence. In order to make this argument, we need to examine what adult human languages are like – to tackle the issue of cross-linguistic variation. That is, we need to look at the samenesses and differences that human languages offer, and then to look at the challenges that the task of learning a first language poses. After that, we will examine the progress children make with learning different types of language, and the stages children typically pass through. Although the data from many languages is sparse, the conclusion we can draw is that roughly by age 3 years, the fundamentals of the language the child is learning have been acquired. The combination of the intricate complexity of adult languages and the seeming ease with which children get to grips with the fundamentals of their language forms a basic argument for an innate learning capacity. We will then consider in more detail the alternative(s) to the claim that language acquisition is possible only by virtue of human biology. Such alternative proposals rely on abstraction from the speech available to children, and fail to account for properties of child language, including the creativity that children display and the disparity in some individuals between general cognitive ability and linguistic ability. At the end of the chapter, we examine some ongoing questions in child language research, focusing on the role of mechanisms for speech comprehension and production in explaining language development.

## 12.2 What has to be acquired: some things every child has to learn

Here is a very short (i.e. seriously non-exhaustive) list of what the child has to master before he/she can be said to have a full knowledge of his/her native language:

1. Word order facts – does the child's language have a basic order and what is it?
2. Inflectional properties – does the language mark as affixes properties such as subject and object on nouns and properties such as tense and aspect (activity completed or not) on verbs?
3. The realization of embedding – what sentence types can be included inside one another, including complements to verbs, adverbial clauses and relative clauses?
4. Lexical restrictions on syntactic configurations.
5. Impermissible sentence types, even within the restrictions of permissible word order.
6. Conventions of usage – pragmatics

We can divide languages into three basic word order types from the possible combinations of S(ubject), V(erb) and O(bject): SVO, SOV and VSO. Examples are English, Japanese and Modern Irish respectively. A distinction that correlates with word order is the nature of hierarchical structure. A **right-branching language** builds up hierarchical structures by expanding the right side of a structure, whereas a **left-branching language** builds structure by expansion on the left side, as schematically shown in (1):

(1) a. Right-branching syntax (English) b. Left branching syntax (Japanese)

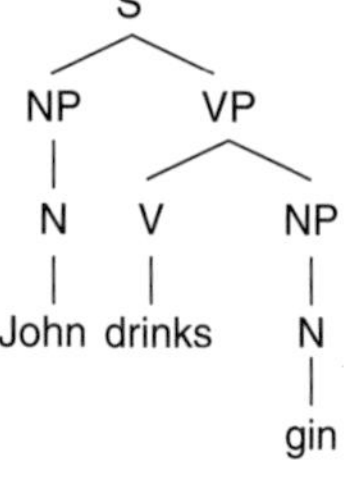


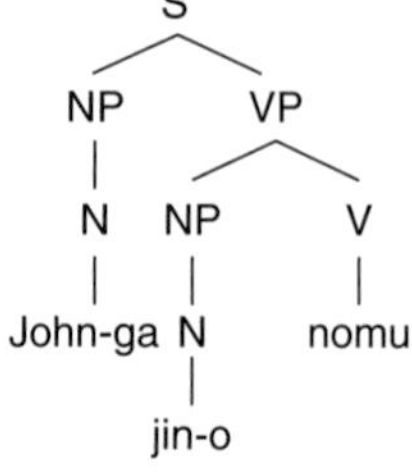

(S = sentence; NP = Noun Phrase; VP = Verb Phrase; N = Noun; V = Verb; ga = nominative [subject] marker; o = accusative [object] object marker)

SVO and VSO languages are right branching, and SOV languages are left branching. This is shown in the trees above, with the object following the verb (head of the phrase) in English and the object preceding the verb in Japanese. If a relative clause modifies the object NP, it follows the head in English, and precedes the object in Japanese. Following the same pattern, if a sentence is embedded inside the VP, it is to the right of the verb in a right-branching language (see (3) below), and to the left in a left-branching language.

Other word orders are possible in languages, frequently when the role of words in the sentence is marked by inflection. However, it is the case that one of the three words orders described above is the basic order, from which other arrangements of words are derived. But, some languages appear to have no basic word order, as we will see below.

Sentences can be built by embedding one sentence within another, allowing for potentially infinite length. Thus a complement to a verb such as *know* in English can be embedded within the complement to the same or another verb, and so on, as illustrated in (2):

(2) Jane thought Susan knew Clive expected ...

(... indicates that the structure could be expanded indefinitely by adding one or more embedded sentences).

(3) Structure for (2)

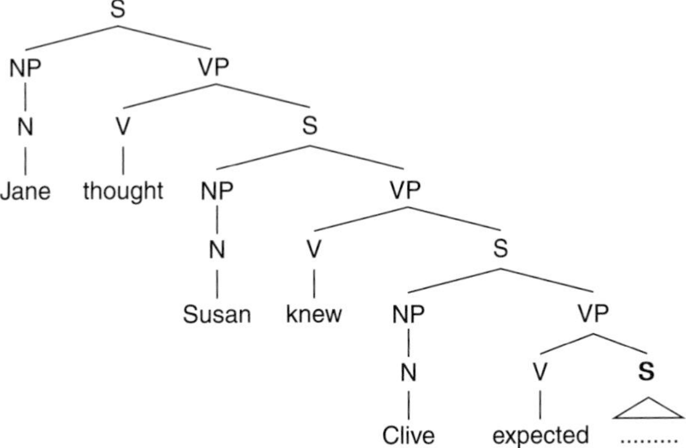


The mapping between individual lexical items and syntactic structure must be obeyed; in (2), we cannot replace *thought* with *encouraged*, for example. *Encourage* cannot take a complement that is tensed (marked for past or present), as illustrated by the ungrammaticality of **Jane encouraged Susan tried to pass the exam.* However, it can take an untensed (infinitival) complement: *Jane encouraged Susan to try to pass the exam.*

Some sentence types are blocked even when the lexical restrictions on syntactic structures are met. For example, we can form a question that targets an embedded clause, moving the object of *expected* to the front of the sentence:

(4) Susan knew in her heart that Clive expected a good outcome.

(5) What did Susan know in her heart that Clive expected _ ?

However, if the embedded clause is itself a question, extraction of the object of that clause is not permitted:

(6) Mary asked who made the cocktails.

(7) *What did Mary ask who made _ ?

Additional restrictions derive from principles of usage. For example, relative clauses can add essential information for the identification of a noun phrase (a restrictive relative, as in (8)), or can add extra information, not essential for the identification of the noun that it modifies (a non-restrictive relative, as in (9)):

(8) No one expected the storm that flooded the valley.

(9) No one expected the storm, which flooded the valley.

It follows from the difference between restrictive and non-restrictive relatives that only non-restrictives can modify a proper name – since a proper name uniquely identifies an individual:

(10) *No one expected John that was the first person to arrive.

(11) No one expected John, who was the first person to arrive.

A pragmatic principle along the lines of 'provide no more information than is necessary' can account for the difference in acceptability between (8) and (10) (see Sperber and Wilson 1995).

## 12.3 When is this knowledge acquired?

It is easy to underestimate children's knowledge, since we are reliant on children's capacity to do experimental tasks and/or their ability to produce language, neither of which may truly reflect the extent of the child's knowledge. So what follows are conservative estimates of children's knowledge.

### 12.3.1 The first year of life

For reasons of space, we will be concerned in this chapter mainly with morphological, syntactic and semantic abilities. Prior to his/her first words, however, the infant shows development in the perception and production of speech. At the earliest stages, babies show sensitivity to the distinction between speech sounds such as [p] and [b], which is signalled by an abrupt shift in Voice Onset Time (the interval between release of a stop consonant and onset of vibration of the vocal chords) at around 25 milliseconds (Eimas et al. 1971). During the first year of life, the child's perception of speech becomes adjusted to the particular language he is exposed to. At around 6 months of age, babies can distinguish those vowel sounds that are prevalent in the speech around them and the perception of vowels is attuned to differences between vowels in, for example, Swedish and English (Kuhl et al. 1992). The perception of consonants shifts towards less typical realizations, including the Spanish Voice Onset Time boundary of approximately zero milliseconds, and the ability to recognize consonant distinctions not found in the language the child is exposed to fades (Werker 1995).

At around 6 months infants begin to produce speech sounds – to babble. Babbling goes (not invariantly) through various stages, and is not confined to speech sounds that a child is exposed to in his/her environment – for example, a velar fricative may be produced in babbling by an English child, although that sound is not part of the repertoire of adult English sounds. The child's early speech is characterized by some characteristic mispronunciations, such as the production of stop consonants in place of fricatives, and the shifting of place of stops from velar [k, g] and labial [p, b] to alveolar [t, d]. See Vihman (1996: ch. 9) and Smith (2010) for a review of child speech errors and their explanation.

## 12.3.2 The acquisition of English

The child learning English produces his/her first recognisable words at around 12 months, and at around 18 months the child begins to combine words. The **two-word stage** shows evidence of obedience to the word order of the language being acquired. In a language such as English, words such as articles, pronouns and prepositions may be omitted – hence the term '**telegraphic speech**' – but in general the word order is correct for the language, and can be shown by filling in the gaps in children's production (Pinker, 1995).

Languages can be divided into those that allow the omission of pronominal subjects (allowing the equivalent of *went to the movies* for *s/he went to the movies*) and those that do not; English does not. Although subjects are omitted in child speech in languages such as English where such omission is ungrammatical, the omission rate is lower than in languages such as Portuguese, which does allow subjects to be dropped. This indicates that early on the child has knowledge that pronoun subject drop is not permitted in English (Valian and Eisenberg 1996).

Between 2 and 3 years, English-speaking children rapidly develop a repertoire of sentence types: declaratives, questions (Stromswold 1995) and commands. And they develop various types of embedded sentence – usually in the order: infinitival complement clauses, tensed complements, adverbial and relative clauses (Limber 1973). There is evidence that at a young age children are aware of syntactic restrictions that, for example, lead to the ungrammaticality of (7) (de Villiers and Roeper 1995; Thornton 1995). Although the data from English are not particularly informative in this regard, we will see below (Section 12.3.3) that tense marking may be omitted at early stages. Passive sentences come into speech and are distinguished from actives (though not all of the time) in the third year (Stromswold n.d.). When the passive is correctly understood, its effect on the interpretation of complement clauses to verbs such as *tell* is also recognized (Maratsos 1974; Goodluck 1981). In (12), *Bill* is the one who jumps, but in (13), it is *John* who jumps:

(12) John tells Bill to jump around.

(13) John is told by Bill to jump around.

Before 5 years of age, children are also aware of such facts as the distinction between restrictive and non-restrictive relative clauses, illustrated in (8–11) above (Fragman et al. 2007) and the constraint on (some) plurals inside compounds – *mice-eater* is an allowable compound, but *rats-eater* is not (Gordon 1985). However, this does not imply that language acquisition is totally complete by that age. Experimental studies show that children take time in learning lexical exceptions, such as *promise*, which does not follow the rule exemplified by verbs such as active *tell*:

(14) Jane promises Bill to jump around. (Jane jumps.)

and the correct assignment of predicates to a class that requires the subject of the main clause to be subject of the subordinate clause (15), and a class that requires the subject to be object of the subordinate clause (16) (Chomsky 1969; Cromer 1987):

(15) Jane is eager to kiss. (Jane wants to kiss.)

(16) Jane is easy to kiss. (Jane is the recipient of kissing.)

Moreover, it is not merely lexical exceptions and lexical restrictions that can take many years to be learned. Although the missing subject of an adverbial clause such as (17) is invariably construed by adults as the subject of the main clause:

(17) Jane kissed Tony before leaving the house.

children may be 8 or older before they develop this rule. (Goodluck (2001) summarizes the non-adult strategies that children use.) And despite the fact that the interpretation of sentences with quantifiers such as *all* and *each* in (18)–(19) does display tendencies that reflect the adult language, children may be well into the school years before they behave in an adult-like way (Brooks and Braine 1996):

(18) a. All the men are building a boat.
b. A boat is being built by all the men.

(19) a. Each man is building a boat.
b. A boat is being built by each man.

In (18a) with *all*, the normal interpretation for adults is for the men to be building one boat together (as opposed to every man building his own boat), whereas for (19a) the opposite is true – the normal interpretation is for every man to be building his own boat. For adults these preferences are modulated by use of passive syntax, with increased proportions of the interpretation that one boat is being built by all the men collectively for both (18b) and (19b). Children may be 5 years of age before they show similar distinctions, and 8 or more before they show levels of performance equivalent to those of adults.

### 12.3.3 Other languages

English has had a dominant place in child language studies because the ground-breaking early studies were of English (most notably Brown 1973). This has changed over the past twenty-five or so years, with a large commitment to cross-linguistic studies. A **configurational language** such as English builds up structure hierarchically, as illustrated by the trees in (1) and (3). Yet within configurational languages there are important differences, as illustrated at an elementary level by differences in basic word order and by properties such as the omission of subjects. A **non-configurational language** such as Warlpiri (spoken in Australia) does not cluster words together in phrases in the same way as English-type languages do, although they may do so at a level of representation more abstract than the linear order of words (Legate 2003). The differences between language types raise important questions for acquisition, which we are only now beginning to answer.

We have already seen one example of the value of cross-linguistic comparison: the development of knowledge that English does not permit overt subjects to be null. Valian and Eisenberg's (1996) study compared English and Brazilian Portuguese and found that although English children omitted subjects they did so to a lesser extent than children speaking Portuguese. This suggested that English-speaking children know that their language requires an overt subject (contrary to what had been supposed by Hyams 1986), but that performance constraints (constraints on the language production system) limited their ability to execute that knowledge.

Another example of the importance of cross-linguistic data is the development of verb inflection. English has a poor inflectional system in the present tense. Only the third-person singular is marked (*s/he sings* vs *I/we/you/they sing*); thus only in the third person can a tensed verb be distinguished from an infinitive (*to sing*). English-speaking children do not reliably command the use of third-person singular agreement until they may be 3 or older (Brown 1973). Other languages have more developed systems, marking person (1st, 2nd, 3rd) and number (singular, plural) more consistently. This permits us to see more readily patterns in the use of inflection. A basic finding is that in some languages, but not others to the same extent, children use an infinitive form of the verb as the main verb (a **root infinitive**), something that is ordinarily ungrammatical in the adult language. There have been various accounts of this phenomenon (including Wexler 1998 and Boser et al. 1992), of which one of the most successful is that of Hoekstra and Hyams (1998). Hoekstra and Hyams assembled the results from studies of spontaneous production of inflection on verbs by children aged approximately 18 months to 36 months in a range of European languages. These studies found that an alternation between use of inflection and use of a root infinitive was not arbitrary. In the examples in

(20), from a child speaking Dutch, the child uses the infinitive form such as *kopen* rather than a tensed form such as present tense *koop*, as required in the adult language. Critically, root infinitives were used for predicates that denoted an event (such as *buy* or *play* in the examples in (20)), not a state.

(20) a. Eerst kaartje kopen!
first ticket buy-infinitive
'We must first buy a ticket!'
b. Niekje buiten spelen.
Niekje outside play-infinitive
'Niek (=speaker) wants to play outside.'
c. Jij helicopter maken.
You helicopter make-infinitive
'You must build a helicopter.'

When the verb denoted a state (e.g. verbs meaning want, please, need and so on), then the verb was inflected for tense. In addition to the requirement that root infinitives denote an event, root infinitives have a modal interpretation – as indicated by the interpretations given in (20), although the effect is more nuanced in some languages (Hyams 2011). Hoekstra and Hyams argue that the use of root infinitives when the verb denotes an event and the modal interpretation of root infinitive utterances are connected. The particular modal meaning associated with root infinitives is deontic, i.e. associated with the necessity or desirability of a future event, and evidence from adult languages points to deontic modality being found in combination with predicates that denote events. It fits with the lack of a dedicated infinitive form in English that there is an absence of restrictions on when bare forms are used in child English – the use of bare forms is not limited to eventive predicates and intended modal meanings. Some examples of English child speech using non-eventive verbs are given in (21) (from Hyams 2011):

(21) a. Becky have puzzle.
b. The baby want a bottle.
c. Ann need Mommy napkin.

What about languages that have an even richer inflectional system than that exemplified by many European languages? Although the number of studies of such languages is limited, the results converge on knowledge of the inflectional system at a very early age. Inuktitut, spoken in Canada, does not have infinitive forms of a verb, and it has a system of verbal affixes that involves approximately 900 combinatorial possibilities (Crago and Allen 2001). Some examples of child use of affixes in the study by Crago and Allen are given in (22):

(22) a. Nirilangannginama (Paul 2;11 [years; months])
niri-langa-nngit-gama (breakdown of morphemes)
eat-FUT-NEG-CVS-1sS (gloss: FUT = future; NEG = negation; CVS = causative; 1sS = first-person singular subject)
'I won't eat.'

b. Piipiapimik tigumialutit (Sarah 1;11)
piipi-apik-mik tigumiaq-lutit (breakdown of morphemes)
baby-DIM-MOD-SG hold-ICM-2sS (gloss: DIM =diminutive; MOD = modalis; SG = singular; ICM = incontemporative; 2sS = second-person singular subject)
'You're holding the baby.'

c. Anaana aarqitait? (Elijah 2;0)
anaana aarqik-jait (breakdown of morphemes)
mother fix-PAR.2sS.3sO (gloss:PAR = participative; 2sS = second-person singular subject; 3sO = third-person singular object)
'Mom, did you fix it?'

Crago and Allen argue that the use of verbal affixes by the child is productive – i.e. not restricted to fixed phrases. Notice that these Inuktitut-speaking children are as young as 23 months. These children's very early knowledge of the verbal inflectional system is remarkable.

**KEY POINTS: A child's progress with language**

- By the age of 3 years, children have learned the basics of their language.
- At that age, children are sensitive to word order patterns and use a variety of embedded sentences.
- Some aspects of children's language (such as lexical restrictions on rules and the adult interpretation of some sentence types) may take into the school years to be mastered.
- Information about the development of non-Indo-European languages is more limited, but some results are quite dramatic – for example, the acquisition of morphological systems in languages with a rich but transparent system of affixes such as Inuktitut.
- The development of non-configurational languages such as Warlpiri remains largely a gap in the literature (but see Bavin 1992).

## EXERCISE 12.1

What is the most probable meaning of *laugh Paul* spoken by an English-speaking child?

## EXERCISE 12.2

Is *Jumping fence a* a plausible child utterance, and if so why (not)?

EXERCISE 12.3

Would a child be able to understand 'baby talk'? I.e. how well would children do when presented with telegraphic speech? (Note: this is a question about how well *a child* would do in understanding sentences in which articles, prepositions, etc. are omitted.)

## 12.4 Theories of language acquisition

### 12.4.1 The input as a basis for learning

So far we have seen that in the course of about one year (2–3 years of age), the child moves from producing utterances that respect some but not all of the properties of the language that he/she is exposed to, to producing well-formed, and complex sentences with many types of embedded clauses particular to the input language. Clearly the child is attuned to the speech around him/her – the **input**. Is attention to the input sufficient for the language to be learned? The general answer is no.

First of all, the child is innovative. Some innovations can be explained as overuse of a regular rule, such as the child who utters *goed* instead of *went*. More difficult to explain in terms of the input are cases in which the child invents a rule/construction not modelled in the adult language. For example, a child studied by Eve Clark made a distinction between the adjective sending with *-y* and *-ed* (Clark 2001):

(23) It isn't crumby [= full of crumbs, speaking of Amarettini biscuits].

(24) My foot is all crumbed [= the bottom of the foot covered with crumbs].

English does not make a distinction between adjectives used to describe permanent properties and those used to describe temporary states, but some languages do. The child's invention can be attributed to access to a general program for what a language can be like (see below, Section 12.4.2).

Another type of innovation involves the child imposing on a sentence an abstract structure that is not the correct one. We saw above that children are often as old as 9 years before they get to know the rule for interpreting the missing subject of an adverbial clause as referring to the main clause subject – *Snowy* not *Leo* is made subject of *dance* in (25):

(25) Snowy pushes Leo before dancing by Ellie.

Children on occasion make the subject of the embedded clause refer to the agent of the first clause (correct for (25), but incorrect for *Snowy is pushed by Leo before* ....), or make the subject of the subordinate clause refer to an entity not mentioned in the sentence, or make the subordinate subject refer to the closest NP (*Leo*). One hypothesis that can cover the range of interpretations given by children to sentences such as (25) is that the child imposes a nominal structure on the subordinate clause, instead of a sentential structure, i.e.

(26) a. Snowy pushes Leo [before [$_{S}$PRO dancing by Ellie]] Correct structure (PRO = phonetically empty subject position)

b. Snowy pushes Leo [before [$_{NP}$ dancing by Ellie]] Child analysis

Nominalization is a mechanism used widely in languages of the world for subordination. A nominal structure allows essentially free reference of the subject of the subordinated structure, whereas the correct (PRO) analysis for English involves restrictions, particularly it requires that the phrase *by Ellie* is given a locative interpretation (the dancing takes place near *Ellie*), not an agentive interpretation (*Ellie* dances). Asked to act out sentences such as (26), children aged 4–6 freely gave an agentive interpretation to the *by* phrase while adults never did (Goodluck 2001), thus providing support contrary to the use of a PRO structure for adverbials in children's grammar and in favour of the nominalization analysis.

A second kind of argument for children's innate ability to learn language is that the input the child receives is purely positive – that is, it contains only grammatical utterances (slips of the tongue aside). So how is the child to work out that, for example, (7) is an ungrammatical question? This is dubbed the **no negative evidence problem**. There has been considerable discussion of 'indirect negative evidence' – the use, for example, of failure by others to comprehend the child's utterances as a clue to the child that he/she has got the grammar wrong. However, this discussion fails to get to grips with the fact that children do innovate, yet they do so only in highly restricted ways. The lack of reinforcement in the input may lead to erroneous grammars such as the adjective example above (*crumby* vs *crumbed*) dying out of the child's grammar. But it remains a fact that children do not innovate 'crazy' systems – systems that are not evidenced in the languages of the world, although not realized in the language the child is exposed to. (For a thorough assessment of the role of negative evidence, see Marcus 1993.)

Third, there are circumstances in which the language acquired does not directly derive from the input. **Creole languages** evolve from pidgins, which are highly restricted systems used for communication between mutually unintelligible languages, usually used for purposes of trade. Creole languages exhibit certain characteristic properties – such as particular tense and aspect systems. Although there is a high degree of controversy concerning the role of child and adult learners of creoles (see DeGraff 1999), it is nonetheless the case that such languages display properties that do not derive from the parent (input) languages. Such properties must derive from the minds of the speakers who create them. Moreover, recent research has focussed on the spontaneous creation of sign languages by deaf communities. The Nicaraguan and Al-Sayyid Bedouin sign languages (see Kegl et al. 1999 and Aronoff et al. 2008, respectively) have developed rapidly, with no access to speech; they display rule-governed properties distinct from the spoken languages around them.

## 12.4.2 An alternative: input with help from biology

For the past fifty years, the theory of first language acquisition that has been most discussed is that advocated by Noam Chomsky, beginning with his book *Aspects of the Theory of*

*Syntax* (1965). Chomsky built on a philosophical tradition, going back *inter alia* to Plato and Descartes, to argue that children process the input with knowledge of a ready-made set of constraints on what a human language can be like: **Universal Grammar** (UG). This enables children to figure out their grammar, and at the same time permits errors that deviate from the target language. In Chomsky's 'principles and parameters' framework (Chomsky 1981), children have to set the parameters for their language type – for example, whether their language is right- or left-branching. And they have to apply principles that restrict what operations languages can use – for example, languages that exhibit hierarchical structure can move elements in the structure, but in general **movement** is only to a position that is 'higher in the tree'. Under this constraint, (27b) but not (27c) can be formed from (27a):

(27) a. In her heart Jane really loved the boy.
b. The boy, in her heart Jane really loved.
c. In, the boy, her heart Jane really loved.

In (27b), the phrase *the boy* is moved to the left and adjoined to the whole sentence:

27b´

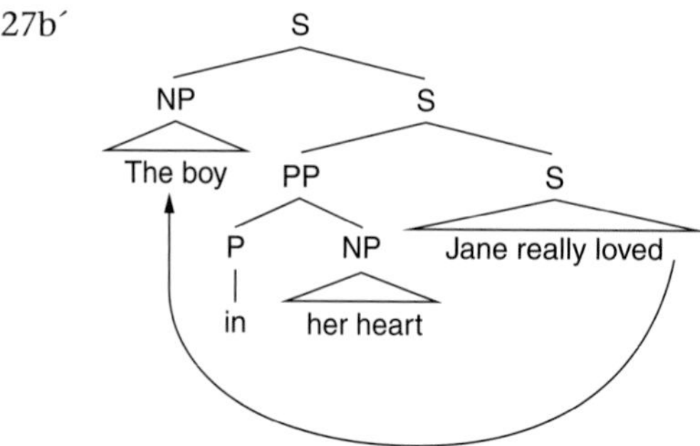


In (27c) the phrase *the boy* is also moved to the left, but is embedded in another phrase *in her heart,*

27c´

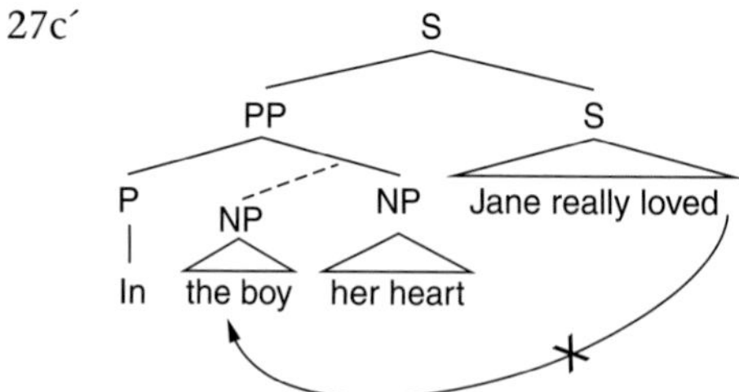


Because of the embedding in another phrase, the movement does not count as movement to a higher position (does not c-command the position from which it has moved; see Chapter 6, this volume).

### 12.4.3 Debates about what role input plays

Children must be exposed to a particular language to learn that language. But there is consistent debate about what degree of biological programming is needed for a child to master his/her language. In the mid-twentieth century, psychology in the United States was largely dominated by the thinking of B. F. Skinner, whose approach to language learning was based on the infant's response to a stimulus, without the aid of a mechanism dedicated to language learning. See Chomsky (1959) for a critique of Skinner's (1957) book *Verbal Behavior*. Despite the power of Chomsky's response, the notion that language acquisition can be accomplished without innate knowledge of Universal Grammar has continued to attract followers. In the 1970s, researchers such as Snow proposed that attention to input diminished the need for an innate component – see, for example, papers in Snow and Ferguson (1977). Prominent among more recent publications is Tomasello's (2003) book *Constructing a Language*, which also purports to challenge the concept of Universal Grammar as a prerequisite for successful language acquisition. There are serious problems with Tomasello's ideas. Take, for example, innovation, which I have claimed above is a sign that children are working with an implicit knowledge of what a human language can be like. Tomasello's account of innovation relies on a model in the input language from which the child can generalize. But no obvious model is available for the examples of innovation cited above (the distinction Clark's child made between *-y* and *-ed* adjectives and the imposition of a nominal structure on adverbial clauses). Another example is the invention of creole and signed languages. Tomasello attempts to dismiss the evidence from the creation of such languages (2003: 287), but the recent studies such as that of Aronoff et al. (2008) clearly support innovation that cannot come from the input language(s).

Why are accounts that attempt to do away with innate knowledge so appealing? Often the seductiveness of such theories is to do with what is taken to be simplicity and elegance – if a theory that doesn't posit an innate knowledge of UG can work, so be it. But for reasons outlined in Section 12.4.1 such a theory *doesn't* work.

In addition, there is a general tension between **top-down theorizing** and **bottom-up reasoning** at work: research that attributes children's success in learning a language to innate knowledge of specifically linguistic properties (a top-down approach) vs. research that relies on properties of the input to explain acquisition patterns (a bottom-up approach). Recent studies in the bottom-up tradition have proposed that the particular input the child receives determines the proportion of root infinitives in the child's speech (the tenseless verbs used in main clauses by children learning languages such as Dutch, see Section 12.3.3 above). Freudenthal et al. (2007) and Freudenthal et al. (2009) carried out simulation studies using corpora of actual speech to children. Their basic observation was that languages in which children use root infinitives also have word orders in which the infinitive form of the verb occurs sentence finally. For example, Dutch (a root-infinitive child language) contrasts with English (a non-root-infinitive child language),

(28) a. Ik ga in het park wandelen
I go-FINITE in the park walk-INFINITIVE
b. I'm going to walk in the park.

Given a simulation mechanism that is biased to process the end of utterances more efficiently than non-final parts of the utterance – i.e. a simulation mechanism that remembers the ends of utterances better – it follows that children learning languages such as Dutch will produce more root infinitive utterances than children learning languages such as English. Moreover, the simulations of Freudenthal and colleagues show that the eventive and modal characteristics of root infinitive constructions can be mimicked.

Does the simulation mechanism described in these papers challenge the top-down analysis of Hoekstra and Hyams (1998), who draw on an innate knowledge of the relation between use of full infinitival forms (as opposed to bare forms such as used for the infinitive in English) and event and modality denoting properties of predicates? Without appeal to an innate mechanism which the child uses to kick-start a grammar forming process based on the linguistic input, it is not clear that simulation studies such as Freudenthal et al.'s can account for what the child acquires. There is a difference between pattern recognition/production and the comprehension of structure. The input the child receives is not coded and analysed in advance for the semantic properties that the child is aware of, according to Hoekstra and Hyams's analysis. Moreover, it is unclear whether the simulation mechanism can handle all languages. Swedish has a robust root infinitive stage (Josefsson 2002), yet it has broadly the same word order in main and subordinate clauses that English has; thus in the simulation model Swedish would be predicted not to display root infinitives, contrary to the facts.

**KEY POINTS: Universal Grammar (UG)**

- The child cannot learn from the input alone.
- UG provides hypotheses about the structures and rules in the ambient language.
- Indirect negative evidence is inadequate to explain the facts of learning: children do innovate, and they create signed languages and may contribute to the creation of creoles.

**EXERCISE 12.4**

Children's first productions of relative clauses seem to be relatives with a gap in object position (e.g. *There's a tractor Alison brought*) despite the fact that relatives with a gap in subject position occur at least if not more frequently in languages of the world. Can you think of any explanation for the early occurrence of object relatives?

**EXERCISE 12.5**

Imagine that a child invents a system in which a question word is placed to the far left of the sentence when the sentence is positive, but is placed two words from the left when the sentence is negative. Thus, the outcome of questioning the object of the verb *eat* would include questions such as:

*What the average dog can eat in one day?*

*John can what not believe the dog eats in one day?*

Is this innovation likely to occur? (Hint: consider the consequence of negating a sentence such as 27a.)

## 12.5 Language learning in special populations

An important source of support for Chomsky's theory of language acquisition comes from persons who learn language very well despite biological constraints. These persons exhibit various aetiologies, including Williams syndrome (a micro-deletion on the long arm of chromosome 7), spina bifida, and other cognitive deficits of unknown or unclear origin. A common thread running through these disorders is an ability with language that exceeds the expectations based on general intelligence. The term '**linguistic savant**' is used to refer to individuals who display this disparity between language ability and other cognitive skills. For example, a man in his thirties (Christopher) studied by Smith and Tsimpli (1995) was found to have a command of English syntax and a remarkable facility to learn foreign languages, despite failing some 'theory of mind' tests and scoring well below average on IQ tests. (The theory of mind test that Christopher failed involved an object being hidden in a certain location in the presence of Christopher and a 5-year-old child, and then being moved to a new location in the child's absence. When asked where he thought the child would look for the object, Christopher indicated the new location.) In addition to frequently cited cases of savants, it has also been shown that some individuals with Down syndrome can achieve a perfect or near perfect command of language (Rondal 1995). Such cases argue for an ability to learn language that is not dependent on general intelligence or other cognitive skills.

**KEY POINTS: Additional evidence for Universal Grammar**

- Special populations and savant persons provide additional motivation for an innate knowledge of universal grammar.
- Intelligence is not a good predictor of ability in the domain of language.
- Language abilities can outstrip other mental capacities.

**EXERCISE 12.6**

Studies have argued that language abilities in special populations are worse than those of age-matched, typically developing children (for example, Grant et al. (2002), for a study of children with Williams syndrome). What bearing does that have on the argument for an innate knowledge of UG?

## 12.6 UG is the right theory – but how to execute learning?

### 12.6.1 The subset principle

A great deal of discussion in the 1980s and early 1990s focussed on how language development took place. It was reasoned that if the child received no correction for errors, then the child must be prevented from making errors in the first place. Thus it has been proposed that children operated under the guidance of the **subset principle**. This principle permits only a gradual expansion of the range of permissible (grammatical) sentences, based on positive evidence from the input (Berwick 1985). Although there remain staunch advocates of the subset principle (Fodor 2009), there are a range of problems with the principle. For example, it is not clear what the mental status of such a principle is. If the child is equipped with an implicit knowledge of UG, why can't he/she use that knowledge to guide the learning process, together with the input, unencumbered by the restriction that he/she must select the most restrictive grammar? And errors are made (adjective formation [*crumby* vs. *crumbed*] is again relevant), so some leeway has to be given to distinguish permissible vs. impermissible errors. Recent research has proposed that the learner reverts to a default grammar, one that generates a smaller output language in the absence of confirming evidence (Biberauer and Roberts 2009). In that sense, the subset principle may be grounded in the facts of development.

### 12.6.2 Language processing and language acquisition

Researchers in language acquisition have usually worked independently from researchers in language processing – the latter being the theory of how sentences and larger units, i.e. discourses, are analysed in the adult mind. But this is changing, and may provide some answers to the puzzle of how the child gets to grips with the structure of his/her language, without the aid of a principle such as the subset principle. We will take three examples: knowledge of restrictions on local syntactic environments for dative sentences; knowledge of syntactic restrictions on definite vs reflexive pronoun interpretation; and knowledge of conditions that block ungrammatical questions in languages such as English.

### 12.6.2.1 Learning dative verbs

Dative verbs (verbs that can take both an object NP and a recipient NP) may allow frames consisting of an NP plus PP (Prepositional Phrase with recipient role) (29), and a double NP (30) inside the VP:

(29) Samson gave a bunch a bunch of roles to me.

(30) Samson gave me a bunch of roses.

However, not all verbs allow both syntactic frames. For example, *whisper* allows only an NP PP frame:

(31) Samson whispered the price to my sister.

(32) *Samson whispered my sister the price.

There are clues to which frames are permitted (for example, in English generally only monosyllabic verbs permit an NP NP frame); see Pinker (1989) for an extensive review. But children do make errors. Thus children may utter sentences such as:

(33) I said her the answer.

How do children in the end get which verbs go with which syntactic frames correct?

Recent research on the command of dative verbs by Joan Bresnan and colleagues gives us an insight into how children achieve the correct word-to-syntax mapping. Adults have been found to vary in their degree of acceptance of sentences such as (34): speakers of American English rate such sentences better than speakers of Australian English (Ford and Bresnan 2012).

(34) Samson whispered me the price.

That is, when the recipient is a pronoun, speakers of one dialect of English (American) judge sentences with an NP NP frame to be more acceptable than speakers of the other dialect. Such factors are not completely arbitrary – in the case of pronominalization of the recipient, this may follow from a short-before-long preference for organization of linear ordering of phrases, itself motivated by efficiency in delivery (Arnold et al. 2000). In the course of development, the child may settle on a particular combination of restrictions that are appropriate for the dialect he/she is learning out of the mental space made available by psycholinguistic and syntactic constraints. An error may simply be a one-off, subject to correction (or not) through the force of frequency in the particular adult language the child is exposed to.

### 12.6.2.2 The interpretation of pronouns

Another area in which children are found not to get things quite right from the outset is the interpretation of definite pronouns (such as *he, him, she, her* . . .) which are subject to **pronominal binding** constraints that impose different restrictions to those that apply to reflexive pronouns (such as *himself, herself, themselves*). Some studies have found that reflexive pronouns cause fewer errors than definite pronouns (see Kaufmann 1994 for a review of the results and tasks used). In (35a and b) the reflexive must refer to the subject *Susan*, and in (36a and b) it may not refer to that person (it can refer to the subject of the higher sentence, *Jane*, or to someone not mentioned in the sentence):

(35) a. Susan criticized herself.
     b. Jane said that Susan had criticized herself.

(36) a. Susan criticized her.
     b. Jane said that Susan had criticized her.

Various accounts (not necessarily disjunctive) have been proposed for why children do worse with definite pronouns than with reflexives. Conroy et al. (2009) suggest that sentence processing theory can contribute to the explanation. Adult subjects have been shown to mentally inspect both legitimate and non-legitimate antecedents for definite pronouns – thus *Susan* as well as *Jane* will be considered as potential coreferents of *her* in (36b). *Susan* will be rejected by adult speakers. But children may select the wrong antecedent because their quantitative processing capacity is less than that of an adult – the child may 'run out of steam' before he/she has completed the sequence of processing operations. Moreover, children have been found to be 'sentence bound' – they have difficulty in accessing the wider discourse (Goodluck 1991; Avrutin 2000), potentially exacerbating the difficulty with (36a).

### 12.6.2.3 Question formation in Akan

We have already seen examples of the benefits of considering languages other than English. Akan, a Kwa language spoken in Ghana, allows a broader range of question types than English does. Although it is very similar to English in word order (SVO) and it can place the question word – as in English – to the left of the sentence, it permits questions equivalent to (7), repeated here as (37b), as well as questions that refer to a position inside a relative clause (38a) and inside an adverbial clause (39a):

(37) a. Dɛn na Mary bisaa sɛ hena na ɔyɛe?
     What FOCUS Mary asked that who FOCUS 3sg:made

     b. *What did Mary ask who made?

(38) a. Dɛn na wohuu onipa ko a otwaae?
     What FOCUS you.saw person SPECIFICITY MARKER RELATIVE CLAUSE 3sg:cut

     b. *What did you see the person that cut?

(39) a. Dɛn na dɔkota no hohoroo ne nsa ho ansa na ɔrefa?
     What FOCUS doctor the washed his hands around before 3sg:took

     b. *What did the doctor wash his hands before he took?

It has been assumed that Akan is different from English in the mechanism that it uses for question formation. Akan uses a pronominal binding mechanism, in which a pronoun is linked to the question word at the beginning of the sentence. In the Akan sentences in (37a–39a) the pronoun is phonetically null. English, by contrast, forms questions by movement of the question word to initial position. English does use pronoun binding in some constructions, such as the *as for* construction, which allows linkage into those constructions for which question formation is forbidden in English:

(40) a. As for Mary, Jane asked who had threatened her.
b. As for the steak, only you saw the person who cut it.
c. As for the scalpel, the doctor washed his hands before he took it.

Goodluck et al. (1995) tested the comprehension of potentially ambiguous questions such as (41) in Akan, following a short story that allowed answers suitable for main clause reference of the question word and subordinate clause reference:

| (41) | Dɛn | na | Sakraman | dii ansa na | ɔrekyerɛw? |
|---|---|---|---|---|---|
| | What | FOCUS | Fox | eat before | 3sg:wrote? |

Both 5–6-year-old Akan-speaking children and adults gave answers that overwhelmingly indicated linking the question word to the main clause position, not the subordinate clause position. Participants showed that they were in principle capable of construing a question word as referring to a subordinate clause, and adults also did a grammaticality judgment task that indicated that questions such as (39a) were indeed grammatical for them (Saah and Goodluck 1995).

What explanation can we give for the fact that in the question response task both the child and adult participants gave answers corresponding to reference inside the main, not the subordinate, clause? In adult sentence processing theory, there is a principle which serves to minimize the load on working memory: the *Active Filler Strategy* (Frazier and Flores d'Arcais 1989). This principle dictates that the first available slot for a question word (a 'filler') is taken. That slot is the position after the main verb in (41). Thus the preference for main clause answers by children and adults to questions such as (41) can be interpreted as an effect of the Active Filler Strategy in online sentence processing.

Notice that the explanation in terms of the Active Filler Strategy offers in this case an alternative to the Subset Principle. The Active Filler Strategy effectively directs the child to a particular answer, which is correct (all languages allow questioning into main clause positions). The input – evidence of the language around the child – will cause the child (if he/she is learning Akan) to unconsciously correct his/her analysis, and posit a more liberal grammar.

**KEY POINTS: Trajectories of learning**

- There is a need for multiple routes from Universal Grammar plus input to mature knowledge of language.
- The child may innovate, but receive no support for his/her innovation (the case of dative verb learning).

- The child may be waylaid due to lack of quantitative processing ability (the case of pronoun interpretation).
- The child may be pushed towards a particular response because of a strategy that is motivated by the need to lessen immediate processing load (the case of Akan question interpretation).

### EXERCISE 12.7

Can you think of a way in which child speakers of Australian English might change their grammar to accept sentences such as (34) more readily?

### EXERCISE 12.8

I stated above that children have problems accessing discourse content. That is, children do better when called on to access only the local syntactic environment. Are there other facts reported in this chapter for which this focus on the local environment can help or hinder help the learner?

### EXERCISE 12.9

Which do you think is more plausible, the grammar of Akan changing to obey the same rules as English, or vice versa (English changing to become like Akan)? (Hint: how frequent do you think questions such as (37)–(39) are in Akan?)

WEBSITE: **Group exercise**

Visit the website and, in a small group, examine data from the Child Language Data Exchange System (CHILDES; MacWhinney 2000). The questions in this exercise ask you to think about the order in which English-speaking children produce question words and complex sentence types. They will also encourage you to compare the amount of null subjects produced by English-speaking children and Spanish- or Italian-speaking children.

## 12.7 SUMMARY

This chapter has outlined some of the bare facts about first language acquisition and the main contender for an explanation of those facts – Universal Grammar, as proposed by

Chomsky and other similarly minded researchers. We have looked at some candidate mechanisms for the mapping between human biology (innate knowledge) and the end product of competence in a native language. The final sections of this chapter on language processing and language acquisition focus on directions that are quite new, and that I feel will greatly benefit the theory of language development.

WEBSITE: **Child language acquisition**

Now go to the website and assess your knowledge of child language acquisition by completing the self-test questions!

## SUGGESTIONS FOR FURTHER READING

Chomsky, N. (1965). *Aspects of the Theory of Syntax*. Cambridge, MA: MIT Press. Section I (pp. 47–59) of the book sketches arguments for an innate linguistic ability.

Guasti, M. T. (2002). *Language Acquisition: The Growth of Grammar*. Cambridge, MA: MIT Press. This textbook is an introduction from the perspective of generative grammar, with the main emphasis on syntactic development.

Snyder, W. (2007). *Child Language: The Parametric Approach*. Oxford University Press. Though in places rather technical, this book offers an introduction to Chomsky's syntactic theory since 1981 (the publication of *Lectures on Government and Binding*), to recent phonological theory, and to the application of theory to child language data.

# ANSWERS TO EXERCISES

### Exercise 12.1

Since we know that basic word order is almost always obeyed, and that subjects may be omitted in child English, the most probable meaning is 'Laugh at/with/near Paul', i.e. a preposition has been omitted.

### Exercise 12.2

Either the order of the article and noun has been reversed (the intended meaning is 'Jumping a fence') or a preposition and noun have been omitted (the intended meaning is something like 'Jumping [a/the] fence [with] a [friend]'. Neither of these errors is typical of child speech, and so this is not a plausible candidate child utterance.

### Exercise 12.3

An easy answer is that children would probably do pretty well, since telegraphic speech contains mainly content words (Nouns, Verbs, Adjectives, Adverbs). We as adults after all understand telegrams. But this raises the question: what if the child doesn't have the full grammar that we use to read meaning into a telegram? Some research has argued that children may have sensitivity to the presence of words that they omit in their own speech (for example, Lleó and Demuth 1999), perhaps suggesting that they may have the capability to supply words that are missing and would do well in understanding telegraphic speech.

### Exercise 12.4

Objects are more frequently inanimate than subjects. Subjects are frequently pronouns or proper names, which cannot head a (restrictive) relative clause (see examples (8)–(10)). This combination of factors may lead to object relatives emerging before subject relatives.

### Exercise 12.5

The innovation is not a plausible one. One reason is that it will generate sentences that violate the condition in Universal Grammar that movement generally takes place to a position higher in the tree. For example, it will generate, *The nice what man cannot believe that a dog eats in a day*.

### Exercise 12.6

It is not necessary that *all* aspects of language ability are superior to those of aged-matched typical children for an argument for innate knowledge of UG to be made. What matters is that the subjects excel in certain areas in a manner not predicted by their general (non-linguistic) cognitive abilities. Williams syndrome individuals develop relatively slowly in the first decade of life; the study by Grant et al. (2002) was of 4–5-year-old Williams syndrome children, who performed worse than their age-matched peers with relative clauses in a repetition task. Overall, the picture from Williams syndrome is a very complex one. Foundational studies (Bellugi et al. 1993) showed vocabulary skills, syntax and pragmatic skills in teenage Williams syndrome subjects that exceeded the expectation based on their mental age and other cognitive skills. Levy and Eilam (2013) review the debate, and contribute fresh data.

### Exercise 12.7

Nothing in UG prohibits (34), and so the child might innovate examples of this kind (however, this doesn't solve the problem of what leads to an innovation 'catching on').

### Exercise 12.8

The rapidity with which children learn the morphological details of languages such as Inuktitut possibly might be aided by a focus on the immediate sentence environment.

### Exercise 12.9

Although we don't have corpus data for Akan, I think that it's plausible that Akan questions such as (37)–(39) are relatively rare in the input. So that might suggest that Akan could change to an English-type grammar, in the absence of evidence in favour of the Akan mechanism.

## REFERENCES

Arnold, J., Wasow, T., Losongco, T. and Grimstom, R. (2000). Heaviness and newness: the effects of structural complexity and discourse on constituent ordering. *Language*, 76, 28–55.

Aronoff, M., Meir, I., Padden, C. and Sandler, W. (2008). The roots of linguistics organization in a new language. *Interaction Studies*, 9, 133–53.

Avrutin, S. (2000). Comprehension of wh-questions by children and Broca's aphasics. In Y. Grodzinsky, L. Shapiro and D. Swinney (eds.), *Language and the Brain: Representation and Processing*. San Diego, CA: Academic Press.

Bavin, E. (1992). The acquisition of Warlpiri. In D. Slobin (ed.), *The Crosslinguistic Study of Language Acquisition*, vol. 3. Hillsdale, NJ: Lawrence Erlbaum.

Bellugi, U., Marks, S., Bihrle and Sabo, H. (1993) Dissociation between language and cognitive functions in Williams syndrome. In D. Bishop and K. Mogford (eds.), *Language Development in Exceptional Circumstances*, pp. 177–89. Hove: Lawrence Erlbaum.

Berwick, R. (1985). *The Acquisition of Syntactic Knowledge*. Cambridge, MA: MIT Press.

Biberauer, T. and Roberts, I. (2009). The return of the subset principle. In P. Crisma and G. Longobardi (eds.), *Historical Syntax and Linguistic Theory*. Oxford University Press.

Boser, K., Lust, B., Santelmann, L. and Whitman, J. (1992). The syntax of VP and CP in early child German: the strong continuity hypothesis. *Proceedings of NELS* 22, 51–65.

Brooks, P. and Braine, M. (1996). What do children know about the universal quantifiers such as all and each? *Cognition*, 60, 235–68.

Brown, R. (1973). *A First Language*. Cambridge, MA: Harvard University Press.

Clark, E. (2001). Emergent categories in first language acquisition. In M. Bowerman and S. Levinson (eds.), *Language Acquisition and Conceptual Development*, pp. 379–405. Cambridge University Press.

Chomsky, C. (1969). *The Acquisition of Syntax in Children from 5 to 10*. Cambridge, MA: MIT Press.

Chomsky, N. (1959). Review of *Verbal Behavior* by B. F. Skinner. *Language*, 35, 26–58.

(1965). *Aspects of the Theory of Syntax*. Cambridge, MA: MIT Press.

(1981). *Lectures on Government and Binding*. Dordrecht: Foris.

Conroy, S., Takahashi, E., Lidz, J. and Phillips, C. (2009). Equal treatment of all antecedents: How children succeed with principle B. *Linguistic Inquiry*, 45, 446–86.

Crago, M. and Allen, S. (2001). Early finiteness in Inuktitut: The role of language structure and input. *Language Acquisition*, 9, 59–111.

Cromer, R. (1987). Language growth with experience without feedback. *Journal of Psycholinguistic Research*, 16, 223–32.

DeGraff, M. (1999). Creolization, language change, and language acquisition: An epilogue. In M. Degraff (ed.), *Language Creation and Language Change*. Cambridge, MA: MIT Press.

De Villiers, J. and Roeper, T. (1995). Barriers, binding and the acquisition of the DP/NP distinction. *Language Acquisition*, 4, 73–104.

Eimas, P., Siqueland. E., Jusczyk, P. and Vigorito, J. (1971). Speech perception in infants. *Science*, 17, 303–6.

Fodor, J. D. (2009). Syntax acquisition: an evaluation measure after all? In M. Piattelli-Palmarini, J. Uriagereka and P. Salabura (eds.), *Of Minds and Language: A Dialogue with Noam Chomsky in the Basque Country*. Oxford University Press.

Ford, M. and Bresnan, J. (2012). 'They whispered me the answer' in Australia and the US: a comparative experimental study. In T. Holloway King and V. de Paiva (eds.), *From Quirky Case to Representing Space: Papers in Honor of Annie Zaenen*. Stanford, CA: CSLI Publications.

Fragman, C., Goodluck, H. and Heggie, L. (2007). Child and adult construal of restrictive relative clauses: knowledge of grammar and differential effects of syntactic context. *Journal of Child Language*, 34, 345–80.

Freudenthal, D., Pine, J., Aguado-Orea, J. and Gobet, F. (2007). Modelling the developmental patterning of finiteness marking in English, Dutch, German and Spanish using MOSAIC. *Cognitive Science*, 31, 311–41.

Freudenthal, D., Pine, J. and Gobet, F. (2009). Simulating the referential properties of Dutch, German and English root infinitives in MOSAIC. *Language Learning and Development*, 5, 1–29.

Frazier, L. and Flores D'Arcais, G. (1989). Filler-driven parsing: a study of gap filling in Dutch. *Journal of Memory and Language*, 28, 331–44.

Goodluck, H. (1981). Children's grammar of complement–subject interpretation. In S. Tavakolian (ed.), *Language Acquisition and Linguistic Theory*. Cambridge, MA: MIT Press.

(1991). Knowledge integration in processing and acquisition. In L. Frazier and J. de Villiers (eds.), *Language Processing and Language Acquisition*. Dordrecht: Kluwer.

(2001). The nominal analysis of children's interpretation of adjunct PRO clauses. *Language*, 77, 494–509.

Goodluck, H., Saah, K., and Stojanovic, D. (1995). On the default mechanism for interrogative binding. *Canadian Journal of Linguistics*, 40, 377–404.

Gordon, P. (1985). Level ordering in lexical development. *Cognition*, 21, 73–93.

Grant, J., Valian, V. and Karmiloff-Smith, A. (2002). A study of relative clauses in Williams syndrome. *Journal of Child Language*, 29, 403–16.

Hoekstra, T. and Hyams, N. (1998). Aspects of root infinitives. *Lingua*, 106, 81–112.

Hyams, N. (1986). *Language Acquisition and the Theory of Parameters*. Dordrecht: Reidel.

(2011). Eventivity effects in early grammar: the case of non-finite verbs. *First Language*, 31, 239–69.

Josefsson, G. (2002). The use and function of non-finite root clauses in Swedish child language. *Language Acquisition*, 10, 273–320.

Kaufmann, D. (1994). Grammatical or pragmatic: will the real Principle B please stand up? In B. Lust, G. Hermon and J. Kornfilt (eds.), *Syntactic Theory and First Language Acquisition: Cross-linguistic Perspectives, vol 2: Binding, Dependencies and Learnability*. Hillsdale, NJ: Lawrence Erlbaum.

Kegl, J., Senghas, A. and Coppola, M. (1999). Creations through contact: Sign language emergence and sign language change in Nicaragua. In M. DeGraff (ed.), *Comparative Grammar Change: The*

*Intersection of Language Acquisition, Creole Genesis and Diachonic Syntax*, pp. 179–237. Cambridge, MA: MIT Press.

Kuhl, P., Williams, K., Lacerda, F., Stevens, N. and Lindblom, B. (1992). Linguistic experiences alter phonetic perception by 6 months of age. *Science*, 255, 606–8.

Legate, J. (2003). The configurational structure of a non-configurational language. *Linguistic Variation Yearbook*.

Levy, Y. and Eilam, A. (2013). Pathways to language: a naturalistic study of children with Williams syndrome and children with Down syndrome. *Journal of Child Language*, 40, 106–38.

Limber, J. (1973). The genesis of complex sentences. In T. Moore (ed.), *Cognitive Development and the Acquisition of Language*. New York: Academic Press.

Lleó, C. and Demuth, K. (1999). Prosodic constraints on the emergence of grammatical morphemes: Crosslinguistic evidence from German and romance languages. In A. Greenhill, H. Littlefield and C. Tano (eds.) *Proceedings of the 23rd Annual Boston University Conference on Language Development*, vol. 2. Somerville, MA: Cascadiilla Press.

MacWhinney, B. (2000). *The CHILDES Project: Tools for Analyzing Talk*, 3rd edn. Mahwah, NJ: Lawrence Erlbaum Associates.

Maratsos, M. (1974). How preschool children understand missing complement subjects. *Child Development*, 45, 700–6.

Marcus, G. (1993). Negative evidence in language acquisition. *Cognition*, 46, 53–85.

Pinker, S. (1989). *Learnability and Cognition: The Acquisition of Verb-Argument Structure*. Cambridge, MA: Harvard University Press.

(1995). Language acquisition. In L. Gleitman and M. Liberman (eds.), *An Invitation to Cognitive Science: Language*, 2nd edn. Cambridge, MA: MIT Press.

Rondal, J. (1995). *Exceptional Language Development in Down Syndrome*. Cambridge University Press.

Saah, K. and Goodluck, H. (1995). Island effects in parsing and grammar. *The Linguistic Review*, 12, 381–409.

Skinner, B. F. (1957)*Verbal Behavior*. New York: Appleton-Century-Crofts.

Smith, N.(2010). *Acquiring Phonology: A Cross-Generational Case-Study*. Cambridge University Press.

Smith, N. and Tsimpli, I. (1995). *The Mind of a Savant*. Oxford: Blackwell.

Snow, C. and Ferguson, C. (eds.) (1977). *Talking to Children*. Cambridge University Press.

Sperber, D. and Wilson, D. (1995). *Relevance: Communication and Cognition*, 2nd edn. Oxford: Blackwell.

Stromswold, K. (1995). The acquisition of subject and object questions. *Language Acquisition*, 4, 5–48.

(no date). Why children understand and misunderstand sentences: an eye-tracking-study of passive sentences. MS, Rutgers University.

Thornton, R. (1995). Referentiality and wh-movement in Child English: juvenile D-linkuency. *Language Acquisition*, 4, 139–75.

Tomasello, M. (2003). *Constructing a Language: A Usage-Based Theory of Language Acquisition*. Cambridge, MA: Harvard University Press.

Valian, V. and Eisenberg, S. (1996). The development of syntactic subjects in Portuguese speaking children. *Journal of Child Language*, 23, 103–28.

Vihman, M.(1996). *Phonological Development: The Origins of Language in the Child*. Oxford: Blackwell.

Werker, J. (1995). Exploring developmental changes in cross-language speech perception. In L. Gleitman and M. Liberman (eds.), *An Invitation to Cognitive Science: Language*, 2nd edn. Cambridge, MA: MIT Press.

Wexler, K. (1998). Very early parameter setting and the unique checking constraint: A new explanation of the optional infinitive stage. *Lingua* 106, 23–79.

# 13 Psycholinguistics

JOHN FIELD

**KEY TERMS**

- attention
- automatic
- buffer
- chunk
- decoding
- discourse construction
- inference
- language processing
- lexical segmentation
- long-term memory
- meaning construction
- parsing
- retrieval
- storage
- working memory

**PREVIEW**

Psycholinguistics studies how the mind enables human beings to produce and understand language. The field is a wide and diverse one; the most important areas it covers are:

- *Language storage.* How is language represented in the mind?
- *Language processing.* What mental processes enable language users to speak, write, listen and read?
- *Neurolinguistics.* Where in the brain are language operations located? What can physical changes in the brain tell us about the way in which language users coordinate the processes they use?
- *First language acquisition.* How does an infant succeed in acquiring a first language in a remarkably short period of time? See Chapter 12.
- *Second language acquisition and use.* How does a learner acquire knowledge about a second language and the ability to apply that knowledge? How are the processes employed different when a language user is operating in a second language?
- *Language impairment.* What can we learn about language processes by studying cases where they do not function in the same way as elsewhere in the population? See Chapter 14.

There is also a set of associated topics where broader questions are raised about language as a phenomenon. They include:

- *The characteristics of language.* To what extent can animal communication be regarded as a type of language? What does this tell us about what is unique in language?

- *The evolution of language.* How did language come about? Does it reflect characteristic ways in which the human brain functions?
- *Thought and language.* Do we need language in order to think? Or do we need to think before we can produce language?

The present chapter will focus chiefly on the first two of these, **language storage** and **language processing**, which lie at the centre of psycholinguistic enquiry. Ideas and research findings in these areas have important implications for enhancing communication skills, for teaching literacy, for understanding how learners acquire a second language, for designing speech therapy, for devising good study techniques, and so on.

The general goals of the chapter are to invite you to view language from a very different perspective to that of the pure linguist and to raise awareness of complex language processes that we tend to take for granted. By the end of the chapter, you should understand better how language is stored in the mind so that it is available for use. You should be able to account for how speech and writing are assembled by people producing language and how meanings are constructed by people hearing and reading it.

## 13.1 INTRODUCTION

The overarching goal of psycholinguistics is to study the information in the mind and the mental processes that enable human beings to perform as successfully as they do when using language. Its ideas and research methods are mainly based upon those of cognitive psychology; but it also draws quite extensively upon areas such as discourse analysis, phonetics, pragmatics, computer modelling and brain imaging. The history of modern psycholinguistics dates back to the 1950s. Before that time, a dominant theory in cognitive psychology known as **behaviourism** discouraged investigation of the human mind, arguing that the only way of understanding its operations was by observing behaviour. This view was even applied to language, with B. F. Skinner claiming as late as 1957 that infants' acquisition of their first language was largely a matter of acquiring habits in return for rewards.

From its outset, psycholinguistics distanced itself from traditional linguistic accounts of language. Its concern was not to describe language; but to identify the means by which language becomes possible. A central concern of psycholinguists is to construct models of how human beings produce and understand language. That does not imply any crude assumption that all human beings and all languages are similar. It is obvious that people vary enormously in the vocabulary they possess and the fluency with which they manage to express themselves. Similarly languages vary greatly in, for example, the word order they adopt and the importance attached to word order as a way of conveying relationships. However, it will be obvious that language-related activities share certain features which are common to all users. For example, reading in any language entails moving the eyes across the page, making sense of black marks on the page and moving from the end of one line of text to the beginning of the next. Educationalists in particular need to understand how readers succeed in turning the marks first into words and then into ideas; and how they carry information forward in the mind when shifting between lines of text.

It is important to note that psycholinguists do not, as is sometimes suggested, ignore context; indeed, in discussing reading and listening, they place particular emphasis upon the way in which context is used to enrich the basic meaning of what has been understood. On the other hand, there are certain areas of psychology which do fall outside psycholinguistics. They include the effects of empathy or personality on how a language user performs and the effects of anxiety or motivation upon how an individual acquires a second language. These issues are better regarded as part of social psychology.

Within psycholinguistics, there are two distinct lines of enquiry. The mainstream one draws largely upon the thinking and research methods used in cognitive psychology. It is driven by evidence: it investigates the processes behind language by means of experiments in which individuals perform particular language tasks. By contrast, a minority of researchers (perhaps better described as 'psychological linguists') set out with a theory of language like Chomsky's phrase structure grammar and attempt to find evidence for it in the speech of language users and in child language.

### EXERCISE 13.1

Consider the sentence: *erm + I sent my sister + an email.* (+ represents a pause). A linguist might analyse it in terms of Subject/Verb/Indirect Object/Direct Object or in terms of types of phrase (NP, VP etc.). Suggest what would interest a psycholinguist.

## 13.2 Storing language: sounds, words and grammar

We first examine the information that enables human beings to produce and understand a piece of language. Here, psycholinguistics considers not only **storage** (how linguistic knowledge is represented in a user's mind) but also **retrieval** (how that knowledge is accessed so accurately and effortlessly). To illustrate the difference, imagine that an individual has suffered a stroke and has language difficulties as a result. Therapists would need to consider whether the language store has been affected or simply the patient's ability to draw upon the store.

Research and theory into how language is stored in the mind have provided insights into a number of questions that concern all linguists. How do we manage to distinguish phonemes, the sounds of a speech system, given how widely they can differ from one word to another and from one speaker to another? How do we store vocabulary in a way that enables us to locate exactly the word we need from a set of 30,000 or more? Can we really assume that we rely on grammatical knowledge in the form of complex rules for assembling accurate sentences, given that a speaker needs to produce these utterances under extreme pressures of time?

### 13.2.1 Phonemes

Speech scientists have long struggled to account for how we manage to recognize phonemes, which have been shown to have no simple one-to-one relationship with the acoustic signals reaching our ears (Nygaard and Pisoni 1995). The way a phoneme is pronounced also varies greatly according to where it occurs in a word and according to the phonemes that come before or after it. Compare the /k/ sounds at the beginning of *cat* and the end of *back*. Or try saying the words *key* and *car* and compare the tongue positions of the /k/. One way of dealing with this issue is to suggest that the syllable rather than the phoneme forms the smallest unit of analysis for a listener or speaker (Segui 1984) as syllables are more consistent in form.

A different solution overturns the traditional idea that listeners hold some kind of perfect version of each phoneme in their minds against which they can roughly match the variations they actually hear in speech. Infants learning to speak come to recognize the sounds of their language as a result of thousands of different encounters – in different voices, different accents and different contexts. It has been suggested that many of these encounters are stored individually as traces in our memory (Bybee 2001; Tomasello 2003). So if an adult listener hears an unusual [e], she matches it not against a standard version but against memories of other people using the same sound.

The **exemplar theory** just suggested may sound improbable. But it ties in with evidence that the human brain has a much greater storage capacity than we ever imagined. It also accounts for the way we are able to adjust to unfamiliar varieties of our own language. Many individuals report that there are accents of their L1 which they have great difficulty in understanding. What seems to make the difference is being exposed, over time, to multiple speakers of that variety. One could interpret this in terms of the need to lay down traces of voices speaking with the accent in question, to which listeners can later refer.

**EXERCISE 13.2**

Here is an example of a piece of psycholinguistic research into the sounds of speech. Morais et al. (1979) studied a group of Portuguese adults who had never learned to read. They asked them to repeat a set of words but without their first sounds. To give an English equivalent, they might have asked them to take the first sound away from GOLD, producing the word OLD. The participants proved unable to do this. What conclusions would you draw from this experiment?

### 13.2.2 Lexis

An important area of psycholinguistic research considers what it means to know a word and how words are connected in the mind (for an accessible overview, see Aitchison 2012). The basic assumption is that a language user possesses a vocabulary store in the mind (a

**mental lexicon**), where content words (nouns, verbs, adjectives) are stored as **lexical entries**. Each entry contains sufficient information about the word to enable us to use it in speech or writing. There is some controversy about whether prefixes such as *dis-* have their own entries or whether a word such as *disagree* is stored as a whole. Function words (*the, of, she, at* etc.) are generally assumed to form a different list and it has been suggested (Grosjean and Gee 1987) that they may be accessed in a different way.

In Levelt's account of speaking (1989: 188), a lexical entry consists of two parts, one relating to form and one to meaning. The first includes details of the word's spoken and written forms, together with information about how it is inflected (e.g. its plural or past tense). The second (known as the **lemma**) represents a range of possible meanings associated with the item. It also includes information on syntactic structure (for example, with the verb ACCUSE,[1] the entry would prescribe a word order of *ACCUSE* + *person accused* + *of* + *reason for accusing*).

The procedure for extracting information from the lexicon varies according to whether one is producing or understanding language. A speaker or writer starts out with a meaning which has to be matched to the most appropriate form; while a listener or reader begins with a form (spoken or written) that has to be matched to a meaning. Early research on word retrieval focused on speaking and studied slips of the tongue (Fromkin 1980) where a wrong word had been chosen. The aim was to compare the wrong word with the intended one to get some idea of what criteria were directing the search. Meaning-related links between the chosen word and the target one were to be expected; but it was noticed that speakers also seemed to be guided by information about the *form* of the word being sought: its first syllable, its stressed syllable, its rhythm and the number of syllables in it. Speakers (and indeed writers) seem to possess an awareness that a given word exists and even some advance knowledge of the form it takes.

Researchers have also studied the information that listeners and readers use in order to recognize a word they hear in a piece of speech or see on the page. The current view is that they do not just try to match the word as a whole but instead draw upon a variety of pieces of evidence. A reader might identify a word by using visual information at several levels: letter features (curves and straight lines), letters, digraphs such as SH or EA, letter order, syllables and whole words (Rastle 2007). A number of possible word matches are weighed against each other in this kind of **competition model**, according to how closely they fit the evidence and according to frequency – until one of the **candidates** wins out over the others. The term **activation** is often used to describe this process: it can be thought of as a type of electrical current that boosts the candidates to varying degrees until one of them finally lights up and we have a word match.

In both retrieving and recognising words, language users are greatly helped by the way lexical entries are organized in the mind. For the purposes of listening or speaking, words are connected according to how they are pronounced. That is why a speaker trying to

[1] This chapter adheres to the convention of using capital letters when referring to an entry in a language user's lexicon, but the normal lower-case italics when referring to an instance of the word in actual speech or writing.

retrieve CONCUBINE might end up with PORCUPINE instead. Similarly, for reading and writing, words are grouped in relation to their written forms. So, for listeners, the word HEAD has links to words such as RED that resemble it phonologically; for readers, it has links to words such as READ which resemble it orthographically.

Other important links between words are based upon meaning rather than form. Early investigations into language psychology in the 1880s made use of **word association** tasks, of the kind often portrayed in the popular press. The method fell into disrepute, partly because it allowed the respondent time to think before replying and partly because it showed a connection between two words but did not show how strong the connection was. Today, psycholinguists prefer a method known as **priming**, where a cue is given to a listener or reader (e.g. *plane*), followed by a non-word (*glork*), a word associated with the cue (*fly*) or a word not associated with it (*cup*). The individual presses a button whenever they hear an actual word rather than a non-word. The time taken to make this response is measured. After hearing PLANE, a respondent would be markedly quicker to recognize *fly* as an existing word than to recognize an unassociated word like *cup*. The method has confirmed some of the findings previously obtained by word association; and has provided evidence that the sense relations of traditional semantics (e.g. similarity and oppositeness of meaning) do indeed have a role in the way the mind organizes words.

These connections are useful to listeners and readers, who benefit from a process of **spreading activation** (Collins and Loftus 1975). After encountering a word such as *plane* in a conversation or text, they automatically anticipate closely linked words such as *fly* or *pilot* and recognize them more easily if and when they occur. Figure 13.1 represents a

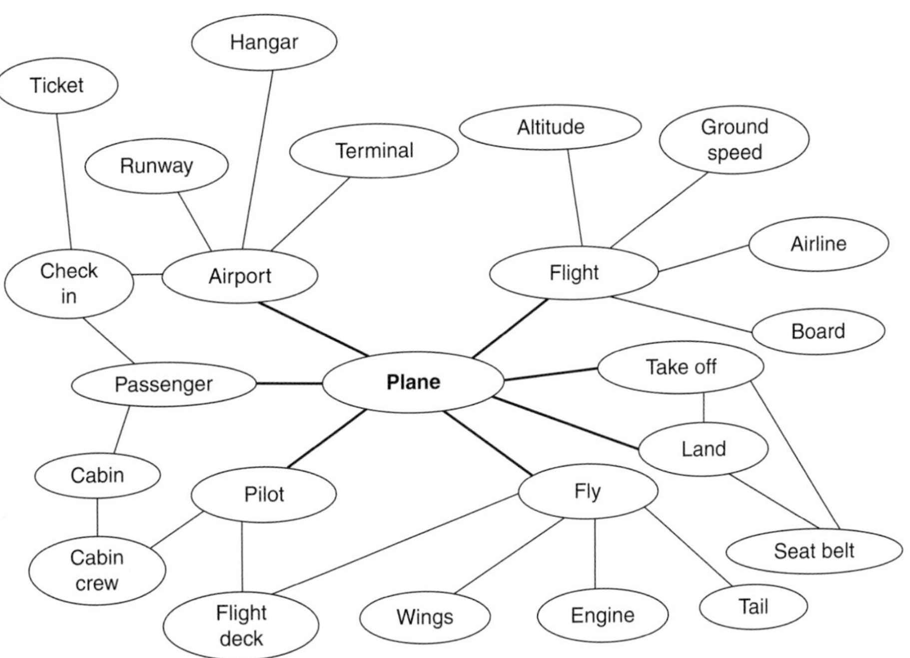


**Figure 13.1** Network of associations for the word PLANE (Field 2005)

network of associations for the word PLANE, with the strongest associations shown as closest to it. There would also, of course, be form-based links to words like PLAIN, PLATE, PLACE.

A further line of lexical research concerns word meanings. It examines, for example, the question of how we manage to classify an unfamiliar object as falling into a group such as FLOWER, DOG, BIRD or FURNITURE. Rosch (1975) suggested that we structure **categories** like these around a highly typical example (in the case of BIRD, a robin and certainly not an ostrich or a penguin). We then decide whether any newly encountered object fits the category by considering its closeness to this **prototype**. However, Rosch's theory has been much challenged – not least by evidence that some people even feel capable of reporting a prototypical even number!

Recent commentators have preferred an exemplar view, where children and adults relate unfamiliar objects to a large number of examples of a category that they have encountered in the past (e.g. creatures classified by other speakers as birds or dogs). Compare the similar theory above on phoneme recognition.

### EXERCISE 13.3

Here are examples of some slips of the tongue (from Fromkin 1973). Compare the word that was chosen with the word that the speaker intended. In what ways does it resemble it? What kinds of cue do the speakers seem to be using when trying to find the word?

(a) *He got hot under the belt (= collar).*

(b) *It's at the bottom – I mean top – of the stack of books.*

(c) *I don't expose (= suppose) anyone will eat that.*

(d) *You can hear the clarinets (= castanets) clicking.*

(e) *white Anglo-Saxon prostitute (= Protestant)*

(f) *The emperor had several porcupines (= concubines)*

WEBSITE: **Group exercise**

Visit the website and, in a small group, attempt the exercise on tip of the tongue phenomena. This exercise will encourage you to think about the way in which words are stored in the lexicon.

## 13.2.3 Grammar

We succeed in assembling speech successfully under very tight pressures of time; and this raises questions about the linguists' idea of a grammar based on applying rules that permit certain combinations of words and exclude others. How are we able to respond so promptly in a conversation if we have to first assemble a complicated grammatical pattern? An alternative, psycholinguistic account (Wray 2002) holds that our ability to produce speech rapidly is dependent upon frequently occurring groups of words being stored in the mind as pre-assembled **chunks**. Thus, we do not have to assemble a sequence such as *I wish I knew*... or *What would you say if*... each time we utter it; but can draw on a unit which is, in effect, part of our stored vocabulary and capable of being produced as a whole.

Traditional ideas about inflections (e.g. past tense endings) have also been challenged. A **connectionist** computer program employed a learning mechanism that strengthened past tense connections that were correct (e.g. WRITE linked to correct past tense WROTE) and weakened those that were not (WRITE linked to regular past tense WRITED). On the basis of this feedback, the program proved capable of 'acquiring' around 500 past tense links (Rumelhart and McLelland 1986). The point is that no abstract grammar rule was necessary; the performance of the program was based upon generalizing from examples and identifying cases that did not fit the norm. However, the extent to which programs such as this can be said to model the real-life acquisition of inflections is open to challenge. The input to the computer concerned only one type of inflection, whereas a child acquiring a language has to deal with many. In addition, the learning process required many repeats before the links were established.

## EXERCISE 13.4

Conventional accounts of grammar give the impression that it is quite a complicated matter to assemble a sentence like *I wish I knew the time* – a main clause with another clause attached to it which requires a past tense verb. Yet speakers manage to do this very rapidly and accurately. Study this piece of speech and underline the groups of words that seem to have been produced as pre-assembled chunks.

> Well I'm still proceeding with the co-operation yes because it's it's right and it's in our interests to do so and again I ++ say to people just discount those type of stories + I mean this is something we've agreed ages ago + and I think it's sensible + if for example in areas like erm + the constitution or indeed in respect of erm education it may be + or any of the issues which matter to the country + you can work with another political party because there are lots of things we have in common with the Liberal Democrats why not do it.
>
> (David Frost interview with Tony Blair, cited in Fairclough 2000)

### KEY POINTS: Storing language

- It is not clear how we manage to identify phonemes, which vary greatly in natural speech. We may possibly keep traces in memory of the many versions that we have heard.
- When searching for a word, we draw on information about its form as well as its meaning.
- Words with similar spoken or written forms are linked in the mind to assist recognition.

- Listeners and readers identify words using many different cues.
- **Semantic networks** help us to recognize words associated with others we have recently read or heard.
- Researchers have studied how we form lexical categories such as BIRD.
- It is difficult to explain how we produce correct grammatical utterances under pressure of time. One solution is that we store frequent chunks of language as if they were vocabulary items.

## 13.3 Using language: basic principles

Accounts of language recognize four major forms of communication – speaking, writing, listening and reading – though we should not overlook the fact that there are other, less widely used forms such as Sign or the use of touch in Braille. We can characterize speaking and writing as **productive** skills; and listening and reading as **receptive** (though the latter are certainly not passive). In psycholinguistic terms, the productive skills require a language user to move from an idea to a form of words, while the receptive skills require the user to move from a form of words to an idea.

We can also characterize the skills by **modality** or form of transmission, with speaking and listening relying upon speech while reading and writing rely upon written text. This has implications for the conditions under which communication takes place. Speech is transitory, while reading and writing have a more permanent form which permits the language user to go back and check. The oral skills thus take place under pressures of time, whereas readers and writers are much freer to decide upon their own pace. Listening is perhaps the most demanding of all the skills because the listener has no option but to listen at a pace that is set by the speaker.

Before examining the four language skills, we need to take note of some basic issues concerning the way in which the human mind operates, as they are critical to understanding the ability to handle speech and writing.

### 13.3.1 Memory

The most quoted model of human memory (Baddeley, Eysenck and Anderson 2009) assumes that it has two major forms. **Long-term memory** is a store holding (for example) our knowledge of past events and knowledge of the world; it also holds our knowledge of language. By contrast, **working memory** deals with short-term operations. It is here that a language user assembles a piece of speech or writing or analyses one produced by somebody else. In order to perform these tasks, the user has to withdraw information about language and about the world from long-term memory. Working memory can also draw upon a record of what has occurred so far in a conversation or a piece of reading.

### 13.3.2 Attention

An important characteristic of human working memory is the way in which it can focus **attention** upon a task in hand and restrict the attention that is given to other parts of the environment (Styles 2005). To give a language-based example, we have an impressive ability to focus upon the voice and words of a single listener even when a noisy party is taking place and there are many other people talking at the same time. Despite this skill, our working memory is limited in how much it can hold. Focusing attention on one area may mean that we do not have enough attention to give to another. Consider, for example, students learning a new language. In the early stages, they may have to give a great deal of attention to recognizing words in a piece of connected speech; this may prevent them from following the speaker's overall line of argument. Attention limitations also explain why it is difficult for an individual to focus on two language tasks at the same time. Students taking notes in a lecture may sometimes find that they have lost the thread because of a conflict between writing and listening.

### 13.3.3 Automaticity

One of the ways in which language users manage to overcome the limitations of working memory is by making many of their basic language processes **automatic** (Schiffrin and Schneider 1977). What this means is that an experienced reader makes an immediate link between the sight of a word on the page and the concept that the word represents, without having to reflect on the process. Similarly, an experienced writer can immediately retrieve the word that he or she needs in order to express a concept. When a process is automatic, it makes minimal demands upon working memory – thus allowing a reader to focus on the ideas of the text or a writer to remember the line of argument that he or she is developing. This explains some of the difficulties faced by children who are learning to read and write. Novice readers have to give so much attention to the words on the page that they may not notice inconsistencies in a text (Oakhill and Cain 2008). Novice writers have to give so much attention to shaping letters that they sometimes lose the thread of what they planned to say (Bereiter and Scardamali 1987). Similarly, second language speakers cannot retrieve words automatically when they need them, and have to give careful thought to assembling grammatical utterances. As familiarity with a language increases, the mapping from idea to word or from word to idea becomes more and more automatic.

**EXERCISE 13.5**

Read the words below. Take no longer than 10 seconds and try to remember as many as possible. Do not look back to revise. Close your book and write down as many of the words as you can.

ground clothes through choose flower empty night
breathe short often twelve scratch dry please friend string

(a) How many words did you remember? If not all of them – why not?

(b) Were you aware of using any particular techniques to help you to remember these words?

**KEY POINTS: Using language**

- The language skills differ according to whether they are productive or receptive and according to modality (speech vs writing).
- Long-term memory stores knowledge of language as well as knowledge of the world.
- Listeners and readers hold language in working memory in order to analyse it; speakers and writers hold language in it that they are about to use.
- Our attention is limited in capacity, which may prevent us from multi-tasking or from focusing simultaneously on different levels of processing.
- If basic operations like word recognition are automatic, it reduces the demands on working memory and enables us to take account of wider meanings.

## 13.4 Using language: the productive skills

### 13.4.1 General processes

There follows a psycholinguistic analysis of what happens when a language user employs each of the four skills, beginning with the productive ones. Models of how the skills operate adopt an **information processing** approach, which aims to show how a piece of information keeps being reshaped by the mind of a language user. For example, a description of listening would consider how sounds reaching the ear are turned into syllables, syllables into words, words into clauses and clauses into ideas.

Information processing models are often presented in flow-chart form, but that does not mean that one stage necessarily waits upon another. Expert language users are able to operate at several different levels at the same time: a reader is capable of interpreting a text at paragraph level at the same time as identifying words and extracting their meanings. Speakers and writers are also flexible and quite often go back and adjust both ideas and language. Writers even change parts of a text while they are producing it.

What does any individual need to do when producing language, whether in speech or writing? They need:

- to have a notion of *where a conversation or piece of writing is leading*;
- to have a *specific idea* that they want to express;
- to construct a *language plan* to express it;
- to *hold the plan* in their mind while they are producing an utterance[2] or sentence;
- to *send out signals* to the relevant parts of their anatomy (speech organs or fingers);
- to *check* on what they have said or written to see if it matches their goals.

[2] It is common to distinguish between an *utterance* in speech (i.e. what is said between two pauses, which may not be a grammatically complete sentence) and a *sentence* in writing, marked by a capital letter at the beginning and a full stop at the end.

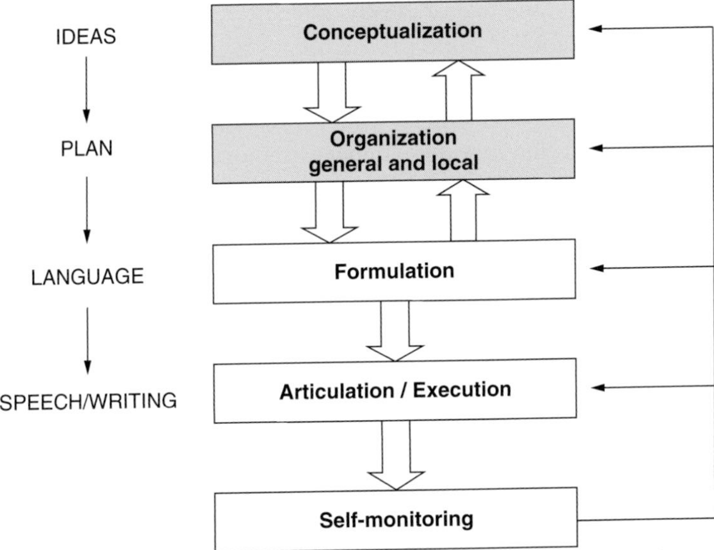


**Figure 13.2** Simplified model of language production

Figure 13.2 illustrates this in the kind of graphic form that psycholinguists favour. It is largely based upon the ground-breaking work of Levelt (1989) on speaking, though Levelt does not make the distinction shown here between *conceptualization* and *organization*.

Speaking and writing employ three distinct phases of planning. The first (marked by grey tones) involves planning for *content*. It is not yet in the form of language; so the second phase involves planning what language to use. The third involves using it.

So how exactly does the translation from idea to language take place? Clearly, it involves grammar and vocabulary, but in what order? The evidence (Garrett 1988) is that grammar comes first. A speaker or writer constructs a grammatical frame, to which words are then added. In doing this, they are helped by their choice of verb, since many verbs have to be followed by a particular syntactic pattern. For example, if you choose the word PUT you have to follow it with (in order) the item that is put and where it is put. Once this kind of pattern has been established, speakers/writers go on to search their lexicon for the right words to insert into it.

The final plan is stored in the mind while the speaker/ writer is producing the words. It is said to be held in a **buffer**, by analogy with the buffer in a printer.

## 13.4.2 Speaking

There are two important differences between the situation of the speaker and that of a writer. Firstly, in many types of speech event, speakers have very little time to plan either content or language. Secondly – and even more obviously – the message has to be delivered in an oral form, which places very different demands upon the language user from a written one.

Planning the *content* of speech depends very much upon the type of speaking being undertaken. If a speaker has to deliver an extended monologue (e.g. a speech or a lecture), he/she usually has ample time to prepare and the ideas may be as neatly organized as they would be in writing. But the situation is very different in the most typical speaking event, a conversation. Here, speakers respond to each other's remarks; so opportunities for forward planning are limited.

As for *language*, speakers have to plan what they are going to say before speaking just as writers do before writing. But they do so under extreme pressure of time. Connected speech contains very brief **planning pauses** of as little as 0.2 seconds, during which a speaker chooses and assembles the next utterance. These pauses often occur at the end of clauses, because the clause is an important unit in planning speech. In a fluent speaker, most pauses fall at grammar boundaries and are relatively brief. By contrast, a less fluent speaker may produce a large number of **hesitation pauses** *within* grammatical structures and may have to revise the original plan because it was not carefully enough thought through or because the speaker lost track of it while engaged in speaking. For an account of pausing in speech, see Laver (1994: 535–9).

Conventional linguistic accounts of language based upon applying rules or tree diagrams are difficult to square with the little time that is available to plan a new utterance. As already noted, planning under time pressure is assisted by the fact that much everyday speech consists of recurrent groups of words. It may not be necessary to assemble a sequence such as *I should have done* word by word; current thinking suggests that the complete sequence may be stored as a chunk in the mind of the speaker, just as a complex vocabulary item such as *on the other hand* is stored. This enables the speaker to produce a complete group of words without having to worry about grammatical accuracy.

The second consideration mentioned was the medium in which the message is transmitted. Connected speech is shaped by how the speaker decides to present it. It is not enough for a speaker simply to assemble a string of words in their standard phonological forms. The speaker has to decide which word in the group is the most important to the message and is to carry intonation stress, and has to downgrade the prominence of other words, especially function words. In addition, speakers often choose to take shortcuts in the way they deliver speech. They might adjust a word to anticipate the word that comes next (*tem pounds*); or they might miss out one or more consonants to deal with difficulties of pronunciation (*next spring* → *neck spring*). This means that speakers have to devise a **phonetic plan** which specifies not just what is in the utterance but how the utterance will be delivered.

The plan is then turned into a set of neural signals to the **articulators** that create the sounds of the language (the lips, tongue, jaw, soft palate and vocal cords). We tend to view this process as straightforward; but, in fact, it is very complex. We have to send instructions to around 100 tiny muscles and their operations have to be closely coordinated.

Finally, while producing an utterance, a speaker **monitors** what he/she is saying. Does it fully represent the original goal in speaking? Does it correspond to the language plan held in the buffer? If there is a mismatch at any level, then the speaker is free to **repair** what has been said. These repairs sometimes take place during speaking, and sometimes immediately following an utterance.

**EXERCISE 13.6**

Imagine a speaker produces the sentence: *I put the cold meat in the* FRIDGE. Explain how she assembled this utterance in terms of:

(a) Planning a grammatical frame

(b) Lexical search

(c) Planning phonologically

(d) Making a phonetic plan

(e) Articulating the sentence

(f) Self-monitoring

### 13.4.3 Writing

The route adopted by a writer largely follows that of a speaker in forming ideas, converting them to linguistic form and checking the end-product. Unsurprisingly, some accounts of writing (e.g. Kellogg 1996) follow Levelt's model of speaking quite closely. The terminology varies a little: what is referred to as *formulation* in speaking is sometimes rather misleadingly called *translation* in writing; the equivalent of *articulation* in speaking is called *execution* in writing.

But again we need to take account of important differences between the two skills. Most obviously, the written rather than the spoken form of the word has to be accessed – and neural signals have to be sent to the fingers, not the articulators. However, perhaps the most important difference lies in the fact that most writing does not suffer from the same time pressures as speaking. That means that there is much greater opportunity for organizing ideas, for planning wording and for **self-monitoring** and revising, all of which play a major role. The lack of time pressures also means that writing is much less sequential than Figure 13.2 might suggest. Monitoring and editing can take place at any time, with the writer looping back to correct text or change decisions at any level (conceptualization, organization, formulation, execution).

There has been some investigation (Hotopf 1983) of problems of *execution* in the form of slips of the pen and keyboard. It demonstrated that writers appear to give reduced attention to function words and that incorrect sequences of letters (THE→*teh*) can become highly automatic and difficult to reverse. The same data also suggest strongly that the plan held in a writer's mind while producing text is in some kind of phonological form. Thus, even among educated writers, the intention to write *20A* might sometimes end up as *28*; *they're* might become *their*.

The investigation of self-monitoring and revising has been greatly assisted by the worldwide use of PCs. This has allowed **keystroke logging** programs (Sullivan and Lindgren 2006), which provide evidence of the editing decisions made when a text does not fulfil a

The ability to plan writing is something that children develop ~~during their first years as writers~~ quite slowly. At first, ~~thye~~ they give ~~a lot of~~ considerable attention to forming letters on ~~teh~~ the page, and tend to say words aloud or to mouth them as they are writing them~~, suggesting~~ . This suggests that much of their ~~mental effort is going into~~ working memory is taken up with the process of forming the words and little ~~of their working memory~~ with the process of planning. The slowness with which ~~thye~~ they write must also make it difficult for them to ~~think ahead~~ organise their ideas. However, aAfter about two years, ~~thye~~ they begin to ~~month~~ mouth not single words but a whole string of words, suggesting that they are now carrying some kind of sentence plan in their heads, which they need to ~~repeat~~ rehearse so as not to ~~loose~~ lose it.

**Figure 13.3** Sample of keystroke logging (Field 2005)

writer's original intentions. It is clear that these decisions operate at all of the levels from conceptualization to execution. As well as correcting typos, changes might relate to overall goals, to the need to foreground important information, to making expression clearer or to failure to identify with the reader's point-of-view. Figure 13.3 provides an example of how a writer edits at different levels.

### EXERCISE 13.7

Look at Figure 13.3. Can you explain the decisions made by the writer? You may find changes that reflect

- conceptualization (changing the angle to be adopted)
- errors of execution
- revisions of style (formality / avoiding repetition of the same words)
- simplifications of syntax
- changes in the writers' view of the reader's understanding of terminology

### KEY POINTS: Productive skills

- Both speakers and writers have to pre-plan the language they intend to use and to hold the plan in a mental buffer while executing it.

- In producing language, we first establish a grammatical framework and then fit words into it.
- Speakers plan speech in brief planning pauses, often at the end of clauses.
- A speaker has to make a phonetic plan which specifies how an utterance is to be produced. This is turned into instructions to the articulators.
- Writers are usually able to give considerable time to planning and revising what they produce. Decisions at any level of processing can be changed during the editing process.
- The language plan in a writer's mind is in some kind of phonological form.

## 13.5 Using language: perception

In accounts of the receptive skills, a distinction is usually made between a *perceptual* phase in which the input is analysed into language and a *conceptual* phase in which a meaning is constructed. At the perceptual level, the demands of listening and reading are clearly very different because of the form in which the language user receives the information. We will therefore examine the two skills separately in this section before going on in the next to consider some shared processes contributing to comprehension.

By way of introduction, Figure 13.4 provides a standard model of language perception which shows some general parallels between the two skills. The first stage (**input decoding**) requires the listener/reader to crack the code in which the message is delivered.

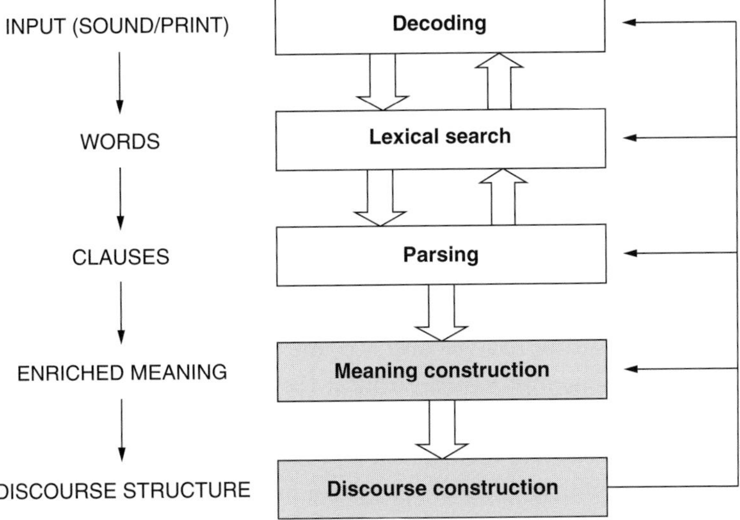


**Figure 13.4** Simplified model of language reception

Listeners have to match acoustic signals reaching their ears to a set of phonemes which represent the sound system of the language; readers have to relate black marks on the page to familiar letter and word forms.

At a second stage, both readers and listeners have to trace connections between the forms they have decoded and words in their lexicon. This provides them with a group of words, in which they then have to recognize a grammatical pattern – a process known as **parsing**. In reading, parsing is assisted by punctuation; in listening it is assisted by intonation patterns. But in both cases, it is a very demanding operation. A listener has to hold an utterance in the mind, retaining the words that were used for long enough to be able to trace a syntactic pattern in them. It might seem that things are easier for the reader, who can after all look backwards to check. Nevertheless, a reader's eyes move across the page so even a reader has to store words in the mind as they are decoded.

### 13.5.1 Listening

A stumbling block in attempting to explain **decoding** in listening lies in the unreliable nature of the speech signal. As already noted, phonemes vary according to the context in which they occur. Even words vary in connected speech, with less important ones reduced in prominence and squeezed in their timing. There is also much variation between speakers, who have different pitch levels, speech rates, precision of articulation and accents. It is remarkable that listeners can adjust to an unfamiliar voice as readily as they do. Traditional accounts envisage listeners as **normalizing** to these features: editing them out in order to focus on the message being conveyed.

In current accounts of **lexical search** (e.g. McQueen 2007), a listener is said to weigh up multiple cues to the identity of a word: drawing upon evidence at phoneme, syllable and word level. But matters are made more complicated by the fact that pauses between words in connected speech are irregular and infrequent, unlike the gaps between words in most writing systems. It is the listener who has to decide where word boundaries are most likely to fall, a process known as **lexical segmentation**. Here, the decisions made are often assisted by rhythmic features of the language being heard. The main strategy in English appears to exploit the fact that 90 per cent of content words in running speech begin with a stressed syllable – so it is relatively safe to work on the assumption that each stressed syllable begins a new word (Cutler 1990). There are of course *fixed stress* languages where one can use this kind of cue to identify word boundaries with 100 per cent certainty.

Descriptions of parsing have to take account of evidence (Marslen-Wilson and Tyler 1980) that listeners attempt to analyse what they hear at a very brief delay behind the speaker of about a quarter of a second. This means that they have to rely upon probability and upon basic syntactic patterns such as Subject–Verb–Object in order to guess the structure of the input they are in the process of hearing. Parsing is assisted by intonation, which often corresponds to syntactic boundaries. But it seems that listening (even in a first language) is a speculative process, with hypotheses constantly being formed and revised.

### EXERCISE 13.8

Consider the kind of utterance that a listener might have to process. It is represented in two ways below. The first format features phonological symbols. The second uses the normal alphabet with bold type indicating stress and bold caps indicating heavy stress.

[ðəˈnekstreɪnfəˈlʌndn] [ɪzðəsebmˈfɔːtɪfrəmplæʔfɔːmeɪt]
thə**necks**trainfə**LON**dən + isthəsebm**FOR**tyfrəm**pla**ˈform**EIGHT** +

ə = schwa, the sound at the beginning of *about, asleep.*

(a) What are the main differences illustrated here between a spoken signal and a written one?

(b) What clues might assist a listener in dividing these utterances into words?

## 13.5.2 Reading

There are three major differences between reading and listening. Firstly, reading is not time-constrained like listening; there is evidence that skilled readers adjust their speed of reading and level of attention to reflect the difficulty of the text and their purpose for reading (Rayner et al. 2012). Secondly, a reading text is not transitory like speech, which means that the reader can look back to check understanding or to confirm that a word has been accurately recognized. Thirdly, decoding in reading is considerably easier than in listening. This is because (a) written text uses standard forms based upon an agreed spelling system; and (b) there are gaps to show where words begin and end.

The use of eye-tracking equipment has led to important insights into the physical process of reading (Rayner et al. 2012). Look at Figure 13.5, which shows how the eye of an efficient reader moves across the page. The reader's eyes move in short sweeps known as **saccades**, which average around 7 to 9 syllables. They then usually rest for around a quarter of a second on a word. The point where they rest is often about a third of the way into the word. Most words are fixated in this way.

Look at the first line of text in Figure 13.5 beginning *Roadside joggers*...The dashes above the words show where the eyes of the reader stopped. The figure above each dash indicates how long in milliseconds the eyes paused (286 = 0.286 of a second). You will notice that the movement of the eyes is not all in one direction: readers go back from time to time. Occasional arrows indicate regressions where the reader looked back. The points that he/she revisited are then shown on a lower line. For example, on line 2, the reader stopped at the word *seem*, then went back and fixated both *healthy* and *body*.

A major component of reading skill is the ability to adjust one's reading style to the type of text being read and to the reader's own goals. So studying a complex text would demand

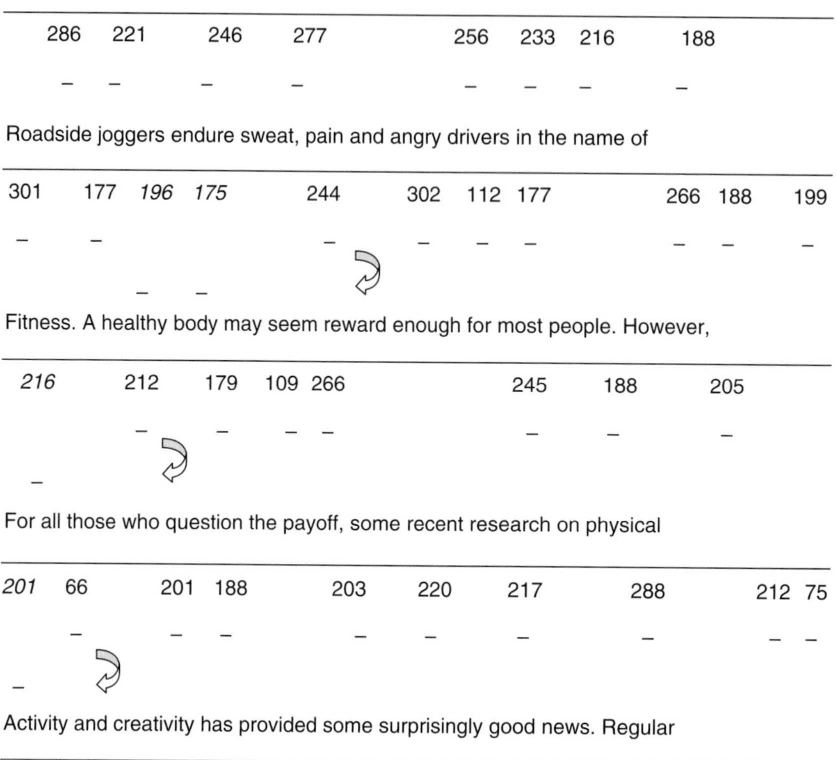


**Figure 13.5** Eye-tracking data (adapted from Rayner et al. 2012: 94)]

shorter saccades and longer fixations, while skimming a newspaper article or reading a crime novel for plot would entail longer saccades and shorter **fixations**.

### EXERCISE 13.9

Look at Figure 13.5.

(a) What type of word does the reader's eye fixate?

(b) What type of word does the reader seem to skip?

(c) Does the reader study each word for the same length of time? If not, which words get studied longer?

(d) Why do you think the reader goes back? To check words, to check understanding or for another reason?

When *parsing* a piece of text, it is necessary for readers to hold decoded words in their minds until the end of a clause or sentence is reached and a syntactic pattern can be imposed on them. The eye has to move across the page, which means that readers have to carry forward information in their minds just as listeners do – particularly when they are moving from the end of one line to the beginning of the next. Here, as with writing, there is evidence that the words are held in some kind of phonological form (Perfetti 1985) – which is why readers sometimes report a 'voice in the head'. This may be a relic of how reading is learned as a child; but it seems more likely that it serves to separate the record of what is stored in the mind from the visual process of identifying new words on the page.

Two issues in reading research have had controversial implications for the teaching of the skill in primary schools. One concerns whether it is useful to teach sound–spelling relationships in a language such as English, which has an irregular alphabetic system. Why not teach children just to recognize whole words instead? In fact, a **dual-route model** of reading (Coltheart 2005), based upon evidence from dyslexia, suggests that a reader has a need for two routes when decoding words – a faster (lexical) one that identifies whole words and a slower (sublexical) one that applies sound–spelling rules to assist word recognition. Even an adult reader has need of the latter in order to deal with unfamiliar names, to match words never seen before in print to words known orally – or to work out how to pronounce words only encountered in writing.

The other controversy was triggered by a claim (Goodman 1967) that good readers employ context and co-text to predict what is to come, so as to avoid having to decode every word they encounter. This led to an approach in which schoolchildren were encouraged to read for pleasure and to guess the meaning of words that they could not recognize. Goodman's claim has been widely discredited (see Gough and Wren 1999). It is not as easy to predict upcoming words as he suggested. In addition, what distinguishes a skilled reader is the ability to decode words and match them to their meanings in a way that is highly automatic. It makes no sense for such a reader to resort to prediction which (unlike decoding) makes heavy demands upon our attention. In point of fact, it is *weak readers* who use context a lot – but they do so to compensate for their problems in recognizing words (Perfetti 1985).

**KEY POINTS: Language perception**

- Listening and reading involve input decoding – lexical search – parsing.
- Listeners have problems with variation in phonemes and words and speakers' voices.
- Listeners have to decide for themselves where word boundaries fall.
- Speech is analysed while it is being produced. This means that listening is a very tentative process with guesses having to be made and revised.
- Skilled readers adjust their reading speed and level of attention to reflect the difficulty of the text and their purpose for reading.
- Readers fixate most content words, but a minority of function words.
- Readers, like listeners, have to carry words forward in their minds so they can parse them.
- Readers need both a lexical and a sublexical route for identifying words.
- Skilled reading depends on automatic word recognition.

## 13.6 Comprehension in listening and reading

In considering comprehension, listening and reading will be discussed together. This is done as a matter of convenience and should not be taken as necessarily supporting the view held by some psycholinguists (e.g. Gernsbacher 1990) that the two skills share the same comprehension route.

The outcome of parsing a piece of text in listening or reading is an 'idea unit'. It is abstract and no longer in the form of language; but it is also rudimentary, in that it takes no account of the context in which it occurs or its relationship to what has been read or heard so far. Two further phases of processing are then necessary. Following Brown and Yule (1983), we will make a distinction between **meaning construction**, building understanding of an utterance or sentence, and **discourse construction**, building understanding of all that has been read or heard so far.

*Meaning construction:*

- enriching a basic 'idea unit' by placing it in a context;
- inferring links between idea units; dealing with reference;
- interpreting the intentions of the speaker or writer.

*Discourse construction:*

- deciding on the relevance of a new piece of information;
- monitoring for consistency with the discourse representation built up so far;
- integrating the new piece of information into the discourse representation;
- building a line of argument that runs through the piece of discourse.

In meaning construction, a listener or reader has to bring in world knowledge, knowledge of the speaker or writer and knowledge of the immediate situation in order to provide a context for a new piece of information. Consider a simple sentence like *Mary phoned her cousin from the station*. We first have to supply world knowledge about family relationships and the function of a station. We also have to expand the notion of *phoned*, which tells us, in a shorthand way, that Mary took out a phone, put in a number and listened to a ringing tone at the other end.

But the process does not end there. Because the call took place away from home, we might form an **inference**, and construct a mental picture of Mary using a mobile. Then suppose that the next sentence is: *It was bad news*. The writer has done nothing to connect this explicitly with the phone call; it is the reader who has to construct the further inference that the cousin gave Mary bad news or vice versa. So inference is used to supply information between sentences as well as within a sentence.

There is also the question of **reference**: the use of words and expressions such as *she, this, the small one, the latter*, which refer to other items in a text. Reference is often straightforward in reading (we have no trouble in associating *her* in the sentence above with Mary). But it tends to be used less precisely in speech (consider an utterance like *The clothes that youngsters wear? I know because I have two of them*). Here, the situation is further complicated by the fact that the listener cannot look back as the reader can.

A further aspect of meaning construction is that we may need to judge the attitude of the speaker or writer whose ideas we are receiving. It may partly be a matter of pragmatics: of understanding the intentions which lie behind a sentence such as *I was wondering if you had five minutes to spare.* It may also be a question of picking up hints from certain words used by a speaker or writer (e.g. words which carry negative connotations) or from patterns of intonation.

Once the basic meaning of the bare idea unit has been enriched in this way, the listener/reader has to decide what to do with the information they have obtained. They need to relate it to a **discourse representation** of what has been mentioned so far in the conversation or the book. The new piece of information can be allowed to decay if it is thought to be trivial or not relevant to the overall text. Or it can be carried forward – either in an imprecise form or with all details retained.

If it is thought worth keeping, it then has to be integrated into the discourse representation. This requires the listener/reader to work out a logical link between the new piece of information and the one immediately before. It also requires the listener/reader to monitor new pieces of information as they come in, to ensure that they are consistent with what has been understood already.

Finally, a listener or reader has to construct an ongoing record of the line of argument that links the various points that occur in a conversation or book. This means distinguishing major points from minor and recognizing the relationships between them. In this way, one builds a structure of topic, subtopic and sub-subtopic rather like the table of contents in a book. It has been suggested (Gernsbacher 1990) that one mark of a skilled listener/reader is the ability to build such structures, whereas unskilled performers tend to link one information point to another without recognizing their relative importance.

## EXERCISE 13.10

This extract comes from a novel. Read it carefully and identify all the places where you have to use your own knowledge of the world in order to fully understand what is happening.

> Rivers folded the paper and ran his fingertips along the edge. 'So they're sending him here?' Bryce smiled. 'Oh, I think it's rather more specific than that. They're sending him to *you.*'
>
> Rivers got up and walked across to the window. It was a fine day, and many of the patients were in the grounds, watching a game of tennis. He heard the *pok-pok* of rackets and a cry of frustration as a ball smashed into the net. 'I suppose he is – "shell-shocked"?'
>
> 'According to the board, yes'. (Pat Barker, *Regeneration* (London: Penguin,1991), p. 4)

### KEY POINTS: Comprehension

- A listener/reader has to add to the bare information obtained from parsing by relating it to a context, using world knowledge, and making inferences about points that a speaker/writer has not explicitly expressed.

- A listener/reader also has to build a discourse representation. This entails deciding which points are relevant, integrating them into what has been heard or read so far and building a line of argument.

## 13.7 SUMMARY

This chapter has drawn on a critical distinction in psycholinguistics between the knowledge of language that we hold in our minds and the processes that we use in employing that knowledge. Instead of adopting a classic linguistic approach of analysing language as a product, we have examined what makes language possible in practical terms.

A number of themes have recurred. One is the importance of automaticity to a great deal of our language behaviour. We need to be able to map rapidly and with minimal efforts of attention from words to their meanings and from meanings to the words that represent them. Without this, it has been suggested, language users become restricted in their capacity to operate at the more sophisticated levels. In the case of speaking and writing, the need to focus upon word retrieval and production may result in the language user losing track of the plan which should be guiding their output. In the case of listening and reading, the need to focus upon decoding words may limit the language user's ability to identify wider patterns of meaning.

A second theme has been the importance of time. Time pressures dictate much of the behaviour of speakers and listeners. The former have to assemble speech in very brief planning pauses; hence our tolerance of much more unstructured discourse patterns in speech than we would accept in writing. The latter have to operate at a speed determined by the speaker and (because speech unrolls little by little) have to make provisional decisions about what they have heard, which may later have to be revised. By contrast, the lack of time constraints in most types of writing gives scope for the extensive planning and editing that is the mark of the skilled writer. Similarly, readers have control over their own timing and can adapt their reading style according to their purpose in reading and to the difficulty of the text.

A third theme has been the variability of spoken input as against the constancy of written. The way in which a piece of speech is delivered is highly flexible and speakers exercise their right to take shortcuts. This causes potential problems for the listener who has constantly to allow for variations in the way the sounds of the speech system are heard, in the way words are pronounced and in the voices of many different speakers. By contrast, the existence of a standard spelling system (even one as quirky as the English one) means that word recognition comes much more easily to a reader than it does to a listener.

It is hoped that this approach to language will have provided some insights into how language users actually operate, even if it has left some questions unanswered. A point not to be missed is that you, the reader, are a language user; and therefore somebody who is capable of testing these insights by identifying examples of them in your own behaviour.

WEBSITE: **Psycholinguistics**

Now go to the website and assess your knowledge of psycholinguistics by completing the self-test questions!

## SUGGESTIONS FOR FURTHER READING

Aitchison, J. (2012). *Words in the Mind*, 4th edn. Chichester: Wiley. This book provides a comprehensive, sound and very readable account of how words are stored and accessed.

Field, J. (2004). *Psycholinguistics: The Key Concepts*. London: Routledge. This reference work defines important terms and issues and is written with linguists in mind.

Field, J. (2014). *Psycholinguistics: A Resource Book for Students*, 2nd edn. Abingdon: Routledge. This university-level coursebook explores in greater depth many of the areas that are covered in this chapter.

# ANSWERS TO EXERCISES

## Exercise 13.1

Psycholinguists are interested in features that linguists might ignore on the grounds that they constitute 'performance' rather than competence. The example might demonstrate how the speaker plans what to say: using *erm* in order to buy time for planning, and making use of short pauses that fall at the ends of phrases and clauses. The shortness of the pieces of speech between the pauses may suggest some problems with planning what to say. A psycholinguist would also be interested in how the speaker was able to assemble this utterance under pressures of time. The use of the verb *sent* might assist. Once the speaker chooses *sent,* it to some extent dictates what comes next – i.e. who it was sent to and what was sent.

## Exercise 13.2

The people studied had never learned to read. So it may be that we are not born with an awareness of the sounds of our language, but only learn to identify phonemes as a result of being taught to read (and possibly as a result of the kind of rhyming games that form part of early education). This is the opposite of what educators tend to assume – which is that they can explain the letters of a language in relation to sounds that children know how to identify. If we cannot naturally separate out phonemes, then it may be that the most important unit of analysis for listeners is the syllable or even the word. It has to be said that this finding has been disputed, though it has also been repeated.

## Exercise 13.3

Evidence from slips of the tongue shows that we search through lexical sets when looking for a word (example a); and that, within these sets, words are linked to their opposites (example b). Sometimes we blend two words from the same set (example c: *expect* + *suppose* = *expose*). There are often similarities of form between the target and the erroneous word; this suggests that when we search for a word, we have some idea about what it sounds like. The wrong word may resemble the target one in several ways:

- the first syllable is often the same (example e); the last syllable is often the same (examples d and f)
- the number of syllables is often the same (examples d, e and f)
- the stress pattern is often the same (examples d, e and f)

Sometimes (example d) the wrong word is similar to the target one in both form and meaning

## Exercise 13.4

*Well I'm still proceeding with the co-operation yes because it's it's right and it's in our interests to do so and again I ++ say to people just discount those type of stories + I mean this is something we've agreed ages ago + and I think it's sensible + if for example in areas like erm + the constitution or indeed in respect of erm education it may be + or any of the issues which matter to the country + you can work with another political party because there are lots of things we have in common with the Liberal Democrats why not do it.*

Note that a few of these chunks are lexical (e.g. *ages ago, in respect of*) but most of them have a pre-set grammatical structure within them, thus saving the speaker from having to assemble it.

## Exercise 13.5

(a) You probably remembered around 7 to 9 of them. This illustrates the limitations of working memory.

(b) To help yourself remember the words, you probably invented contexts that linked two or more words to reduce the load on your memory. More interestingly, you probably also tried to 'say' the words in your mind to help you to remember them – despite the fact that the words were presented to you in written form. Some of the operations that take place in working memory (including holding clauses from reading in our minds until we have worked out their grammar and composing sentences in writing) appear to take place in some kind of phonological form, sometimes referred to as a 'voice in the head'.

## Exercise 13.6

(a) By choosing the verb PUT, the speaker commits herself to a sentence pattern. The most likely is PUT + object + *in/on/under* + receptacle. This sentence pattern is part of her knowledge of the word PUT.

(b) The speaker identifies three concepts to be added to the frame (*cold, meat, fridge*). She then maps from the concepts to the relevant entries in her lexicon (here she is also guided by some intimations about the form of the words (single syllable, perhaps the first sounds).

(c) The speaker extracts the spoken forms of PUT, COLD, MEAT and FRIDGE /pʊt/, (/kəʊld/, /miːt/, /frɪʤ/).

(d) The speaker works out that *fridge* is the most important word and marks it for stress. She gives weak prominence to the function words *I, the, in, the.* She stores a phonetic plan in her buffer.

(e) The speaker has to turn the utterance she has planned into a set of instructions from her brain to tell her lips, her tongue, etc. to form the appropriate sounds.

(f) The speaker may check the plan immediately before she articulates it; she listens to herself speaking and checks that what she says corresponds to what was planned.

## Exercise 13.7

1. The writer changes his mind about the angle to be adopted (*during their first years as writers → quite slowly /think ahead →organize their ideas*) or adds new information (*or to mouth them*).
2 The writer corrects typing errors, where he has perhaps developed a highly automatic but wrong keystroke sequence: *thye → they / month →mouth.*
3. The writer changes to a more formal style: *a lot of → considerable.*
4. The writer makes a syntactic change to avoid a long sentence: *suggesting → This suggests.*
5. The writer assesses the knowledge of his readers, and decides that they will understand the terms *working memory* and *rehearse.*
6. The writer avoids repetition of the same words: *of their mental effort into* (deleted).
7. A link is added to make the logic of the text clear: *However,...*
8. Similar sounding words are confused: *loose →lose.*

## Exercise 13.8

(a) No gaps between words. No punctuation to help mark clause / sentence boundaries. Important words are stressed. Sounds can be missed out. Some sounds are reduced to weak /ə/.

With NEXT and PLATFORM, the speaker has made it easier to say the words by missing out one of the sounds. With SEVEN, the speaker has made it easier to say the word by substituting a /b/ for the /v/. These simplifications make life easier for the speaker but harder for the listener.

(b) Listeners can identify a word more easily if it occurs before or after a pause, because its ending or beginning is marked. They can listen out for prefixes like *pre-* or *re-* and suffixes like *-ing* or *-ment*, which also mark the beginnings and endings of words. They can listen out for the stressed syllables of words, which are clearer than others and often give a good clue to the identity of a word.

### Exercise 13.9

(a) The reader fixes attention on almost every content word in the text (*roadside, joggers, endure, sweat*).

(b) The reader skips many function words *and, in, the, of, for* etc. The reader also skips some other short words (*pain, may,most*). These words are usually very frequent and easily recognized. Their shortness enables a reader to identify them in advance when they are seen at the right hand edge of his/her vision.

(c) Longer and less frequent words (*roadside, fitness, reward, payoff*) may take longer to recognize than shorter ones. This tells us that readers do not just recognize words by their shapes; they also take account of letters within the word and the sequence of the letters.

(d) This reader regresses very little, and does so twice to check the first word on a new line. This shows the demands of having to carry forward information from one line to the next while at the same time decoding words.

### Exercise 13.10

*fold* creates an *edge.*
*sending* suggests that somebody did not come of their own free will.
a *window* is something that Rivers can look through.
*fine* weather allows people to play sports outdoors.
*patients* suggests that this is a hospital.
*rackets* and a *net* are used in tennis.
*shell-shocked* suggests that the person being discussed is a soldier. There are special associations with the First World War.

## REFERENCES

Aitchison, J. (2012). *Words in the Mind*, 4th edn. Chichester: John Wiley.

Baddeley, A., Eysenck, M. and Anderson, M. C. (2009). *Memory*. Hove: Psychology Press.

Bereiter, C. and Scardamalia, M. (1987). *The Psychology of Written Composition*. Hillsdale, NJ: Erlbaum.

Brown, G. and Yule, G. (1983). *Discourse Analysis*. Cambridge University Press.

Bybee, J. (2001). *Phonology and Language Use*. Cambridge University Press.

Collins, A. M. and Loftus, E. F. (1975). A spreading-activation theory of semantic processing. *Psychological Review*, 82, 407–28.

Coltheart, M. (2005). Modeling reading: the dual-route approach. In M. J. Snowling and C. Hulme (eds.), *The Science of Reading: A Handbook*, pp. 6–23. Malden, MA: Blackwell.

Cutler, A. (1990). Exploiting prosodic possibilities. In G. Altmann (ed.), *Cognitive Models of Speech Processing: Psycholinguistic and Computational Perspectives*, pp. 105–21. Cambridge, MA: MIT.

Fairclough, N. (2000). *New Labour, New Language?*. London: Routledge.

Field, J. (2005). *Language and the Mind*. London: Routledge.

Field, J. (2014). *Psycholinguistics: A Resource Book for Students*, 2nd edn. Abingdon: Routledge.

Fromkin, V. A. (1973). *Speech Errors as Linguistic Evidence*. The Hague: Mouton.

Fromkin, V. A. (ed.) (1980). *Errors in Linguistic Performance: Slips of the Tongue, Ear, Pen and Hand*. New York: Academic Press.

Garrett, M. F. (1988). Processes in language production. In F. J. Newmeyer (ed.), *Linguistics: The Cambridge Survey, vol. 3: Language: Psychological and Biological Aspects*, pp. 69–96. Cambridge University Press.

Gernsbacher, M. A. (1990). *Language Comprehension as Structure Building*. Hillsdale, NJ: Erlbaum.

Goodman, K. S. (1967). Reading: a psycholinguistic guessing game. *Journal of the Reading Specialist*, 6, 126–35.

Gough, P. B. and Wren, S. (1999). Constructing meaning: the role of decoding. In J. Oakhill and R. Beard (eds.), *Reading Development and the Teaching of Reading*, pp. 59–78. Oxford: Blackwell.

Grosjean, F. and Gee, J. (1987). Prosodic structure and spoken word recognition. *Cognition*, 25, 135–55.

Hotopf, W. N. (1983). Lexical slips of the pen and tongue: what they tell us about language production. In B. Butterworth (ed.), *Language Production, vol. II: Development, Writing and Other Language Processes*. London: Academic Press.

Kellogg, R. T. (1996). A model of working memory in writing. In C. M. Levy and S. Ransdell (eds.), *The Science of Writing*, pp. 57–71. Mahwah, NJ: Erlbaum.

Laver, J. (1994). *Principles of Phonetics*. Cambridge University Press.

Levelt, W. J. M. (1989). *Speaking*. Cambridge, MA: MIT Press.

Marslen-Wilson, W. and Tyler, L. K. (1980). The temporal structure of spoken language understanding. *Cognition*, 88, 1–71.

McQueen, J. (2007). Eight questions about spoken word recognition. In G. Gaskell (ed.), *Oxford Handbook of Psycholinguistics*, pp. 37–53. Oxford University Press.

Morais, J., Carey, L., Alegria, J. and Bertelson, P. (1979). Does awareness of speech as a sequence of phonemes arise spontaneously? *Cognition*, 50, 323–31.

Nygaard, L. C. and Pisoni, D. B. (1995). Speech perception: new directions in research and theory. In J. L. Miller and P. D. Eimas (eds.), *Speech, Language and Communication*, pp. 63–96. San Diego, CA: Academic Press.

Oakhill, J. and Cain, K. (2008). Introduction to comprehension development. In K. Cain and J. Oakhill (eds.), *Children's Comprehension Problems in Oral and Written Language*, pp. 3–40. New York: Guilford Press.

Perfetti, C. (1985). *Reading Ability*. New York: Oxford University Press.

Rastle, K. (2007). Visual word recognition. In M. G. Gaskell (ed.), *The Oxford Handbook of Psycholinguistics*, pp. 71–88. Oxford University Press.

Rayner, K., Pollatsek, A., Ashby, J. and Clifton, C. (2012). *The Psychology of Reading*, 2nd edn. Hove: Psychology Press.

Rosch, E. (1975). Cognitive representations of semantic categories. *Journal of Experimental Psychology: General*, 104, 192–233.

Rumelhardt, D. E, McClelland, J. L. and the PDP Research Group (1986). *Parallel Distributed Processing, vol. 1*. Cambridge, MA: MIT Press.

Segui, J. (1984). The syllable: a basic perceptual unit in speech processing. In H. Bulmer and D. G. Bauhaus (eds.), *Attention and Performance, X*. Hillsdale, NJ: Erlbaum.

Shiffrin, R. M. and Schneider, W. (1977). Controlled and automatic human information processing: II. *Psychological Review*, 84, 127–90.

Skinner, B. F. (1957). *Verbal Behavior*. Acton, MA: Copley.

Styles, E. A. (2005). *Attention, Perception and Memory: an Integrated Introduction*. Hove: Psychology Press.

Sullivan, K. and Lindgren, E. (2006). *Computer Key-stroke Logging and Writing: Methods and Applications*. London: Elsevier.

Tomasello, M. (2003). *Constructing a Language: a Usage Based Approach*. Cambridge MA: Harvard University Press.

Wray, A. (2002). *Formulaic Language and the Lexicon*. Cambridge University Press.

# 14 Clinical linguistics

LOUISE CUMMINGS

**KEY TERMS**

- aphasia
- cleft lip and palate
- dysarthria
- hearing loss
- language disorder
- laryngectomy
- specific language impairment
- speech disorder
- speech and language therapy
- verbal dyspraxia
- voice disorder

**PREVIEW**

This chapter examines the many ways in which language and communication can break down in children and adults. These so-called communication disorders are usually the result of illness, disease and injury. These medical and traumatic events can compromise speech and language or the ability to produce voice, and have their onset in the developmental period or childhood, or adulthood and later life. You will be introduced to various stages in the communication cycle, and the specific disorders that result when these stages are disrupted. By locating disorders at different points in this cycle, you will see that quite different processes are involved in communication disorders. Several clinical distinctions that are integral to the study of communication disorders and to the work of speech and language therapists will be examined. They include the distinction between a receptive and an expressive language disorder, a developmental and an acquired communication disorder and an important clinical distinction between a speech disorder and a language disorder. You will then see how these disorders are manifested in children and adults through a discussion of speech, language and voice in two developmental and two acquired communication disorders: cleft lip and palate, and specific language impairment in children, and aphasia and laryngectomy in adults. By the end of the chapter, you will have knowledge of an important clinical application of linguistics, as well as an awareness of the work of **speech and language therapy**.

## 14.1 INTRODUCTION

For a significant number of children and adults, speech and language skills are disordered to such an extent that they pose a significant barrier to effective communication. The Royal College of Speech and Language Therapists estimates that 2.5 million people in the UK have a communication disorder. Of this number, some 800,000 people have a disorder that is so severe that it is hard for anyone outside their immediate families to understand them. In the US, the National Institute on Deafness and Other Communication Disorders estimates that one in every six Americans has some form of communication disorder. These large figures convey something of the extent of the burden of communication disorders on society as a whole. They should not, however, serve to distract from the personal impact of these disorders, an impact that is most often experienced as reduced quality of life as well as educational and occupational disadvantage.

The clinicians and researchers who study, assess and treat communication disorders do so from within a branch of linguistics called 'clinical linguistics'. This is a broad area of academic and clinical investigation that overlaps with medical and other fields of study (e.g. neurology, psychology) and that demands a sound understanding of language at all of its levels. In this chapter, you will be introduced to some of the disorders that are examined by clinical linguists. You will encounter new terminology – much of it linguistic in nature, but some of it from other disciplines – that is used to characterize these disorders and their impact upon communication. A number of communication disorders will be examined in detail to give you a sense of how they manifest in the children and adults who develop them. These disorders have been chosen in order to represent the main clinical areas of speech, language, hearing and voice (a further area of clinical work, swallowing disorders, will not be considered in this chapter). By the end of the chapter, you should be able to identify and describe some of the many disorders that can affect human communication across the lifespan. But first, it is necessary to examine the different ways in which human communication can be disrupted.

## 14.2 Breakdown in the communication cycle

Human communication is a remarkably complex process that draws upon a diverse set of linguistic, cognitive and motor skills. Before we even utter a single word, we must decide what message we want to communicate to a listener or hearer. Deciding what that message should be is itself a complex process that requires knowledge on the part of the speaker of the context in which a verbal exchange is occurring, the relevance of the message to that context and the goals of a particular exchange. Having successfully made these assessments, the speaker will have a clear **communicative intention** in mind which he or she will wish to convey to the hearer (see Figure 14.1). In most communication between people, that intention is conveyed through language, although it may also be conveyed through non-verbal means (e.g. gesture, facial expression). To the extent that a linguistic utterance is to be produced, the speaker needs to select the phonological, syntactic and semantic structures that will give expression to this intention. As can be seen in Figure 14.1, this is achieved in a stage of the communication cycle called **language encoding**.

A linguistically encoded intention is an abstract structure that still has some way to go before it is in a form that can be communicated to a listener. The speaker must select from the range of motor activities that the human speech mechanism is capable of performing those that are necessary to achieve the transmission of the utterance to a listener. It is

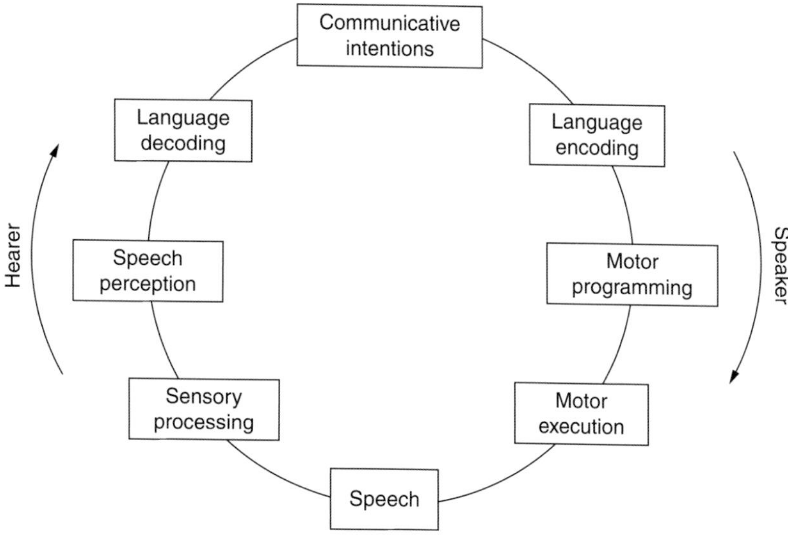


**Figure 14.1** The human communication cycle
(from Cummings 2008; reproduced with permission from Edinburgh University Press)

during the stage of **motor programming** that these selections are made (subconsciously, of course) and certain motor routines are planned in relation to the utterance. Motor programs can only be realized if anatomical structures (e.g. lips, tongue, vocal folds) receive nervous signals instructing them to perform particular movements. Figure 14.1 shows that these movements are carried out during a stage in communication called **motor execution**. Assuming all preceding stages have been performed competently, the result of these various processes is audible, intelligible speech.

Thus far, we have only described the processes that lead to the production of a linguistic utterance. Yet human communication is not just about producing utterances but is also about receiving or understanding them. It can be seen in Figure 14.1 that the first step in this receptive part of the communication cycle is called **sensory processing**. This is the stage during which sound waves are converted in the ear from mechanical vibrations into nervous impulses which are then carried to the auditory centres in the brain. The auditory centres are responsible for recognizing or perceiving these impulses as speech sounds on the one hand or non-speech (environmental) sounds on the other hand (e.g. the bark of a dog). When recognition of speech sounds is involved, this stage of the communication cycle is called **speech perception**.

Having recognized or perceived speech sounds, the task of attributing significance or meaning to the utterance begins. As depicted in Figure 14.1, rules begin to analyse the phonological, syntactic and semantic structures in the linguistic utterance in a stage called **language decoding**. Amongst other things, these rules tell the hearer the grammatical constructions used in the utterance (e.g. passive voice rather than active voice) as well as the semantic roles at play in the utterance (e.g. if a particular noun phrase is the agent in the sentence). The outcome of linguistic decoding of the utterance is not necessarily the particular communicative intention that the speaker intended to convey by way of producing the utterance (only sometimes is the literal meaning of the utterance the meaning that the speaker intended to convey). Quite often, further processing that is pragmatic in nature is needed to recover the particular intention that the speaker intended to communicate, for example, that the speaker who utters *Can you open the window?* is requesting the window to be opened. It is only when the speaker's intended meaning is recovered by the hearer that the communication cycle in Figure 14.1 can be said to be complete.

The complex nature of the human communication cycle means that there is a multitude of ways in which this cycle may be disrupted in people with communication disorders. The adult with schizophrenia who has thought disorder may have difficulty formulating an appropriate communicative intention, that is, one which is relevant, fulfils the goals of a particular communicative exchange, and so on. The adult with non-fluent **aphasia** (or dysphasia) has impaired language encoding skills, one consequence of which is the use of syntactically reduced utterances (see Section 14.5.1). The child or adult with **verbal dyspraxia** may struggle to select specific motor routines during the motor programming of the utterance. The child with cerebral palsy or the adult who sustains a traumatic brain injury may both experience **dysarthria**, a disorder that disrupts the execution of speech on account of failure of nervous impulse transmission to the articulatory musculature.

Sensory processing of the speech signal may be disrupted in the individual with **hearing loss**. This loss may be either congenital (present from the time of birth) or acquired (as a result of an infection, for example) and may be conductive or sensorineural in nature (conductive hearing loss describes a failure of speech sound conduction in the middle ear, while sensorineural hearing loss is the result of damage to auditory centres in the brain or to any of the auditory nerves carrying nervous impulses to the brain). The child with Landau-Kleffner syndrome, who experiences language impairment in the presence of a seizure disorder, has intact hearing but is unable to recognize or perceive spoken words. The resulting **auditory agnosia** is often mistaken for deafness. The child with specific language impairment (SLI) and the adult with Down syndrome and intellectual disability (or learning disability) may lack some of the language decoding skills required to understand the syntactic and semantic structures in the utterances spoken by others. Finally, the child with an autism spectrum disorder (ASD) may have impaired pragmatic skills and may fail to recover a speaker's communicative intention in producing an utterance. These conditions and many others not mentioned here (stammering, **voice disorder**, etc.) form the complex array of communication disorders that are examined by clinical linguists. In the next section, key clinical distinctions adopted by these linguists will be discussed.

## EXERCISE 14.1

The human communication cycle is depicted in Figure 14.1. It portrays communication as a complex process involving eight stages. Read each of the scenarios presented below. Then decide which of the eight stages in the communication cycle is impaired in the client described. Your answer may include one stage or more than one stage.

(a) Sally is a sociable 5-year-old who attends primary school. The school's speech and language therapist has assessed Sally's communication skills and has found that her use of phonology is more typical of a 3-year-old child. In all other respects her communication skills are normal.

(b) Bill is 49 years old and has been diagnosed with a brain tumour in his left cerebral hemisphere. Formal assessment of his language skills reveals that his comprehension and production of syntax is disrupted. His speech is also somewhat slurred and mildly unintelligible.

(c) Frank is 65 years old and has been diagnosed with Alzheimer's disease. His participation in conversation has steadily diminished as he has found it increasingly difficult to make relevant contributions to verbal exchanges with others. An assessment of his communication skills reveals relatively intact structural language skills (i.e. syntax, semantics) but marked difficulty in generating appropriate messages for communication.

(d) Felicity is 6 years old. She was born with Möbius syndrome which has affected a number of the cranial nerves used in speech production. She is attending regular speech and language therapy where the focus is on improving the intelligibility of her speech.

(e) Toby is 7 years old and is in recovery following severe bacterial meningitis. The infection has caused bilateral damage to the cochlea in his inner ear. Audiological assessment has revealed significant sensorineural hearing loss. His language skills are age appropriate.

(f) Rose is 50 years old and is two years into her recovery from a traumatic brain injury that was sustained in a road traffic accident. Her expressive and receptive language skills are relatively intact. However, she has marked difficulty in sequencing the articulatory movements that are needed to produce speech and her vowels are severely distorted. The speech and language therapist diagnoses acquired verbal dyspraxia.

## 14.3 Significant clinical distinctions

The discussion of the communication cycle in Section 14.2 introduced a number of terms that are central to work in clinical linguistics. The cycle drew a distinction between the expression or production of utterances (**expressive language**), and the reception or understanding of utterances (**receptive language**). This distinction pervades the assessment and treatment of communication disorders. For example, the clinician who is asking a client with aphasia to point to the picture in which 'The man, who is crossing the road, is tall' is assessing that client's understanding of relative clauses. The child with Down syndrome who is asked to describe a picture in which 'The ball is on top of the box' is having an aspect of his or her expressive syntax (i.e. use of locative prepositions) assessed. Similarly, the clinician who is using exercises designed to eliminate the phonological processes of stopping (e.g. [tup] for 'soup') and fronting (e.g. [tat] for 'cat') in the speech of a 5-year-old child is working on expressive phonology, while the clinician who is asking the adult with dementia to organize pictures according to semantic fields is focusing on an aspect of receptive semantics in therapy.

The receptive–expressive distinction allows clinicians to characterize a number of different scenarios. One such scenario is where there is a mismatch in receptive and expressive skills in a client, that is, where one set of skills is significantly better than the other. For example, in the adult with non-fluent aphasia receptive language skills are typically superior to expressive language skills. Another scenario is where one set of language skills deteriorates more rapidly than the other in a client. For example, in the child with Landau-Kleffner syndrome receptive language skills are first to be affected. Expressive deficits usually occur later in the disorder and are thus considered to be secondary to the receptive impairment (Honbolygó et al. 2006).

A second important clinical distinction is that between a developmental and an acquired communication disorder. For a significant number of children, speech and language skills are not acquired normally during the developmental period. This may be the result of an anatomical defect or neurological trauma sustained before, during or after birth. The impact of these events on the development of speech and language skills varies considerably across the babies and children who are affected by them. The group of **developmental communication disorders** is thus a large and diverse one including children with cleft lip and palate (anatomical defect in the pre-natal period), children with brain damage due to oxygen deprivation during labour (neurological insult in the perinatal period) or children with cerebral palsy as a result of meningitis contracted at 6 months of age (neurological damage in the post-natal period).

The group of **acquired communication disorders** is equally large and diverse. Previously intact speech and language skills can become disrupted for a range of reasons including the onset of disease, trauma or injury affecting the anatomical and neurological structures that are integral to communication. An adult may develop a neurodegenerative condition like motor neurone disease, multiple sclerosis, Parkinson's disease or Alzheimer's disease. He or she may sustain a head injury in a road traffic accident, violent assault, sports accident or as a result of a trip or fall. A previously healthy adult may sustain a stroke (known as a cerebrovascular accident or CVA). He or she may succumb to infection (e.g. meningitis) or develop benign and malignant lesions on any of the anatomical structures involved in speech production (e.g. larynx, tongue). Any one of these events will disrupt communication skills leading to disorders such as acquired aphasia and dysarthria.

A third distinction that is integral to work in clinical linguistics is that between a **speech disorder** and a **language disorder**. These are not the same thing notwithstanding everyday usage (people tend to use 'speech disorder' to refer to both speech and language disorders). The distinction between a speech and a language disorder can be best demonstrated by referring to the diagram of the communication cycle in Figure 14.1. Breakdown in the boxes in this diagram labelled 'language encoding' and 'language decoding' typically leads to a language disorder. So the adult with aphasia and the child with specific language impairment have a language disorder because they are unable to encode and decode aspects of language (e.g. syntax, semantics). However, breakdown in the boxes labelled 'motor programming' and 'motor execution' typically lead to speech disorders, verbal dyspraxia (or apraxia) and dysarthria, respectively.

Traditionally, the speech–language distinction has been taken to reflect a distinction between non-symbolic and symbolic aspects of communication with only language dealing with symbolic aspects of communication (i.e. those that convey meaning). Crystal (1997: 267) explicitly articulates this distinction when he states that 'the former [language disorders] refer only to the "symbolic" aspects of communication, i.e. those concerned with the formulation and structuring of meaning … The latter [speech disorders] refer to the "non-symbolic" aspects, that is, those concerned only with the use of sounds seen as a set of meaningless phonetic entities'. Although the distinction is still in widespread clinical use, it has attracted some criticism (e.g. it leaves the status of phonology somewhat indeterminate between speech and language). Of course, notwithstanding the distinction between speech and language disorders, it is not uncommon to find both types of disorder in a single client. For example, the adult who sustains a CVA may develop both aphasia and dysarthria.

All three clinical distinctions are integral to the discussion of communication disorders in Sections 14.4 and 14.5.

## EXERCISE 14.2

This exercise is intended to get you thinking about three important distinctions in clinical linguistics: (1) receptive vs expressive communication disorders, (2) developmental vs acquired communication disorders and (3) speech vs. language disorders. Each of the scenarios below examines one of these three distinctions. You need to state which distinction within your answer.

(a) Landau-Kleffner syndrome (LKS) is a rare disorder in children that has a peak incidence between 4 and 7 years of age (Temple1997). It leads to sudden or gradual loss of language skills in the presence of a seizure disorder (the children who develop LKS experience seizures as they sleep). Another term for LKS is '*acquired* epileptic aphasia'. Why is the term 'acquired' used of this disorder when it is exclusively children who develop the condition?

(b) Patrick is 59 years old. He is aphasic following a CVA some six months earlier. His communication skills have been assessed by a speech and language therapist using the Boston Diagnostic Aphasia Examination (Goodglass, Kaplan and Barresi 2001), amongst other assessments. This has revealed that Patrick struggles to understand certain syntactic constructions (e.g. relative clauses and passive voice) and that he produces semantic paraphasic errors when asked to name pictures (i.e. his errors are semantically related to the target word, e.g. he says 'eye' for ear). Are Patrick's difficulties with syntax and semantics expressive or receptive in nature?

(c) Penelope is 8 years old and she has a severe communication disorder. Her problems with communication are so severe that she is unable to attend mainstream school and must attend a special school that has a team of speech and language therapists. Penelope's therapist has extensively assessed her communication skills and has noted the following:

some slurring of speech, reports of unintelligibility from caregivers and teachers, age-appropriate performance on the Clinical Evaluation of Language Fundamentals (Semel, Wiig and Secord 2003). Does Penelope have a speech disorder, a language disorder, or both?

(d) John is 27 years old and has schizophrenia. His communication skills are bizarre, which has led to withdrawal and social isolation from everyone other than close family members. Informal observation by a speech and language therapist reveals marked impairment in the pragmatics of language. Specifically, John fails to understand humour and irony used by others and he interprets many utterances literally (e.g. he responds 'yes' to indirect speech acts such as 'Can you tell me the time?'). Also, he contributes many irrelevant utterances in conversation and produces utterances that are poorly related to each other. Are John's problems with pragmatics receptive or expressive in nature?

(e) Frank is 45 years old. He is currently under the supervision of a speech and language therapist who is treating him for a speech disorder (dysarthria) that he developed as a result of a head injury sustained in a motorbike accident. This is not Frank's first contact with speech and language therapy. When he was 5 years old, he was diagnosed with grammatical delay by a therapist at the primary school he attended. Frank has experienced two communication disorders to date. Are these disorders developmental or acquired in nature?

(f) Paul is a lively 6-year-old who has a number of cognitive and communication problems caused by his mother's excessive consumption of alcohol during pregnancy (he has been diagnosed as having foetal alcohol syndrome by a paediatrician). His expressive syntax is severely delayed – he is still only at the two-word stage of language production. An analysis of his expressive phonology reveals a number of immature phonological processes. However, his articulation skills are intact. Does Paul have a speech disorder, a language disorder or both?

## 14.4 Developmental communication disorders

Now that we are clear about the distinction between developmental and acquired communication disorders, we can begin to examine a few of these disorders in detail. The communication problems that attend **cleft lip and palate** and a disorder called **specific language impairment** (SLI) will be used to demonstrate how factors in the developmental period can adversely affect communication. Despite the fact that both conditions are developmental disorders, cleft lip and palate and SLI are significantly different in several other respects (hence, the reason for their selection). Firstly, a clear organic aetiology (or medical cause) in the pre-natal period is responsible for the anatomical malformations in cleft lip and palate. No similar or other cause for the severe language impairment in SLI can be found. Secondly, language disorder is the primary communication disorder in SLI. In cleft lip and palate, however, such language disorder as occurs is normally secondary to the severe speech disorder in cleft children. Thirdly, hearing is also often impaired in children with cleft lip and palate. By definition, the child who is diagnosed with SLI cannot have any hearing loss. The combination of these two disorders will give you a comprehensive overview of the different ways in which communication disorders can manifest themselves in the developmental period.

### 14.4.1 Cleft lip and palate

In some children, the tissues that form the upper lip, upper gum and hard and soft palates do not fuse properly during early pre-natal development. The result is a cleft of one or more of these structures. Although there is some small variation in the rate of occurrence of cleft lip and palate, figures suggest that this birth defect is found in between 1 in 700 births (Sargent 1999) and 1 in 750 births (American Cleft Palate-Craniofacial Association). Cleft lip and palate affects males and females in a ratio of 2:1 (Sargent 1999).

The anatomical defect in cleft lip and palate is believed to have a multifactorial aetiology which includes genetic factors (evidenced by aggregation of the condition in families), certain medications (e.g. anticonvulsive drugs), heavy alcohol consumption and smoking. Another indication that genetic factors are at work in this disorder is that over 150 syndromes have the defect as part of their differential diagnosis. Two such syndromes are velocardiofacial syndrome (the syndrome most commonly associated with cleft palate) and Pierre Robin syndrome (Sargent 1999). Whatever factors cause the embryological malformations in cleft lip and palate to occur, what is clear is that they have their effect in the first trimester of pregnancy (see Cummings (2008) for further discussion). Sargent (1999) reports that 21 per cent of all orofacial clefts have a (unilateral and bilateral) cleft lip only (see Figures 14.2 and 14.4), 46 per cent have a cleft lip and palate (see Figure 14.3), and 33 per cent have a cleft palate alone. Stengelhofen (1993) states that an isolated cleft of the palate is the only type of cleft which occurs more commonly in females.

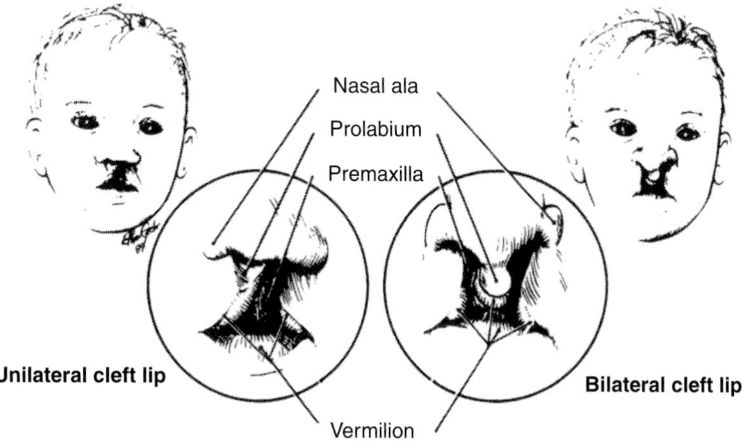


**Figure 14.2** The cleft lip and nose (reprinted with permission from the Cleft Palate Foundation, www.cleftline.org)

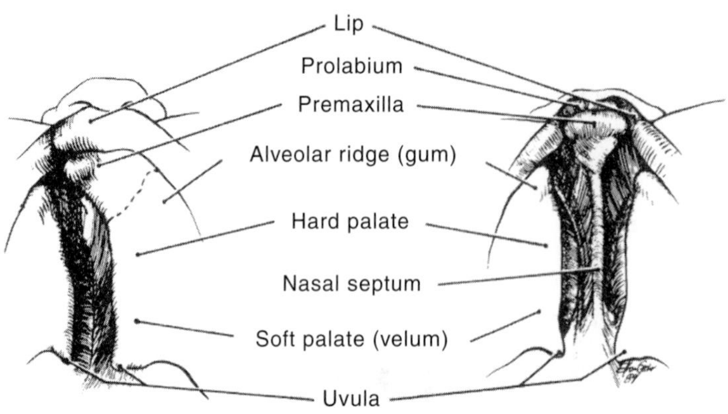


**Figure 14.3** Unilateral and bilateral cleft lip and palate (reprinted with permission from the Cleft Palate Foundation, www.cleftline.org)

The child who is born with a cleft lip and palate faces considerable hearing, speech and language problems (Cummings 2008, 2014a). A significant number of cleft children experience severe and persistent ear infections with concomitant hearing loss. Van Cauwenberge, De Moor and Dhooge (1998) report that over 50 per cent of children with cleft palate have recurrent episodes of acute otitis media (a middle ear infection that is commonly known as 'glue ear'). When one considers the anatomical and physiological defect in cleft palate, it is easy to see why cleft children are particularly prone to middle ear infections and hearing loss.

The Eustachian tube connects the middle ear to the nasopharynx (region of the throat behind the nasal cavities). Through its opening, the middle ear is ventilated. Opening of the Eustachian tube is achieved through the contraction of the tensor veli palatini muscles. This pair of palatal muscles is abnormal in the child with cleft palate with the result that the middle ear is inadequately ventilated. In the absence of adequate ventilation, fluid accumulates in the middle ear leading to the development of otitis media. If this fluid becomes infected, pus may develop which then ruptures through the tympanic membrane (ear drum). This sequence of events may be avoided through a surgical procedure known as myringotomy. In this procedure, a small pressure-equalizing tube, which functions by ventilating the middle ear, is inserted into the ear drum.

The principal speech defect in cleft palate stems from failure to achieve sufficient intra-oral air pressure for speech production. Even when the cleft in the palate is surgically repaired in a procedure known as palatoplasty, pulmonary air may escape into the nasal cavities on account of inadequate closure of the velopharyngeal port (a surgically repaired soft palate may lack the mobility and length required to close this port). The result is excessive nasal resonance during speech production (hypernasal speech). The cleft child engages in a number of compensatory strategies in order to achieve the necessary build-up of air pressure for speech. These strategies involve a general backward shift in the place of articulation of speech sounds as the child attempts to gain closure at other locations in the vocal tract. Some of these aberrant articulations are described below.

The oral plosives /p,b,t,d,k,g/ may be substituted by glottal stops /ʔ/ as the glottis is the only point in the vocal tract where the child can achieve a build-up of air pressure. There

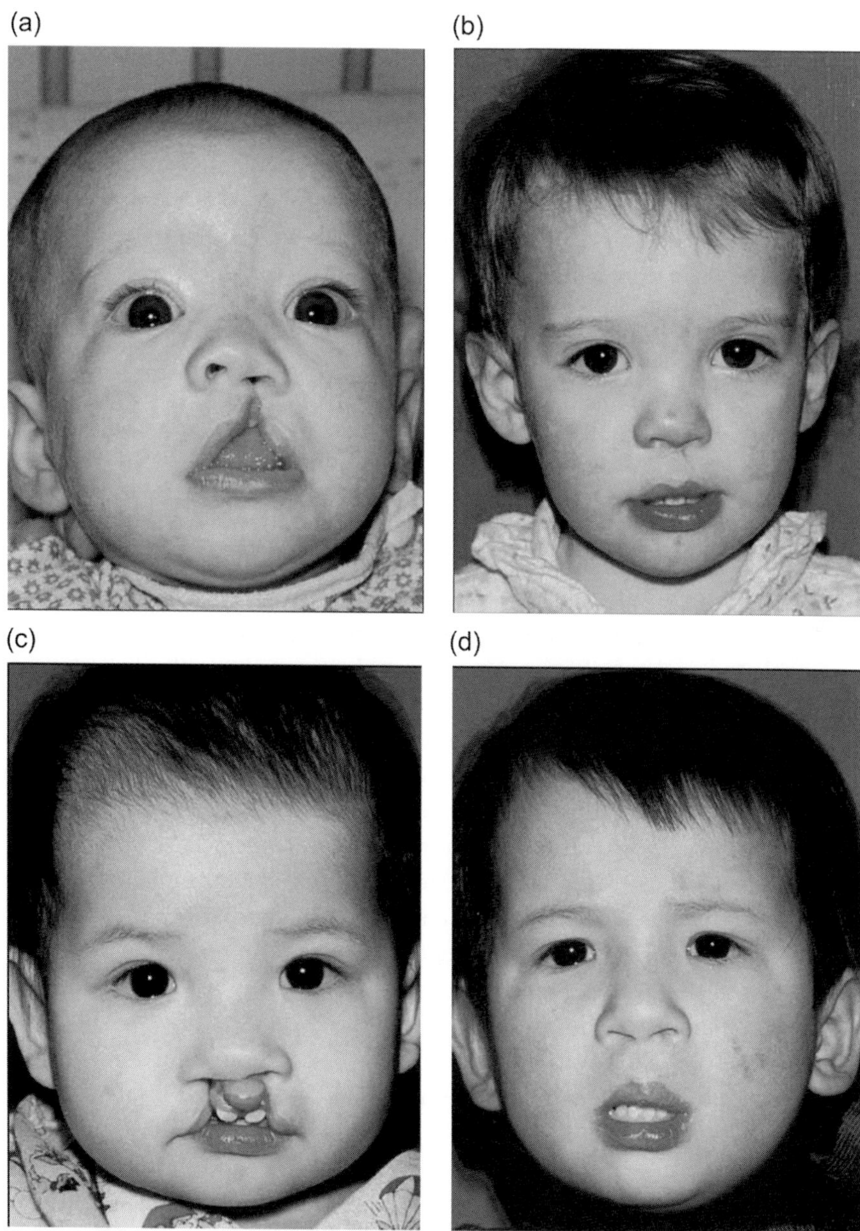


**Figure 14.4** Diagrams showing unilateral cleft lip (A) pre-operatively and (B) post-operatively, and bilateral cleft lip (C) pre-operatively and (D) post-operatively. These excellent surgical results appear in the *Craniofacial Surgery Book* (1999) by Larry A. Sargent, MD, the operating surgeon in both cases. Dr Sargent's permission to reproduce these images is gratefully acknowledged.

may be substitution of palato-alveolar fricatives /ʃ,ʒ/ with palatal /ç,ʝ/, velar /x,ɣ/ or pharyngeal /ħ,ʕ/ fricatives. Secondary articulations (e.g. pharyngealization, velarization and nasalization) and double articulations (e.g. alveolar and glottal contacts) are common. The result of these various phonetic defects is a marked reduction in the intelligibility of the cleft child's speech. Other strategies include increased activity at the level of the larynx as the child attempts to compensate for the loss of air through the velopharyngeal port. For example, the child may accommodate to a new speaking volume or strain the voice in other ways. Finally, the exit of air from the nasal cavities during speech can produce audible nasal emissions. These may mask articulations in the oral cavity, further reducing the intelligibility of the child's speech. One of these deviant articulations – the use of glottal stops in place of fricatives and plosives – is evident in the following data from Howard (1993). These are the productions of a 6-year-old girl called Rachel, who was born eleven weeks prematurely with a central cleft of the hard and soft palates:

'yes' [jɛʔ]
'go' [ʔəʊ]
'toy' [ʔɔɪ]

The phonetic defects in the cleft child's speech have an adverse effect upon the child's developing phonological system. Many of the sound contrasts that are found in the speech of non-cleft children are lacking in the speech of the cleft child. For example, if the alveolar and post-alveolar consonants /d,t,z,ʃ,ʧ,ʤ/ are all realized as [g], the child is unable to signal any difference in meaning between words like '*tin*', '*chin*', '*shin*', '*din*' and '*gin*'. This process of backing, which originates initially in the child's speech as a result of the particular constraints imposed on articulation through abnormalities in anatomy and physiology, can eventually become an organizing principle within the child's phonological system. Backing can become so well established in the child's phonological system that even when the alveolar fricatives /s,z/ emerge, they too can undergo backing to the velar fricatives /x,ɣ/. The extent of phonological impairment in the cleft child reflects the range of sounds that a child can articulate. For example, the cleft child who has a phonetic inventory consisting only of nasals /m,n,ŋ/, the velar fricatives /x,ɣ/ and the glottal stop /ʔ/ has a much reduced system of sound contrasts and a correspondingly severe phonological impairment.

Beyond phonology, there is evidence of other language impairments in cleft children. Studies have revealed delays in lexical development in cleft palate children (Broen et al. 1998). Scherer and D'Antonio (1995) report significantly lower frequencies for both the total number of words (a measure of vocabulary use) and the number of different words (a measure of vocabulary diversity) in a study of thirty cleft children aged between 16 and 30 months. Cleft children have also been found to have a reduced mean length of utterance (MLU is a measure of grammatical development). For example, the fifteen children with unilateral or bilateral cleft lip and palate in a study by Chapman (2004) had an average MLU of 2.80 morphemes. Typically, children of 39 months (the age of the cleft subjects in Chapman's study) have a MLU of 3.5 morphemes. There may be various reasons for the language delay in cleft children, including the speech defect, hearing loss, cognitive deficits (particularly in cleft children with syndromes in which there is intellectual disability) and prolonged periods of hospitalization during which the cleft child lacks appropriate stimulation.

**KEY POINTS: Cleft lip and palate**

- Found in approximately 1 in 700 births with males and females affected in a ratio of 2:1.
- Compromises speech, language, hearing, feeding and dentition.
- Chief communication defect is hypernasal speech which is due to velopharyngeal incompetence.
- Backed articulations are common as the child attempts to compensate for loss of air pressure through the velopharyngeal port by finding a position further back in the vocal tract where closure can be achieved.
- General backward shift in place of articulation has an adverse effect on the child's developing phonological system.
- Conductive hearing loss is common due to repeated episodes of otitis media ('glue ear'); treated by insertion of pressure-equalizing tubes in the ear drum.

### 14.4.2 Specific language impairment

For some children, there is a severe and specific deficit in the acquisition of language. Other aspects of development (e.g. motor skills) are normal and there is no known cause for the impairment in language. Although a number of terms have been used in the past to describe this population of children, the diagnostic label specific language impairment (SLI) is now in widespread clinical use. The SLI label has been called a diagnosis by exclusion. Thus, Craig (1991: 166) remarks that 'the SLI diagnostic label is applied on the basis of well-accepted exclusion criteria'. These criteria include a range of conditions (e.g. hearing loss, neurological damage, anatomical defects) that are known to cause language impairment in children.

Leonard (1998: 10) defines criteria for the application of the SLI label. Children with SLI must have language test scores of –1.25 standard deviations or lower and a performance IQ of 85 or higher. Their poor language skills must place them at risk for social devalue. They must pass hearing screening at conventional levels and have no recent episodes of otitis media with effusion. There should be no neurological dysfunction (no evidence of seizure disorders, cerebral palsy or brain lesions) and the child must not be taking medication for the control of seizures. There must be no structural anomalies in the oral cavity and the child must pass screening for oral motor function using developmentally appropriate items. The child must not exhibit symptoms of impaired reciprocal social interaction or restriction of activities (this criterion excludes children with an autism spectrum disorder). Despite intact skills and performance in each of these areas, the child with SLI exhibits a language disorder that is so severe that he or she typically receives education within special language units.

Deficits may occur at all language levels in SLI, but are most pronounced in syntax and semantics. Phonology may be disrupted in SLI but should not be the only impaired language level – Leonard (1998: 13) states that 'children with phonological disorders are included in the category of SLI only if they perform poorly on other measures of language'. Aguilar-Mediavilla, Sanz-Torrent and Serra-Raventos (2002) examined the phonology of 3-year-old children with SLI and found, amongst other things, that these children used more syllabic and nonsyllabic cluster reduction and initial and final consonant deletions than age controls. Children with SLI also deleted medial consonants significantly more often than age controls and deleted unstressed syllables in initial position significantly more than control subjects. Aguilar-Mediavilla et al. (2002: 573) state that these results suggest that 'the development of SLI phonology is deviant'.

There are extensive reports of deficits in morphosyntax in children with SLI, with tense-marking morphemes particularly vulnerable to impairment. Rice, Wexler and Hershberger (1998) found that morphemes which share the property of tense marking (third-person singular *-s*; past tense *-ed*; *be* and *do*) are mastered by age 4 years in typically developing children and after 7 years in children with SLI. Other grammatical findings in SLI are also noteworthy. They include higher production and acceptance rates of past tense over-regularizations (e.g. *he falled*) than in age-matched controls, greater use and acceptance of infinitive forms in finite positions (e.g. *he fall off*) and greater acceptance of finite form errors in VP complement positions (e.g. *he made him fell*) (Redmond and Rice 2001). Rice, Wexler and Cleave (1995) found that children with SLI used non-finite forms of lexical verbs and omitted *be* and *do* more frequently than controls matched for age and mean length of utterance (MLU). The following data are taken from Moore (2001), who studied twelve children with expressive SLI. The mean age of these children was 4 years, 6 months. Errors in these children's spoken utterances include the omission of the auxiliary verb *is* and the use of an incorrect personal pronoun (*her* instead of *she*):

Child aged 4 years, 2 months: *And her painting now*
Child aged 4 years, 10 months: *Her's painting a flower*
Child aged 5 years, 4 months: *He eating*

The semantics of language is also disrupted in children with SLI. These children have been found to produce more errors in naming pictures than children with no language impairment with proportionally more of these errors the names of objects associated with the pictured object (e.g. shoe/foot) and phonologically related to the target (Lahey and Edward 1999). McGregor et al. (2002) found that children with SLI made significantly more errors when naming age-appropriate objects than typically developing age-matched controls with semantic misnaming and indeterminate responses (e.g. *don't know* or non-specific responses) forming the predominant error types for both groups of subjects. McGregor et al. (2002: 998) state that 'this study demonstrates that the degree of knowledge represented in the child's semantic lexicon makes words more or less vulnerable to retrieval failure and that limited semantic knowledge contributes to the frequent naming errors of children with SLI'.

The issue of whether children with SLI experience pragmatic difficulties is an area of considerable debate (Cummings 2009, 2014b). Traditionally, it has been assumed that if pragmatic difficulties do exist, they must be secondary to the child's structural language impairment (the child who lacks the grammatical competence to achieve inversion of the subject pronoun and auxiliary verb in *Can you open the window?* will not be able to form the indirect speech act of request, for example). Bishop and co-workers have argued that there exists a subgroup of children with SLI in whom pragmatic difficulties are not simply the consequence of poor structural language skills (Bishop 1998, 2000; Bishop et al. 2000). Formerly known by the diagnostic label 'semantic pragmatic disorder', children with pragmatic language impairment are described as being poor at inferencing, over-literal, neglectful of their listener's perspective and as displaying a tendency to use socially inappropriate and/or stereotyped conversational responses (Bishop 2000).

**KEY POINTS: Specific language impairment**

- Severe language disorder in children: language skills -1.25 standard deviations or greater below mean.
- Diagnosis by exclusion: language disorder in the absence of hearing loss, psychiatric disturbance, intellectual disability, etc.
- Deficits particularly evident in syntax and semantics; errors in morphosyntax are common.
- Phonology may be disrupted but should not be the only impaired language level.
- Debate surrounds status of pragmatic deficits, primary or secondary in nature (latter related to structural language problems).

WEBSITE: **Group exercise**

Visit the website and, in a small group, examine the data from children with specific language impairment. Discuss the linguistic errors committed by these children. Then answer the five questions based on the data.

**EXERCISE 14.3**

Babies and children with cleft lip and palate face considerable hearing, speech and language problems. Speech difficulties involving articulation and resonation persist in many cases long after surgery (lip and palate repair) has been performed. Using your knowledge of the anatomical and physiological defects in cleft lip and palate and your knowledge of phonetics, explain why the following groups of sounds pose particular problems for the cleft child:

PLOSIVES: /p,b,t,d,k,g/
FRICATIVES: /f,v,θ,ð,s,z,ʃ,ʒ/
VOWELS: heavily nasalized

**EXERCISE 14.4**

Specific language impairment is a complex diagnostic category in which there is a diverse pattern of linguistic deficits. The following statements are designed to test your understanding of this diagnostic label and the language problems manifested by children with SLI. Indicate which of these statements are true and which are false.

(a) Children with SLI have poor articulation skills and low speech intelligibility.

(b) The diagnostic label SLI excludes language impaired children with brain damage.

(c) There is evidence of deviant phonology in children with SLI.

(d) SLI is used of the language impaired child with a history of otitis media.

(e) The label SLI is applied to language impaired children with craniofacial defects.

(f) Children with SLI are slow to acquire tense-marking morphemes (e.g. past tense *-ed*).

(g) Limited semantic knowledge is responsible for naming errors in children with SLI.

(h) Pragmatics is an area of intact language performance in children with SLI.

(i) A diagnosis of specific language impairment is based upon exclusionary criteria.

(j) The child with cerebral palsy can be diagnosed with SLI.

## 14.5 Acquired communication disorders

Individuals with previously intact speech and language skills can develop a communication disorder. An adult may sustain a stroke and develop a language disorder known as aphasia. The adult with dementia or mental illness may also experience disruption to their language skills. A neurodegenerative condition like motor neurone disease and Parkinson's disease can cause deterioration in speech skills leading to dysarthria. Benign and malignant lesions may compromise the neurological and anatomical structures that are involved in communication. Thus, an adult may develop a brain tumour or laryngeal tumour and experience communication problems as a result. In this section, two of these disorders will be examined in detail. The first disorder is aphasia, a language problem that results from damage to the language centres in the left hemisphere of the brain. The second disorder is communication following **laryngectomy**, a surgical procedure in which the speaker's larynx is removed. The different methods of communication available to the laryngectomee client following this operation will be considered.

### 14.5.1 Aphasia

Aphasia is an acquired language disorder that results from damage to the language centres in the left hemisphere of the brain. Although a range of neurological diseases and traumas can cause aphasia, the main cause of the disorder is cerebrovascular accidents or strokes. Aphasia can compromise language at all levels including phonology, morphology, syntax, semantics and pragmatics. It affects language in all its input and output modalities. So, as well as having problems producing and understanding spoken language, the adult with aphasia may struggle to produce and understand written language (acquired dysgraphia and dyslexia, respectively) or produce and comprehend signs (if the client with aphasia is a user of British Sign Language, for example). The disorder thus has far-reaching consequences for communication in the affected individual.

Historically, a number of different terms have been used to characterize aphasia. Some of these labels reflect neurological criteria such as the site of the lesions in the brain that cause aphasia (e.g. Broca's aphasia, Wernicke's aphasia). Other labels reflect the fact that the production or comprehension of language can be chiefly affected in aphasia (e.g. expressive or receptive aphasia). In this section, the dominant classification system will be adopted – certainly the one used by the National Aphasia Association in the US – in which aphasia is broadly classified into fluent and nonfluent types.

In fluent aphasia, there is a severe impairment in the comprehension of language in the presence of effortless, fluent speech. Utterances are well articulated and the intonational and other suprasegmental features of normal speech are also present. This can give the person with fluent aphasia the appearance of being a reasonably competent communicator. However, language output is often very incoherent due to the extensive use of jargon by the client (hence, the term 'jargon aphasia' to describe this type of aphasia). The person with fluent aphasia displays poor monitoring and correction of incoherent language output. Other linguistic features of the disorder include echolalia (the client echoes back another speaker's utterance), circumlocution (the person with aphasia is unable to produce a target word on account of lexical retrieval problems and proceeds to talk around it), and perseveration, where the speaker with aphasia continues to produce a linguistic form beyond what is appropriate. Finally, the person with fluent aphasia may also produce errors known as phonemic paraphasias (e.g. the use of *canerdillar* for 'caterpillar').

Jargonistic output in fluent aphasia can take several forms. The person with fluent aphasia can link English words together to produce meaningless utterances (e.g. the jargon speaker who described a daughter's holiday as 'She's got a rainbow, you know, three monthly rainbow going to Alaska', Marshall et al. 2001). Often, however, the client will create new words or 'neologisms'. When neologisms are used infrequently, the resulting utterance may still be understood by the listener (e.g. the jargon speaker, who wants to go for a walk in the park, utters 'We have to go to the pargoney', Robson et al. 2003). However, if neologisms dominate output, the result is completely meaningless language (e.g. the jargon speaker who described what he had done during the week as 'Oh I kegde treychoinge and cortlidge, oh erm partlie chulz, potiler crediss my children ringer', Robson et al. 2003).

The person with nonfluent aphasia displays a quite different pattern of linguistic impairments. In this type of aphasia, comprehension is relatively intact. However, the client displays considerable struggle in producing utterances and is both aware of, and frustrated by, his or her expressive difficulties. On account of his or her restricted output, the person with nonfluent aphasia tends to speak in short intonation units with the result that the suprasegmental features of speech are disrupted. Lexical-semantic disturbances are common in nonfluent aphasia and may manifest themselves in errors known as semantic paraphasias. In these errors, the word uttered by the speaker with aphasia is often semantically related to the target lexeme (e.g. *watch* for 'clock').

The most significant linguistic feature in nonfluent aphasia is that the syntactic structure of utterances is often considerably reduced and incomplete. For example, when asked to describe a picture in which a girl is handing a bouquet of flowers to her teacher, the person with nonfluent aphasia may struggle to produce 'Girl ... flower ... teacher'. Nonfluent output, which includes the retention of content words (e.g. nouns, verbs and adjectives) and the loss of function words (e.g. definite and indefinite articles, auxiliary verbs, prepositions), can give spoken language the appearance of a telegram (hence, the use of the term 'agrammatic aphasia' to describe this type of aphasia). When expressive problems are particularly acute, the person with nonfluent aphasia may use stereotypical forms (e.g. *that's right, OK then, you know*) to hold onto the floor during conversation and maintain the interaction.

The following data illustrate some of these linguistic errors in aphasia. The extract below was produced by a 61-year-old man with fluent jargon aphasia who was studied by Conroy et al. (2009). This man is describing the cookie theft picture from the Boston Diagnostic Aphasia Examination (Goodglass et al. 2001). This speaker engages in circumlocution when he says *going to the ground* for 'falling'. A semantic paraphasic error occurs in the use of *bowl* for 'sink':

> She's filling the bowl of water. He's slipping off the [unintelligible utterance] on the ground, having to say, he's going to the ground. I think there's only two things to manage. He is, he is, she is going to ... going to say 'surprise', look she is noticing.

The extract below is produced by a man called Roy who was studied by Beeke et al. (2007). Roy was in his mid-to-late 40s at the time of data collection. He had sustained a left-hemisphere cerebrovascular accident while waterskiing seven years earlier:

> um ... so s- er skiing ... er waterskiing ... yeh uh Greenbridge ... yeah? uh Kent ... uh ... uh ... four of them ... uuuhh ... blokes y'know ... uh ... uhhh ... boat ... and ... anyway ... sort of ... waterskiing ... and strange! ... sort of ... and then ... ur ... bang! [mimes falling over] ... funny ... and all of a sudden ... bang.

Roy's expressive output is typical of nonfluent aphasia. It is littered with pauses and fillers (*um, uh*), retains content words such as nouns (e.g. *boat*) and adjectives (e.g. *strange*) and omits all function words with the exception of the preposition *of* and the conjunction *and*. Roy also uses mime to compensate for his limited expressive language.

**KEY POINTS: Aphasia**

- Acquired language disorder which is most often caused by cerebrovascular accidents (strokes).
- Affects the production and comprehension of spoken, written and signed language.

- Several aphasia syndromes, broadly classified into fluent and non-fluent types.
- Fluent aphasia (includes Wernicke's aphasia) is characterized by severe comprehension deficit and jargonistic verbal output.
- Non-fluent aphasia (includes Broca's aphasia) is characterized by relatively intact comprehension and agrammatic output (content words are retained and function words lost).
- Other linguistic deficits found in aphasia include word-finding difficulties, circumlocution, perseveration and echolalia.

### 14.5.2 Communication after laryngectomy

Laryngeal cancer is a significant cause of communication disability in the adults who develop this disease. In 2006, there were just over 1,800 new cases of laryngeal cancer diagnosed in the UK (Cancer Research UK). The disease occurs more often in men than in women and is most often found in people over 60 years of age (it is rarely diagnosed in people under 40). A number of factors have been linked to the development of laryngeal cancer, including smoking and alcohol consumption, gastro-oesophageal reflux disease, immunosuppression (in HIV/AIDS and transplant recipients), infection with certain viruses (e.g. human papillomavirus 16) and bacteria (e.g. helicobacter pylori), and a history of head and neck cancer in first-degree relatives.

Depending on the size and nature of a tumour at diagnosis, a range of different treatment techniques may be employed. Radiotherapy is a standard part of all treatment protocols. In terms of surgery, if the tumour is confined to a specific laryngeal region, a partial laryngectomy may be performed. However, if the tumour is advanced and has invaded surrounding tissues, more extensive surgical procedures involving a total laryngectomy will be required. Given that the larynx is removed in a total laryngectomy, a person who undergoes this procedure must employ some method other than phonation to achieve the production of voice. In the rest of this section, the three main methods that can be used to achieve communication in people who undergo a total laryngectomy will be examined.

During a total laryngectomy, the trachea is directed onto the neck to create a stoma (see (A) in Figure 14.5). An individual permanently breathes through this stoma, as there is no longer a connection between the lungs and the oral and nasal cavities. Voice production after surgery can be achieved through the use of an artificial (electronic) larynx, oesophageal voice or a voice prosthesis (speaking valve). As can be seen in Figure 14.5, an artificial larynx is held against the neck and vibrates the air in the oral cavity (in an intra-oral artificial larynx, sound is fed into the mouth via a small tube). This vibrated air is then shaped into speech sounds by the movement of the articulators as normal. The resulting voice lacks intonation and has a certain robotic quality. Also, immediately after surgery and radiotherapy, neck tissues may be too tender for the pressure of this device. In oesophageal voice production, an individual can be taught how to take air down into

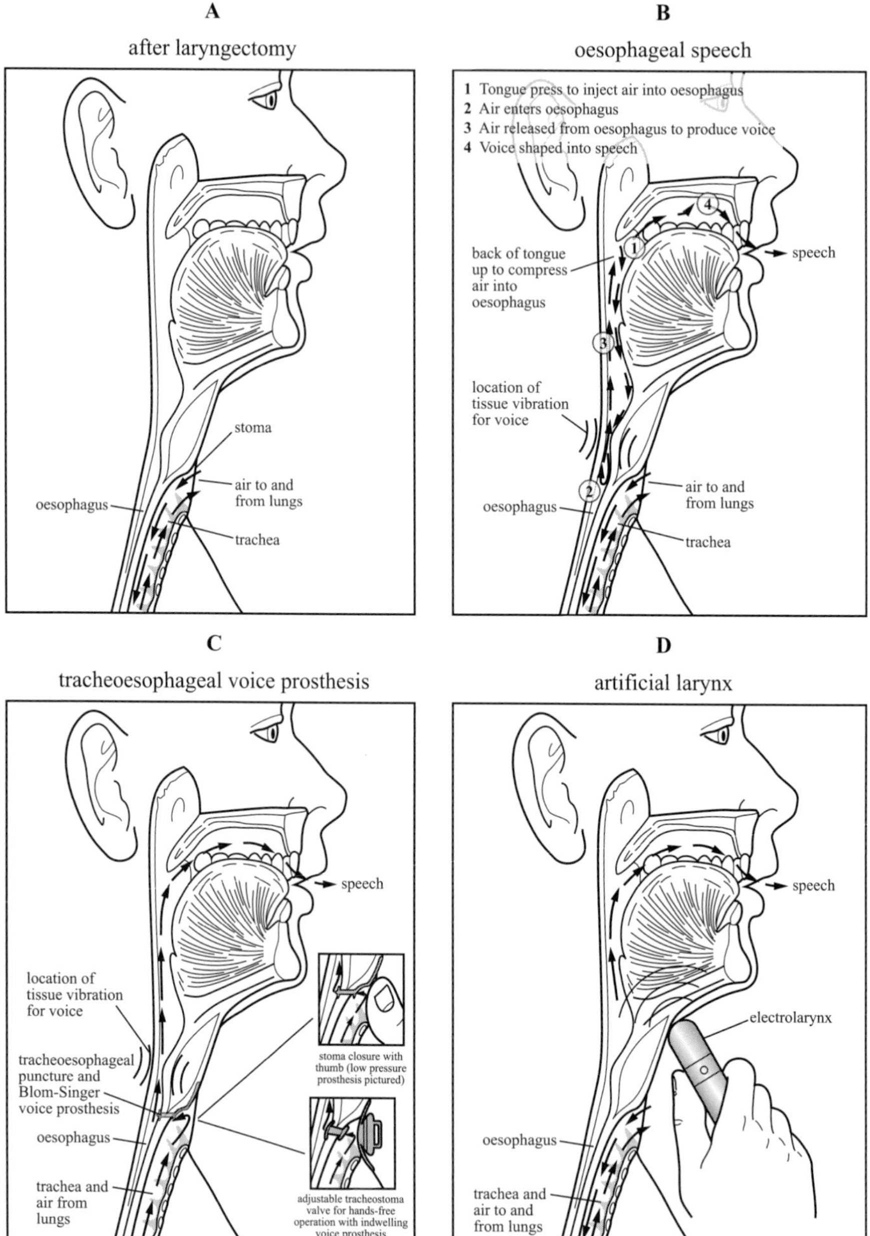


**Figure 14.5** Diagrams showing (A) anatomical structures after laryngectomy and various methods of post-laryngectomy voice production: (B) oesophageal voice, (C) tracheoesophageal voice prosthesis and (D) artificial larynx (reprinted with permission from InHealth Technologies, www.inhealth.com)

the oesophagus and bring it up again under voluntary control (see (B) in Figure 14.5). The exiting air causes the sphincter at the top of the oesophagus (the cricopharyngeus muscle) to vibrate. Excellent speaking voices can be achieved through this method of communication, although in some cases the voice is rather deep and has a 'wet' quality.

Nowadays, most people who undergo laryngectomy are being offered the opportunity to have a voice prosthesis fitted at the same time as the operation is performed. Although different valves are available (e.g. Provox, Blom-Singer), they all operate by shunting air from the trachea into the oesophagus where it is used to produce oesophageal voice (see (C) in Figure 14.5). Some valves require the laryngectomee client to block the stoma with the thumb, while an adjustable tracheostoma valve may be used with other prostheses permitting hands-free operation. Because a pulmonary airstream is involved (as opposed to air being gulped back into the oesophagus as in standard oesophageal voice), the laryngectomee client can maintain a longer flow of speech and achieve greater volume using a voice prosthesis.

**KEY POINTS: Laryngectomy**

- Surgical removal of the larynx either in part (partial laryngectomy) or in whole (total laryngectomy).
- Performed in order to treat laryngeal cancer (more common in individuals with a history of heavy smoking and alcohol consumption).
- Three methods of communication after laryngectomy: (1) artificial larynx, (2) oesophageal voice (OV) and (3) voice prosthesis (speaking valve).
- An artificial (electronic) larynx vibrates air in the oral cavity; in OV, the sphincter (cricopharyngeus) muscle at the top of the oesophagus is vibrated; a speaking valve directs pulmonary air from the trachea into the oesophagus where it vibrates the cricopharyngeal segment.

## EXERCISE 14.5

A number of linguistic errors can occur in the verbal output of speakers with aphasia. Using the labels 'phonemic paraphasia', 'semantic paraphasia', 'neologism' and 'circumlocution', characterize the type of error that has occurred in the following utterances:

(a) 'She checks blood pressure and pushes medicine trolley' (target word *nurse*)

(b) 'It was sore when I first broke my arm' (target word *leg*)

(c) 'I saw him take money from the tillery' (target word *till*)

(d) 'The king was pleased to live in a [kastil]' (target word *castle*)

(e) 'Many soldiers died in the tankert' (target word *tank*)

(f) 'My family has one and it goes round and round' (target word *microwave*)

(g) 'Life was tough and men died in the [trɛntɪs]' (target word *trenches*)

(h) 'It was all good when I was a young boy' (target word *girl*)

### EXERCISE 14.6

Listen to the audio file 'Communication after laryngectomy'. You will hear the voices of six people (five men and one woman) who have undergone laryngectomy. Two of the speakers are using an artificial larynx to communicate. A further two speakers are communicating using oesophageal voice. There are also two speakers who are communicating using a speaking valve. Your task is to:

(a) Identify the method of communication for each of the six speakers.

(b) Identify the speaker whose tongue nerve was severed during laryngectomy. A clue to help you is that this person struggles to say the word 'communication'.

(c) State which speech sound in 'communication' is particularly problematic for the speaker you identify in part (b).

## 14.6 SUMMARY

This chapter has provided the reader with a comprehensive overview of clinical linguistics. This linguistic discipline examines the many ways in which language and communication are disrupted in children and adults with communication disorders. The chapter has highlighted the points in the communication cycle at which breakdown may occur, and described the specific communication disorders that arise from damage at each of these loci. Clinical linguists observe several key distinctions in their study of communication disorders. These distinctions include the difference between a receptive and an expressive language disorder, a developmental and an acquired communication disorder, and a speech and language disorder. These distinctions were fundamental in the consideration of the communication difficulties that attend cleft lip and palate and specific language impairment in children, and aphasia and laryngectomy in adults. A sound understanding of communication disorders is vital for the successful assessment and treatment of these disorders by speech and language therapists.

WEBSITE: **Clinical linguistics**

Now go to the website and assess your knowledge of clinical linguistics and communication disorders by attempting the self-test questions!

### SUGGESTIONS FOR FURTHER READING

Cummings, L. (2013). Clinical linguistics: a primer. *International Journal of Language Studies*, 7, 1–30. This article examines how knowledge of each of the branches of linguistics is essential to understanding speech and language disorders. Clinical data are used to illustrate disorders at the levels of phonetics, phonology, morphology, syntax, semantics, pragmatics and discourse.

Cummings, L. (2014). *Communication Disorders*. Basingstoke: Palgrave Macmillan. This book will give you further information on each of the four communication disorders examined in this chapter: cleft lip and palate (section 2.2), specific language impairment (section 3.3), aphasia (section 5.2) and laryngectomy (section 7.5).

Plante, E. M. and Beeson, P. M. (2007). *Communication and Communication Disorders: A Clinical Introduction*, 3rd edn. Boston: Allyn and Bacon. This introductory textbook presents an overview of human communication and its disorders across the life span. Case illustrations of specific communication disorders are included.

# ANSWERS TO EXERCISES

### Exercise 14.1

(a) language encoding
(b) language encoding; language decoding; motor execution
(c) communicative intentions
(d) motor execution
(e) sensory processing
(f) motor programming

### Exercise 14.2

(a) The term 'acquired' in *acquired* epileptic aphasia relates to the fact that a significant amount of language acquisition has taken place prior to the onset of Landau-Kleffner syndrome.
(b) Patrick's problems with syntax are receptive in nature. His difficulties with semantics are expressive.
(c) Penelope has a speech disorder.
(d) John has receptive and expressive pragmatic problems.
(e) Frank's grammatical delay is developmental, while his dysarthria is acquired.
(f) Paul has a language disorder.

### Exercise 14.3

Sounds requiring build-up and control of intra-oral air pressure (i.e. plosives and fricatives) or an oral articulation (i.e. vowels) will be most adversely affected in cleft children. The cleft child's anatomical and physiological defects contribute directly to the loss of air pressure in the oral cavity. Firstly, the cleft child may experience velopharyngeal incompetence whereby air leaks from the oral cavity via the velopharyngeal port into the nasal cavities creating hypernasal speech. This may occur because the soft palate (or velum) is somewhat immobile after palatoplasty (surgical repair of the palate) or because it is not long enough or large enough to make posterior and lateral contact with the pharyngeal wall. Secondly, oro-nasal fistulae (holes) can develop in the area of the palatal repair. Some smaller fistulae have little or no impact on speech production. However, larger fistulae can be a significant cause of air leakage into the nasal cavities.

### Exercise 14.4

True statements: (b), (c), (f), (g), (i)
False statements: (a), (d), (e), (h), (j)

### Exercise 14.5

(a) circumlocution
(b) semantic paraphasia

(c) neologism
(d) phonemic paraphasia
(e) neologism
(f) circumlocution
(g) phonemic paraphasia
(h) semantic paraphasia

### Exercise 14.6

(a) Bert and John (artificial larynx); Don and Stan (oesophageal voice); Joan and Derek (speaking valve)
(b) John
(c) voiceless velar plosive /k/

## REFERENCES


Aguilar-Mediavilla, E. M., Sanz-Torrent, M. and Serra-Raventos, M. (2002). A comparative study of the phonology of pre-school children with specific language impairment (SLI), language delay (LD) and normal acquisition. *Clinical Linguistics and Phonetics*, 16, 573–96.

Beeke, S., Wilkinson, R. and Maxim, J. (2007). Individual variation in agrammatism: A single case study of the influence of interaction. *International Journal of Language & Communication Disorders*, 42, 629–47.

Bishop, D. V. M. (1998). Development of the children's communication checklist (CCC): A method for assessing qualitative aspects of communicative impairment in children. *Journal of Child Psychology and Psychiatry*, 39, 879–91.

(2000). Pragmatic language impairment: A correlate of SLI, a distinct subgroup, or part of the autistic continuum?. In D. V. M. Bishop and L. B. Leonard (eds.), *Speech and Language Impairments in Children: Causes, Characteristics, Intervention and Outcome*, pp. 99–113. Hove: Psychology Press.

Bishop, D. V. M., Chan, J., Adams, C., Hartley, J. and Weir, F. (2000). Conversational responsiveness in specific language impairment: Evidence of disproportionate pragmatic difficulties in a subset of children. *Development and Psychopathology*, 12, 177–99.

Broen, P. A., Devers, M. C., Doyle, S. S., Prouty, J. M. and Moller, K. T. (1998). Acquisition of linguistic and cognitive skills by children with cleft palate. *Journal of Speech, Language, and Hearing Research*, 41, 676–87.

Chapman, K. L. (2004). Is presurgery and early postsurgery performance related to speech and language outcomes at 3 years of age for children with cleft palate? *Clinical Linguistics and Phonetics*, 18, 235–57.

Conroy, P., Sage, K. and Ralph, M. L. (2009). Improved vocabulary production after naming therapy in aphasia: Can gains in picture naming generalise to connected speech? *International Journal of Language & Communication Disorders*, 44, 1036–62.

Craig, H. K. (1991). Pragmatic characteristics of the child with specific language impairment: An interactionist perspective. In T. M. Gallagher (ed.), *Pragmatics of Language: Clinical Practice Issues*, pp. 163–98. San Diego, CA: Singular Publishing Group.

Crystal, D. (1997). *The Cambridge Encyclopedia of Language*, 2nd edn. Cambridge University Press.

Cummings, L. (2008). *Clinical Linguistics*. Edinburgh University Press.

(2009). *Clinical Pragmatics*. Cambridge University Press.

(ed.). (2014a). *Cambridge Handbook of Communication Disorders*. Cambridge University Press.

(2014b). *Pragmatic Disorders*. Dordrecht: Springer.

Goodglass, H., Kaplan, E. and Barresi, B. (2001). *Boston Diagnostic Aphasia Examination*, 3rd edn. Baltimore, MD: Lippincott Williams & Wilkins.

Honbolygó, F., Csépe, V., Fekésházy, A., Emri, M., Márián, T., Sárközy, G. and Kálmánchey, R. (2006). Converging evidences on language impairment in Landau-Kleffner syndrome revealed by behavioral and brain activity measures: A case study. *Clinical Neurophysiology*, 117, 295–305.

Howard, S. J. (1993). Articulatory constraints on a phonological system: A case study of cleft palate speech. *Clinical Linguistics & Phonetics*, 7, 299–317.

Lahey, M. and Edwards, J. (1999). Naming errors of children with specific language impairment. *Journal of Speech, Language, and Hearing Research*, 42, 195–205.

Leonard, L. B. (1998). *Children with Specific Language Impairment*. Cambridge, MA: MIT Press.

McGregor, K. K., Newman, R. M., Reilly, R. M. and Capone, N. C. (2002). Semantic representation and naming in children with specific language impairment. *Journal of Speech, Language, and Hearing Research*, 45, 998–1014.

Marshall, J., Pring, T., Chiat, S. and Robson, J. (2001). When ottoman is easier than chair: An inverse frequency effect in jargon aphasia. *Cortex*, 37, 33–53.

Moore, M. E. (2001). Third person pronoun errors by children with and without language impairment. *Journal of Communication Disorders*, 34, 207–28.

Redmond, S. M. and Rice, M. L. (2001). Detection of irregular verb violations by children with and without SLI. *Journal of Speech, Language, and Hearing Research*, 44, 655–69.

Rice, M. L., Wexler, K. and Cleave, P. L. (1995). Specific language impairment as a period of extended optional infinitive. *Journal of Speech and Hearing Research*, 38, 850–63.

Rice, M. L., Wexler, K. and Hershberger, S. (1998). Tense over time: The longitudinal course of tense acquisition in children with specific language impairment. *Journal of Speech, Language, and Hearing Research*, 41, 1412–31.

Robson, J., Pring, T., Marshall, J. and Chiat, S. (2003). Phoneme frequency effects in jargon aphasia: A phonological investigation of nonword errors. *Brain and Language*, 85, 109–24.

Sargent, L. A. (1999). *The Craniofacial Surgery Book*. Chattanooga, TN: Williams.

Scherer, N. J. and D'Antonio, L. L. (1995). Parent questionnaire for screening early language development in children with cleft palate. *Cleft Palate-Craniofacial Journal*, 32, 7–13.

Semel, E., Wiig, E. H. and Secord, W. A. (2003) *Clinical Evaluation of Language Fundamentals*, 4th edn. Australia: Psychological Corporation.

Stengelhofen, J. (1993). The nature and causes of communication problems in cleft palate. In J. Stengelhofen (ed.), *Cleft Palate: The Nature and Remediation of Communication Problems*, pp. 1–30. London: Whurr.

Temple, C. (1997). *Developmental Cognitive Neuropsychology*. Hove: Psychology Press.

Van Cauwenberge, P. B., De Moor, S. E. G. and Dhooge, I. (1998). Acute suppurative otitis media. In H. Ludman and T. Wright (eds.), *Diseases of the Ear*, pp. 353–60. London: Arnold.

# 15 Language and ideology

LESLEY JEFFRIES

**KEY TERMS**

- constructed opposition
- critical discourse analysis (CDA)
- critical stylistics
- deixis
- ideational meaning
- ideology
- *langue* and *parole*
- modality
- naturalization
- negation
- textual-conceptual functions
- transitivity

**PREVIEW**

This chapter builds upon the basics of language structure and functions (Chapters 2–9) to demonstrate how texts (spoken or written, long or short) present a particular view of the world which reflects the ideological position of one (or more) of the perceived producers of the text. The chapter takes a neutral view of what ideology means, seeing it as referring to sets of values (and also, in some cases, beliefs) that are held by a group of people, often a society as a whole. You will be introduced to the framework of critical stylistics, which allows you to analyse the hidden and implicit ideologies inherent in textual construction. The basis of this framework is the 'textual-conceptual function' which demonstrates how the text is constructing different aspects of the world of the text by processes such as naming, negating, hypothesizing and enumerating. This approach shares with critical discourse analysis (CDA) the idea that ideology is present in all texts, but unlike CDA it is politically neutral rather than taking an explicitly socialist or Marxist stance in itself.

## 15.1 INTRODUCTION

Although we tend to assume that there is some kind of abstract linguistic system in place, underpinning the things we say and write, linguistics has long recognized that there are also discrepancies between this 'idealized' system which is made up of items (phonemes, morphemes, words, phrases, clause elements etc.) and the rules for how they combine into texts (the phonological rules and the grammar) – and the way in which the system is 'realized' when it is used. Famously, Saussure (see also Chapter 1), often seen as the founder of modern linguistics, labelled this distinction (in French) **langue** (language) and **parole** (speech) and much of the effort of early linguistic description went into describing how the *langue* worked. Later, when it became evident that there was regular patterning even in the apparently messy reality of *parole*, subdisciplines of linguistics (e.g. sociolinguistics, pragmatics, conversation analysis) grew up to try and map out the regularities in usage as much as in the system itself. Later, the cognitive approach to human language represented in Chomsky's transformational-generative grammar recognized a similar distinction between the abstract underlying system of the language – here seen as part of human cognition and therefore labelled 'competence' – and the usage of the system which was labelled 'performance' (see also Chapter 1).

This potted history of linguistics leaves out a lot of detail, but it is useful here as the background to an amended view of how human language works, which adds a third strand into the binary pair of system and use (*langue* and *parole*; competence and performance) that has dominated linguistics since the 1920s. This third strand is not only relevant to discussions of language and ideology (it can also be used to explain stylistic effects), but it does allow for the partially systematic nature of textual meaning to be explored in isolation from the underlying linguistic *system* and also separately from the interactive aspects of communication (*use*).

There are some linguistic approaches (most notably Halliday's systemic-functional grammar) which take the opposite approach and try to merge the two traditionally separated aspects of *system* and *use* by describing the functions of items and structures at the same time as describing their form and meaning. This seems to me to make the task of linguistic description harder, because the models that are produced end up being at least as complex as the data that they describe. This tendency to produce over-complex models of language runs counter to one of the principles of scientific description which requires the analyst to choose the simplest model that adequately describes the data and thus has the power to explain how the data work. This is not to argue that systemic function linguistics (SFL) has provided no insights into the workings of language. On the contrary, this chapter uses many such insights from SFL. It is the approach that differs; SFL and other approaches, such as many discourse analytic approaches, are trying to explain all the facets of communication in a unitary model, whereas the framework provided here aims to separate out strands of linguistic structure and meaning to explain them separately, often drawing on established models and frameworks for each of these strands.

So, the approach presented here adds the idea of 'textual meaning' into the space between the idealized *system* of language (*langue*/competence) and its *use* (*parole*/performance). This textual meaning depends on the underlying system of items and rules of combination (i.e. lexis and grammar with phonology for the spoken language). The systematic *linguistic* meaning of the items and structures in a language have partly regular form–function relationships, so speakers of a language know what a (grammatical) combination of words means even when it is not used in context. *Textual* meaning has a less clear set of form–function relationships than linguistic meaning, yet it is still grounded in the words that are spoken or written, rather than in the context of situation, participant relations or other more pragmatic meanings.

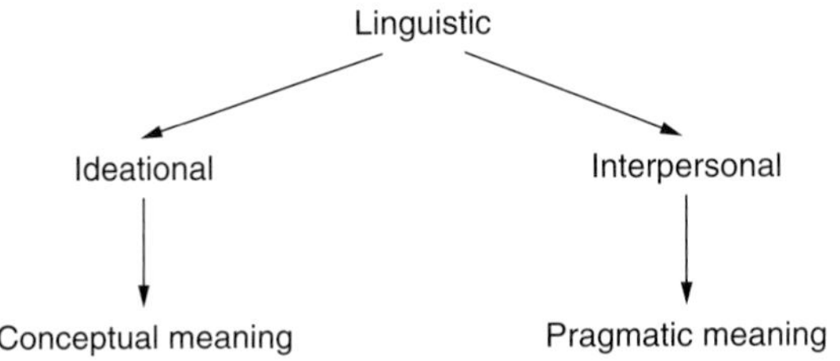


**FIGURE 15.1** The main strands of human linguistic behaviour

This third strand, which I am calling textual meaning, differs from linguistic meaning in referring to language as it appears in textual context, though stopping short of considering the full range of contextual aspects of its potential interpersonal meaning. There are some important ways in which this approach overlaps with an influential stylistic theory of recent years: Text World Theory (Gavins 2007). Text World Theory is an approach to fictional (and other) texts which attempts to model the process that takes place in the reader's brain in reading novels, plays, poems and other texts (e.g. news reports) and which allows the reader to 'envisage' the world of, for example, an Edward Lear nonsense poem such as 'The Pobble who had no toes', the world of a fantasy text such as in the *Harry Potter* novels – or even real places and events that we do not experience directly, as encountered, for example, in the news reports of uprisings in the Middle East. Text World Theory was developed in relation to the reading of literary texts and has so far not been widely used a great deal to address the question of how we process non-fiction texts in relation to ideology. Critical stylistics (Jeffries 2010) draws on this metaphor of a 'text world' to investigate the construction of ideological meaning in all texts and suggests the theoretical position such meaning may occupy in a theory of language.

The framework described above (and set out in diagram form in Figure 15.1) allows the analyst to consider the specific role that textual meaning plays in producing ideological effects, whether or not the producer of the text intends them consciously and irrespective of whether readers allow them to influence their own outlook, either temporarily or permanently. The rest of this chapter will attempt to give the reader some analytical tools to help decipher the ideological content of texts whilst acknowledging that text producers may be unwitting in their ideological content and readers may react differently to textual meaning of this kind. In other words, we may read a text which makes racist, feminist or other ideological assumptions and be subtly, strongly or not the least influenced in our own views by the ideological content. Nevertheless, there is a widespread view that repetition of the same ideology across many texts does cause readers to begin to assimilate that ideology, albeit subconsciously. This process, when it is widespread across society is called '**naturalization**' and can result in the ideology being accepted as being 'common sense'. The debate about how texts influence readers in this piecemeal way will need to be taken up when we have more information on the cognitive reactions of readers to texts.

This chapter assumes that the underlying system of language is fundamental to both the meaning of texts, for which I have borrowed Halliday's term 'ideational', and the interactive purpose of communication, for which again I borrow a term, 'interpersonal', from Halliday. Figure 15.1 represents this relationship schematically. The basics of grammar, phonology, morphology, semantics and even some fundamental textual concepts, such as cohesion and sentence-linking structures all belong in the linguistic system. The meanings produced by a text conceptualize the world (whether it's the real world or a fictional one) at the ideational level and it is here that naturalized ideologies feature in language use. It is this, ideational, function of language which will concern us for the remainder of this chapter as it is the basis of what I call '**critical stylistics**'.

**KEY POINTS: Concepts in language and ideology**

- The introduction has explained that in addition to the abstract system of items and rules of combination (lexis and grammar) there is not just one, but two further types of meaning produced in the use of human language. These are the ideational (textual) level of meaning and the interpersonal (contextual) level of meaning.
- The metaphor of the text world is used here to explain the level of textual meaning which creates the conditions for readers (and listeners) to conceptualize the viewpoint of a particular text. There is a difference between this conceptual potential and what readers actually do, of course.

**EXERCISE 15.1**

There are ten linguistic 'events' described below. For each one, decide whether the event is being described as part of the linguistic, the ideational, or the interpersonal level of meaning:

1. The Subject of the sentence is 'John', the verb is 'ate' and the Object is 'a cake'.
2. The blog assumed that all NHS reform is a bad thing.
3. Jason interrupted Sheila who had been speaking for five minutes non-stop.
4. The Prime Minister described a non-existent scenario to frighten us.
5. 'Hot' is the opposite of 'cold'.
6. There are more than five nouns in English which refer to chairs.
7. Bertrand made it sound as though pizza was the opposite of cake!
8. Masie upset Susie by telling her she was wrong.
9. In English noun phrases, adjectives go before the noun.
10. The newspaper told the story without mentioning that the government were to blame.

## 15.2 Ideology

Before the framework of critical stylistics is explained in more detail, it is useful to consider the meaning and significance of the word ideology. There are many popular uses of this word, for example when we want to criticize someone because we disagree with their ideas and their political outlook. Thus, we might accuse someone of being 'ideological' when we do not agree with them and we somehow accuse them of having unacceptable ideas. This is very often the kind of criticism that the tabloid (right-wing) newspapers in the UK will produce against more socialist or left-wing speakers or writers. The assumption is that there is something shameful and unacceptable about people holding such views and often that they are morally worse for holding them. This can – and does – also occur in reverse, with the left wing holding the view that people with ultra-conservative views are morally repugnant. As there is more power – and news organization ownership – held in western democracies by those with right-wing views, the vested interests of news organizations tend to represent the former, more often than the latter point of view.

A more neutral view of what ideology means would be to see it as referring to sets of values (and also, in some cases, beliefs) that are held by a group of people, often a society as a whole. This definition, which is the one I will assume in this chapter, sometimes leads to the notion that ideology is found *in all texts at all times* – not just those which are clearly at odds with the mainstream or explicitly prejudiced against or for certain people or ideas. This view, though often stated, is harder to follow through in practice, and can lead to ideology being seen as little more than the surface meaning of a text. Such textual meaning, though clearly supporting the framework proposed here, somewhat undermines the usefulness of the word ideology by making it too general to be of much use in discovering how people use and abuse the power of language. If we take the following (invented) sentences, for example, some are harder to link to systems of values (i.e. ideologies) than others:

(1) No gay couples welcome here.

(2) Those children ought to be told to behave properly.

(3) I had fish and chips for dinner last night.

(4) Do you like my new coat?

Sentence (1) is relatively easy to link to an anti-homosexual ideology which will often be held at the same time as a range of other views (that heterosexual couples should be married rather than living together; that children should be raised by their biological, heterosexual parents etc.). Sentence (2) is a little more subtle, but does seem to imply that adults in charge of children have a duty to control them in order not to inconvenience other adults. It may be held alongside other ideologies such as the view that children should be taught self-control or that children are naturally anarchic and need to be controlled by rules. Sentence (3) is less clearly ideological, but does rest on the assumption that eating fish is acceptable, which is common sense (naturalized ideology) in a largely omnivorous mainstream society. The sentence itself, of course, is not intended as an attempt to spread such ideologies – it is simply a statement of fact about a particular person's experience on a single day. But the repeated assumption of norms (like *eating fish is fine*) does reinforce the underlying ideological system too. Sentence (4) is hard to link to ideology at all, though at a push I would say that it demonstrates the ideology that looking good is an important part of how we value ourselves as human beings. In a later section,

I will explore the nature of 'naturalized' ideologies, which are those which have become so embedded in a culture that they seem to be common sense and are therefore difficult to spot at times.

For now, we will begin with the notion that ideology is more than ideation. **Ideation** is the creation of a particular text world along a number of dimensions (see Section 15.4) which show the reader what the world of the text looks like, who inhabits it and how they behave. This will work for both fictional and (allegedly) non-fictional worlds. Although there is, in a sense, only one non-fictional world, the different viewpoints that we all inhabit mean that our descriptions of that one 'real' world are likely to differ in small and large ways. Ideation is the construction of a particular description of the world through language.

Where ideology enters the picture, then, is where these ideational processes in texts produce worlds which have values attached to them. The following short (invented) text can be used to illustrate the difference between the two:

(5) I was in the café at the community centre last week and the place was heaving with young mothers (but only a *few* fathers!) with small babies and toddlers. The children were all crawling around on the floor, spreading their food under the chairs and leaving toys in the doorway where other customers were entering and leaving. It was the nursery from hell, not a civilized place to have a coffee.

Much of this text creates a place (*café*) and time (*last week*) and describes the people in the situation (*mothers, babies, toddlers, fathers*). It also describes the activities of the children (*crawling, spreading, leaving*) and the position of items (*under the chairs, in the doorway*). So far, this description of the text is ideational but not ideological. It simply draws a picture of the scene. However, interspersed with the descriptions are hints of ideological attitudes such as *but only a* few *fathers!*, which may be taken to imply that feminism hasn't done as much for gender equality as one might expect, and *spreading their food under the chairs and leaving toys in the doorway where other customers were entering and leaving*, which hints at values relating to respect for others' comfort and safety and the importance of cleanliness. The final sentence makes clear, by contrasting two different scenes, what was only implicit earlier, that the scene was not conducive to pleasure for adults. It is worth keeping in mind that ideation and ideologies are delivered by the same set of textual features. What makes ideation ideological is the value assigned to it.

### 15.2.1 Explicit and implicit textual meaning

The discussion of ideological meaning has so far assumed that the difference between implicit and explicit ideologies in texts is clear. Critical stylistics, like critical linguistics and **critical discourse analysis**, is more interested in the implicit than the explicit ideologies in texts. This is because the latter are easy to spot, easy to critique or disagree with and as a result are less likely to be used manipulatively or in an underhand way. They are also self-consciously and sincerely held views which are less likely to be used either unwittingly or mischievously in order to persuade others without their consent, though they may be malicious or unpleasant in themselves.

Linguistically, one can link explicit ideology to the propositional basis of the sentences and utterances produced. Explicit ideological ideation is thus linked closely to the semantic meanings of the basic structures of the language. So, the following sentences set out explicit ideologies on a range of topics and from different political viewpoints:

(6) I think animals should have the same rights as human beings.

(7) I believe that only men (/ land-owners / white people / indigenous citizens) should have a democratic vote.

(8) I think having sex outside of marriage is wrong.

(9) I believe that there are no supernatural beings, such as gods.

(10) I think evolution should not be taught as fact in schools.

The ideologies in these examples are produced by the normal workings of the basic linguistic system and they are clearly both explicit and also intentionally produced as a result. Note that although these examples all begin with an explicit statement of opinion (*I think, I believe*), they would still be explicitly ideological without this clause.

The question of intention in the case of implicit ideological construction in texts is more difficult to pin down. This is partly because the producer of the ideology could be the speaker or writer themselves but it could also be the person who commissioned the text (such as a politician who has speech writers or the owners of a newspaper) or it could even be the presented view of a third party, such as a character in a novel or someone being quoted by the actual speaker or writer of the text. These questions of authorial ownership of ideology belong to the contextual aspects of language study (specifically participation frameworks; Goffman 1981), and though they are not traditionally included in interpersonal models, which tend to focus on the immediate participants in spoken interactions, these aspects of text production seem to me to belong under the interpersonal heading.

What follows in this chapter is a focused assessment of how ideologies turn up in texts (written or spoken) and very little consideration of the people who produce or the people who consume them, important though these are (see Chapters 8 and 9 for some discussion of these issues). The question of how strongly the ideologies in a text may influence the outlook of the reader is partly a personal question and partly a question of psychology, which will be left for other publications to explore.

**KEY POINTS: Ideology**

- This section discussed the meaning of ideology in the context of critical stylistic analysis. For our purposes, it is the agreement across a community that some ideas are valued and some are not.
- This section also distinguished between the creation of ideational meaning in texts, which may not have ideological value attached, and ideology which implies a value.
- Section 15.2.1 also distinguished between implicit and explicit ideology in texts. Explicit ideology is less linguistically complex and also less likely to be abused. Implicit ideology is more interesting as well as being more open to misuse.

**EXERCISE 15.2**

For the following sentences, work out what is ideational and what might also be said to be ideological. Say whether any ideology you see is explicit or implicit. (Hint: there may not be only a single answer in some cases!)

1. Women should stay at home to look after children once they are married.
2. The house was full of people; each room had three or four beds in it.
3. There was no where to sit and every surface was piled high with papers.
4. It wasn't fair how the money was divided out.
5. The expensive elderly generation is growing fast.
6. She looked up and saw the sun beginning to rise out of the sea.
7. Most of the girls over 12 on the island were mothers.
8. They spoke about the terrible rise in teenage pregnancies in Britain.

## 15.3 Implicit textual meaning

Most of the concern that people express about ideology in texts is about implicit ideological messages being included and the danger of them affecting the viewpoint of readers without the reader consciously taking on these ideologies. In other words, what people fear is something like brainwashing, where you are not aware that your views are being subtly altered and manipulated. The dangers of extreme forms of brainwashing of this kind are probably overstated, because we can teach ourselves – and others – to be critical readers and sceptical readers. Nevertheless, we may fear, for example, that more vulnerable readers than ourselves (e.g. children) could be overly influenced by the ideologies of the texts they read. This is true, for example, of parents worried about their children reading (or watching) narratives with excessive or graphic violence, though evidence is mixed about whether this necessarily creates violent young people in itself. There has also always been a tendency for religious leaders to fear that exposure of their followers to texts depicting unorthodox or 'sinful' actions might corrupt them. It may be that the distinction between explicit and implicit ideology could be helpful here. Perhaps it is more insidious when a text incorporates hidden – or naturalized – ideologies – because they are harder to spot and thus harder for the reader to consciously question.

### 15.3.1 Naturalized ideologies

Naturalized ideologies are those values that have become so ingrained in the thinking of a particular community or society that they are no longer recognized as ideological at all and are taken to be common sense. The ideology that says society should protect and care for the vulnerable (young, old, infirm), for example, is widespread in many of the world's societies nowadays, though it has not always been so and there remain places in the world where people with learning difficulties or physical disabilities, for example, are left without basic needs, because they are valued less than the able. It is also a matter of ideology whether you think that governments should be responsible for this type of care, with the money raised through taxation – or whether you believe that such care for vulnerable people should be carried out by voluntary and charity organizations, or even by the immediate neighbours of the people concerned, but the answers to these questions are less naturalized as they form part of the active political debate of many societies.

We can sometimes witness ideologies becoming naturalized in our society as opinions shift. For example, attitudes to homosexuality, common law relationships, single parents, abortion, race, class and women's roles in society have all changed dramatically in the last fifty years. Nevertheless, these ideological changes are not uniform across all members of society and there remain pockets of resistance to the naturalization of liberal attitudes to these issues. On the whole, however, they are now becoming so widely accepted that they seem almost common sense and are included alongside the much longer-standing ideologies that you should not kill people and you should not steal other people's things.

What the ideational features of texts often manage to do is to effectively help to naturalize ideologies by presenting them as assumed and therefore as common sense. The rest of this chapter will largely present the different ways in which texts manage to take ideologies for granted, as part of their normal production of meaning – and thus make them more likely to become naturalized as a result.

### 15.3.2 Textual-conceptual functions

So far, this chapter has introduced the notion that there is a level of textual meaning intermediate between the language system (its phonology, grammar etc.) and the language use (what it is 'doing' in relation to the discourse participants). It is at this level of meaning that **ideational meaning** – the construction of a particular worldview – takes place and can produce naturalized, or at least assumed, ideologies. This textual level of meaning refers to the ways in which the text constructs the world along a number of dimensions. These dimensions are each described in some detail in Section 15.4. Here, I will introduce the general idea of the 'textual-conceptual function' which is the label given to these dimensions of textual meaning.

**Textual-conceptual functions** refer to the different aspects of the text world which the text produces. Thus, they include, for example, what the text producer chooses to name; how s/he chooses to present the actions, events and states of being that form the processes of the narrative; how definite or hypothetical the text producer makes the world of the text; what things (or people) the text producer decides are 'opposites' for the purposes of the text world and what the text producer assumes or takes for granted. There are a small number of additional textual-conceptual functions explored in Section 15.4, alongside those listed here. There may not be an infinite number of these functions, but it is possible that a few more will be added as the framework develops. They all answer the question 'what is the text doing?' in relation to the emerging text world. By contrast, the linguistic level of meaning answers the question 'what do these morphemes/words/phrases/clauses/sentences mean out of context?' and the interpersonal level of meaning answers the question 'what is happening between the participants as a result of this utterance/these utterances?'.

**KEY POINTS: Implicit textual meaning**

- This section discussed the question of whether ideological texts were likely to brainwash their readers, and concluded that it is not as simple as that. Longer and repeated exposure to certain ideologies may, however, affect the reader of such texts.
- The chapter introduced the idea of naturalization, the process by which ideologies become so regularly assumed that they are finally seen as common sense.
- Finally, the notion of the 'textual-conceptual function' was introduced as the basis of critical stylistic analysis. These functions describe the way that texts construct a conceptual world for the reader to either assimilate or reject.

**EXERCISE 15.3**

Think of three naturalized ideologies that are so ingrained for you that you had to work hard to 'see' them as anything other than the 'truth'.

See if you can visualize a society in which those ideologies are reversed in polarity – so that things that we value are seen as bad and bad things are seen as good.

Do you know of any (current or past) societies in which those polarities are indeed reversed?

## 15.4 The textual-conceptual functions

What follows below is a brief introduction to each of the different ways in which a text constructs a conceptual world, using the basic linguistic system to represent participants, actions and so on in a way that may introduce assumed ideologies into the text. Each of the textual-conceptual functions is a complex network of form–function relationships in itself, and may require further reading to fully assimilate.

### 15.4.1 Naming and describing

One of the important things that texts do is to name things in the world of the text. Thus, a news article may name a police officer in a case (*Chief Superintendent, Chris Badger*) and a 'true life' story in a women's magazine may name the protagonist (*depressed, out-of-work single mother, Sue Foster*), whilst a politician may name a policy (*these vital reforms of the health service*). Notice that in each of these examples, it is the noun phrase that is being identified as a 'name'. This is because naming as a textual-conceptual function refers to the whole nominal element of the clause as though it provides a label for the referent, including descriptors such as adjectives which become an intrinsic part of the referent as a result. Thus, whilst it may well be a simple fact that Chris Badger is a police superintendent, and this naming practice is therefore completely factual, the description of Sue Foster as depressed is less open to scrutiny by the recipient of the text and could potentially be the opinion of the producer rather than being an official assessment of her mental health. By contrast, her status as unemployed and a single mother may be more factual, though the decision to package all this information into a single noun phrase could have its own consequences as Sue Foster's identity becomes more wrapped up with her marital/parental status and her lack of work. The text's producer could, of course, have made any of these identifying characteristics a feature not of the naming process, but of the description of the *processes, actions and states of being* that we will consider next. In this example, that could mean that more than one sentence is needed in order to fit in the following clauses: *Sue Foster doesn't have a job. Sue Foster is a mother. Sue Foster is depressed.* Though less elegant and (in this form) highly repetitive, the latter version presents each of Sue's characteristics as the proposition of the sentence, meaning that not only is she less closely identified by these characteristics but the recipient can also question the truth of these propositions more easily. The question of why her marital, parental and employment statuses might even be relevant in a story about (for example) successful slimming produces additional insights into the ideologies of the text. Thus, it is implied, women who do not reach the ideal of being successful career women at the same time as producing children and holding onto their partners are more likely to put on weight and need the help of experts to slim down to the idealized shape of womanhood.

### 15.4.2 Presenting processes, actions and states of being

The way in which texts present processes, actions and states can be analysed using the descriptive tool of transitivity. **Transitivity** has been well recognized in the critical discourse analysis (CDA) literature (see, for example, Fairclough 1989). This label comes from Halliday's systemic-functional grammar, whose insights include the distinction between the ideational and interpersonal metafunctions of language, which I am borrowing here. Halliday (1984) and his followers noticed (as others have also done) that there is not a clear one-to-one relationship between the form of linguistic structures (such as clauses or sentences) and their meaning. Thus, in English, for example, although we think of the grammatical subject of a clause as the 'actor' who intentionally performs the 'action', this is not always the case (*John was astonished by the snow in March*) and in fact the grammatical role taken by the verb is not always an 'action' at all (*John was a teacher*).

Grammatical descriptions of English (and other languages) have long recognized a set of verb categories that depend on their grammatical properties. So, for example, some (intransitive) verbs need only a subject (*she died*); some (transitive) require an object (*he ate the sausage*) and still others (ditransitive) require two objects (*she sent me a letter*) or an

**TABLE 15.1** Model of transitivity (adapted from Simpson 1993)

| Main category | Subcategories | Participants | Example |
|---|---|---|---|
| Material action processes | Intention<br>Supervention<br>Event | Actor, goal | *buy, eat*<br>*fall*<br>*occur* |
| Verbalization processes | | Sayer, verbiage<br>Goal | *say, tell* |
| Mental cognition processes | Cognition<br>Reaction<br>Perception | Senser phenomenon | *think*<br>*hate*<br>*hear* |
| Relational processes | Intensive<br>Possessive<br>Circumstantial | Carrier<br>Attribute | *Be*<br>*have*<br>*be* |

adverbial (*he <u>was</u> in the bath*) to be complete. This basic difference of grammatical co-occurrence was later developed into a semantic categorization when it was recognized that these verb groups tend to be semantically linked. The resulting transitivity system is partly based on grammatical and partly on semantic similarities, as can be seen from the model of transitivity presented in Table 15.1.

When speakers or writers produce texts, they have to choose how to represent the scenario they are describing and that includes the choice of which kind of verb to use. The reason that making choices between these different categories matters textually is that the choice of one transitivity category over another will cause the rest of the clause to be altered and the consequence can be a different viewpoint on the same basic scenario. For example, if the government decides to cut spending on the health service, this could be presented in a number of different ways, depending on your ideological viewpoint:

(11) The government <u>has cut</u> the amount spent on free health care. (*material action, intention*)

(12) Citizens <u>are losing</u> money in their health care system. (*supervention*)

(13) Healthcare <u>is shrinking</u>. (*event*)

(14) The government <u>thinks</u> free health care needs cutting. (*mental cognition*)

Whilst some of the above are simply innocuous alternatives, there is nevertheless a shift in focus between the different versions. Examples (12) and (13) both delete the actor (the government) from the clause, with the result that there is less emphasis on the intentional actor in the situation. Whilst it may not be difficult for a reader to recover the original actor from a sentence using this kind of transitivity choice, it would require a conceptual effort which is not always convenient during the process of reading. The default situation for the reader is, therefore, to accept the text world's view of the situation, in which the cuts to health care are in focus, but the actors are not. It is not difficult to see why governments taking unpopular measures, for example in relation to cuts in spending, may welcome texts which put their role into the background by the careful choice of particular transitivity categories.

### 15.4.3 Hypothesizing

The contribution of modality to the meaning of a text is often mentioned by critical discourse analysts. **Modality** concerns the text producer's view of whether their statements are certain (or not) and whether they are desirable (or not). Although at first sight, these two strands of meaning seem rather different (*what you want* and *what you think is true*), they share modal meaning, which amounts to the notion that the situation described is hypothetical. The prototypical delivery mechanism in English for modality is the modal verb (*may, might, can, could, shall, should, will, would, must, ought to*), though this can differ in other languages. In English, modal verbs are auxiliary verbs which must occur before a main verb (e.g. *must improve, should be, could have been, shall arrive*).

As well as modal verbs, there are a number of other forms which add a modal dimension to the text. These include the modal adjectives (*possible, probable, certain, desirable*), the modal adverbs (*possibly, probably, certainly, hopefully*) and some main lexical verbs (*want, think, desire, hope, expect*). The main effect of modality on a reader/listener is to undermine the certainty of the propositional content of the utterance. Unlike categorical statements devoid of modality (e.g. *John has taken the cake*), modalized forms of texts bring to mind the doubtfulness of scenarios, even when they are presented as very certain (*I am sure John took the cake*). The very mention of the speaker's (or writer's) view of the certainty of a fact is enough to make it seem much weaker than an unmodalized (categorical) version.

Modality affects the ideational meaning of texts by moderating the certainty or desirability of the situation(s) being described. This can provide the text with two main ways of influencing the reader/listener:

- The apparent honesty of the text's producer who is not being categorical, but admitting that they are not certain (*I think the government should...; I want the US to...*) can make them seem sincere.
- The modality allows the text producer to construct an alternative hypothetical world in which the scenario they hypothesize is necessarily conceptualized by the recipient, whether for good (*I want a world where my children can breathe unpolluted air*) or for ill (*I think that climate change is going to bring millions of refugees into Europe*). This can have a powerful effect in causing the reader to visualize alternative worlds – either to fear them or to aspire to them.

To some extent, the statement of desirability (or obligation) which is produced by some modals (e.g. *You should not own a car; I want nuclear weapons to be abolished*) is both more obviously interpersonal and more explicit than other textual-conceptual functions and it demonstrates that there are no absolute boundaries between categories in linguistic systems. However, at the same time, modalized utterances are also producing an ideational structure of how the world might be – and it is this kind of textual meaning which is ideational – and may also be ideological.

### 15.4.4 Contrasting

The textual-conceptual functions already introduced have covered some of the most important textual meanings: naming of participants and things in the text world, the choice of transitivity and its consequences for the meaning – and the introduction of hypothetical text worlds through modality. There are, however, other important dimensions of the conceptual worlds created by texts which are more sporadic in their occurrence, but vital to understanding the ideational features of the text. These include the capacity of texts to create one-off opposites which are not conventional opposites, such as *hot–cold* or *alive–dead,* but instead have the status of opposites simply in that textual context.

There are a number of ways of triggering constructed opposites of this kind. Most common is the use of **negation** to contrast two different options which may (*It was honey, not gravy*) or may not (*It was a sunset, not a lasagne*) belong to the same semantic field. The resulting opposites usually have some other, more conventional opposites underpinning them, depending on the context in which they are used. So, the first pair here clearly exemplify the more conventional opposite *sweet/savoury* and would presumably be used to refer to this distinction either literally or metaphorically (that song she sang was so touching, though her usual lyrics are pretty strong; it was honey, not gravy). The second pair (*sunset/lasagne*) are harder to imagine as opposites, though the regular use of sunsets to indicate romantic, idealistic moments might suggest that lasagne is seen as everyday and mundane by comparison (*our honeymoon was all sunsets and no lasagne!*).

Other ways of causing opposites to be constructed in texts include the following:

Explicit triggers (despite X, Y; X as opposed to Y)
Parallel structures (He thought X. She thought Y)
Comparative structures (More X and less Y)
Replacive structures (X instead of Y)

In each case, the items filling the X and Y slots are not the conventional opposites of the language, but they become oppositional by their juxtaposition in these frames. The conventional linguistic opposites include a number of different types of opposite, such as gradable antonyms (*tall–short*), which have intermediate values as well as the extremes and are usually adjectives. These are common and taught to children at a young age. However, the default opposite type is mutually exclusive complementarity, where the opposites have no intermediate value and the denial of one implies the confirmation of the other. Thus, if you are not *dead,* you are *alive* and vice versa.

The textual construction of opposites depends on the reader understanding, in general, what opposites are and also knowing the conventional opposites of the language which are being implied in the **constructed opposition**. The construction of oppositional meaning in texts has potential for creating naturalized ideologies where two groups of people are seen as having mutually exclusive interests and such oppositions are to be found wherever opinions are being formed.

An example from the political debates in the UK, for example, demonstrates the insidious nature of constructed opposition. In the months prior to early 2013, there had been a number of politicians and right-wing newspapers talking about two groups of people using the nouns *skivers*[1] and *strivers*. Whilst this distinction was also lexicalized in other ways (e.g. *shirker* vs *worker*), the *striver/skiver* pair seemed to catch on, so that in January 2013, Zoe Williams (in the *Guardian*, 9 January 2013) noted that the Labour Party were complicit in this construction of what appeared to be a complementary opposite where people had to be one or the other:

(15) The skiver, in opposition parlance, is always unmentioned, yet he lurks; Labour won't tolerate him either, this feckless bogeyman of Westminster's devising.

This observation, that the constructed opposition is now so well known that you only need to mention one word for the other to be invoked, demonstrates that textual meaning can and does become more widespread social meaning at times. In a tea shop recently, a group of friends and I split into two groups to sit at different tables that would accommodate us. As I sat down, one of the people on my table said 'We're the skivers. They're the strivers.' This constructed opposition has taken hold and is now part of social banter. The consequences of dividing the world into two for people caught in poverty and benefit-dependency is stark and damaging to all of us, as was George W. Bush's pronouncement after the events of 11 September 2001 that 'Either you are with us or you are with the terrorists' which divided the world in a new and dangerous way.

## 15.4.5 Negating

One of the main ways in which a text can construct an ideational world is by telling the reader what it isn't. Negating is one way of making the reader understand what the options could have been, since the very act of negating creates the mental image of both the positive and the negative scenarios for the reader. If you are told *This is a rabbit*, you imagine a rabbit. If you are told *This is not a rabbit*, you probably still imagine a rabbit, since you cannot tell what else it might be from this statement alone, so you don't go through all of the other items in the world imagining them, but instead you imagine a rabbit and then you might also mentally 'cross it out' or make it disappear.

There are a number of different ways of negating things in texts. In English, there are the basic core negators of nouns (*no*) and verbs (*not*) as in *There are no biscuits* and *I did not eat the last biscuit*. There are also a number of intrinsically negating words, mostly adverbs and

[1] For readers not familiar with *skiver*, it is a word used in British English to describe someone who avoids work where possible, and is therefore a close synonym to *shirker*, which has a wider usage.

pronouns, such as *never, nowhere, nobody, no one, nothing* as well as, in English at least, morphological affixes all of which produce some kind of negating effect: e.g. *uncomfortable, insubstantial, de-stress, anti-oxidant, car-free, humourless.* As well as these clearly negating forms, there are many lexically negative words such *as lack, fail, omit,* which have negation as part of their semantic make-up. Beyond this, of course, human beings have many non-linguistic ways of negating, such as by shrugging or shaking the head.

Like modality, negating has the capacity to bring hypothetical scenarios to mind, as explained above, because the negated situation is imagined despite the negation (Nahajec 2009). An example of the use this might have for those with ideological as well as ideational intentions comes from a newspaper interview in 2008 with Ken Livingstone, at that time a candidate for being elected as Mayor of London. Livingstone made the comment 'This election is not a joke', though there was nothing in the previous conversation that indicated it was a joke. Livingstone's assertion, however, perversely brings to mind the very scenario it is denying, implying as a result that someone (maybe his rival Boris Johnson?) does indeed think that the election is a joke. The ideology that democracy is not only very important, but is also a serious business that should not be treated light-heartedly, is one that is very widespread in British society, though the election of the 'clownlike' Boris Johnson may demonstrate that not all voters feel the same way. Livingstone's strategy, therefore, of trying to undermine his rival by implying that it was all a game to him, did not seem to work.

### 15.4.6 Enumerating and exemplifying

As we have seen in this chapter so far, texts name things in the conceptual world that they are constructing; they choose ways to represent processes and actions; hypothesize about what might be or should be; create one-off opposites and make us think about things that aren't as if they were. In addition, they sometimes give us individual cases of categories, either in order to specify the complete list of members of that category (enumerating) or in order to exemplify the kinds of things belonging to that category (exemplifying). There is a lot of scope here for not only ideational construction of meaning (what categories exist in this world and what members do they have?) but also ideological naturalization (what is assumed to be a member of which category?).

Just like with the construction of opposites, texts can 'play' with the background social and linguistic assumptions about what belongs in which category, so that the reader is obliged, whilst reading the text at least, to conceptualize the world in which, for example, ostriches belong to the category not of flightless birds (with penguins and emus) but of African symbols:

(16) We brought back photos of all the African symbols of our journey: ostriches, rondavels, ant hills, elephant droppings and other amazing things.

What is noticeable about this list is first of all that the items in the list are a purely personal record of an individual's trip, so the category of 'African symbols' is not a universal one.

The other thing to notice is that the list ends with a rather vague miscellaneous category (other amazing things). This is a very common way to end categories where itemizing each member of the category would become boring, uninformative or irrelevant. This means that there is not always a clear division between exemplifying and enumerating, since the catch-all final item could be said to include everything that had not been individually mentioned.

The tendency for three-part lists to have significance beyond their apparent structure has been well documented, not least in the discussion of political language (Atkinson 1984). Three-part lists seem to embody the concept of completeness, implying that any list that has three items in it is in some sense covering the whole of the category it represents. Whether there are deep psychological or evolutionary reasons for this is still under debate, but there are consequences that have ideational and sometimes also ideological effects.

Some lists are clearly complete, as for example in the case of this instruction in a self-assembly pack of furniture: *Check all bolts, screws, legs and castors regularly to make sure they haven't loosened*. It would be unsafe and possibly illegal to put an exemplary list in this text: *Check all the bolts, screws and other fixings regularly*. In other contexts which seem at first sight rather similar, however, exactly this kind of list is used. Here is one from a women's magazine on the topic of cosmetic surgery: *It is thus possible to improve long-term facial contours, for example, by augmenting the cheekbones, the chin, the jaw-line or any other area that lacks definition*.

Not only does the choice of the verb *improve* presuppose that the reader will have problems with her looks, the list itself finishes with a catch-all (*any other area that lacks definition*) which by definition will include almost every reader. The **ideology** of bodily (in this case facial) perfection underlies the insidious use of such lists to draw the unwary reader into thinking that perhaps, after all, she (usually she) does need some kind of cosmetic surgery.

The three-part list is ubiquitous in advertising, politics and religious texts (this is one too!). Here is an example from a UK government website:

(17) We would all like to be part of a *safe, prosperous and healthy* community. A community where everyone has the right to the same *opportunities, freedom and respect*. Somewhere we can be proud of.

Many such lists are gestures towards the ideological common ground in society; no one will argue against the idea that we want to be *safe, prosperous and healthy* or have rights to the same *opportunities, freedom and respect*. However, these lists are not really enumerating the essentials of human life, so much as symbolizing the category and indicating by the three-part list that all members of the category are implied. The writer could have chosen three other similarly vague absolutes, such as *cohesive, equal and sustainable* for the first list. This would have slightly shifted the ideological emphasis (in a more liberal or left-wing direction), but the job of the list would have been the same; to indicate that we all have the same needs, which the text goes on to say are being supplied by the government in power.

### 15.4.7 Presenting others' discourse

The power of the language user to present other people's words and thoughts is another way in which texts present the world through a particular viewpoint. Speech and thought presentation (often now called discourse presentation) has long been studied by stylisticians interested in the way that literary texts present the speech and thought of characters, and how this interacts with the thoughts and attitudes of the narrator or author. Leech and Short (1981, 2007) first proposed a model of speech and thought presentation and it is still being developed. Here, we will use a version based on Short (1996):

| NRS | NRSA | IS | FIS | DS |
|---|---|---|---|---|
| Narrative Report of Speech | Narrative Report of Speech Act | Indirect Speech | Free Indirect Speech | Direct Speech |

The model represents a range between the version which is most faithful to the original language used (DS) at one extreme and the version which is least faithful at the other (NRS). Another way of putting this is that there is most authorial interference at the left-hand end of the range and least interference at the right-hand end. The use of narrative reports of speech (*he spoke at length*) and speech acts (*he complained bitterly*) leave the reader/listener with little independent judgement of the words actually spoken whereas direct speech (*he said 'I was not to blame'*) give the recipient the closest experience to actually having heard the words spoken without having been there.

The model as presented above includes only speech, but if we also include the presentation of thought in the same series of categories, we can see that there is a 'norm' marked at different places on the two sets:

| | | | | norm<br>↓ |
|---|---|---|---|---|
| NRS | NRSA | IS | FIS | DS |
| NRT | NRTA | IT | FIT | DT |
| | | ↑<br>norm | | |

As Short points out, the norm for presenting speech is direct speech, because it is the most faithful way of repeating the original speech. In thought presentation, however, since we cannot be witnesses to other people's actual thoughts, the norm is indirect thought presentation (*he thought that she should have helped him*) rather than direct thought presentation (*he thought 'She should help me'*). The direct presentation of thought requires the author to put into words the thoughts of the person concerned, and this appears to give the author a different kind of interference possibility, as it seems that s/he has privileged access to the mind of the person whose thoughts are being reported.

The ideological implications of this model are relatively clear; if you are the producer of a text, such as a news report, you have the power to present the words and thoughts of those you agree with and disagree with through the different categories explained above. Though this ability to skew the words and thoughts of others can be used consciously and deliberately, it is probably also natural that an author will unconsciously slant a report of others' words to serve their own viewpoint. This is all part of the way that human beings tell stories and is often neither malicious nor manipulating. It may, however, cause certain attitudes to be naturalized as common sense over a period of time and across a range of texts. Here is an extract from the *Daily Mail* online about newly issued guidance for employers (in April 2013) from the Equality and Human Rights Commission:

(18) It says that genuine beliefs held by vegetarians, ecologists and druids should be treated the same as religious beliefs by bosses. Employers should also consider giving time off to druids and pagans for a pilgrimage to Stonehenge or Glastonbury.

This text uses indirect presentation of the original by including the reporting clause (it says) and the implication of this presentation method is that there is a reasonable level of faithfulness to the original, just as there would be, for example, in the DS/IS pair of sentences below:

(19) a. He said 'I am sorry to hear your news'.
b. He said that he was sorry to hear my news.

The normal expectation is that indirect representation of speech or writing would change the tense (*am – was*), the person (*I – he*) and little else. However, as we can see below, one relevant part of the original text mentions minority belief systems (or none) in passing, but does not give the specific example of trips to Stonehenge or Glastonbury, which are not mentioned anywhere in the document:

(20) The law protects adherents to all the generally recognised religions, as well as druids and pagans, for example. It also protects people without any religion or belief, including humanists and atheists.

Here we see the representation of a written text illustrating the tendency of the tabloid press to make liberal laws such as the European Human Rights Convention seem silly in order to undermine them.

### 15.4.8 Assuming

One of the strongest ways that a text can produce ideological effects in its readers is by making assumptions that the reader or listener will find difficult to argue with. We have already seen that noun phrase packaging (naming) of things and people in a text world can be difficult to contest. The use of definite noun phrases to produce existential presuppositions of this kind can make it hard for even critical readers to question the assumptions that the text is making:

The textual-conceptual function of assuming is sometimes seen as belonging in the domain of pragmatics (see Chapter 8) because of the implicit nature of the meaning involved. However, presuppositions are present in the fabric of the text itself, even though they are hard to pin down as they do not form the proposition of the sentence, but are taken for granted as being in the text world. The result is that you cannot negate presuppositions by negating the sentence as a whole. Here is a sentence from an article by the British Prime Minister, David Cameron, in the *Sun* newspaper (6 April 2013):

(21) And we are ending the crazy situation where people could have a bigger income by choosing to stay on benefits rather than work.

This sentence has a proposition which can be summarized as 'We are stopping X' where X refers to the very long noun phrase starting with *the crazy situation* and running to the end of the sentence. This noun phrase presents a concept which is presupposed by the sentence. We can test it by negating the sentence:

(22) And we are not ending the crazy situation where people could have a bigger income by choosing to stay on benefits rather than work.

The presupposition that there is indeed a crazy situation as described in the noun phrase remains intact, even if the proposition of the sentence is now negated.

There are other ways in which assumptions are produced, as well as through the naming practices that we saw earlier. There are a range of 'triggers' of logical presupposition which include, for example, change of state verbs (e.g. *stop, start*) and 'factive' verbs which both presuppose the truth of the clause following them:

(23) You should stop being racist. (assumes the addressee is racist)

(24) Jane realized that she was hungry. (assumes that Jane is hungry)

A longer discussion of logical presupposition triggers can be found in Chapter 8, but here the important thing to notice is that this is another way in which texts produce meaning – by putting some of it into the (assumed) background of the propositions in its sentences.

### 15.4.9 Constructing a time–space envelope

The final textual-conceptual function we will encounter here is the one that is most often discussed in relation to text worlds; the construction of a world with dimensions of space and time. This function of texts draws upon the 'deictic' properties of human language which developed to serve the purposes of face-to-face communication but which have become fundamental to the way in which we imagine the constructed worlds of texts even at a distance in space and time from the world envisaged. Deixis is what enables us to cognitively 'move around' within the London of Dickens's time when we're reading one of his books as well as the mechanism for our conceptual construction of the unreal worlds of Harry Potter and Star Wars.

The way that **deixis** works is that some words and phrases link to the context in a specific – and variable – way. So, for example, the referent of the first-person pronoun *I* or the second-person pronoun *you* varies depending on who is speaking to whom. Likewise, in relation to time and space, the adverbs *here, there, now* and *then* all refer to different actual places and times, depending on who uses them and when. In face-to-face interaction, these words will be understood by the participants by referring to the context. In texts that are received in a different space and time from the one they are produced in, the recipient has to work out what these deictic words refer to. The process of doing so is part of constructing a mental map of the world described by the text concerned (McIntyre 2007). Thus, readers are able to identify more closely with protagonists in fictional texts by positioning themselves in relation to the deictic terms. This may mean, for example, seeing the narrative through the eyes of one or more first-person narrators or viewing the spatial layout of a fictional (or real) village or town as the characters move through the scenes.

For non-fictional texts, such as news articles, the mechanisms are the same, but the effect may be to present a place like Afghanistan or London; a time period, like the 1960s or a person or group of persons, like a government, through a particular viewpoint. This viewpoint may be simply descriptive, but it will often also be ideological. I recently took a taxi tour of the trouble spots of Belfast following the thirty years of sectarian troubles in Northern Ireland. The commentary by the taxi driver tried to be as even-handed as possible to the two communities involved in the conflict. However, there were small deictic indications that our guide was from the Catholic, Republican community as he used the first-person plural (our) more readily when talking about this group than he did when presenting the views of the Protestant, Loyalist community. The facts were not given in a biased way at all, but the viewpoint was partly skewed.

**KEY POINTS: The textual-conceptual function**

- This section introduced each of nine textual-conceptual functions, which are the basis of critical stylistic analysis, and illustrated their ideological potential.
- The nine text-conceptual functions are:
  - Naming and describing
  - Presenting processes, actions and states of being
  - Hypothesizing
  - Contrasting
  - Negating
  - Enumerating and exemplifying
  - Presenting others' discourse
  - Assuming
  - Constructing a time–space envelope.

## EXERCISE 15.4

The following passages come from a number of newspaper websites responding to the April 2013 death of Margaret Thatcher, who was British Prime Minister in the 1980s:

1. Margaret Thatcher's bluntness, strong character, sharpness and sternness were reflected in the words that helped earn her the nickname the Iron Lady, and many quotes from Britain's radical former prime minister, who died today at age 87, will go down in history.

2. 'I am not a consensus politician. I'm a conviction politician.' 1979
3. 'Where there is discord, may we bring harmony. Where there is error, may we bring truth. Where there is doubt, may we bring faith. Where there is despair, may we bring hope.' (Quoting St Francis of Assisi, on her 1979 election victory)
4. 'This woman is headstrong, obstinate and dangerously self-opinionated.' (ICI personnel department assessment, rejecting job application from the then Margaret Roberts in 1948)
5. 'I suspect there are thousands of people who think that having a party is not enough. They want to be there at her state funeral. They want to protest at the injustice of Thatcher parading her wealth and status through the streets of London, when so many live and die in poverty as a result of her policies.'
6. The Metropolitan Police has asked groups planning to demonstrate during or in advance of Margaret Thatcher's funeral to make themselves known to officers so that their 'right to protest can be upheld'.

For each example, comment on the textual-conceptual functions that provide the ideational meaning and explain the nature of the ideological content where relevant.

WEBSITE: **Group exercise**

Visit the website and, in a small group, examine the texts provided there. For each text, discuss the ideation produced by the text and to what extent it produces some implicit ideology. Work out which of the textual conceptual functions are in play (there may be more than one) and discuss which members of the group have a naturalized ideology matching the one in the text.

## 15.5 SUMMARY

This chapter has introduced the framework of critical stylistics (Jeffries 2010) as a way to approach the analysis of ideology in texts. Ideology is seen here as a socially constructed system of values which are largely shared across a community, often to the extent that they become naturalized as 'common sense'.

The chapter argues that there are three strands of meaning inherent in the use of human language. The first is *linguistic meaning*, which refers to the basic systems and structures of the language and their de-contextual functions or meaning. The second is *textual meaning*, which is where texts present their text worlds through a number of textual-conceptual functions, such as naming, negating and hypothesizing. The ideational meaning that is produced in this way is potentially the source of implicit ideological meaning, which is the subject of this chapter. The final strand of meaning inherent in human language is interpersonal meaning. This includes pragmatic meanings such as implicature and face and also conversational meanings like openings and closings.

The difference between ideation and ideology and the nature of implicit versus explicit ideology were explored here before the textual-conceptual functions by which texts create worlds were explained and illustrated with reference to ideological production of meaning. The textual-conceptual functions are labelled in non-technical ways (e.g. naming, negating, contrasting) to emphasize the fact that they refer to what a text is *doing* when it constructs a conceptual 'world' of ideation and ideology.

WEBSITE: **Language and Ideology**

Now go to the website and assess your knowledge of language and ideology by completing the self-test questions!

## SUGGESTIONS FOR FURTHER READING

Fairclough, N. (2010). *Critical Discourse Analysis: The Critical Study of Language*, 2nd edn. London: Longman. This recent exposition of critical discourse analysis has a very good discussion of ideology and argues for the relevance of CDA analysis to modern politics.

Jeffries, L. (2010). *Critical Stylistics*. Basingstoke: Palgrave. This textbook is the place for you to see each of the textual-conceptual functions in more detail and see more illustrations of how each one works.

Jeffries, L. (2014). Critical stylistics: discerning power and ideology in texts. In M. Burke (ed.), *The Routledge Handbook of Stylistics*, pp. 408–20. London: Routledge. This chapter in a specialist stylistics handbook is a slightly higher-level exposition of the framework underlying critical stylistics. It may help some readers to read another explanation of the linguistic-textual-interpersonal model of linguistic meaning.

# ANSWERS TO EXERCISES

## EXERCISE 15.1

| | Type of meaning | Commentary |
|---|---|---|
| 1. | Linguistic | The general rules of grammar are part of the language system underlying its usage. |
| 2. | Ideational | This sentence describes the kind of meaning produced by an actual text. |
| 3. | Interpersonal | The interruption here is part of the ongoing interaction between two people. |
| 4. | Ideational | The scenario here, though denied (non-existent) by the speaker, is the ideational meaning of the Prime Minister. The subordinate clause (to frighten us) could also be seen as interpersonal. |
| 5. | Linguistic | The conventional opposites (hot/cold) are part of the underlying system of the language. |
| 6. | Linguistic | The lexis of a language – all the words that belong to it and how they relate to each other – is part of the underlying system of the language. |
| 7. | Ideational | This sentence shows Bertrand creating a 'new' opposition between pizza and cake and it is therefore ideational as it gives a particular view of the world. |
| 8. | Interpersonal | The main clause here (Maisie upset Susie) is concerned with the interaction between them. The subordinate clause (by telling her she was wrong) could also be seen as ideational. |
| 9. | Linguistic | The placing of adjectives in noun phrases in English are part of the systematic set of rules of grammar. |
| 10. | Ideational | This is ideational because it describes the newspaper as setting out a view of the world in which the government's role is downplayed. |

## Exercise 15.2

1. This is clearly explicitly ideological because the modal verb (*should*) indicates that it is the producer's view and it concerns a value judgement.
2. This appears to be purely ideational as it creates the concept of a house with lots of people in it – including many beds. Any ideological meaning would be contributed by the reader who may have views as to the ideal circumstances for human beings to live in which are drawn from experience.

3. The negation (*there was nowhere to sit*) brings an implicit ideological content into an otherwise ideational sentence. The reason for the negation is that it produces an expectation in the reader that there ought to be places to sit in a house.
4. This sentence is an explicitly ideological one, with the concept of fairness being at the centre of that ideology.
5. There is an implicit ideology here about the value of citizens. In this case, there is a label (*the expensive elderly generation*) which implies that non-productive older people are a burden to society.
6. This sentence is ideational because it produces a conceptual space and time, but it does not confer any values on the scene and there is therefore no ideological content.
7. This sentence is ideational as it describes a society in which young girls get pregnant. Any feelings that a western reader might have about whether this should happen are drawn from experience and not from the text.
8. By contrast with sentence 7, this sentence allows for the ideology that young girls should not be sexually active and are not ready to be mothers. The ideology is provided by the evaluative adjective, *terrible*.

## Exercise 15.3

Here are a few ideologies that seem to be quite naturalized:

(a) It is right not to steal from others.
(b) Small children should not be sent out to work.
(c) Telling the truth is the right thing to do.
(d) We should treat people the same, whatever their own ideologies.
(e) It is right to have only one sexual partner at any one time.

(a) This is one of the hardest ones to imagine away because it is so deeply ingrained in all human culture. However, there may be some occasions where stealing is legitimated in order to put right a larger wrong. Whether you agree with that or not, some people certainly think this way. The big question is how to judge when stealing becomes legitimate in this way.

It is probably only some kinds of subcultures (e.g. thieves) that see stealing as straightforwardly legitimate, though there may be those who see the moral value of stealing as a gradable offence which is mitigated by need (e.g. stealing to feed your children). There are and have been, however, societies which see stealing from other states or communities as legitimate within war.

(b) This is an absolute value in our society, but it is possible to imagine that other societies and other times might see small children as potential workers. Victorian Britain certainly included many children amongst the work force in factories, mills and domestic service. The needs of families in many impoverished societies around the world are still supplied to a great extent by the children working in factories, on rubbish heaps or at markets.

(c) Like stealing, this one seems to be a universal ideology that most human societies share. Most adults realize that there are some occasions when lying may be appropriate, to prevent a larger problem or to protect the vulnerable from truth that could hurt them. It is difficult to imagine a community where lying was praiseworthy, though it is common in all walks of life and people sometimes seem to admire those who get away with it.

(d) This seems like a simple question of equality, but it is proving difficult for many societies to make sure that all groups of people are treated equally. Where individual rights (to faith, to behaviour, to sexuality etc.) may clash with others' rights or with the general good, problems arise. This has been evidenced in cases taken to the European Court for Human Rights for example, which has to make judgements about the rights of individuals, for example, to bar homosexual couples from their Bed and Breakfast premises, to wear religious items of jewellery at work and so on. This ideology demonstrates that they may be fine in theory, but the practice can be difficult to implement.

(e) There is a very long-standing ideology that supports monogamy in much of human culture, though there are also some cultures which officially recognise polygamy (the right of men to have more than one wife). Note that this ideology clashes with the last one, as women are not granted the same right as men to marry multiple partners in polygamous societies.

## Exercise 15.4

1. This example contains a four-part list (*bluntness, strong character, sharpness and sternness*) which seems to indicate that it is not a symbolic, but a real list. However, the last two items (*sharpness and sternness*) are not particularly different in meaning, so it also seems as though it is a list that is straining to be taken seriously, so it makes an effort to avoid being a three-part list, which could be seen as only symbolic. Either way, these four nouns form the head of a long noun phrase with the possessive (*Margaret Thatcher's*) which presuppose that she was indeed all of these things. This naming practice does not invite the reader to contest it.

The other feature worth noting in this example is the noun phrase 'Britain's radical former prime minister' which presupposes that she is radical and does not allow for this aspect of her character to be questioned.

2. This is Margaret Thatcher inventing new opposites. We may think of consensus as normally opposing words like *autocrat* or *dictator*, both of which are normally valued negatively compared to the more positive consensus. However, in this statement, Thatcher manages to create a new opposite for the word *consensus* – *conviction*. Because conviction has a positive value, the result of this constructed opposition is that consensus is obliged to take up the negative value of the pairing.
3. These are not Thatcher's own words, of course, but they are interesting because they only partly depend on conventional opposites. *Discord* and *harmony* are well-established opposites, often used metaphorically to refer to conflict between people. The pairings of *doubt/faith* and *despair/hope* are also conventional and therefore familiar. The surprising pairing here is between error and truth. These each have their own conventional opposite (*error/correctness* and *falsehood/truth*) but she chooses to pair the perhaps less aggressive *error* with truth, as though she wants to indicate that her predecessors in government are more mistaken than malicious.
4. This insightful assessment of the as-yet-unmarried Thatcher by a prospective employer uses the convenience of a three-part list to damn her: *headstrong, obstinate and dangerously self-opinionated.* This seems to be a symbolic list aimed mainly at making it clear that she was not wanted for the job as the three parts of the list overlap considerably in their semantics and are therefore not clearly making different points about her qualities – or lack of them.
5. This part of a commentary on the emerging tendency for people to hold street parties to celebrate the passing of Margaret Thatcher uses modality to allow the speculation to follow. After the initial 'I suspect', everything else is the product of the writer's imagination and though it may be based on some inside information, it is presented here as a hypothetical situation which the reader is invited to believe as it is produced by an honest journalist who lets us know that s/he isn't certain of the facts.
6. This example illustrates the use of a very short stretch of apparently direct speech to bring credibility to the whole sentence and to contrast, perhaps, the request by the police for protestors to identify themselves (and thus putting themselves at risk of pre-emptive arrest) with the purported reason for this request, which is to defend their right to peaceful protest.

## REFERENCES


Atkinson, M. (1984). *Our Masters' Voices: The Language and Body Language of Politics*. London: Routledge.

EHRC (2013). Religion or belief in the workplace: a guide for employers following recent European Court of Human Rights judgments.

Fairclough, N. (1989). *Language and Power*. London: Longman

Gavins, J. (2007). *Text World Theory: An Introduction*. Edinburgh University Press.

Goffman, I. (1981). *Forms of Talk*. Philadelphia: University of Pennsylvania Press.

Halliday, M. A. K. (1994). *An Introduction to Functional Grammar*, 2nd edn. London: Edward Arnold.

Jeffries, L. (2010). *Critical Stylistics*. London: Palgrave Macmillan.

Leech, G. and Short, M. ([1981] 2007). *Style in Fiction: A Linguistic Introduction to English Fictional Prose*. London: Pearson Education.

McIntyre, D. (2007). Deixis, cognition and the construction of viewpoint. In M. Lambrou and P. Stockwell (eds.), *Contemporary Stylistics*, pp. 118–30. London: Continuum.

Nahajec, L. (2009). Negation and the creation of implicit meaning in poetry. *Language and Literature*, 18(2), 109–27.

Short, M. (1996). *Exploring the Language of Poems, Plays and Prose*. London: Longman.

Simpson, P. (1993). *Language, Ideology and Point of View*. London: Routledge.

# 16 Media discourse

PHILIPPA SMITH AND ALLAN BELL

**KEY TERMS**

- critical discourse analysis
- discourse
- ideology
- media
- media literacy (literate)
- modes of communication
- news
- newsworthy
- social practice
- text

**PREVIEW**

This chapter looks at media discourse – that is, how the media use language and images to construct meaning in society. We are interested in how media discourse can influence the way we think and we emphasize the need for greater critical awareness of the messages we are exposed to daily by analysing discourse found in media texts. The concept of investigating media discourse is closely linked with discourse analysis and we recommend that this chapter should be read in conjunction with Caldas-Coulthard's comprehensive examination of this topic in Chapter 9. We provide some context for the emergence of media discourse within the field of discourse analysis, as well as describing some theoretical approaches and methods that have been used to study media texts whether news reports, advertisements or broadcast interviews. But as former journalists, and now academics whose main body of research lies in the study of media texts, we focus in particular on the language of the news to exemplify how critical analysis and interpretation are crucial in becoming media literate. This chapter will give you a greater appreciation and understanding of media and their significance.

## 16.1 INTRODUCTION

**Discourse** surrounds us. It is the meaning that lies behind everyday conversations, letters, signs in shop windows, speeches, paintings, photographs, a tweet, a slogan on a t-shirt, a television programme, a product brand, a website or even a car's personal registration plate. The text is what we actually read, see or hear – in other words the 'observable product' that carries meaning (Talbot 2007: 9). Discourse is 'a form of knowledge' (Devereux 2003: 158) that is conveyed through text. One way to grasp the concept of discourse is to think of the commonly used phrase 'reading between the lines' where we seek to understand what is being implied rather than explicitly said.

Although **media discourse** can relate in today's terms to any form of medium of communication such as weblogs or social networking sites, in this chapter we are concerned specifically with the discourse that is constructed and conveyed through **news** organizations. As we will demonstrate, news discourse is a complex phenomenon that plays an important role in 'wider processes of social and cultural change and in wider power relations and ideological processes in society' (Fairclough 1995: 201).

Our objective in this chapter is to develop your understanding about what media discourse is, how it is produced, its effects and how you might analyse it. We will look at media discourse as a field of research and highlight some frameworks for analysing news texts. Using a lead story from a news website as a case study for analysis we demonstrate the construction of discourse through various modes such as text, layout and visuals. Our intention is that rather than just being consumers of **media**, you become competent researchers with the capability to see and understand the meaning behind the text.

## 16.2 Media discourse in the news

Media discourse involves a social action whereby many different beliefs, attitudes and opinions can be communicated from the producer to you, the consumer, through texts in a range of genres from news stories and advertisements to phone texts, tweets, podcasts, weblog posts, or live chat on social networking sites. We are living in a media-saturated world where we are bombarded by thousands of messages on a daily basis. While it is easy to be passive and simply absorb these messages and accept them as true, becoming more critically aware of their underlying meanings is crucial to understanding the power of the media. Fortunately there are ways of systematically analysing media discourse that help us to achieve this. However, with our focus on the news in this chapter, it is important to look at what we mean by news before proceeding to look at how to analyse it.

### 16.2.1 What is news?

The purpose of print, broadcast and, more recently, digital news media, is to gather information and package it in a way that makes it **newsworthy** and attractive to its intended audience. The process of constructing news stories involves a number of individuals – the news editor or chief reporter who assigns stories to journalists; the photographers and videographers who obtain visual content; the journalists themselves who gather information (through tip-offs, research, interviews, observations, official documents and public relations releases) and then write the copy (the text); the sub-editors and/or web editors who write headlines, edit stories and position them amongst other stories on pages, websites or broadcast bulletins; and editors who may do final checks. In the case of visual media there are also the news readers and presenters who, through their facial expressions and tone of voice, will affect how a story is perceived by the audience. Online platforms mean that boundaries between newspapers, radio and television are being blurred.

The roles of staff in newsrooms are less standardized across the board than they were in the twentieth century, so it is not possible to describe just one way in which the flow of news works. However, it is important to recognize the input of many different individuals who contribute to the way a story is written and presented, which will influence the audience's reception and interpretation of communicative events.

### 16.2.2 Constructing reality

A key question that is frequently raised by academics in examining media texts is: do media offer a window on the world that reflects reality, or do they actually construct reality? Are, for example, the images of war that we see on television just as they happen, or are they presented from a particular perspective that may lead us to support one side as opposed to the other?

It is impossible for any text to be ideologically neutral. That is, texts will always present a particular version of reality that promotes 'certain kinds of beliefs about the world and certain kinds of power relationships between people' (Jones 2012: 49). To illustrate this we can look at an example of media discourse surrounding New Zealand's largest immunization programme of children in 2004 and 2005, which was launched to combat alarming rates of the meningococcal B disease. Medical researchers tracked the headlines in the New Zealand print media assessing their accuracy against the content of the articles (Turner, York and Petousis-Harris 2009). In one case study where two recently immunized children were hospitalized with a different strain of the disease, 50 per cent of the thirty headlines analysed were identified as misleading and 20 per cent were ambiguous. None of the misleading headlines such as 'Immunized children catch killer disease' and 'Sick children no surprise to anti-jab campaigner', nor the ambiguous ones such as 'Vaccine not 100 per cent effective', are ideologically neutral: the language used presents a negative impression of the vaccine even though it was not produced to cover this particular strain of the disease. The anti-vaccination discourse within these headlines may well influence people's perception about vaccinations as a whole and dissuade them from immunizing their children. But even this headline, 'Vaccinated child catches different meningitis strain', deemed accurate by the researchers, still presents an ideological viewpoint. The language used is factual, but rather than emotive or seemingly accusatory as in the other examples, it suggests that the child is still protected from a specific strain of meningitis covered by the vaccination.

### 16.2.3 Why study the language of news?

There are many reasons why linguistic scholars should study the news. Firstly, its availability means there is a wealth of texts to analyse – sometimes researchers are challenged to limit themselves to manageable amounts of data! Secondly, it is interesting to see how the media use language, images and a wide range of **modes of communication** such as colour, design and layout. But, as you can see from our example, looking at vaccination headlines, analysing media discourse is important 'for what it reveals about a society and . . . contributes to the character of society' (Bell 1998: 65). Media discourse analysis can help us to be **media literate**, that is, you are able to have a 'clearer perspective to see the border between your real world and the world manufactured by the media' (Potter 2013: 10). This is about having a 'set of competencies' to be able to interpret the media and institutions (Hoechsmann and Poyntz 2012: 1) and the discourses that are constructed and conveyed. But understanding exactly how this happens requires sound **discourse analysis**.

**KEY POINTS: Media discourse**

- Media discourse involves social action between the newsmakers and the audience.
- A range of people within media organizations have input into the construction of a news story.
- All texts have a perspective and cannot be ideologically neutral.
- Media discourse can be transmitted through a range of communication modes.
- Media discourse analysis helps us to become media literate and see how reality can be constructed.

## EXERCISE 16.1

We talked about understanding discourse using the metaphor of 'reading between the lines' – a way of understanding what is really being said whether this is articulated by visual or linguistic means. Below there are seven news headlines from different media organizations. They all cover the same story – Russian President Vladimir Putin's speech to Eastern European leaders on 10 April 2014 announcing possible consequences for their countries if Russia stopped subsidizing Ukraine's gas debt. Read and compare these headlines and the words that they use. Pay attention to which media organization they come from and in which country they are based. Then consider the following questions:

1. Which of these headlines might be considered ideologically neutral?
2. Do these headlines offer a window on the world that reflects reality, or do you think the media actually construct that reality?

(a) From Al Jazeera news organization based in Doha, Qatar, owned by the government of Qatar (Source: Associated Press):

'Putin: Ukraine gas debt could affect Europe'

(b) From Itar-Tass, major news agency in Russian:

'President Vladimir Putin's letter to leaders of European countries. Full text'

(c) From *Kyiv Post*, Ukraine's leading English newspaper. By Interfax-Ukraine:

'Putin's letter to European leaders: Russia subsidized Ukraine for four years'

(d) From the BBC (British Broadcasting Corporation). By Daniel Sandford:

'Putin warns Europe of gas shortages over Ukraine debts'

(e) From Television New Zealand, a publicly owned broadcaster in New Zealand (Source: Associated Press):

'Putin: Ukraine debt threatens Europe gas supplies'

(f) From ABC News (American Broadcasting Corporation), a commercial television network in the United States (Source: Associated Press):

'Putin: Ukraine debt threatens Europe gas supplies'

(g) From the *Financial Times*, a British international daily newspaper. By Jack Farchy in Moscow and Joshua Chaffin in London:

'Europe supply in jeopardy as Putin warns of Ukraine gas cut'

## 16.3 Media discourse analysis

Section 16.2 highlighted the significance of media discourse and the language of news, setting out reasons why analysis of **texts** is both important and academically interesting. We now turn to look at media discourse analysis as a field of research. While discourse analysis gained popularity in the 1970s when an interest in the structure and form of words, phrases and sentences was overtaken by a desire to analyse discourse as language in use (van Dijk 1983), it took some time for researchers to recognize the value in examining media texts. In this section we look at the rise of media discourse analysis and some frameworks for studying news.

### 16.3.1 Researchers and the mass media

Prior to the 1970s researchers of mass media – print, film, radio and television – had largely ignored discourse as an area for study. They had mainly followed a more sociological or cultural studies approach by examining macro-phenomena such as the relations between media institutions, culture and society as well as the effects on the audience and the public (van Dijk 1985). However, with the growth of discourse analysis in latter decades of the twentieth century (see Chapter 9), the media soon came to be recognized as providing a wealth of data from which social meanings and stereotypes could be identified through the modes of language and communication (Bell 1991). As van Dijk (1985: 5) states:

> Discourse is no longer just an 'intervening variable' between media institutions or journalists on the one hand, and an audience on the other hand, but also studied in its own right, and as a central and manifest cultural and social product in and through which meanings and ideologies are expressed or (re-)produced.

The burgeoning interest in discourse analysis (including media discourse) has been evident in a range of different disciplines from psychology, education and health to politics and commerce using a myriad of different methodological approaches. These include genealogical analysis, discursive psychology, narrative analysis, interactional social linguistics, speech act theory, critical linguistics, literary analysis, cognitive linguistics, conversational analysis, pragmatics, ethnography of communication, genre analysis, narrative analysis and critical discourse analysis (see also Chapter 9).

Examples of subjects to have come under the discursive knife of researchers interested in news texts include the representation of immigrants, controversial newspaper cartoons, political discourse on radio talkback, crime reporting in the news, journalists' coverage of climate change and the framing of obesity in the media. However, the changing nature of news production, and its public dissemination as a result of advancing communications technology, has greatly increased the number of texts and variety of new genres accessible for study. While some researchers, for example, have compared traditional news formats with their online counterparts to assess the impact of digital change on journalist discourse (Bell and Smith 2013), others have looked at subjects such as the growth of news weblogs as a form of online journalism (Matheson 2004), or the quoting of tweets in newspaper coverage (Broersma and Graham 2012).

But it is not just the journalists who are under scrutiny when it comes to analysing news discourse. Of particular interest has been the role of the active reader/viewer in contributing to the construction of the news particularly in audience feedback columns on media websites or social network sites, and the public's submission of videos, photographs and tweets direct from their mobile devices. The inclusion of audience-generated material in news coverage of events such as the 9/11 World Trade Centre attack, the tsunamis in Malaysia in 2009, or the rise of the Arab Spring in 2011, are examples of what Pavlik refers to as the 'profound transformation' of the content of news being 'largely enabled, if not driven, by technological change' (2000: 231).

It is also important to point out that technology has assisted in the ways discourse analysis can be conducted. **Corpus-based discourse analysis** can be used for gathering data on linguistic aspects of news using computer software that can search a huge corpus (a collection of texts saved electronically) for patterns in language such as the repetition of specific words, or the frequent sequencing of words or terms together (collocations). More recently, web-based text analysis toolkits have been developed that can capture and archive vast amounts of text directly from blogs or social networking sites on the internet, making it accessible for coding and analysis. This has brought a more quantitative aspect to discourse analysis but it is often combined with qualitative methods to provide a more comprehensive investigation of a research topic.

We have highlighted a range of approaches to the analysis of media discourse whether this involves the gathering of data or theoretical approaches to analysis, but understanding how you might research texts yourself requires a knowledge of frameworks which we move on to in the next section.

**KEY POINTS: Media discourse analysis**

- Media discourse analysis emerged in the later decades of the twentieth century.
- It is easy to access a range of media texts for analysis through print, broadcast and digital platforms.
- The audience has a more participatory role in news making now that comments, photographs and videos can be submitted using digital technology.
- A wide range of academic disciplines use discourse analysis to study media texts.
- There are numerous methodological approaches to discourse analysis.

**EXERCISE 16.2**

Imagine that you are a journalist and you have been assigned to cover a story about a suspicious fire at a school overnight. It's the third suspicious fire in the area in two weeks. Who would you interview to find out details about what happened and what information would you be looking for based on the key journalistic questions of what, why, when and how? List your sources of information and other aspects of the story you might want to cover that will make it newsworthy.

Now view this story from a researcher's perspective. What research questions could you use to analyse this story that might give insight into the way it was constructed? Consider the subject of the fire and the journalist's desire to write a newsworthy story and whether the story provides a balanced view point about what happened or whether it enables some 'voices' to dominate over others. Think about the range of linguistic devices and modes of communication the journalist might use to make it newsworthy.

## 16.4 Frameworks for analysis

We now move on to looking at how to analyse news discourse. This requires the implementation of specific frameworks which we consider briefly in this section before presenting our case study as an example.

Our own definition of discourse analysis in relation to the news highlights its complexity:

> Discourse analysis requires close examination of the news text, both the linguistic form and other modalities such as its visual aspect. It focuses on the form of the text and how it is used in a social context – its construction, distribution, and reception. It aims to understand what are the meanings and social significance of the text. (Smith and Bell 2007: 78)

Given this complexity it is not surprising that there are numerous ways that news discourse might be analysed. Perhaps the three most influential frameworks developed since the 1980s are those of Bell, who focuses on the structure of news stories, van Dijk, and Fairclough, who apply **critical discourse analysis** approaches to media discourse.

Bell's (1991, 1998) work on the language of news media focuses on the concept that journalists write in a certain way by telling a 'story' to attract readers or viewers. In analysing news items he offers a step-by-step guide to demonstrate how journalists apply a particular structure to report an event, to reveal what has happened, where it occurred, how and why. In a close analysis of a story's text he looks at particular aspects of a journalist's interpretation of an event such as the news angle they use, how social actors are identified, what sources of information are quoted (eye witnesses or other news organizations), the inclusion of personal narratives, and the sequence in which aspects of the events are described. Consideration is also given to news processes that might influence a story's production such as deadlines, competing news stories, how much space might be available on a page, audience interpretation and what technology might be used.

One particular study of Bell's (2003), for example, compared the news coverage of three separate expeditions to the South Pole – Captain Scott in 1912, Sir Edmund Hillary in 1958, and Peter Hillary in 1999. Analysis of each of these news stories showed how the various technologies available at the time (telegraph/newspaper, then radio, and finally satellite phone and television) influenced reporting of the stories including their use of tense and chronological sequencing of events. Overall Bell's framework for analysing the language of the news enables insights into a story's construction that can highlight inconsistencies, incoherence, gaps and ambiguities, thereby determining more clearly what the story is really saying.

Studies of media discourse conducted by Teun van Dijk and Norman Fairclough involve their own particular approach of critical discourse analysis (CDA). CDA is concerned with the relationship between language, ideology and power, although it has been criticised as not having one existing theory or specific method of analysis. However, viewed from another perspective, CDA has also been acknowledged for being a 'flexible school of thought, rigorous in debate' that embodies a range of approaches and theoretical backgrounds (Bhatia 2013: 2). Its strength lies in its commonality of programmatic principles in that it is concerned with research that is problem oriented, and with inequality and abuse of power through language as **social practice**. Most importantly it considers context as a relevant part of analysis. The use of the term 'critical' in CDA is not applied in the sense of criticizing, but rather in seeking to explain social phenomena in order to have an emancipatory effect. That is, the objectives of CDA are to highlight issues that are often opaque or hidden, to create awareness about the production and reproduction of power of discourse, and ultimately to make a positive impact on a situation that has major ideological effects.

Van Dijk, in his sociocognitive approach to critical discourse studies (as he prefers to call it), is interested in the structure of the news when it comes to examining media texts. Rather than focusing on micro-analysis of language he pursues a more thematic investigation by combining two different types of analysis – semantic and syntactic. **Semantic analysis** is concerned with the structure and strategies of a text including the overall topic and the social or political context in which it is used. **Syntactic analysis**, on the other hand, involves the detailed analysis of the overall organization of a news story and its themes. This involves looking at features such as sentence structure, headlines, and lead paragraphs. Van Dijk is also interested in the ideological effects of discourse, and his media research is perhaps best known for its studies of racism, inclusion and exclusion in the news (see, for example, 1991, 1992, 2000).

Fairclough's approach reveals 'dialectical relations between language, power and ideology' (Ouyang 2013: 1) and is based on a three-dimensional framework for discourse analysis. Developed in the 1980s, this is useful in studying media texts because it recognizes the relationship between text, discourse practice and socio-cultural practice. Figure 16.1 shows our adaption of Fairclough's framework into a convenient diagram to explain the interconnectedness of each level in the analysis of news discourse.

The text is at the centre of analysis, whether it is a specific news story, a video or the home page of a news website, or simply a headline or an image. This is where we examine the semiotic 'tools' that help to create meaning. The analysis of text can be conducted on several levels and it is up to the researchers to decide the depth they may wish to go to depending on their research question/s. For example, research might focus on individual words and phrases or metaphors, or, alternatively, explore a broader level such as themes of persuasion or argumentation. **Discourse practice** is concerned with a text's production, distribution and consumption. It takes into account aspects such as organizational structures of a news organization, journalistic practice in writing stories, staff hierarchy in a news room, and methods of publication and distribution (online or hard copy) as well as how stories are received or consumed by the audience. Finally, social practice involves the context in which news as a communicative event takes place. Historical, social, political and cultural discourses exist in society that may affect our interpretation and understanding of a news story. In addition, other discourses such as those of institutions or governments may exist within news stories and their repetition and reproduction can see them

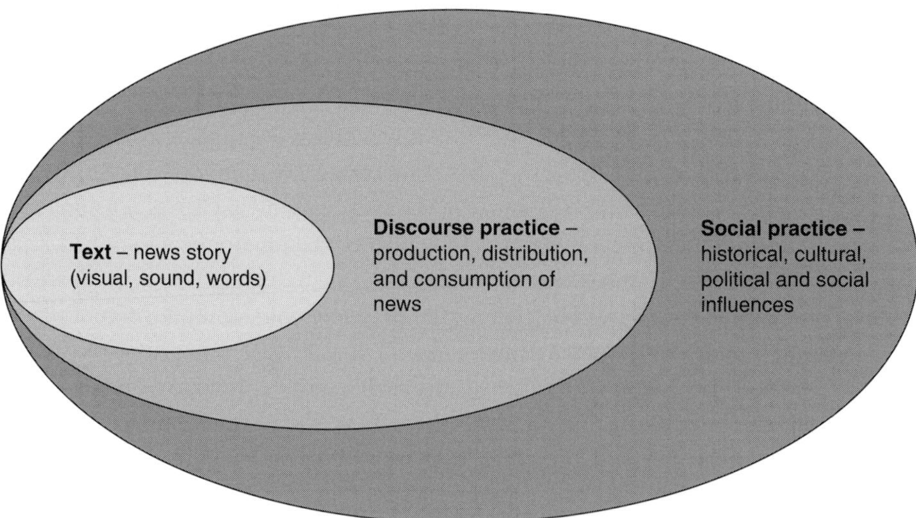


**Figure 16.1** Fairclough's three-dimensional framework for analysis adapted in the context of a news story

become regarded as 'normal' in society. The process whereby dominant ideologies achieve the status of common sense is known as '**naturalization**'. Examples of how Fairclough (1995) has used this three-dimensional approach to media texts include examination of television programmes such as *Crimewatch UK*, the *Oprah Winfrey Show* and *Medicine Now*, but also the current affairs programmes *Panorama* and *Today*.

While limitations of space make it impossible to provide a complete outline of the analytical steps within each of these three frameworks in this section, the list of recommended readings and references at the end of the chapter will guide you to books authored by these academics which provide more detailed information.

## 16.4.1 Case study

Let's now put our theory into practice and analyse a news story about a commonly recurring class of story, exemplified in the news of a military helicopter crash in Afghanistan as it appeared as a lead story in the online version of *The Telegraph* in the United Kingdom. Although the story first appeared at 5.02pm on Saturday 26 April, it is still the lead story on the home page of *The Telegraph* website the following morning Sunday 27 April (see Figure 16.2). The full story appears on its own page (Figure 16.3) and is

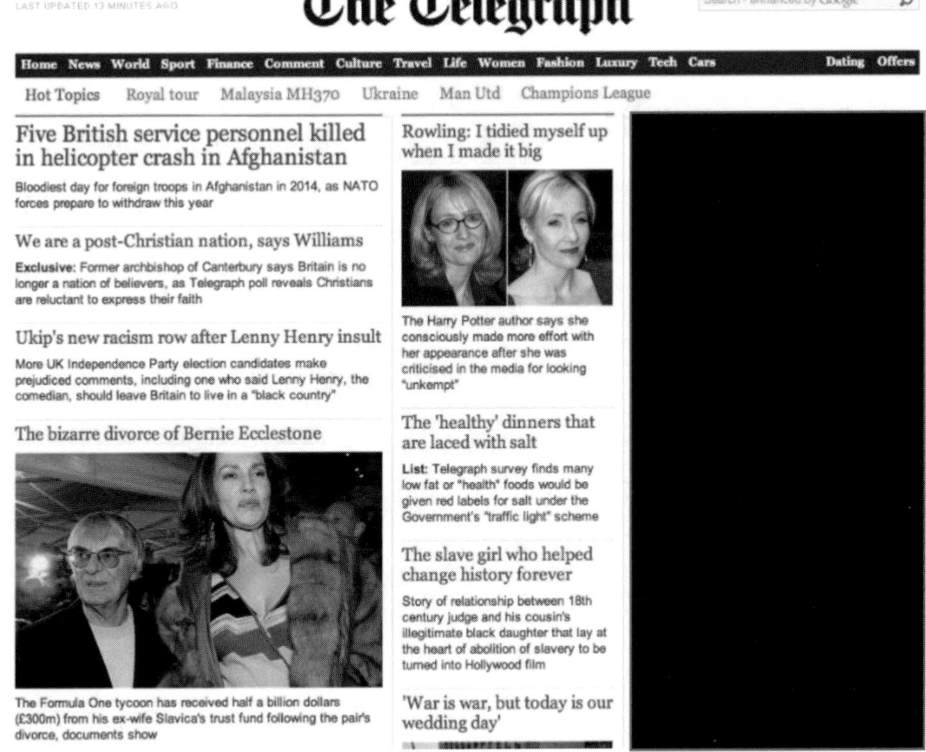

SUNDAY 27 APRIL 2014
LAST UPDATED 13 MINUTES AGO

The Telegraph

Search - enhanced by Google

Home News World Sport Finance Comment Culture Travel Life Women Fashion Luxury Tech Cars Dating Offers

Hot Topics Royal tour Malaysia MH370 Ukraine Man Utd Champions League

**Five British service personnel killed in helicopter crash in Afghanistan**

Bloodiest day for foreign troops in Afghanistan in 2014, as NATO forces prepare to withdraw this year

**We are a post-Christian nation, says Williams**

Exclusive: Former archbishop of Canterbury says Britain is no longer a nation of believers, as Telegraph poll reveals Christians are reluctant to express their faith

**Ukip's new racism row after Lenny Henry insult**

More UK Independence Party election candidates make prejudiced comments, including one who said Lenny Henry, the comedian, should leave Britain to live in a "black country"

**The bizarre divorce of Bernie Ecclestone**

The Formula One tycoon has received half a billion dollars (£300m) from his ex-wife Slavica's trust fund following the pair's divorce, documents show

**Rowling: I tidied myself up when I made it big**

The Harry Potter author says she consciously made more effort with her appearance after she was criticised in the media for looking "unkempt"

**The 'healthy' dinners that are laced with salt**

List: Telegraph survey finds many low fat or "health" foods would be given red labels for salt under the Government's "traffic light" scheme

**The slave girl who helped change history forever**

Story of relationship between 18th century judge and his cousin's illegitimate black daughter that lay at the heart of abolition of slavery to be turned into Hollywood film

**'War is war, but today is our wedding day'**

**Figure 16.2** Home page of *The Telegraph* (reproduced with permission from Telegraph Media Group Limited 2014; copyright restrictions prevent the reproduction of advertisements and the cartoon that appear on this page)

The Telegraph

Home | News | World | Sport | Finance | Comment | Culture | Travel | Life | Women | Fashion | Luxu

USA | Asia | China | Europe | Middle East | Australasia | Africa | South America | Central Asia | E

Afghanistan | Pakistan | India | North Korea | South Korea | Japan | Kazakhstan

HOME » NEWS » WORLD NEWS » ASIA » AFGHANISTAN

British troops killed in helicopter crash in Afghanistan

Five British service personnel have been killed in a helicopter crash in Afghanistan, the Ministry of Defence discloses

British Royal Air Force, KAF Air Field in Kandahar, Afghanistan in May 2010 Photo: Rex

By Ben Farmer, Defence Correspondent and Miranda Prynne
5:02PM BST 26 Apr 2014

Five British service personnel were killed when the helicopter they were travelling in crashed in southern Afghanistan.

The Lynx helicopter crashed during a routine flight in Kandahar province, the Ministry of Defence (MoD) said.

Three of the servicemen were from the Army Air Corps, based at RAF Odiham in Hampshire. One was a Royal Air Force serviceman also based at RAF Odiham. One was a member of the Army Reserve from 3 Military Intelligence Battalion, based in London.

The Taliban had tried to claim responsibility for the deaths but Major General Richard Felton, Commander Joint Helicopter Command, said on Saturday night that the crash appeared to be a "tragic accident".

He said: "It is with great sadness that we must confirm that five UK service personnel have been killed in this incident which, at this early stage, would appear to have been a tragic accident.

Related Articles

- Ironing becomes casualty of Afghanistan withdrawal 26 Apr 2014
- Three Americans shot dead by Afghan guard at Christian missionary hospital 24 Apr 2014
- Afghan guard shoots dead three foreigners at hospital 24 Apr 2014
- Interview: Steve McCurry's memories of Afghanistan 24 Apr 2014
- US troop numbers in Afghanistan may drop below 10,000 22 Apr 2014
- Afghan poll risks grow as Abdullah Abdullah strengthens lead in preliminary results 20 Apr 2014

"Events like this, whilst mercifully rare, remind us of the risks our personnel face in their work in Afghanistan as we approach the conclusion of the combat mission later this year.

"Our thoughts are with the families and loved ones of those who have lost their lives."

David Cameron, the Prime Minister, said his "heart goes out to the families and friends of those killed in this terrible tragedy".

Mr Cameron said: "Every British fatality is a source of deep sadness. This latest incident, which has cost the lives of five UK service personnel, brings home to us all once again how our armed forces continue to put their lives on the line to help the people of Afghanistan.

"I cannot pay high enough tribute to each and every one of them for the job that they do and the sacrifices that they make."

Ed Miliband, the Labour leader, said: "This is a tragic and poignant reminder of the sacrifices made by our Armed Forces in serving our country with bravery and distinction. I pay tribute to them and their continuing work in Afghanistan, elsewhere abroad, and here at home

Print this article | Share 168 | Facebook 91 | Twitter 77 | Email | LinkedIn 0 | +1 0

Afghanistan
News » Defence »
UK News »
Ben Farmer »
Miranda Prynne »

In Afghanistan

Anja Niedringhaus 1965 - 2014

Afghan tour winds down

Navy photographer awards

Afghan Red Cross attacked

**Figure 16.3** A screenshot showing the first half of the full story web page including photographs and links to stories and videos (reproduced with permission from Telegraph Media Group Limited 2014)

reached by clicking the cursor on the headline. None of the text on the home page or story page has been altered overnight – only a photograph has been replaced by a video, which we will discuss later. We will apply discourse analysis to examine both web pages as complementary components that construct the overall story on this particular day. We look at headlines and the lead sentence (story introduction), the story's event structure (the order in which the story gives us information), as well as other features such as the attribution of sources, specification of time and place, and the ways language and images are used that might affect our interpretation of the crash.

## Headlines

Beginning with the home page we see that our story features first in a list of stories each with its own headline and **standfirst** (secondary headline) prominent at the top left. The headlines are stand-alone units that summarize the story. They are usually written separately by a sub-editor or news editor who will be placing the story on the page. However, in some organizations journalists now write their own headlines, though we do not know whether this is the situation in our case study. The purpose of headlines is to attract and hold the attention of readers so that they will continue to read the main body of the story. In the case of the online news format this requires the reader to be interested enough to click and open another web page. However it is also important to note that while headlines are brief, they are a reader's first introduction to the story and are influential in framing perspectives and interpretation from the outset.

The larger size of the headline font reinforces the lead positioning of this story. It is blue in colour, which differentiates it from the standfirst, in black type, indicating that it contains the most important information. The colour and the size of the headline also help it to compete for attention amongst the multiple stories that appear on the home page (some featuring celebrities), the colour photographs, a cartoon and other headlines designed to bait readers with words such as 'racism', 'bizarre divorce' and 'slave girl'. However, it is likely that the news value and the serious content of our story is the reason for its prominence.

The headline 'Five British service personnel killed in helicopter crash in Afghanistan' would have a significant impact on its local UK readers, particularly those who are likely to be concerned about their own nationals fighting in a foreign land. The headline alone has all the elements of drama and tragedy. Firstly it indicates the 'who' – that is, the five British personnel who have been killed. The label 'service personnel' appears to underplay the victims (they are not 'air crew', for example). We find later in the story that they are probably described in this way because they are from different parts of the British military – the airforce, the army air corps and the army reserve. The 'where' of Afghanistan is also included in the headline (a location readers already associate with war and conflict), as well as the 'what' (a helicopter crash resulting in deaths).

The standfirst beneath the headline intensifies the drama by providing more detail: 'Bloodiest day for foreign troops in Afghanistan in 2014, as NATO forces prepare to withdraw this year.' The superlative 'bloodiest' is graphic. It is the lexicon of battle not of an accidental crash, which reinforces an aversion to the loss of life in the circumstances of this story. The reference to NATO (the North Atlantic Treaty Organization, the intergovernmental military alliance based on the North Atlantic) also introduces the wider significance of the crash by reinforcing the sense of unity between British troops and their NATO allies who, together, must bear the consequences of this long and drawn-out war. The tragedy and the irony of the circumstances are accentuated when we are told that the NATO forces are close to withdrawing from the area. The framing of this standfirst in the context of withdrawal, while evoking sympathy that these deaths have occurred just a few months prior, works in two additional ways. Firstly, it softens the blow of this news for the British public as it puts a time limit on the involvement of their troops in Afghanistan. But secondly, it also serves the interests of the politicians, whose decision it has been that the UK military should be in Afghanistan, by indicating the upcoming end of involvement. The reason for the helicopter crash is not stated on the home page, though the words 'crash', 'Afghanistan' and 'bloodiest' appearing in close proximity to each other hint that this may well have been the result of a planned attack. To seek more information the readers must move to the full story on its own web page, which we turn to examine next. Because of its size, we are able to reproduce a screenshot of only part of the web page, though this includes some of the important features to which we refer in our analysis. However, in the next section we have extracted the text and numbered the paragraphs for easy reference.

The web page in Figure 16.3 featuring the full helicopter crash story, written by *The Telegraph's* defence correspondent and another journalist, has its own headline and standfirst. They focus on the fact that it is British troops who have died and the repetition of the word 'killed' in both sentences reinforces a sense of tragedy. It is the first time that the Ministry of Defence is named as the source of the story, indicating that the news is official. But it is also interesting that the verb 'disclose' is used in relation to the MoD rather than 'announce', implying there has been some sort of secrecy around this event, perhaps because of a delay in its confirmation. Remember our discussion earlier of social practice in the framework of discourse analysis, based on Fairclough's work. This news article sits within a discourse environment where many readers would already be familiar with the war against al Qaeda and the Taliban in Afghanistan that began in 2001 and the deaths of troops from the United States, Britain and forty-six countries who were part of the International Security Assistance Force. Readers' perceptions about what happened from what has been revealed so far, in both sets of headlines on the home page and the story web page, may well lead them to assume that the helicopter crash resulted from an intentional attack on British troops by the Taliban.

The photograph directly beneath the headlines showing an armed jeep and troops walking with guns in the KAF Air Field in Kandahar, Afghanistan, is an archived image taken four years earlier. It provides a visual element to the story in the absence of any current photographs and serves to reinforce a discourse of war and an atmosphere of tension relating to the living and working conditions of the British troops. However, in an updated version of the story which appeared at 8.00am on 27 April, the photograph is replaced by a video (lasting 1 minute, 38 seconds) showing an airforce commander in the UK confirming the accident in an official statement to the media. This illustrates how the insertion of video into news stories, as another mode of communication made possible through the internet, can bring a greater sense of reality, dynamism and emotion in contrast to the traditional limitations of the hard copy format using print and photographs only.

So far, from these headlines, we are aware of the helicopter crash, where it happened, and who was involved. Still to be answered are the questions as to *when* it actually happened and *why*. We now move to examine the event structure of the rest of the story to establish what the story tells us has happened and whether it will reveal the cause of the crash.

## Event structure

In examining the event structure of the story we want to see how the journalists relate what has happened. Included in this investigation is not just the identification of events as they occurred and the specific order in which they are presented, but also the people involved (the news actors), locations and times. The full text of the *Telegraph* story is reproduced below. For ease of reference, each paragraph (some of which are just one sentence long) has been numbered.

### Full text of the *Telegraph* story

1 Five British service personnel were killed when the helicopter they were travelling in crashed in southern Afghanistan.

2 The Lynx helicopter crashed during a routine flight in Kandahar province, the Ministry of Defence (MoD) said.

3 Three of the servicemen were from the Army Air Corps, based at RAF Odiham in Hampshire. One was a Royal Air Force serviceman also based at RAF Odiham. One was a member of the Army Reserve from 3 Military Intelligence Battalion, based in London.

4 The Taliban had tried to claim responsibility for the deaths but Major General Richard Felton, Commander Joint Helicopter Command, said on Saturday night that the crash appeared to be a 'tragic accident'.

5 He said: 'It is with great sadness that we must confirm that five UK service personnel have been killed in this incident which, at this early stage, would appear to have been a tragic accident.

6 'Events like this, whilst mercifully rare, remind us of the risks our personnel face in their work in Afghanistan as we approach the conclusion of the combat mission later this year.

7 'Our thoughts are with the families and loved ones of those who have lost their lives.'

8 David Cameron, the Prime Minister, said his 'heart goes out to the families and friends of those killed in this terrible tragedy'.

9 Mr Cameron said: 'Every British fatality is a source of deep sadness. This latest incident, which has cost the lives of five UK service personnel, brings home to us all once again how our armed forces continue to put their lives on the line to help the people of Afghanistan.

10 'I cannot pay high enough tribute to each and every one of them for the job that they do and the sacrifices that they make.'

11 Ed Miliband, the Labour leader, said: 'This is a tragic and poignant reminder of the sacrifices made by our Armed Forces in serving our country with bravery and distinction.

I pay tribute to them and their continuing work in Afghanistan, elsewhere abroad, and here at home.

12 'I mourn with all those who have lost loved ones, their grief is shared by people right across Britain at this very sad time.'

13 The helicopter, a Lynx Mk9, crashed on Saturday morning close to Kandahar Airfield.

14 The accident was the deadliest air disaster for UK service personnel in a war zone for almost eight years and took the total number of British casualties in the country to 453.

15 It comes just a few months before British forces are due to withdraw from Afghanistan and hand over security to local forces.

16 The MoD said the crash was under investigation. The next of kin of all five servicemen have been informed.

17 The Westland Lynx Mk9 is being phased out and replaced, although its reliability has not previously been questioned.

18 Saturday's incident was the worst for British troops since March 6, 2012, when a Warrior armoured vehicle was blown up by a roadside bomb. Six soldiers from the Yorkshire Regiment died in the blast.

19 In September 2006, a Nimrod aircraft crashed after a catastrophic fire on board, killing 14 crew members. An official inquiry blamed the crash on systemic failings and cost-cutting by the MoD.

20 A spokesman for the Nato-led International Security Assistance Force (ISAF) said it was investigating yesterday's helicopter crash. 'ISAF is still in the process of reviewing the circumstances to determine more facts,' the spokesman said.

21 A local police spokesman said the wreckage was in the Chaghrai area of Kandahar province's Takhta Pul district, about 30 miles from the Pakistan border.

22 Said Ahmad Zia Durrani, a spokesman for Kandahar's police chief, told the Sunday Telegraph that the helicopter was on a 'training flight' and it was unclear why it had crashed. But the same spokesman also told the news agency Agence France Presse: 'It was doing military exercises and crashed as a result of a technical fault.'

23 A spokesman for the governor of Kandahar, which neighbours Helmand, said he believed a technical failure was to blame.

24 The crash marked the bloodiest day for all foreign troops in Afghanistan in 2014. In December, another Nato helicopter – a Blackhawk – was shot down by the Taliban in the southern province of Zabul, killing six American personnel onboard.

25 Immediately after that crash, US officers suggested the helicopter had come down due to a mechanical failure but that the crew may then have come under fire. Officials later said that Taliban militants had brought down the aircraft.

26 Lynx helicopters are light utility aircraft used for a wide range of operational capabilities, including transport and resupply. They usually carry a crew of three, including a gunner. It is thought that the other two military personnel on board could have been travelling as passengers.

27 Paul Beaver, a defence analyst, said: 'It is difficult to speculate on what has happened, but it sounds like this was a flying accident instead of a case of the aircraft being shot down.

28 'It could be weather-related, it could be dust or it could have been trying to avoid birds, for example, or it could be some kind of mechanical failure.'

29 Investigators will examine the helicopter's log books and other documentation, weather conditions and if it was carrying out an authorized job according to its capabilities.

30 Nato forces are currently preparing to withdraw combat troops by the end of this year, with responsibility for fighting the Taliban insurgency handed over to the Afghan army and police.

31 The International Security Assistance Force (ISAF) coalition of international forces said earlier today in a statement: 'Five International Security Assistance Force service members died as a result of a helicopter crash in southern Afghanistan today.

32 'ISAF is still in the process of reviewing the circumstances to determine more facts. Our thoughts and prayers go out to the family and friends affected this tragic event.' (Reproduced with permission from Telegraph Media Group Ltd)

The lead sentence (paragraph 1) is the introduction to the main story and here we are provided with much the same information already given in the headlines. However, it is interesting that the past tense 'were killed' is used here rather than the present perfect 'have been killed' in the standfirst above. The past tense conveys a greater sense of time lapse, and it is possible that this relates to a delay in the official confirmation of the crash and consequential late publication of the story, as we suggested earlier.

It is in paragraphs 2–7 where we learn several facts from the quoted sources of the Ministry of Defence and Major General Richard Felton, Commander Joint Helicopter Command (possibly one and the same source). These facts are: that the helicopter (identified as a Lynx model) was on a routine flight; that the servicemen came from different divisions within the British army and air force based in Odiham and London; and that the crash was most likely an accident rather than the result of combat. In paragraph 4, uncertainty surrounds the inclusion of information about possible Taliban responsibility for what happened. The words that state they had 'tried to claim' responsibility for the deaths indicate that enough time has elapsed since the crash for them to do so – which is another clue to delay in the official confirmation of the deaths. It is not clear who reported the Taliban's claim, but the repetition by General Felton in both paragraphs 4 and 5 that the crash both 'appeared' and 'would appear' to be a 'tragic accident' serves to counteract any other suggestion until further information is obtained.

Felton, in his reported quotes in paragraphs 5–7, uses conventionalized expressions of sympathy that we would associate with official military discourse: 'It is with great sadness that we must confirm…' and 'Our thoughts are with the families…'. He uses the collective pronouns of 'we' and 'our' as he speaks officially on behalf of the British services (and to a certain extent the British public, who may share the sentiments) in expressing 'great sadness' for the victims and their families. Felton is also the same spokesperson who features in the updated story video clip mentioned earlier where he stands outside the Odiham air force base to deliver a statement using similar words to those published in the story. However, when questioned by a journalist at the end of the video about the cause of the accident, the General responds that he is neither willing to answer questions nor to speculate about why the crash happened when an investigation is ongoing.

The expressions of sympathy continue in paragraphs 8 to 12 with the reported responses from British politicians, the Prime Minister David Cameron and Leader of the Opposition Ed Miliband (presumably provided from released statements to the media). Both, besides offering condolences to the friends and families of those who have been killed, use emotive language about the tragedy of the crash, the bravery of British armed forces, and focus on the theme of service to the United Kingdom and the Afghan people. Again the words 'tragic' and 'tragedy' are repeated and relate closely to others that are used: 'grief', 'sadness' and 'sacrifice'. Although from opposing political parties, the common discourse of nationalistic compassion from both Cameron and Miliband in showing respect for the nation's defence force personnel and their families would be an appropriate response in the eyes of the British public. Such reporting of the comments of political leaders in times of national significance would also be an expectation of the readers of a British online newspaper. From this point on there seems to be little new information to report on the actual helicopter crash, particularly as it appears that the only factual information available has come through the official sources. Rather there is now a move in the story to speculate on the cause of the crash – probably the most burning question for the journalists and their readers. At this stage the media are able to only add further information by drawing on what they can find out about the design and make of the helicopter, other historical incidences of casualties in Afghanistan, and comments from other sources.

Paragraph 13 repeats information about the crash and, for the first time, the timing of the accident on the previous day – 'Saturday morning' – is actually stated. More detail is provided on both the model of the helicopter – a Lynx Mk9 – and the location of the incident 'close to the Kandahar Airfield' (which features in the photograph). Paragraph 14 intensifies the seriousness of the crash by placing it in a historical context and describing it as 'the deadliest air disaster for UK service personnel in a war zone for almost eight years'. Numerical information is included in the same sentence as we are told that the total number of British casualties in Afghanistan now stands at 453 as a result of this crash. This information in paragraph 14 serves to heighten the stakes in the story, although this may be counteracted somewhat in paragraph 15 where, once again, the intent is stated 'to withdraw British forces and hand over security to local forces' in the coming months. This raises hope that perhaps this will be the last loss of life among British troops in Afghanistan before they depart.

It is in the first sentence of paragraph 16, however, that readers are told for the first time that the crash is 'under investigation'. This is followed by another sentence stating simply that 'the next of kin of all five servicemen have been informed'. The placing of these two sentences together is ambiguous as it is not clear whether the next of kin have been informed about the investigation or merely of the deaths. If the latter, the story does not include the servicemen's names, which are usually released once next of kin have been notified. It is possible that these details are not yet known, though we cannot be sure. However, another story that appeared on *The Telegraph* website at 10pm on 27 April is devoted to this aspect. It identifies the servicemen and publishes their individual photographs (sourced from the MoD, according to its reference). This follow-up story also provides information about the servicemen's specific duties and includes tributes in the body of the text from their families or commanding officers.

The notification of the investigation half way through the story, however, offers a turning point in its narrative as it launches into speculation about the possible cause of the crash. This is done either through the provision of information that implies a possible cause or by way of the reported speech from other sources. Sentences 17–19 offer a mix of information that does not flow cohesively. The sentences jump back and forth in the topics they cover, either by stating details about Lynx helicopters, what they are used for, and potential technical problems, or by highlighting other attacks on British or foreign troops – which seems to imply that an attack by the Taliban should not be discounted. Information about the fatal crash of a Nimrod aircraft in 2006, for example, is noted by an official inquiry as being due to 'systemic failings and cost-cutting by the MoD', and this opens the possibility that the Ministry might be at fault. The mention of an official inquiry also appears to link to the next paragraph (20) which identifies the Nato-led International Security Assistance Force (ISAF) as the body investigating this latest crash.

The next paragraphs from 21 on include several sources commenting on the crash. These include a local police spokesman on behalf of Kandahar's police chief, who gives contradictory information. The story reports in paragraph 22 that, on the one hand, the spokesman told *The Sunday Telegraph* (the Sunday edition of *The Telegraph*) that the reason for the crash during a 'training flight' was unclear, while on the other hand, he told the news agency Agence France Presse that it occurred as a result of a technical fault while involved in military exercises. Another spokesman, this time for the governor of Kandahar, suggests in paragraph 23 that technical failure was to blame, while a 'defence analyst' in paragraphs 27 and 28 (no credentials are cited), evaluates a range of possible causes other than being shot down, such as the weather, dust, avoidance of birds or mechanical failure. Paragraph 29 states that the investigators will examine helicopter documentation including log books, check weather conditions and whether the helicopter was 'carrying out an authorised job according to its capabilities'. This information is not attributed as coming from any particular person, but may possibly have been the suggestion of the defence analyst, or the ISAF, or the journalists who have written the story.

Interspersed amongst the news sources offering their opinions are several paragraphs that provide information not directly related to this crash. Yet they still imply that there are possible causes to be considered. These include details about the operational capabilities of the Lynx helicopters as well as the description of another incident five months earlier involving the crash of a NATO Blackhawk helicopter. The US officers, we are told, who originally reported that this crash resulted from mechanical failure, later announced that Taliban militants were responsible for shooting it down. The implication is that this may, too, prove to be the case in this latest crash.

The final paragraphs of the story are rather oddly placed: 30 repeats information about the withdrawal of NATO forces from Afghanistan, and paragraphs 31 and 32 return to the ISAF announcing this latest helicopter crash, their reviewing of circumstances to 'determine more facts', and offering sympathy to friends and family affected. It is possible that the ISAF might have been the first to confirm that the crash had occurred, and that this was followed by an official statement from the British commander.

Additional information to be noted on this web page are the availability of links to related stories and videos for readers wishing to access more information. Even though they must navigate to these, titles such as 'Afghan tour winds down', 'Afghan Red Cross attacked' and 'Afghan guard shoots dead three foreigners at hospital' contribute to the overall discourse about the war in Afghanistan, the dangers that abound and the need to withdraw troops.

## Overview

After this analysis of the text we are in a better position to comment on the overall story and how it has been constructed on a news organization's website. The story topic is deemed important enough in the eyes of *The Telegraph* to give it top billing: the majority of its readers would be British and would therefore have a vested interest in the story of the death of five British troops. As a result the story features prominently as the lead story on the home page, with the full story appearing on a separate web page complete with text and photographs (and a video in a follow-up story) and links to related stories and videos.

The initial focus is on the official confirmation of a helicopter crash in Afghanistan where five British servicemen have been killed. As is usual practice for journalists, the story begins with the most newsworthy information first, which is then embellished with additional information that often serves to background the story. This story has been written by two journalists who have pieced together information provided through official sources – the Ministry of Defence in Britain and the International Security Assistance Force – both of which state that the crash was a 'tragic' event but do not give its cause. The story, while devoid of direct commentary from the journalists, intimates an atmosphere of secrecy from the official sources, and it appears there has been some delay in receiving the information, suggesting that it has had to do the rounds of top military and political people before being released, as well as notifying next of kin.

While the story features expressions of sympathy from two key British political figures, the real story that we determine the journalists are after is that there is a need to find out who or what is responsible for the crash. This highlights the ongoing news value of the story which moves to speculate on causes. By drawing on an interesting diversification of news actors as sources whether a spokesman in Afghanistan, a 'defence analyst' or the media agency Agence France Presse, the story points to several possible causes including misuse of the helicopter, a technical failure, Ministry of Defence budget cuts, atmospheric conditions, or an attack by militants. Although this offers a smorgasbord of possibilities, it is the possibly faulty helicopter and a Taliban attack that receive the most attention in this story. The rather jumbled mix of reported statements, facts on helicopters and references to other incidents that happened in 2006, 2012 and 2014, shows a lack of cohesion in the story structure. This is quite typical of early reports about such events and may well be indicative of the pressure on journalists to be first with a story in the face of fierce media competition – particularly with online platforms enabling instant publication. It is interesting to note how this story incorporates earlier incidents, whether crashes caused by combat or technical failure, or the repeated mention of the upcoming withdrawal of troops. This cross-referencing impacts on readers' overall understanding and ownership of a situation which involves the loss of British lives during war and may influence their attitudes towards long-running distant conflicts like Afghanistan. Overall this story is constructed in such a way that it uses the minimal official information available on the crash, but investigates it further by looking at possible causes using other sources and references to related stories.

**KEY POINTS: Frameworks for analysis**

- Three influential frameworks for analysing news, developed since the 1980s, are those of Bell, van Dijk and Fairclough.
- Analysis of news discourse requires a close reading of the text and identification of certain features such as language, sources, images and event structure.
- Critical discourse analysis is concerned with language, power and ideology.
- Discourse practice is concerned with the production, distribution and consumption of a text.

WEBSITE: **Group exercise**

Many modes of communication are used on a news organization's home page. Go to the website where, in a small group, you can identify and discuss the various modes located in a news home page of your choice. A list of questions is provided to guide you in your analysis.

## EXERCISE 16.3

1. Find a news story on a website to analyse.
2. Read it as you would normally at one go without stopping to review.
3. Then look away and write down a quick summary of what you think the story is about.
4. Now go back and do a more detailed analysis of it. If possible print out a copy of the page and number the paragraphs for easy reference.
5. Pay attention to where the story first appears on the website. Is it placed in a prominent position? What makes it stand out – does it have a heading and a standfirst? What colour and size are the fonts and are there photographs, diagrams, or videos included?
6. Who is the story written by – the organization's journalists or is it provided from another agency? What are the sources of the story and how has the news organization come by this information?

7. Is the story interesting on a local, national or international level? If so, why?
8. Examine the event structure of the story. What information is reported on first? Are the events in chronological order? If not, why do you think this is done? Does this affect the cohesion of the story?
9. What sort of language is used in the story? Look at the quoted speech of sources as well as the way situations are described. Does the story involve emotion? How is this expressed and how might this effect the readers' interpretation?
10. Are there links to related stories on the web page? What further information do they provide and is this useful for the reader?
11. What evidence can you find of any referencing to earlier stories or events used to explain or provide background for the current story?
12. Finally, go back to the notes you took about the story at the beginning. How do these compare now that you have analysed the story? How influential was the story in your understanding of the situation? Do you agree with it?

## 16.5 SUMMARY

Our objective in this chapter has been to make you more critically aware of the construction of news in today's society and how meanings that are conveyed through words and images can influence us in the ways we think. There is no doubt that the media perform an important function in our daily lives in bringing us the news whether in print, by broadcast, or through digital platforms. We have an expectation that the media will provide us with stories that will keep us informed about the world around us, that they will probe and investigate by asking the questions behind occurrences, and that they will bring us the truth behind stories.

However, we have been concerned with showing you how the media construct reality through certain forms and conventions of journalistic practice within news organizations, and how various discourses are produced that may influence the way we think about various topics and form impressions of others. We have shown you the complexity surrounding the construction of news stories as various semiotic dimensions come into play drawing on Wodak's (2006: 4) description of these as:

> texts, images, the link between text and image, the production of texts by journalists and news agencies, intended and optional readings (i.e. the *dialogicality of news*), the ideological and economic interests of the newspapers, broadcasting and TV companies, and their owners, the presupposed knowledge of the readers, historical (national) traditions of news reporting, recent global influences, and so forth.

Our example of the analysis of a news story, as well as the various exercises in this chapter, have been designed to give you the skills for you to make your own judgements when it comes to understanding the media and their messages. The French philosopher Ricoeur once stated that 'language does not speak, people do' (1976: 13). This chapter has given you a foundation to see the reality behind these words.

WEBSITE: **Media discourse**

A list of multiple-choice questions on media discourse can be found on the website. This is a good way to test your knowledge about what you have learned from this chapter!

## SUGGESTIONS FOR FURTHER READING

Bell, A. and Garrett, P. (eds.) (1995). *Approaches to Media Discourse*. Oxford: Blackwell. This edited book provides insight into the main approaches to media discourse. Included are chapters by the academics we have referred to in our 'Frameworks for analysis' section – Allan Bell, on the discourse structure of news stories, Norman Fairclough, on an analytical framework to examine political discourse in the media, and Teun van Dijk, on opinions and ideologies in the press. Further information on these authors' frameworks can be found in their publications under references in this chapter.

Cotter, C. (2010). *News Talk: Investigating the Language of Journalism*. Cambridge University Press. This books draws on the author's knowledge of linguistics and journalism to trace news stories from start to finish. She looks at the processes behind the production of news and the speech events and social practice of the media community to demonstrate how these shape the language of news.

Matheson, D. (2005). *Media Discourses: Analysing Media Texts*. Maidenhead: Open University Press. For those students wishing to explore media discourse beyond the news, this book ventures into areas such as reality television, broadcast interviews, sports commentary, consumer magazine, and new media genres.

# ANSWERS TO EXERCISES

## Exercise 16.1

1. None of these headlines is ideologically neutral – though some are stronger in the way they frame the story than others.
   (a) Aljazeera's headline provides a soft approach in using hedging language 'could affect' – to indicate the *possibility* of a negative outcome of the gas debt on the rest of Europe, but it does embody a warning.
   (b) The headline from the Russian news agency Itar-Tass might appear to be ideologically neutral because it simply announces that it is publishing the full text of Putin's speech. However this, in fact, serves a political purpose for Putin in simply reproducing his political discourse about the situation without any critique, paraphrasing or commentary. In effect Itar-Tass acts as a 'mouthpiece' for Putin and leaves readers to make their own judgement.
   (c) The headline of Ukraine's English-language newspaper presents Putin as making a veiled threat to European countries, implying that the possible end of Russia's subsidizing of Ukraine will affect them.
   (d) The BBC's use of 'warns' and (e) TVNZ and (f) the ABC network's use of 'threatens' in their identical headlines indicate Putin's negative attitude towards Ukraine and its debt to Russia. Note here that TVNZ and the ABC networks' source for this story is a news agency, the Associated Press, so that the angle of this headline used by both is likely to have been reproduced from there.
   (g) The order of the words in this headline from the *Financial Times* is interesting because it foregrounds 'Europe supply' as the focus of the story rather than the 'Ukraine gas cut'. The juxtapositioning of Europe and Ukraine puts greater pressure on the European leaders in taking responsibility for Ukraine's debt – but this can be seen as an ultimatum from a powerful Putin.
2. The headlines in this exercise demonstrate how the news media construct reality in different ways. Those that use words such as 'warn', 'threaten', 'jeopardy' and 'cut' create an atmosphere of concern, while Aljazeera's hedging raises less anxiety. The reproduction of Putin's speech might be considered 'real', however it is this Russian leader's own discourse and version of reality that dominates.

## Exercise 16.2

A journalist would seek out as much information as possible for this story by contacting official sources such as the police and the fire department. He/she would aim to find the most newsworthy angle by establishing the facts behind the fire by asking the 'who, what, when, how and why' questions. But of particular interest would be whether the fire was caused by an arsonist and whether anyone died or was hurt. In looking for story angles the journalist might attend the scene of the fire to speak with people onsite for their comment or even find eye witnesses who can give their account of what happened. Follow-up stories could include the school's response to the fire and how this has affected the students, what evidence there is to show any connection with the other fires, and whether anyone is arrested as a result.

The discourse analyst would look at how the text of the fire story was presented. Questions that would be asked are: what has the journalist seen as the most newsworthy angle and how has he/she used language to describe what has happened? Has the journalist interviewed people as sources that provide interesting quotes, what type of language is used to describe the effects the fire has had on the school, teachers, neighbours etc.? Does the journalist provide background information on the other fires and attempt to suggest a link between them all? What images are used to support this story? After analysing the text the researcher would be in a better position see what sort of discourse was being conveyed. This might relate to a lack of support from the authorities in catching an arsonist, or one of heroism in the community if someone demonstrated bravery. More broadly, the analyst might ask: why has the fire been reported at all?

### Exercise 16.3

As we are unable to comment on the individual text you have chosen to examine for this exercise, it would be useful for you to have a fellow discourse analyst examine the same text as you to see if they agree with your findings. Have you interpreted the story in the same way? Have you highlighted the same discoursal features (language, cohesion, images) of the story? What beliefs, attitudes or ideological assumptions do you both have that might affect the same or different interpretations of the text?

## REFERENCES

Bell, A. (1991). *The Language of News Media*. Oxford: Blackwell.

(1998). The discourse structure of news stories. In A. Bell and P. Garrett (eds.), *Approaches to Media Discourse*, pp. 64–104. Oxford: Blackwell.

(2003). A century of news discourse. *International Journal of English Studies*, 3(1), 189–208.

Bell, A. and Smith, P. (2013). News discourse. In C. Chapelle (ed.), *The Encyclopedia of Applied Linguistics* (online edition). Oxford: Blackwell.

Bhatia, A. (2013). Critical discourse analysis: history and new developments. In C. Chapelle (ed.), *The Encyclopedia of Applied Linguistics* (online edition). Oxford: Blackwell.

Broersma, M. and Graham, T. (2012). Social media as beat: tweets as a news source during the 2010 British and Dutch elections. *Journalism Practice*, 6, 403–19.

Devereux, E. (2003). *Understanding the Media*. London: Sage Publications.

Fairclough, N. (1995). *Media Discourse*. London: Edward Arnold.

Hoechsmann, M. and Poyntz, S. (2012). *Media Literacies: A Critical Introduction*. Malden, MA: Blackwell.

Jones, R. (2012). *Discourse Analysis: A Resource Book for Students*. New York: Routledge.

Matheson, D. (2004). Weblogs and the epistemology of the news: some trends in online journalism. *New Media & Society*, 6(4), 443–68.

(2005). *Media Discourses*. Maidenhead: Open University Press.

Ouyang, H. (2013). Fairclough, Norman. In C. Chapelle (ed.), *The Encyclopedia of Applied Linguistics* (online edition). Oxford: Blackwell.

Pavlik, J. (2000). The impact of technology on journalism. *Journalism Studies*, 1(2), 229–37.

Potter, W. (2013). *Media Literacy*. London: Sage Publications.

Ricoeur, P. (1976). *Interpretation Theory: Discourse and the Surplus of Meaning*. Fort Worth: Texas Christian University Press.

Smith, P. and Bell, A. (2007). Unravelling the web of discourse analysis. In E. Devereux (ed.), *Media Studies: Key Issues and Debates*, pp. 78–100. London: Sage Publications.
Talbot, M. (2007). *Media Discourse: Representation and Interaction*. Edinburgh University Press.
Turner, N., York, D. and Petousis-Harris, H. (2009). The use and misuse of media headlines: lessons from the McNZB immunisation campaign. *The New Zealand Medical Journal*, 122(1291), 22–7.
van Dijk, T. (1983). Discourse analysis: its development and application to the structure of news. *Journal of Communication*, 33(2), 2–43.
(1985). Introduction: Discourse analysis in (mass) communication research. In T. van Dijk (ed.), *Discourse and Communication: New Approaches to the Analysis of Mass Media Discourse and Communication*, pp. 1–9. Berlin: Walter de Gruyter.
(1991). *Racism and the Press*. London: Routledge.
(1992). Discourse and the denial of racism. *Discourse and Society*, 3(1), 87–118.
(2000). New(s) racism: a discourse analytical approach. In S. Cottle (ed.), *Ethnic Minorities and the Media: Changing Cultural Boundaries*, pp. 33–49. Buckingham: Open University Press.
Wodak, R. (2006). Images in/and news in a globalised world: introductory thoughts. In R. Wodak and G. Myers (eds.), *Discourse Approaches to Politics, Society and Culture, DAPSAC 18*, pp. 4–16. Amsterdam: John Benjamins.

## ELECTRONIC SOURCES

Farchy, J. and Chaffin, J. (10 April 2014), 'Europe supply in jeopardy as Putin warns of Ukraine gas cut', *Financial Times*. Retrieved 12 April 2014 from www.ft.com/cms/s/0/04c551ce-c0b6–11e3-a74d 00144feabdc0.html#axzz2yX1DprOH
'President Vladimir Putin's letter to leaders of European countries. Full text' (10 April 2014), Itar-Tass news agency. Retrieved 12 April 2014 from http://en.itar-tass.com/russia/727287
'Putin: Ukraine debt threatens Europe gas supplies' (10 April 2014), *American Broadcasting Corporation News*. Retrieved 12 April 2014 from http://abcnews.go.com/International/wireStory/pro-russians-call-east-ukraine-region-independent-23266278
'Putin: Ukraine debt threatens Europe gas supplies' (10 April 2014), *Television New Zealand*. Retrieved 12 April 2014 from http://tvnz.co.nz/world-news/putin-ukraine-debt-threatens-europe-gas-supplies-5909135)
'Putin: Ukraine gas debt could affect Europe' (10 April 2014), *Al Jazeera*. Retrieved 12 April 2014 from www.aljazeera.com/news/europe/2014/04/putin-ukraine-gas-debt-could-affect-europe-2014410172010575368.html
'Putin's letter to European leaders: Russia subsidized Ukraine for four years' (10 April 2014), *Kyiv Post*. Retrieved 12 April 2014 from www.kyivpost.com/content/ukraine/putins-letter-to-european-leaders-russia-subsidized-ukraine-for-four-years-342908.html
Sandford, D. (10 April 2014). 'Putin warns Europe of gas shortages over Ukraine debts', *British Broadcasting Corporation*. Retrieved 12 April 2014 from www.bbc.com/news/world-europe-26975204)

# 17 Literary linguistics

MICHAEL BURKE

**KEY TERMS**

- alliteration
- assonance
- consonance
- deixis
- discourse presentation
- foregrounding
- formalism
- functionalism
- metre
- multimodality
- point of view
- pragmatics
- rhetoric
- semantics
- style

**PREVIEW**

This chapter explores how language, grammar and rhetoric can be employed as critical tools in text analysis, and in particular, in the analysis of literary texts. The logical point of departure in literary linguistics is that since prose and poetry are made up of words, phrases, clauses and sentences, the most appropriate way to analyse those texts is by means of linguistic frameworks. Just as an art critic might come to a balanced interpretation by observing and commenting on patterns of things like colour, depth and form, so the literary linguist can attain a grounded understanding of the textual object of investigation, as it were, by detecting and reporting on perceptible lexical, syntactic and discoursal patterns within a given context.

In this chapter, you will first be introduced to the historical background of literary linguistics as it developed in the twentieth century. Thereafter, we will consider some of the directions the field is taking today. Lastly, and moving on to a more practical side, you will be introduced to a range of literary linguistic tools and methods. The focus here will be on analysis up to and including the sentence level. It is here that we will be exploring the notion of foregrounding at the levels of language. The goal is to anchor our literary interpretations and evaluations in concrete linguistic description. By the end of the chapter, not only will you have acquired a firm knowledge of the history, tools and methods of literary linguistics, you will also be able to bring what you have learned to bear on your own literary linguistic analyses.

## 17.1 INTRODUCTION

The term 'literary linguistics' is often used interchangeably with 'stylistics'. Literary linguistics does not engage solely in the analysis of literary texts, but in other discourse forms too, including political discourse, advertising discourse, legal discourse and even everyday conversation. The reason for this is that the notions of creativity and innovation in language are not just confined to the realm of literature. Just look at the world around you: the internet, the television, even the public texts on display on your university campus.

Most definitions of literary linguistics focus on method (see, for example, Simpson 2004 or Nørgaard, Busse and Montoro 2010). They emphasize that an analysis should be evidence-based and therefore recoverable. It is for this reason that a substantial part of this chapter will be devoted to what we might call 'literary linguistics in practice'. It is also here that we see that literary linguistics is very much a form of 'applied' linguistics.

The literary linguist is a kind of empirical/forensic discourse critic who goes in search of language-based evidence in order to either support or challenge the interpretations and evaluations of literary critics and/or cultural commentators. The tools that are brought to bear in this stylistic analysis come from the domains of morphology, phonology, lexis, syntax, **semantics**, as well as from the various discourse and pragmatic models.

Literary linguistics is of significance in language studies because it can arm you, as students, with critical, descriptive linguistic tools. In addition to this, there is a second angle to literary linguistics, namely, that it provides what we call an evidence-based model that will assist you in your learning of English grammar. If you have always struggled to understand dry constituent categories like nouns, verbs, tenses, adverbs, adjectives, prepositions, etc., then literary linguistics will give you the opportunity to encounter, play around with and ultimately learn all of these through the accessible and pleasurable framework of creative texts.

## 17.2 The development of literary linguistics in the twentieth century

Now we have had a taster of what literary linguistics is, let us explore its roots. Although the real origins of literary linguistics are to be found in classical **rhetoric**, as alluded to at the end of the previous section, the modern ones are firmly located in the twentieth century, and especially in Charles Bally's 1909 treatise on French stylistics and in Leo Spitzer's 1928 'Studies in Style'. These authors, however, wrote in their own languages for relatively restricted audiences. For this reason, it is Roman Jakobson, who we should refer to as the father of modern literary linguistics. He was a leading figure in the Russian Formalist movement of the early twentieth century, which was also known as the 'Moscow Linguistic Circle'. While there, he worked with many other prolific scholars. One of these was Viktor Shklovsky, who claimed in his work that the function of art was to make people see the world in novel and stimulating ways. This was to be achieved, he said, through a process called 'defamiliarization'. Another important affiliate of this group was Vladimir Propp, whose focus was primarily on the narrative structure and morphology of texts and in particular folk tales. Much of the groundwork for modern literary linguistics was laid down by these Russian scholars. Owing to the political and social upheavals that were taking place just after the First World War and the Communist Revolution, Jakobson fled Russia and found refuge in the country known in those days as Czechoslovakia, where he became a founding member of the 'Prague Linguistic Circle', also known as the 'Prague School' or the 'Prague Structuralist Movement'. At the outbreak of the Second World War, he found himself fleeing politics and war once again, this time to end up in the United States. It was only then that we in the West started to find out about his work, as it was translated into many languages including French, German and especially English. Throughout the entire period of his life, Jakobson and his colleagues conducted research and developed theories on language communication. Jakobson was particularly interested in 'the poetic function of language', which is why he is so important for literary linguistics.

Just like the ancient rhetoricians before him who explored the nature of *kairos* and the rhetorical situation of a discourse act, Jakobson was interested in mapping the constitutive factors of any speech event or act of verbal communication. Following up on Bühler's earlier 1934 claim that there are three parts to any discourse act (a speaker, a message and a hearer), Jakobson suggested that there are in fact six basic functions to any act of communication. He said that in any situational context there is an addresser (1), who sends a message (2), to an addressee (3). Further, the message requires a context (4), and needs to be in a code (5), that is common to both the speaker and hearer. Finally, there needs to be contact (6), a physical and psychological connection, including voice quality and gestures, between the speaker and hearer that enables them to partake in the communication. Table 17.1 presents an overview of how Jakobson modelled these six basic functions at the time.

He later went on to complete this six-part basic scheme with what he called an associated 'function of language' for each part. This can be seen in Table 17.2.

Jakobson said that although all the functions play a role, one of them had to be dominant in any given context. He first thought that this would be the addresser, or the addressee or the message. He concluded later, however, that the dominant function of speaking and writing is on the message itself, namely, on its **style** (Jakobson 1960). Here we see how the message/text rises to the top in terms of importance in meaning making. We call this strong emphasis on the linguistic form '**formalism**' or 'textualism'.

While working in the Prague School in the 1920s and 1930s Jakobson became interested in the notion of **foregrounding**, a concept which had been developed by Jan Mukařovský, who was a key figure in the Prague School (see Garvin 1964). Put simply, foregrounding highlights the poetic function of language and in particular its ability to deviate from the linguistic norm and to create textual patterns. This idea not only built on Shklovsky's earlier work on 'making strange' (defamiliarization), but was, in effect, a

**TABLE 17.1** Jakobson's six basic functions of any communicative act

| | | |
|---|---|---|
| | (4) CONTEXT | |
| (1) ADDRESSER | (2) MESSAGE | (3) ADDRESSEE |
| | (6) CONTACT | |
| | (5) CODE | |

**TABLE 17.2** Jakobson's six associative functions of language

| | | |
|---|---|---|
| | (D) REFERENTIAL | |
| (A) EMOTIVE | (B) POETIC | (C) CONATIVE |
| | (F) PHATIC | |
| | (E) METALINGUAL | |

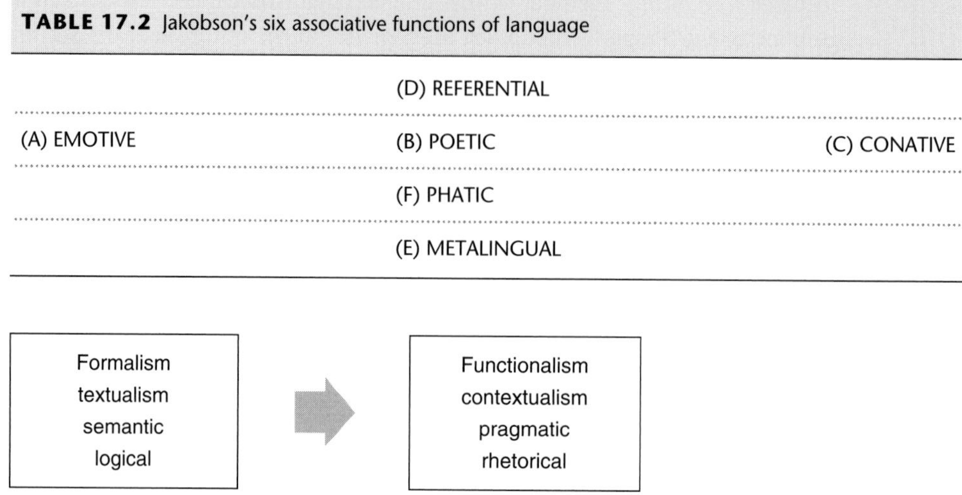


**Figure 17.1** The shift in meaning making from formalism to functionalism

modern description, at a meta-level, of the basic workings of schemes and tropes from classical rhetoric. In addition to this, the Prague School moved away from formalism, where the emphasis in meaning making was mainly on the logical and semantic message/text, to something called functionalism, which, in addition, considered the context too in the process of rhetorical and pragmatic meaning making. Figure 17.1 above shows this development at four different levels.

**KEY POINTS: The development of literary linguistics in the twentieth century**

- Roman Jakobson, and his fellow Russian Formalists, set out much of the textual framework for modern literary linguistics.
- Jakobson was primarily interested in language communication and in particular the poetic function of language with an emphasis on the text/message.
- The Jakobsonian model has six parts: the addresser, the message, the addressee, the context, the code and the contact (as well as the six associative functions of language).
- The Prague structuralists added a functional dimension to formalism. They also developed the key literary linguistic notion of 'foregrounding'.

## EXERCISE 17.1

1. Which of these concepts does not fit within the framework of formalism, and why?
   (a) Logic
   (b) Text
   (c) Rhetoric

(d) Grammar

(e) Propositional meaning

2. Which of these concepts does not fit within the framework of functionalism, and why?

(a) Rhetoric

(b) Pragmatics

(c) Context

(d) Discourse

(e) Logic

## 17.3 The main branches of literary linguistics today

As we have seen, for much of the twentieth century literary linguistics was chiefly a formalist affair, with the form of the text and language playing a dominant role. This is not surprising, since literary linguistics takes its methodological prompts from both the dominant literary and the prevailing linguistic theories of the time. In many ways then, literary linguistics is sandwiched between the two disciplines, with one foot in literary theory and the other in linguistic theory, as you can see in Figure 17.2.

So, for example, in the 1950s and 1960s, when the 'pure' textual approach of new criticism from literature was in vogue, together with the universality of generative/transformational, Chomskyan grammar from linguistics, literary linguistics was primarily a formal matter too. As time went on, however, this kind of narrow textualism came in for serious criticism, chiefly because it ignored contextual factors such as the reader/listener and his/her mental input in meaning making. Formalist approaches in literary linguistics were to last up to the early 1970s. After this period, the content, the reader and the role of nurture began to assert a hold (it was also at this time that the functionalist work of the Prague School was being discovered in the West, owing to translations from the Czech language). This led to so-called phenomenological and reader-response approaches in literary theory, which were interested in subjective experience rather than objective reality.

**Figure 17.2** The main theoretical influences on literary linguistics

In linguistic theory, a similar development took place, which led to a more functionalist approach. This meant a move away from the dominant Chomskyan notions of 'deep structure' and 'universalism' in grammar and language. Literary linguistics, as you might be able to predict by now, followed suit and started to look at the context as well as the text.

The main literary linguistic tools employed in this period in the analysis of literary texts were taken from Michael Halliday's theory of 'systemic functional grammar' (Halliday 1985). The 'system' that is alluded to in the name does not involve a rigid or universal one-to-one mapping, but rather it includes various options and the construal of meaning, and all this depends on the contexts in which words find themselves. We could say that it does not just look internally to formal grammatical properties, but also externally to higher-level systems of discourse interaction. It is now that contextual factors like genre, register and ideology come into play. The notion of transitivity is important in literary linguistic analysis. The way Halliday refers to this concept is not in its default grammatical sense of whether a verb takes an object or not, but rather within the framework of his notion of 'ideational' meaning, i.e. how language, through such things as nominals, verbals and adverbials, represents participants, processes and circumstances in the experiential world (see Halliday 1985).

You might say as well that, in general, a contextualized approach to literary linguistics also considers what might be termed the sociocultural context of any given reading situation. Key questions here pertaining to the text are 'who speaks?', 'to whom?', 'where?', 'when?', 'how?'. In posing these questions, notions like **deixis**, **point of view** and social relationships now start to play a role. The text is no longer paramount. Rather, it is the text in conjunction with the context that counts in meaning creation.

Towards the end of the twentieth century, a further development took place in linguistic scholarship as it started to move from functionalist approaches to cognitive ones. This allowed for extra contextual dimensions to be explored. This primarily pertained to what goes on in a reader's mind and body when he/she reads as well.

If we look back to the last thirty years or so, a number of developments that are particular to literary linguistics can be mapped out. A major expansion concerns discourse and pragmatic approaches which look at how literary language functions in regard to both text and context (see Verdonk 1993). Studies in this area ordinarily focus on such things as characterization, power relations, conversation structures, **discourse presentation**, etc. Many of the key analytic concepts that are employed here come from the field of **pragmatics**, about which you have already read extensively in Chapter 8. These include the cooperative principle, inferencing, politeness, presupposition, relevance theory, speech act theory, turn-taking. This opens up lots of analytic potential for the literary linguist. For example, in his/her analysis, a literary linguist might now explore such literary pragmatic phenomena as impoliteness in Shakespeare's *Julius Caesar*, or conversational implicature in Ian McEwan's *Atonement*, or presupposition in the short fiction of Grace Paley, or code-switching in Jane Austen's *Persuasion*.

Another major branch of literary linguistics in this period is critical literary linguistics (Fowler 1986; Jeffries 2010), which also includes a feminist variant (Mills 1995; Jeffries

2007; Montoro 2011). These critical approaches draw heavily on the Hallidayan toolkit that we spoke about earlier from systemic functional grammar. One of the main objects of such an analysis is to look at how social patterns of language can influence how it is perceived and understood. Feminist approaches also build on earlier work done in feminist literary criticism to provide a gender perspective for the critical analysis of literary and other texts.

Pedagogical approaches to literary linguistics also emerged in this period. They tend to focus either on how useful literary linguistic analysis is for teaching the language of literature or on how productive literary linguistics is for teaching grammar and proficiency to both second language learners and first language speakers. In this second sense, it takes on the role of language learning through the analysis of creative discourses, such as literature. Here, it is very close to its old classical rhetorical roots (Widdowson 1992; Clarke and Zyngier 2003; Burke 2010a, 2010b; Burke et al. 2012).

A relatively recent, but very productive advance in literary linguistics is a corpus approach, developed from computational and corpus linguistics. It uses large text corpora, such as the British National Corpus (BNC), together with so-called concordancers (corpus tools) like *Wordsmith* (Scott 2004), in order to gain evidence-based empirical insights into language usage and patterning (Semino and Short 2004; Stubbs 2005; Mahlberg 2007).

Further recent approaches to literary linguistics include new historical ones, which look diachronically at changing styles in literary language (Busse 2010); **multimodality** approaches which seek to push stylistic scholarship out of beyond the printed word to encounter how other semiotic modes such as images help to construct meaning (McIntyre 2008; Montoro 2010; Nørgaard 2010) and cognitive ones, which attempt to describe and account for what happens in the minds of readers when they interface with (literary) language (Stockwell 2002). Cognitive literary linguistic studies are productive and taking their cues from both cognitive linguistics and cognitive psychology have explored a whole range of phenomena. These include conceptual metaphor theory (Freeman 1995), schema theory (Cook 1994; Semino 1997), contextual frame theory (Emmott 1997), parabolic functions (Burke 2003), blending theory (Dancygier 2006) and text world theory (Lahey 2006; Gavins 2007). More recently, there has been a turn in cognitive literary linguistics towards the concept of emotion and what happens in both the mind and brain during literary discourse processing. In this neuroscientific domain, the focus is on both style in the mind and style on the page/screen (Burke 2011, 2013; Hogan 2013, 2014).

This then concludes the overview of what literary linguistics is, how and why it developed the way it did and what its main branches and approaches are today. In the next section, we will look at what constitutes a literary linguistic analysis. We will be focusing on what happens at and below the level of the sentence, rather than what happens above the sentence level, which has already been alluded to when we discussed such pragmatic models as inferencing, politeness theory, turn-taking and speech act theory. Most importantly – and in line with the adage that 'real learning is doing' – in this next section you will learn how to conduct your own literary linguistic analysis.

**KEY POINTS: The main branches of literary linguistics today**

- Formalist approaches and analyses in literary linguistics gave way to Hallidayan functional approaches.
- The functional turn in literary linguistics led to a range of discourse and pragmatic approaches being adopted in literary linguistic scholarship.
- In the late twentieth century many new approaches developed including critical and cognitive ones.
- Current popular methods in the field of literary linguistics in the twenty-first century include multimodal, corpus and emotive approaches.

**EXERCISE 17.2**

1. Which of the following concepts below would you say does not primarily fall within the framework of a cognitive literary linguistic analysis, and why?
   (a) Text world theory
   (b) Blending theory
   (c) Conceptual metaphor theory
   (d) Schema theory
   (e) Feminist theory
2. Which of the following concepts below would you say does not primarily fall within the framework of a pragmatic literary linguistic analysis, and why?
   (a) Corpus methods
   (b) Politeness theory
   (c) Speech act theory
   (d) Conversational implicature
   (e) Turn-taking

## 17.4 Literary linguistic method: foregrounding and analysis

Foregrounding in language usually entails one or more of three things: repetition, parallelism or deviation. The deviation in question is either from some internal or external norm. Foregrounding can take place visually or from an auditory perspective. The act of foregrounding also prompts readers and listeners to search for additional levels of meaning and to look for semantic links within the recurrent lexical items. Much of this work initially happens subconsciously. There is also a strong affective aspect to foregrounding in both the pleasant satisfaction of noticing it at work and in being unknowingly moved by it.

Strategic acts of foregrounding in language, as indeed in music and pictorial art, can lead to powerful emotions in readers, listeners and viewers alike.

We can make a general division in literary linguistic analysis of, on the one hand, a foregrounding analysis of the linguistic levels and, on the other, the application of pragmatic frameworks. In the previous section, we were introduced to some of the many pragmatic and discourse tools which can be applied to literary texts to bring forth new aspects of meaning for further interpretation. As mentioned, we will not expand further on these in the rest of this chapter. Our analytic focus from here on in will be on a foregrounding analysis of the linguistic levels both under and at the sentence level. We will have a particular focus on deviation rather than parallelism and repetition, although all three will play a role. Brief overviews of the grammatical categories will be given just to refresh your memory. However, you are encouraged to go back and reread the relevant parts of earlier chapters in this volume on phonetics, phonology, morphology, grammar, syntax and semantics.

A question that you as a budding literary linguist always need to pose yourself at this initial stage is at what linguistic level is the repetition, parallelism or deviation occurring? For this, you will need to have a good grasp of the grammatical basics. In Table 17.3 a number of linguistic phenomena are listed. These are also the tools that go into your literary linguistic toolkit. They are listed here from 1–8 in broadly ascending order of size. (By 'size' I mean that when we are talking about a morpheme or a phoneme, we are looking at something that is much more discrete in actual, physical scope than say a discourse act or a pragmatic utterance).

It should be noted that although these linguistic levels are represented as individual units here, they are dependent on one another in a text. Our focus for now will be on the six smaller units; the ones operating at or below the sentence level, that is, from the phonological level up to the syntactic one. We will consider the first three together – phonology, graphology and **metre** – as they are closely related when encountered in written form. We will then look at morphology, followed by lexis/semantics and finally

**TABLE 17.3** The linguistic levels of analysis

| |
|---|
| 8. Pragmatic |
| 7. Discoursal |
| 6. Syntactic |
| 5. Lexical/Semantic |
| 4. Morphological |
| 3. Metrical |
| 2. Graphological |
| 1. Phonological |

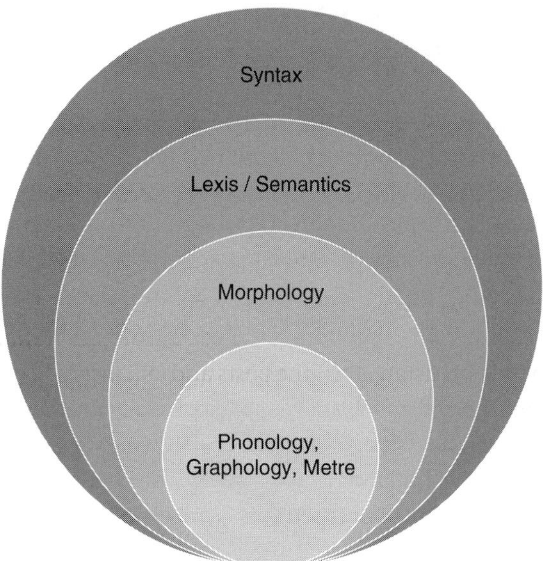


**Figure 17.3** Linguistic levels of foregrounding (at or below the sentence level)

syntax. Once you have seen how a literary linguistic foregrounding analysis is done, you should be able to embark on one yourself. Just to help you understand these levels a little more clearly, in Figure 17.3 they are reproduced in a more accessible manner.

Foregrounding is often present in all good prose and poetry. However, it is by no means limited to the poetic genre. Indeed, there is arguably just as much linguistic deviation, repetition and parallelism going on in the persuasive world of advertising, political discourse, legal discourse, etc. Let us look at several examples now beginning with the smaller linguistic units that we have placed together here for practical purposes: phonology, graphology and metre.

### 17.4.1 Phonological, graphological and metrical foregrounding

Literature is mostly on the page. It is a visual phenomenon. On top of that, the vast majority of fiction reading done these days takes the mode of a silent procedure. Conversely, linguistic sounds are in the auditory world of speech. In light of this, the question can be posed as to whether literary linguistics can have a phonological dimension at all. Well, arguably, it can, and this is where foregrounding in graphology and patterns in metre and rhyme come in. Foregrounding certainly occurs in prose. However, it is arguably more common in poetry. In this section we will consider a number of categories including **alliteration**, **consonance**, **assonance**, sound symbolism, graphology and rhyme and metre.

Let us take the first three together. Alliteration, consonance and assonance are all figures of speech from classical rhetoric. Alliteration is the repetition of consonants in two or more words. The consonants in question are usually in the initial position of a word and fall on stressed syllables. Alliteration occurs in poetic language but it is also prevalent in idiomatic expressions such as 'as blind as a bat' or 'as dead as a dodo'; in tongue twisters such as 'round the ragged rocks the rascal ran' or 'she sells sea shells on the sea shore' and in advertising discourse such as 'You'll never put a better bit of butter on your knife' (from Country Life Butter) or 'In touch with tomorrow' (from Toshiba Electronics).

Consonance is similar to alliteration, except it is the repetition of consonants that are stressed in the same place in different words but with different vowels. Moreover, consonance is usually at the end position of words. In this sense we can see it as a kind of end alliteration or in some cases an instance of half rhyme. The famous advertising slogan 'Beanz, meanz Heinz' is a good illustration of this. There are examples from literature too, such as the sentence 'he thrusts his fists against the posts and still insists he sees the ghosts' which is from Stephen King's horror novel *It.*

Assonance pertains to the rhyming of vowels and diphthongs, rather than consonants. It also does not take the close location of consonants into account, as is the case in consonance. It is also known as half rhyme or partial rhyme. Below we can see how some of the vowels and/or diphthongs rhyme in the words 'lonely/floats', 'high/hills', 'host/golden', 'beneath/trees', etc. from the famous poem 'Daffodils' by William Wordsworth.

I wandered lonely as a cloud
That floats on high o'er vales and hills,
When all at once I saw a crowd,
A host, of golden daffodils;
Beside the lake, beneath the trees,
Fluttering and dancing in the breeze.

When delivered orally, the foregrounding of sounds is certainly an aid to memory for the speaker and also the hearer. It also gives emphasis to that particular part of the word, and in doing so, brings it to our attention. Such cases of what we might term 'sound symbolism' can have onomatopoeic affects.

Just like alliteration and assonance, onomatopoeia is also a style figure from the classical world of rhetoric. Onomatopoeia is a word that in its pronunciation suggests the sound of the object or the process that it is describing. For example, when you put your bacon in a frying pan it 'sizzles', when a bird takes flight its wings 'flutter', when you quickly need a carton of milk you might 'zip' down to the shops. All of these words, and many more, like the sounds animals are said to make, are onomatopoeic in English.

In literature, all these things we have just mentioned can have pleasing effects. Consider the alliteration in the following lines, from the prologue to Act 1 of William Shakespeare's *Romeo and Juliet.*

From forth the fatal loins of these two foes;
A pair of star-cross'd lovers take their life.

However, alliteration can also have a much more 'representative' or sound-symbolic effect and in doing so help create meaning in the poem. For example, the repetition of the letter 's' in the opening lines of George Macbeth's poem 'Scissor-Man' below onomatopoeically gives off a palpable sense of danger and menace. The oppressive and foreboding atmosphere is brought about to a large extent by this foregrounded sound symbolism. From a graphological perspective, the lines appear to stick out erratically in a thrusting fashion, and as such are foregrounded, which may add to the palpable sense of a threat established by the alliterative 's'.

I am dangerous
    in a crisis
with sharp legs and a screw
    In my genitals.

Alliteration can also be found in many a newspaper headline where it is often employed playfully.

> Petrol, pasties and the politics of panic: No.10 shambles over drivers hoarding fuel, and the tax on takeaway food (*The Daily Mail*, 27 March 2012)

Such examples of foregrounding lead readers to make subconscious inferences about what their purpose might be in a text. In a sense, linguistic deviation employed in creative texts has priming effects.

Alliteration, assonance and consonance all have the effect of clustering sounds and in this sense we can see how rhyme, metre and even rhythm are categories that can be dealt with here in this section on phonology. It is a fact that all language has rhythm. You may not have thought about it this way before, but it does. English happens to be what is called a 'stressed-timed' language. This means you can keep adding syllables to a sentence and as long as they are not stressed it won't make much different to the duration of utterance. That may sound a bit strange, but if you don't believe me, try reading aloud the sentences below.

Students write papers

The students write papers

The students write the papers

The students are writing the papers

The students have been writing the papers

You would think that by adding syllables the sentence would take you increasingly longer to say aloud. However, this doesn't really happen, does it? The reason for this is that in all these sentences there are just three stressed syllables, namely 'students', 'write' and 'papers' and this doesn't change. So it takes approximately the same length of time to read these sentences aloud. This works for stressed-timed languages like English, but not for so-called 'syllable-timed' languages, like, for example, French, where every syllable takes approximately the same amount of time to be pronounced. This implies that the longer the sentence, the longer it will take you to read it aloud. These may seem like subtle variations, but they are important. Indeed such distinctions in prosody are worth bearing in mind when you are learning a new language, like French, as it will also account for why English speakers find the French language so difficult to articulate (and vice versa).

Let us now look at a related matter, namely, rhyme. Rhyme takes place when two words (or more than two in some cases) end in stressed syllables. It is usually the final consonant and vowel sounds that are the same, e.g. 'people' and 'steeple' or 'coffee' and 'toffee' or 'running' and 'stunning'. Metre, a phenomenon often mentioned in relation to rhyme, refers to patterns in poetic discourse and more specifically to the patterns of both stressed and unstressed syllables. It is thus concerned with periodic units of rhythm in a line. Traditionally metre (also referred to sometimes as 'metrics' or 'prosody') has been the domain of the literary theorist rather than the linguist, but the literary linguist must also take it into consideration as one of his/her stylistic analytic tools.

A 'foot' is what we call a metrical unit in verse. A foot has two parts. The first part comprises of one stressed syllable, known traditionally as 'ictus', which is often represented visually in the following way [/]. The second part of the foot comprises of one or more unstressed syllables. The customary name for this is a 'remiss' and it is often represented visually with the following symbol [X]. Let us try this out. If you were to say aloud 'di-dum, di-dum, di-dum' (X /, X /, X /), you are pronouncing, on three occasions, an unstressed syllable, i.e. a remiss marked 'X', followed by a stressed syllable, that is, an ictus marked '/'. You would also be articulating the most common foot which is known as the 'iamb'. You might have heard of the phrase 'iambic pentameter' somewhere before. Pentameter means 'five feet' (*pente* is the Greek word for five). Consider the following line from the poem 'To Autumn' by John Keats.

To swell the gourd, and plump the hazel shells.

We can now 'scan' this line ('scan' is from the term 'scansion' meaning to read the beats in the words/lines). You can see in Table 17.4 that it is in perfect iambic pentameter, namely, two beats – one unstressed followed by one stressed – repeated five times. I have also included the accompanying scansion ictus and remiss marks in the table in order to make it clearer for you.

There are more patterns at a poet's disposal than just iambs and all of these can appear in two, three, four, five, six or even more feet. If you can remember a bit of Greek from school, then you might be able to work out that these are called 'dimeter' (two feet), 'trimeter' (three feet), 'tetrameter' (four feet), 'pentameter' (five feet), 'hexameter' (six feet), etc. Let us briefly look at some of these other patterns.

If you were to invert the iambic structure, pronouncing the stressed syllable first, then you would be using the second most common foot which is called the 'trochee'. Try saying

**TABLE 17.4** A scanned line of poetry in iambic pentameter

| X / | X / | X / | X / | X / |
|---|---|---|---|---|
| To swell | the gourd | and plump | the ha- | -zel shells |

aloud 'dum-di, dum-di, dum-di, (/ X, / X, / X) just to get the feeling of trochaic metre. Both the iamb and the trochee are made up of one stressed and one unstressed syllable. However, two other common feet in English poetry are made up of three 'beats', as it were, rather than two. The first of these has two weak (unstressed) syllables followed by one strong (stressed) one, or to put it in the jargon of prosody, two remises followed by an ictus, as in 'di-di-dum, di-di-dum, di-di-dum' (X X / | X X / | X X/). This is known as an 'anapest' in the discourse of prosody. It sounds a bit like a galloping horse, doesn't it? The second of these three-beat metres comprises a stressed syllable followed by two unstressed ones as in 'dum-di-di, dum-di-di, dum-di-di' (X X | / X X | / X X), which is known as a 'dactyl'. You can remember this pattern by thinking of certain names. The actors Jennifer Aniston and Christopher Eccleston both have double dactylic names, as does the UK long jumper Christopher Tomlinson. Dactyls have the onomatopoeic effect of appearing to 'trip up', as it were, which is not handy if you happen to be an actor or a long jumper.

These four then (the iamb, the trochee, the anapest and the dactyl) are the most common metrical forms in English poetry. Two others that come up on a semi-regular basis, often used as 'fillers', are the so-called 'pyrrhic foot', which is made up of two unstressed syllables 'di-di, di-di, di-di' (X X, X X, X X) and the 'spondaic' foot which, counter to the pyrrhic metre, has two stressed syllables 'dum-dum, dum-dum, dum-dum' (/ /, / /, / /).

Foregrounding in metre can be achieved quite easily and at different levels as long as the writer is skilled and knows how and when she/he wishes to deviate from the norm that he/she has set up. For example, a line in dactylic hexameter, which also happens to be the main metre of classical Greek prose, might only stay true to its pattern until the sixth unit, where a poet might employ an anapest, purposely upsetting the metrical apple cart, as it were, and bringing the semantic content of this part of the line to the reader's or hearer's attention. A person could also do this in the middle of a line, on say the third or fourth unit. Alternatively, a poet could produce foregrounding at a 'higher level' than the single line by having the first three lines of a short four-line poem – or advert or song lyric for that matter – in iambic pentameter and then have the final line in, say, iambic hexameter (to highlight the final two 'extra' beats of the line) or in trochaic pentameter (to highlight and thus foreground the entire line against the rest of the text). Such instances of deviation from a steady pattern can alert readers and listeners and draw them in.

Finally in this section, we will briefly consider foregrounding at the graphological level which we alluded to briefly when we discussed the 'Scissor-man' poem. Text, unlike oral performance, is silent. However, a writer can choose to speak or even shout in a text by utilizing the formatting tools at his/her disposal. Imagine you were to open your literary linguistics syllabus/ course manual and you see the following instructions presented in this way.

ALL assignments must be handed in <u>personally</u>.

Late assignments will **not** be marked.

You should see that your lecturer is kind of 'shouting' i.e. emphasizing – by means of capitalization, underlining and the use of a bold font – that (a) it concerns every assignment you write, (b) you have to show up yourself to hand them to him/her, and (c) the assignments must be on time otherwise your lecturer won't look at them at all, resulting in a very low grade.

In creative texts, like fiction, poetry and advertising discourse, such graphological foregrounding draws your attention and suggests extra levels of meaning. Consider the line below from the second stanza of Ted Hughes' poem 'The Crow's First Lesson':

'No, no', said God. 'Say Love. Now try it. LOVE.'

Here we see how his use of capitalization foregrounds the already highlighted concept of love.

If you are a fan of the *Discworld* novels by Terry Pratchett you might have noticed how the recurring character 'Death' always speaks in small capitals, as such his discourse is foregrounded against that of other characters.

In this next example, from the novel *The Curious Incident of the Dog in the Night-Time* by Mark Haddon, the graphological foregrounding, in the use of a bold font, both highlights, and helps perform, as it were, the autism of the main character:

> Mother was a small person who smelt nice. And she sometimes wore a fleece with a zip down the front which was pink and had a tiny label which said **Berghaus** on the left bosom. (2004, p. 24)

Another more traditional form of graphology is so called 'concrete poetry' inspired perhaps by George Herbert's poem 'Easter Wings' from 1633, whereby the layout of the text in the poem is manipulated on the page to project the form of the subject matter of the poem. So a poem about a horse would be in some equine shape, a poem about crying would be in the shape of a tear streaming down a person's cheek and a poem about birds migrating would place the words of the poem in the small shapes of distant migrating birds. Such poems are not really foregrounded internally but externally as they go against the norms of other more regular poetic forms (more about this internal–external division later). Graphological considerations these days come under the remit of multimodal analysis, which seeks to add to the literary linguistic toolkit by using things such as images, colour, layout, typography and other semiotic modes.

**KEY POINTS: Phonological, graphological and metrical foregrounding**

- The smallest units of foregrounding involve phonology, graphology and metre/rhyme.
- Phonological foregrounding (repetition, parallelism or deviation) can find form in alliteration, consonance, assonance, sound symbolism, onomatopoeia, etc.
- Graphological foregrounding (repetition, parallelism or deviation) can find form in typography, font, colour, layout, etc.
- Metrical foregrounding (repetition, parallelism or deviation) depends on the type of metre (e.g. iambic, trochaic, anapestic, dactylic, etc.) and the length of the foot (e.g. trimeter, tetrameter, pentameter, etc.).

**EXERCISE 17.3**

1. Which of the three (alliteration, consonance or assonance) is most prevalent in the examples of advertising slogans below. Motivate your answer.
   (a) Don't dream it. Drive it [Jaguar cars]
   (b) It beats as it sweeps as it cleans [Hoover vacuum cleaners]
   (c) Your potential. Our passion [Microsoft computer software]
2. Which metres are these two lines in? Speak them aloud slowly over and again. Now write them out and try scanning them using the ictus and remiss symbols.
   (a) 'Come live with me and be my love'
   (Christopher Marlowe,'The Passionate Shepherd to his Love')
   (b) 'Half a league, half a league, half a league, onward'.
   (Alfred, Lord Tennyson 'The Charge of the Light Brigade')
3. What is the main metre of all limericks?

## 17.4.2 Morphological foregrounding

Morphemes, as you probably know from the extensive description in Chapter 4, are the building blocks of words. There are two main kinds of morphemes: free morphemes and bound morphemes. Many words in the English language are made up of both free and bound morphemes. The three main ways of generating new words in general is by inflection, derivation or compounding. The words that make up free morphemes can stand alone; they are words in their own right. Free morphemes are either grammatical or lexical. Lexical free morphemes are probably the most common. Some examples are 'henhouse', 'bookshelf', 'mousetrap', 'armchair, 'yearbook', etc. These examples have been generated through the process of compounding, rather than that of inflection or derivation and are therefore known as 'compound words'. Lexical free morphemes rely on open-class, content words, like nouns and lexical verbs, which carry meaning. Grammatical free morphemes are made up of closed-class, function words, like prepositions and pronouns.

The other main type of morpheme is known as a bound morpheme. In English, bound morphemes can only appear as part of a larger word. For example, the word 'unbound ' uses the bound morpheme 'un'. You can also have larger combinations, such as the word 'unfortunately' which has four morphemes one free ('fortune') and three bound ('un', 'ate' and 'ly'). Standard bound morphemes are affixes, which can be defined as a morpheme attached to a word stem or root (essentially a free morpheme) to form a new word. In English the most common affixes are prefixes and suffixes. Prefixes, as the word suggests, appear before a stem or word. Indeed, the element 'pre' in the word prefix is, in fact, a prefix. Other prefixes include bound morphemes like 'un' as in 'unnatural, 'dis' as in 'disused' and 'im ' as in 'imperfect', etc. Suffixes appear after a stem or word. Examples of these are bound morphemes like 'ness' as in 'kindness', -'ation' as in 'combination' and 'ment' as in 'shipment'.

All this sets the scene as to how words might deviate at a morphological level in literary linguistics analysis. The answer is by adding a beginning or an ending (or even in some cases a middle, known as an 'infix') to a word that it would not normally have. Some well-used examples in literary linguistics classrooms come from the pen of the twentieth-century poet E. E. Cummings. For example, in his poem 'from spiraling ecstatically this' he writes the following line:

The whole perhapsless mystery of paradise

Here the word 'perhaps' which ordinarily has no suffix, acquires one and in doing so becomes foregrounded against the background of more regular discourse in the poem. He might have written 'perhapsship' or 'perhapsment' or 'perhapness' or even 'perhapslessness' instead. More examples, again from Cummings, can be found in his poem 'pity this monster manunkind'. Indeed, even in the title line there is the infix –'un-', which is unusual in English except in humourous expletives, such as 'abso-bloody-lutely' and 'fan-f**kin-tastic'. The –'un-' in 'manunkind' also has the function of a prefix to the word 'kind'. Later in the same poem we encounter the foregrounded word 'unwish' and indeed, in other poems by Cummings you will come across words like 'unhearts', 'unminds', 'unselves', 'unlives', 'undeaths', 'unfree'.

Both literary writers and corporate advertisers know that there is huge scope for extending words with prefixes, like for example 'un', or suffixes, like for example, 'less', and that we as consumers of language (and the products they represent) somehow implicitly know this. For instance, a word like 'homeless' is in common usage, while 'houseless', although acceptable, is far less common. Words like 'maybe-less', 'alongsideness' and 'sandwichness' are clearly not frequently deployed and as a result would therefore be stronger examples of foregrounded language if found in texts.

Other words can be extended, as it were, with suffixes. A common example of this is the word 'proof', in the sense of 'impervious to penetration', as in the common word 'waterproof'. Similar words in the same field include 'weatherproof', 'dampproof' and 'rainproof'. Extended, but still acceptable, terms include 'foolproof', 'childproof' and 'soundproof'. Creative, and thus foregrounded, terms might be words like 'Gruffalo-proof', 'cricketproof', 'ironyproof' and 'grammarproof', as in:

- I've told my two-year- old daughter that the new wallpaper in her bedroom is definitely *Gruffaloproof.*
- My mother is 100% *cricketproof.*
- I am afraid that my new boss is terminally *ironyproof.*
- The young man who always sits at the back during his literary linguistics class is irredeemably *grammarproof.*

**KEY POINTS: Morphological foregrounding**

- Morphology is a relatively 'lower' level of foregrounding involving free and bound morphemes.
- Free morphemes can be lexical or grammatical. They are words in their own right. Bound morphemes are not words in their own right. They involve, for example, affixes being attached a word stem (essentially a free morpheme) to form a new word.
- With free morphemes, foregrounding can occur when two or more lexical items are brought together to make new, but recognizable, creative compounds. With bound morphemes, foregrounding can occur when unusual affix–word combinations are produced.
- Infixes are not usually found in regular English, but can be made use of for humorous or creative effects.
- Once a suffix is in broad use, it can be expanded almost exhaustively across the language (as the 'proof' example in the text shows)

**EXERCISE 17.4**

1. Which of the following is not an example of a free morpheme? Motivate your answer. Once you have found it, try expanding it with affixes in order to foreground it.
   (a) Doghouse
   (b) Textbook
   (c) Boyish
   (d) Carport
2. The lines below are all from different poems by E. E. Cummings. As best you can, using the discourse of an analytic linguist, try to describe the morphological foregrounding that is taking place in these examples.
   (a) The mouth reacts curvingly
   (b) The guests arrive floatingly
   (c) Bits tumble hushingly
   (d) The world floats away crylaughingly

## 17.4.3 Lexical and semantic foregrounding

Lexical deviation can take several forms in literary linguistic analysis. We cannot consider them all, but some of the ones we will look at here include neologisms (invented words), functional conversions (the process of converting one word from one grammatical class to another) and style/genre breaking (the taking of a word or form that would normally occur in a specific register of English and putting it where it ordinarily does not belong). Interestingly, such unexpected variations and deviations in lexical style can indirectly point you as a reader to a possible anomaly or crisis, either ongoing or upcoming, in the world of the story or in the mind and/or life of the character involved.

Neologisms draw our attention and trigger us to start searching either consciously or subconsciously for added layers of meaning. Consider stanza thirteen below from Gerard Manley Hopkins's famous long poem 'The Wreck of the Deutschland', which laments the sinking of a German passenger ship in 1875 and the huge loss of life.

Into the snows she sweeps,
Hurling the haven behind,
The Deutschland, on Sunday; and so the sky keeps,
For the infinite air is unkind,
And the sea flint-flake, black-backed in the regular blow,
Sitting Eastnortheast, in cursed quarter, the wind;
Wiry and white-fiery and whirlwind-swivelled snow
Spins to the widow-making unchilding unfathering deeps.

Coinages such as 'flint-flake' and 'Eastnortheast' arguably exhibit a playfulness of language which can engage and even delight readers in spite of the seriousness of the poetic story content. Perhaps the most powerful neologisms, however, in this stanza occur in the final line. Premature death and the tragedy of not being able to experience parenthood are excruciatingly painful enough for an involved person who is looking on to endure, but the coinages 'unchilding' and 'unfathering', which can also be classed as forms of morphological foregrounding, somehow, in their newness and deviation from the norm, contain an added intensity of driving home the tragedy of what we might call, in fitting neologistic style, 'unparented loss'.

The stanzas preceding this one arguably do not contain as many new word forms as this one does, nor do the ones that follow. In this sense then, we could infer that this stanza might itself very well be foregrounded at a lexical level within the context of the entire poem, drawing our attention to it in an act of secret discourse that says 'Hey, I am significant, pay more attention to me ... I have something extra to share about the meaning of this poem that only attentive and engaged readers may get access to'. Sometimes such foregrounding has a so called 'iconic' element to it, that is, the form seems to reflect part of the semantic notion of the surrounding textual content as in the two examples below from James Joyce's *Ulysses*:

Davy Byrne smiledyawnedandnodded all in one

Just mix up a mixture of theolologicophilolological

Popular culture abounds with neologisms, arguably none more so than cartoon show *The Simpsons* where during almost every episode you can come across deviant lexical items embedded in ordinary discourse. Some examples include 'sacrilicious' (which is Homer's description of a waffle landing in his mouth while he is praying), 'safen-up' (Homer's order to his factory coworkers to work less recklessly in front of the new German factory owners), 'Saudi-Israelia' (uttered by Bart's date when she tells him that sex on prom night is just as American as our 51st state, Saudi-Israelia).

Of course, over time some neologisms enter the lexicon and in doing so are no longer viewed as new or foregrounded. All of the following words, expressions and phrases are said to have been coined by Shakespeare and used for the first time in his plays, e.g. 'frugal', 'horrid', 'obscene', 'the milk of human kindness', 'foregone conclusion', 'green-eyed monster', 'a sorry sight', one fell swoop', 'cruel to be kind', and many, many more: hundreds, in fact. Today, however, none of the lexical items or phrases would seem new or strange. There is no deviance in their usage in expected contexts. We might conclude that Shakespeare's lexical dexterity and creativity has become our everyday normality and it is this path that most neologisms inevitably take, unless they disappear as quickly as they arrived. The reason for this is that language is anything but a static object to be pinned down and logically appraised. Rather, language is a mobile phenomenon to be chronicled and marvelled at.

We can also see this with so-called 'functional conversions' whereby words that are originally only used as nouns or verbs or adjectives cross boundaries, as it were, and grammatical classes. Many words in English have both verb and noun grammatical functions. For example, you can 'bank (v) your money in the Bank of Dave in Burnley' (n) or you might 'strike (v) a police officer during a strike (n)' or you could 'drink (v) a drink (n) at a drinking (a) party'. Not all English words are as grammatically flexible as these are, and this leaves room for the creative juices of writers to flow, whether they are those of poets, fiction writers, advertising designers or political speech writers. Take for instance the noun 'table' which has relatively recently crossed grammatical boundaries to act as both a verb and an adjective in the context of, 'he tabled a motion' and 'the committee rejected his tabled motion'. Interestingly, the word 'table' does not yet appear with ease in other regular discourse contexts. If you were to say 'He tabled a contract' or 'He tabled a CV' or even the more literal 'He tabled a cup and saucer', these will still be foregrounded.

Some nouns are already very flexible in contexts. The noun 'eye', for example, can be used almost ubiquitously as a verb, albeit in slang English. This is not the case for all human body parts. For example, as I write sitting here in my study at home on a Sunday morning I can 'eye' the ring dove sitting on the garden shed in my back garden, but I cannot 'ear' the blackbird sat on the opposite wall. Creative writers can exploit such deviations. For example, a new novel about a linguistics student at university might open with a scene where she is 'i-padding' her way across a number of theories or 'Kindling' her sources for a paper or 'Facebooking' her way to an F grade.

A further form of lexical foregrounding is style/genre breaking, that is, taking a word that would normally occur in a specific register of English and putting it with a register where it ordinarily does not belong. For example, if you have ever read any poetry by Phillip Larkin you will see that coarser words like expletives occur amid the most poetic and deeply philosophical of poetic lines. Try reading poems like 'Vers de Société', 'High Windows' and 'This Be the Verse' to see what I mean.

Semantic deviation is similar and yet different to lexical deviation. The difference lies in the fact that it has a strong paradoxical aspect to it. Consider the opening line to George Orwell's acclaimed novel *1984*:

It was a bright cold day in April and the clocks were striking thirteen.

The line is already in a highly foregrounded position in that this is the opening discourse to the novel. Impressions you as a reader might get upon reading this opening line include (a) clocks don't strike thirteen, even twenty-four-hour clocks, (b) thirteen is an unlucky number, (c) April days are not supposed to be cold, because if they are, then the newborn of the spring will die of exposure. In short, there is a semantic inconsistency which draws you in and sends you subconsciously reeling in search of added meaning. You might be thinking, something is not quite right here or even something not too nice may be about to happen to the main character or his world.

The poet Emily Dickenson is no stranger to semantic paradox, as many lines from her work attest. Look at the following three lines from different poems:

1. This is the hour of lead
2. I felt a funeral in my brain
3. Pain has an element of blank

Semantic deviation plays on presupposition and inference, concepts, as we saw, that are prevalent in the field of pragmatics. We expect certain words to appear in certain contexts because of their meaning and our past experience of them. Let me take one of the examples from above to show what I mean. In the line 'This is the hour of lead', it is the word 'lead' that is foregrounded. We do not expect it, and as such it strikes us along with all its connotational and analogical values of 'dark', 'heavy' and 'harmful'. What we might expect is something like 'This is the hour of judgement' or 'This is the hour of destiny' or 'This is the hour of truth'. These are quite abstract nouns compared with something as material and tangible as lead. The use of such a concrete noun in a linguistic setting that usually prefers abstract ones might act to heighten the strength of the foregrounding effects.

**KEY POINTS: Lexical and semantic foregrounding**

- Lexis is a mid-range level of foregrounding in the range of levels running from phonemes to syntax.
- It involves a number of lexical phenomena including neologisms, functional conversions and style/genre breaking.
- Semantic foregrounding has a paradoxical dimension to it that plays on the pragmatic notions of inference and presuppositions.

## EXERCISE 17.5

1. You can say he 'legged it', and even he 'elbowed it', but not he 'armed it' (in the sense of 'the use the arm in a throwing movement'). Which of the following functional conversions, also related to body parts, can be said to be in everyday usage and which would still be considered creative or foregrounded language use. Motivate your answers where necessary.

(a) He eyed the girl across the road

(b) She eared the telephone receiver

(c) He headed the ball

(d) She lipped the boy next door

(e) She footed her way across the lawn

(f) He handed the gun over to the policeman

2. You saw in the text an example of a poem by Emily Dickenson with the foregrounded line 'I felt a funeral in my brain' whereby the word 'funeral' in this context was the foregrounded element. Consider the following six alternatives and say to what extent they are foregrounded or not. Put them in order and motivate your choices.
   (a) I felt a banging in my brain

   (b) I felt a murmur in my brain

   (c) I felt a fairground in my brain

   (d) I felt a pulsing in my brain

   (e) I felt a blizzard in my brain

   (f) I felt a garden in my brain

### 17.4.4 Syntactic foregrounding

You have already read extensively about syntax in Chapter 6 to which you can refer if necessary. Here, however, is a very brief overview for the specific purpose of this chapter. English, as you probably now know, has a relatively straightforward syntactic structure, namely, 'Subject–Verb–Object' [SVO]. This is the case in both the mainclause and the subclause. Consider the fictive sentence below:

Juliet [S] acquired [V] a new lover [O], *(main clause),*

because she [S] doesn't like [V] Montagues [O] *(sub clause)*

Almost all English sentences follow this basic SVO 'She doesn't like him' pattern. This is not the case for all languages. For example, some might have a SOV ('She him doesn't like') design or a VSO ('Doesn't like she him') arrangement. There are other possible combinations too, but these are the most frequent. People who produce creative language seek to exploit the 'simplicity' of English syntax. Before we look at this we should note that this is not new. There is a Greek term known as 'hyperbaton', which literally means 'to step over' or 'transpose'. It is a style figure, known as a 'scheme' from classical rhetoric. It is also sometimes used synonymously with another term known as 'anastrophe', which means 'a turning back'. This too is a style figure from classical rhetoric that involves the transposition of words in sentences, so that they appear in position that is unusual and is not strictly speaking grammatically correct. In being moved around like this into unfamiliar grammatical positions, the word or words in question strike our attention. In literary linguistic terms, and as you can guess by now, we would say such a word or phrase becomes syntactically foregrounded and, as a result, becomes 'charged' to take on extra significance and extra meaning that in turn can colour and/or affect our ongoing sense of meaning-making that we as readers might have already built up about a particular story or text that we are reading. Ancient Greek was a much more complex language, grammatically speaking, than English is today, and as such there was perhaps far more scope for the wordsmiths of ancient Athens than there is now for English-speaking writers and advertisers. Nonetheless, English has produced some rich examples of syntactic deviation in its creative discourses. Consider Adriana's utterance in William Shakespeare's *Comedy of Errors* who, on the subject of men, poses the following question:

Why should their liberty than ours be more?

Here, the question gains much more significance due to the unusual grammatical order in the line. Indeed, we might say that a double foregrounding is at work when we read the text in its original context, as this line is in turn foregrounded against the co-text of the surrounding sentences, which are structured in a more default English word order pattern. The effect of this might very well be that the readers or listener ponder the utterance far more deeply than otherwise might have been the case. Given the social nature of the utterance, it might even lead to a challenging of beliefs in readers. Consider another example again by Shakespeare but this time from his play *Henry IV, Part 2*.

Uneasy lies the head which wears a crown

Here, in this line the word 'uneasy' is heavily foregrounded, which is very apt for the context of looming civil war and potential regicide. If the sentence were to have been written in a regular pattern it would have read something like 'the head which wears a crown lies uneasy', which you may agree has a much less oppressive or prognostic effect than the syntactically foregrounded original.

We have thus far only looked at literary examples. However, as we have already learned, literary linguistics analyses all modes of creative discourse production, not just literature. Consider, therefore, the three utterances below made by the character Yoda from the *Star Wars* film series. The first is from *Star Wars V: Episode V – The Empire Strikes Back* (1980), the second from *Star Wars: Episode VI – Return of the Jedi* (1983) and the third from *Star Wars: Episode II – Attack of the Clones* (2002).

- Always in motion the future is
- When nine hundred years old you reach, look as good, you will not
- Truly wonderful the mind of a child is

As a character, Yoda makes for an interesting syntactic phenomenon, as it were, as he almost always speaks in the foregrounded syntax of hyperbaton. As a result, in his own discursive world, his displaced word-order language can be said to be not foregrounded at all, since he uses it all the time. However, compared to the language usage of the other characters, it most certainly is. Here is another example from the real world. A colleague of mine used to have the following message on his office door on an A-4 sheet of paper.

Even without the skull and crossbones the regular imperative sentence 'Do not disturb!' does not have the same powerful effect as the syntactically foregrounded version 'Disturb me not!' which now has the added quality of a seemingly overt threat.

Below is a line that a student in my creative writing class once came up with in a poem:

Shimmers the moonlight on the evening sea

Here, the verb 'shimmers' has been foregrounded for emphasis. The writer has arguably attempted to bring it to our attention. Indeed, the author may be hoping that we can now almost see it; that the new emphasis that it has been afforded almost brings it 'before our eyes'. The sentence now has a VSO order, when under normal circumstances it would have a SVO order as in the sentence 'the moonlight shimmers on the evening sea'. But here, in this regular word order version, the shimmering is both dimmed and diminished. The radiance is arguably not brought before our eyes and we are not encouraged to imagine its brilliance. Hence, we are also unlikely to engage emotionally with this piece of discourse, whereas in the foregrounded version, and set within the context of a full poetic text, we might very well do so.

Finally, if you happen to be a non-native speaker of the English language you should remember that these word-order patterns that deviate from the norm would not be considered acceptable English usage. Indeed, depending on which country you are from, and what the sentence structure is like in your own language (e.g. SOV, VSO, etc.) your utterance might be viewed as a form of 'contamination' or 'interference' from your mother tongue. In short, and to paraphrase Winston Churchill, who may or may not have been related to Yoda, 'this sort of English, up with, your lecturer is unlikely to put'.

**KEY POINTS: Syntactic foregrounding**

- Syntax is at the upper-range level of foregrounding.
- It involves deviations from the structured English Subject–Verb–Object word order.

- Much of what goes for syntactic foregrounding can be found under the rhetorical notions of hyperbaton and anastrophe meaning 'to transpose' and 'to turn (back)' respectively.

## EXERCISE 17.6

1. Read the lines below from 'The Tell Tale Heart' by Edgar Allan Poe. What is the word order of those parts that are underlined? Which words are foregrounded? What effect, if any, might it have on a reader?
   It is impossible to say how first the idea entered my brain; but once conceived, it haunted me day and night. Object there was none. Passion there was none.
2. What is the word order here in these examples? What gets foregrounded?
   (a) One swallow does not a summer make
   (b) Yet I'll not shed her blood. Nor scar that whiter skin of hers than snow. (Shakespeare, *Othello* Act V, Scene 2)
   (c) Sometimes too hot the eye of heaven shines (Shakespeare, 'Sonnet 18')

WEBSITE: **Group exercise**

Visit the website and, in a small group, attempt the exercises that are designed to encourage you to think about the method of analysis used in literary linguistics.

## 17.5 SUMMARY

This brings us to the end of our journey into the realm of literary linguistics. In this chapter we have considered the Russian formalist roots of literary linguistics. Here, we focused on the main theories of Roman Jakobson and especially on his scientific ideas of acts of human communication and on the poetic function of language. We also looked at literary linguistics as it has emerged in more recent times, through the functionalism of the Prague structuralists and into the pragmatics scholarship of the present. We have, however, primarily looked at 'literary linguistics in practice', which constituted how foregrounding takes place at a number of linguistic levels. These levels included the phonological, the graphological, the metrical, the morphological, the lexical, the semantic and the syntactic. Many examples were given here from different cultural domains, both high and low, in order to help you to better understand both the process and the theory of foregrounding. One thing that we were not able to delve into more deeply, owing to space constraints, was the discourse and pragmatics side of literary linguistic analysis. Hopefully, you will now go on to do more self-study both in this area and in the ones you have already read about in this chapter. (See Burke 2014.)

Remember that you only really begin to understand how literary linguistics works when you start doing things for yourself, by means of real hands-on experience. So go ahead and conduct your own literary linguistic analysis. It doesn't matter if it doesn't work out the first time around. Only practice makes perfect. Afterwards, try your hand at creating your own foregrounded discourse that deviates from some norm. It is fun and if you practise often enough, you will slowly see how the very stuff of linguistics and grammar gets into your bones, just by playing around with creative language. This is a pleasant byproduct, as it were, of literary linguistics: you get to learn about the workings of grammar through the enjoyable filter of imaginative texts.

If this pedagogical grammar-learning side is an offshoot of literary linguistics, then the main part is to arm students like yourself with the grammatical tools to become efficient and effective linguistic-forensic sleuths; for it is only such linguistic knowledge that can bring empirical, evidenced light to the oftentimes impenetrable fog of literary interpretation.

WEBSITE: **Literary linguistics**

Now go to the website and evaluate your knowledge of literary linguistics by answering the self-test questions!

## SUGGESTIONS FOR FURTHER READING

Burke, M. (2010). Rhetorical pedagogy: teaching students how to write a stylistics paper. *Language and Literature*, 19(1), 77–92. If you are stuck as to how to start writing a literary linguistic paper/essay for your module/course, then this is the article for you, as it takes you through the entire process, step-by-step, of researching, analysing and writing up a literary linguistics essay

(ed.). (2014). *The Routledge Handbook of Stylistics*. London: Routledge. This is the most up-to-date overview of all aspects of literary linguistics (thirty-two chapters in total). This handbook, which also functions as a textbook, takes you from classical rhetoric to cognitive neuroscience and in doing so shows you how to conduct every kind of literary linguistic analysis imaginable. The chapters are written by experts from all over the world.

Nørgaard, N., Busse, B. and Montoro, R. (2010). *Key Terms in Stylistics*. London: Continuum. This is a resource book, which offers a very handy overview of the field. It introduces you very succinctly to the key branches, key terms, key thinkers and key texts in stylistics.

# ANSWERS TO EXERCISES

## Exercise 17.1

1. The answer here is (c) 'rhetoric'. The others all fit within the idea of a framework of a text-based autonomous or independent system of language, something that formalism adheres to. Rhetoric, on the other hand, is very much a pragmatic model of meaning making that comes into being in context as shown by the two thousand year old rhetorical notion of *kairos*.
2. The answer here is (e) 'logic'. The others all fit within the idea of a framework of a context-based, dependent system of language, something that functionalism adheres to. Logic, on the other hand, is a very much a semantic or textual model of meaning making that comes into being as a result of the text as seen in the logical, propositional notions of deductive, internal validity.

## Exercise 17.2

1. The answer is (e) 'feminist theory'. The others are clearly cognitive phenomena as they are all interested to a lesser or greater extent in finding out what happens in a reader's mind when he/she engages with a literary text. Feminist theory, on the other hand, falls mainly within the framework of a critical, rather than a cognitive, approach to literary linguistics. As such, it is much more concerned with contextual factors like how social patterns of language can influence how language is perceived and understood. Feminist approaches also tend to employ aspects of systemic function grammar as an analytic methodology.
2. The answer is (a) 'corpus methods'. The others are clearly pragmatic phenomena as they are all interested to a lesser or greater extent in finding out what happens within the context of a discourse utterance within a communicative situation. Corpus methods, on the other hand, fall mainly within the framework of a computational, rather than a pragmatic, approach to literary linguistics. As such, they are much more concerned using large text corpora together with concordancers in order to gain empirical insights into language usage and patterning.

## Exercise 17.3

1. (a) This is an example of alliteration as it involves the repetition of consonants in two or more words in the initial position on stressed syllables. In this particular case, one could argue that there is also an aspect of sound symbolism at work here, as the alliterative 'd' also has onomatopoeic (i.e. engine-like) effects, which act to reinforce the meaning of the product, almost bringing it to audible life.

   (b) This is an example of assonance (also known as half rhyme or partial rhyme) as it involves the repetition of rhyming of vowels and/or diphthongs, rather than consonants. Unlike consonance, the close location of consonants is not an issue. Here again one could argue that there is also an aspect of sound symbolism at work in the clean, crisp, swishing vowel sounds that are repeated. The strange thing is that this is not the engine-like sound of a vacuum cleaner, but the traditional clear sound of a broom as can be seen in the name of the popular 'swiffer' dusters that are on sale these days.

(c) This example, like (a), is also a case of alliteration, as it involves the repetition of consonants in two or more words in the initial position on stressed syllables. Unlike (a), however, and also (b), there is no apparent extra sound symbolism at work here.

2. (a) iambic tetrameter – It is clearly iambic (X /) and there are four feet

(b) dactylic trimeter followed by a single trochee. Here the dactylic metre can be said to add to the effect of the galloping horses (remember, dactyls have the effect of skipping and tripping along). Arguably, had the poet used anapests instead of dactyls this effect might have been felt even stronger.

3. All limericks are anapestic. They employ three feet (trimeters) in the three main/longer lines (1, 2 and 5) and a combination of an anapest and an iamb (dimeter) in the two shorter lines (3 and 4).

## Exercise 17.4

1. The answer is (c) 'boyish'. The other three are free morphemes because the word stems can appear independently in other linguistic contexts (e.g. dog, house, text, book, car, port). The word 'boyish' is a bound morpheme. 'Boy' is the stem and 'ish' the suffix. Indeed, you could extend this with yet another suffix 'ly' as in 'boyishly'. However, you could not extend it with a third 'less' or a fourth 'ness', as in 'boyishlylessness', unless of course you were seeking to foreground this word in specific context for a definitive persuasive end.
2. The first three examples are all similar. They are manner adverbs that are formed with a word stem, the present participle suffix 'ing', and the adverbial suffix 'ly'. It is the addition of the second 'ly' suffix that produces the creative foregrounding. The fourth example is different in that although it too has the present participle suffix 'ing' followed by the adverbial suffix 'ly', it has two stems 'cry' and 'laugh' that are brought together in a compound, free morpheme fashion, even though 'crylaugh' is not a free morpheme in everyday English. The reason it works though here is because although these two words are opposites, the poet knows that they are also very similar. For instance, for some people, and especially in the case of children, crying can turn to laughter and vice versa in an instant. Hence, their literal linguistic proximity.

## Exercise 17.5

1. Sentences (a), (c) and (f) are functional conversions that are clearly in common everyday usage. Sentences (b), (d) and (e) are not and can therefore be used in a foregrounded way in certain contexts. It is interesting to note that the words 'lipped', 'footed' and 'eared' are real/acceptable words but can only be used in other contexts and with other grammatical, mainly compound adjectival, functions, as in 'fleet-footed', 'tight-lipped' and 'long-eared'.
2. There are roughly speaking three natural/expected examples and three arguably foregrounded/creative ones. The expected ones are (a), (b) and (d). Example (d) is perhaps the least obvious and example (a) is the most default. The three creative/foregrounded ones are (c), (e) and (f). All are strongly foregrounded, but perhaps the garden and/or fairground example is the most deviant in this context.

## Exercise 17.6

1. It should read 'There was no object. There was no passion', but this regular word order is inverted. Note here that we are not talking about an SVO inversion, but rather about an inversion of what we call an existential clause [*there* + verb, typically 'be'] and the noun. In the original version the nouns 'object' and 'passion' get transposed to the beginning of the sentences and become foregrounded.

The effect of this could be an increased sense of feeling, especially with the foregrounding of the word 'passion'.

2. (a) Here, the words 'does not make a summer' are presented as 'does not a summer make'. The verb 'make' is thus foregrounded in this SOV syntactic deviation.
   (b) The inversion here is not as simple as the previous example. Here, the line 'Nor scar that skin of hers that is whiter than snow' is presented in a foregrounded manner as 'Nor scar that whiter skin of hers than snow'. The words 'white' and 'skin' change places. Interestingly, the word 'snow' is still in final position, but in the foregrounded version it receives much more emphasis than it would in the accepted English version, as does, by default, the whiteness of the woman's skin.
   (c) Here the words 'the eye of heaven (i.e. the sun) shines too hot' are presented in the following syntactically deviant manner: 'too hot the eye of heaven shines'. Here, the basic Subject–Verb elements 'the eye of heaven' and 'shines' stay in place. It is the adverbial 'too hot' which when transposed from the end of the sentence, where it is adjacent to its verb, to the beginning of the sentence, where it is distanced from it, that it becomes foregrounded. The effect is to make the scene seem even hotter than it already is.

## REFERENCES

Bally, C. (1909). *Traité de stylistique française*. Heidelberg: Carl Winters.

Bühler, K. (1934). *Sprachtheorie: Die Darstellungsfunktion der Sprache*. Jena: Fischer.

Burke, M. (2003). Literature as parable. In J. Gavins and G. Steen (eds.), *Cognitive Poetics in Practice*, pp. 115–28. London: Routledge.

(2010a). Rhetorical pedagogy: teaching students how to write a stylistics paper. *Language and Literature*, 19, 77–92.

(2010b). Why care about pedagogical stylistics? *Language and Literature*, 19, 7–11.

(2011). *Literary Reading, Cognition and Emotion: An Exploration of the Oceanic Mind*. New York: Routledge.

(2013). The rhetorical neuroscience of style: on the primacy of style elements during literary discourse processing. *Journal of Literary Semantics*, 42, 000.

(ed.) (2014). *The Routledge Handbook of Stylistics*. London: Routledge.

Burke, M., Csábi, S., Week, L. and Zerkowitz, J. (eds). (2012). *Pedagogical Stylistics: Current Trends in Language, Literature and ELT*. London: Continuum.

Busse, B. (2010). Recent trends in new historical stylistics. In D. McIntyre and B. Busse (eds.), *Language and Style*, pp. 32–54. Basingstoke: Palgrave.

Clarke, U. and Zyngier, S. (2003). Towards a pedagogical stylistics. *Language and Literature*, 12, 339–51.

Cook, G. (1994). *Discourse and Literature: The Interplay of Form and Mind*. Oxford University Press.

Dancygier, B. (2006). What blending can do for you. *Language and Literature*, 15, 5–15.

Emmott, C. (1997). *Narrative Comprehension: A Discourse Perspective*. Oxford University Press.

Fowler, R. (1986). *Linguistic Criticism*. Oxford University Press.

Freeman, D. C. (1995). Catch(ing) the nearest way: Macbeth and cognitive metaphor. *Journal of Pragmatics*, 24, 689–708.

Garvin, P. L. 1964). *A Prague School Reader on Esthetics, Literary Structure and Style*. Washington, DC: Georgetown University Press.

Gavins, J. (2007). *Text-World Theory: An Introduction*. Edinburgh University Press.

Halliday, M. A. K. (1985). *An Introduction to Functional Grammar*. London: Arnold.

Hogan, P. C. (2013). *'Ulysses' and the Poetics of Cognition*. New York: Routledge.
(2014). Stylistics, emotion and neuroscience. In M. Burke (ed.), *The Routledge Handbook of Stylistics*, pp. 000. London: Routledge.
Jakobson, R. (1960). Closing statement: linguistics and poetics. In T. A. Sebeok (ed.), *Style in Language*, pp. 350–77. Cambridge, MA: MIT Press.
Jeffries, L. (2007). *Textual Construction of the Female Body: A Critical Discourse Approach*. Basingstoke: Palgrave.
(2010). *Critical Stylistics: The Power of English*. Basingstoke: Palgrave.
Lahey, E. (2006). (Re)thinking world-building: Locating the text-worlds of Canadian lyric poetry. *Journal of Literary Semantics*, 35, 145–64.
McIntyre, D. (2008). Integrating multimodal analysis and the stylistics of drama: a multimodal perspective on Ian McKellen's *Richard III*. *Language and Literature*, 17, 309–34.
Mahlberg, M. (2007). Corpus stylistics: bridging the gap between linguistic and literary studies. In M. Hoey, M. Mahlberg and M. Stubbs (eds.), *Text, Discourse and Corpora*, pp. 219–46. London: Continuum.
Mills, S. (1995). *Feminist Stylistics*. London: Routledge.
Montoro, R. (2010). A multimodal approach to mind style: semiotic metaphor vs multimodal conceptual metaphor. In R. Page (ed.), *New Perspectives on Narrative and Multimodality*, pp. 31–49. London: Routledge.
(2011). *The Stylistics of Chick Lit: An Analysis of Cappuccino Fiction*. London: Continuum.
Nørgaard, N. (2010). Multimodality: extending the stylistics toolkit. In D. McIntyre and B. Busse (eds.), *Language and Style*, pp. 433–48. Basingstoke: Palgrave.
Nørgaard, N., Busse, B. and Montoro, R. (2010). *Key Terms in Stylistics*. London: Continuum.
Propp, V. ([1928] 1968). *Morphology of the Folktale*. Austin: University of Texas Press.
Semino, E. (1997). *Language and World Creation in Poems and Other Texts*. London: Longman.
Semino, E. and Short, M. (2004). *Corpus Stylistics: Speech, Writing and Thought Presentation in a Corpus of English Narratives*. London: Routledge.
Scott, M. (2004). *WordSmith Tools Version 4*. Oxford University Press.
Shklovsky, V. ([1925] 1990). *Theory of Prose*. Elmwood Park, IL: Dalkey Archive Press.
Simpson, P. (2004). *Stylistics: A Resource Book for Students*. London: Routledge.
Spitzer, L. (1928). *Stilstudien*. Munich: Max Hüber.
Stockwell, P. (2002). *Cognitive Poetics: An Introduction*. London: Routledge.
Stubbs, M. (2005). Conrad in the computer: examples of quantitative stylistics methods. *Language and Literature*, 14, 5–24.
Verdonk, P. (ed.) (1993). *Twentieth Century Poetry: From Text to Context*. London: Routledge.
Widdowson, H. G. (1992). *Practical Stylistics: An Approach to Poetry*. Oxford University Press.

# GLOSSARY

**accent:** the pronunciation of a linguistic variety. Accents can tell us about where a speaker is from, but can also give us social information about a speaker's social class or education.

**acquired communication disorder:** a communication disorder which has its onset after the period in which speech and language is normally acquired. Such a disorder can be found in adolescents and adults.

**acronym-formation:** non-morphemic word-formation process forming new words by reducing compounds and phrases to their initials; acronyms, in the narrow sense, are products of this process which can be pronounced like normal words, e.g. *NATO, AIDS.*

**activation:** the likelihood that a word matches the available evidence. Evidence in favour of a word increases its activation; evidence against reduces it.

**actuation:** the initiation of a linguistic innovation.

**adjective:** a word that can function as a modifier within the noun phrase, where, in English, they typically appear between the article and the noun. This is called their attributive use. It is illustrated by the word *blue* in *I bought a blue balloon.* Adjectives also have a predicative use, exemplified by *blue* in *The balloon is blue.*

**adverbial:** a clause element which generally refers to less central circumstances of actions, states and events, such as the location, timing, manner, cause, effect or reason. They respond to *wh-* word questions such as *Why…, Where…, When.., How…* etc. and they can be represented by adverb phrases: *I saw him (very) briefly. (How long…?)* or prepositional phrases: *I saw him in the garden. (Where…?).*

**age grading:** differences between age groups which repeat as each generation ages – that is to say, all speakers in a particular community will use a particular variant at a particular age.

**agglutinating language:** a type of synthetic language (e.g. Turkish) which is rich in inflectional morphemes and produces long words by concatenating sequences of morphemes that do not overlap and typically have a one-to-one relation of form and meaning.

**airstream:** an airstream is the moving air used to produce speech. This is usually controlled expulsion of lung air, the egressive pulmonic airstream. Other airstreams used in speech are the egressive and ingressive pharyngeal/glottalic airstreams and the ingressive oral/velaric airstream.

**Aktionsart:** a German term for situation type.

**alliteration:** a style figure (a trope) from classical rhetoric (tropes deviate at the semantic level, unlike schemes, which deviate at the syntactic level). It represents the repetition of consonants in two or more words. The consonants in question are usually in the initial position of a word and fall on stressed syllables.

**allomorph:** a different formal realization of a morpheme, especially inflectional ones.

**allophone:** the surface form of a particular phoneme; the allophones of a specific phoneme are in complementary distribution with each other.

**alveolar:** a consonant produced at the alveolar ridge, a bony structure on the roof of the mouth, located between the top teeth and the hard palate, e.g. [t], [d], [n].

**analytic language:** type of language which does not encode grammatical categories by means of inflectional morphemes affixed to stems but by other means such as word order, auxiliaries and particles.

**analytic truth:** another term for linguistic truth.

**antonymy:** words in a semantic opposition, including binary, gradable, relational and reverse antonyms.

**aphasia:** an acquired language disorder that is most often caused by a stroke in the left hemisphere of the brain. Language in all its spoken, written and signed modalities may be impaired to varying degrees.

**apparent-time change:** this assumes that people's grammar is relatively unlikely to change during adulthood, so studies that use this approach will compare speakers of different ages in a community and use it to describe language change over time, see real-time change.

**appositional compound:** a type of two-headed, non-determinative compound combining two different descriptions of the same referent (e.g. *singer-songwriter*).

**approaches to discourse analysis:** non-critical approaches describe discursive phenomena mainly in terms of structure; critical approaches not only describe but also show how discourse is shaped by relations of power and ideologies.

**arbitrariness:** the design feature of human language whereby there is no necessary connection between the sign, or word, and what it signifies. The connection between the two is random. The opposite to arbitrariness is a 'motivated' connection, as with onomatopoeic words.

**articulation:** the physical and mental process of producing speech.

**articulator:** organ involved in producing speech.

**aspect:** a semantic system which allows speakers different viewpoints on the time profile of an event or situation, for example by choosing between a perfective and imperfective verb form.

**aspiration:** a voiceless interval (see VOT), sounding like [h], at the beginning of a vowel when this immediately follows the end of a previous consonant (generally a plosive, fricative or affricate). In English /p/, /t/ and /k/ are aspirated, e.g. [phi:] *pea/pee/P.*

**assonance:** a style figure (a trope) from classical rhetoric pertaining to the rhyming of vowels and diphthongs. Unlike consonance it does not take the close location of consonants into account.

**attention:** the ability to focus the mind narrowly on a particular task or activity – or a particular aspect of language.

**auditory agnosia:** a disorder in which the ability to recognize or perceive the spoken forms of words is compromised. It can be a feature of several conditions including Landau-Kleffner syndrome in children.

**automatic:** describes a process that can be carried out rapidly and with minimal attention (an example is mapping from word to meaning and from meaning to word).

**back-formation:** typically word-class-changing word-formation process involving the deletion of a suffix or suffix-like element (e.g. *to babysit* ← *babysitter*).

**bahuvrihi compound:** type of exocentric compound where the meaning of the compound stands for a property or part of the head (e.g. *paleface* 'person who has a pale face').

**behaviourism:** a theory (current in the first half of the twentieth century) that the human mind is unknowable and that the focus of study for psychologists should be human behaviour.

**bilabial:** a consonant produced with the closure of the top and bottom lip, e.g. [p], [b].

**blending:** type of non-morphemic word-formation process involving the merging or telescoping of two lexemes into one.

**bottom-up reasoning:** the approach to problem solving that takes data and uses the data to build a theory/explanation.

**bound morpheme:** type of morpheme that cannot occur by itself but only as an affix to a free morpheme.

**buffer:** a storage device in the mind which (a) holds a planned clause that a speaker/writer is currently producing; (b) holds a group of words that has been heard or read, while the listener/reader traces a grammatical pattern in them.

**c-command:** in a syntactic tree, a given node c-commands its sister and all nodes dominated by its sister.

**candidate:** a word that partly or completely fits the evidence considered by a listener/reader and forms a possible match with what has been heard or read.

**Cardinal Vowels:** sixteen fixed values learned and memorized by phoneticians, established to facilitate an auditorily based method of vowel description.

**case:** a linguistic system used in some languages to indicate the grammatical function (e.g. subject, object, etc.) of words in a sentence by the addition of morphological inflections to nouns, pronouns and adjectives.

**category:** the group of objects which falls within the meaning range of a particular word.

**causative:** a semantic and grammatical category that identifies a causal role of a referent in relation to an event or state described by a verb.

**chain shift:** a model from historical linguistics to explain sound changes in language by imaging phonemes to be like links in a chain; when one moves position, the others inevitably move too so that each phoneme ends up sounding like the one before it prior to the change.

**chunk:** a group of two or more words that commonly occur together. They can be stored in the mind as a whole and produced already assembled.

**cleft lip and palate:** an embryological malformation that results in a failure of the tissues of the upper lip, gum and hard and soft palates to fuse normally during pre-natal development. Speech, hearing, and language can all be compromised to varying degrees.

**clipping:** a type of non-morphemic word-class-preserving word-formation process involving the deletion of parts of the source lexeme at the end (back-clipping, e.g. *photo* ← *photograph*), front (front-clipping, e.g. *bus* ← *omnibus*) or on either side (e.g. *flu* ← *influenza*).

**coda:** in syllable structure the coda is a consonant or consonants following the nucleus.

**communication:** the activity of living participants that exchange information and meaning through semiotic systems (speech, writing, gestures, images, sound, etc.).

**communicative intention:** the mental state that motivates the production of an utterance and which must be recovered in order for a hearer to be said to have understood what a speaker meant by an utterance.

**comparative linguistics:** a branch of linguistics that compares different languages (or varieties of language). Traditionally, the focus has been on comparing languages historically. Typically, this has been done by considering the forms of related languages and drawing hypotheses about possible ancestor languages. Thus, families of languages, such as the Proto-Indo-European (PIE) family tree, are reconstructed. Historical comparative linguistics is comparative philology.

**competition model:** a theory that listeners and readers identify words by matching the evidence at different levels of detail (e.g. phoneme, syllable, word, phrase) against a possible set of word matches.

**complementary distribution:** the distribution of allophones of a single phoneme, which are found in different contexts; compare ‘contrastive distribution’.

**complex lexeme:** lexeme consisting of more than one lexical morpheme.

**compositional:** where the meaning of a complex meaning is predictable from its parts.

**compounding:** type of morphemic word-formation process involving the combination of at least two free lexical morphemes, i.e. lexemes.

**conditioning factor:** with respect to a phonological alternation, a conditioning factor refers to the context associated with a particular allophone; a conditioning factor may be phonetic context alone, or in combination with a specific morphological operation or lexical class.

**configurational language:** a language that displays hierarchical structure, embedding phrases and sentences one within the other.

**conjunction:** a word class whose members function to join clauses. 'Co-ordinating' conjunctions (*and, but, or*) join two equal clauses, e.g. *She left but he stayed,* while 'subordinating' conjunctions indicate that the following subordinate clause is part of another clause, e.g. *She left when he arrived.* Here *when he arrived* is a subordinate clause functioning as an adverbial.

**connectionist:** a type of computer modelling which shows that links between grammatically related words can be achieved by being exposed to examples without the need to acquire grammar rules.

**consonance:** a style figure (a trope) from classical rhetoric that is similar to alliteration, except it is the repetition of consonants that are stressed in the same place in different words but with different vowels. Consonance usually occurs at the end position of words.

**consonant:** sound with a relatively narrow constriction or complete closure in the vocal tract such as [p], [m], [s], [t͡ʃ], [ɾ].

**constative utterance:** an expression used by Austin to refer to utterances that report or describe states of affairs in the world and are true or false.

**constituent:** a group of words that occur next to each other in a sentence and act as a unit. In syntactic tree diagrams, constituents are represented by subtrees rooted at a particular node.

**construal:** a speaker's choices in characterizing a situation for communication.

**constructed opposition:** one of the textual-conceptual functions which are recognized in critical stylistics as answering the question 'what is the text doing in constructing the text world?' In this case, texts may construct oppositional meaning which is not conventionally recognized in the language in general. There are 'triggers' (such as 'X, not Y') which help to construct these one-off opposites.

**content word:** words that convey the main meaning in a sentence, such as nouns, verbs, adjective or adverbs, as opposed to function words.

**context:** any aspect of a language user's knowledge, physical environment and social relationships to others may shape the production and interpretation of utterances and form part of their context. These aspects include physical context (e.g. setting of a conversation), social context (e.g. social standing of speaker and hearer), epistemic context (background knowledge of speaker and hearer), and linguistic context (e.g. preceding utterances in a conversation).

**context of culture:** the outside context where ways of doing things according to specific cultural rules happen.

**context of situation:** the immediate location of events that determines ways of interacting (things going on in the world outside the text which make the interaction what it is).

**contingent truth:** something that depends on the way the world is and that could have been false.

**contradiction:** a sentence that is false by its meaning, irrespective of context.

**contradictory:** a relation between two sentences where the truth of one entails the falseness of the other and vice versa.

**contrastive distribution:** the distribution of phonemes, found in identical contexts and capable of forming minimal pairs; compare 'complementary distribution'.

**conventional implicature:** a type of implied meaning that is attached by convention to particular lexical items. For example, the word *but* in the utterance *Frank is overweight but healthy* generates an implicature to the effect that it was not expected that Frank would be healthy.

**conversion:** a type of typically word-class-changing word-formation process which transposes a lexeme to a new word-class without the addition of an overtly marked suffix (e.g. *empty* V ← *empty* Adj).

**cooperative principle:** a principle proposed by Grice to capture certain rational expectations between participants in verbal and non-verbal exchanges. This principle is the basis upon which speakers and hearers can derive implied meanings from utterances in conversation.

**copulative compound:** a type of two-headed, non-determinative compound denoting the sum of two meanings (e.g. *bitter-sweet*).

**corpus** (plural *corpora*): an electronic database of text, usually sampled to be maximally representative of a particular language or language variety. Used to test hypotheses and/or construct theories of language.

**corpus-based discourse analysis:** the analysis of discourse that uses a corpus, which is a large collection of texts saved electronically. Various types of computer software enable the search for words or patterns of language.

**count noun:** a noun which can have a plural form and which can be preceded by *a*, e.g. *a horse, horses*, as opposed to a noncount noun. Also called 'countable noun'.

**covert prestige:** when speakers use or judge varieties positively that differ from the standard variety, opposite to overt prestige.

**creole language:** a language that emerges from a pidgin, and displays properties distinct from the native languages of adults who know the pidgin. It displays a larger number of grammatical features than the pidgin from which it developed, and also has an expanded lexicon. Unlike a pidgin, it is spoken as a first language.

**critical discourse analysis (CDA):** an approach to language which associates linguistic text analysis with social meanings of language in political and ideological processes. It may be used to reveal the ideological effects of language and power.

**critical stylistics:** this is a deliberate departure from CDA, which aims to retain the insights and strengths of a scientific and rigorous approach to text analysis whilst also accepting that text producers have power over text recipients (i.e. readers/listeners). The approach is based on a conviction that there is an identifiable level of textual meaning which affects readers variably, but which constructs a text world ideationally and to some degree also ideologically.

**crossing:** when speakers use features of language which are associated with another ethnic group.

**daughter:** in a syntactic tree, the daughters of a given node (if any) are those nodes that can be reached by following a single edge of the tree downward.

**decoding:** recognizing language sounds and word forms in reading or listening.

**deixis:** a word from Greek meaning 'pointing' or 'showing' which refers to how utterances are anchored in person, space and time, e.g. person deixis (*us* vs *them*), space deixis (*here* vs *there*), time deixis (*now* vs *later*), etc. Deixis stresses the importance of the context of a discourse utterance.

**demonstrative:** demonstratives are elements of the noun phrase. They often encode number distinctions and deictic distinctions having to do with proximity. English has four demonstratives, cross-classified as singular versus plural and proximal versus distal:

| | Proximal | Distal |
|---|---|---|
| singular | this | that |
| plural | these | those |

**denotation:** the relation between a linguistic expression and its extension.

**dental:** a consonant with a place of articulation at the teeth, e.g. [θ].

**derivational morpheme:** type of morpheme involved in the creation of new lexemes, typically close to the stem and subject to productivity restrictions.

**derivational morphology:** branch of morphology dealing with word-formation types using prefixes and suffixes.

**descriptive and prescriptive approaches:** modern linguists aim to describe the patterns of language which they encounter in actual usage. They do not engage in prescriptive practices, i.e. telling speakers what is 'correct' or 'incorrect' usage.

**design features for language:** a list of key features of human language, and taken together, they distinguish human language from other forms of animal communication.

**determinative compound:** type of endocentric compound exhibiting a modifier–head relation between the constituents.

**developmental communication disorder:** a communication disorder which has its onset in the developmental period, a time when children are undergoing speech and language acquisition.

**diachronic:** from the Greek *diachronous*; diachronic linguistics is concerned with the study of language as it develops over time; see also 'synchronic'.

**dialect:** a particular variety of a language and considers pronunciation, word choice and grammatical structure as well as particular elements of discourse.

**dialect continuum:** varieties of a language fall along a continuum rather than being discrete entities. Varieties which are nearer each other tend to be more similar, with varieties at both extreme ends of the continuum being most different.

**dialect levelling:** the process whereby regional varieties of a language may become more similar over time.

**discourse (singular):** the ways people use different semiotic resources, or different signs, to communicate meanings. When we study discourse, we study the way a text creates meaning and reflects the views and ideology of its producer and his/her society. All discourse is essentially interactive and dialogic. All discourses are placed in social contexts.

**discourses (plural):** the term refers to the discourses of institutions with their rules and regulations (legal discourses, media discourses) or ideologically motivated discourses (sexist discourse, racist discourse).

**discourse analysis:** studies all types of interactions and their semiotic realization in order to demonstrate that they are systematically structured and socially organized.

**discourse construction:** building a discourse representation.

**discourse domain:** the socially recognized context within which the discourse takes place (scientific discourse takes place within the domain of science, for example).

**discourse identities:** our gender, age, profession and social relations, our nationality, our religion are realized in multiple ways through the ways we interact with others.

**discourse practice:** the processes of text production, distribution and consumption. This may involve institutional processes or routines such as those found in journalistic practice.

**discourse presentation:** also known as 'speech and thought presentation', discourse presentation is the arrangement of the words and/or thoughts of others by a narrator. This can range from a simple narrator's report of speech to indirect speech, free indirect speech, direct speech and free direct speech. The differences are usually highlighted with linguistic markers, such as a shift in tense, pronoun or deixis.

**discourse representation:** recall by a language user of what has been said or written so far, into which new information is integrated.

**discreteness:** the design feature of human language whereby the elements of the language can be analysed and identified.

**displacement:** the design feature of human language whereby speakers are able to refer to objects and events which are not concurrent with the present time or place. Speakers can refer to past or future time, and can also refer to events happening in other places.

**dominate:** in a syntactic tree, a given node dominates all nodes that can be reached by following a connected strictly downward path through the tree.

**dual-route model:** an account of reading which stresses the importance of both recognizing whole word forms and recognizing letter–sound relationships.

**duality of patterning:** the smallest segments of a language are combined to make larger and larger elements. For example, phonemes in a language combine to make morphemes, which combine to make words.

**dvandva compound:** a type of compound which has two heads (e.g. *bitter-sweet, actor-director*).

**dysarthria:** a developmental or acquired speech disorder which is caused by neurological damage (e.g. a stroke). Speech is unintelligible to varying degrees.

**economy:** a potential explanation for why languages change over time; centred on the notion that speakers develop their language in order to be more economical, e.g. through reduction and lenition.

**empirical truth:** truth that derives from correspondence to a set of affairs, gained by experience.

**endocentric compound:** a type of compound where one constituent, in English usually the final one, encodes the grammatical and semantic head.

**entailment:** a relation between sentences where the truth of one guarantees the truth of the other, so *John broke the window* entails *The window broke.*

**ethnolect:** an ethnic variety of a dialect or language.

**exchange structure:** a sequence of linked utterances. The typical exchange structure has three parts, where the third part functions to evaluate or comment upon the fit between the first and the second, and it is sometimes optional – Initiation, Response, Follow-up.

**execution:** the physical and mental process of producing written text on the page or screen.

**exemplar theory:** the theory that listeners store multiple examples of words and of chunks of language in their minds, encountered at different times and in different voices.

**exocentric compound:** type of compound whose grammatical and semantic head is encoded by neither of the constituents but 'lies outside' the compound (e.g. *redbreast*).

**expressive language:** the production or formulation of language. Expressive language is most closely identified with the stage of language encoding in the communication cycle.

**expressiveness:** a potential explanation for why languages change over time centred on the notion that speakers develop their language in order to be more expressive and creative, e.g. through the addition of new words to the language's vocabulary.

**extension:** a thing or set of things that a linguistic expression can be used to refer to.

**extrametricality:** a state in which phonetic material is invisible to a particular phonological operation, such as stress assignment.

**felicity condition:** a condition on the appropriate performance of a speech act. Felicity conditions specify who must say and do what and in what circumstances in order for a speech act to be performed felicitously. If these conditions are not met, a speech act is infelicitous.

**fixation:** point at which a reader's eyes stop in order to identify a word.

**flapping:** the articulation of a /t/ or /d/ as a 'tap' or 'flap', involving quick contact between the tip of the tongue and the alveolar ridge; it is characteristic of various dialects of English and symbolized as [ɾ].

**foregrounding:** a term that pertains to the poetic function of language and its ability to deviate from linguistic norms and also to create textual patterns (repetitions or parallelisms).

**formalism:** a term that stresses a focus on language as an autonomous system with emphasis on such things as propositional meaning and grammatical forms. When applied to literary linguistics, formalism refers to the dependence on formal linguistics criteria in detecting stylistic patterns in texts. Things like pragmatic functions and the general communicative context or situation play no role.

**forms of discourse:** our communications will depend not only on cultural and situational contexts but also on our socialization patterns, on our beliefs and values (ideologies) and on the ways we use our face and politeness systems.

**free morpheme:** type of morpheme that can occur as a free form.

**free variation:** where a speaker's choice of forms of language to use is arbitrary – opposite to structured variation.

**function word:** words that have a grammatical function, for example, to relate two other words and show the relationship between them, e.g. *the King <u>of</u> Spain*. Function words are generally short and frequent, as opposed to content words.

**functional view of language:** language is different in different situations. A functional view focuses on what makes a piece of language different from another.

**functionalism:** a term which in many senses is the opposite of formalism. Functionalist approaches to literary linguistics consider the pragmatic function of language in meaning making as well as in the communicative context.

**fundamental frequency:** abbreviated as 'f-zero' (written f0) and measured in Hertz (Hz), this is the measurable rate of vibration of the vocal folds. Relating to perceived pitch, f0 is responsible for intonation and lexical tones.

**fusional language:** type of language (e.g. Latin) which is rich in inflectional morphemes frequently encoding several meanings in one form.

**garden path sentence:** a sentence which the hearer starts to parse assuming one structure, which in fact turns out to be wrong, necessitating a re-parsing.

**gender-exclusive language:** features of language which tend only to be used by one gender or another.

**gender-preferential language:** features of language which are more likely to be used by one gender or another.

**generalized conversational implicature:** a type of implied meaning that does not require any special context for its generation. For example, the indefinite article *a* in *Bill is meeting a woman this evening* generates an implicature to the effect that the woman Bill is meeting is not his mother, sister, wife, etc.

**genitive:** a form of the noun which in writing is represented by adding *-'s* for the singular and *-s'* for the plural, e.g. *the winner's/winners' speech*. In speech these forms are indistinguishable from the plural. It is sometimes referred to as the 'Saxon genitive' or 'apostrophe *-s*'. Genitives do not always indicate a possessor; they cover a wide range of relationships between their noun and the following head noun.

**genres:** socially acceptable ways of using language in connection with a particular kind of social activity. When texts share the same obligatory and optional structural elements, they belong to the same genre. The four broad generic structures are narrative, expository, hortatory or behavioural, and procedural.

**gloss:** a word-by-word or morpheme-by-morpheme translation of foreign language examples. Glosses are usually written below the foreign language examples and aligned with them. Linguists now usually follow the Leipzig glossing rules: www.eva.mpg.de/lingua/resources/glossing-rules.php

**grammar:** a grammar is a characterization of all the rules (syntactic, morphological, phonological, semantic, etc.) needed to characterize a given language together with the lexicon for that language. More narrowly, the syntactic rules that characterize the grammatical sentences of the language with their meanings are sometimes referred to as its grammar. A grammar that is explicit is called a generative grammar.

**grammatical morpheme:** type of morpheme encoding grammatical meanings and relations.

**grammaticalization:** the gradual process by which items undergo development to become more grammatical in character.

**Great Vowel Shift:** a sound change that occurred in English between approximately 1400 and 1650 and which resulted in the raising of the seven long vowels of Middle English.

**head:** the most important word in a phrase, the one which is obligatory. The term is most commonly applied to noun phrases, for example *the tall <u>girl</u> standing over there*, but it can also be applied to phrases derived from other word classes: verbs, adjectives, adverbs and prepositions.

**hearing loss:** a reduction in hearing that can be partial or complete, and that can be conductive (middle ear dysfunction) or sensorineural (cochlea or brain damage) in nature. Hearing loss is assessed and managed by audiologists.

**hesitation pause:** a pause where a speaker changes or loses track of a speech plan.

**homographs:** distinct lexemes sharing spelling but not pronunciation.

**homonymy:** the relationship between words that are identical in form but belong to different lexemes.

**homophone:** distinct lexemes sharing pronunciation but not spelling.

**hyberbole:** a traditional label for exaggeration viewed as a rhetorical figure of speech.

**hyponymy:** a relationship in the lexicon between more specific and more general terms. The more specific term is the hyponym and the more general is either called the superordinate or the hyperonym.

**ideation:** ideational meaning is used to describe the production of text worlds by texts. Though ideation may also have values attached and thereby become ideology, it can also be fairly neutral and descriptive.

**ideational meaning:** the way that texts create a cognitive world which is reflected in the language chosen. This includes the kind of world (real, imagined, historic) that is described in the text, and the people, places and activities typical of that world. It also includes the ideological landscape of the world, for example, attitudes towards the genders, towards different races, views of wealth and sociopolitical hierarchies.

**ideology:** the way we view the world based on ideas, beliefs, attitudes and values that we share with others. To be ideologically neutral would be where an ideological base or perspective is believed to be absent.

**idiolect:** the personal variety of an individual speaker.

**illocutionary act:** one of three acts proposed by Austin that are performed in the speaking of any utterance. This act is closest to the meaning of the utterance intended by the speaker and can include promises, threats, and apologies.

**imperative:** a type of full clause which has a verb but no surface subject, e.g. *Listen to me!* Imperatives are often said to refer to orders, but in fact a whole range of directive functions can be realized by them, for example wishes (*Have a nice day!*), invitations (*Take a seat*) or offers (*Try this*).

**implicature:** a type of implied or implicated meaning that goes beyond what is said by an utterance. Grice recognized the following types of implicature: generalized conversational implicatures (includes scalar implicatures), particularized conversational implicatures and conventional implicatures.

**inchoative:** a semantic and grammatical category in verbs that identifies a change of state in an entity.

**indirect speech act:** a speech act can be performed directly (e.g. *Open the window!*) or indirectly (e.g. *Can you open the window?*). The choice of speech act is determined by politeness considerations, amongst other factors. An indirect speech act is often produced by questioning one of the preparatory conditions on the performance of a speech act (in the case of the above directive, that the hearer *can* undertake the requested action).

**inference:** supplying information that a speaker or writer has not made explicit.

**inflectional morpheme:** type of bound morpheme creating word forms and marking grammatical categories and relation, typically positioned at the very end of words.

**inflectional morphology:** branch of morphology dealing with the bound morphological markers of grammatical categories and relations.

**information processing:** an approach to analysing performance as a series of phases, at each of which a piece of information is changed in form.

**initialism:** product of acronym-formation which is pronounced as a sequence of individual letters (e.g. *IRC←internet relay chat*).

**input:** the speech that a child hears, augmented by the speech situation, including gestures.

**input decoding:** matching sensations reaching the ear to the sounds of the language.

**intersubjectivity:** in general linguistics terms, a concept that describes the communicative necessity of paying attention to an addressee's position and face needs. In theories of semantic change, a concept that describes cases where lexical items develop meanings which encode attitudes towards the addressee (e.g. the use of honorifics such as *sir* or *madam*).

**intonation:** intonation refers to identifiable tunes or melodies used in speech over 'chunks' of speech called intonational phrases (IPs). English IPs are usually quite short – seven words or less.

**intonational phrase:** intonational phrase (IP) is the 'chunk' of speech spanned by an identifiable intonation tune; in English, IPs are usually quite short – seven words or less.

**intransitive verb:** a verb that has no object, for example *fall*.

**IPA:** the IPA or International Phonetic Association is a representative organization for phoneticians, established in 1886. The IPA's alphabet, summarized in the IPA Chart (page 26) and discussed in detail in the *Handbook* (IPA 1999), is used for the transcription of speech. For full details, go to www.langsci.ucl.ac.uk/ipa/index.html

**isogloss:** an imaginary boundary or line on a map which shows where different linguistic features are used.

**keystroke logging:** recording the changes that a writer makes to a text while working on it.

**labiodental:** a consonant produced with the lower lip and the upper teeth, e.g. [f], [v].

**language:** a semiotic system (or code) for making meaning.

**language decoding:** the stage in the human communication cycle in which linguistic rules are used to analyse the syntactic structure and semantic content of utterances.

**language disorder:** a breakdown in the formulation or production of language (expressive language disorder) or the comprehension or understanding of language (receptive language disorder). In clinical terms, a language disorder is distinct from a speech disorder in that only the former deals with symbolic aspects of communication.

**language encoding:** the stage in the human communication cycle in which phonological, syntactic and semantic elements are selected in order to give linguistic expression to a communicative intention.

**language processing:** term used generally for the processes which enable language users to speak, listen, write and read; sometimes used more narrowly to refer only to listening and reading.

**language storage:** how language is represented in the mind.

**langue:** the abstract system all speakers have the knowledge of, which is a social contract, and not the property of an individual.

**laryngectomy:** surgical removal of either the whole larynx (total laryngectomy) or part of the larynx (partial laryngectomy). This procedure is usually necessitated by the presence of a laryngeal carcinoma (cancer).

**larynx:** a cartilaginous structure (the cricoid, thyroid cartilage and two arytenoid cartilages) located at the top of the trachea (or windpipe) and containing the vocal folds.

**left-branching language:** a configurational language in which phrasal material is built up by embedding on the left-hand side of the phrase being expanded.

**lemma:** part of a lexical entry that contains the meaning of word and the syntactic functions associated with it.

**lenition:** a phonological process whereby consonants become weaker, based on the idea that consonants can be compared in terms of relative strength. Examples might include a voiceless stop changing to a voiceless fricative, or a voiced fricative changing to a liquid.

**lexeme:** a semantic word; the basic unit of lexical semantics.

**lexical entry:** the grouping of related senses of a word in a published dictionary; or a hypothetical organizational level of lexemes in a mental lexicon.

**lexical morpheme:** type of morpheme encoding rich conceptual meaning.

**lexical relations:** the semantic relations between lexemes in the same language, such as synonymy, antonymy, hyponymy, etc.

**lexical search:** matching a word that has been identified to a word in one's vocabulary.

**lexical segmentation:** identifying word boundaries in connected speech.

**lexical semantics:** the study of word meaning and meaning relations between words.

**lexicalization:** the gradual process by which items undergo development to become more lexical in character.

**lexicon:** a speaker's knowledge about individual morphemes and words.

**lexis:** the level of language concerned with words or vocabulary. The entire stock of words in a language is known as the lexicon.

**linguistic reconstruction:** the reconstruction of a language (or aspects of a language, e.g. its phonology) based on indirect evidence. Linguistic reconstruction is necessary in cases where little or no primary data exist of the language in question.

**linguistic savant:** a person whose linguistic abilities well outstrip his/her intelligence and other mental abilities, such as the ability to pass Theory of Mind tests.

**linguistic truth:** truth that derives from linguistic meaning, regardless of context.

**linguistic variable:** a feature of language usage which separates speakers; see also 'social variable'.

**literal meaning:** the hypothesis that there is a regular, transparent use of sentences and words, which is different from and more basic than non-literal or figurative uses like metaphor, metonymy, irony, etc.

**loan:** a lexical item borrowed (i.e. copied) from another language.

**locutionary act:** one of three acts proposed by Austin that are performed in the speaking of any utterance. This act captures the sense and reference of the linguistic expressions in an utterance and is closest to the traditional, semantic notion of meaning.

**long-term memory:** the part of memory where permanent knowledge is stored about (a) the world, the individual's past experiences, routine events; (b) language and how to use it.

**manner of articulation:** the kind of approximation or constriction made between the active and passive articulators and the type of sound this produces, such as plosive [p, b], fricative [s, z, ʃ], etc. Manners are listed on the vertical axis of the IPA Chart (page 26).

**maxim:** a proposal of Grice in which four maxims of quality, quantity, relation and manner are used to give effect to the cooperative principle. Maxims can be flouted or not observed in various ways often with a view to generating implied meanings.

**meaning construction:** adding to the bare information extracted during listening and reading by drawing on world knowledge, context and inference.

**media:** the communication channels through which information can be disseminated such as television, radio, newspapers and the internet.

**media discourse:** the discourse inherent in media texts.

**media literate:** to have the ability to interpret the media and their messages.

**mental lexicon:** the vocabulary store in a language user's mind.

**metalinguistic negation:** when a speaker, rather than denying an assertion, rejects the assertion's assumptions or implications.

**metaphor:** in traditional terms, a figurative use of language based on an implicit identification of resemblance or analogy. In cognitive linguistics it is seen as a linguistic reflection of a more general and systematic psychological process of analogical mapping between two domains of knowledge, one being a source domain and the other a target domain.

**metonymy:** in traditional terms, a figurative use of language where reference is achieved by identifying something associated with the referent. So the place name *Washington* can be used to refer to the US government. In cognitive linguistics it is seen, like metaphor, as a mapping, but within a single domain of knowledge. The expression used (here *Washington*) is called the vehicle and the intended referent, the target (the US government).

**metre:** a phenomenon often mentioned in relation to rhyme. It refers to patterns in poetic discourse and, more specifically, to the patterns of both stressed and unstressed syllables. It is thus concerned with periodic units of rhythm in a line.

**minimal pair:** two words which differ in meaning and which also differ by a single segment, e.g. *cat* vs *pat, hat* vs *heat, bit* vs *bid*.

**modality:** 1. form of input to a language user (spoken versus written, also Sign and Braille); 2. the textual-conceptual function which produces doubt about the certainty of a proposition. Though prototypically delivered by modal verbs (*might, can, should*), it can also be delivered by adjectives (*possible, likely*) and adverbs (*possibly, probably*).

**modes of communication:** the various ways meaning can be communicated whether through language (written or spoken), image, signs or sounds. This can also include smell, texture and colour.

**modifier:** constituent of a complex lexeme which specifies the head.

**monitor:** check your own speech or writing to see if it (a) is accurate (b) meets your goals.

**morpheme:** smallest meaning-bearing unit of a language.

**morphological conditioning:** dependence of the choice of allomorphs on the final morpheme of the stem; pertains to 'irregular' allomorphs, e.g. *sang* or *mice*.

**mother:** in a syntactic tree, the mother of a given node is the single node (if any) connected to it by a single edge going up.

**motor execution:** the stage in the human communication cycle in which the muscles of the articulators perform the various articulatory movements required to produce speech.

**motor programming:** the stage in the human communication cycle in which there is planning of the movements of the articulators.

**movement:** the syntactic operation of moving a phrase to another position in the sentence.

**multimodality:** multimodality is concerned with the different semiotic modes other than language (but also including language) that go to make up a communicative act. For example, meaning making in a pictorial advertisement is about more than just the words used. It also concerns the images, colour, movement, layout, typography, etc.

**multiword unit:** semantic unit consisting of more than one word whose meaning is not compositional.

**mutual intelligibility:** if people speaking different varieties of a language or dialect can understand one another, they are said to be mutually intelligible.

**nasalized:** a nasalized sound occurs when the velum is in the lowered (open) position and there is no closure in the oral cavity so that air flows simultaneously through the oral and nasal cavities. This process is called nasalization. Intentionally nasalized vowels are found in many languages, for example French.

**naturalization:** the process whereby dominant ideologies are constantly repeated and reproduced in the news to the extent that they achieve the status of common sense and become regarded as 'normal' in society.

**negation:** the process by which texts create an alternative (denied or refused) worldview. It can be delivered by a number of textual means (typically *not* or *no*) but its relevance as a textual-conceptual function is its ability to retrospectively produce the expectation of something which is actively denied by the text itself.

**neutralization:** the state of affairs in which two phonemes fail to contrast in a specific context, e.g. the /t/ and /d/ in *atom* vs *Adam* in American English.

**news:** the production of information relating to recent events.

**newsworthy:** the aspects of a story that journalists believe will attract readers' attention are considered to be newsworthy or to have news value. Some examples of categories of newsworthiness are the proximity of an event to readers (e.g. a local story), the prominence of people involved (e.g. a celebrity), or how unexpected an event might be (e.g. an earthquake).

**no negative evidence problem:** the challenge of devising a theory of acquisition in which the child does not receive overt correction of his/her errors, and yet succeeds in deducing the rules of his/her language.

**non-configurational language:** a language in which hierarchical clusters are not present in the surface order of words.

**noncount noun:** a noun which cannot have a plural form and which cannot be preceded by *a*, e.g. *a money*, as opposed to a count noun. Also called 'uncountable noun'. Some words which are noncount in English have equivalents in other languages which are count, e.g. *information*.

**non-literal meaning:** the hypothesis that there are figurative uses of language like metaphor, metonymy, irony, etc. that are distinct from the regular, transparent use of sentences and words, which is termed literal meaning. Traditionally non-literal meaning is seen as requiring extra effort to understand.

**normalizing:** adjusting to the voice of a speaker in terms of pitch, speech rate, accent, etc.

**noun:** member of an open class of words whose members occur as the main word of subjects and objects of sentences and of objects of prepositions. The British logician Peter Geach proposed a cross-linguistically stable semantic definition of nouns which is based on the fact that adjectives like *same* can modify nouns, but no other kinds of parts of speech. Not only that, but there also do not seem to be any other expressions with similar meaning that can modify verbs and adjectives. Consider the following examples:

a. John and Bill participated in the same fight.
b. *John and Bill samely fought.

Geach proposed that nouns and only nouns are predicates with identity criteria. Even in languages where something like (b) is grammatical, it cannot mean the same as (a). Instead of meaning that Bill and John participated in the same fight it means that they fought in the same way. The property of being a predicate with identity criteria can be used as a cross-linguistic diagnostic for being a noun.

**noun phrase:** a noun and all the words that 'go' with it, for example *the tall girl standing over there*. Noun phrases in English may be very long with multiple instances of recursion.

**nucleus:** in syllable structure the nucleus is the core, obligatory part of a syllable; a nucleus is typically a vowel, though some languages allow non-vowels to be nuclei, e.g. the final [n] in English *button* when pronounced [ˈbʌtn̩]

**number:** a grammatical category that expresses the distinction between the singular and plural forms of nouns, pronouns and determiners and encompasses the grammatical agreement of these with verbs. Number can be indicated by inflection (e.g. *chairs*, *babies*) or a change in word form (e.g. the distinct pronominal forms *I* [singular] and *we* [plural] in English).

**numeral:** many languages distinguish between cardinal numerals (*one, two, three, four, five*... and ordinal numerals (*first, second, third, fourth, fifth*,... — ')' . Cardinal numerals are used to describe quantities, ordinal numerals to pick out a position on an explicit or implicit list.

**object:** a clause element required by transitive verbs, for example: *They last saw the thieves in a stolen car*. It can form the subject of a passive, e.g. *The thieves were last seen in a stolen car*. Most grammarians recognize at least two types of object: direct and indirect. The above example is a direct object. Direct objects most typically indicate things or people affected by or resulting from actions.

**obstruent:** the class of consonants including stops, fricatives and affricates.

**onset:** in syllable structure the onset is a consonant or consonants occurring before the nucleus.

**overt prestige:** when speakers use or judge varieties positively that are similar to the standard variety, opposite to covert prestige.

**paradigmatic:** a paradigmatic analysis would identify all the possible choices of e.g. words which can fit a particular slot in the sentence. For example, the italicized choices can all fit in the same slot before a noun, and as a result, are said to all be determiners in grammatical terminology: *the, these, those, some, all, few* BOOKS.

**parameter:** a point of restricted variation characterizing the differences between the grammars of different languages.

**parameter setting:** the theory that language acquisition is facilitated by the fact that languages are structured by an innate Universal Grammar which admits just a few variations. These parameters, or variations, limit the amount by which languages differ from one another.

***parole*:** the actualization of an abstract system, an individual's behaviour regulated by language, or particular instances of speech.

**parsing:** the analysis of the structure of the sentence into grammatical elements using terminology such as subject, verb, object.

**participant role:** see semantic role.

**particularized conversational implicature:** a type of implied meaning that requires a particular context for its generation. This meaning is recovered through the combined operation of the cooperative principle and maxims.

**passive voice:** a construction in which the object of a transitive verb becomes its subject, with changes to the verb phrase (and optionally with a *by* phrase to indicate the original subject), e.g. *was surprised by his behaviour (cf. His behaviour surprised me).* Passives are used when – for various reasons – an object needs to be presented at the beginning of a clause, or a subject needs to be omitted.

**patois:** referring to a non-standard variety that tends to be linked to a creole, for example Jamaican patois.

**pedagogic grammar:** grammar for teaching purposes. Since learners cannot be confronted with the full complexity of grammar, the information that is presented to them by teachers and in textbooks will be highly selective and simplified, though it should not be inaccurate.

**performative utterance:** an expression used by Austin to describe utterances that perform actions. These utterances do not report or describe states of affairs and are not true or false, as constative utterances are.

**perlocutionary act:** One of three acts proposed by Austin that are performed in the speaking of any utterance. A perlocutionary act only comes about when a hearer changes his behaviour or course of action in response to an utterance. For example, a hearer may understand an utterance to be a warning not to enter a field, but proceed to do so anyway.

**philology:** the study of historical texts produced at a particular time and in a particular context, drawing on insights from linguistics, literary studies and history. Philology was an important precursor to the current discipline of historical linguistics.

**phoneme:** an abstract representation of a speech sound which may be associated with one or more allophones; phonemes occur in contrastive distribution and may be indentified through minimal pairs.

**phonetic plan:** a speech plan in which words have been bound together as a group. This entails simplifying transitions between words (*tem pounds*) and within words (*hambag*).

**phonological conditioning:** dependence of the choice of allomorphs on the final phoneme of the stem; pertains to 'regular allomorphs', e.g. *kissed* or *dogs*.

**phonotactics:** the allowable combination of speech sounds in a particular language, such as those sounds which may occur together in an onset or coda.

**place of articulation:** the point in the vocal tract at which the primary obstruction to the airstream occurs, such as bilabial [p], palatal [j], glottal [h] and [ʔ], etc. Places are listed along the horizontal axis of the IPA Chart (page 00).

**planning pause:** a brief pause where a speaker plans the form of the next utterance.

**point of view:** in literary linguistics, point of view refers to the filter or the perspective through which the events of a story are perceived. The narratological equivalent is the term 'focalizer' (meaning the angle of vision through which a story is focused, often by a narrator or main character). In point of view, the focus is often either on space and time, ideology or psychology.

**polysemous/polysemy:** these terms are used when a word has distinct but related meanings.

**possessive compound:** type of exocentric compound based on a possessive relation between the meaning encoded by the compound constituents and the meaning of the exocentric head (e.g. *redbreast* 'a bird that has a red breast').

**postmodifier:** part of a noun phrase that comes after the head. Prepositional phrases and relatives clauses are common postmodifiers, e.g. *a crisis of immense proportions*; *a crisis which has stunned the world*. In written English postmodification may be extensive, leading to long noun phrases.

**pragmatics:** the study of language use in contexts. It is concerned with the meaning of utterances that emerge during interpersonal situations, rather than on the propositional meaning of sentences. In this sense it is clearly descended from classical rhetoric and the idea of *kairos*, a locative notion of time pertaining to the most opportune moment/circumstances for the success of a persuasive discourse utterance.

**predicative:** a clause element whose function is to describe something already mentioned as subject or object, rather than to introduce a distinct entity (as is the case with objects). Adjectives as well as noun phrases are common as predicatives: *He's rich/a banker* (subject predicatives); *They drove her crazy* (an object predicative).

**prefixation:** type of typically word-class-preserving word-formation process involving the attachment of a bound lexical morpheme at the front of a base (e.g. *unfair, disagree*).

**premodifier:** in noun phrases, the part that comes between the determiner and the head. Adjectives are common, but so are nouns: *a keen student, a business student.*

**prescriptive grammar:** an approach to grammar which relies on certain self-appointed authorities to dispense advice on certain grammatical issues. Their decisions are not based on evidence, as opposed to descriptive grammar, and therefore may be unrelated to primary grammar. Though unpopular in linguistics, their pronouncements are still influential among some native speakers of English.

**presupposition:** this describes information which is assumed, taken for granted or in the background of an utterance. Presuppositions reduce the amount of information that a speaker must explicitly state and are triggered by certain lexical items and constructions.

**primary data:** examples of language as it is (or was in the past) actually used, e.g. newspapers, fiction, letters, etc.

**primary grammar:** the grammar that all native speakers of a language possess and utilize unconsciously in order to communicate accurately and effectively in speech and writing (and which learners of the language may also partially possess).

**priming:** modern alternative to the *word association* task, where a researcher presents a word to a language user, followed by a target word which may or may not be connected to the word.

**principle:** a property or property of rules that characterizes all human languages.

**productive:** involving speaking or writing.

**productivity:** the design feature of human language whereby the language is able to accommodate new combinations of the elements of the language, and this allows for new meanings to be expressed.

**pronominal binding:** definite pronouns and reflexive pronouns are subject to syntactic constraints, that ensure for example that definite pronouns ordinarily cannot refer to an NP in the same simple sentence, whereas reflexive pronouns must refer to an NP in the same simple sentence.

**propagation:** the spread of a linguistic innovation, such as a new word or a sound change, to all speakers of the language in which the actuation occurred.

**proposition:** a unit of meaning expressed by a sentence or utterance and which can be true or false. Traditionally, propositional meaning has been studied in semantics. Increasingly, theorists are recognising a role for pragmatic factors in propositional meaning.

**Proto-Indo-European (PIE):** a hypothetical, reconstructed ancestor of Indo-European languages. PIE was first proposed by the British philologist Sir William Jones, who was moved to postulate its existence after noticing a significant number of similarities between Sanskrit and Classical Greek and Latin.

**prototype theory:** a theory proposed by the cognitive psychologist Eleanor Rosch, in which concepts have a complex structure containing a central prototype and other more marginal elements.

**real-time change:** a study which samples a particular community over time; see 'apparent-time change'.

**reanalysis:** a type of linguistic change whereby (i) a word's surface form remains the same but its part-of-speech changes or (ii) the morphological structure of a word is reanalysed by speakers (e.g. *heli* + *copter* as opposed to Greek *helico* [helix] + *pter* [wing]).

**receptive:** involving listening or reading.

**receptive language:** this refers to the comprehension or understanding of language. Receptive language is most closely identified with the stage of language decoding in the human communication cycle.

**reduplication:** non-morphemic word-formation process involving the repetition of a word or word-like element in unchanged form (e.g. *hush-hush*), with a different vowel (e.g. *hip-hop*) or a different consonant (e.g. *boogie-woogie*).

**reference:** the act of using linguistic expressions to identify things in the world.

**referent:** the thing identified by an act of reference.

**repair:** correcting one's own spoken language; dealing with breakdowns of understanding.

**retrieval:** how a language user accesses language (especially vocabulary) in the mind.

**rhetoric:** in its classical (Greek/Roman) form the forerunner of literary linguistics. It is concerned with finding and generating material, arranging that material, stylizing it and then memorizing and delivering it. Literary linguistics is mostly concerned with the 'stylizing' part of classical rhetoric in which such things as appropriateness, clarity, deviation and patterning are to be found.

**rhyme:** in syllable structure the rhyme refers to the combination of nucleus together with the coda.

**right-branching language:** a configurational language in which phrasal material is build up on the right-hand side of the phrase being expanded.

**root compounds:** type of compound consisting of free lexical morphemes only, as opposed to synthetic compounds (e.g. *doorknob, lamppost*).

**root infinitive:** in general, all main clause (root) verbs in adult languages must be tensed. This is not the case for a stage in child language, in which a non-tensed verb may be used.

**RP:** the standard form of British English pronunciation which is closely linked to the written variety of Standard English.

**saccade:** sweeping movement of a reader's eyes.

**scalar implicature:** a type of generalized conversational implicature that is generated by a set of terms which differ in informational strength. For example, the word *some* in the utterance *The thief stole some of the jewels* generates the implicature that the thief did not steal all the jewels (*some* is semantically weaker than *all*).

**scientific grammar:** a type of secondary grammar that is intended for academic study rather than teaching. Compared to pedagogic grammar, scientific grammar can be complex and extensive in its attempt to capture the subtleties of native speakers' primary grammar.

**secondary data:** contemporary commentaries on how language is (or was in the past) actually used, e.g. dictionaries, grammars, guides to usage, etc.

**secondary grammar:** conscious knowledge and descriptions of grammar (including both pedagogic and scientific) that attempt to describe primary grammar and which are codified in grammar books or in the rules of thumb given by teachers.

**self-monitoring:** checking language which is about to be produced, is being produced or has just been produced to see if it meets one's goals, and is appropriate. Checking whether understanding of a new piece of information is consistent with what was heard/read before.

**semantic analysis:** examination of the meanings of words and phrases taking into account social and political contexts.

**semantic network:** a complex set of associations in the mind between words which belong to the same lexical group (*hat, coat*), share similar or opposite senses, occur together frequently (*drive, car*) or collocate with each other (*heavy* + *smoker*).

**semantic role:** a semantic relation an argument takes in relation to a verb, such as AGENT, PATIENT, THEME, INSTRUMENT, LOCATION, SOURCE, GOAL, etc.

**semanticity:** the design feature of human language whereby the words, and combinations of words, in the language are meaningful. The signs in the language can be linked with objects, people, places or experiences in the world.

**semantics:** in many senses the reverse side of the pragmatics coin. It is concerned with the study of textual, linguistic meaning and as such largely eschews the context. In this sense, unlike pragmatics, its roots are not in rhetoric but in the philosophy of logic/dialectic.

**semiologist:** one who studies signs and symbols.

**semiotic:** meaningful signs or symbols such as language or illustrations.

**sense:** sense is used in lexical semantics to identify the distinct lexemes linked by homonymy, so an ambiguous word like *bark* is said to have more than one sense. Similarly, the related meaning distinctions identified in polysemy are also called senses, so a polysemous word like the noun *run* (a fast pace, a race, an errand, continuous production, sequence of cards, score in cricket, etc.) is also said to have multiple senses.

**sensory processing:** the stage in the communication cycle in which sound waves are converted from mechanical vibrations in the middle ear to nervous impulses which travel to the auditory centres in the brain.

**sentence stress:** the audible prominences or beats (derived from word stresses) that make up the rhythm of an utterance; each intonational phrase has its own rhythm, e.g. *the 'word was polysyl'labic* || or: *it was a 'polysyllabic 'word* ||.

**signifier and signified:** the signifier is the sign itself, characterized by its arbitrary relationship with the meaning it designates – the signified. A sign is then said to be comprised of two halves: signifier and signified. This is an insight from Saussure.

**simple lexeme:** lexeme consisting of one lexical morpheme only.

**sister:** in a syntactic tree, any nodes that share the same mother are sisters.

**situation type:** a categorization of events and situations encoded in the lexical items of a language, allowing distinctions, for example, between static and dynamic types, and within the latter between durative and punctual. One influential classification distinguishes between accomplishments, activities, achievements and semelfactives

**social practice (also known as sociocultural practice):** social, cultural and political aspects that contribute to the overall understanding of a communicative event such as a news story.

**social practices:** things that people (social actors) do with/to other people, in specific places following conventions/rules in time and space.

**social semiotics:** the study of the nature of signs in society. It incorporates the following components: culture, other semiotic systems alongside verbal language; *parole* (the act of speaking); diachrony (time, history), process and change and the material nature of signs.

**social variable:** a factor such as class, gender or ethnicity which is used to identify groups of people.

**sonorant:** the class of consonants which includes nasals, liquids, and approximants.

**specific language impairment:** a developmental language disorder in which there is severe impairment of expressive and receptive language skills in the absence of predisposing conditions such as hearing loss, intellectual disability and craniofacial anomalies.

**speech act:** a term used by Austin and later Searle to describe utterances which perform acts or actions. Both Austin and Searle recognized different types of speech acts such as assertives (e.g. statements) and directives (e.g. requests).

**speech and language therapy:** the profession that assesses and treats communication and swallowing disorders in children and adults. In the United States, the term 'speech-language pathology' is used.

**speech disorder:** an impairment of the production of speech sounds which may be developmental or acquired in nature. A speech disorder may arise as a result of disruption in the motor programming and/or execution stages in the human communication cycle.

**speech perception:** the stage in the communication cycle during which speech sounds are recognised or perceived. Disruption to speech perception is the basis of the disorder called auditory agnosia in Landau-Kleffner syndrome.

**speech role:** the role a speaker adopts for himself/herself and in so doing assigns to the listener a complementary role that s/he wishes him/her to adopt in his/her turn. The addresser–addressee are the main speech roles.

**spreading activation:** an automatic process whereby hearing, reading or producing a word makes links with other associated words in the mind. This assists listeners and readers to anticipate words that they may encounter later and speakers and writers to retrieve words that they may later need.

**Standard English:** the codified variety of English (used in dictionaries and grammar books), and tends to be linked to education, media and official language usage.

**standfirst:** a subheading, line or brief paragraph that summarizes a news story and is located immediately above or below the headline.

**stress:** the prominence of a particular syllable in a word; English stress typically involves both higher pitch and greater volume of the prominent syllable.

**structured variation:** where a speaker's choice of forms of language to use is not arbitrary, but linked to other factors – opposite to free variation.

**style:** style in language can be said to be either motivated or non-motivated (i.e. conscious or subconscious) choices of (authorial) expression that come about in a particular context.

**subject:** a clause element which usually occurs before the verb (e.g. *I know*), may determine its form (e.g. *he thinks*), and inverts with part of the verb phrase to form questions (e.g. *Can I stay?*). Subjects may indicate the 'doer' of an action, but they have several other roles.

**subjectification:** a gradual process of semantic change whereby the meanings of an item come to express the speaker's beliefs or attitudes more closely.

**subset principle:** the principle whereby the child's grammar expands to include a larger range of grammatical sentences; it is called the subset principle because each prior grammar permits a smaller range of sentences to the next grammar in the language.

**suffixation:** type of typically word-class-changing word-formation process involving the attachment of a bound lexical morpheme at the end of a base (e.g. *fairness, agreement*).

**surface phonetics:** in phonology a surface form refers to the phonetic shape, i.e. the actual pronunciation, of a word, affix, phrase, etc. Compare 'underlying phoneme'.

**SVO language:** a typological description of a language in which the syntactic structure subject–verb–object is the most common order of sentence elements (cf., for example, SOV and VOS).

**syllable:** a phonological concept which organizes speech sounds into larger units; recognition of syllables is useful in expressing phonotactic restrictions and assigning stress, among other things.

**synchronic:** from Greek *synchronous*; synchronic linguistics is concerned with the study of language at a particular point in time (as opposed to the study of the development of language over time); see also 'diachronic'.

**synecdoche:** a traditional label for PART FOR WHOLE and WHOLE FOR PART metonymies.

**synonymy:** having the same meaning; of two sentences defined as entailing one another.

**syntactic analysis:** a detailed analysis of a text and how it is organized. In a news story this would involve looking at aspects such as headlines, standfirsts, and event structure.

**syntagmatic:** the relations of combination that elements of a language enter into. For example, taking the words *men hats green old in,* there are a number of possibilities of combination which include: *old men in green hats* and *green men in old hats*.

**synthetic compound:** type of compound consisting of at least three morphemes, among them one bound morpheme and one encoding a verb (e.g. *washing-machine, dog owner*); many synthetic compounds cause problems for analyses based on binary branching.

**synthetic language:** type of language which encodes grammatical categories by means of inflectional morphemes.

**synthetic truth:** a proposition true by correspondence to a set of affairs.

**telegraphic speech:** children aged around 2 years omit 'small' words such a prepositions and (in)definite articles, in a manner reminiscent of adults when writing a telegram. (In the days when telegrams were sent, they were charged by the word; the message could be conveyed effectively by using only nouns, verbs, adjectives and adverbs.)

**teleological mechanisms:** mechanisms that preserve the internal balance of the linguistic system, including such phenomena as analogy (linguistic copying) or hole-filling to help enhance uniformity.

**tense:** a semantic and grammatical system that allows speakers to situate events in time. Tense is deictic since it relates fundamentally to the time of an act of speaking or writing.

**text:** what we read, see or hear in an observable product whether a book, a news article, a film, a television programme or a street sign. It is the object that carries meaning.

**textual-conceptual functions:** the ways in which texts create different dimensions of their text world, from the construction of a time–space 'envelope' via deixis to the construction of particular binary opposites for this particular text world.

**thematic role:** see 'semantic role'.

**tone:** or **lexical tone:** the melodic rising or falling of pitch affecting the meaning of words. Tones can be contour tones (with pitch change, e.g. Modern Standard Chinese (MSC) Tone 4 high-to-low falling [ʃu˥˩] 'tree') or register tones (where pitch remains level e.g. MSC Tone 1 high level [ʃu˥] 'book').

**top-down theorizing:** the approach to problem solving that starts from an hypothesis and develops predictions that can be tested.

**transcription:** the writing system developed to commit speech sounds to paper, using the specially devised alphabet of symbols and diacritics summarized in the IPA Chart. A symbol represents always and only the same one sound. Transcription can be narrow/phonetic (using many diacritics and enclosed in square brackets, e.g. *pine* [phä̝ɪ̯̃n]) or broad/phonemic (using basic symbols with very few diacritics and enclosed in slant brackets, e.g. *pine* /paɪn/).

**transitive verb:** a verb which has an object, and which can be turned into the passive voice, e.g. *They scolded me.* / *I was scolded by them.* Most transitive verbs in English can occur without an object given the right circumstances, e.g. *I can't understand (this sentence).* Some verbs, for example *run*, have different meanings when they are transitive and when they are intransitive, e.g. *She runs every day* (intransitive) / *She runs an IT company* (transitive).

**transitivity:** the effect that choosing a verb has on the rest of the clause and the resulting viewpoint of the scenario being described. Some verbs indicate actions and others are more descriptive of states, but stylistic choice sometimes allows either to be chosen, with consequent effects on the presentation of the text world.

**tree diagram:** a syntactic tree diagram is a picture of the structure of a sentence representing both word order and hierarchical organization into constituents. Standard trees also have the following properties: No node in a tree has more than one mother. Every tree contains exactly one node without a mother, the root. No edges (branches) cross. The words of the sentence do not dominate any further nodes; they are the leaves of the tree.

**truth-value:** being true or false; the value of a declarative sentence in a given context.

**two-word stage:** children aged around 2 years tend to produce utterances that contain two words. Some words may be favoured in particular (first, second) position.

**underlying phoneme:** in phonology an underlying form is an abstract representation consisting of the phonemes of a specific word, affix, phrase, etc. Compare 'surface phonetics'.

**Uniformitarian Principle:** the notion that the general properties of language were the same in the past as they are in the present. The Uniformitarian Principle places restrictions on linguistic reconstruction, such that reconstructions cannot posit forms and possibilities that could not have been the case at some past time.

**Universal Grammar:** the theory proposed by Chomsky that a set of innate, underlying principles set limits on how languages can be structured. This set of principles is hard-wired into the brain. This allows the child to deduce the patterns of the language they are learning.

**variety:** a neutral term for a language or a dialect.

**velar:** a velar consonant is one produced with the back of the tongue and the velum or soft palate, e.g. [k], [g] and [ŋ].

**verb phrase:** a verb and all the auxiliaries that may 'go' with it, e.g. *(We) have been waiting.*

**verbal dyspraxia:** a disorder of speech motor programming which may be developmental or acquired in nature. Volitional speech is more impaired than automatic speech, and both vowels and consonants are affected.

**verbal repertoire:** the set of language variety/varieties a speaker has access to.

**vernacular:** a social dialect with features different to the standard variety which tends to have little prestige.

**vocal tract:** the interconnected system of lungs, trachea, larynx, pharynx and the nasal and oral cavities, used to produce speech.

**voice:** modal/normal voice is generated by the vibrating of the vocal folds and is used in speech to distinguish voiced sounds, e.g. [m], [z], etc. from voiceless sounds, e.g. [p], [s], etc.

**voice disorder:** any disorder that compromises the structure and function of the phonatory mechanism. This includes structural anomalies (e.g. vocal nodules and polyps), misuse of the laryngeal mechanism (e.g. muscle tension dysphonia) and psychological factors (e.g. conversion aphonia).

**VOT:** Voice Onset Time, abbreviated VOT, is the term used when describing the time it takes for voicing to commence in a voiced sound immediately following a voiceless consonant. This causes aspiration (a h-sound) when the affected sound is a vowel. English /p t k/ are followed by a long VOT.

**vowel:** sound in which there is unimpeded airflow and which occurs at the centre of a syllable, e.g. [ɔː] as in *board* /bɔːd/.

**word association:** traditional psychological method, where a researcher says a word and a language user has to respond with the first word that comes into his or her mind.

**word class:** a grouping of words according to their formal (structural and morphological) characteristics. Not all the characteristics of a word class are shared by all its members; thus there are some words which are fully typical of their class, and others which are less so.

**word-formation:** cover term for morphemic and non-morphemic processes involved in the creation of new lexemes on the basis of existing morphemes and lexemes; branch of morphology dealing with these processes.

**working memory:** the part of memory which controls current operations – including producing language and analysing language that has been heard or read.

**zero-morpheme:** theoretical construct used, among other things, to explain conversion as a form of derivation comparable to (overt) suffixation, e.g. *empty* V ← *empty* Adj + {Ø}.

# INDEX